The Earthscan Reader in
Sustainable Cities

The Earthscan Reader in Sustainable Cities

Edited by David Satterthwaite

Earthscan Publications Ltd, London and Sterling, VA

First published in the UK and USA in 1999 by
Earthscan Publications Ltd

Copyright © David Satterthwaite, 1999

Reprinted 2001

A catalogue record for this book is available from the British Library

ISBN: 1 85383 601 x (paperback)
       1 85383 602 8 (hardback)

Typesetting by Composition & Design Services, Minsk, Belarus
Printed and bound by Creative Print and Design Wales, Ebbw Vale
Cover design by Andrew Corbett

For a full list of publications, please contact:

Earthscan Publications Ltd
120 Pentonville Road
London N1 9JN
Tel: (0171) 278 0433
Fax: (0171) 278 1142
email: earthinfo@earthscan.co.uk
http://www.earthscan.co.uk
22883 Quicksilver Drive, Sterling, VA 20166-2012, USA

Earthscan is an editorially independent subsidiary of Kogan Page Ltd and
publishes in association with WWF-UK and the International Institute for
Environment and Development

This book is printed on elemental chlorine free paper

Contents

Contents

List of Tables, Boxes and Figures

Tables

Boxes

List of Tables, Boxes and Figures

Figures

About the Authors

Alan AtKisson is president of AtKisson + Associates, Inc., a consulting firm that focuses on sustainability and cultural change, and Director of Arts & Culture for the Sustainability Institute in Vermont, USA. He is also a Senior Fellow on sustainability policy with Redefining Progress. His first book, on the human response to global trends, will be published by Chelsea Green Press in 1999. AtKisson was a co-founder of *Sustainable Seattle*, and has since been a consultant to government agencies and community forums on sustainable development issues all over the world. He is also a professional singer and songwriter. He can be contacted by email at AtKisson@aol.com.

Jeb Brugmann is Secretary General of the International Council for Local Environmental Initiatives (ICLEI) and is based at its World Secretariat, City Hall, 8th floor, East Tower, Toronto, Ontario M5H 2N2, Canada, email: ibrugmann@iclei.org.

Scott Campbell teaches at the Urban and Regional Planning Program of the College of Architecture and Urban Planning, University of Michigan, 2000 Bonisteel Blvd, Ann Arbor, Michigan 48109-2069, USA, email: sdcamp@umich.edu.

Herbert Girardet, a UN Global 500 Award recipient, is visiting professor for environmental planning at Middlesex University, London, and chair of the Schumacher Society, UK. He is author of *The Gaia Atlas of Cities* and co-author of *Making Cities Work* which was published by Earthscan for Habitat II and of the Report *Creating A Sustainable London* (1996). His documentary on London's metabolism, *Metropolis*, was shown on British Television (Channel 4) in 1994. Most recently he wrote *Creating Sustainable Cities*, Green Books, Dartington, Devon, UK, 1999.

Jorge E Hardoy founded the Instituto Internacional de Medio Ambiente y Desarrollo (IIED-América Latina) and was its President until his death in 1993. He also founded the Human Settlements Programme of the International Institute for Environment and Development (IIED) in 1977 and was its Director. He was also President of the National Commission for Historic Monuments in Argentina and Editor of the journal *Medio Ambiente y Urbanizacion.* Qualifying as an architect in 1950 with a Masters and PhD from Harvard University in City and Regional Planning, he wrote widely on both historical and contemporary urban issues, but mostly in Spanish. Among his publications with Earthscan are *Squatter Citizen: Life in the Urban Third World* (with David Satterthwaite), published in 1989, *The Poor Die Young; Housing and Health in Third World Cities* (edited with Sandy Cairncross and David Satterthwaite), published in 1990 and *Environmental Problems in Third World Cities* (with Diana Mitlin and David Satterthwaite) published in 1992. He was a former President of the Inter-American Planning Society, twice a Guggenheim fellow and advisor of the World Commission on Environment and Development (the Brundtland Commission).

Graham Haughton is head of the Centre for Urban Development and Environmental Management (CUDEM) at Leeds Metropolitan University. His research interests include sustainable development, urban development and labour markets. Recent books include *Sustainable Cities* (1994, with Colin Hunter, Jessica Kingsley Publishers and 1999, Stationary Office) and an edited collection, *Community Economic Development* (1999, Stationary Office). Address: CUDEM, Leeds Metropolitan University, Calverley Street, Leeds LS1 3HE, UK, email: g.haughton@lmu.ac.uk.

Michaela Hordijk is a geographer specializing in urban environmental management and is external assessor of the *Cities for Life Forum* in Peru. She is currently finalizing a PhD study on the role of local initiatives in urban environmental management in a low income area in Lima, Peru (University of Amsterdam, Department of Human Geography, Centre of Latin American Studies and Documentation, and the Institute for Housing and Urban Development Studies – IHS – in Rotterdam). Address: University of Amsterdam, Nieuwe Prinsengracht 130, 1018 VZ Amsterdam, Netherlands, email: mhordijk@knoware.nl.

Marianne Kjellen is a researcher at the Stockholm Environment Institute (SEI), and a doctoral student at the Department of Human Geography of the University of Stockholm. Her research focus is currently environment and water issues in Southern cities. She has coordinated the multi-city study on household environments in Accra, Jakarta, São Paulo and Port Elizabeth for the past three years, and based a number of publications on this work. Address: Stockholm Environment Institute, Box 2142, 10314 Stockholm, Sweden, email: marianne.kjellen@sei.se.

Ritu Kumar is an economist working with the Commonwealth Science Council, Science and Technology Division, Commonwealth Secretariat, London, UK. She has worked with UNIDO for ten years and has developed and implemented projects relating to industry and environmental policy in a number of Asian and African countries. She is currently developing a programme on eco-efficiency and energy conservation for the Commonwealth Science Council. Address: Science and Technology Division, Commonwealth Secretariat, Marlborough House, Pall Mall, London SW1Y 5HX, UK, email: ritukumar@aol.com.

Gordon McGranahan directs the Urban Environment Programme of the Stockholm Environment Institute (SEI). Trained as an economist, he has been working on environment and development issues for the last 20 years. His work on urban environmental issues is represented in a range of SEI publications, edited books and journals, the last including *Environment, Habitat International, Environment and Urbanization, World Development* and the *Journal of Environmental Planning and Management*. He initiated the Sida-funded studies of Accra, Jakarta, and São Paulo on which the paper included here draws. Address: Stockholm Environment Institute, Box 2142, 10314 Stockholm, Sweden, email: mcgranahan@sei.se.

Donella Meadows is an adjunct professor of environmental studies at Dartmouth College and director of the Sustainability Institute. She was one of the co-authors of *The Limits to Growth* (1972) and *Beyond the Limits* (1992) and a founder of the Balaton Group. She is presently designing an eco-village and organic farm in Hartland, Vermont. Her email: Donella.H.Meadows@dartmouth.edu.

Liliana Miranda is the National Coordinator of the *Cities for Life Forum* and the Executive Secretariat of the Peru Urban Management Education Programme (PEGUP). Both are located in ECOCIUDAD a Peruvian NGO where she is the vice-president. Trained as an architect, she previously taught urban planning and management at different Peruvian universities. Address: Foro Ciudades para la Vida, Ecociudad, Vargas Machuca 408, San Antonio, Miraflores, Lima 18, Peru; email: foro@ciudad.org.pe.

Diana Mitlin is an economist working in the Human Settlements Programme at the International Institute for Environment and Development (IIED). Her current interests include NGOs, urban community development, sustainable development, housing finance for low-income groups and the use of participatory methodologies in urban areas. Recent activities include contributing to UNCHS, *An Urbanizing World: the Global Report on Human Settlements 1996*, (Oxford University Press) and coordinator of an IIED research project on community environmental initiatives in Karachi and Manila. Recent publications she has co-authored include *Funding Community Initiatives*, Earthscan, 1994 and *Environmental Problems in Third World Cities*, Earthscan, 1992. For the last five years, she has been managing editor of *Environment and Urbanization*. She is also on the advisory board of *Third World Planning Review*, a Trustee of Intermediate Technology Development Group and a former chair of the British charity Homeless International.

Joe Nasr is vice-president of The Urban Agriculture Network. His 1996 *Urban Agriculture: Food, Jobs and Sustainable Cities* (co-authored by Jac Smit and Annu Ratta) will appear in a 2nd edition soon. He is currently setting up new research programmes on urban agriculture methods and data, and on the agriculture-urbanization in coastal Lebanon (his country of birth). Address: The Urban Agriculture Network, 1711 Lamont Street, NW, Washington DC 20010, USA, email: joenars@compuserve.com.

Peter Newman is Professor of City Policy and Director of the Institute for Science and Technology Policy at Murdoch University in Perth, Australia. He has written widely on urban and transport issues, including *Cities and Automobile Dependence: An International Sourcebook*, Gower Technical, 1989 and *Sustainability and Cities: Overcoming Automobile Dependence*, Island Press, Washington DC, 1999 (co-authored with Jeffrey R. Kenworthy). This paper is based on a background paper prepared by the author for UNCHS (Habitat), *An Urbanizing World; The Global Report on Human Settlements 1996*, Oxford University Press, 1996. Address: Institute for Science and Technology Policy, Murdoch University, Perth 6150, Australia; email: newman@central.murdoch.edu.au.

William Rees has taught at the University of British Columbia since 1969–70 and is currently Professor and Director of the University's School of Community and Regional Planning. His teaching and research emphasize the public policy and planning implications of global environmental trends and the necessary ecological conditions for sustainable socioeconomic development. Much of his work is in the realm of ecological economics and human ecology. He is best known in this field for his invention of 'ecological footprint analysis', a quantitative tool that estimates humanity's ecological impact on the ecosphere in terms of appropriated ecosystem (land and water) area. This research reveals the fundamental incompatibility between continued material economic growth and ecological security, and has helped to reopen debate on human carrying capacity as a prime consideration in sustainable development. Dr Rees is currently a co-investigator in the 'Global Integrity Project', oriented toward determining the necessary ecological conditions for biodiversity preservation. Dr

About the Authors

Rees was recently awarded a UBC Killam Research Prize (1996) in acknowledgment of his research achievements. Address: UBC School of Community and Regional Planning, 6333 Memorial Road, Vancouver, BC, Canada V6T 1Z2.

Nick Robins is Coordinator of the Sustainable Consumption and Trade Initiative at the International Institute for Environment and Development (IIED). He is co-author of *Unlocking Trade Opportunities* (1997), a case study report profiling pioneering producers in the South who have benefited from rising social and environmental expectations in their export markets. He is currently working in a collaborative research project with partners in the South to analyse the dynamics of critical supply chains and pinpoint opportunities for introducing more sustainable practices. Over the past five years, he has worked on the sustainable consumption agenda at the global level, with the Norwegian Ministry of Environment and others to accelerate international cooperation on the issue. Address: IIED, 3 Endsleigh Street, London WC1H 0DD, UK, email: nick.robins@iied.org.

Joan Roelofs is a professor of political science at Keene State College in New Hampshire and member of the Greens/Green Party USA. She teaches both political theory and public administration, which, along with the influence of Charles Fourier, William Morris, and Ebenezer Howard, inspired her book *Greening Cities* from which the extract in this Reader is drawn. Professor Roelofs is also on the editorial board of *Capitalism, Nature, Socialism*, a red-green journal. Address: Department of Political Economy, Keene State College, Keene NH 03435-3400, USA, email: jroelofs@keene.edu.

David Satterthwaite directs the Human Settlements Programme at the International Institute for Environment and Development (IIED) and teaches a course on The City and the Environment at the Institute of Latin American Studies (University of London). He founded the international journal *Environment and Urbanization* with Jorge E. Hardoy in 1989 and has been its Editor since then. He is a co-author of four previous Earthscan books: *The Environment for Children* (1996), *Funding Community Initiatives* (1994), *Environmental Problems in Third World Cities* (1992) and *Squatter Citizen* (1989). He was also editor and principal author of *An Urbanizing World: Global Report on Human Settlements, 1996* published for the U.N. Centre for Human Settlements by Oxford University Press (1996). He also worked with Jorge E Hardoy as an advisor to the World Commission on Environment and Development (the Brundtland Commission). Address: IIED, 3 Endsleigh Street, London WC1H 0DD, UK, email: david@iied.org.

Jac Smit is president of The Urban Agriculture Network. His first urban agriculture project was in 1968 in Calcutta; he first published on the subject in 1978. He pioneered both the inclusion of urban agriculture in urban plans and its use as a development intervention for low-income food-deficient countries. His current focus is how policies can be adopted by local and national governments to capture the full potential of urban agriculture. Address: The Urban Agriculture Network, 1711 Lamont Street, NW, Washington DC, 20010, USA, email: urbanag@compuserve.com.

Jacob Songsore is Full Professor and temporary Head at the Department of Geography and Resource Development at the University of Ghana-Legon. He has worked on both urban and rural development issues in Ghana, and published extensively on urban health and sustainability, including contributions to *World Development,*

Environment, Environment and Urbanization, and the *World Health Statistics Quarterly.* He led the field study in Accra for the comparative analysis of Accra, Jakarta and São Paulo presented in the paper included here. Address: Department of Geography and Natural Resource Development, University of Ghana, Box 59, Legon-Accra, Ghana.

Luz Estella Velásquez is Associate Professor and researcher at the Institute of Environmental Studies (IDEA), National University of Colombia, Manizales. She has also been closely involved in developing the Agenda 21 in Manizales. The chapter in this Reader is drawn from a longer report prepared as part of a research programme coordinated by the International Institute for Environment and Development, supported by the Swedish International Development Cooperation Agency (Sida). Address: Faculdad de Architectura, IDEA: Universidad Nacional Manizales, El Cable, Manizales, Colombia, email: bioluz@emtelsa.multi.net.co.

Acknowledgements

Many friends have helped in the preparation of this Reader, especially through commenting on the initial list of papers to be included and suggesting how they should be organized. Special thanks are due to Graham Haughton, Gordon McGranahan, Diana Mitlin, Yvonne Rydin and members of the Balaton Group. Special thanks too to Luz Stella Velásquez, Liliana Miranda, Michaela Hordijk and Maria Elena Foronda for their leadership in showing what local action rooted in participatory models can achieve. Also to my colleagues at IIED's Human Settlements Programme, Cecilia Tacoli, Jane Bicknell, Sheridan Bartlett (who is also with the Children's Environment Research Group) and, again, Diana Mitlin for their help. I am also grateful to my students at the Institute of Latin American Studies who helped in the selection of the literature included here and from whose questions and discussions I have learnt much. There is also, inevitably, a great intellectual debt to Jorge E. Hardoy, who directed IIED's Human Settlements Programme until his death in 1993 and to Barbara Ward, with whom I first worked on 'sustainable city' issues during the 1970s.

Thanks are also due to all the authors who allowed their work to be reprinted - and, where the originals were published in journals or books, to the publishers that permitted their reproduction. Special thanks are due to the Editors of *Urban Studies*, *The Journal of the American Planning Association* and *The Journal of Planning and Education Research* for allowing this, without charge – which helped to keep down the price of the Reader. Special thanks are also due to The World Health Organization, the UN Centre for Human Settlements and the UN Environment Programme for permitting extracts to be taken from their publications.

Special mention should also be made of the international agencies that support the work of IIED's Human Settlements Programme. The Swedish International Development Cooperation Agency (Sida) has long supported our work – and the case studies of Manizales and of the 'Cities for Life' Forum in Peru came from a work programme they funded which is reviewing innovative local agenda 21s. The European Commission also supports this work programme and the preparatory work for this programme was invaluable in helping to prepare this Reader. Thanks are also due to the UK Government's Department for International Development (DFID), the Dutch Government's Directorate-General for International Cooperation, the Swiss Agency for Development and Cooperation and Danish Cooperation for Environment and Development (DANCED) for their support of our work.

Earthscan staff also deserve special thanks, particularly Jonathan Sinclair Wilson for suggesting this Reader and Ruth Coleman and Paul Field for editing and preparing the manuscript. They also helped shape the Reader. Earthscan has been a most valuable and supportive part of our work; this is now the sixth Earthscan book that has come out of IIED's Human Settlements Programme since 1989 and these form such an essential part of our efforts to disseminate the findings of our work.

David Satterthwaite
Human Settlements Programme
International Institute for Environment and Development (IIED)
10 February 1999

Part I
Sustainable Cities:
An Introduction

Chapter 1

The Key Issues and the Works Included

David Satterthwaite

WHAT THE READER COVERS

The last five years have brought a considerable growth in the literature on how cities (or urban development in general) can be made compatible with sustainable development goals. This Reader brings together a diverse range of published articles and extracts from books which cover the key issues on this topic. It includes not only general works but also papers focusing on cities and environmental justice, health, transport, industry, agriculture, planning, designing with nature and waste management. The Reader includes case studies of cities with innovative sustainable development plans (usually called local agenda 21s – see Box 1.1) and papers discussing how best to assess, measure and monitor progress towards the achievement of sustainable development goals at city and national levels. It also has papers considering the ethical underpinnings of sustainable development and cities and how 'sustainable cities' need to be considered within a regional and global context.

Various factors influenced the choice of the pieces included in this Reader. The first was simply what I and those who I consulted find most interesting, stimulating and relevant. Other factors include: a desire to mix conceptual works with case studies; a need to cover as many of the key topics that fall within the theme of sustainable cities; and a desire to ensure strong coverage of regions and continents other than Europe and North America. It is surprising how many books on urban issues claim to have a world coverage and yet have so little material on Asia, Africa and Latin America, and so rarely draw on the rich and diverse urban literature by specialists from these regions.

This Reader has works that take different perspectives from my own research programme on 'sustainable development' and on 'sustainable cities'. It includes some which make points that I disagree with. It would seem inappropriate for any compiler of a Reader covering a subject as broad and important as this to include only works that reflect their own perspectives. However, as discussed in more detail below, the term sustainable development was taken to imply a simultaneous commitment to meeting human needs and to 'sustaining' or keeping intact environmental capital, so this Reader does not include works which choose to use the term sustainable development to mean other things.

The selection of works reproduced here was much helped by the suggestions of a wide range of people (whose help is acknowledged in the Preface), including the assessments of what the students taking a course I teach[1] on 'The City and

Box 1.1 *A guide to some of the acronyms and phrases used in this Reader*

Agenda 21: This is the most substantive document formally endorsed by all the government representatives attending the United Nations Conference on Environment and Development (UNCED) held in Rio de Janeiro in 1992; see Box 1.2 for more details about this and its link to local agenda 21.

Brundtland Commission: The term often given to the World Commission on Environment and Development since it was chaired by Gro Harlem Brundtland, former Prime Minister of Norway and now Director General of the World Health Organization. See 'Sustainable Development' below.

Ecological Footprints: A concept developed by William E Rees through which to make evident the large land area on whose production the inhabitants and businesses of any city depend for food, other renewable resources and the absorption of carbon to compensate for the carbon dioxide emitted from fossil fuel use. Many chapters use this concept while Box 20.7 has a summary of the concept.

Environmental capital: A term used interchangeably with natural capital – see below.

ICLEI: The International Council for Local Environmental Initiatives is an association of local governments dedicated to the prevention and solution of local, regional and global environmental problems through local action. Some 300 cities, towns, counties and their associations are members. ICLEI was launched in 1990 as the international environmental agency for local governments and has had a major role in helping to develop and implement the concept of local agenda 21s (see Box 1.2).[2]

IIED: The International Institute for Environment and Development, a non-profit policy research institute founded in 1971 which helped to develop the concept of sustainable development during the 1970s and which has sought to ensure that it is applied at local, regional, national and global levels ever since.[3]

Local Agenda 21: This is the name often given to sustainable development plans developed within particular cities or localities. The term Local Agenda 21 comes from Chapter 28 of Agenda 21, which was the principal output of the United Nations Conference on Environment and Development (UNCED). See Box 1.2 for more details.

Natural capital: Also termed environmental capital, this is the stock of natural assets which includes renewable resources (living species and ecosystems), non-renewable resources (for instance, fossil fuels) and the waste-assimilation capacities of ecosystems or of the whole planet. William E Rees describes and discusses natural capital in Chapter 2. It is also discussed in Donella Meadows' paper on indicators and information systems for sustainable development (Chapter 17).

Sustainable development: There is no agreement as to a definition but most agree with the World Commission on Environment and Development's 1987 definition that it is 'meeting the needs of the present without compromising the ability of future generations to meet their own needs'.[4] However, the term sustainable development was in use at least ten years earlier than this and the discussion of the need to join these two basic principles goes back at least to the early 1970s – for instance, in the books and articles of Barbara Ward, the founding President of IIED – the International Institute for Environment and Development (see note 17 at the end of this chapter for more details).

Box 1.1 *(continued)*

The South (and the North): 'The South' is a term widely used when there is a need to refer to all the low- and middle-income nations of Africa, Asia and Latin America and the Caribbean, in preference to the conventional United Nations terms of 'developing' or 'less-developed' countries. The term 'the North' came to be used for Europe, North America and high-income countries in Asia and Oceania, instead of the UN term 'developed countries'. Geographic inaccuracy (as many countries in 'the South' are in the Northern Hemisphere and as Australia and New Zealand are considered part of 'the North') is preferred to the UN terminology which implies that countries in Europe, North America and Australasia are superior ('developed') to other ('developing' or 'less developed') countries. The level of per capita income reached by countries is also rather a limited (and inaccurate) basis by which to classify countries as 'developed' and 'developing' (or less developed). An alternative would be to replace the term 'the South' with the 'non-industrialized' countries but this is also inaccurate as certain Asian and Latin American countries are among the world's major industrial producers and include some with higher proportions of their labour force in industry than North America and most European countries. However, there is such diversity within the countries in 'the South' that, where possible, generalizations about 'the South' are avoided.[5]

Third World: It encompasses the same group of countries as the term 'the South' – see above. The term is less widely used since the demise of the Soviet Union and other centrally planned economies (which were the Second World). Although the term 'Third World' is sometimes interpreted as having pejorative implications, its original use (especially by the non-aligned nations themselves) and its origins (the term based on 'the third estate' as they contained most of the world's population) never had this intention.

---

the Environment' have found useful. But there were limits to the length of this Reader. There are many fine and important works that I had hoped to include but that had to be left out, although hopefully the lists of Further Reading after Parts II, III, IV and V help to highlight these.

The Reader includes papers that focus on particular sectors that are important within 'sustainable development and cities' such as transport or industry, but the limits on length meant that only one work could be included within each sector. It is also perhaps inaccurate to characterize many of these as sectoral – for instance, as the paper on health by the World Health Organization stresses, 'creating healthy cities' is not about health programmes but about ensuring that all sectors include concerns for health. Other papers such as those on urban design, planning and indicators for sustainable development are also not sectoral but about how to ensure that the relevant intersectoral linkages are understood and acted on.

DEFINING THE BOUNDARIES FOR 'SUSTAINABLE DEVELOPMENT AND CITIES'

One of the difficulties in choosing literature for this Reader is knowing where to draw the boundaries. Virtually all work on sustainable development has relevance for cities, if sustainable development includes an interest in reducing ecological disruption or damage and protecting natural capital, given that a high proportion of the world's production, consumption and waste generation is concentrated in cities. In addition, all works on meeting human needs (including those focusing on poverty reduction) have relevance to the theme of this Reader, if sustainable development includes an interest in meeting human needs, since close to half the world's population and a large proportion of all poverty and the deprivation associated with it are concentrated in urban areas.[6]

It did not seem necessary to include in this Reader a paper on the scale of the world's urban population, but Table 1.1 is included to show the distribution of this population between different regions and each region's level of urbanization. It is a reminder of how much of the world's urban population is outside Europe and North America. For instance, although more than three-fifths of Asia's population may still be in rural areas, Asia now contains close to half the world's urban population. The scale and level of urbanization in Asia is also probably understated in Table 1.1 as some of the most populous Asian countries use definitions for urban centres that understate their urban populations.[7] By 1990, Asia also had 44 of the world's 100 largest cities.[8] Latin America now has a much larger urban population than North America and more of the world's 100 largest cities. Even Africa, which is generally perceived as so unurbanized, now has a larger urban population than North America. Table 1.1 also includes data on the regional distribution of the world's 100 largest cities in the years 1800 and 1900 to emphasize the point that, historically, Asia has always had a high proportion of the world's largest cities, and that South and Central America and North Africa have also long had large cities.[9]

However, as many papers in this Reader discuss, it is not so much the size of a country's urban population but the production structure and the consumption levels within urban areas and the quality of environmental management at city, regional and national level that affects the extent to which sustainable development goals are met in cities. In addition, although the growth rates of urban populations in Africa, Asia and Latin America or the rate of increase in their levels of urbanization are sometimes cited as a factor in their unsustainability, these growth rates are not unprecedented.[10] Many countries in the North had periods when their level of urbanization increased as rapidly.[11] In addition, many cities in North America figure among the world's fastest growing cities during the 20th century.[12] And some of the fastest growing cities in Latin America and Asia are also among those with among the best performance in meeting sustainable development goals.[13] Various papers in this Reader stress how a city's rapid growth or an increasingly urbanized population within a nation need not be incompatible with sustainable development goals and how urbanized populations bring important potential advantages for meeting human needs and reducing resource use and wastes (see especially Chapter 3).

In choosing literature for this Reader, there is also the problem that virtually all works on environmental problems in cities can be considered as relevant to the theme of sustainable cities. In addition, as most papers in this Reader emphasize, the key issue is not really 'sustainable cities' but cities whose built form, government structure, production systems, consumption patterns and waste generation and management systems are compatible with sustainable development goals for the city, its wider region and the whole biosphere.

There is also the difficulty of knowing what meaning to ascribe to the term sustainable development. As various papers in this collection discuss, many interpretations are given to the term, but the main differences in interpretation are not so

Table 1.1 *Some basic urban statistics*

	Urbanization level		Proportion of the world's urban population		Number of the world's 100 largest cities			
	1950	1995	1950	1995	1800	1900	1950	1990
Africa	14.7	34.4	4.5	9.7	4	2	3	7
Eastern Africa	5.3	21.7	0.5	1.9	0	0	0	0
Middle Africa	14.2	33.2	0.5	1.1	0	0	0	1
Northern Africa	24.7	45.9	1.8	2.9	3	2	2	5
Southern Africa	38.2	48.1	0.8	0.9	0	0	1	0
Western Africa	10.3	36.6	0.9	3.0	1	0	0	1
Americas	52.8	74.9	23.7	22.5	3	21	26	27
Caribbean	35.4	62.4	0.8	0.9	1	0	1	0
Central America	39.8	68.0	2.0	3.3	1	1	1	3
Northern America	63.9	76.3	14.4	8.6	0	16	18	13
South America	43.2	78.0	6.5	9.6	1	4	6	11
Asia	16.8	34.6	32.0	46.4	64	23	33	44
Eastern Asia	16.7	36.9	15.2	20.3	29	16	18	21
South-central Asia	16.6	28.8	13.7	15.4	24	5	9	13
South-eastern Asia	14.8	33.7	1.2	6.3	5	1	5	8
Western Asia	26.7	66.4	1.8	4.3	6	1	1	2
Europe	52.2	73.6	38.8	20.7	29	51	36	20
Eastern Europe	39.3	70.4	11.8	8.4	2	9	7	4
Northern Europe	72.7	83.7	7.7	3.0	6	16	6	2
Southern Europe	44.2	65.1	6.5	3.6	12	8	8	6
Western Europe	67.1	80.5	12.8	5.6	9	18	15	8
Oceania	61.6	70.3	1.1	0.8	0	2	2	2
World	29.3	45.2						

Source: The statistics for 1950 and 1995 were taken or derived from data in United Nations *World Urbanization Prospects: the 1994 Revision,* Population Division, New York, 1995. The data on the distribution of the world's 100 largest cities is taken from Satterthwaite, David, *The Scale and Nature of Urban Change in the South,* IIED, London, 1996, which drew on the IIED cities database that combines the data on city populations from 1950 to 1990 from United Nations 1995, op cit with recent and historic data drawn from around 250 censuses and from Chandler, Tertius and Gerald Fox, *3000 Years of Urban Growth,* Academic Press, New York and London, 1974

much in what is covered as in the extent to which emphasis is given to one or more of three aspects: meeting human needs; sustaining or keeping intact natural capital (including both natural resources and ecosystems) at local, regional and global level; and ensuring that human activities or values can be 'sustained' (for instance, as in discussions of economic or social 'sustainability').

Some works on sustainable development concentrate almost entirely on one of these three aspects. A review of the literature on sustainable development in 1992 commented that many works on sustainable development are about ecological sustainability, not development (in terms of meeting human needs)[14] and this is still true for many works published more recently. The paper in this Reader by Gordon McGranahan, Jacob Songsore and Marianne Kjellén highlights the difficulties and inconsistencies that arise if 'meeting human needs' are discussed only from an ecological sustainability perspective.

There are also many works whose interest in sustainability is not related to reducing ecological damage and avoiding the depletion of stocks of natural capital but to making sure that some human activity 'keeps going' or some building or form of infrastructure – for instance, a water supply system – keeps functioning. The interest of these works is in the social or institutional means to ensure these keep going – and mostly without a consideration of the environmental aspects of this. There is little in common between these and the works that concentrate on ecological sustainability.

Most of the works that use the term sustainable development for 'keeping human activities going' or infrastructure functioning come from international agencies. This can be seen as their appropriation of the term sustainable development to highlight the long-standing problem they face of ensuring that the projects they fund – for instance, the road, bridge, irrigation system, power station, water supply system – continue to function after the project is completed and their support ends. The concern of such agencies is largely about institutional structures within the recipient country that are able to manage and maintain the infrastructure. This problem of external agencies funding projects which rapidly deteriorate or cease to work soon after completion had been recognized long before the international agencies began using the term sustainable development to highlight the need to address this. It then became common for discussions of sustainable development at international conferences to proceed with no recognition that the term sustainable development was being used in two very different ways – by those concerned about environmental problems to mean ecological sustainability and by those from most development co-operation agencies to mean ensuring the projects they funded continued to function.

The two very different meanings given to the term sustainable development help explain the confusions and contradictions within some of the international declarations about sustainable development. For instance, consider the different implications that these two different meanings have for the link between sustainable development and economic growth. If sustainable development is taken to mean the institutional capacity to manage the maintenance and repair of, say, roads, water supplies, drains and power stations, then there are enormous potential complementarities between economic growth and sustainable development as wealthier enterprises (and hopefully households) can afford to pay more for well functioning and maintained infrastructure. But the nature of the relationship between sustainable development and economic growth is very different if sustainable development includes a concern for ecological sustainability.[15] This is especially so if the term sustainable development is being used only to mean ecological sustainability (ie with no component about meeting human needs).

This Reader takes as its reference point the Brundtland Commission's statement that sustainable development is about 'meeting the needs of the present without compromising the ability of future generations to meet their own needs'.[16] The two key principles within this statement were also the basis on which my own Institute, the International Institute for Environment and Development, was founded in 1971.[17] Thus, perhaps the single most important defining characteristic of the diverse works included here is their interest in combining 'the meeting of human needs' in cities with minimizing or halting the transfer of costs from city-based production, consumption or waste generation to other people or ecosystems, both now and in the future.

THE WORKS INCLUDED IN THE READER

The Context

The first work included in this Reader, William E Rees' paper on 'Achieving Sustainability: Reform or Transformation', is not specifically about cities. It was chosen because it summarizes so well the key sustainable development issues within which a consideration of sustainable cities must take place. As such, it helps to link debates about sustainable cities to the broader debates about sustainable development. The paper describes how many of the contradictions associated with sustainable development can be traced to differing fundamental beliefs and assumptions about the nature of the human-environment relationships. It highlights the differences between the 'expansionist' and the steady-state (ecological) worldviews. In the first, the assumption is made that getting the 'prices' right allows market forces to address any resource scarcities or ecological limits and that technological developments can allow substitutes to be developed for natural capital. In the second, there is a recognition that the economy is dependent on the ecosphere for energy and material resources and for breaking down or assimilating wastes and that many of this ecosphere's life-support services cannot be substituted by technological innovation. ('...only the foolhardy would trust in markets and technology to find substitutes for such eco-essentials as photosynthesis and climate regulation, the ozone layer and natural biodiversity' – pp 31–32). In addition, the paper points out that the ecosphere is a complex system whose behaviour is not governed by market forces but by evolutionary forces, complex systems dynamics and thermodynamic laws.

This paper is also valuable for any collection of works on sustainable cities because it exposes the reader to the ideas of authors who have been important in debates about sustainable development but who have not written much specifically about cities – for instance, the work of Herman E Daly. The tendency for debates about sustainable development and sustainable cities to develop independent of each other can be seen in the fact that so few authors have worked within both of these. William E Rees is one important exception to this.

It may surprise some people that William E Rees' 1992 paper on 'Ecological footprints and appropriated carrying capacity: what urban economics leaves out'[18] is not also included. But the reader will find him- or herself exposed to the key points made in this important paper since so many of the other works included here draw on it or on work developed from it – for instance, the book by Mathis Wackernagel and William E Rees entitled *Our Ecological Footprint – Reducing Human Impact on the Earth* (New Society Publishers, 1995). The last paper included in this Reader (pp 426–460) includes a summary of Rees' 1992 paper, while the paper by Herbert Giradet (pp 394–425) uses the conceptual basis suggested by Rees in describing London's ecological footprint.

David Satterthwaite

Linking Sustainable Development and Cities

This section opens with a short extract from *An Urbanizing World: Global Report on Human Settlements 1996*, the official UN report prepared for the 1996 UN Conference on Human Settlements (also called Habitat II or the City Summit). This emphasizes the potential advantages that cities have for addressing sustainable development goals. Although the concentration of people, enterprises and motor vehicles (and their wastes) in cities is often seen as 'a problem', high densities and large population concentrations also bring certain advantages for meeting human needs and for environmental management. These include lower costs per household and per enterprise for the provision of the infrastructure and services that minimize environmental hazards – for instance, systems for piped water supplies and the removal of household and human wastes – and that reduce or recycle wastes. The concentration of enterprises reduces the unit costs of enforcing environmental legislation, including regulatory agencies making regular checks on plant and equipment safety, as well as on occupational health and safety, pollution control and the handling of hazardous wastes. Cities with well-managed transport and land use policies should allow a high proportion of all people's trips to be made by walking, bicycling or public transport. The text also stresses how 'good governance' is at the centre of more effective responses and this includes key roles for city and municipal authorities, citizens and their community-based organizations and NGOs and the private sector.

Many other works in this Reader emphasize both the potential advantages of cities for the achievement of sustainable development goals and the extent to which 'good governance' is central to realizing this potential. This stress on the potential of cities is important in that so many general works on sustainable development see cities as 'the problem' and choose not to consider how urban development can be made compatible with sustainable development goals, despite the increasing concentration of the world's production and population in urban areas. The stress on governance is also important, not least because it shows that addressing sustainable development goals is not achieved simply by 'technical fixes'.

This extract from *An Urbanizing World* is followed by Graham Haughton's paper on 'Environmental Justice and the Sustainable City'. This considers how different policy approaches to sustainable cities address the five equity principles which are central to sustainable development – intergenerational and intragenerational equity, transfrontier responsibility (so environmental costs are not transferred across boundaries), interspecies equity and procedural equity. Procedural equity is needed to ensure that all people's legal rights to, among other things, a safe and healthy living and work environment are respected, that they are fairly treated and that they can engage in democratic decision-making processes about the management of the urban centre in which they live. This helps to clarify why conflicts can arise between different groups, each of which see themselves as committed to sustainable development but each with different priorities in regard to which of these equity principles they stress. For instance, those who give priority to improving environmental health in cities (often called the brown agenda) tend to emphasize intragenerational equity and procedural equity. Those who give priority to ecological sustainability (often called the green agenda) tend to emphasize intergenerational equity and transfrontier equity, while some emphasize interspecies equity.[19]

The paper on 'Environmental Justice and the Sustainable City' is followed by my own paper on 'Sustainable Cities or Cities that Contribute to Sustainable Development?' It was included because I thought it important to stress the different kinds of environmental problems that have to be addressed if sustainable development goals are to be met – ie:

- controlling infectious and parasitic diseases;
- reducing chemical and physical hazards within the home, workplace and wider city;
- achieving a high-quality city environment;
- minimizing the transfer of environmental costs to the inhabitants and ecosystems surrounding the city; and
- 'sustainable consumption' or minimizing the transfer of environmental costs to more distant people and ecosystems or into the future.

This paper seeks to outline the differences between these in terms of who is responsible for the problem, who is most affected by them, and how the problems can be addressed and by whom. It also discusses how these different environmental agendas fit within the economic, social and political goals of sustainable development.

After this a paper by Gordon McGranahan, Jacob Songsore and Marianne Kjellén shows how the primary environmental concerns of the most disadvantaged urban dwellers are not issues of 'sustainability' and how a stress on sustainability can mean inadequate attention to reducing poverty and eliminating the severe health hazards that so many low income urban dwellers face in Africa, Asia and Latin America. This paper also discusses how environmental problems differ between cities, according to their level of affluence, drawing on detailed empirical studies of household level environmental problems in Accra, Jakarta and São Paulo in which the authors were involved.[20]

Different Sectoral Programmes that Contribute to the Achievement of Sustainable Development Goals in Cities

It is obviously important for any discussion of sustainable cities to include a detailed discussion of health, transport, production, agriculture, urban design, urban planning and resource conservation and management. But it was also only possible to include one work on each of these large, important and complex subjects.

For health, the World Health Organization's paper on *Creating Healthy Cities in the 21st Century* was chosen because it summarizes so many of the key issues in regard to health in cities, but not only in terms of an absence of disease or injury but also in terms of well-being. It also includes strong sections on water and sanitation and urban air pollution and on the particular environmental problems that affect children and women in cities.

For transport, Peter Newman's paper on 'Reducing Automobile Dependence' was included in part because this goes to the core of one of the most difficult issues for sustainable cities – how to reduce automobile dependence in wealthy cities – in part because of its broad perspective as it discusses transport issues in a great variety of cities in all the world's regions. This paper also includes short case studies of cities that have sought to reduce automobile dependence in Asia, Latin America, Europe, North America and Australia.

For the piece on production structures, I had to cheat a little and persuade Nick Robins and Ritu Kumar to write the paper reproduced in this Reader on 'Producing,

Providing, Trading: Manufacturing Industry and Sustainable Cities'. Readers are meant to bring together and reproduce works that have been already published, but no paper could be found that discussed the urban dimensions of production, including the role of companies, local authorities and national governments, with an interest in both the North and the South. As this paper describes, most discussions of sustainable industrial development have not been linked to considerations of urban development, as if such development can be pursued free of context and location. This paper also goes beyond the discussion of 'clean production' to consider what sustainable development goals imply for industry's sourcing of raw material inputs and for products (including the environmental implications of their use and disposal).

For urban design, a chapter on this topic from Joan Roelofs' book on *Greening Cities: Building Just and Sustainable Communities* is included not only because this covers the issue but also because it will encourage the reader to go to the book from which it is drawn and benefit from its coverage of other aspects of 'Green Cities'.[21] This chapter is also a reminder of the historic roots of discussions of green cities (a subject that perhaps deserves more attention than it is given in this Reader) and of the innovation shown by many households and enterprises in Europe and North America towards production and consumption patterns that are more compatible with the goals of sustainable development.

For urban planning, Scott Campbell's paper on 'Green Cities, Growing Cities, Just Cities? Urban Planning and the Contradiction of Sustainable Development' was chosen because it discusses the core dilemma for any urban planner – how to reconcile the need for all urban centres to have prosperous economies, an equitable distribution of the benefits of this prosperity and protection of the environment (within the urban centre and with regard to environmental cost transfers). The paper also recognizes the limited 'room for manoeuvre' that planners inevitably have and stresses their role in assisting groups with different perspectives to understand other groups' perspectives and priorities. As the paper notes, 'All too often, the economists speak of incentives and marginal rates, the ecologists speak of carrying capacity and biodiversity, the advocate planners speak of housing rights, empowerment and discrimination and each accuses the others of being "out of touch"' (p 264). The paper also reveals the difficulties in narrowing the gap between theory and practice as it stresses how using terms such as sustainable planning or sustainable zoning do not necessarily imply that one knows what these mean.

For urban agriculture, although there is a large and rapidly growing literature, few people bring the depth and range of experience in this of Jac Smit and Joe Nasr of the Urban Agriculture Network. I also hope that their paper on 'Urban Agriculture for Sustainable Cities: Using Wastes and Idle Land and Water Bodies as Resources' will encourage the reader to go on to the book these two authors subsequently wrote with Annu Ratta on *Urban Agriculture: Food, Jobs and Sustainable Cities.*[22]

For resource conservation and waste management, a second extract from *An Urbanizing World: The Global Report on Human Settlements 1996* is included as this summarizes the range of opportunities for resource conservation and waste reduction in urban areas, especially in the more affluent ones. It also discusses the potential economic benefits of a transition to more resource-efficient cities, including the employment-generating benefits. It also discusses the shift in thinking from waste management to recognizing wastes as resources and how waste minimization can be a key part of waste management.

Seeking Action at City Level

This section had to include material on Local Agenda 21 for two reasons. First, virtually all the world's governments committed themselves to implementing local agenda 21s at the UN Conference on Environment and Development in Rio de Janeiro in 1992. These are meant to be the means by which each locality (including each city and town) develops its own sustainable development plan (see Box 1.2 for more details). But this is not a sufficient reason in that governments have been making commitments on key environment and development issues at international conferences since the 1972 UN Conference on the Human Environment in Stockholm and then ignoring them. It makes for depressing reading to go back to the declarations and commitments made by governments at United Nations Conferences held during the 1970s and 1980s and to see how little progress has been made in many of them. To give but one example, if commitments made by governments during the 1970s in regard to water and sanitation had been fulfilled, virtually all the world's population would have had adequate provision by 1990; the WHO paper in Chapter 7 describes just how large the shortfalls in provision remain. But the second reason for giving attention to Local Agenda 21 is the evidence of innovation in developing such local agendas among many urban areas. There are many examples of cities where

---

Box 1.2 *Local Agenda 21*

The term 'Local Agenda 21' is used so frequently in this Reader that it deserves some introduction. Those who use it sometimes forget to explain what it means; one city official was recently heard to ask, 'If we are now on to Local Agenda 21, what happened to the previous 20 local agendas?'[23]

The term Local Agenda 21 comes out of Agenda 21, which was the principal output of the United Nations Conference on Environment and Development (UNCED), which was also known as the Earth Summit. Agenda 21 was intended as 'an action plan for the 1990s and well into the 21st Century'.[24] Among its 40 chapters are many that are particularly pertinent to sustainable cities, including those on combating poverty (Chapter 3), changing consumption patterns (Chapter 4), protecting and promoting human health (Chapter 6), promoting sustainable human settlements development (Chapter 7), and environmentally sound management of toxic chemicals, hazardous wastes, and solid wastes and sewage-related issues (Chapters 19, 20 and 21).

Local Agenda 21 comes from Chapter 28 entitled 'Local Authorities' Initiatives in Support of Agenda 21' and it states why local governments have such an important role in implementing Agenda 21:

Because so many of the problems and solutions being addressed by Agenda 21 have their roots in local activities, the participation and cooperation of local authorities will be a determining factor in fulfilling its objectives. Local authorities construct, operate and maintain economic, social and environmental infrastructure, oversee planning processes, establish local environmental policies and regulations and assist in implementing national and sub-national environmental policies. As the level of governance closest to the people, they play a vital role in educating, mobilizing and responding to the public to promote sustainable development (28.1).

Box 1.2 *Continued*

Chapter 28 lists four objectives:

a   By 1996, most local authorities in each country should have undertaken a consultative process with their populations and achieved a consensus on 'a local Agenda 21'.
b   By 1993, the international community should have initiated a consultative process aimed at increasing cooperation between local authorities.
c   By 1994, representatives of associations of cities and other local authorities should have increased cooperation and coordination to enhance the exchange of experience and information between them.
d   All local authorities should be encouraged to implement and monitor programmes which aim to ensure that women and youth are represented in decision-making, planning and implementation processes.

The goals of Chapter 28 are not so much on what local agenda 21s should include but on how they should be organized, especially the local consultation processes to ensure that all groups are involved and that the key environment and development issues outlined in other chapters of Agenda 21 are brought down to local level.

Sources: Robinson, Nicholas A (ed), *Agenda 21: Earth's Action Plan*, Oceania, New York, London, 1993 and Lafferty, William M and Katarina Eckerberg (eds), *From the Earth Summit to Local Agenda 21: Working Towards Sustainable Development*, Earthscan, London, 1998

---

innovative local agenda 21s have been developed and within this are many of the most interesting examples of cities trying to move towards the achievement of sustainable development goals. However, as discussed in more detail below, much of this innovation is a result of local initiatives, not national initiatives – and in many instances, local non-governmental initiatives.

It was difficult to choose which papers to include in this Reader about Local Agenda 21. This section had to include a strong case study of an innovative Local Agenda 21 and although there are more examples of innovation in Europe than any other region, the case of Manizales in Colombia by Luz Estella Velásquez was chosen. One reason for this is that it is a particularly interesting case study of how a Local Agenda 21 was developed and became integrated into the municipal development plan and budget. Another reason is that it also shows the importance of the national context for supporting innovation at city level – in this instance, the importance of democratization, decentralization and other national level changes which have provided more scope for local government initiatives in Colombia. The paper on 'Let us build cities for life: the national campaign of Local Agenda 21s in Peru' by Liliana Miranda and Michaela Hordijk was chosen because it describes a national initiative that brought together the efforts of many different groups to support the development of local agenda 21s in a wide range of urban centres. It also helps to highlight the political dimensions of the changes needed for cities to move towards sustainable development goals and the extent to which it must ensure that national frameworks allow a lot of scope for local initiatives and actions.

The above papers include a strong focus on participation. So, implicitly or explicitly, do most of the other papers in this Reader, and it is a central theme of the paper by Scott Campbell. It is difficult to see how 'human needs' will be met for lower income groups (or for other groups whose needs are ignored or who face discrimination) without participation in the sense of political systems which respect their rights and ensure that their demands receive the attention they deserve.

I would have liked to include some works in this Reader that focus specifically on this theme – for instance, Mike Douglass' 1992 paper on 'The political economy of urban poverty and environmental management in Asia[25] or his 1994 paper written with Malia Zoghlin on 'Sustaining cities are the grassroots' which included a case study from Bangkok.[26] There is also the fascinating case study from Mexico City on how illegal settlers sought to justify their land occupation through the promotion of an urban development model that was 'socially necessary, ecologically sound and economically viable' – in Keith Pezzoli's book *Human Settlements and Planning for Ecological Sustainability: The Case of Mexico City.*[27] There are also some important new case studies of community-level local agenda 21s – for instance, Michaela Hordijk's case study of the development of a Local Agenda 21 in Pampas, a low-income community in Lima, Peru, and a case study of the Local Agenda 21 developed in Olivares, the lowest income district (*comuna*) of Manizales by Luz Stella Velásquez (also the author of the case study of Manizales in Chapter 14).[28] But these do not fit easily in any existing section. While I would have liked to add another section to this Reader on 'Seeking action at community level', the Reader was already too long without such a section.

This section on 'Seeking Action at City Level' had to have good coverage of indicators for sustainable development. The case study of Manizales is also interesting on this subject for the decentralized monitoring system that has been developed for each of Manizales' 11 *comunas* to track progress in social conditions, community involvement, natural resource use, energy efficiency and waste management. The paper also describes the means for ensuring community involvement in the development of the indicators and their measurement and interpretation. The case study of Seattle in the USA by Alan AtKisson is included because of the innovation shown in developing sustainable development indicators through a public process that sought to involve all facets of civil society. The paper by Jeb Brugmann was chosen because it stresses how sustainable development indicators have to be built into the official planning process if they are to be effective. This paper critically reviews the experience in Seattle and contrasts this with examples from the state of Oregon and the city of Santa Monica in the US where the development of indicators was more fully integrated into local government plans and activities. But to provide a more general discussion of indicators for sustainable development, a work whose focus is broader than sustainable cities was chosen – an extract from *Indicators and Information Systems for Sustainable Development* by Donella Meadows. This was included because discussions of indicators for cities have to be considered within the broader sustainable development context, otherwise the indicators fail to consider the environmental impacts of the production and consumption concentrated in cities on people and ecosystems outside cities, both now and in the future. The extract was also chosen because the starting point of the document from which it is drawn is not indicators but why indicators are needed and what kind of information system indicators are meant to serve.

The extract by Donella Meadows describes a framework for sustainable development indicators which considers the ways in which natural capital (the stocks and flows in nature – 'ultimate means' since all life and economic transactions depend on this) are drawn on by 'built capital' (the production structure which produces economic output) and 'human and social capital' (which includes knowledge, wealth, health, trust, fair and democratic political and legal systems...) to address well-being ('ultimate ends' which includes happiness, fulfilment, self-respect...). Most economic and social indicators concentrate only on built capital and human and social capital. Sustainable development is a call to expand the economic calculus to include natural capital and to ensure that well-being is the ultimate end rather than 'adequate' per capita incomes or levels of consumption which are necessary but not sufficient conditions for well-being. The extract stresses how the three most basic aggregate measures of sustainable development are the sufficiency with which well-being ('ultimate ends') are realized for all people, the efficiency with which natural capital ('ultimate means') are translated into ultimate ends and the sustainability of the use of natural capital.

I had hoped to include in this section another paper by Graham Haughton which reviews the many different tools and methods available to urban authorities who commit themselves to better meeting sustainable development goals.[29] But the Reader was already too long. The section on Further Reading at the end of Part IV has some suggestions on this.

Sustainable Development for Cities Within a Regional, National and Global Context

Choosing papers for this section was difficult because there are various important and interesting case studies of particular city-region interactions but few international overviews. One solution would have been to include several case studies from different regions of the world, but there was not enough room for this. In the end, just two works were chosen. The first is Herbert Giradet's paper on 'Sustainable Cities: A Contradiction in Terms?' as it looks at London's large and international ecological footprint. The second is a chapter from a book I co-authored with Jorge E Hardoy and Diana Mitlin on 'The rural, regional and global impacts of cities in Africa, Asia and Latin America'.[30] Compilers of Readers should perhaps be more modest about including works to which they contributed, but I could find no other international overview of this subject (that is so central to the theme of sustainable cities) which gave sufficient attention to Africa, Asia and Latin America (which now contain most of the world's urban population). This chapter is also useful for a Reader in that it includes summaries of some of the most interesting case studies of city-region interactions – for instance:

- Mike Douglass' paper on 'The environmental sustainability of development – coordination, incentives and political will in land use planning for the Jakarta metropolis';[31]
- A World Bank study of *Towards a Sustainable Urban Environment: The Rio de Janeiro Study;*[32] and
- Philip F Kelly's paper on 'The politics of urban-rural relationships: land conversion in the Philippines'.[33]

This chapter also includes a summary of William E Rees' paper on 'Ecological footprints and appropriated carrying capacity – what urban economics leaves out'.[34]

I would have liked to include another subsection in this Reader on national frameworks to support moves by city authorities and other groups towards better meeting sustainable development goals. There is some discussion of this in the papers included, especially in the papers by William E Rees, Donella Meadows and Nick Robins and Rita Kumar. The paper by Liliana Miranda and Michaela Hordijk describes the kind of national movement needed to support the development of local agenda 21s.

If Earthscan had allowed me to flout even more the length limits to this Reader, I would have liked to include extracts of *From the Earth Summit to Local Agenda 21: Working Towards Sustainable Development* edited by William M Lafferty and Katarina

---

Box 1.3 *The most significant factors affecting the implementation of Local Agenda 21 in eight European countries*

A review of the experience with Local Agenda 21 in eight European countries (Finland, Sweden, Norway, Germany, Austria, the Netherlands, the United Kingdom and Ireland) suggests that each of the factors listed below appears to have had positive effects on Local Agenda 21 implementation. Any combination of factors should have a cumulative positive effect.

- A previous involvement on the part of representatives of local authorities in the process of the 1992 UN Conference on Environment and Development (the Earth Summit).
- An active positive attitude on the part of responsible central government officials to the Local Agenda 21 idea.
- Central government initiatives and campaigns to disseminate information on Local Agenda 21.
- The availability of central government financial resources to subsidize Local Agenda 21 initiatives.
- Enough local government autonomy to render the Local Agenda 21 idea interesting and possible.
- Membership in cross-national environment-and-development alliances and charters – for instance, the European Campaign of Sustainable Cities and Towns.[37]
- A previous history of international 'solidarity' orientations and activities at the local level.
- Previous municipal involvement in environmental and sustainable development pilot projects.
- Previous experience with 'co-operative management regimes' (among social partners and stakeholders such as the important role of various NGOs in Sweden, the Netherlands and the UK).
- Active individual 'firebrands' for Local Agenda 21 at the local level.
- Perceived possibilities for coupling Local Agenda 21 with the creation of new jobs.
- Perceived conditions of 'threat' to local environment-and-development conditions from external sources.

(NB This review also highlights the difficulties in making cross-country comparisons and the many factors, particular to each country, which influenced the extent of Local Agenda 21 development.)

Source: Eckerberg, Katarina and William M Lafferty, 'Conclusions: comparative perspectives on evaluation and explanation', in Lafferty, William M and Katarina Eckerberg (eds), *From the Earth Summit to Local Agenda 21: Working Towards Sustainable Development*, Earthscan, London, 1998, pp 238–262.

Eckerberg[35] with its assessments of progress in the development of local agenda 21s in eight different European countries. Box 1.3 presents a list of some of the most significant factors affecting the implementation of local agenda 21s in these countries. The International Council for Local Environmental Initiatives also has an interesting study on National Obstacles to Local Agenda 21.[36]

The list in Box 1.3 helps to stimulate a consideration of what conditions within nations and cities help to encourage the development of local agenda 21s. Some of the points mentioned in this Box are relevant to the development of some of the local agenda 21s in Latin America – for instance, 'perceived conditions of threat to local environment-and-development conditions from external sources' were important for the Local Agenda 21 in Ilo (Peru) with the high level of contamination caused by the Southern Peru Copper Corporation[38] and in Chimbote (Peru) from a steel processing firm and also from local fishmeal processing industries.[39] 'Enough local government autonomy' was also important, and also for the case of Manizales included in this Reader. Other factors identified as important for supporting the implementation of local agenda 21s in the eight European nations are obviously important in other nations – for instance, a well-established environmental policy at national or regional level. The European study also points to how the limited power and resources available to local authorities in the UK helped to encourage local authority partnerships with community organizations, NGOs and local business; this also appears as a factor important in encouraging multistakeholder partnerships in some local agenda 21s outside Europe. But care is also needed in assuming that the factors listed in Box 1.3 are necessarily relevant or among the most significant factors in other countries. When considered in relation to innovation in local agenda 21s in Latin America (or to forms of environmental management which address some of the main issues within local agenda 21s), the importance of decentralization and democratic reform at municipal level (and, for many countries, a return to democracy at national level) need to be stressed. The paper included in this Reader about the National Campaign for Local Agenda 21s in Peru also shows how it need not be a national government body that serves as the catalyst and supporter of local agenda 21s within urban authorities.

How Useful is this Volume?

If this Reader proves popular, Earthscan, the publishers, will be encouraged to publish an updated edition at some point in the future. It would be very valuable to receive readers' assessments of this volume, including which works they found useful and those which were of less interest. It would also be very useful to receive suggestions for works that should have been included or deserve inclusion in a new edition. Comments can be sent to David Satterthwaite, Human Settlements Programme, International Institute for Environment and Development, 3 Endsleigh Street, London WC1H ODD, UK, e-mail: david@iied.org

NOTES AND REFERENCES

1   I teach a course on The City and the Environment within a masters programme at the Institute of Latin American Studies, University of London, and the selection of papers here has been much helped by what the course participants have found useful

2   For more details, see http://www.iclei.org./about.htm

3   For more details, write to IIED, 3 Endsleigh Street, London WC1H ODD, UK, or see its web page: http://www.iied.org

4   World Commission on Environment and Development, *Our Common Future*, Oxford University Press, 1987, p 8

5   For a discussion of the implications that this invention of a single category for such a large and diverse range of countries and cultures has had, along with a critique of other terms and concepts that are used within 'development', see Escobar, Arturo *Encountering Development: The Making and Unmaking of the Third World*, Princeton Studies in Culture/Power/History, Princeton University Press, Princeton, New Jersey, 1995

6   For a discussion as to why global estimates of urban poverty have greatly underestimated the scale and the extent of deprivation in urban areas of Africa, Asia and Latin America, see Satterthwaite, David, 'Urban poverty: Reconsidering its scale and nature', *IDS Bulletin*, Vol 28, No 2, April 1997, pp 9–23. See also Wratten, Ellen, 'Conceptualizing urban poverty', *Environment and Urbanization*, Vol 7, No 1, April 1995, pp 11–36

7   For instance, China has a large population living in 'rural' settlements which are of a size, population and economic base that would make them qualify for classification as urban centres in virtually all other countries. See UNCHS (Habitat), *An Urbanizing World: Global Report on Human Settlements 1996*, Oxford University Press, Oxford and New York, 1996; also Satterthwaite, David, *The Scale and Nature of Urban Change in the South*, IIED, London, 1996

8   Although estimates or projections for individual city populations for 1995 and 2000 are available, the fact that very few countries have had a census since 1990 or 1991 make these speculative

9   See, for instance, Chandler, Tertius and Gerald Fox, *3000 Years of Urban Growth*, Academic Press, New York and London, 1974; also Bairoch, Paul, *Cities and Economic Development: From the Dawn of History to the Present*, Mansell, London, 1988

10   Preston, Samuel H, 'Urban growth in developing countries: a demographic reappraisal', *Population and Development Review*, Vol 5, No 2, 1979, pp 195–215 stressed this and other points in regard to the rate of urban change in the South not being unprecedented. Satterthwaite 1996 (op cit) reviewed the evidence from the many censuses held between 1979 and 1993 and these supported the points made by Preston's 1979 paper and also showed how much the annual average growth rates of many of the South's largest cities had dropped during the 1980s

11   Preston 1979, Satterthwaite 1996, UNCHS 1996, op cit

12   Satterthwaite 1996, op cit

13   For instance, Curitiba in Brazil, which is often cited as one of main success stories in good environmental management, is one of the world's fastest growing cities in recent decades. So too in Porto Alegre, also in Brazil. For a case study of Curitiba, see Rabinovitch, Jonas, 'Curitiba: towards sustainable urban development', *Environment and Urbanization*, Vol 4, No 2, October 1992, pp 62–77. For a case study of Porto Alegre, Menegat, Rualdo, 'Environmental management in Porto Alegre', *Environment and Urbanization*, Vol 11, No 2, 1999

14   Mitlin, Diana, 'Sustainable development: a guide to the literature', *Environment and Urbanization*, Vol 4, No 1, April 1992, pp 111–124

15   There is some further discussion on this in the final section of the paper on 'Sustainable Cities or Cities that Contribute to Sustainable Development?' in Part II. See also Mitlin, Diana and David Satterthwaite, 'Sustainable development and cities', in Cedric Pugh (ed), *Sustainability, the Environment and Urbanization*, Earthscan Publications, London, 1996, pp 23–61 and Brugmann, Jeb, 'Is there a method in our measurement? The use of indicators in local sustainable development planning' (Chapter 18)

16   World Commission on Environment and Development, *Our Common Future*, Oxford University Press, 1987, p 8

17   The principles on which IIED was founded in 1971 were very similar to the Brundtland Commission's definition. The conceptual underpinnings of sustainable development were widely discussed and described in the early 1970s and possibly earlier. The term sustainable development arose primarily to acknowledge the development needs of low-income groups and low income countries within the growing interest in local, national and global environmental issues in the North and the understanding of the international dimensions of environmentalism. The need to reconcile these two aspects was widely discussed before and during the UN Conference on the

Human Environment at Stockholm in 1972, even if this was not called sustainable development at that time. The Brundtland Commission's stress on 'meeting the needs of the present without compromising the ability of future generations to meet their own needs' had been a central theme in the writings of Barbara Ward (IIED's first President) throughout the 1970s, although this was usually phrased as meeting the 'inner limits' of human needs and rights without exceeding the 'outer limits' of the planet's ability to sustain life, now and in the future. See, for instance, *The Cocoyoc Declaration* adopted by the participants of the UNEP/UNCTAD symposium on 'Pattern of Resource Use, Environment and Development Strategies' in 1974 that was drafted by Barbara Ward and republished in *World Development*, Vol 3, Nos 2 and 3, February–March 1975. See also Ward, Barbara and René Dubos, *Only One Earth: The Care and Maintenance of a Small Planet*, André Deutsch, London, 1992, Ward, Barbara, 'The inner and the outer limits', The Clifford Clark Memorial Lectures 1976, *Canadian Public Administration*, Vol 19, No 3, Autumn 1976, pp 385–416, and Ward, Barbara, *Progress for a Small Planet*, Penguin, 1979, subsequently republished by Earthscan Publications, London

18 Published in *Environment and Urbanization* Vol 4, No 2, 1992, pp 121–130
19 See McGranahan, Gordon and David Satterthwaite, 'Environmental Health or Ecological Sustainability? Reconciling the Brown and Green Agendas in Urban Development' in Cedric Pugh (ed), *Sustainability in Cities in Developing Countries: Theories and Practice at the Millennium*, Earthscan Publications, 1999
20 These include: Songsore, Jacob, *Review of Household Environmental Problems in the Accra Metropolitan Area, Ghana*, Working Paper, Stockholm Environment Institute, Stockholm, 1992; Songsore, Jacob and Gordon McGranahan, *Women and Household Environmental Care in the Greater Accra Metropolitan Area (GAMA), Ghana*, Urban Environment Series Report No 2, Stockholm Environment Institute in collaboration with Sida, Stockholm, 1996; Jacobi, Pedro, *Environmental Problems Facing the Urban Household in the City of São Paulo, Brazil*, Stockholm Environment Institute, Stockholm, 1995; Surjadi, Charles, L Padhmasutra, D Wahyuninsih, G McGranahan and M Kjellén, *Household Environmental Problems in Jakarta*, Stockholm Environment Institute, Stockholm, 1994; and Songsore, Jacob, John S Nabila, A T Amuzu, K A Tutu, Yvon Yangyuoru, Gordon McGranahan and Marianne Kjellén, *Proxy Indicators for Rapid Assessment of Environmental Health Status in Residential Areas: the Case of the Greater Accra Metropolitan Area (GAMA)*, Urban Environment Series Report No 4, Stockholm Environment Institute in collaboration with Sida, Stockholm, 1998. Summary papers have also been published in *Environment, Environment and Urbanization* and *World Development*. For further details, write to Stockholm Environment Institute, Lilla Nygatan, Box 2142, 103 14 Stockholm, Sweden
21 Roelofs, Joan, *Greening Cities: Building Just and Sustainable Communities*, The Bootstrap Press, New York, 1996
22 Smit, Jac, Annu Ratta and Joe Nasr, *Urban Agriculture: Food, Jobs and Sustainable Cities*, Publication Series for Habitat II, Volume One, UNDP, New York, 1996
23 Liliana Miranda, one of the authors of Chapter 15, told me of this comment
24 Robinson, Nicholas A (ed), *Agenda 21: Earth's Action Plan*, Oceania, New York, London, 1993, p xx
25 This was published in *Environment and Urbanization*, Vol 4, No 2, 1992, pp 9–32
26 This was published in *Third World Planning Review*, Vol 16, No 2, pp 171–200
27 Published by the MIT Press, 1998
28 Hordijk, Michaela, 'A dream of green and water: Community-based formulation of a Local Agenda 21 in peri-urban Lima, Peru', *Environment and Urbanization*, Vol 11, No 2, October 1999. Luz Stella Velásquez's study of Olivares is also to be published in this issue
29 Haughton, Graham, 'Key policy domains for improving the urban environment', *Environment and Urbanization*, Vol 11, No 2, October 1999
30 Chapter 4 of *Environmental Problems in Third World Cities* published by Earthscan in 1992. The text is drawn from a revised and updated version of the original Chapter 4 which will be within a new edition of this book that Earthscan will publish in 2000
31 Douglass, Mike, 'The environmental sustainability of development – coordination, incentives and political will in land use planning for the Jakarta metropolis', *Third World Planning Review*, Vol 11, No 2, 1989, pp 211–238

32   Kreimer, Alcira, Thereza Lobo, Braz Menezes, Mohan Munasinghe and Ronald Parker (eds), *Towards a Sustainable Urban Environment: The Rio de Janeiro Study*, World Bank Discussion Papers No 195, World Bank, Washington DC, 1993

33   Kelly, Philip F, 'The politics of urban-rural relationships: land conversion in the Philippines'*Environment and Urbanization*, Vol 10, No 1, 1998, pp 35–54

34   Rees, William E, 'Ecological footprints and appropriated carrying capacity – what urban economics leaves out' *Environment and Urbanization*, Vol 4, No 2, October 1992, pp 121–130

35   Earthscan Publications, London, 1998

36   ICLEI, *Study on National Obstacles to Local Agenda 21*, International Council for Local Environmental Initiatives (ICLEI) and CAG Consultants in collaboration with the UNDESA Division for Sustainable Development, Background Paper No 31, DESA/DSD/1998/31, 98–10870 for the Sixth Session of the UN Commission on Sustainable Development held 20 April-1 May 1998, New York, 1998

37   A campaign launched at the First European Conference on Sustainable Cities and Towns which took place in Aalborg, Denmark, in 1994. The Conference was jointly convened by the city of Aalborg and the European Commission, and prepared by ICLEI (the International Council for Local Environmental Initiatives). The Charter of European Cities and Towns Towards Sustainability (also known as the Aalborg Charter) was signed at the Conference by 80 European local authorities (to date over 380 local authorities have signed it) and this commits them to drawing up and implementing long-term action plans towards sustainability, notably through Local Agenda 21 processes. The campaign seeks to support European local authorities in the development and implementation of Local Agenda 21 and similar processes. For more details, see http://www.sustainable-cities.org and http://www.iclei.org./la21/eurola21.htm#1section

38   Díaz, Doris Balvin, José Luis López Follegatti and Michaela Hordijk, 'Innovative urban environmental management in Ilo, Peru', *Environment and Urbanization*, Vol 8, No 1, April 1996, pp 21–34

39   Foronda F, Maria Elena, 'Chimbote's Local Agenda 21: initiatives to support its development and implementation', *Environment and Urbanization*, Vol 10, No 2, Oc tober 1998, pp 129–147

Chapter 2

Achieving Sustainability:
Reform or Transformation?

William E Rees

(From *Journal of Planning Literature,* Vol 9, No 4, May 1995, pp 343–361. Reprinted by permission of Sage Publications, Inc.)

Summary: We have reached a unique juncture in human ecological history, one requiring a radical reconfiguration of planning values and goals. The 'ecological footprint' of the global economy is already larger than the planet, yet a quarter of humanity still lives in proverty, the human family is expanding by 90 million a year, and material demands everywhere are rising. An unlikely tenfold reduction in the energy and intensity of economic activity would be required to accommodate anticipated economic growth safely, posing an enormous challenge to planners in facilitating the transition to sustainability. Failure enhances the considerable possibility of global disaster.

INTRODUCING THE CONUNDRUM

The modern era might be described as a global techno/economic hegemony in which humanity's material purpose has become its only purpose. Indeed, some observers argue that modern technology 'has become totalizing, one dimensional, planetary, and terrifyingly normalizing...' and that the resultant ascendancy of 'acquisitive man' or 'economic man' (*Homo oeconomicus*), whose ethos is rooted in 'growthmania and... conspicuous consumption,' has become the distinguishing feature of our age (Jung and Jung 1993, p 86).

This is strong language. Yet it is increasingly difficult to argue with at least one major consequence of the situation as described: humankind, thoroughly alienated from nature, is set on an unsustainable course which certainly degrades the natural 'environment' and which could plausibly end with the ecological razing of the Earth. As Terry Barker (1994) points out, this sobering conclusion 'is not that of a "deep green" minority. It is the scientific, political, and economic consensus as expressed by the UN Intergovernmental Panel on Climate Change, The Brundtland Report, the [UN] Conference on Environment and Development in Rio de Janeiro, the Business Council for Sustainable Development, and the World Resources Institute' (p 1).

The Changing Global Context

> Humanity stands at a defining moment in history. (Preamble, *Agenda 21*,
> United Nations, 1992)

Because of its exponential population growth, humankind has gone in just a few decades from playing a bit part to becoming the major player on the world's ecological stage. The four- to fivefold increase in world economic activity since the Second World War has produced an unprecedented level of material and energy exchange between the ecosphere and the human economic subsystem. As a result, humankind is now a major consumer species in all the significant ecosystems of the world. The human enterprise already appropriates or otherwise diverts 40 per cent of terrestrial and 25 per cent of coastal marine photosynthesis to its own use and the economic demand for non-renewable energy and material commodities is rising apace (Vitousek et al 1986). Of course, the laws of energy conservation and mass balance dictate that the entire energy and material flux through the human economy must return in altered form – as pollution and waste – to the ecosphere. The sheer volume of these human-induced flows is accelerating the deterioration of major ecosystems and is now capable of seriously disrupting global life-support functions essential to the maintenance of life itself.

A growing number of ecologists and ecologically minded economists interpret the seeming convergence of the economy with the ecosphere as implying a new type of constraint on economic expansion. Such symptoms as ozone depletion, atmospheric change, global deforestation and rising extinction rates have convinced these analysts that 'current *throughput* growth in the global economy cannot be sustained' (Goodland 1991, p 15, emphasis added). Herman Daly (1991a) argues that this new reality requires a perceptual transition from 'empty-world to full-world economics,' (p 29) a shift which he terms 'an historical turning point in economic development' (p 29). Similarly, Caldwell (1990) argues that 'the world is passing through a (*sic*) historical discontinuity' (p 191) requiring a reorientation of previous goals and values and a radical reconfiguration of the way people relate to the Earth.

Meanwhile, millions have yet to benefit from the old ways. Despite surging growth in the newly industrializing countries, humanity remains 'confronted with a perpetuation of disparities within and between nations, a worsening of poverty, [continuing] ill health and illiteracy' (Quarrie1992, p 47) and a population growing at 90 million per year. In response to this continuing poverty and inequity, *Agenda 21*, the far-reaching accord on sustainable development reached at the UN's 1992 Earth Summit in Rio de Janeiro, ostensibly launched humanity on 'a global partnership for sustainable development' designed to achieve 'the fulfillment of basic needs, improved living standards for all, better protected and managed ecosystems, and a safer, more prosperous future' (Quarrie, p 47). Of course, the goals of *Agenda 21* themselves reflect the contradiction many see in the term 'sustainable development' – how can we produce the growth deemed necessary to '[improve] living standards for all' and provide a 'more prosperous future' while simultaneously protecting ecosystems, when historic patterns of material growth seem responsible for present unsustainable levels of ecological disintegration?

William E Rees

Purpose and Premises

This paper examines the sustainability debate with the intent of clarifying for planners some of the more controversial environment-economy conundrums. I start from the premise that with the onset of human-induced global change we have, in fact, reached a unique juncture in history and that planning for ecologically sustainable economic development requires revisiting many of the assumptions upon which prevailing planning and development models are based. I argue that mainstream approaches to sustainability have failed to ask fundamental questions and to undertake analyses vital to understanding the physical dimensions of the problem, to say nothing of their political and social implications. Consequently, to borrow the inverted logic of an anonymous wag, sustainability measures taken to date 'appear to have great depth on the surface, but deep down are as shallow as hell'.

Readers unfamiliar with the debate may find the analysis and conclusions provocative. This is a major potential value of the paper – to present a minority but increasingly tenable perspective on the implications of sustainability for further discussion and evaluation. The development of theory relevant to planning requires a thorough examination of important starting assumptions and subsequent analyses; if the former are reasonable and the latter consistent with accepted facts and real-world experience, we should think twice before rejecting disquieting conclusions.

SEEING THROUGH DIFFERENT LENSES

Many of the contradictions associated with 'sustainable development' can be traced to differing fundamental beliefs and assumptions about the nature of humankind-environment relationships. These differing pre-analytic visions (or paradigms or

Table 2.1 *Comparing competing paradigms*

Property or quality	Expansionist worldview	Steady-state (ecological) worldview
Epistemological and scientific origins	Modern roots in the enlightenment and accompanying scientific revolution (Copernicus, Galileo, Bacon, Décartes, Newton) of 16th to 18th centuries; Newtonian analytic mechanics	Rooted in 20th century physics and biology; Prigoginian self-organization (dissipative structures), non-equilibrium thermodynamics, complex systems theory, deterministic chaos and systems ecology
Central scientific premise	Nature is knowable through reductionist analysis, observation and experimentation; the observer is separate from the observed; nature is thus objectified (the origin of 'objective' knowledge)	The behaviour of natural systems is unknowable (unpredictable) at the whole systems level[a]; uncertainty is large and irreducible within wide margins; holistic approaches provide the best understanding of global change but whatever our investigative stance, humankind is an integral part of the ecosphere; there is no truly objective knowledge

Table 2.1 *Continued*

Structure of analytic models	Models tend to be simple, linear, deterministic and single equilibrium-oriented; management strategies assume smooth change and complete reversibility	Models are complex, non-linear, dynamic and characterized by multiple equilibria; management strategies therefore recognize abrupt discontinuities, dynamic boundary conditions and potential irreversibilities
Attitude towards people and the future	Emphasis on the individual and immediate national interests; primary concern for the present generation; comfortable with time and space discounting	Greater emphasis on community and collective interests generally; concerned about present and future generations; cautious about conventional discounting
Perspectives on Nature	Humankind is the master of nature; people can adapt 'the environment' at will to serve their wants and needs. Nature is valued mainly as a source of resources and sink for wastes	Humanity lives in a state of obligate dependency on the ecosphere; resources ultimately control people; there are few examples of industrial 'man' successfully managing or controlling resource systems sustainably (eg fisheries, forests, agricultural soils). In addition to production value, nature has intrinsic worth, value for its own sake
Economic paradigm and connectedness to ecosphere	Neoliberal (neoclassical) economics: treats the economy as separate from and independent of nature; analytic models are generally 'inorganic' and mechanical, lacking any physical representation of the material and energy transformations and the structural and time-dependent processes of the ecosphere (see Christensen 1991)	Ecological economics: sees the human economy as a fully contained, dependent, integral sub-system of the ecosphere that should be analysed as an extension of human metabolism. Understanding the physical/material transformations that bind the economy and ecosystems, maintaining essential ecosystems functions, and recognizing the lags and thresholds characterizing ecosystems behaviour is paramount to sustainability
Starting point for analysis	The circular flows of exchange value between firms and households (with money as the metric)	The unidirectional and irreversible flows of low-entropy energy/matter from nature through the economy and back in degraded form[b]. (Physical measures of stocks and flows should at least supplement money as the metric)
Role and ecological efficacy of markets	Free markets stimulate (through rising scarcity value and corresponding prices) both the conservation of depletable assets and the search for technological substitutes; free markets and technology can therefore help to decouple the economy from nature	Markets work as described for a limited range of familiar non-renewable resource commodities but prices for renewable flows are inadequate indicators of ecological scarcity. Market prices reveal only exchange value at the margin and do not reflect the size of remaining natural capital stocks, whether there are critical minimal levels below which stocks cannot recover, nor the ultimate contribution of such stocks to human existence or survival. Most important, there are no markets for many biophysical

Table 2.1 *Continued*

		goods (eg the ozone layer) and essential life-support services (eg photosynthesis and waste assimilation) which have immeasurable positive eco nomic value
On the substitutability of natural capital	Natural capital and manufactured capital are near-perfect substitutes. Technology can make up for any depleting natural resource. (Typical quote of proponents: 'Exhaustible resources do not pose a fundamental problem' (Dasgupta and Heal 1979, p 205))	Natural capital is complementary to and often prerequisite for human-made capital. Given the market failures noted above, the standard measures of scarcity (prices and costs) may fail absolutely to induce either the conservation of vital stocks or technological innovation. In any case, it is unlikely that humans will devise technological substitutes for many ecospheric life-support functions whose loss would be irreversible and potentially catastrophic
Attitude towards economic growth a) social role of growth	Growth in both the rich and poor countries is essential as the only practical means available to alleviate human poverty within nations and to address material inequities between countries	Any available ecological space for growth should be allocated to the Third World. In any event, growth cannot be relied upon as the only means to relieve poverty. People must face up to the need for significant intra- and international redistribution of wealth and access to nature's services. Political, social, economic and institutional reform are needed to facilitate the necessary behavioural, value and attitudinal changes. This in turn calls for sophisticated public education programmes on sustainability issues
b) ecological role of growth	Growth in the developed world will increase the market for the products of developing countries. This will in turn enrich the Third World, helping to provide the surpluses needed for the rehabilitation and future sustainable use of natural capital. (This paradigm often sees depletion of natural capital and local pollution as a Third World problem)	We cannot safely grow our way to sustainability, particularly in the First World – the global economy is already running a massive hidden ecological deficit, attributable mostly to industrialized countries. Far from providing the surpluses needed to rehabilitate natural capital, material growth based on current economic assumptions and available technology depends on its further depletion, increas- ing the sustainability deficit and leading to accelerated ecological decline. Real wealth is measured by enduring cultural artefacts, supportive sociopolitical institutions, growing natural capital stocks and long-term ecological security
c) nature of limits	There are practical limits on human population, but no constraints on economic growth (ie on per capita GDP); technology can generally substitute for	There are real biophysical constraints on both population and material through- put growth; humankind must live on the natural income generated by

Table 2.1 *Continued*

	depleted natural capital and, over time, the economy can be 'dematerialized' by increases in economic and technological efficiency	remaining stocks of natural capital. Total human impact or load is a product of population times average per capita material consumption (including waste output) and cannot be reduced below critical maximum safe levels by efficiency gains in the foreseeable future
Stance on carrying capacity[c]	There are no limits to regional or global carrying capacity; trade can relieve any locally significant limiting factors and technological advances will alleviate more general scarcities (see above)	Carrying capacity is finite and declining and should become a fundamental component of demographic and planning analysis. Trade and technology only appear to increase local carrying capacity, while actually reducing it on a global scale. Meanwhile, all trading regions exceed their own territorial capacities, become dependent on imports of depletable resources, and ultimately reach the same limiting factor. (At this stage, there are no further safety valves)
On GDP as welfare indicator	GDP (or per capita GDP) is an imperfect indicator, but correlates well with standard measures of population health and remains the best overall measure we have of human welfare	GDP is woefully inadequate as a measure of social and ecological welfare. It says nothing about the distribution of the benefits of growth – per capita GDP can rise while the money income of many people falls in real terms. Worse, GDP includes both the depreciation of manufactured capital (ie decreases in the value of capital)[d] and defensive expenditures against pollution or other forms of ecological decline as positive entries, and says nothing at all about the depletion of natural capital. GDP can therefore continue to increase, creating the illusion of increasing well-being while economic, ecological and geopolitical security are all being eroded (Herman Daly's '"anti-economic growth" – ie growth that makes us poorer rather than richer' [Daly 1991b, p 242])
Attitude toward economic globalization	Deregulation, global markets and free trade will enhance economic efficiency and contribute to greater social equity and international security through expansive growth in world product (GWP)	Deregulation, expanding markets and free trade will indeed increase gross global product, but under prevailing assumptions and terms of trade they will also increase income disparities and accelerate the depletion of natural capital, thereby decreasing both ecological and geopolitical security

a Includes social and economic systems, ie any complex self-organizing system. b Even 100% material recycling would consume net energy and matter. c Carrying capacity is usually defined as the maximum sustainable population in a given area, but is better thought of as the maximum sustainable human 'load' (population × resources consumption). See Catton 1986. d The rationale is that capital depreciation is ultimately a cost of doing business.

worldviews) define and delimit any significant problem to be analysed and determine the scope, depth and direction of our thinking about it.

Because we acquire a particular worldview simply by living, growing up and being educated in a particular sociocultural milieu, we are often unconscious that we even have one and that we operate from it in virtually everything we do. Most of us are therefore generally unaware of the subtle ways in which the prevailing paradigm shapes our understanding of, and approach to, societal problems or that there may be more viable alternatives. Indeed, when we think that 'the world is flat' was once a self-evident paradigmatic truth, it raises the unsettling possibility that much of even our present cultural worldview may consist largely of shared illusions!

Many scientists, policy analysts, and even politicians argue that sustainability will require a 'paradigm shift' or a 'fundamental change' in the way we do business but few go on to describe just what needs to be shifted or any implications for the *status quo*. To help clarify matters, Table 2.1 details the 'expansionist' and 'steady-state' worldviews, the two major paradigms competing for attention on the sustainable development stage today. (See Ayres [1993] for a review of a fuller range of cornucopian to neo-Malthusian arguments.) The table provides a detailed guide to the comparative analysis which follows. The main argument is that many of our so-called 'environmental problems' stem from flaws in the prevailing expansionist paradigm that can be remedied only by a global shift toward the ecological steady state. In this light, sustainability poses a far more serious challenge to many of society's most basic beliefs and analytic concepts than most mainstream planners and policy makers have been prepared to contemplate so far.

The Expansionist Paradigm

Technological expansionism clearly occupies centre-stage in the eyes of most contemporary governments and official development organizations. This worldview is associated with neoclassical economics which treats the economy as an independent,

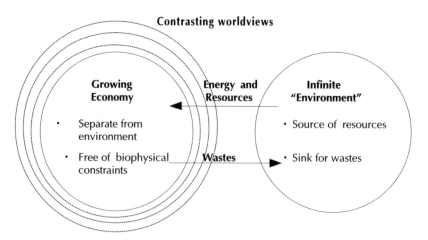

Figure 2.1a *Expansionists treat the economy as an open, growing, independent system lacking any fundamentally important 'connectedness' to an infinite environment*

self-regulating and self-sustaining system whose productivity and growth are not seriously constrained by the environment (Figure 2.1a). Adherents believe that humankind has achieved mastery over relevant parts of the natural world and through technology will be able to compensate for the depletion of any important natural resources. Even the UN's ground-breaking World Commission on Environment and Development (the Brundtland Commission) can be placed in this camp. The Commission assumed that any limits on the environment's ability to meet human needs were imposed not so much by nature as 'by the state of technology and social organization' (p 43) and that while future expansion would have to be qualitatively different from present forms of growth, 'a five- to tenfold increase in world industrial output can be anticipated before the population stabilizes [at about twice the present numbers] sometime in the next century' (WCED 1987, p 213).[1]

Prevailing economic rationality relies heavily on the assumed simple mechanics of free and open markets to ensure sustainability. This naturally leads to great emphasis on 'internalizing the externalities' and 'getting the prices right' as an essential first step. Many conventional economists place great confidence in price as an indicator of scarcity and on the mechanics of the marketplace to relieve it – rising prices for scarce resources automatically leads to conservation of the affected resources and stimulates the search for substitutes. And as Nobel Laureate Robert Solow has observed: 'If it is very easy to substitute other factors for natural resources, then... The world can, in effect, get along without natural resources...' (Solow 1974, p 11).

In fact, these mechanisms seem to be working, at least for commonly traded non-renewable resources. With the exception of timber, the real prices of all resources examined – including rural land – have shown a significant drop over this century implying *increasing* economic availability (Barnett and Morse 1963), although a levelling of this trend may have occurred around 1970 (Nordhaus 1992). Since real prices for appropriable resources show no major turn towards scarcity, economists generally 'tend to be at the relaxed end of the spectrum' of those concerned about environmental constraints on growth (Nordhaus 1992, p 5).

As suggested by the emphasis on money price, the conceptual starting point for conventional economic analysis is the 'circular flow of exchange value' (Daly 1991b, p 195). Most standard economic textbooks feature a standard circular diagram of economic process as 'a pendulum movement between production and consumption within a completely closed system' (Georgescu-Roegen 1971). Value embodied in goods and services flows from firms to households in exchange for spending by households (national product). An equal value, reincarnated in factors of production, flows back to firms from households in exchange for wages, rents, profits, etc (national income). Unfortunately, this model is problematic when it comes to assessing ecological sustainability since there is no connection in these money flows to biophysical reality. Indeed, 'it is impossible to study the relation of the economy to the ecosystem in terms of the circular flow model because the circle flow is an isolated, self-renewing system with no inlets or outlets, no possible points of contact with anything outside itself' (Daly 1991c, p 196).

It follows that sustainability sometimes seems a simple business from the expansionist perspective. If there are no general environmental constraints on the economy and we can find technological substitutes for particular resources, then the shortest route to sustainability is to stay our present course. If we continue freeing up markets, privatizing resources and government services, and eliminating barriers to trade, a new round of growth in both rich and poor countries will provide the wealth needed both to redress poverty and inequity and to generate the

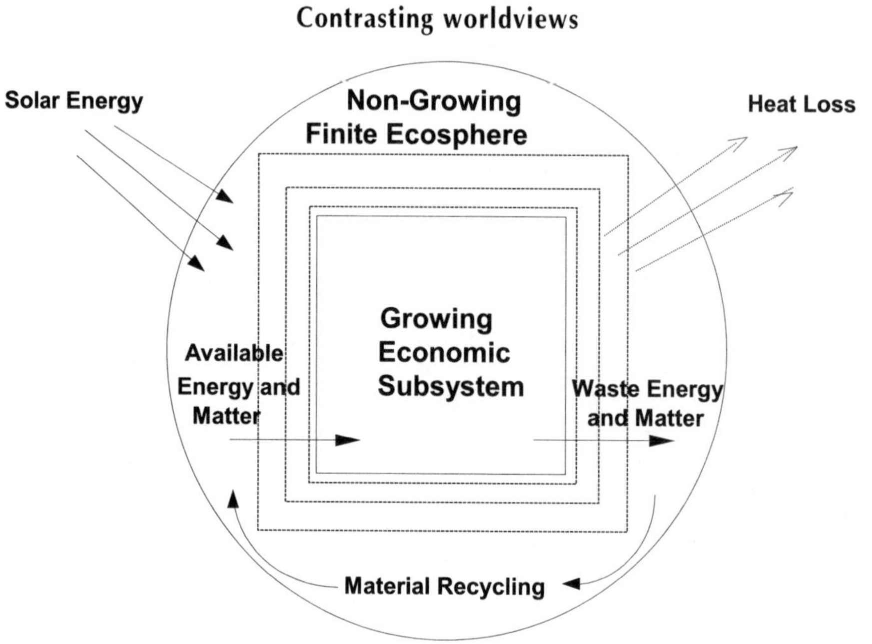

Contrasting worldviews

Figure 2.1b *Ecological economics sees the economy as an open, growing, wholly dependent subsystem of a materially closed, non-growing, finite, ecosphere (Daly 1992)*

economic surpluses needed, particularly in the developing world, better to husband the natural environment (see Beckerman 1974 for a full exposition). In short, '...the surest way to improve your environment is to become rich' (Beckerman 1992, p 491 as cited in Ekins 1993, p 267).

The Steady-State (Ecological) Alternative

By contrast, ecologists and ecological economists argue that many of the assumptions and beliefs of conventional economics are responsible for, or at least aggravate, the sustainability crisis. They see the economy not in isolation, but rather as an inextricably integrated, completely contained, and wholly dependent subsystem of the ecosphere (Rees 1990) (Figure 2.1b). Moreover, both the economy and the ecosphere are complex self-organizing systems whose behaviour is ultimately governed not by the simple mechanics of neoclassical analysis but by evolutionary forces, complex systems dynamics, and thermodynamic laws. Indeed, the second law of thermodynamics as applied to open far-from-equilibrium systems provides an important theoretical and heuristic foundation upon which to rebuild our understanding of economy-environment interaction.[2]

From this perspective, the economy is seen as a highly ordered, dynamic system maintained by available energy/matter (essergy) 'imported' from the ecosphere. In this respect, industrial metabolism becomes an extension of biological metabolism. Like our bodies, the economy consumes energy and material produced by nature,

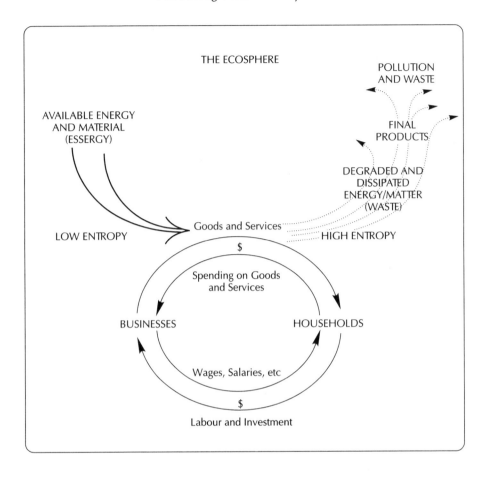

Figure 2.2 *The linear throughput of energy/matter. The linear throughput of low-entropy energy and matter (upper part of diagram) sustains the economy and drives the circular flows of exchange value (lower part of diagram), yet is invisible to conventional economic analysis*

transforms the 'available' portion of it into useful goods and services, and returns the entire material and energy flux to the environment as waste. Like all such processes in nature, economic transformations are subject to the Second Law: every energy/material transformation produces an increase in net entropy – a permanent degradation of available energy and the dissipation of matter (resource depletion and pollution). In thermodynamic terms then, nature is the real producer; all economic activity involves consumption and invariably contributes to the human 'load' on the environment.

It follows that the ecologically important flows in the economy are not the circular flows of money but rather the unidirectional and thermodynamically irreversible flows of useful matter and energy from the ecosphere through the economic subsystem and back to the ecosphere in degraded form (upper part of Figure 2.2).[3] This linear throughput is what fuels the economy – despite our technological wizardry, human society remains in a state of obligate dependence on the ecosphere for both the production of usable energy/matter and for waste assimilation (as well as other life-support services).

Sustainability is clearly a more complex problem from the ecological perspective than it appears to be from the economic mainstream. The economy apparently exists in a quasi-parasitic relationship with the ecosphere, ultimately dependent on material flows to and from nature and on life-support services, many of which are *invisible* to monetary analyses. Money prices are therefore unreliable indicators of ecological scarcity and can have only a limited role in fostering sustainability. In any event, only the foolhardy would trust in markets and technology to find substitutes for such ecoessentials as photosynthesis and climate regulation, the ozone layer and natural biodiversity. Finally, growth in national product (and national income) is ultimately constrained by systemic limits on the flows of ecological goods and services (natural income). Certainly when the economy has reached the maximum sustainable level of material throughput, flow rates should be held constant or in 'steady-state'.

NODES OF TENSION BETWEEN THE EXPANSIONIST AND STEADY STATE PARADIGMS

It should be obvious even from this brief comparison that the development policies flowing from such differing paradigms will be as different as the paradigms themselves. The critical point is that any paradigm is only a model and the policies it suggests can only be as good in coping with reality as the original model is in capturing the essence of that reality. This begs the question of which of our competing paradigms provides the better guide to policy for sustainability. The following sections explore some of the most important characteristics of the natural world that are reflected in the ecological worldview but are missing from the prevailing expansionist model.

The Economy as Dissipative Structure

Modern formulations of the second law of thermo dynamics suggest that all highly ordered complex systems develop and grow (increase their internal order) 'at the expense of increasing the disorder at higher levels in the system's hierarchy' (Schneider and Kay 1994, p 2). In other words, complex systems maintain their internal order and remain in a dynamic non-equilibrium state through the continuous dissipation of available energy/matter extracted from their host environments. The reduced entropy of the local system is achieved at the cost of increased entropy of the global system within which the local system is embedded. Because they feed upon and degrade available energy/matter from outside themselves, such self-organizing non-equilibrium systems are called dissipative structures (Nicolis and Prigogine 1977).

The human economy is one such highly ordered, dynamic, far-from-equilibrium dissipative structure. Its internal order and complexity continuously increase as it grows and develops, particularly through the formation of manufactured capital made from natural capital (resources). However, because the economy is an open growing subsystem of the materially closed, non-growing ecosphere (Daly 1992), beyond a certain point the increasing order (negentropy) of the former can be purchased only by increasing the disorder (entropy) of the latter. The second law thus provides both a necessary condition for sustainability and a nearly sufficient explanation of the physical mechanisms behind the present ecological crisis. Economic activity is ecologically sustainable as long as the consumption of essergy by the economy is less than its production in nature (ie, there is no continuous net entropy increase). Today's population and material growth is unsustainable because an expanding economy necessarily appropriates an ever greater share of the low entropy energy/matter continuously being formed in the ecosphere. Through economic growth, humans displace other species from their habitats and take over their ecological niches, meanwhile impeding the productivity of remaining natural systems through pollution. All this accelerates the destruction of the world's major ecosystems, and is driving the greatest extinction episode since the natural catastrophes at the end of the Paleozoic and Mesozoic eras (Wilson 1988).

The deconstruction of ecosystems becomes problematic when we consider the conditions that must be satisfied for the ecosphere to continue regenerating itself (Rees 1990). The ecosphere, like the physical processes and living species it comprises, is a self-producing system. The organizational property that enables living systems to produce and maintain themselves is known as autopoiesis and depends on the complex interdependent relationships linking the system's major components. The critical point is that the structural integrity of these relationships is essential not only for the functioning of the system, but also for the production and maintenance of the participating components themselves (Maturana and Varela 1988).

Here the important question for sustainability is: At what point does the erosion of ecosystems and the entropic 'disordering' of the ecosphere begin to interfere with its capacity for self-production? This is a nearly intractable question for ecology and conventional economic rationality does not even raise the question. Implications of the second law are generally not part of economic analysis. Even William Nordhaus, who does briefly consider entropy in a modified production function focuses only on energy supply, not on systems organization and integrity. This leads him to conclude that 'because virtually all the stock of negentropy is contained in appropriable energy resources' any drag on economic growth associated with increased entropy would already be accounted for 'in the growth drag from [more costly] energy resources. Any further correction would be double-counting' (Nordhaus 1992, p 34). In short, conventional analysis leaves the destabilizing effects of simplified ecosystems and the disruptive impacts of waste accumulation unaccounted for, yet these issues are at the heart of ecological sustainability.

The Constant Natural Capital Stocks Criterion

One of the most significant contributions of neoclassical environmental economists to the sustainability debate has been the shift from treating natural resources as mere free goods of nature to recognizing that 'resources' comprise a unique class of productive capital capable of producing a stream of income indefinitely into the future (see Box 2.1). This enables greater analytic rigour by elevating so-called natural capital to the same theoretical status as the more familiar manufactured or human-made capital (physical plant, machinery, infrastructure, etc) and human/social capital (knowledge, skills, social infrastructure, etc).

There is general agreement that no development path is sustainable if it depends on the depletion of productive assets. From the perspective of capital theory, society can be said to be economically sustainable if it passes on an undiminished per capita

---

Box 2.1 *Natural capital*[4]

Natural capital refers to 'a stock [of natural assets] that yields a flow of valuable goods and services into the future'. For example, a forest or a fish stock can provide a flow or harvest that is potentially sustainable year after year. The stock that produces this flow is 'natural capital' and the sustainable flow is 'natural income'. Natural capital also provides such services as waste assimilation, erosion and flood control, and protection from ultra-violet radiation (the ozone layer is a form of natural capital). These life-support services are also counted as natural income. Because the flow of services from ecosystems often requires that the latter function as intact self-producing systems, the integrity of such systems is an important attribute of natural capital.

There are three classes of natural capital: *Renewable* natural capital, such as living species and ecosystems, is self-producing and self-maintaining using solar energy and photosynthesis. These forms can yield marketable goods such as wood fibre, but may also provide unaccounted essential services when left in place (eg, climate regulation). *Replenishable* forms of natural capital (eg, ground water and the ozone layer) is non-living but, like living forms, is often ultimately dependent on the solar engine for renewal. Finally, *non-renewable* types of natural capital, such as fossil fuel and minerals, are like inventories in that any use implies liquidating part of the stock.

This paper takes the position that since adequate stocks of self-producing and replenishable natural capital are essential for life support (and are generally non-substitutable), these classes of natural capital are generally more important to sustainability than are non-renewable forms.

---

stock of capital from one generation to the next (Pearce 1994a, Solow 1986, Victor 1991). Ecologists and economists are therefore debating various interpretations of a 'constant capital stock' condition for sustainability in which the major bone of contention is the degree to which manufactured capital can be substituted for natural capital.

Traditional environmental economists assume close substitutability and favour a weak sustainability criterion in which the aggregate stock of manufactured and natural capital must be held constant (Nordhaus 1992, Pearce et al 1989, 1990; Pezzey 1989). By this criterion, it is of little consequence if natural capital assets are depleted provided that part of the returns are invested in creating an equivalent value of manufactured capital. Weak sustainability is favoured explicitly by most economists and implicitly by most development planners today.[5]

On the other hand, *ecological* economists generally regard natural and manufactured capital to be complements rather than substitutes – for example, more fishboats are no substitute for a depleted fish stock[6] – and also believe there are many essential life-support services for which there is little possibility that technology could find an adequate substitute. The ecologically minded therefore support a strong sustainability criterion in which both renewable natural capital and manufactured capital must be held intact separately (Costanza and Daly 1992, Daly 1990, Rees 1990, Victor et al 1994). This more risk-averse version of the constant capital stocks criterion can be stated as follows:

> Each generation should inherit an adequate per capita stock of both manufactured and self-producing natural assets no less than the stock of such assets inherited by the previous generation.

Manufactured capital aside for the moment, this version of the constant capital stocks criterion implies that humankind must learn to live on the annual income (the 'interest') generated by remaining stocks of essential natural capital (Rees 1990). These physical flows are related to Hicksian (or sustainable) income, the level of consumption that can be maintained from one period to the next without reducing real wealth (productive capital).

Economists generally approach the constant stock problem using customary accounting methods and the monetization of capital depreciation/appreciation. This raises two additional flaws in weak sustainability, both associated with stock valuation. First, the ecosphere provides at least four categories of goods and services to the economy: material and energy resources, waste assimilation, life support services, and aesthetic and spiritual values (Jacobs 1991). Of these, markets deal reasonably well with only the first category, mainly non-renewable resources. As noted in Table 2.1, many of the biophysical stocks, flows and functions associated with the other types of natural capital are difficult to quantify and price and others are simply invisible to conventional analysis (Rees 1991, Rees and Wackernagel 1994, Schulze 1994). Indeed, some stocks now thought to have immeasurable positive economic value had not previously been recognized by economists at all (eg, the ozone layer). For such reasons, economists Vatn and Bromley (1993) argue that efforts to derive hypothetical values for natural income and capital stocks – essential inputs to conventional analysis – are inevitably undermined by 'a non-trivial loss of information' and conclude that 'so-called "contingent valuing" therefore... may contribute minimally – if at all – to the revelation of values' (p 130). This poses a frustrating dilemma to a culture accustomed to linear science being able to provide unequivocal answers to technical problems. 'If we cannot reliably measure whether a given current management practice is sustainable, or predict whether an alternative would be more or less sustainable, how can we move toward sustainability?' (Carpenter 1990, 1994a, 1994b).

The second problem is as fundamental. Assuming the problems with measurement and valuation were overcome, it is still questionable whether price can provide a valid indicator of ecological scarcity. For ecologically essential goods and life-support services, it is not the money value but rather the physical quantity of natural capital stocks and flows that is key to sustainability. Rising prices for these factors could, therefore, create the illusion of constant natural capital (measured in terms of stable income or total stock value) even as the physical stocks are reduced below critical levels.

Because of these fundamental weaknesses, the prevailing system of costs, prices and market incentives fails absolutely to measure ecological scarcity or to determine the appropriate levels of natural capital stocks. Since certain of these critical 'assets' maintain the life-support functions of the ecosphere, the risks associated with their depletion are unacceptable and there may be no possibility for technological substitution. Some environmental economists have noted that '*conserving what there is* could be a sound risk-averse strategy' (Pearce et al 1990, p 7 [emphasis added]).

THE ECOLOGICAL FOOTPRINT OF THE HUMAN ECONOMY

The fundamental question for ecological economics is whether remaining stocks of natural capital (species populations, ecosystems and related biophysical processes) are adequate to provide the resource flows and waste sinks that will be required by the anticipated human population into the next century while simultaneously maintaining the general life support functions of the ecosphere. As noted, this question is not amenable to monetary analysis and can only be approached through measures of physical stocks and flows.

The author and his students have addressed this issue by using land (ecosystem) area as a proxy for natural capital. We estimate the area of productive land (agricultural land, forest land, etc) required to produce/absorb the material/energy flows associated with particular patterns of consumption. This approach suggests that the average Canadian (or American) needs between 4 and 5 hectares (approximately 10–12 acres) to support his/her consumer lifestyle.[7] Using such data, we can estimate the 'ecological footprint' of an entire population or economy, defined as the aggregate area of land required continuously to produce the resource inputs and to assimilate the waste outputs of that population/economy wherever on Earth the land may be located (Rees 1992, 1994a; Rees and Wackernagel 1994).

Our analyses show that industrial regions, and even whole countries, survive by appropriating the carrying capacity of an area of land vastly larger than the areas they physically occupy. While they may seem economically prosperous, industrial economies are running massive 'ecological deficits' with the rest of the planet which are not revealed in their trade balances or current accounts. The problem is that in a finite world not every region or country can be a net importer of biophysical goods and services. Extrapolation of the present North American lifestyle to the entire world population of 5.7 billion would require about 24 billion hectares of ecologically productive land using existing technologies. Since there are only 8.8 billion hectares of such land on the planet, we would need at least two additional Earths to bring just the present human population up to North American ecological standards. These data provide some measure of both global ecological limits and North–South inequity, the primary challenges confronting *Agenda 21*.[8]

Optimal Sustainable Scale

The possibility that the human enterprise has already exceeded the long-term carrying capacity of the Earth leads us to ask whether the economy has an optimal size (see Daly 1991b). We can approach this question theoretically by considering the gradual 'development' of the ecosphere in a total social benefit:cost framework (Figure 2.3). At each stage in the process, there are both real benefits and real costs. Generally speaking, the tangible benefits of development – jobs, money income, the value of services provided by manufactured and some natural capital – are relatively easily estimated in dollar terms from market prices. By contrast, while it may be possible to estimate some pollution damage costs and defensive expenditures, many ecological costs (such as the value of natural income sacrificed as a result of natural capital depletion and the entropic degradation of ecosystems) will be impossible either to quantify or monetize for reasons explained earlier.

As development proceeds to maturity, the marginal social value of additional increments begins to fall – the hundredth forestry project is not quite as important to a regional (or global) economy as the first. At the same time, we should be able to show that at a certain stage in the process the marginal costs of development increase rapidly. The curves will therefore intersect when falling marginal benefits just equal rising marginal costs and at this point growth in economic throughput should stop. Unfortunately, since we are unable in practice to assign a price to

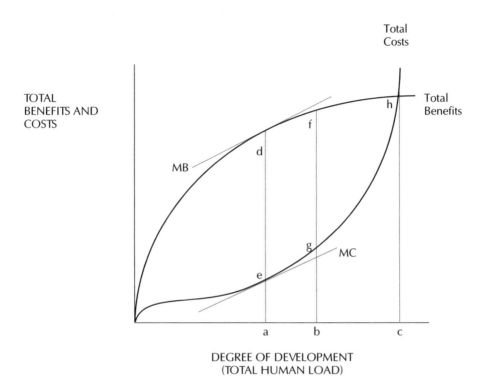

Figure 2.3 *Optimal economic scale. Point 'a' represents that stage in the develop-ment of the ecosphere at which net total benefits (total benefits minus total costs) are maximized. At this point, falling marginal benefits just equal rising marginal costs (slope MC = slope MB). Throughput growth beyond 'a' is therefore counterproductive. Indeed, by point 'c,' ecocatastrophe has cancelled all the benefits of development (figure adapted from Daly 1991c)*

many ecological losses, the increasing scarcity value of natural capital goes unac-counted. The attention of both decision-makers and ordinary citizens is therefore focused on the benefits of past development and the potential for continuous eco-nomic gain from more of the same. Indeed, there is no perceived limit on the *dollar* value of developmental benefits. Meanwhile, we forget that the accelerating losses of ecological capital and the life-support services they provide – which should be a major factor on the cost side of the equation – are being subtracted from a finite *physical* quantity[9] which is near maximum at the beginning of the 'development' sequence and is reduced at each subsequent stage of the process.

Figure 2.3 illustrates this analysis by showing the long-term theoretical[10] rela-tionship between total benefits/costs and the progressive development of the eco-sphere (the latter corresponds closely with total human load). Most significantly, point 'a' represents that point in the development process when the difference be-tween total benefits and total costs of development is maximized. At this stage the slopes of the total costs and benefits curves are equal (declining marginal gains [MB] just equal increasing marginal costs [MC]). Point 'a' therefore represents the theoretically optimal size for the aggregate human enterprise.[11] Development beyond 'a' produces no additional *net* benefit. Indeed, at 'b,' although total benefits have increased, costs have risen even more steeply and have more than cancelled gains ([ad-ae] > [bf-bg]). In short, development beyond 'a' is both ecologically unsustainable and uneconomic; further growth simply cannot be justified.

As long as the measurement of ecological costs remains elusive, this must remain a theoretical analysis. However, we should note that the inability to measure something does not mean it does not exist. For any level of technological sophistication and pattern of demand there is an ecologically optimal size for the aggregate economy. Thus, there is a current optimum and while its exact magnitude may elude us, global change is a plausible indication that it may already have been exceeded, at least in particular dimensions.

Self-Organizing Systems and Global Change

> Global change represents a new class of problems that severely challenges our ability to achieve sustainable development. These problems 'are fundamentally nonlinear in causation and discontinuous in both their spatial structure and temporal behavior'. They are 'more and more frequently caused by local human influences... that accumulate to trigger sudden changes directly affecting the health of people, the productivity of renewable resources, and the vitality of societies'.
> (Holling 1994, p 57)

Ecological and complex systems theory suggest that cumulative losses of ecosystems function or components may reach (invisible) critical points of no return beyond which systems structure and behaviour change critically and irreversibly. Ecosystems thus provide prime examples of Prigoginian self-organization (Nicolis and Prigogine 1977). Such systems do not maximize for anything in particular but function as an optimal dynamic balance of all the forces acting upon them. If there is too much development of any one type, 'the system becomes overextended and brittle' and therefore primed for seemingly chaotic change (Kay and Schneider 1994, p 35). A key feature of such 'self-organization' is that there may be little warning that the system is approaching a bifurcation point where profound reorganization may occur and no way of predicting the subsequent state of the system before the fact. To complicate matters, complex systems behaviour is often characterized by significant lags between cause and effect.

The cumulative 'brittleness' and delayed responses of exploited ecosystems reveal a major weakness in our previous analysis. Figure 2.3 describes a potentially manageable static equilibrium system characterized by continuous smooth change and implicit reversibility. However, if the behaviour of real-world ecosystems under stress is more often characterized by discontinuities and systemic lags, the cumulative cost curve is more likely to break unexpectedly and rapidly upward and to the left with little hope of an orderly return to stable predictability. The greater the lag, the further beyond any economic optimum development will proceed before spontaneous systems self-(re-)organization. Such overshoot describes the recent collapse of the North Atlantic ground-fish stocks and may be a widespread phenomenon. In a recent review, Ludwig et al (1993, p 17) found that while 'there is considerable variation in the details, there is a remarkable consistency in the history of resource exploitation: resources are inevitably overexploited, often to the point of collapse or extinction'.

Complexity and self-organization theory thus undermine many prevailing assumptions about humanity's capacity to manage the ecosphere for sustainability. Indeed, if systemic, discontinuous (or 'catastrophic') change were to be induced in some globally critical system, civilized existence might no longer be possible for much of humankind. As noted, ecosystems have no inherent, single, 'preferred' state. The ecosphere may well be able to thrive in any number of alternative steady-state configurations which are not necessarily conducive to human physical or social well-being. Thus, if the behaviour of a sub-system (eg, the human economy) does not conform to the functional parameters of the super-system of which it is a part (the ecosphere), it may well be selected against (Kay and Schneider 1994). Such an outcome could result from, for example, massive stratospheric ozone depletion or erratic climate change, both of which could occur as cumulative effects of our present growth-bound way of life. The possibility of such ecocatastrophe is weakly represented in Figure 2.3 by the stage of global development reached at 'c' (and beyond). All the benefits of development are wiped out by cumulative (mostly environmental) costs.

A second reason for concern in this new climate relates to prevailing human economic behaviour. Western industrial culture and the logic of expansionist economics encourage individuals and nations alike to behave as self-interested utility maximizers. While this philosophy might be sustainable in an unlimited world – as indeed it seemed to be through most of human history – the inevitable result of everyone trying to maximize his/her use of resources on a finite planet is the competitive over-exploitation of common-pool resources (see Ophuls and Boyan 1992, Ch 4). As noted, global change is, in fact, prime evidence that many of the ecosphere's abundant sources are over-used and its sinks filled to over-flowing.

The central mechanism of this 'tragedy of the commons'[12] is that while each individual's (or nation's) share of the damage costs to the common-pool may be relatively small, the benefits of maximizing private gains are comparatively large. Even if one recognizes the looming collective problem, 'self-restraint is unprofitable and ultimately futile unless one can be certain of universal concurrence' (pp 198–199). Thus, we may be propelled to the brink of ecological and social chaos 'not so much by the evil acts of selfish people as by the everyday acts of ordinary people whose behavior is dominated, usually unconsciously, by the remorseless self-destructive logic of the commons' (Ophuls and Boyan 1992, p 199).

LINES OF CONVERGENCE

The ecological perspective has begun to influence expansionist analyses. Most economists and development planners still insist that global sustainability is achievable only through large increases in the consumption of goods and services in both the rich and poor countries. This is seen as the only politically feasible and economically viable means to alleviate poverty and inequity both within countries and between rich and poor countries. At the same time, many now accept the fact of limits on *throughput* growth. The only way to achieve both rising incomes/consumption and reduced energy/material use is dramatically to reduce the ratio of resource use per unit GDP. The needed increase in consumption might be sustainable if accompa-

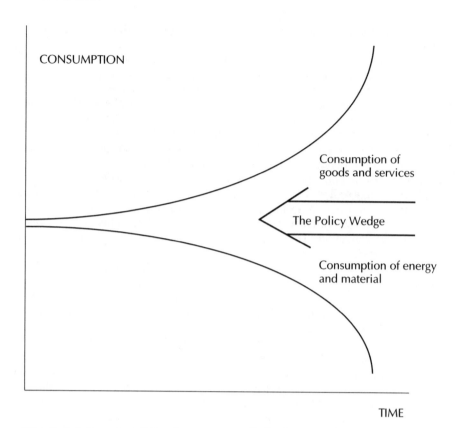

CONSUMPTION

Consumption of
goods and services

The Policy Wedge

Consumption of energy
and material

TIME

Figure 2.4 *Dematerializing the economy. At the limits to material throughput, sustainability requires that growth in the consumption of goods and services be accompanied by a proportional decline in the energy and material intensity of that consumption (figure adapted from Pearce 1994b)*

nied by a corresponding reduction in the material and energy content of goods and services (Pearce 1994b; Figure 2.4). The growth ethic has finally engaged biophysical reality.

Various studies suggest that even present emissions of carbon dioxide should be reduced by a minimum of 60 per cent and those of many other air pollutants by from 50 per cent to 90 per cent (RMNO 1994; Young and Sachs 1994; IUCN/UNEP/WWF 1991; MOHPPE 1988). If the material dimension of welfare is to be maintained in the face of such massive cut-backs, substantial gains will have to be made in the technological efficiency of energy and material use in coming decades. Assuming a doubling of population and a quadrupling of world output over the next 50 years (2–3 per cent growth per year), sustainability demands that the resource/environmental impact per unit consumption be reduced by 91 per cent. This scenario assumes continued GDP growth in both the North and South, 'which remains the principal, practically unchallenged global aspiration' (Ekins and Jacobs 1994, p 10). Other studies reach similar conclusions (Ekins 1993, RMNO 1994b, Schmidt-Bleek 1993a, b). Even the Business Council for Sustainable Development seems to have accepted that: 'Industrialised world reductions in material throughput, energy use, and environmental degradation of over 90 per cent will be required by 2040 to meet the needs of a growing world population fairly within the planet's ecological means' (BCSD 1993, p 10).

The needed order of magnitude reduction in the material intensity of economic output would result in what some analysts refer to as the 'factor-10 economy'. There is obviously much room for debate over whether this degree of economic demateri-alization is possible, but optimists are united with pessimists 'in arguing that it can only be approached by determined government policy' (Ekins and Jacobs 1994, p 14). The extreme risks associated with the unavoidable market failures outlined above argue persuasively for government having a major role in guiding society toward sustainability using a combination of regulatory and incentive-based instruments.

What should be included in the 'policy wedge' to be driven between the con-sumption of goods and services and the use of energy and material (Figure 2.4)? Achieving a factor-10 economy will require major changes in industrial strategy, fis-cal and taxation policy, and consumer-corporate relations. Many analysts agree that an essential first step is ecological tax reform. This would include replacing exist-ing corporate subsidies by a system of resource use and depletion taxes, and mar-ketable quotas, off-set by corresponding reductions in other taxes (Brown, L, et al 1991; Costanza and Daly 1992; von Weizsäcker 1994). By raising prices closer to the full social cost of goods and services, higher taxes on energy and material inputs should stimulate conservation, substitution and more efficient manufacturing tech-nologies; meanwhile, significant reductions in value-added and income taxes would reduce upward pressure on wages and salaries. Since both measures increase the attractiveness of labour relative to capital, a positive side effect of sustainability reform should be to increase the demand for labour.

There is more potential good news. Higher taxes and prices on energy and ma-terials favour reuse, repair, reconditioning and recycling, all of which are less ma-terial- and more labour-intensive than replacement manufacturing. In particular, product-life extension activities 'are a substitution of the transformation and service activities of extractive industries and base material production and thus a replace-ment of large-scale, energy- and capital-intensive units by smaller-scale, labour- and skill-intensive, independent, locally integrated work units' (Stahel and Jackson 1993, p 270). In summary, if managed properly, the net effect of the coming transition to sustainability could be not only less consumption and waste but also more employ-ment opportunities and greater regional self-reliance (Rees 1994b).

PLANNING FOR SUSTAINABILITY

Clearly, professional planners should reassess the paradigm which lies behind most professional planning education and practice today. The prevailing expan-sionist worldview could neither anticipate nor can it explain the pace of global eco-logical change. By contrast, the ecological paradigm provides a nearly sufficient ex-planation of increasing global entropy (as evidenced by such diverse phenomena as ozone depletion and the loss of biodiversity) and promises more unpleasant sur-prises ahead. If these observations are indicative of the relative 'degree of fit' of the two competing visions to the reality they purport to model, then future planning and development should look more to the ecological worldview for inspiration. Even the 'factor-10' economy, while clinging to the growth ethic and the technological fix, is a singular concession to the ecological imperative now confronting humanity.

Given the anticipated growth of the human population and rising material expectations everywhere, the end-of-pipe environmental reforms that swept the developed world in the 1970s and 1980s are no longer an adequate response to ecological concerns. Environmental assessment, pollution control and environmental standards legislation, growth management strategies, and similar measures are steps in the right direction and can produce positive local effects. However, they remain largely reactive, are often plagued by problems of interjurisdictional co-ordination, and are frequently undermined by indifferent implementation and lax enforcement. Indeed, it is probably fair to say that while the instruments currently available for environmental planning and management have had important cosmetic effects, they have not significantly changed fundamentally unsustainable environment-economy relationships. Global change has accelerated throughout the period of reform, energy and material throughput has expanded, and the ecological footprint of the human economy now spans the entire Earth.

All this suggests that sustainable development is a new kind of development requiring a transformation of both human-to-nature and people-to-people relationships on the local to global scales. There is more to be gained from changing behaviour and values than there is from technological fixes. Table 2.2 presents a minimal set of 'necessary conditions' for sustainability which stress the need to reconcile the ecological, cultural and economic dimensions of human well-being. Were society to take even these few conditions seriously, the result would be the most significant socioeconomic revolution since the enlightenment. Unfortunately, none of these criteria is being fully met in any 'developed' country, nor for the world as a whole today.

A Special Role for Planners

Achieving sustainability will thus require that global society becomes self-consciously engaged in its own reconstruction. This may well be a historic first – the

Table 2.2 *Necessary conditions for global sustainability*

Ecological stability requires that:

*   Consumption by the economy of the products and services of nature be compatible with rates of production by the ecosphere.
*   The production of wastes by the economy remain within the assimilative capacity of the ecosphere.
*   Economic activity protect the essential life-support functions of the ecosphere, and preserve the biodiversity and resilience of the Earth's ecological systems.

Geo-political security requires that:

*   Society satisfy basic standards of material equity and social justice.
*   Governance mechanisms be in place to enable an informed citizenry to have an effective participatory role in decision-making.
*   People share a positive sense of community cohesion (local and global) and a sense of collective responsibility for the future.

first intentional paradigm shift in the entire history of our species. Humanity has grown to fill the Earth and now must shift its focus from a youthful emphasis on growth to mature attention to development. The challenge to planners during this transition is exceeded only by the scope of opportunity to participate in shaping the coming of age of humankind.

Planners, by the very nature of their profession, are uniquely positioned to play a leadership role in this transition. In this increasingly fragmented and specialized world, planning is the one academic discipline and professional pursuit that explicitly attempts to be holistic or at least integrative at the level of society as a whole. At its best, planning provides a context in which the specialized knowledge of others comes together and begins to make unified sense.

The challenge of sustainability for the developed world is how to reduce our ecological footprints while satisfying the economic aspirations and sociocultural needs of society. Whatever specific activities and actions are sanctioned by the planning process, they can only be considered to be sustainable if they contribute to any of the following goals without significantly violating the others: reduced energy and material use, lower levels of waste production, the enhancement of natural capital stocks, and greater social justice and equity in an increasingly crowded world.

For regional and resource planners, the emphasis will be on the biophysical indicators. Development that produces no net loss of natural capital will itself require a revolution of thought and practice. Similarly, growth accompanied by an order of magnitude reduction of resource consumption and waste output per unit GDP represents an extraordinary technical and regulatory challenge (Rees 1994b).

For urban planners, sustainability means developing and promoting plans that contribute to more efficient urban form and to stronger social fabric. Our communities must become at once both more compact yet more habitable, more productive yet more efficient (Rees and Roseland 1991; Roseland 1992).

Cities may be the most magnificent of human achievements. They are certainly the engines of national economic growth, the centres of social discourse and the living repositories of human cultural achievement. But in ecological terms they are also nodes of pure consumption, the entropic black holes of industrial society. This means, paradoxically, that while there is no hope for the city *per se* to achieve sustainability independent of its vast and scattered global hinterland, it is in cities that the greatest opportunities exist to make the changes necessary for general sustainability. Most people in the industrial world live in cities, most consumption takes place in cities, and there are enormous potential material and energy savings through the economies of scale inherent in high urban densities. In addition, local governments tend to be in closer contact with their constituents and generally more immediately accountable than are state/provincial or federal politicians. All of this means that policies for sustainable development gain their greatest leverage in cities.[13] Many useful sources for policy and design guidance are available, ranging from the new journal *The Urban Ecologist*, through Girardet's *The Gaia Atlas of Cities* (1992), Roseland's *Toward Sustainable Communities* (1992) and Milbrath's *Envisioning a Sustainable Society* (1989), to Mollison's *Permaculture* (1990), the most comprehensive guide to the ecological restructuring of society.

A single urban example will suffice. It is commonplace to argue that the private automobile must give way to public transportation in our cities and just as commonplace to reject the idea as politically unfeasible. But how many planners or citizens have thought through the effect of reallocating a significant proportion of the considerable direct and indirect public subsidy to private automobiles – up to $2500 per year per vehicle – to public transit? Such a shift in incentives would be not only ecologically more sustainable but also both economically more efficient and socially more equitable. (It *should* therefore appeal to both the political right and left.) Over time, it would also contribute to better air quality, improved public health, greater access to the city, more affordable housing, more efficient land use, the hardening of the urban fringe, the conservation of food lands, and levels of urban density at which at least direct subsidies to transit become unnecessary. In short, because of complex systems linkages, seriously addressing even a single issue in the city inevitably forces attention on to many related contributing factors. This might be called the 'urban sustainability multiplier'.

Of course, none of this is relevant if people are uninformed or deliberately misinformed on the issues, unconvinced of the need to change or too parochial to appreciate their role in the global play. Also, from the political perspective, the actionable 'facts of the matter' are confused by a combination of scientific uncertainty and analytic blindness that mitigates against significant policy action. All this feeds into a subconscious seam of social denial. Not far below the surface in any discussion of global sustainability is a collective fear and loathing of the implications and potential consequences of taking 'our common future' and the ecological crisis seriously. Planners therefore have an unprecedented opportunity to practise their procedural skills as educators, as facilitators and as mediators between politicians and citizens in shaping the sustainability agenda.

This reminds us that achieving sustainability is not only, or even primarily, a technical issue. Indeed, a crucial role for planners is in helping to set the policy and planning goals that provide social context and public purpose for new regulatory regimes and technical fixes alike. What are the appropriate public policy instruments and economic incentives for change? Who benefits and who pays? What are the distributional effects? Does society have an obligation to compensate those whose jobs may no longer be sustainable (or who have lost their livelihoods with the collapse of some crucial ecosystem)?[14] Who should be responsible for relocation or retraining? In short, what kind of social safety net do we need to ensure equitable distribution of the costs and benefits of the shift to sustainability? All these questions suggest that achieving sustainability may have more to do with the substitution of social capital for material capital than it does with the substitution of technology for nature.

Student planners may face additional moral and ethical considerations more sweeping than any encountered by their predecessors. For example, do North Americans have an inherent right to continue appropriating the ecological services of five ha of land per capita, and a vastly disproportionate share of other ecosystemic functions, in a crowded, impoverished world where an equitable distribution of natural income would limit us to the output of 1.5 hectares? (Note that this says nothing of the needs of the millions of other species with which we share the planet.) Humanity may have to recognize that the stream of ecological goods and services produced by many forms of natural capital in the global 'common pool' is simply inadequate to satisfy present, let alone anticipated, demand. Once again, if there isn't enough natural capital to go around the problem is not technical but sociopolitical. Social and resource planners have a key role to play in the design and implementation of both national conservation plans and the international treaties that will be required to allocate the world's finite ecological budgets fairly.

The Do Nothing Alternative: How Plausible is Eco-Disaster?

Approaching sustainability from the assumptions of the ecological paradigm clearly assigns professional planning a significant role in the reconstruction of national and global society. The major alternative, supported by expansionist beliefs, is to continue as at present with planners acting as little more than developmental traffic cops. This latter stance assumes that the sustainability crisis is overdrawn and requires no special response. Given the scientific uncertainty around global change, the seeming political impracticality of necessary action, popular cynicism towards the political process and a strong element of social denial, this is the preferred path of many educated professionals and ordinary citizens alike (and support for this position will receive a substantial boost in the US by the recent swing towards the conservative right).

At the same time, we should keep in mind that the properties and behaviour of the ecosphere are indifferent to human beliefs and values and in this sense our community and collective interests in sustainability are apolitical. Should we vote for the *status quo* and the assumptions of the ecological perspective hold true, we may well be setting the stage for an era characterized by increasing local civil disorder and growing geopolitical instability – the by-products of unarrested ecological deterioration.

There is little doubt that global ecological change is real and threatening. At the same time many analysts argue that there is still time to make a reasonably smooth transition to sustainability. Certainly, the environmentally decoupled 'optimal utilization' economy described above is theoretically attractive and is obviously the most politically palatable of solutions for today's material world. However, typical of expansionist 'solutions', it is a purely technical response to a systemic crisis, one that ignores social and cultural context and accepts unquestioned the fundamental values of the consumer society. Quite apart from the (unasked) question of whether a fourfold increase in GDP in the rich countries will really make anyone happier, there are a number of reasons for concern that such a single-minded approach to sustainability will not succeed.

First, as already suggested, the current level of public understanding, irreducible scientific uncertainty, the power of vested interests, and the large potential costs associated with required structural adjustments to the economy all present barriers to the decisive political action required for the 'factor-10' scenario. How receptive would today's politically cynical electorate be to any suggestion of massive tax reform? Yet without public intervention to drive the efficiency revolution and to tax away the gains, technological advance will be slow and may actually work against sustainability. History suggests that spontaneous efficiency gains in the economy result in increased profits (income) or lower prices, both of which lead to *increased* consumption and accelerated resource depletion (Rees 1994b). Economists call this the 'rebound' effect. For example, US data reveal that despite the increasing fuel efficiency of automobiles, aggregate fuel consumption continues to increase as more cars are used more frequently for longer trips. It seems that under prevailing circumstances, growth eventually overwhelms gains from efficiency (Brown et al 1991). In any case, there are technical and economic limits to efficiency in practice – food, cars and television sets cannot be completely dematerialized. A good cup of coffee needs some minimal number of beans. Many such political, economic and technical factors may have contributed to de Bruyn's and Opschoor's (1993) finding for 20 European countries, that while there was some evidence of environment-economy delinking between 1966 and the early 1980s, material consumption in well-developed countries has since risen faster than GDP.

All this means that while the efficiency revolution promises a great deal, our social and political institutions may not be able to deliver the technological goods. Given the mounting pressure of population growth and accelerating ecological decline in much of the world, sustainability may require after all that the presently rich accept lower material standards in exchange for enhanced ecological and geopolitical security.

What might this look like? In *Beyond the Limits* Meadows et al (1992) suggest that to reduce the human load on the earth to within carrying capacity, we should 'aim for an [universal] industrial output per capita of $350' (about one-fifth the present world average) beginning in 1995 (p 198). Assuming perfect birth control – two children per couple – and gradually improving technological efficiency, the world population would level off at about 7.7 billion around the year 2050 'with enough food, consumer goods, and services to support every one of them in material comfort' (p 201).

Meadows and her colleagues consider this to be a scenario 'the world could actually attain' (p 201). But to begin serious movement in this direction would require a reassessment of fundamental social values; it also raises moral and ethical questions that are so far only on the margins of the sustainability debate. The primary question, of course, is whether under any circumstances short of imminent (and evident) global collapse, the presently rich would be willing to consider any significant reduction in their own material prospects that the poor might live at all.[15] As Lynton Caldwell (1990) observes:

> The prospect of worldwide cooperation to forestall a disaster... seems far less likely where deeply entrenched economic and political interests are involved. Many contemporary values, attitudes, and institutions militate against international altruism. As widely interpreted today, human rights, economic interests, and national sovereignty would be factors in opposition. The cooperative task would require behavior that humans find most difficult: collective self-discipline in a common effort. (p 173)

In this light, empirical evidence on the relationship between ecological decline and sociopolitical stability provides cold comfort. Recent studies suggest that 'in many parts of the world, environmental degradation seems to have passed a threshold of irreversibility' and 'that renewable resource scarcities of the next 50 years will probably occur with a speed, complexity, and magnitude unprecedented in history' (Homer-Dixon et al 1993, p 38). Meanwhile, work on environmentally related social strife suggests that 'so long as [ecological] decline is seen as temporary, advantaged groups are likely to accept policies of relief and redistribution as the price of order and the resumption of growth. Once it is accepted as a persisting condition, however, they will increasingly exert economic and political power to regain their absolute and relative advantages' (Gurr 1985, pp 38–39). In short, the increasing disordering of regional ecosystems and the ecosphere must inevitably be accompanied by increasing social entropy – the breakdown of civil order within countries and increasing turbulence in international relations. Global change and social inertia clearly make poor bedfellows and both factors increase the likelihood of ecological collapse accompanied by geopolitical chaos.

EPILOGUE: WHICH IS THE GOOD NEWS STORY?

On balance, the tack taken here has been fairly optimistic; it is at least technically possible to conceive of an ecologically stable world characterized by economic sufficiency and true social development. At the same time we must recognize that present ecological trends, prevailing sociopolitical values and the dominant economic paradigm all enhance the plausibility of an ecological disaster scenario. While there is much that planners can do to help to engineer sustainability, a strong argument can be made that they might better spend their time planning for ecological failure and the subsequent socioeconomic crash.

As recent history shows, any prediction about the pace of social or technological change is hazardous and we have only begun to probe the depth of our ignorance about global change. Given this uncertainty, every individual – planner and ordinary citizen alike – will have to make a personal decision on where to stand in the sustainability debate. Even if one accepts the fact of an ecological crisis, some equivocation about how to respond is understandable. Fortunately, many measures that might be taken to achieve sustainability will be the more necessary if we are unable to avoid catastrophe, so at least there is some overlap among the objectives of pre-emptive and disaster planning.

Of course, how skilful planners are in communicating the message of sustainability is crucial to the political success of any scenario. People will only support policies and plans if they believe such plans will ultimately improve their general welfare and, if well-informed, they are generally capable of making intelligent decisions and trade-offs. Planners therefore have an urgent professional duty to consider the evidence supporting various alternatives with exceptional care before committing to a particular sustainable development path.

Table 2.3 *A consequences matrix*

...and we act according to the	What if... the natural world behaves according to the	
	Expansionist worldview	*Ecological worldview*
Expansionist worldview	Continuation of present trends: increasing per capita GDP but greater income disparity, increasing social tension and deteriorating global environmental quality	Possible global ecological disaster Geopolitical instability, resource wars Economic chaos
Ecological worldview	A better world: greater social equity, improved environmental quality	Enhanced ecological resilience Improved chances for geopolitical security Economic stability

Ecological sustainability is often presented as a singular option requiring uncomfortable change and economic sacrifice. This is a strategic error by sustainability proponents – sacrifice is always a hard sell! The public must be confident that the future as shaped by policies for sustainable development will be more attractive than that offered by any alternative development strategy. Indeed, this paper argues that to the extent the assumptions and prescriptions of the ecological paradigm are a better reflection of reality than those of mainstream models, it is a *good* news story. Certainly there will wrenching adjustments for many. However, acting in accordance with the ecological paradigm is the surest path to long-term ecological stability and sociopolitical security if the basic assumptions of the model hold. In fact, one could make the case that even if the assumptions of the expansionist paradigm are correct, we would be better off if we acted in accordance with the ecological model. By contrast, there can be little doubt that we would be very much worse off if we acted as expansionists in an ecologically constrained world.

It is worth noting here that where there is great uncertainty about the state of the world and the stakes are high, it makes sense to opt for the strategy that generates the most favourable worst case outcome. As illustrated in Table 2.3, the ecological steady-state satisfies this MaxiMin criterion. In this light, the *bad* news is that even as evidence mounts in support of the ecological perspective, most of the world seems committed as never before to the well-worn expansionist path.

NOTES

1   Ironically, some members of the expansionist school regard the Brundtland Commission as being excessively 'nervous' about the state of the natural world (see Nordhaus 1992). Being seen by conservative economists as relatively radical and by hard core environmentalists as excessively conservative is evidence of the fine line walked by the Commission and of the ambiguity inherent in the 'sustainable development' concept it popularized
2   Binswanger (1993) lists recent treatments of this topic
3   Some of the dissipated matter can be recycled in nature by photosynthesis. However, degraded energy is permanently lost into space
4   Liberally adapted from Costanza and Daly (1992)
5   Nevertheless, surprisingly few major countries meet the weak criterion (and none likely meet the strong criterion – see Pearce and Atkinson 1992, 1993)
6   Even 'complementarity' does not go far enough in some situations. Since human-made capital is made from natural capital and requires natural capital to function, we should say that natural capital is *prerequisite* to manufactured capital
7   This estimate assumes the land is being used sustainably and is therefore a conservative underestimate
8   The world may actually be abandoning the challenge. Even the relatively modest commitments made under *Agenda 21* now appear 'little more than a memory' as proposed projects 'wither for lack of interest on the part of wealthy protagonists' (Stackhouse 1994)
9   Or rather from many finite quantities – the 'environment' encompasses an array of inherently incommensurable ecological goods and services
10 'Theoretical' because Figure 2.3 assumes all costs and benefits can be identified, quantified and monetized
11 The existence of such an optimum does not imply that it should necessarily become a developmental objective. There are any number of reasons why a civilization living below the maximum level of sustainable economic throughput of its habitat might be preferable to one existing right at the cusp. On the other hand, there is no virtue and much hazard associated with life beyond the optimum

12   Garrett Hardin's classic essay, 'The Tragedy of the Commons' (1968) popularized this problem. However, since the traditional 'commons' actually implied group property rights which limited over-exploitation, the 'tragedy of the commons' might better have been called 'the tragedy of open access'

13   The city of Vancouver's landmark *Clouds of Change* report on the potential role of an individual municipality in addressing global atmospheric change is an excellent example (Vancouver 1990)

14   Thousands of fishers' families are now being compensated by the state in Canada following the recent precipitous collapse of North Atlantic ground-fish stocks

15   Ironically , one of the effects of global restructuring under the expansionist paradigm has been a marked *increase* in income disparity in many countries, including the US (see *The Economist* 5–11 November 1994 for several articles on 'slicing the cake')

REFERENCES

Ayres, Robert U 1993. Cowboys, cornucopians and long-run sustainability. *Ecological Economics* 8:189–207

Barker, Terry 1994. Is green economic growth possible? In *Energy-Environment-Economy Modelling Discussion Paper No 7.* Cambridge, UK: Department of Applied Economics, University of Cambridge

Barnett, H and C Morse 1963. *Scarcity and Growth: The Economics of Natural Resource Scarcity.* Baltimore: Johns Hopkins Press

BCSD 1993. *Getting Eco-Efficient.* Report of the BCSD First Antwerp Eco-Efficiency Workshop, November 1993. Geneva: Business Council for Sustainable Development

Beckerman, W 1974. *In Defence of Economic Growth.* London: Jonathan Cape

Beckerman, W 1992. Economic growth and the environment: whose growth? whose environment? *World Development* 20:4:481–496

Binswanger, Mathias 1993. From microscopic to macroscopic theories: entropic aspects of ecological and economic processes. *Ecological Economics* 8:209–234

Brown, Lester, Christopher Flaven, and Sandra Postel 1991. *Saving the Planet: How to Shape an Environmentally Sustainable Global Economy.* Washington, DC: Worldwatch Institute

Brown, Lester, Sandra Postel and Christopher Flavin 1991. From growth to sustainable development. In *Environmentally Sustainable Economic Development: Building on Brundtland.* R Goodland, H Daly, S El Serafy and B von Droste (eds) Paris:UNESCO

de Bruyn, S M and J B Opschoor 1993. De- or relinking economic development with the environment (draft manuscript). The Netherlands: Department of Spatial and Environmental Economics, Free University and Tinbergen Institute

Caldwell, Lynton Keith 1990. *Between Two Worlds: Science, the Environmental Movement, and Policy Choice.* Cambridge, UK: Cambridge University Press

Carpenter, R A 1990. Biophysical measurement of sustainable development. *The Environmental Professional* 12:356–359

Carpenter, R A 1994a. Pers comm

Carpenter, R A 1994b. Can we measure sustainability? *Ecology International Bulletin* 21:27–36

Catton, William 1986. Carrying capacity and the limits to freedom. Paper prepared for Social Ecology Session 1, XI World congress of Sociology. New Delhi, India (18 August, 1986)

Christensen, Paul 1991. Driving forces, increasing returns, and ecological sustainability. In *Ecological Economics: The Science and Management of Sustainability* (R Costanza, ed) New York: Columbia University Press

Costanza, Robert and Herman E Daly 1992. Natural capital and sustainable development. *Conservation Biology* 1:37–45

Daly, Herman E 1990. Sustainable development: from concept and theory towards operational principles. *Population and Development Review* (special issue). Reprinted in Herman E Daly 1991. *Steady State Economics* (2nd ed). Washington: Island Press

Daly, Herman E 1991a. From empty world economics to full world economics: recognizing an historic turning point in economic development. In *Environmentally Sustainable Economic Development: Building on Brundtland* R Goodland, H Daly, S El Serafy and B von Droste (eds) Paris:UNESCO

Daly, Herman E 1991b. The concept of a steady-state economy. In H Daly *Steady-State Economics* (2nd ed) Washington: Island Press

Daly, Herman E 1991c. The circular flow of exchange value and the linear throughput of matter-energy: a case of misplaced concreteness. In H Daly *Steady-State Economics* (2nd ed) Washington: Island Press

Daly, Herman E 1992. Steady-state economics: concepts, questions, policies. *Gaia* 6:333–338

Economist, The 1994. November 5–11

Dasgupta, P and D Heal 1979. *Economic Theory and Exhaustible Resources* London: Cambridge University Press

Ekins, Paul and Michael Jacobs 1994. Are environmental sustainability and economic growth compatible? In: *Energy-Environment-Economy Modelling Discussion Paper No 7* Cambridge, UK: Department of Applied Economics, University of Cambridge

Ekins, Paul 1993. 'Limits to growth' and 'sustainable development': grappling with ecological realities *Ecological Economics* 8:269–288

Georgescu-Roegen, Nicholas 1971. *The Entropy Law and the Economic Process* Cambridge, MS: Harvard University Press

Girardet, Herbert 1992. *The Gaia Atlas of Cities: New Directions for Sustainable Urban Living* Anchor/Doubleday

Goodland, Robert 1991. The case that the world has reached limits. In *Environmentally Sustainable Economic Development: Building on Brundtland.* R Goodland, H Daly, S El Serafy and B Von Droste (eds). Paris: UNESCO

Gurr, Ted R 1985. On the political consequences of scarcity and economic decline. *International Studies Quarterly* 29:51–75 (p 58)

Hardin, G 1968. The tragedy of the commons. *Science* 162:1243–48

Holling, C S 1994. New science and new investments for a sustainable biosphere. In *Investing in Natural Capital: The Ecological Economics Approach to Sustainability* (A-M Jansson, M Hammer, C Folke and R Costanza, eds) Washington: Island Press

Homer-Dixon, Thomas F, Jeffrey H Boutwell and George W Rathjens 1993. Environmental change and violent conflict. *Scientific American*, February 1993

IUCN/UNEP/WWF 1991. *Caring for the Earth: A Strategy for Sustainable Living.* Gland, Switzerland: World Conservation Union/United Nations Environment Program/World Wide Fund for Nature

Jacobs, Michael 1991. *The Green Economy* London: Pluto Press

Jung, H Y, and P Jung 1993. Francis Bacon's philosophy of nature: a postmodern critique. *The Trumpeter* 10:3:86–89

Kay, James and Erik Schneider 1994. Embracing complexity: the challenge of the ecosystem approach. *Alternatives* 20:3:32–39

Ludwig, Donald, Ray Hilborn, and Carl Walters 1993. Uncertainty, resource exploitation, and conservation: lessons from history. *Science* 260:17+36

Maturana, Humberto R and Francisco J Varela 1988. *The Tree of Knowledge.* Boston: New Science Library

Meadows, Donella H, Dennis L Meadows, and Jørgen Randers 1992. *Beyond the Limits* Toronto: McClelland & Stewart

Milbrath, Lester 1989. *Envisioning a Sustainable Society (Learning Our Way Out)* Albany, NY: Suny Press

MOHPPE 1988. *To Choose or Lose: National Environmental Policy Plan.* The Hague, The Netherlands: Ministry of Housing, Physical Planning and Environment

Mollison, Bill 1990. *Permaculture: A Designer's Manual* New South Wales: Tagari Publications

Nicolis, G and I Prigogine 1977. *Self-organization in Nonequilibrium Systems* Chichester: J Wiley and Sons

Nordhaus, William D 1992. Lethal Model 2: the limits to growth revisited. *Brookings Papers on Economic Activity* 2:1–43

Ophuls, William and A Stephen Boyan, jr 1992. *Ecology and the Politics of Scarcity Revisited: The Unraveling of the American Dream* New York: W H Freeman and Company

Pearce, David and Giles Atkinson 1992. *Are National Economies Sustainable?: Measuring Sustainable Development* CSERGE Discussion Paper GEC 92–11. London: University College Centre for Social and Economic Research on the Global Environment

Pearce, David W and Giles D Atkinson 1993. Capital theory and the measurement of sustainable development: an indicator of weak sustainability *Ecological Economics* 8: 103–108

Pearce, David, Anil Markandya and Edward Barbier 1989. *Blueprint for a Green Economy* London: Earthscan Publications

Pearce, David 1994a. *Valuing the Environment: Past Practice, Future Prospect.* CSERGE Working Paper PA 94-02. London: University College Centre for Social and Economic Research on the Global Environment

Pearce, David 1994b. *Sustainable Consumption Through Economic Instruments.* Paper prepared for the Government of Norway Symposium on Sustainable Consumption, Oslo, 19–20 January, 1994

Pearce, David, Edward Barbier and Anil Markandya 1990. *Sustainable Development: Economics and Environment in the Third World* Aldershot: Edward Elgar

Pezzey, John 1989. *Economic Analysis of Sustainable Growth and Sustainable Development* Environment Department Working Paper No 15. Washington: World Bank

Quarrie, Joyce, ed 1992. *Earth Summit '92* London: Regency Press. See United Nations 1992

Rees, William and Mark Roseland 1991. Sustainable communities: planning for the 21st century. *Plan Canada* 31:3:15–26

Rees, William E 1991. Economics, ecology, and the limits of conventional analysis. *Journal of the Air Waste Management Association* 41:10:1323–1327

Rees, William E 1992. Ecological footprints and appropriated carrying capacity: what urban economics leaves out. *Environment and Urbanization* 4:2:121–130

Rees, William E 1994a. Revisiting carrying capacity: area-based indicators of sustainability. Paper presented to the International Workshop on *Evaluation Criteria for a Sustainable Economy,* 6–7 April 1994 (proceedings forthcoming).Graz, Austria: Institut für Verfahrenstechnik, Technische Universität Graz

Rees, William E 1994b. *Sustainability, Growth, and Employment: Toward an Ecologically Sustainable, Economically Secure, and Socially Satisfying Future.* Paper prepared for the IISD Employment and Sustainable Development Project. Winnipeg: International Institute for Sustainable Development

Rees, William E and Mathis Wackernagel 1994. Ecological footprints and appropriated carrying capacity: measuring the natural capital requirements of the human economy. In *Investing in Natural Capital: The Ecological Economics Approach to Sustainability* (A-M Jansson, M Hammer, C Folke, and R Costanza, eds) Washington: Island Press

Rees, William E 1990. The ecology of sustainable development. *The Ecologist* 20:1:18–23; or Sustainable Development and the Biosphere: Concepts and Principles. *Teilhard Studies Number 23* Chambersburg, PA: Anima Books (for American Teilhard Association for the Future of Man)

RMNO 1994b. *Sustainable Resource Management and Resource Use: Policy Questions and Research Needs* Publication No 97. Rijswijk, The Netherlands: Advisory Council for Research on Nature and Environment (RMNO)

RMNO 1994a. *Toward Environmental Performance Indicators Based on the Notion of Environmental Space.* Publication No 96. Rijswijk, The Netherlands: Advisory Council for Research on Nature and Environment (RMNO)

Roseland, Mark 1992. *Toward Sustainable Communities* Ottawa: National Round Table on the Environment and the Economy

Schmidt-Bleek, F 1993a. MIPS – A universal ecological measure. *Fresenius Environmental Bulletin* 1:306–311

Schmidt-Bleek, F 1993b. MIPS revisited. *Fresenius Environmental Bulletin* 2:407–412

Schneider, Eric D and James J Kay 1994. Life as a manifestation of the second law of thermodynamics. *Advances in Mathematics and Computers in Medicine* (in press)

Schulze, Peter C 1994. Cost-benefit analysis and environmental policy. *Ecological Economics* 9:197–199

Solow, Robert 1974. The economics of resources or the resources of economics. *American Economics Review* 64:2:1–14 (Papers and Proceedings of the 86th Annual Meeting of the American Economic Association)

Solow, Robert 1986. On the intergenerational allocation of natural resources. *Scandinavian Journal of Economics* 88:1

Stackhouse, J 1994. Rio summit little more than a memory. *Globe and Mail* (Toronto, 10 December, 1994)

Stahel, Walter and Tim Jackson 1993. Optimal utilization and durability. In *Clean Production Strategies* (T Jackson, ed) London: Lewis Publishers (for the Stockholm Environment Institute)

United Nations 1992. *Agenda 21* New York: United Nations (United Nations Conference on Environment and Development)

Vancouver 1990. *Clouds of Change: Final Report of the City of Vancouver Task Force on Atmospheric Change* Vancouver: City of Vancouver

Vatn, Arild and Daniel W Bromley 1993. Choices without prices without apologies. *Journal of Environmental Economics and Management* 26:129–148

Victor, Peter A 1991. Indicators of sustainable development: some lessons from capital theory *Ecological Economics* 4:191–213

Victor, Peter A, Edward Hanna and Atif Kubursi 1994. How strong is weak sustainability? Paper prepared for a symposium on Models for Sustainable Development (Paris, March 1994) Forthcoming in Silvie Faucheux, Jan van der Straaten and Martin O'Connor, eds. *Sustainable Development: Analysis and Public Policy* Dordrecht: Kluwer Academic Publishers

Vitousek, Peter, Paul R Ehrlich, Anne H Ehrlich, and P Matson 1986. Human appropriation of the products of photosynthesis. *BioScience* 36:368–374

WCED 1987. *Our Common Future* Oxford: Oxford University Press for the UN World Commission on Economy and Environment

von Weizsäcker, Ernst U 1994. *Earth Politics* London: Zed Books (see Chapter 11: Ecological Tax Reform)

Wilson, E O 1988. The current state of biological diversity. In *Biodiversity* (E O Wilson, ed) Washington, DC: National Academy Press

Young, John and Aaron Sachs 1994. *The Next Efficiency Revolution: Creating a Sustainable Materials Economy* Worldwatch paper 121: Washington: The Worldwatch Institute

Part II
Linking Sustainable Development and Cities

Chapter 3

Cities as Solutions in an Urbanizing World

UN Centre for Human Settlements

(Reprinted from Chapter 13 (pp 417–421) of UNCHS (Habitat), *An Urbanizing World: Global Report on Human Settlements 1996*, Oxford University Press, Oxford and New York, 1996 with permission from The UN Centre for Human Settlements)

MOVING AWAY FROM A NEGATIVE VIEW OF CITIES

Cities have long been blamed for many human failings. Capital cities are often blamed for the failures or inadequacies of the government institutions located there. The wealthiest cities are often blamed for the inequalities in income that the contrasts between their richest and poorest districts make visible. Cities in general and industrial cities in particular are blamed for environmental degradation. Images such as 'exploding cities' and 'mushrooming cities' are often used to convey a process of population growth and urbanization that is 'out of control'. Cities are often blamed for corroding the social fabric. Within the current concern for 'sustainable development', cities are often cited as the main 'problem'.

Yet this Report, in surveying the evidence, found little substance to these criticisms. These criticisms forget the central role that cities and urban systems have in stronger and more stable economies that in turn have underpinned great improvements in living standards for a considerable portion of the world's population over the last few decades. Average life expectancy, worldwide, grew by more than 12 years between 1960 and 1992, while in many countries it grew by 18 or more years.[1] Data presented in earlier chapters showed the close association between urbanization and economic growth and the fact that urbanization is not 'out of control'; it also showed the high concentration of the world's largest cities in the world's largest economies. The tendency to consider 'rapid urbanization' as a problem forgets that the world's wealthiest nations also underwent periods of rapid urbanization and that the rate of increase in the level of urbanization in countries in the South is rarely larger than that experienced in earlier decades by countries in the North.[2] While it is true that many cities have grown very rapidly, this is largely a reflection of the rate at which their economies grew.[3]

The attempts to imply a link between 'exploding cities' and 'rapid population growth' in the South ignore the fact that those who live in or move to cities generally have smaller families than those living elsewhere and that the countries with the largest increase in their level of urbanization over the last 20–30 years are also generally those with the largest falls in population growth rates.[4] Chapter 1 also noted that cities are not 'mushrooming'; indeed, most of the world's largest cities have long histories and a high proportion of the major cities that do not are in North America and Australia. This hardly suggests that the appearance of major new cities is associated with poverty.

Many cities certainly have a high concentration of poverty. The scale of urban poverty and its depth in terms of the deprivation, ill health and premature death it causes have been greatly underestimated.[5] But worldwide, the scale and depth of poverty in rural areas remains higher, if sometimes less visible. In general, the higher the level of urbanization in a country, the lower the level of absolute poverty.

Anti-city polemic also obscures the real causes of social or ecological ills. It fails to point to those responsible for resource overuse and environmental degradation and fails to perceive the great advantages (or potential advantages) that cities offer for greatly reducing resource use and wastes. It is not cities that are responsible for most resource use, waste, pollution and greenhouse gas emissions, but particular industries and commercial and industrial enterprises (or corporations), and middle and upper income groups with high consumption lifestyles. Most such enterprises and consumers may be concentrated in cities but a considerable (and probably growing) proportion are not. In the North and in the wealthier cities or regions of the South, it is the middle or upper income household with two or three cars living in rural areas or small towns or low density outer suburbs of cities that has the highest consumption of resources – generally much more so than those with similar incomes living within cities.

The Positive Role and Advantages of Cities

Cities have the potential to combine safe and healthy living conditions and culturally rich and enjoyable lifestyles with remarkably low levels of energy consumption, resource-use and wastes.[6] The fact that cities concentrate production and population gives them some obvious advantages over rural settlements or dispersed populations.

The first advantage is that high densities mean much lower costs per household and per enterprise for the provision of piped, treated water supplies, the collection and disposal of household and human wastes, advanced telecommunications and most forms of health care and education. It also makes much cheaper the provision of emergency services – for instance, fire-fighting and the emergency response to acute illness or injury that can greatly reduce the health burden for the people affected. The concentration of people and production may present problems for waste collection and disposal, but these are not problems that are insuperable, especially where a priority is given to minimizing wastes. There are also the long-established traditions in many cities in the South which ensure high levels of recycling or re-use of wastes on which government's solid waste management can build.[7] Within the largest cities, the concentration of population can make the treatment and disposal of sewage problematic given the volume of excreta and waste water that needs to be disposed of. But this is rarely a major problem in smaller cities and towns, where most of the world's urban population lives. There are many examples of the successful and safe utilization of sewage for intensive crop production.[8] There are also an increasing number of examples of effective sanitation systems that do not require high volumes of water, including some that require no water at all[9] (although water is always needed for hand washing and personal hygiene in general). The techniques for enormously reducing the use of fresh water in city homes and enterprises, including recycling or directly reusing waste waters, are well known, where freshwater resources are scarce,[10] although it is agriculture, not cities, that dominates the use of fresh water in most nations.[11]

The second advantage that cities provide is the concentration of production and consumption, which means a greater range and possibility for efficient use of resources – through the reclamation of materials from waste streams and its reuse or recycling – and for the specialist enterprises that ensure this can happen safely. Cities make possible material or waste exchanges between industries. The collection of recyclable or reusable wastes from homes and businesses is generally cheaper, per person served. Cities have cheaper unit costs for many measures to promote the use of reusable containers (and cut down on disposable containers) or to collect chlorofluorocarbons from fridges and other forms of cooling equipment.

The third advantage is that a much higher population concentration in cities means a reduced demand for land relative to population. In most countries, urban areas take up less than 1 per cent of the national territory. The entire world's urban population would fit into an area of 200,000 square kilometres – roughly the size of Senegal or Oman – at densities similar to those of high-class, much valued inner city residential areas in European cities – for instance, Chelsea in London.[12] In most cities around the world, there are examples of high-quality, high-density residential areas. In the central districts of certain cities, the popularity of housing has increased, as governments controlled private automobiles, improved public transit and encouraged a rich and diverse street life.[13] Although unchecked urban (or more often suburban) sprawl is often taking place over valuable agricultural land, this can often be avoided. And in many cities in the South, the scale of urban agriculture is such that a significant proportion of city-consumption of food is also produced within the city.[14]

The fourth advantage of cities in climates where homes and businesses need to be heated for parts of the year is that the concentration of production and residential areas means a considerable potential for reducing fossil-fuel use – for instance, through the use of waste process heat from industry or thermal power stations to provide space heating for homes and commercial buildings. Certain forms of high-density housing such as terraces and apartment blocks also considerably reduce heat loss from each housing unit, when compared to detached housing. There are also many measures that can be taken to reduce heat gain in buildings to eliminate or greatly reduce the demand for electricity for air-conditioning.[15]

The fifth advantage of cities is that they represent a much greater potential for limiting the use of motor vehicles, including greatly reducing the fossil fuels they need and the air pollution and high levels of resource consumption that their use implies. This might sound contradictory, since most of the world's largest cities have serious problems with congestion and motor-vehicle generated air pollution. But cities ensure that many more trips can be made through walking or bicycling. They also make possible a much greater use of public transport and make economically feasible a high-quality service. Thus, although cities tend to be associated with a high level of private automobile use, cities and urban systems also represent the greatest potential for allowing their inhabitants quick and cheap access to a great range of locations, without the need to use private automobiles.

Cities are also among societies' most precious cultural artefacts. This can be seen in the visual and decorative arts, music and dance, theatre and literature that develop there and in the variety and diversity of street life evident in most cities. In most cities, there are buildings, streets, layouts and neighbourhoods that form a central part of the history and culture of that society. Some of the most lively expressions of popular culture are evident in many of the poorer areas in cities, both in art[16] and in music.[17] Many cities or particular city districts demonstrate how cities can provide healthy, stimulating and valued housing and living environments for their inhabitants without imposing unsustainable demands on natural resources and ecosystems.

Cities are also places in which the 'social economy' has developed most, and where it must prosper, not only for the benefits it brings to each street or neighbourhood but also for the economic and social costs it saves the wider society.[18] The social economy is a term given to a great variety of initiatives and actions that are organized and controlled locally and that are not profit-oriented. It includes many activities that are unwaged and unmonetized, including the work of citizen groups, residents' associations, street or *barrio* clubs, youth clubs, parent associations that support local schools and the voluntary workers who help ensure that a preventive focused health-care system reaches out to all those in need within its locality. It includes many voluntary groups that provide services for the elderly, the physically

---

Box 3.1 *Local exchange trading systems (LETS)*

Many cities have various forms of community exchanges operating within particular localities. During the 1980s and early 1990s, Local Exchange Trading Systems became increasingly popular as formal systems by which people in any locality or neighbourhood could exchange goods and services without money. These serve to, in effect, increase the purchasing power of those involved and the range of goods and services they can afford while also retaining value within the locality.

LETS schemes function by publishing a list of goods and services offered for sale by its members, priced in particular units of account set up by that scheme. This allows members to exchange goods and services with no money changing hands. As a member provides goods or services to another member, so they run up credit that is recorded by the scheme. A member who 'purchases' these goods or services has a debit that is then paid off by providing goods or services to another member. All members receive regular statements to keep them informed of their position.

There are LETS groups in many countries, including more than 200 LETS groups in the UK and close to 200 in Australia. Some have grown to a considerable size – for instance, one in the Blue Mountains in Australia has 1000 accounts involving more than 2000 people. A survey in the UK found that the average membership is 70 and that groups tend to double in size in a year until they reach a membership of around 250, when their growth rate slows down. In this same survey, 25 per cent of members were unemployed and 12 per cent worked part-time. Over a third of the LETS have businesses as members, rather than individuals.

Sources: Graham Boyd, 'The urban social economy', *Urban Examples*, UNICEF, New York, 1995; and Long, Peter, *Let's Work; Rebuilding the Local Economy*, Grover Books, Bristol, 1994

---

disabled or other individuals in need of special support. It often includes many initiatives that make cities safer and more fun, helping to provide supervised play space, sport and recreational opportunities for children and youth. It may provide formal or informal supervision or maintenance of parks, squares and other public spaces. But it includes enterprises and initiatives that have paid workers and sell goods and services – for instance, local enterprises which combine social as well as commercial aims, owned by people within a defined locality or who share other forms of common interest. It also includes initiatives to support such enterprises – for instance, the many community enterprise development trusts set up in recent years and the local-exchange trading systems that are now in evidence in more than 20 countries (see Box 3.1).

The social economy within each locality creates a dense fabric of relationships that allow local citizens to work together in identifying and acting on local problems or in taking local initiatives.[19] Its value to city life is often enormous, but this is often forgotten by governments and international agencies, as it is almost impossible to calculate its value in monetary terms. A considerable proportion of the economic growth in the wealthier countries in recent decades has come from shifting functions from the social economy where their value was not counted in economic terms (and not recorded in GNP statistics) to the market economy. Energies once invested in developing and maintaining family and community relationships and in building or supporting local initiatives and institutions had to be redirected to earn sufficient income to pay the taxes that then funded government responses to the problems the social economy had helped to address or keep in check – for instance, structural unemployment, insecurity, vandalism, crime and a sense, among many low-income households and youth, of being excluded from social and political processes.

The Role of Governance

Perhaps the single most important – and difficult – aspect of urban development is developing the institutional structure to manage it in ways that ensure that the advantages noted above are utilized, and also done in ways that are accountable to urban populations. Most of the problems described in this Report in terms of very poor housing, lack of piped water and provision for sanitation and drainage, the lack of basic services such as health care, the serious and often rising problem of urban violence, the problems of traffic congestion and air and water pollution arise largely from a failure of government institutions to manage rapid change and to tap the knowledge, resources and capacities among the population within each city. Indeed, governments have often helped to destroy or stifle the 'social economy' in cities that is so central to their prosperity and to the capacity of the inhabitants in each locality to identify and act on their own priorities.

Making full use of the potential that cities have to offer requires 'good governance'. The evidence of the 1980s and early 1990s is that 'good governance' can bring major economic and social gains, and much less environmental degradation. This can be seen in the extent to which such critical social indicators as infant mortality and life expectancy vary between countries with comparable levels of per capita income or between cities of comparable size and prosperity. For nations with relatively low incomes per person, 'good governance' at the level of a city or nation can deliver a 10- to 15-year increase in levels of life expectancy above the average.[20] There is also no contradiction between high social achievement and good economic performance; indeed, the link may be that high social achievement is associated with better than average economic performance.

'Good governance' can also be assessed in the extent to which city, regional and national governments ensure that people within their boundaries have safe, sufficient water supplies, provision for sanitation, education and health care. Although, in general, the proportion of the population with access to these rises, the wealthier the city and the higher the country's per capita income, there is great variation in performance between nations and cities with comparable levels of per capita income. In most nations, there has also been a failure to consider the economic costs – as well as the immense social costs – of not ensuring basic service provision to their populations.

A successful city is one where the many different goals of its inhabitants and enterprises are met, without passing on costs to other people (including future generations) or to their regions. It is also one where the social economy is allowed to thrive. But in the absence of 'good governance', cities tend to be centres of pollution and waste. Even when pollution levels are much reduced in the city – as they have been in most cities in the North – this is often because environmental costs are being passed on to other regions – for instance, through acid rain and water pollution and dumping wastes generated within the city outside its boundaries. City enterprises and households can also pass on costs to future generations through overuse of scarce resources and through their contributions to greenhouse gas emissions. Worldwide, city-based enterprises and consumers account for a high proportion of all resource use. They also produce a high proportion of all wastes, including toxic and hazardous wastes and air and water pollution.

In the absence of 'good governance', cities can be unhealthy and dangerous places in which to live and work. Each household and enterprise can reduce their costs by passing their environmental problems of solid and liquid wastes and air pollution on to others. At least 600 million urban dwellers in the South live in very poor conditions – many of them in illegal settlements – with very inadequate provision for water, sanitation, drainage, garbage collection and other basic services. Meanwhile, in the absence of a planning framework, city expansion takes place haphazardly and often with urban sprawl over the best quality farmland. Hundreds of millions of low income households live in illegal or informal settlements that developed on land ill-suited to housing – for instance, on flood-plains or steep slopes with a high risk of landslides or mudslides. They live here because these are the only land sites which they can afford or where their illegal occupation will not be challenged because the land site is too dangerous for any commercial use. Hundreds of millions of city inhabitants have been forced to find or build homes in illegal settlements, where the threat of forced eviction is always present.

NOTES AND REFERENCES

1   More details of this were presented in Chapter 3 of the *Global Report* from which this extract is drawn

2   See, for instance, Preston, Samuel H, 'Urban growth in developing countries: a demographic reappraisal', *Population and Development Review*, Vol 5, No 2, 1979 and Satterthwaite, David, 'The scale and nature of urban change in the South', IIED Working Paper, London, 1996

3   There are some exceptions, as described in Chapters 1 and 2, but most rapidly growing cities are also cities whose economy is growing

4   The countries with the largest increases in levels of urbanization during the 1980s are also generally those with the largest increase in their economies, as described in Chapters 1 and 2. These chapters also described how population growth rates are generally lowest in the countries with the highest per capita incomes and the highest levels of urbanization. Over the last 15–20 years, population growth rates have also generally declined most in the countries with the most rapid economic growth, although there are important exceptions – see Cleland, John, 'Population growth in the 21st century; cause for crisis or celebration', Paper presented to the 21st Century Trust meeting on *Population Growth, Health and Development: Problems and Prospects for the 21st Century*, Oxford, 1995

5   More details of this were presented in Chapter 3 of the *Global Report* from which this extract is drawn

6   This section draws from Satterthwaite, David, 'Sustainable Cities', *Resurgence*, Issue 67, November/December 1994, pp 20–23

7   More details of this are given in Chapter 8 of the *Global Report*

8   Smit, Jac and Joe Nasr, 'Urban agriculture for sustainable cities: using wastes and idle land and water bodies as resources', *Environment and Urbanization*, Vol 4, No 2, October 1992; Mara, Duncan and Sandy Cairncross, *Guidelines for the Safe Use of Wastewater and Excreta in Agriculture and Aquaculture*, World Health Organization, Geneva, 1990

9   Winblad, Uno and Wen Kilama, *Sanitation without Water*, Macmillan, Basingstoke, 1985; Pickford, John, *Low-cost Sanitation: a Survey of Practical Experience*, Intermediate Technology Publications, London, 1995

10   See, for instance, The Water Program, *Water Efficiency: A Resource for Utility Managers, Community Planners and other Decision Makers*, Rocky Mountain Institute, Snowmass, 1991

11   See Table 22.1, pp 330–331 in World Resources Institute, *World Resources 1990–91: a Guide to the Global Environment*, Oxford University Press, Oxford, 1990

12   The example of Chelsea was chosen because it combines very high-quality housing, very little of which is in high rises (and most of which is pre-20th century) with a diverse economic base, large amounts of open space and among the best educational and cultural facilities in London. With a population density of around 120 persons per hectare, it is an example of how relatively high density need not imply overcrowding or poor quality living environments. The world's urban population of around 2.6 billion in 1995 would fit into an area of land similar to that of Senegal (197,000 square kilometres) or Oman (212,000 square kilometres) at a density comparable to that of Chelsea

13   See Chapter 9 of the original *Global Report*

14   The scale of agricultural production in any city is obviously dependent on where the boundaries are drawn. Many cities and most metropolitan areas have boundaries that are considerably larger than the central highly built-up core and include large areas which are intensively farmed

15   Chapter 12 of the *Global Report* gave more details of this

16   See as one example the street art developed by young people in Dakar, Senegal, that is shown in ENDA, *Set setal: des murs qui parlent – nouvelle culture urbaine a Dakar*, No 143 in series Etudes et Recherches, ENDA, Dakar, 1991

17   Examples would include the schools of samba within the *favelas* of Rio de Janeiro and the strength and diversity of so much modern African music that originates from poorer areas of African cities, a small proportion of which has found a wider international audience in recent years

18   This material on the social economy is drawn largely from Korten, David C, *Civic Engagement to Create Just and Sustainable Societies for the 21st Century*, A Conference Issues Paper prepared for Habitat II, 1995; and Boyd, Graham, 'The urban social economy', *Urban Examples*, UNICEF, New York, 1995

19   Korten 1995, op cit

20   See Chapter 3 of the *Global Report*

Chapter 4

Environmental Justice and the Sustainable City

Graham Haughton

(Reprinted from the *Journal of Planning Education and Research* Vol 18, No 3, 1999, pp 233–43 © Association of Collegiate Schools of Planning)

JUSTICE, EQUITY AND SUSTAINABILITY

Recent years have seen a re-emergent interest in issues surrounding social justice and environmental justice, with the two increasingly seen as interlinked (Friedmann 1989; Harvey 1992; Hofrichter 1993; Smith 1994; Hay 1994; see Harvey 1973, and Berry and Steiker 1974 for earlier discussions). This resurgent interest in examining justice issues has been accompanied by a more general reawakened interest in normative theoretical approaches within planning and geography, with detailed examination of values (rights, ethics, quality of life) being reinserted with renewed confidence into recent work within these disciplines (Beatley 1994; Bourne 1996; Smith 1997; Sayer and Storper 1997). The need to re-evaluate the ethical underpinnings of policy and analysis has been given additional impetus by the emergence of sustainable development debates – Lipietz (1996 p 223), for instance, argues that the greatest achievement of the 1992 Rio Earth Summit and related conferences may well be the widespread popular and political acknowledgement of the need for 'new rights and obligations to be incorporated within social norms', involving 'the recognition, at first moral, of new rights, new bearers of rights and of new objects of rights'. In this view, the discourse of sustainable development has enlarged consideration of rights through its explicit attention to the rights of future generations, of present-day socially marginalized groups to a 'good' environment, and also to the need to consider 'Other' (non-human) dimensions of the natural world as having rights to continued existence, as recognized in biodiversity treaties.

Reflecting theoretical debates over local-global dimensions of economic restructuring, social justice and environmental justice debates involved equity issues at a range of scales, from the local to the global, and also the broader economic, social and political systems which foster and perpetuate inequalities between different social groups and different areas. In environmental terms this requires looking both at systems which generate environmentally degrading activities and also at differential access to environmental 'goods' and environmental 'bads,' notably as expressed in differential impacts on different social groups, sectors and geographical areas. A particularly powerful illustration is provided by environmental racism debates which have highlighted how cases of environmental dumping, such as the concentration of toxic waste incineration plants found in poor areas, have exercised disproportionate adverse impacts on areas with large concentrations of people of colour in many instances (Bullard 1990; 1993). Environmental justice and social justice are seen as intrinsically connected in such analyses, with both treated in this article in this larger conception of addressing both the underlying systemic *causes* of injustice and the more traditional distributive justice concerns of seeking to redress inequalities of outcome. This is important since some commentators have begun to question whether a narrow 'equity' concern with distributional aims (eg decisions on who comes to be most polluted and where) may have the unintended perverse effect of overshadowing more broadly constituted 'justice' concerns with addressing underlying structural issues – that is, engaging with systems to reduce or prevent pollution rather than distribute it more equitably (Young 1990; Pulido 1994; Heiman 1996; Lake 1996).

This article sets out a small number of interlinked principles for sustainable development which derive from these concerns, and then moves on to assess how four different sets of approaches to creating a sustainable city measure up against them. One of the basic premises of the analysis here is that a sustainable city cannot be achieved purely in internal terms: a sustainable city is essentially one which contributes effectively to the global aims of sustainable development, where sustainable development is seen as much as a process as an end-product. With the emergence of ever-thickening and extending patterns of global economic trading, and increasingly global exchanges of environmental resources and waste streams, it is futile and indeed virtually meaningless to attempt to create a 'sustainable city' in isolation from its broader hinterland area. Moreover, it is necessary to see that cities make other contributions to global well-being which make a purely local focus on their environmental impacts potentially unhelpful. Or, to put it another way, a densely developed, highly populated city could well be deemed 'unsustainable' if looked at solely at the local level, in terms of its dependence on the appropriated environmental assets of other regions: alternatively, at a regional or even global scale, this form of city may be preferable to sprawling, low density, low-level developments, consuming considerable agricultural land and requiring considerable energy for transportation between dispersed activities. In a global sense then, a high-density city which overcrowds and displaces the already transformed 'natural' environment at the local level may be preferable to lower density forms of urban development where at the local level 'nature' survives rather better. In part, how one makes a judgement on such issues depends on whether a weak or strong definition of sustainability is adopted – that is, the extent to which it is seen as acceptable to replace natural capital with human capital, and in particular the approach taken to preserving critical natural stocks. In the four approaches to sustainable urban development outlined below, it becomes clear that each embodies a different perspective in this respect, although the issues are not teased out in full here – the emphasis is rather on equity and justice issues. In urban management terms, these tensions in defining what the sustainable city is, or might be, are important in guiding attention to the need to look at the underlying philosophical bases of local actions in support of sustainable development, whilst also directing attention to look globally as well as locally when assessing the overall impacts of policies in support of sustainable urban development.

It is valuable to begin by elaborating on what sustainable development actually means and on some of its tensions. Ultimately sustainable development means the long-term survival of the planet and its processes of dynamic evolution, including the wide range of species which currently live on it, not least humankind. For humans, it specifically requires achieving a position which allows us to live in harmony with the rest of the planet, so that we neither destroy ourselves nor the systems which support other life-forms. The essential threat to sustainable development is that the human species is attempting to live beyond the capacity of the Earth to sustain both humans and other species, most notably as we destroy the natural balance of critical natural protective systems, from depletion of the ozone layer to the creation of the greenhouse effect. Moving towards sustainable development requires achieving economic and social systems which encourage environmental stewardship of resources for the long-term, acknowledging the interdependency of social justice, economic well-being and environmental stewardship. The social dimension is critical since the unjust society is unlikely to be sustainable in environmental or economic terms in the long-run, since the social tensions which are created undermine the need for recognizing reciprocal rights and obligations, leading in all manner of ways to environmental degradation and ultimately to political breakdown.

The tensions between economic development and environmental stewardship are a central feature of the sustainable development debate, with controversy surrounding the Brundtland Commission's (WCED 1987) declared view that economic development is essential in order to meet the social goals of sustainable development. The critics of this view hold that economic growth within the current dominant market-driven capitalist mode is largely responsible for environmental degradation, therefore we need to question whether continued economic expansion of this type is either desirable or acceptable (Seabrook 1990; O'Connor 1993, 1994). It is precisely because the Brundtland Commission's growth-compatible vision of sustainable development version is more politically palatable that its definition gained so much political support, whilst more radical views have remained a marginalized part of the sustainable development discourse.

This brings the analysis back to the varying possible interpretations of sustainable development: these have been described as running along a spectrum from 'very weak' or 'light green' versions to 'very strong' or 'deep green' interpretations (Turner, Pearce and Bateman 1994). Proponents of the weak version are held to have a largely anthropocentric worldview, which sees considerable scope for technological solutions to environmental problems, and in particular for the substitutability of natural capital with human capital – for instance, replacing fossil fuel-derived energy with new technologies for creating nuclear energy or capturing tidal energy. Versions of 'environmentalism' which support 'sustainable profits' or 'sustainable accumulation' by private enterprises are generally regarded as 'light green' in that they tinker at the edges with the existing system of accumulation, rather than seek radical transformations in favour of preserving natural assets. By contrast, proponents of deep-green sustainability views tend to emphasize that market-led systems of capitalist growth reductively consign nature to a role of mere market 'inputs' or 'outputs', limited only by the capacity of the market to make profits out of these natural assets, in the process inevitably leading to environmental degradation. The strong version of sustainability holds a more nature-centred worldview, which seeks to prevent destruction of natural assets beyond their regenerative capacities by reducing overall consumption levels and to avoid unnecessary high risks associated with some untested quick-fix technological solutions. In particular, the strong sustainability perspective argues against wholesale 'substitutability' of natural with human assets, involving a more widely constructed definition of critical natural stocks – that is, those natural assets which cannot be used beyond their natural regenerative capacities without major damage to the integrity of ecosystems.

In order to move towards sustainable development it is essential to address the way in which our current political, economic and social systems allow widespread cost-transference to take place, where many of the negative environmental and related impacts of the activity of a person, company or even region, are in effect displaced elsewhere (Haughton 1998). At the urban level resource demands can exercise major impacts on other areas – for instance, in the valleys where reservoirs are built to supply cities, whilst urban pollution of water can have negative impacts on downstream users and natural aquatic ecosystems. We have currently evolved sophisticated systems for hiding our responsibilities for the deleterious effects of our behaviour patterns, whilst embarking on a series of risky technology-driven projects without full consideration and knowledge of their impacts (from the introduction of CFCs to the development of nuclear energy). Indeed, it can even be argued that much of the recent growth of Western capitalism can be traced to the ability of corporations (and governments) to externalize more and more of their social and environmental costs in pursuit of cost-cutting competitive gains, even at the same time as achieving efficiencies in energy and raw material usage (O'Connor 1991; O'Connor 1993). Such externalities can effectively divorce people, businesses and governments from responsibility for their actions, fostering irresponsible behaviour patterns. Extending rights and obligations to ensure that externalities are brought into the decision-making frame, whether through the market mechanism (via the pricing mechanism, eg adopting 'green' taxes), legal sanction or other means, is essential to moving away from current patterns of widespread profligacy in resource usage and unthinking disposal of wastes.

At two levels, then, we need to change our ways. Firstly, we need improved political, economic, regulatory and legal systems, allied to enhanced information and educational systems, which bring home to individuals and groups the way in which their activities exercise direct and indirect impacts beyond the local scale and over a very long time horizon. Secondly, and related, we need to devise systems which ensure that those responsible for making environmental demands assume the main responsibility for the consequences of their activity – they should not expect other people, other species or other places to absorb the associated costs of environmental and social breakdown. New systems are needed which not only require those who cause environmental problems to share in their remediation, but which also move beyond this to requiring changes in behaviour patterns to reduce or halt environmentally degrading activities. Sustainable development, then, is about recognizing and accepting our responsibilities not just for the places where we live, but more widely for the environment at a global scale. In order to do this we need to look beyond the environment itself, to the broader economic, social and political systems within which human decisions are made. Fundamentally, sustainable development is about altering behaviour patterns not just directly in relation to the environment, but about changing the broader systems which shape human behaviour.

FIVE CENTRAL EQUITY PRINCIPLES FOR SUSTAINABLE DEVELOPMENT

In trying to establish what it is that makes a concern for sustainable development different from the existing concerns of environmental planning, it is helpful to highlight five interconnected 'equity' principles which move to centre place in any discussion of sustainable development, representing the essential environmental justice dimension of the concept. I would argue strongly that if these equity conditions are not addressed singly and collectively, then inevitably the ability to move towards sustainable development will be critically undermined. This said, each of these 'equity' principles in themselves represent contestable goals since no clear definitive state of final 'achievement' recognizable by all is ever likely to occur – it is the process of moving towards them, of changing human practices in the spirit of them, which is important, not some elusive readily quantifiable end-goal. This initial analysis provides the beginnings of a normative framework for environmental justice against which it is possible to evaluate different approaches to fostering the sustainable city, a task which is undertaken in subsequent sections.

Firstly, there is the principle of *intergenerational equity*, or the principle of futurity as it is sometimes known. This is perhaps the most widely acknowledged ingredient of sustainable development, drawing from the Brundtland definition of sustainable development as being 'development which meets the needs of the present without compromising the ability of future generations to meet their own needs' (WCED 1987). A second principle is also alluded to in this statement, and more fully elsewhere in the Brundtland report, that of *intragenerational equity*, or, more generally, contemporary social equity or social justice. As argued earlier, since equity and justice can be argued to have different emphases for some commentators, the emphasis here is on the wider conception of social justice – that is, seeking to address the underlying causes of social injustice, not simply dealing with redistributive measures. Whilst not without some ambiguity, it is possible to introduce these two principles here just briefly since they have been so fully developed elsewhere in the literature (see, for instance, WCED 1987; Haughton and Hunter 1994).

The third key principle for sustainable development is that of *geographical equity*, or transfrontier responsibility. Transfrontier responsibility requires that local policies should be geared to resolving global as well as local environmental problems. All too often, decision-makers adopt a parochial concern for protecting localized corporate or environmental interests whilst effectively ignoring external impacts of their decisions (Beatley 1991). Of particular concern is that too often, external impacts which affect areas outside the particular jurisdictional domain of the host polluter can be ignored if the polluter feels no responsibility for the recipient area and is beyond formal systems of legal sanction, such as liability to pay compensation. In a variant of the old saw 'out of sight, out of mind', activities are effectively encouraged which degrade distant areas, creating major environmental externalities – that is, uncompensated costs which are passed on to someone or somewhere else, and the further afield they are, the more administratively and politically separate their legal system, the easier it is to perpetrate such transfers of costs.

Geographical equity concerns are apparent from the neighbourhood level to the global, from issues of environmental dumping and concern over environmental racism to transfrontier acid deposition and degradation of the Amazon rainforests. As consumers, when we have information about the products of tropical rainforests, whether they are taken from a sustainably managed resource or a short-term commercial pillaging of an area, we can all take part in this process. The policy need is to go beyond current systems to ensure that environmental information is more widely available and that systems are in place to prevent trade in resources from non-sustainable sources. In addressing these concerns, it is essential to ensure that political or jurisdictional boundaries are not to be used to shield individuals, companies and governments from the negative impacts of their activities, as argued in the first section of this paper.

This in turn relates to a fourth principle, that of *procedural equity*. This principle holds that regulatory and participatory systems should be devised and applied to ensure that all people are treated openly and fairly. In its narrowest interpretation, this concern with procedural equity is applied solely within a particular legal jurisdiction, which can create problems in an increasingly globalized economy and in an era when environmental impacts are increasingly large-scale in impact, paying no regard to political boundaries. Pulido (1994), for instance, charts the way in which south-western US firms have sought to evade local environmental regulations by threatening to move across the border to Mexico, effectively transferring the problem rather than solving it. In the present broader definition of procedural equity, which links closely to geographical equity, a central concern is that political boundaries should not be used to allow polluters to be immune from prosecution by affected people in other jurisdictions. Those affected by pollution in other countries, for instance, should have the same rights to legal standing to defend themselves against polluters as those in the host country would (Haughton and Hunter 1994). Critical to making this form of equity operational is a right of equal access to information, and beyond this a more general right of access to information for all interested parties on activities which exert deleterious environmental impacts, locally and globally. Added to this is a concern over which decision-making processes procedural equity might cover, given that to be involved solely over how the environmental burdens of contemporary society are equitably distributed would be a highly truncated definition. Procedural equity requires an extended definition which encompasses engagement with 'the gamut of prior decisions affecting the production of costs and benefits to be distributed' (Lake 1996, pp 164–166).

The concern with procedural equity here also covers what is sometimes referred to as the principle of participation. In general I have tended to be cautious about adopting this as a separate principle, reflecting my deep concern that some forms of participation can undermine rather than support democratic processes of engagement – for instance, middle-class community groups lobbying to prevent homes for the mentally ill opening in their neighbourhoods, or tenacious mavericks who seek to usurp community participation channels for narrow sectarian interests or even to pursue personal grudges and vendettas. Alternatively, it is clear that participation is central to achieving effective and sustainable processes of regeneration, owned and mobilized by the general public as well as state authorities.

Reflecting these concerns, it is possible to argue that procedural equity is about much more than legalistic and bureaucratic procedures for establishing and enforcing obligations and rights. In addition, it needs to embrace wider processes of public engagement, where multiple democratic and participative forms and channels are brought into play to foster participation and engagement with processes of change. People need an appropriate framework of democratic political processes, and with this responsibilities, ranging from the local, urban, regional and national scales, to multinational decision-making bodies. This concern suggests that all people should have access at different points into public decision-making processes (in particular at the junction of public and private decision-making, for instance over corporations siting hazardous waste facilities). This requires a balancing of democratic and participative methods of engagement with decision-making, rather than a displacement of necessary democratic responsibilities by other bodies.

The earlier discussion on different interpretations of sustainable development contrasted those who hold what might be termed largely anthropocentric views with those with more nature-centred values. Following on from this, there is a view that more attention needs to be paid to what might be termed *interspecies equity* – that is, placing the survival of other species on an equal basis to the survival of humans. This is not to suggest the moral equivalence of humans with other life-forms, rather to highlight the critical importance of preserving ecosystem integrity and maintaining biodiversity. Other species have intrinsic rights, though these are not necessarily the same as those for humans. In a sense, then, the argument is that nature has certain rights, whilst humans also have obligations, to nature and to each other, to ensure that individual animal species and indeed whole ecosystems are not degraded to the point of non-sustainability. It is in this latter sense, then, that I incorporate a concern with interspecies equity here, to reflect a broader concern with environmental stewardship.

FOUR APPROACHES TO ACHIEVING SUSTAINABLE URBAN DEVELOPMENT

The literature about promoting sustainable urban development in Western nations can be broadly categorized into four approaches. These approaches, or models, are far from being mutually exclusive, and indeed it is possible to see that whilst at times the advocates of the different approaches appear to be in 'ideological' conflict with each other, in reality there is a fairly strong shared base of common assumptions and common policy directions. This said, each approach has its own distinctive traits, its own ways of rationalizing its policy stances and its own sets of priorities for both how a city should be laid out and managed. In this sense each model in fact embodies distinctive assumptions of what creates non-sustainable behaviour patterns in cities and, more broadly, from this, how policies in support of sustainable urban development should be framed.

Self-reliant Cities

The self-reliant city approach is centred on attempts to reduce the negative external impacts of a city beyond its own bioregion, seeking to: reduce overall resource consumption; use local resources where possible; develop renewable resource-based consumption habits, always in a sustainable fashion; minimize waste streams; and deal with pollution *in situ* rather than 'exporting' it to other regions (Morris 1982, 1990). Whilst coming in many guises, perhaps the most distinctive variants of the self-reliant city are those propounded by West Coast bioregionalists in the USA. The bioregion is usually seen as a central construct, replacing artificial political boundaries with natural boundaries, based typically on river catchment areas, geological features or distinctive ecosystem types, although it is readily conceded that precise boundaries are usually difficult to define (Register 1987; Andruss et al 1990). Urbanization in a bioregional context is usually argued as best being smaller in scale and more decentralized, whilst calling for greater efforts to design with nature – that is, designing cities in ways which bring 'nature' into the city, from open spaces to urban forests and roof gardens.

The politics of the bioregion are similarly usually envisaged as more decentralized and openly participative than conventional politics (Bookchin 1974, 1980, 1992; Berg 1990), bringing a direct concern with the 'equity of engagement' issues discussed earlier. Callenbach's (1975) novel *Ecotopia,* for instance, talks of decisions being arrived at only by debate and consensus, with no formal voting. Social equity issues are a dominant theme, encouraging people to realize their full potential and accept the need to act responsibly to others and towards the natural environment more generally. In this version of the self-reliant city, the intention is to build ecocities which blend into their natural environment and which enhance 'life, beauty and equity' (Register 1987, p 13); quite explicitly, this critique holds that cities 'built for maximum profit... or to confer maximum wealth on all citizens equally' cannot emerge as ecocities (ibid). The distinctive approach to interspecies equity becomes one of respecting the need to preserve external habitats and also to encourage a more complex urban ecology, where cities are designed to 're-establish or permit natural life forms to co-exist with the city by giving them sizable slices of their natural habitat around the city (greenbelt instead of suburbia), and within it (in parks, along restored creeks and shorelines)' (Register 1987, p 18). A preservationist stance to critical natural resources is dominant, together with a commitment to encouraging biodiversity at all spatial scales, based on a belief that natural ecosystems tend towards complexity, characterized by increasing numbers of life-forms complexly interrelated. This is carried forward into a widely held belief that cities need to emulate this complexity by fostering environmental, social and economic diversity, avoiding social and economic 'monocultures' as much as environmental ones.

Given its considerable political agenda for fundamental institutional transformation in the quest for sustainability, the self-reliant city is the most radical of the approaches outlined here. The main problem with this approach is the danger of taking regional autarky to unacceptable levels. Wallner et al (1996, p 1770) capture something of this in their discussion of islands of sustainability, arguing that cities need to balance the need to build internally and connect externally, since areas which are wholly self-reliant may survive but 'do not make any contribution to the evolution of the whole economic system towards sustainability', neither learning from nor sharing with other regions. Alternatively, the great strength of the self-reliant approach is its explicit concern with equity issues. In particular, relative to the other models of sustainable urban development, what the self-reliant city approach adds is a clear emphasis on interspecies equity, procedural equity and also social equity, bringing these to the forefront of both problem diagnosis and the processes of devising policies for the sustainable city.

Redesigning Cities

This is perhaps the dominant approach adopted by most Western planners and architects. In essence the environmental problems of cities are seen to be linked intrinsically to poor design of the urban fabric, in particular 20th-century additions predicated on the assumption of cheap and readily available fossil fuels for homes, work and transport. Of special concern are the problems associated with the rise of the motor vehicle, from the spread of low-density residential sprawl to the need to build a substantial infrastructure, including road systems and parking lots. From this perspective, a central feature of moving towards sustainable development has to be the redesigning of the city, including the very layout of the city at the regional scale – should we opt for concentrated decentralization, eg in new towns, corridors of urban expansion, or continue to sprawl (Breheny and Rookwood 1993; Haughton and Hunter 1994)? At more local scales, there are important issues of building design, promoting higher residential densities, and attempts to foster greater mixed land use, the latter widely advocated in order to minimize the need to undertake long journeys from home to work, school, shops and leisure facilities. Using the land resource more effectively through reshaping the city, it is argued, can lead to substantial energy savings (Owens 1986; see Breheny 1995 for a critique), whilst more localized efforts to improve building insulation and to aligning buildings to capture more natural sunlight can also bring significant energy savings.

The redesigning the city movement can be seen as essentially concerned with an approach which focuses less on bringing nature back into the city itself and more on creating a city on human-terms – that is, one which is socially and economically vibrant and viable, creating and celebrating distinctive built environments with their own cultural assets and aesthetics. With the emphasis on higher residential density developments in particular, the intention is less to create a fabric which embraces 'nature' within the city, rather to create a vital urban centre in its own terms, which exercises less impact on external areas – for instance, by reducing rural land take for expansion and more generally by reducing energy consumption. Natural capital is assumed to be substitutable with human capital, within certain limits, so that preserving an ancient cathedral may be more valuable that creating a new wildlife habitat; this said, this is substitutability within limits, with critical natural stocks preserved as far as possible and technologies generally being reorientated to work *with* rather than *against* nature. In terms of equity considerations, most are indirectly present – that is to say, implicit rather than explicit. However, the emphasis on sorting out the problems of the city from within does mean that external impacts are not unpacked in any detail – it is just assumed that reducing land take and energy usage will have desirable impacts elsewhere. Little attention is paid to what the impacts might be of the remaining imported resources flows and exported waste streams of the city.

Externally Dependent Cities

Conventional economists within what Rees (1995) refers to as the 'expansionist' paradigm, tend to argue that the best way to address environmental concerns is to pursue the current dominant Western path of high economic growth which, it is said, will provide the wealth to address social inequalities and come up with solutions to environmental problems. This is in marked contrast to the 'steady state' approaches of ecological economics which emphasize the interconnectedness of economy and ecology within a context of finite possibilities offered up by the ecosphere, in terms of resource availability and ability to absorb wastes. Ecological economics tends to argue that the environment should be seen as providing both opportunities and limits to economic growth, so that growth needs is shaped to ensure that it does not exceed local and global environmental carrying capacities (Ekins and Max-Neef 1992).

The externally dependent city essentially follows the conventional or 'neoclassical' view that environmental problems can be addressed effectively through improving the workings of the free market within existing capitalist systems. Typically, light-green approaches emphasize the power of economic growth to generate problem-solving technologies, as opposed to problem-creating technologies, with the implicit assumption of considerable substitutability between human and natural capital stocks. For example, Simon (1981) challenges the view that loss of agricultural land to an out-of-town shopping mall is necessarily a bad thing, since the market is sending clear signals that the land is worth more commercially developed for retailing than it is for selling crops, reflecting overall consumer preferences and utilities. He also argues that although the loss of land may be associated with considerable 'externality disutilities', there are also evident externality benefits to those who use the mall or those with adjacent land which rises in value.

In the free-market model, it is generally assumed that critical natural stocks can be adequately protected by the market itself supported by a minimalist regulatory system, setting minimum standards in respect of preservation. Following in the footsteps of Coase (1960), advocates of the free-market approach generally envisage expanding the areas of human activity subject to 'market disciplines' by pricing externalities and extending property rights, aiming to use market disciplines, backed by legal sanction, to change human behaviour patterns in support of resource conservation and reduced pollution. For instance, extending property rights to cover ambient air quality could discourage factories from emitting pollutants if they were subject to paying compensation for any environmental deterioration experienced by other property owners, provided that this made it economically cheaper to purchase equipment to reduce pollution at source than to pay compensation (LeGrand et al 1992).

For the advocate of using the market system to address environmental problems, the essential problems are usually seen as those of inadequate pricing, underdeveloped systems of property ownership, poorly constructed markets, overregulation, poor regulation and no regulation. These can all lead to market failures, which in turn lead to environmental problems. Central to this critique are market externalities – that is to say, aspects of behaviour not adequately captured by conventional market pricing signals and not readily amenable to formal regulatory intervention. So, excessive petroleum usage in cars in this view is connected directly to the fact that certain impacts of this usage are not captured in the pricing mechanism. These externalities might include the costs of pollution in terms of, for instance, impacts on asthmatics, contributions to the greenhouse effect, and the costs of road deaths and accidents. If such costs were calculated and added to the price of petrol, this ought to lead people to prefer more petrol-efficient cars, sending signals in turn to car manufacturers to produce less energy-profligate vehicles. Considerable intellectual energy is currently being expended by economists to find ways of shadow pricing such externalities and bringing them into appropriate pricing systems, within the inevitable political constraints – for instance, voter resistance to governments which push up petroleum taxes rapidly (Pearce, Markandya and Barbier 1989). It should be noted that it is not just conventional economists who see merit in this approach – some radical commentators also argue for altering pricing systems to incorporate externalities more effectively – the main differences perhaps relate to the relative emphasis on the role of state regulatory systems (Jacobs 1991). Alternatively, there is a strong radical critique which holds that pricing reform is essentially ephemeral, since capitalist market systems are inherently incapable of moving towards sustainable development – in this view, more far-reaching transformations of the economy and its regulation are required (O'Connor 1993).

In a similar vein, from the perspective of many conventional economists pursuing a market-centred approach, the environmental problems of the city are fundamentally ones of market failure or government failure. In the externally dependent city, trading around the world is seen as essentially unproblematic as long as market externalities can be identified, assessed and brought into the market mechanism by some means. Urban environmental problems are seen to be related not so much to cities themselves, rather to more general market failures. Cities just happen to be major generators of market externalities by virtue of their size, which leads to concentrations of environmental problems in them (Button and Pearce 1989). The free market view is most evident in the work of the World Bank in trying to address the environmental problems of Third World cities. Here, the environmental problems of cities are reduced to issues of improving the city overall: '[t]he challenge of urban policy is, in abstract terms, how to maximise the agglomeration economies and their positive externalities while minimising the diseconomies and their negative externalities' (World Bank 1991, p 53; see also Button and Pearce 1989).

Following from this problem identification, the World Bank's (1991) proposed solutions flow rapidly in terms of measures to improve market efficiency; for instance, introduce land reforms, including land registers, and use the market to provide incentives to alter behaviour patterns. In particular it is argued that pricing policies may need to be changed since '[b]y pricing resources and services at cost, excessive resource use can be discouraged and costly investments postponed... especially in countries with seriously distorted prices, improved pricing policies can be an incentive for more efficient resource use and reduced air and water pollution' (ibid, p 74). Whilst equity considerations are not absent from such analyses (see Pearce 1992), they are sometimes in practice reduced to secondary elements for policy concern, where it is assumed that appropriate market adjustment would in any case begin to address inequities.

Fair Shares Cities

The final approach to sustainable urban development is one which I term Fair Shares cities, which sets out to ensure that environmental assets are traded on a fair basis, with a particular view to ensuring that exchange does not take place in ways which degrade donor environments, economies and societies. To achieve this, it is important to ensure that adequate compensation is provided for the transfer of environmental assets. Similarly, waste streams which effectively 'appropriate' the environmental health of other areas need to be regulated so that they do not impact adversely on recipient area ecosystems, economies and societies, and, to the extent that they do, adequate compensatory mechanisms should be established. Given the emphasis on reducing use and pollution streams, many elements of the self-reliant city, redesigning the city and externally dependent city policy directions are present. In the Fair Shares model, however, the additional dimension is to bring about institutional transformations which directly link the actions of those responsible for degrading environments, within the city and beyond, to the means of repairing or compensating for this damage. As a precondition for trading in environmental externalities it is essential to take into account the carrying capacity and tolerance levels of host and recipient environments. In this model, critical natural stocks are preserved, whilst there is a conditional form of substitutability in other respects, where environmental exchanges are subject to increased concern about ensuring that adequate compensation is made for any damaging environmental impacts. In overall policy terms, then, it is important in the first instance to seek to minimize adverse impacts in aggregate, and to ensure that access to environmental assets is equitably distributed, and in the second instance to ensure that adequate compensatory mechanisms are in place to compensate for the transfer of environmental externalities between individuals, groups and geographical areas.

The two dimensions of change are very much interconnected. If negative externalities can be identified and attributed to their source, requiring full compensation under the principles of geographical and procedural equity in particular, this will lead to some changes in behaviour patterns. Such sentiments are easy to express, yet they remain surrounded by ambiguities which make it difficult to begin to see how they can be converted from broad principle into operational practice. Realistically, there will always be some trading of environmental goods and bads. For instance, a city may well 'export' a small amount of air pollution to a neighbouring underdeveloped region which still has sufficient natural assimilative capacity to absorb and neutralize the pollution. In this case the environment of the recipient area remains largely undamaged and it might be possible to devise compensation mechanisms for the usage of this spare capacity, which could help to develop the area concerned. These need not be financial – they might also include preferential rights to market access of polluter countries or changes to migration rights for people in the recipient areas (White and Whitney 1992). The danger remains, however, of socially unacceptable impacts arising, as demonstrated by regular protests by those opposing exports of nuclear or other toxic wastes. What is deemed an 'underpolluted' area by one person, may well be someone else's preferred pristine environment. Clouding the issue still futher, there will also be instances of tension between environmental and social equity – for instance, where a poor nation pollutes a richer one, making the notion of 'transfer' compensation payments more politically difficult to negotiate. In addition, there will be many instances of ambiguity over where a pollutant is sourced from and the relative impacts of different sources – for instance, among West European nations causing acid deposition problems in Scandinavia.

If we accept that some exchanges of environmental value are both inevitable and potentially beneficial, the policy imperative becomes to identify and in some sense measure these exchanges, and then to devise systems to provide adequate compensation for any adverse impacts. These might be simply changes to pricing systems, but as the distribution of resulting income tends to be geographically and socially unconnected to where impacts are felt (contributions to the general tax base or feeding the profits of large multinationals, for instance), then it is also likely to require some form of linked system for reparations. White and Whitney (1992), for instance, take the view that it should be possible to devise systems of reparations which link areas benefiting from an exchange of environmental value to those degraded by it.

It needs to be emphasized that there are enormous practical and conceptual difficulties in isolating and gauging the net impacts of these flows. The word 'net' here is important, since cities will inevitably generate a series of positive impacts on parts of their hinterland areas, providing much needed investment and jobs, for instance (Jacobs 1984). Reducing the calculus to environmental inputs and outputs is immensely problematic in this sense. Even if restricted solely to environmental considerations alone, there remain practical difficulties of measuring the multiplicity of tangible environmental flows involved and also their interactions – for instance, accidental combinations of air pollutants from different sources (Haughton 1997). There are problems, too, in identifying how revenues would be raised, and also in respect of precisely who should pay for, and who should receive, any reparations.

Given the problems of identifying externalities and trade-offs plus workable compensatory mechanisms at anything other than a large scale, the 'fair shares' approach is one which is perhaps easier to operate at the level of the nation state rather than at the individual city, except where strong city-states exist, such as Hong Kong or Singapore. This said, it is possible to see ways in which cities can begin to work out their 'ecological footprint' as one first step towards increasing awareness of hinterland impacts and developing the policies to address them. Even small neighbourhood areas within cities can set up trading relationships with hinterland areas on more favourable terms or engage in targeted remedial action. An example of this is the Halifax EcoCity proposal in Adelaide, which envisages buying and restoring rural land in its hinterland area as part of a 'remedial-compensatory' approach (Downton 1997).

In terms of equity considerations, the 'fair shares' approach potentially seeks to address all dimensions given that it is constructed here as building on the best of each of the other models. It is strongest in addressing geographical and procedural equity issues, whilst the attention to local and global carrying capacities signals a strong concern for interspecies equity. Where the model falls down perhaps is in its preoccupation with institutional transformation which mirrors the similarly problematic technical and design solutions of the redesigning the city approach and the overemphasis on economic tools in the externally dependent city model.

EQUITY PRINCIPLES AND MODELS OF SUSTAINABLE URBAN DEVELOPMENT

It is difficult to provide a definite set of judgements on the relative merits of each of the four approaches to sustainable development outlined here, not least because in practice there is often considerable overlap between the policies adopted under each approach – the shifts towards higher residential densities and mixed land uses advocated under the 'redesigning the city' approach, for instance, are also clearly central to the self-reliant cities approach. As in this example, what differentiates the approaches is sometimes as much what is *not* present as what is, in terms of both intellectual baggage and practical policy approaches. The approach here is to reflect on some of the equity criteria outlined earlier to begin the process of evaluating how the four approaches match up to the equity principles underpinning notions of sustainable development. There are problems here, too, since in truth to be meaningful the principles need to be seen not separately but in combination, given that they are all interrelated to some degree. It also needs to be admitted from the start that these equity principles represent just one way in which the various approaches could be evaluated, and undoubtedly others would prefer to highlight various dimensions of economic efficiency, political accountability or social viability, for instance.

Despite the necessarily crude nature of trying to judge each model in a reductive fashion which reduces complex trade-offs to one person's (ie my) judgement, it is a valuable exercise to begin to see how each of the four models of sustainable urban development embodies different sets of concerns. Figure 4.1 provides a summarized version of how each model of sustainable urban development might be seen to fare when judged against the main principles for sustainable development outlined earlier. The intention here is not to *prove* or *assert* any one model as better than another; rather, it is to **highlight** the key areas of concern in relation to fundamental principles for sustainable development which I see as being linked to each model. In a sense, it is for other people to use their own judgement to undertake similar exercises since I do not claim this as in any way being a definitive view – even for myself, there are tensions and contradictions which I recognize still need to be explored. For all its problems, this initial analysis does begin to highlight some of the possible weak points and the strengths of each approach to sustainable urban development.

Having briefly alluded to some of the key equity issues associated with each model in the previous section, the present section reworks this by providing a brief overview of each principle in turn, reflecting on the relative merits of each model. In terms of intergenerational equity, I tend to give the proponents of each approach the benefit of the doubt and assume that it is an overriding concern for all of them, although this appears to me to be largely implicit in the case of the externally dependent city model and more explicit in the other models. It should be said that, in practice, whilst intergenerational equity may be very much a concern for those who are seeking to integrate sustainable development considerations into the free-market approach, such work represents just a small part of the totality of work in this vein, much of which continues seemingly oblivious to the challenges raised by sustainable development.

The most problematic area in respect of social equity concerns extreme versions of the free-market model which rely heavily on the market mechanism rather than state regulation to achieve their distributive goals. This said, it is clear that transforming markets to reduce externalities and associated cost-transferring activities is likely to be a central ingredient in shifting towards processes of sustainable development within existing capitalist systems. As such, simply rejecting the market modification approaches would be short-sighted; alternatively, expecting the market approach to bring about social equity goals without major 'directive' transformations and regulatory intervention would be unrealistic. Whilst both self-reliant and fair shares approaches invariably put social equity considerations to the fore, this is not always true of 'redesigning the city' approaches, which sometimes tend towards tinkering with technocratic systems of doing things for people or making people do things differently (which is also one reason why this model achieves slightly less than topgrading in respect of procedural equity).

In terms of geographical equity, I have a concern that extreme versions of the self-reliant city approaches could have detrimental impacts on regions which formerly relied on income gained from trade with them, so for this reason I rate it as having potentially (but not necessarily) perverse implications in respect of this principle. Similarly, there is a residual concern that areas which become too introspective and look to solutions from some romanticized low technology past will miss out on some of the benefits of emergent technologies – an isolated community stuck in a time-warp of 50 years ago would be stuck with a lot of energy-inefficient technologies, for instance. Whilst externally dependent city approaches have the potential to create policies which address spatial inequities, as a general rule the tools of the free-market economist tended to limit consideration of geography to the 'friction of distance effects' associated with location decisions, whilst underplaying the way in which space is used in the creation of certain externalities.

My analysis of procedural equity in each of the models follows that for geographical equity, with the exception that implicitly at least self-reliant cities are more coherently committed to setting in place systems which reduce or compensate for adverse external impacts, whilst being very clearly committed to improving internal procedural issues, in particular participation mechanisms.

With respect of interspecies equity, as noted earlier, judgements on potential impacts of urban development approaches may well vary according to which spatial

Equity concern	City type			
	Externally dependent	Self-reliant	Redesigning cities	Fair shares
1 Intergenerational	✓✓	✓✓	✓✓	✓✓
2 Social	?	✓✓	✓	✓✓
3 Geographical	?	??	=	✓✓
4 Procedural	?	✓✓	=	✓✓
5 Interspecies	=	✓✓	?	✓

✓✓	Positive
✓	Implicit
=	Neutral/unclear
?	Potentially perverse

Figure 4.1 *Environmental justice and models of sustainable urban development*

scale is used in studying the city-region and the personal judgements about whether it is better to encourage natural areas, agriculture and wildlife habitats closer to the city centre (self-reliant city) or to protect hinterland environments by building more compact cities with only limited public open space. One example of such tensions in terms of redesigning the city approaches concerns attempts to build higher density, more compact cities, which may well lead to the loss to residential development of valuable brownfield open space sites, for instance, which once hosted considerable wildlife activity. Alternatively, such policies may well forestall or even prevent residential encroachment on greenfield sites at the edge of the city. It very much reflects my personal beliefs that I see more problems with 'concreting' over the city than with approaches which encourage the extension of green areas within the city; for this reason, the redesigning the city and the externally dependent city models both appear as potentially problematic in Figure 4.1, since in some versions both undervalue the role of encouraging greenspace in the city either by relegating it in importance or, in the case of the free-market approach, relying on commercial land values to reflect broader aesthetic values.

The question of which approach overall is 'best' is evidently more tricky than it seems, made more problematic in that so many of the features of the different models are in practice shared. The approach which appears to emerge most favourably is the Fair Shares city, although by imbuing it with most of the positive qualities of the other models, I have perhaps begun to give it a degree of concreteness and desirability that it does not really yet have. In practice, my view is that each of the models is in a sense dominated by particular professions, often linked into specific policy and academic disciplinary areas (eg ecologists, planners or economists).

In conclusion, the main value of highlighting the differences in approach is to draw attention to the parallel possibilities which exist in addressing the urban contribution to sustainable development, to try to ensure that policy myopia does not set in. This seems particularly important to planners: we do not have all the tools necessary to move towards sustainable development, just some of them. We can see aspects of the Tinbergen principle at work here – for a policy to achieve its goals policy-makers require at least as many tools as there are goals. Too often policies have been framed which are too ambitious relative to the resources and instruments available to implement them.[1] This needs to be recognized in our training of planners too, as we seek to integrate ecological and economic perspectives more thoroughly into our curricula. So I am not against any of these approaches which are, after all, rather artificially constructed here to highlight the different prevalent schools of thought; rather, I would argue that all bring particular insights of value to the goal of moving towards the sustainable city and sustainable development more generally. The challenge is to draw on their respective concerns and strengths towards a more integrated policy approach for the future.

ACKNOWLEDGEMENTS

This work benefits from various discussions with comments from anonymous referees of this journal, two of whom provided particularly useful and detailed advice for which I am grateful. The paper derives from work undertaken under ESRC project (grant L320 25 3186). An earlier working of the sustainable urban development models can be found in the journal *Cities* (Haughton 1997); the current article briefly summarizes the arguments found there and extends the analysis by examining the equity implications of each. Thanks also to Simon Guy, Simon Marvin and Joe Ravetz for comments on earlier drafts of this paper. Responsibility for the contents remains mine alone.

NOTES

1   I am grateful to one of the referees of this paper for this comment

REFERENCES

Andruss, V, Plant, C, Plant, J and Wright, E, eds 1990. *Home! A bioregional reader* Philadelphia: New Society Publishers

Beatley, T 1991. A set of ethical principles to guide land use policy. *Land Use Policy*, 8 (1), January: 3–8

Beatley, T 1994. *Ethical Land Use: principles of policy and planning*. Baltimore: John Hopkins University Press

Berg, P 1990. Growing a life-place politics. In *Home! A bioregional reader*, eds Andruss, V *et al* 137–44. Philadelphia: New Society Publishers

Berry, D and Steiker, G 1974. The concept of justice in regional planning: justice as fairness. *Journal of the American Institute of Planners* 6 (4): 414–21

Bookchin, M 1974. *The Limits of the City*. New York: Harper Colophon

Bookchin, M 1980. *Towards an Ecological Society*, Montreal, Canada: Black Rose Books

Bookchin, M 1992. *From Urbanization to Cities: towards a new politics of citizenship*, London: Cassell

Bourne, L S 1996. Normative urban geographies: recent trends, competing visions, and new cultures of regulation. *The Canadian Geographer*, 40 (1), 2–16

Breheny, M 1995. The compact city and transport energy consumption *Transactions of the Institute of British Geographers*, NS 20 (1): 81–101

Breheny M and Rookwood, R 1993. Planning the sustainable city region. In *Planning for a Sustainable Environment*, ed, A Blowers, 150–89. London: Earthscan

Bullard, R 1990. *Dumping in Dixie: race, class and environmental quality*. Boulder, Colorado: Westview Press

Bullard, R, ed 1993. *Confronting Environmental Racism: voices from the grassroots.* Boston, Mass: South End Press

Button, K and Pearce, D 1989. Improving the urban environment: how to adjust national and local government policy for sustainable urban growth. *Progress in Planning* 32 (3): 135–184

Callenbach, E 1975. *Ecotopia.* Berkeley, CA: Banyan Tree Books

Coase, R H 1960. The problem of social cost. *Journal of Law and Economics*, 3: 1–44

Downton, P 1997. Ecological community development. *Town and Country Planning*, 66 (1), January: 27–29

Ekins, P and Max-Neef, M, eds 1992. *Real-life Economics: understanding wealth creation*, London: Routledge

Friedmann, J 1989. Planning, politics and the environment. *Journal of the American Planning Association*, Summer: 334–341

Harvey, D 1973. *Social Justice and the City*, London: Edward Arnold

Harvey, D 1992. Social justice, postmodernism and the city. *International Journal of Urban and Regional Research*, 16 (4): 588-601

Haughton, G 1997. Developing sustainable urban development models. *Cities* 14 (4): 189–195

Haughton, G 1998. Geographical equity and regional resource management: water management in southern California *Environment and Planning B*, 25 (2): 279-98

Haughton, G and Hunter, C 1994. *Sustainable Cities.* London: Jessica Kingsley Publishers

Hay, A 1995. Concepts of equity, fairness and justice in geographical studies. *Transactions of the Institute of British Geographers* NS 20 (4): 500–508

Heiman, M 1996. Race, waste and class: new perspectives on environmental justice. *Antipode* 28 (2): 111–121

Hofrichter, R, ed 1993. *Toxic Struggles: the theory and practice of environmental justice.* Philadelphia: New Society Publishers

Jacobs, J 1984. *Cities and the Wealth of Nations*, Harmondsworth, UK: Penguin

Jacobs, M 1991. *The Green Economy: environment, sustainable development and the politics of the future.* London: Pluto Press

Lake, R W 1996. Volunteers, NIMBYs, and environmental justice: dilemmas of democratic practice. *Antipode*, 28 (2): 160–174

LeGrand, J Propper, C and Robinson, R 1992. *The Economics of Social Problems.* Third edition, Basingstoke, UK: Macmillan

Lipietz, A 1996. Geography, ecology, democracy. *Antipode*, 28 (3): 219–228

Morris, D 1982. *Self-Reliant Cities: energy and the transformation of urban America.* San Francisco: Sierra Club Books

Morris, D 1990. The ecological city as a self-reliant city. In *Green Cities*, ed D Gordon, pp 21–35. Montreal, Canada: Black Rose Books

O'Connor, J 1991. Socialism and ecology. *Capitalism, Socialism, Nature*, 2 (3): 1–12

O'Connor, M 1993. On the misadventures of capitalist nature. *Capitalism Socialism Nature*, 4 (3): 7–40

Owens, S 1986. *Energy, Planning, and Urban Form.* London: Pion

Pearce, D 1992. Economics, equity and sustainable development In *Real-life Economics: understanding wealth creation* eds P Ekins and M Max-Neef, pp 69–76, London: Routledge

Pearce, D, Markandya, A and Barbier, E B 1989. *Blueprint for a Green Economy*, London: Earthscan

Pulido, L 1994. Restructuring and the contraction and expansion of environmental rights in the United States. *Environment and Planning A* 26 (6): 915–936

Ravetz, J 1994. Manchester 2020 – a Sustainable City Region Project. *Town and Country Planning* 63 (3): 181–185

Rees, W 1995. Achieving sustainability: reform or transformation? *Journal of Planning Literature* 9 (4): 343–361

Register, R 1987. *Ecocity Berkeley: building cities for a healthy future*, Berkeley, CA: North Atlantic Books

Sayer, A and Storper, M 1997. Guest editorial essay. Ethics unbound: for a normative turn in social theory. *Environment and Planning D* 14 (4): 1–17

Seabrook, J 1990. *The Myth of the Market.* Bideford, Devon, UK: Green Books

Simon, J L 1981. *The Ultimate Resource.* Oxford, UK: Martin Roberston

Smith, D M 1994. *Geography and Social Justice.* Oxford: Blackwell

Smith, D M 1997. Back to the good life: towards an enlarged conception of social justice. *Environment and Planning D* 15: 19–35

Turner, R K, Pearce, D, and Bateman, I 1994. *Environmental Economics.* Hemel Hempstead, UK: Harvester Wheatsheaf

Wallner, H P, Narodoslawsky, M, and Moser, F 1996. Islands of sustainability: a bottom-up approach towards sustainable development. *Environment and Planning A* 29 (10): 1763–1778

WCED (World Commission on Environment and Development) 1987. *Our Common Future,* Oxford, UK: Oxford University Press

White, R and Whitney, J 1992. Cities and environment: an overview. In *Sustainable Cities: urbanization and the environment in international perspective,* eds R Stren, R White, and D Whitney, pp 8–52. Boulder: Westview Press

World Bank 1991. *Urban Policy and Economic Development: an agenda for the 1990s.* World Bank policy paper, Washington DC: World Bank

Young, I M 1990. *Justice and the Politics of Difference.* Princeton, NJ: Princeton University Press

Chapter 5

Sustainable Cities or Cities that Contribute to Sustainable Development?

David Satterthwaite

(Reprinted from *Urban Studies* Vol 34, No 10, 1997, pp 1667–1691)

Summary: This paper outlines a framework for assessing the environmental performance of cities in regard to the meeting of sustainable development goals. It also
considers how the environmental goals fit with the social, economic and political
goals of sustainable development and the kinds of national frameworks and international contexts needed to encourage city-based consumers, enterprises and governments to progress towards their achievement. In a final section, it considers the
extent to which the recommendations of the Habitat II Conference helped to encourage national governments and city and municipal authorities in this direction.

INTRODUCTION

The last ten years have brought examples of considerable innovation among city and
municipal authorities in most parts of the world in regard to sustainable development.
In Europe and North America, many cities have put in place long-term programmes
to improve their environment, reduce resource use and reduce waste (Mega 1996a,
UNCHS 1996, European Commission 1994). A growing number of cities have local
authorities who have committed themselves to sustainable development goals – as
in the European Campaign of Sustainable Cities and Towns – and have shown a
greater willingness to share knowledge and experiences with other city authorities
(Mega 1996a, UNCHS 1996). Certain cities in Latin America have also put in place
long-term programmes to address environmental problems – as in, for instance,
Curitiba in Brazil (Rabinovitch 1992) and Ilo in Peru (Díaz et al 1996) – while in many
cities in all regions of the world, there has been considerable innovation by city authorities in addressing environmental problems. There is also a worldwide movement
of 'healthy cities' in which local authorities in more than 1000 cities have sought new
ways to work with the many different actors and interests within their boundaries
in the promotion of health and prevention of disease (WHO 1996).

The discussion of sustainable development in regard to cities has also gained
greater official recognition. For instance, the terms 'sustainable cities' and 'sustain-

able human settlements' were much in evidence at Habitat II, the second UN Conference on Human Settlements (also known as the City Summit) held in Istanbul in June 1996. Despite the disagreements between the different groups represented at the Conference – for instance, between the European Union, the Group of 77 and the United States – all government delegations appeared to support the idea of 'sustainable human settlements' or 'sustainable urban development'.

But this apparent unanimity is misleading because there was no clear, agreed definition as to what the terms 'sustainable cities' and 'sustainable human settlements' mean. Such a diverse range of environmental, economic, social, political, demographic, institutional and cultural goals have been said to be part of 'sustainable development' that most governments or international agencies can characterize some of what they do as contributing towards sustainable development. This can include goals whose achievement in one sector or location implies a move away from the achievement of sustainable development goals in another sector or location. For instance, one reason why the environmental quality of wealthy cities can improve is because the consumers and producers they concentrate can import all the goods whose production requires high levels of resource use and usually includes high levels of waste (including serious problems with hazardous wastes), pollution and environmental risk for their workforce (Satterthwaite 1997).

Governments in the world's wealthiest nations can also support the notion of 'sustainable cities' without admitting that it is consumers and enterprises in their cities that need to make the largest reductions in resource use and waste generation. Most governments in the North also continue to view economic growth as the main means by which unemployment is to be reduced and incomes increased and it is difficult, if not impossible, to combine these with significant falls in the use of non-renewable resources and the generation of greenhouse gases, unless there is an explicit linking of employment generation with such goals. The simultaneous achievement of the social and environmental goals inherent in the Brundtland Commission's definition of sustainable development (meeting the needs of the present without compromising the ability of future generations to meet their own needs) implies very different policies to reduce unemployment and increase incomes among those with inadequate incomes – that address more directly the problem than 'trickle down' from economic growth and that support reduced resource use and waste. And while many national governments may claim that they are promoting sustainable development, few have begun to put in place the fiscal and institutional framework that supports a move towards the achievement of the complete set of sustainable development goals in the urban (and rural) areas within their boundaries (see, for instance, O'Riordan 1989, Haughton and Hunter 1994).

This lack of progress among the nations in 'the North' discourages progress among nations in 'the South'. The fact that 'the South' includes three-quarters of the world's population and a large and growing share of its economic activity and high-level consumers also means a large and growing share in global resource use, waste generation and greenhouse gas emissions. But despite the diversity of nations within 'the South', they can collectively point not only to higher levels of resource use, waste and greenhouse gas emissions per person in the North but also to much higher historic contributions to these problems. Without a strong commitment by governments in the North to reduce resource use, waste and greenhouse gas emissions, and to support the achievement of sustainable development goals in the South, the governments in the South are reluctant to act. This delays the actions that could make the (often) rapidly urbanizing nations' settlement patterns and transport systems less dependent on high levels of private automobile use and their buildings less dependent on high levels of energy for lighting and heating or cooling. As will be discussed in more detail later, it is difficult to adjust buildings, settlement patterns and transport systems that developed during a long period of cheap oil and (generally) growing prosperity to much lower levels of fossil fuel use. But in nations which are urbanizing rapidly, putting in place the institutional and regulatory framework that encourages energy conservation in all sectors, minimizes the need for heating or cooling in buildings and encourages settlement patterns that limit the need for high levels of private automobile use can ensure the development of cities that are more compatible with some of the main sustainable development goals. A framework encouraging efficient use of water within all sectors and promoting the reuse of waste water where appropriate can also considerably reduce the prospect of water scarcity.

The ambiguity as to what 'sustainable cities' or 'sustainable human settlements' means also allows many of the large international agencies to claim that they are the leaders in promoting sustainable cities when in reality they have contributed much to the growth of cities where sustainable development goals are not met. For instance, most international agencies give a low priority to directly meeting human needs – for example, in supporting provision of safe and sufficient supplies of water and provision for sanitation, primary education and health care. Most also give a low priority (or allocate nothing) to improving garbage collection and disposal, energy conservation and public transport in cities, despite their importance for the achievement of sustainable development goals.[1]

This paper contends that to progress towards the achievement of sustainable development goals, the environmental performance of cities has to improve not only in terms of improved environmental quality within their boundaries but also in terms of reducing the transfer of environmental costs to other people, other ecosystems or into the future. This presents considerable institutional difficulties for city and municipal authorities whose official responsibilities are to the citizens within their boundaries. Within a competitive world market, it is difficult for city authorities to reconcile the need to attract or retain new investment with a commitment to the full range of sustainable development goals, especially those sustainable development goals that raise costs within the city to reduce environmental costs for people outside these cities. This is a subject to which this paper will return, after describing a framework for assessing the environmental performance of cities.

A FRAMEWORK FOR CONSIDERING THE ENVIRONMENTAL PERFORMANCE OF CITIES

The Difficulties of Comparing Environmental Performance Between Diverse Urban Centres

Perhaps the main difficulty facing any researcher or institution intent on comparing the environmental performance of different cities (including those in the North and the South) is the range of problems that are 'environmental'. For instance, from the perspective of environmental health, cities in the North perform much better for their inhabitants than most cities in the South, as can be seen in the much smaller role of environmental hazards in illness, injury and premature death (WHO 1996, UNCHS 1996). But from the perspective of average levels of resource use or waste or greenhouse gas emissions per person, most cities in the South have much lower levels than cities in the North (Hardoy et al 1992, UNCHS 1996).

There is also the difficulty of knowing how to judge the environmental perfor-mance of cities when the achievement of a high quality environment in many cities is in part achieved by transferring environmental problems to other people or locations. For instance, sewage and drainage systems that take the sewage and waste water out of the city bring major environmental advantages to city-dwellers and city-busi-nesses, but if disposed of untreated in nearby water bodies, this usually brings se-rious environmental and economic costs to others – for instance, through damage to local fisheries or to water bodies that are then unfit for use by communities down-stream. The transfer of environmental costs can also be over much greater distances or into the future.

This suggests the need to distinguish between different kinds of environmen-tal problems when making comparisons between cities, so like can be compared with like. But there is a danger that this reduces intercity comparisons on environ-mental performance to those indicators that are easily measured. For instance, it is easier to get information on the concentration of certain air pollutants such as sulphur dioxide in major cities in the South than the proportion of their population with adequate provision for piped water and sanitation or the contribution of mo-tor vehicle accidents to injury and premature death. This means that discussions of sulphur dioxide concentrations probably gets more prominence than they deserve within the discussions of environmental hazards in cities, while the inadequacies in provision for water and sanitation and in limiting traffic accidents get insufficient at-tention. In assessing the environmental performance of cities, there is a need both to distinguish between different environmental problems and to seek a more compre-hensive coverage of all environmental problems, including those for which there is often little data. There is also a need to ensure that improved environmental perfor-mance in one area is not at the expense of improved performance in another.

Within a commitment to sustainable development, there are five broad catego-ries of environmental action within which the performance of all cities should be assessed. These are:

1   Controlling infectious and parasitic diseases and the health burden they take on city populations, including reducing city populations' vulnerability to them. This is often termed the 'brown agenda' or the sanitary agenda as it includes the need to ensure adequate provision for water, sanitation, drainage and garbage collection for all city-dwellers and businesses. It should include more than this – for instance, in controlling the infectious and parasitic diseases that are not associated with inadequate water and sanitation, including acute respiratory infections (the single largest cause of death worldwide) and tuberculosis (the single largest cause of adult death worldwide) and the many diseases that are transmitted by insect or animal vectors;
2   reducing chemical and physical hazards within the home, workplace and wider city;
3   achieving a high quality city environment for all city inhabitants – for instance, in terms of the amount and quality of open space per person (parks, public squares/plazas, provision for sport, provision for children's play) and the pro-tection of the natural and cultural heritage;

4   minimizing the transfer of environmental costs to the inhabitants and ecosystems surrounding the city; and

5   ensuring progress towards what is often termed 'sustainable consumption' – ie ensuring that the goods and services required to meet everyone's consumption needs are delivered without undermining the environmental capital of nations and the world. This implies a use of resources, a consumption of goods imported into the city and a generation and disposal of wastes by city enterprises and city dwellers that are compatible with the limits of natural capital and are not transferring environmental costs on to other people (including future generations).

The first three categories can be considered as the environmental aspects of meeting city dwellers' needs. These fit within the conventional mandate of local authorities, although there is great variety in the ways in which local authorities promote their achievement. The fourth and fifth are more problematic since they are concerned with environmental impacts that generally occur outside the jurisdiction of the local authorities with responsibility for environmental management in cities.

Separating a consideration of the environmental performance of cities into these five categories allows a consideration of the common elements that all cities share within an understanding of how priorities must differ. For instance, perhaps the main environmental priority in most cities in the North is to reduce levels of resource use, wastes and greenhouse gas emissions while also maintaining or improving the quality of the city's environment. But this does not mean neglecting the other aspects – for instance, in most cities, much remains to be done to reduce physical hazards (for instance, those caused by motor vehicles) and chemical pollutants – and, as outlined below, there are also new threats to be confronted in the control of infectious diseases. In addition, in most cities in the North, there is still a proportion of the population that live or work with unacceptable levels of environmental risk. By contrast, the environmental priorities in most small cities in the lower income countries of the South will centre on the first two categories, although building into their urban plans a concern for a high quality urban environment, efficient resource use, good management of liquid and solid wastes and a minimizing of greenhouse gas emissions will bring many long-term advantages. Considering cities' environmental performance across the five categories also helps to clarify how environmental problems change for cities that become increasingly large and/or wealthy (see Bartone et al 1994, Satterthwaite 1997).

Controlling Infectious and Parasitic Diseases

By concentrating people and economic activities, cities have many advantages over a more dispersed settlement pattern for the control of infectious and parasitic diseases, especially the concentration of people which lowers the unit costs of most forms of infrastructure (including piped water, drainage and most kinds of sanitation) and services (including health care, emergency services and garbage collection). With good management in public health and environmental health and with all sectors of a city's society contributing to health, cities can be among the most healthy places to live in, work and visit (WHO 1996).

But in the absence of such management, there are many infectious and parasitic diseases that thrive when provision for water, sanitation, drainage, garbage collection and health care is inadequate or where it breaks down. As a result, cities can become among the most health-threatening of all human environments as disease-causing agents and disease vectors multiply, as the large concentration of people living in close proximity to each other increases the risk of disease transmission, and as health-care systems become unable to respond rapidly and effectively. If provision for sanitation, drainage and garbage collection breaks down or fails to keep up with a city's expanding population, this greatly increases health hazards, especially from the many diarrhoeal and other diseases spread by human excreta and from diseases spread by vectors who breed or feed on uncollected garbage or breed in standing water – for instance, malaria, filariasis, yellow fever and dengue fever, in the climates where the mosquito species that are their vectors can survive. At any one time, close to half of the urban population in the South is suffering from one or more of the main diseases associated with inadequate provision for water and sanitation (ibid). If health-care systems break down or fail to keep up with the growth in population, the health problems of those who catch diseases are much magnified – for instance, acute respiratory infections are among the main causes of infant and child death, although they are easily cured if diagnosed and treated appropriately. In addition, if health-care systems cannot implement immunization programmes, diseases such as measles and diphtheria can become major causes of death.

Most cities also concentrate large numbers of people who are particularly vulnerable to infection. For instance, most cities in the South have high proportions of infants within their populations and these have immune systems that have not developed to protect them from common infectious diseases. In many such cities, a large proportion of infants and young children (and adults) have immune systems that are compromised by undernutrition and worm infections. Many cities or particular city districts in the North and some in the South also have a high concentration of older people who are more vulnerable to many infectious diseases. Most cities also have a constant movement of people in and out of them which can mean the arrival of newcomers who bring new infections to which the city population has no immunity (ibid).

There are also two further problems. The first is the growing number of what are usually termed 'new' or 'emerging' diseases, of which AIDS is the best known and one of the most widespread. These are new in the sense that they only recently became a significant public health problem, but in most instances it is their incidence and geographic range that is new, as they previously existed either in nature or in isolated communities (ibid). The second is the re-emergence of well-known infectious diseases that until recently were considered under control. For instance, cholera and yellow fever are now striking in regions that were once thought to be safe from them. Malaria and dengue fever have become among the most serious health problems in many urban centres. Tuberculosis remains the single largest cause of adult death in the world, and its incidence has been increasing rapidly over the last decade, in the North as well as the South. The main reason why emerging and re-emerging diseases have become such a serious problem is the low priority given by most governments and international agencies to public health and health care. But part of the reason is also the greater difficulties in preventing and controlling infectious diseases as societies urbanize and as population movements increase (including the very rapid growth in the number of people crossing international borders), and as disease-causing agents develop resistance to public health measures or adapt to changing ecological circumstances in ways that increase the risks of infection for human populations. For instance, the control of malaria has become more difficult in many places as the *Anopheles* mosquitoes can no longer be killed by many insecticides and many of the drugs used to provide immunity or to treat malaria are no longer effective. Various species of the anophelines have also proved able to adapt to urban environments (WHO 1992, WHO 1996). Similarly, many bacterial disease-causing agents, including those that cause pneumonia, tuberculosis and typhoid fevers, and some diarrhoeal diseases and forms of food poisoning have become resistant to many antibiotic drugs (WHO 1996). Meanwhile, the development and distribution of new antibiotics cannot keep up with the speed at which many disease-causing agents develop a resistance to them, especially in the lower income countries in the South (Leduc and Tikhomirov 1994).

Urbanization can also create foci for disease vectors and new ecological niches for animals which harbour a disease agent or vector. This may be the result of the expansion of built-up areas, the construction of roads, water reservoirs and drains, and land clearance and deforestation (WHO 1992) or the result of increased volumes of human excreta, garbage or waste water that are not cleared away. In addition, as cities expand, it is common for low-income groups to develop settlements on land subject to flooding or on or beside wetlands, as this land has less commercial value and the inhabitants have more chance of being permitted to stay there. But this may also mean close proximity to places where various insect vectors can breed and so putting their inhabitants at risk from, for instance, malaria (from *Anopheles* mosquitoes) or dengue fever or yellow fever (from *Aedes* mosquitoes).

The means to enormously reduce these problems are well known and have long been applied in cities in the North and in some cities in the South. In such cities, although some of the emerging or re-emerging diseases are causing serious difficulties for public authorities, the contribution of infectious and parasitic diseases to ill health and premature death has been enormously diminished. The speed of this transformation in the health of urban populations is often forgotten. It is only in the last 100 years or so that societies have developed the knowledge, capacity and competence to protect against diseases that formerly thrived, especially in cities. This can be seen in the infant mortality rates that existed only 100 years ago in the world's most prosperous cities. Today, infant mortality rates in healthy, well-served cities are around 10 per 1000 live births and it is very rare for an infant or child to die from an infectious or parasitic disease. Most prosperous European cities 100 years ago still had infant mortality rates that exceeded 100 per 1000 live births; in Vienna, Berlin, Leipzig, Naples, St Petersburg and many of the large industrial towns in England, the figure exceeded 200 and in Moscow it exceeded 300 (Bairoch 1988, Wohl 1983).

In most of the South, much remains to be done. Infant mortality rates of 100 or more per 1000 live births still remain common in cities in the South or in the city areas where low-income groups live. Even higher infant mortality rates are common in the informal or illegal settlements where there is inadequate provision for water, sanitation and health care. A 1990 estimate suggested that 600 million urban dwellers in the South lived in shelters and neighbourhoods where their lives and health were continually threatened because of the inadequate provision of safe, sufficient water supplies, sanitation, removal of solid and liquid wastes, and health care and emergency services (Cairncross et al 1990, WHO 1992).

Reducing Chemical and Physical Hazards Within the Home, Workplace and Wider City

The scale and severity of many chemical and physical hazards increases rapidly with increasing industrial production and with the growth in road traffic. While controlling infectious and parasitic diseases or reducing city populations' vulnerability to them centres on provision of infrastructure and services to entire city populations (whether through public, private, NGO or community organization provision), achieving progress in this second category is largely achieved by regulating the activities of enterprises and individuals. Probably the most important factor in terms of improving health is controlling occupational hazards that includes people's exposure to dangerous concentrations of chemicals and dust, inadequate lighting, ventilation and space, and a lack of protection from machinery and noise. Action is needed in these areas from the large factories down to small 'backstreet' workshops (WHO 1996).

One of the most serious chemical hazards in many cities is indoor air pollution from smoke or fumes from open fires or inefficient stoves (WHO 1992). This is especially so when coal or biomass fuels are used as domestic fuels. High levels of indoor air pollution can cause inflammation of the respiratory tract which, in turn, reduces resistance to acute respiratory infections, while these infections in turn enhance susceptibility to the inflammatory effects of smoke and fumes. There are also many other health problems associated with high levels of indoor air pollution (ibid).

There is also a need to reduce to a minimum the risk from accidents within the home and its immediate surrounds. Accidents in the home are often among the most serious causes of injury and premature death, especially in cities in the South where it is common for a high proportion of the population to live in accommodation with three or more persons to each room in a shelter made from temporary (and inflammable) materials and with open fires or stoves used for cooking and (where needed) heating. It is almost impossible to protect occupants (especially young children) from burns and scalds in such circumstances.

There are also tens of millions of urban dwellers in the South who are at high risk from floods, mudslides or landslides. In most cities in the South, a considerable proportion of the population live on land sites that are subject to floods, mudslides or rockfalls. Low-income households choose such hazardous sites because they are often the only sites within easy reach of employment that are available to them. Safer sites are too expensive and any attempt to occupy these illegally and develop housing on them would result in eviction.

As in the control of infectious and parasitic diseases, a good primary health-care system and provision for emergency services are also important so that those who are injured or poisoned can rapidly get appropriate treatment. There is also a need for traffic management which minimizes the risk of motor vehicle accidents and which protects pedestrians and for ensuring an adequate provision for play and recreation for the entire city population. Clean, safe and stimulating playgrounds for children are needed most in the poorest residential areas where there is the least space within and around homes for children to play. Citywide, there is an urgent need for a full range of measures to promote healthy and safe working practices in all forms of employment and to penalize employers who contravene them.

There is also a need to control air and water pollution. As cities become larger, more industrialized and wealthier, so there is a growing need for more comprehensive and effective control of emissions and wastes from industries and motor vehicles. Worldwide, more than 1.5 billion urban dwellers are exposed to levels of ambient air pollution that are above the recommended maximum levels and an estimated 400,000 additional deaths each year are attributable to ambient air pollution (WHO 1996). Once problems of indoor air pollution are greatly reduced by the use of cleaner fuels and better stoves and ventilation, and occupational hazards are greatly reduced by effective enforcement of health and safety regulations, governments usually have to turn their attention to reducing ambient air pollution. If industrial pollution has been much reduced, it is usually motor vehicles that become the main source of urban air pollution.

Achieving a High Quality City Environment

Action in the two categories above is essentially to reduce or remove the health problems that arise from the concentration of people, enterprises and motorized transport systems within a city. Their focus is on prevention and on rapid and effective treatment for any illness or injury. This third category is qualitatively different in that it centres on ensuring provision of those facilities that make city environments more pleasant, safe and valued by their inhabitants. It includes ensuring sufficient area and quality of open space per person (for instance, in terms of parks, public squares/plazas, provision for sport and provision for children's play) and a concern that all city dwellers have access to such provision. Integrated into this would also be a concern to protect natural landscapes with important ecological and/or aesthetic value – for instance, wetland areas or river banks or coasts. It includes a concern to preserve a city's cultural heritage. There are obvious links between this and the first two categories. For instance, ensuring adequate provision for children's play in each neighbourhood of a city that is safe, well-maintained, accessible and managed in ways to serve the needs of different income groups and age groups can greatly reduce accidents as fewer children play on roads, garbage tips or other unsafe areas. Such provision can also contribute much to children's physical, mental and social development (Hart 1997). Such provision is particularly important in the lower income areas of cities in the South which lack adequate provision for water, sanitation and drainage and where housing is generally overcrowded, as it allows children to play without exposing them to the risk of faecal contamination or garbage or infection from disease vectors (Satterthwaite et al 1996).

There are also many other ways in which improving the urban environment can be combined with reducing environmental hazards. For instance, provision for water bodies in parks and the protection of wetlands can be integrated into systems for treating stormwater and for reducing the risk of flooding or limiting flood damage when it occurs. Planting trees in cities and suburbs can not only be justified for their aesthetic value but also for their contribution to, among other things, reducing cooling costs, absorbing pollutants and acting as windbreaks and noise barriers. Support for urban agriculture can be integrated into provision for open space and the reuse of waste waters, and can prove particularly important for improving the diets and livelihoods of low-income groups in most urban centres in the South (Smit et al 1996).

Ensuring provision for public space within each neighbourhood in ways which respond to the diverse needs and priorities of the different groups within the population is rarely given much attention in rapidly growing cities in the South. As a result, little or no provision for public space becomes built into the urban fabric and as all land sites are developed for urban activities, it becomes almost impossible to remedy this deficiency. In addition, pressure from middle- and upper-income groups for public action to address this may be much lessened as their purchasing power allows them exclusive access to such resources, through purchasing or renting homes with gardens or homes in areas with good provision for open space or through membership of clubs which allow members access to open space or beaches or provision for sports. The capacity of middle- and upper-income groups to pay for such provision may not only reduce the pressure from such groups for more public provision but the country clubs, sports clubs, golf courses and private beaches may also pre-empt land and natural resources that had previously been open to use by all city inhabitants.

Minimizing the Transfer of Environmental Costs to the Inhabitants and Ecosystems Surrounding the City

The fourth and fifth categories for environmental action are both about minimizing the transfer of environmental costs to the ecology and the people living outside the city. The fourth category concentrates on the transfer of costs to the 'city-region' while the fifth concentrates on the transfer to more distant peoples and ecosystems (including those in different nations) and to the future. The distinction between the two is important in that improved performance in the former is often achieved at the expense of the latter.

The ecology of the region around large and prosperous cities has generally been much changed by the demand for resources and the generation of wastes concentrated within the cities. As Ian Douglas has described, the development of cities transforms the ecology of their region as land surfaces are reshaped, valleys and swamps filled, large volumes of clay, sand, gravel and crushed rock extracted and moved and water sources tapped, and rivers and streams channelled (Douglas 1983, 1986). This rearrangement of water, materials and stresses on the land surface combined with the natural tendency of city-dwellers and city-businesses to dispose of their wastes in the region around the city brings damaging consequences. Changes brought to the hydrological cycle by the city's construction and its system for water, sanitation and drainage usually bring damaging consequences 'downstream'. In addition, as provision for sewers and drains improves in the city, the impact of the waste water on the wider region increases, as it is disposed of untreated into a river, estuary or sea, close to the city. Solid wastes (including toxic and hazardous wastes) are often disposed of on land sites around the city, often with little or no provision to prevent these from contaminating local water resources. Air pollution from city-based industries, space heating, thermal power stations and motor vehicles often results in acid precipitation that damages terrestrial and aquatic ecosystems outside the city. Tall smokestacks for thermal power stations and city enterprises can also simply transfer environmental costs from in and around the power station and enterprise to 'downwind' of the city, although the impact may be pushed far beyond the city-region. There is also the damage to vegetation arising from ozone generated by the complex photochemical reactions involving urban air pollutants and sunlight, with ozone concentrations often higher downwind of large and wealthy cities than over the city itself (Conway and Pretty 1991).

It was only in the 1960s that this aspect of cities' environmental impact began to be addressed in the North. The growth in environmentalism from the 1960s onwards pressed for major reductions in air pollution, for large investments in the treatment of liquid wastes and in the management of solid wastes (with special provision for hazardous wastes) and in more controls on the extraction of building materials in the city surrounds. In the world's wealthier nations, this has considerably reduced the environmental impact of city-based production and consumption on the region around cities. It has also begun to set limits on the environmental impact that city-based demand for freshwater can inflict on local or increasingly distant watersheds. However, in most major cities in the South, much remains to be done to lessen the transfer of environmental costs to the region surrounding the city. In addition, at least part of this problem has been solved by transferring the environmental costs to more distant peoples and ecosystems.

Sustainable Consumption

The fifth category for environmental action in any city is reducing or eliminating the transfer of environmental costs to people and ecosystems beyond the city-region, including their transfer into the future. This could be considered as ensuring the environmental performance of the people and businesses the city concentrates becomes compatible with the goals of sustainable development at national and global levels.

For the largest and wealthiest cities, a large part of the transfer of environmental costs to their region has now been transferred to other regions and to global systems. The demands they concentrate for food, fuel and raw materials are largely met by imports from distant ecosystems with much less demand placed on the surrounding region, which makes it easier to maintain high environmental standards in this region and, for instance, to preserve forests and natural landscapes. In addition, the goods whose fabrication involves high levels of fossil-fuel consumption, water use and other natural resource use, and dirty industrial processes (including the generation of hazardous wastes) and hazardous conditions for the workforce can be imported. The possibilities for enterprises and consumers to import such goods is much helped by the low price of oil.

Other cost transfers are into the future. For instance, air pollution may have been cut in many of the world's wealthiest cities but emissions of carbon dioxide (the main greenhouse gas) remain very high and in most cities may continue to rise – for instance, because of increasing private automobile ownership and use. This is transferring costs to the future through the human and ecological costs of atmospheric warming. The generation of hazardous non-biodegradable wastes (including radioactive wastes) and non-biodegradable wastes whose rising concentrations within the biosphere are having worrying ecological consequences are also transferring costs to the future. So too are current levels of consumption for the products of agriculture and forestry where the soils and forests are being destroyed or degraded and biodiversity reduced.

While there is disagreement as to where the limits are for the use of non-renewable resources, the exploitation of soils and forests, and the use of the global sink for greenhouse gases, it is clear that the level of waste and greenhouse gas emissions per capita created by the lifestyles of most middle- and upper-income households in the North could not be sustained if most of the world's population were to have comparable levels. Wealthy households in the South may have comparable levels of consumption, but it is the concentration of the world's high consumption households in the North and the much greater historic contribution of the population in the North to existing global environmental problems that makes this a North–South issue.

When judged only in terms of resource use and waste generation, most urban centres in the lower income nations of the South perform well in that the low levels of economic activity and limited consumption levels of most of the population en-sure that figures for resource use per person are very low. So too are per capita lev-els of greenhouse gas emissions and stratospheric ozone depleting chemical emis-sions. Low-income urban citizens are also models of 'sustainable consumption' in that they use very few non-renewable resources and generate very little waste. They are also among the most assiduous collectors and users of recycled or reclaimed materials. But these are also generally the people who face the most serious poverty and have the most serious environmental problems in terms of exposure to infectious and parasitic diseases and to chemical and physical hazards. This is a reminder of the need to assess the environmental performance of cities in all five of the above categories.

Assessing Cities' Regional and Global Ecological and Human Footprints

It is difficult to estimate the ecological costs that arise from producing the large and diverse range of raw materials, intermediate goods and final goods that meet the de-mands of city producers and consumers. Certain concepts have helped to map out and to begin to quantify the scale and nature of these interregional or international transfers of environmental costs. One is the calculation of cities' 'ecological footprints' developed by William Rees (Rees 1992; Wackernagel and Rees 1996) which makes evident the large land area on whose production the inhabitants and businesses of any city depend for food, other renewable resources and the absorption of carbon to compensate for the carbon dioxide emitted from fossil fuel use. Rees calculated that the lower Fraser Valley of British Columbia (Canada) in which Vancouver is located has an ecological footprint of about 20 times as much land as it occupies – to produce the food and forestry products its inhabitants and businesses use and to grow veg-etation to absorb the carbon dioxide they produce (Rees 1992). London's ecological footprint is estimated to be 125 times its actual size, based on similar criteria (Jopling and Giradet 1996). However, care is needed in comparing the size of different cities' ecological footprints. One reason is that the size of the footprint as a multiple of the city area will vary considerably, depending on where the city boundary is drawn, and this is the main reason why London's inhabitants appear to have a much larger indi-vidual ecological footprint than the inhabitants of the Fraser Valley.[2] A second is dif-ferences between cities in the quality and range of statistics from which a city's eco-logical footprint is calculated. Finally, the calculation of ecological footprints for cities should not obscure the fact that particular enterprises and richer income groups con-tribute disproportionately to these footprints. For example, Wackernagel and Rees (1996) calculate that the average ecological footprint for the poorest 20 per cent of Canada's population is less than a quarter that of the wealthiest 20 per cent.

The concept of ecological footprints can also be applied to particular activities – for instance, Wackernagel and Rees (1996) consider the ecological footprint of different kinds of housing, different commuting patterns, road bridges and different goods (including tomato production and newspapers). Another concept that helps to reveal the reliance of wealthy cities on non-renewable resources is through calcu-lating the 'material intensity' of the goods consumed in that city (or what is some-times termed these goods' ecological rucksack). The material intensity of any good can be calculated, relative to the service it provides, as a way of providing a quick and rough estimate of its environmental impact (Schmidt-Bleek 1993). This calculation can include all the energy and material inputs into any good from the extraction or fabrication of materials used to make it through its use to its final disposal. It can also include consideration of how much service that good provides, including how long it lasts – so, for instance, a fridge or car that lasted 20 years would have less material intensity than one that lasted 10 years. It has been calculated that a home fridge designed to lower its 'material input:intensity of service ratio' could be constructed with available technologies and materials to achieve a resource productivity of roughly six times that of currently available models (Tischner and Schmidt-Bleek 1993). There is also the long-established practice of calculating the energy-intensity of different goods which also take into account the energy used in their fabrication, transport, preparation for sale, sale, use and disposal. Since in most instances, most or all of the energy input comes from fossil fuels, this allows an idea of how the use of this good contributes to the use of fossil fuels and the generation of carbon dioxide (the largest contributor to atmospheric warming), and perhaps also some idea of the air pollution implications of its fabrication, use and disposal.

While these concepts have helped to make apparent the extent to which modern cities generate environmental costs far from their boundaries, it is difficult to quantify all such transfers. For instance, the long-term health and ecological consequences of many chemical wastes are unknown, including those arising from the accumulation of certain persistent chemicals. It is also difficult to estimate the scale of the health risks faced by the workers and their families who make the goods which the consumers and enterprises within wealthy cities use. It is also difficult to adjust the calculations for a city's 'ecological footprint' to take account of the goods and services that its enterprises produce for those living outside its boundaries. To take an extreme example, a city which produced high fuel efficiency buses or solar panels would have the fossil fuel inputs into their fabrication taken as part of the city's ecological footprint but no allowance made for these goods' contribution to reducing the ecological footprint in other locations.

Constraints on Action in the Five Categories

The distinction between the five categories for environmental action outlined above is reflected in the historical evolution of government intervention in the urban environment, as the first category became a major concern during the second half of the 19th century (and is often referred to as the sanitary revolution), with the second and third following soon after, although progress on many aspects of these had to wait until citizen pressure helped to ensure that safeguarding environmental quality became an accepted part of governments' responsibilities. The fourth and fifth are more recent in terms of their widespread discussion among governments and international agencies, although there is a literature dating back at least 20 years on the need to move in this direction (see, for instance, Ward 1976 and the discussions about a Conserver Society within Canada during the mid 1970s[3]). This should not be taken to imply that environmental action in cities has to go through these five categories sequentially, and there are many long-term advantages for city authorities in recognizing the validity of all five, as long as their priorities do not become distorted (as in a concern for 'sustainable consumption' detracting from more pressing and immediate needs for improved environmental health).

This distinction between these five categories is also useful in considering the political economy of environmental problems since there are differences between the categories in terms of who is responsible for the problems, who is most affected by them, the possibilities for those who are affected to get the problems addressed, how the problems are addressed and by whom. Addressing the environmental problems in the first category has long been understood as the responsibility of public authorities – in public health and environmental health – even if many of the actions may be delegated or contracted to private enterprises, non-government organizations or community-based organizations. In category 2, it is again recognized as the role of public authorities to set standards and enforce them, with unions and other worker organizations having a major role in promoting solutions for occupational health and safety, and consumer groups and democratic political structures having importance in getting action on other chemical and physical hazards. Democratic political structures also have great importance in category 3 in ensuring that the environmental priorities of all the city's populations get addressed.

There are obvious vested interests that oppose public action in each of these categories as they imply higher costs for certain enterprises or citizens or controls over what they can do within their enterprise or on land that they purchase or with the wastes they generate. But in categories 1–3, at least city authorities can seek compromises between those involved; it is one of their central functions to do so. In most cities, there are areas of broad agreement among diverse groups for the promotion of health, prevention of disease and achievement of environmental quality, and it is developing and promoting this common agenda that is at the core of Healthy City programmes (WHO 1996).

One important institutional difficulty arises if environmental problems or costs are being transferred from one area to another and the local authority structure is made up of different, largely autonomous local authorities with no mechanisms to manage intermunicipality disputes and resource transfers. The transfer of environmental costs from richer to poorer areas within nations or regions is what underlies what is often termed 'environmental racism' as polluting industries or wastes are systematically located in lower-income areas. There is also the institutional difficulty in addressing environmental problems in category 4, where city authorities have no jurisdiction in the wider region and where the power of the city-based vested interests to use resources or sinks in the region around the city in environmentally damaging ways is generally greater than that of its inhabitants.

The institutional difficulties in categories 1 to 4 have greater possibilities of being resolved since they fall within the boundaries of one nation. For category 5, most do not and it is difficult to foresee how to prevent such transfers. There has been some progress on this front in recent years, mostly through pressure brought on governments and business by consumer groups or NGOs (see, for instance, Harrison 1997). For example, what is termed 'green consumerism' where purchasers choose goods whose fabrication or use has less damaging environmental consequences which is supported by 'eco-labelling' has put pressure on many manufacturers to address the environmental implications of their products' fabrication, use and disposal. 'Fair trade' campaigns and the sale of 'fair-trade' goods have helped to raise issues such as the wages and/or working conditions of those who make the goods or the human rights records of their governments. These have also put pressure on producers and retailers to take what is usually termed 'ethical sourcing' more seriously – for instance, to avoid the use of goods produced in countries or by companies with poor human rights or environmental records. Many companies' unethical investments or products or poor environmental performance have been exposed by campaigns – for instance, to promote consumer boycotts of their products – or by environmental or human rights campaigners purchasing some shares and bringing pressure on the company at shareholder meetings. There are examples of companies (including multinational corporations) which have made explicit commitments to improve environmental performance or better wages and working conditions for their workforce or for those working in major subcontractors, and even a few that allow independent audits to check on their claims. There are examples of governments which have promoted or supported eco-labelling and the control of certain imports for ethical or environmental reasons. But the people who are affected by the international transfer of environmental costs have no direct political influence on the governments of the nations into which the goods they helped to produce are imported.

There is some international action to prevent the most obvious and blatant international transfer of environmental costs, as in the controls on the export of hazardous wastes and on the trade of endangered species or products derived from them. But the basis of international trade would be threatened if action extended to address all such transfers – for instance, through governments in the North only permitting imports from countries in the South where good standards of occupational health and safety were maintained. Or where the import of goods produced by multinational corporations was only permitted if the corporation and its main subcontractors met agreed standards for good environmental practice in the use of resources, and generation and management of wastes in all its operations in different countries, with independent groups allowed to monitor their performance. Such controls appear at odds with the process of globalization, but it is difficult to foresee how to prevent this transfer of environmental costs to other people or ecosystems without such measures (see Goodland 1995; Redclift 1996). The initiatives to promote green consumerism and fair trade can only have limited impact if the goods they promote have to compete with those whose lower price reflects the inadequate wages and poor working conditions of those who made them and the avoidance of costs through no attention to pollution control and waste management.

INTEGRATING IMPROVED ENVIRONMENTAL PERFORMANCE INTO THE SOCIAL, ECONOMIC AND POLITICAL GOALS OF SUSTAINABLE DEVELOPMENT

One of the more contentious issues in discussions of 'sustainable development' is what the 'sustainable' refers to. A review of the literature on sustainable development found that much of it was almost exclusively concerned with ecological sustainability, with little or no mention of 'development' in the sense of the meeting of human needs (Mitlin 1992). Perhaps partly in reaction to this, there are also discussions of sustainable development that focus almost exclusively on meeting human needs with little consideration of ecological sustainability – as in, for instance, the Habitat II documents, as will be discussed later. There is also a third set of literature, most of it coming from international agencies, where the term 'sustainable development' is used in discussions about whether the projects of international agencies will continue to function after the removal of foreign aid; here too, little or no consideration is generally given to ecological sustainability. Perhaps what makes the Brundtland Commission's statement so important is its insistence that meeting human needs must be combined with ecological sustainability (to meet 'the needs of the present without compromising the ability of future generations to meet their own needs' (World Commission on Environment and Development 1987, p 8).

In previous work with Jorge Hardoy and Diana Mitlin, we suggested that the 'sustainable' part of sustainable development be considered as avoiding the depletion of environmental capital (or concentrating on ecological sustainability), while the 'development' part of sustainable development be considered the meeting of human needs (see, for instance, Hardoy et al 1992, Mitlin and Satterthwaite 1996). This led to an elaboration of the social, economic and political goals, based on the Brundtland Commission's statement given above, within a commitment to limit or stop the depletion of the four kinds of environmental capital (see Box 5.1). The upper part of this box summarizes the social, economic and political goals inherent in meeting human needs; these will not be elaborated here, since the purpose of this paper is to concentrate on the environmental aspects of sustainable development.[4]

However, some mention should be made of the issue of population growth since this affects both the 'sustainable' and the 'development' components, and the issue of population growth is rarely given much attention within the discussions of sustainable development and cities (Drakakis-Smith 1996). Discussing population growth is complicated by the scale of the differentials between the largest and the smallest consumers in terms of their contribution to the depletion of natural capital. There is a tendency to assume that the size of a city's, nation's or region's population is the main influence on its depletion of natural capital and that the rate of population growth is the main influence on the rate of change in this depletion. But a significant proportion of the urban population in the South (including many of the people in cities which have had rapid population growth rates in recent decades) have consumption levels that are so low that they contribute little or nothing to the use of non-renewable resources and the generation of wastes, including the generation of greenhouse gases. Worldwide, most resource use and waste generation arises from the consumption patterns of middle and upper income households (most with very low fertility rates) and the enterprises who produce the goods they consume. In addition, countries in the South which have had the fastest growing economies in recent decades are also likely to be the countries with the most rapid growth in the use of natural capital and generally the largest decreases in population growth.[5] In regard to sustainable development, perhaps the most important issue to stress is that meeting human needs as outlined in Box 5.1 which includes meeting the sexual and reproductive health needs of men and women also supports a rapid decrease in fertility rates in countries with high population growth rates (see for instance Sen et al 1994). But it may also provide the basis for far more people to choose high consumption lifestyles, which is why the meeting of human needs has to be combined with considerations of how to minimize the depletion of environmental capital.

This distinction between the 'ecological sustainability' and the 'development' components of sustainable development has the advantage of avoiding the ambiguities inherent in such terms as 'economic sustainability', 'social sustainability' and 'cultural sustainability' where it is not certain what is to be sustained and how sustaining it would affect environmental capital. For instance, the concept of social sustainability might be taken to mean the sustaining of current societies and their social structures when the meeting of human needs without depleting environmental capital implies major changes to existing social structures. If social sustainability is taken to mean the social measures needed to prevent social disruption or conflict, and the reduction of poverty justified by this, as McGranahan, Songsore and Kjellén

Box 5.1 *The multiple goals of sustainable development as applied to cities*

Meeting the needs of the present ...

- *Economic needs* – includes access to an adequate livelihood or productive assets; also economic security when unemployed, ill, disabled or otherwise unable to secure a livelihood.
- *Social, cultural, environmental and health needs* – includes a shelter which is healthy, safe, affordable and secure, within a neighbourhood with provision for piped water, sanitation, drainage, transport, health care, education and child development. Also a home, workplace and living environment protected from environmental hazards, including chemical pollution. Also important are needs related to people's choice and control – including homes and neighbourhoods which they value and where their social and cultural priorities are met. Shelters and services must meet the specific needs of children and of adults responsible for most child-rearing (usually women). Achieving this implies a more equitable distribution of income between nations and, in most, within nations.
- *Political needs* – includes freedom to participate in national and local politics and in decisions regarding management and development of one's home and neighbourhood, within a broader framework which ensures respect for civil and political rights and the implementation of environmental legislation.

... without compromising the ability of future generations to meet their own needs

- *Minimizing use or waste of non-renewable resources* – includes minimizing the consumption of fossil fuels in housing, commerce, industry and transport plus substituting renewable sources where feasible. Also, minimizing waste of scarce mineral resources (reduce use, reuse, recycle, reclaim). There are also cultural, historical and natural assets within cities that are irreplaceable and thus non-renewable – for instance, historic districts and parks and natural landscapes which provide space for play, recreation and access to nature.
- *Sustainable use of finite renewable resources* – cities drawing on freshwater resources at levels which can be sustained (with recycling and reuse promoted). Keeping to a sustainable ecological footprint in terms of land area on which city-based producers and consumers draw for agricultural and forest products and biomass fuels.
- *Biodegradable wastes not overtaxing capacities of renewable sinks* (eg capacity of a river to break down biodegradable wastes without ecological degradation)
- *Non-biodegradable wastes/emissions not overtaxing (finite) capacity of local and global sinks to absorb or dilute them without adverse effects* (eg persistent pesticides; greenhouse gases and stratospheric ozone-depleting chemicals).

Source: Developed from Mitlin, Diana and David Satterthwaite, *Cities and Sustainable Development*, the background paper to Global Forum '94, Manchester City Council and IIED, June 1994

point out, the legitimate objection to poverty is not because it undermines 'social sustainability' as the poor protest but the suffering the poverty causes (McGranahan et al 1996).

Phrases such as 'sustainable cities', 'sustainable human settlements' and 'sustainable urbanization' are also unclear for similar reasons.[6] It is not cities or urbanization that sustainable development seeks to sustain but to meet human needs in settlements of all sizes without depleting environmental capital. This means seeking the institutional and regulatory framework in which democratic and accountable city and municipal authorities ensure that the needs of the people within their boundaries are addressed while minimizing the transferring of environmental costs to other people or ecosystems or into the future. This in turn requires consideration of the kinds of national policies and legal and institutional frameworks, and the kinds of international agreements that encourage city and municipal authorities in this direction.

THE LOCAL, NATIONAL AND INTERNATIONAL FRAMEWORKS FOR PROMOTING SUSTAINABLE DEVELOPMENT AND CITIES

The beginning of this paper noted the many examples of progress by city and municipal authorities in different regions of the world towards sustainable development goals. There are examples of innovations by such authorities in all five of the categories of environmental action described above. This highlights the relevance for all cities of the point made by the European Commission's report on *European Sustainable Cities* (European Commission 1994) that local governments with their many and varied roles are in a strong position to advance the goals of sustainable development as direct or indirect providers of services, regulator, leader by example, community informer, advocate, adviser, partner, mobilizer of community resources and initiator of dialogue and debate. There are also examples of how what might be termed a 'sustainable consumption' logic can be institutionalized in building codes and zoning and subdivision regulations, in planning for transport, water supply and waste water disposal, recreation and urban expansion, in local revenue-raising (through environmental taxes, charges and levies) and through local authorities bringing in environmental considerations when budgeting, purchasing and tendering.

But there are also the limits on the capacities of city and municipal authorities to act. This is especially so in most of Africa, Asia and Latin America where their powers and the resources at their disposal severely limit their capacity to act on the five categories outlined above. Although there has been some decentralization of decision-making power and considerable progress in more democratic and transparent urban authorities in many nations in the South over the last 10–15 years, most urban authorities have very limited funds for capital investment at their disposal (UNCHS 1996). They depend on higher levels of government or international development assistance (negotiated through higher levels of government) for this and it is obviously difficult to develop a long-term programme to improve their environmental performance without an assured source of funding. Privatizing public services can draw on another source of capital for investment, although private enterprises are generally only interested in those aspects of environmental improvement for which the beneficiaries can be charged and can pay. In addition, the extent to which privatization is able to compensate for weak and ineffective local authorities in the South has been exaggerated (see, for instance, Sivaramakrishnan 1997). Ironically, although privatization was seen as a solution to weak and ineffective city authorities, privatization is likely to work best where the local authorities are able to set appropriate terms for private sector enterprises and monitor the cost and the quality of any services they provide, and, where needed, to enforce compliance with agreed standards and prices.

In the North, city and local authorities generally have far more resources, better trained staff and a more assured source of capital investment, although city and municipal authorities in the poorest urban areas face particular problems. But all city and municipal authorities are limited in what they can achieve in regard to the fifth category, 'sustainable consumption', although sustainable development cannot be achieved if there is no progress on this category. The reviews of recent experiences in European cities point to a large range of environmental innovations – for instance, expanding the pedestrianization of streets, in public transport, in waste management (including recycling and waste reduction) and urban 'greening' (European Commission 1994, Mega 1996a, 1996b). They point to many examples of good governance as city authorities become more explicit in their goals to improve health and environmental performance, more transparent and co-operative in the ways they work and with a greater commitment to environmental auditing (ibid). However, much of what is being done is only local and regional in scope and thus covering only the first four categories in which action is needed. Improving each city's environment and protecting its cultural heritage (and by doing so increasing its attraction to new investment and tourism) and reducing the environmental damage done to the surrounding region do not necessarily reduce greenhouse gas emissions (although some of the initiatives can do so by reducing fossil-fuel use).

This implies the need for international agreements that set enforceable limits on each national society's consumption of scarce resources (or resources whose use implies unacceptable ecological costs) and their use of the global sink for wastes. But it is also clear that most action to achieve sustainable development has to be formulated and implemented locally. The fact that each village, province or city and its insertion within local and regional ecosystems is unique implies the need for optimal use of local resources, knowledge and skills for the achievement of development goals within a detailed knowledge of the local and regional ecological carrying capacity (see, for instance, Drakakis-Smith 1996). As Pugh (1996) notes,

> At all levels of policy and programme application (for government agencies), there are situational complexities in endeavouring to balance economic efficiency, the operation of markets, regard to the public goods and economic externality aspects of the environment, and attention to issues affecting poverty and social justice. (pp 234–235)

This requires a considerable degree of local self-determination, since centralized decision-making structures have difficulty in implementing decisions which respond appropriately to such diversity. Nevertheless, national and international frameworks are needed to ensure that individual cities or countries do not take advantage of others' restraint. Cities where businesses, consumers and local authorities improve their environmental performance, including reducing their transfer of environmental costs to other locations, need to be rewarded, not penalized as enterprises and consumers who want to avoid good environmental performance move elsewhere.

There is the danger that Redclift (1996) highlights – that the 'solution' to what are perceived as global problems may be forms of global environmental management. But these global problems are caused by the aggregation of production and consumption, much of it concentrated within the world's urban centres. Redclift suggests that we cannot 'manage' the environment successfully at the global level without first achieving progress towards sustainability at the local level. 'We are in effect inventing new institutional structures for managing the environment which bear little or no relation to the processes through which the environment is being transformed' (ibid, p 1). But it is also difficult to see how local decisions will incorporate global responsibilities without international agreements among governments to take responsibilities for addressing global problems within their boundaries. If the governments of nations within the North commit themselves to reduced levels of greenhouse gas emissions, they will have to develop the incentives and regulations that support reduced greenhouse gas emissions within each locality, but with local decisions about how best to achieve this. And as Redclift (1996) also points out, this must be done in ways that incorporate a knowledge of the consequences of our behaviour into the behaviour itself rather than seeking to invent management techniques to combat the contradictions of development (Redclift 1996). We need to recover control over consumption rather than set up new institutions to manage its consequences (ibid).

National governments have the main responsibility for ensuring that local authorities address categories four and five, as well as the first three. Internationally, they have the responsibility for reaching agreements to limit the call that consumers and businesses within their country make on the world's environmental capital. But there is little evidence of national governments setting up the regulatory and incentive structure to ensure that the aggregate impact of the economic activities within their boundaries and their citizens' consumption is not transferring environmental costs to other nations or to the future, although a few governments in Europe have taken some tentative steps towards some aspects (see European Commission 1994; UNCHS 1996; Mega 1996b). What is also noticeable is the extent to which urban issues are given little attention in most national sustainable development strategies, despite the prominent role of city-based production and consumption in most nations' resource use, waste generation and greenhouse gas emissions and despite the great potential for cities and for urban policies to contribute to addressing sustainable consumption (Mitlin and Satterthwaite 1996; UNCHS 1996). Much of the general literature on national environmental and sustainable development plans also ignores or gives very little attention to urban issues.[7]

The kind of incentive and regulatory structure that is needed to promote the achievement of sustainable development goals in cities is relatively easy to conceive as an abstract exercise. Certainly, human needs can be met and poverty greatly reduced without an expansion in resource use and waste generation which threatens ecological sustainability. It is also possible to envisage a considerable reduction in resource use and waste generation by middle- and upper-income households without diminishing their quality of life and in some aspects enhancing it (see, for instance, the many studies showing how fossil-fuel use in the North can be cut considerably without reducing living standards, as in Leach et al 1979). The work of the Rocky Mountain Institute in the United States (among other groups) has highlighted the extent to which resource use and waste can be cut within prosperous economies, without compromising living standards (see, for instance, Lovins and Lovins 1991). There is also considerable potential for employment creation in a shift to lower levels of resource use and waste, although some employment in certain businesses or sectors will suffer.[8]

It is also possible to envisage the poorer nations achieving the prosperity and economic stability they need to underpin secure livelihoods and decent living conditions for their populations and the needed enhancement in the competence and accountability of their government without a much increased call on environmental capital. The knowledge exists on how to develop more productive and sustainable agriculture (see, for instance, Pretty et al 1992), forestry management (see, for instance, Sargent and Bass 1992), industrial production (Robins and Trisoglio 1992) and settlement patterns (Breheny 1992; Haughton and Hunter 1994; Blowers 1993; UNCHS 1996). But the prospects for translating what is possible into the needed national frameworks and international agreements remains much less certain. Powerful vested interests oppose most, if not all, the needed policies and priorities. Richer groups will oppose what they see as controls on their right to consume or higher costs that arise from changed pricing structures to encourage conservation and waste reduction. Technological change can help to resolve this – for instance, moderating the impact of rising gasoline prices through the relatively rapid introduction of increasingly fuel-efficient automobiles and the introduction of alternative fuels derived from renewable energy sources. But if combating atmospheric warming does demand the scale of reduction in greenhouse gas emissions that the IPCC's most recent assessment suggests, this will imply changes in people's right to use private automobiles which cannot be met by new technologies and alternative ('renewable') fuels – at least at costs which at present would prove politically acceptable. As Professor O'Riordan recently commented, 'as the scientific case to curb global warming has strengthened, so the politicians have retreated' (in Pearce 1997, p 12).

There are also the difficulties in converting buildings, settlement patterns, urban systems and energy, transport and waste-disposal systems that developed during the last 40 years of low oil prices which are not easily modified for much reduced fossil fuel use. So many existing commercial, industrial and residential buildings and urban forms – for instance, low-density suburban developments and out-of-town shopping malls – have high levels of energy use built into them and these are not easily or rapidly changed (Gore 1991). This means a number of critical consumption areas that are not determined by consumer preference, as individuals are locked into relatively high consumption patterns by physical infrastructure over which they have little or no control – energy, housing, transport and waste-collection systems are prime examples (Robins and Roberts 1996). It is difficult for urban households to maintain a commitment to recycling if it is difficult for them to take the separated materials to recycling points. In many cities in the North, it is difficult for households to avoid purchasing a car, as urban forms have changed to serve car users and not pedestrians, bicyclists and public transport users. Many of the lowest income households in the North have the worst insulated housing and the least capacity to pay for addressing this. Many also rent their accommodation and are reluctant to invest in improvements from which the landlord will draw most benefits. There are also consumption habits that have developed among the world's middle and upper income groups that are probably incompatible with sustainable development, if extended to more than a small minority of the world's population – for instance, the much increased use of air transport and the widespread use of private automobiles for leisure.

AN INITIAL ASSESSMENT OF THE OUTCOME OF HABITAT II FOR PROMOTING SUSTAINABLE DEVELOPMENT AND CITIES

In the light of the above discussion, the two key documents that came out of the Habitat II Conference (the Istanbul Declaration on Human Settlements and the

Habitat Agenda) can be assessed for the extent to which they addressed the two central points of sustainable development in regard to cities: a strong priority to meet human needs within a strong commitment to minimize the depletion of the four different kinds of environmental capital listed on the bottom half of Box 5.1.

In making this assessment, it must be remembered that these large global conferences seek a consensus among the representatives of all governments present. Both the Declaration and the Habitat Agenda had to be acceptable to the representatives of some 180 government delegations and with considerable pressure being brought to bear on government delegations from groups as diverse as the Catholic Church, the US government's delegation (and their strong opposition to housing being considered a human right through much of the preparatory process) and feminist and human rights coalitions. It is easy to point to a lack of precision in some of the language used, the repetition and the tendency to have long lists of 'problems' with little consideration of their linkages (and often their underlying causes). But these are to be expected in a document that had to cover such a large subject area, including many issues which are controversial, and to be endorsed by representatives of so many different governments with diverse positions, and in which so many groups demanded or promoted additional text or changes to the draft text. Where the wording of a paragraph on some controversial issue appears unclear or imprecise, this may be because greater clarity or precision prevented agreement by some government representative or representative of some group of countries. One of the persons involved in drafting the document admitted that on the first day of the Conference itself, nearly seven hours were spent in deciding whether sustainable settlements 'promote' or 'should promote' human rights and this is a reminder of how complex it can be to reach agreement among so many interested parties (Kakakhel 1996).

A first impression of the treatment of sustainable development and cities within the two key documents could be favourable. Both the Istanbul Declaration on Human Settlements and the Habitat Agenda make frequent mention of 'sustainable human settlements' or 'sustainable human settlements development' – sustainable urban development is also mentioned several times. Sustainable human settlements development is one of the two major themes for the conference, the other being 'adequate shelter for all'. In addition, both documents give a high priority to the meeting of human needs in cities (and other human settlements), including the need for a strong priority for poverty reduction. They also stress the need to address environmental problems and acknowledge the important health components in doing so. There is also a strong stress on the need to strengthen city and municipal authorities.

However, the documents are weakest where they needed to be strongest – in agreeing on the kind of national and international frameworks that would ensure sustainable development goals are addressed in cities (and other settlements). As one of the World Bank's most experienced urban specialists noted:

> The biggest gap in the Istanbul discussions was the lack of progress in operationalizing the notion of environmentally sustainable development [and] while the term 'sustainable development' was mentioned repeatedly, little progress was made in suggesting how it could be operationally applied to urban areas. (Cohen 1996, p 4)

The Habitat II documents make little mention of the kinds of frameworks needed to achieve significant reductions in the depletion of environmental capital from the people and enterprises who at present contribute most to these (a high proportion of which are concentrated in cities in the North). It also made little mention of the new resources that need to be directed to the meeting of human needs in the nations where there are insufficient resources to achieve this.

There is also considerable confusion within the Habitat II documents as to what sustainable development is meant to sustain – whether it is settlements or settlement policies or particular activities within settlements. This was not a confusion that arose from the search for consensus at the Conference itself for it was present in earlier drafts of what became the Habitat Agenda. Within the text, sometimes it is human settlements that are to be sustainable – for instance, 'sustainable human settlements' or 'sustainable urban centres' or 'sustainable communities' – or aggregates of human settlements as in sustainable spatial development patterns. In other instances, it is society in general or living conditions that are to be 'sustainable'. In others, it is particular activities within urban areas that are to be sustainable, as in sustainable shelter markets and land development or sustainable transport, sustainable agriculture, sustainable livelihoods, sustainable resource use, sustainable water supply or sustainable energy use. 'Sustained economic growth and equity' are also mentioned as part of sustainable development; clearly, 'sustained economic growth' is not part of sustainable development, although one suspects that what the delegates meant was that the promotion of sustainable development should not inhibit lower income countries achieving higher incomes and greater economic prosperity and stability.

The worry of government delegates from the South that environmental measures might be the means by which the North inhibit their economic development is still strong in these global meetings – after surfacing as long ago as the 1972 UN Conference on the Human Environment in Stockholm which initiated the cycle of global UN Conferences on environment and development issues. The closest the Habitat II documents come to addressing the loss of environmental capital arising from high consumption lifestyles is several references to 'unsustainable consumption and production patterns, particularly in industrialized countries'[9] but these are not addressed in the recommendations. And, despite the length of the Habitat II documents, there is no mention of the dangers posed to settlements by global warming or of the need to curb greenhouse gas emissions. Perhaps the delegates felt that this was unnecessary, since the Habitat II documentation endorsed the recommendations of previous conferences, and that this was an issue covered by Agenda 21, coming out of the Earth Summit (the UN Conference on Environment and Development in 1992).

The Habitat II documents also have many examples of where it is not human settlements or activities in human settlements but the development of human settlements that should be sustainable, or particular human settlements policies as in sustainable land-use policies or more sustainable population policies. Sometimes it is broader than this as in sustainable economic development and social development activities. In regard to what constitutes sustainable development, the documents often refer to this being a combination of economic development, social development and environmental protection.[10] These are mentioned as 'interdependent and mutually reinforcing components of sustainable development'.[11] This highlights another flaw in the documents – the assumption that a concern for environmental quality within cities is all that is needed to achieve the environmental component of sustainable development goals. What this misses is the many means by which enterprises and those with high consumption lifestyles transfer some of their environmental costs to other people, other regions or into the future, as outlined in earlier sections.

Although much of the literature on sustainable development can be criticized for emphasizing the sustaining of environmental capital to the virtual exclusion of any consideration of human needs, the Habitat II documents do the opposite. Two factors help to explain this. The first, already noted, is the way in which many development agencies came to use the term sustainable development as the label given to ensuring that their development projects continued to operate when these agencies' external support was cut off at the 'end of the project'. Although this is a problem that was recognized before the term sustainable development became widely used, many international agencies borrowed the new terminology, without taking on board its original meaning. The second is the desire of the United Nations Centre for Human Settlements which was responsible for organizing the Habitat II Conference and the government ministries which deal with this UN agency (mainly ministries of housing[12]) to put human needs at the centre of 'sustainable development', partly in reaction to the failure of so much of the sustainable development literature to do so. But in doing so, they gave little attention to the fact that sustainable development is also about addressing the depletion of environmental capital (and not just promoting environmental quality in settlements). Perhaps the avoidance of clear positions and specific recommendations that address the more contentious issues within sustainable development is the cost that had to be paid for achieving consensus. But this means that the Habitat II documents include no recommendations on many of the key points in regard to what needs to be done to ensure sustainable development goals are met in cities (and other settlements).

CONCLUSIONS

This paper has outlined a framework for a more comprehensive accounting of cities' environmental performance within a commitment to other sustainable development goals. It stressed the importance of taking account of the environmental costs generated or imposed by city-based activities on people or ecological resources outside city boundaries or displaced into the future. It also stressed the importance of integrating the discussions about cities and sustainable development with the general discussions about sustainable development and ensuring that urban issues are fully considered within national environmental plans and national sustainable development strategies.

Given the tendency for many environmentalists to view cities only as places which generate environmental costs, a greater attention to cities' environmental problems might also ignore the benefits that city-based enterprises and consumers provide (or can provide) for people, natural resources and ecosystems outside their boundaries. Of course, these include the goods purchased by city businesses, governments and consumers which provide incomes from those living outside the city and the goods and services provided by city-enterprises to those living outside the city. Also, care must be taken in ascribing blame to 'cities' for environmental costs transferred from within cities to other ecosystems or people in that it is particular groups in cities (mostly the higher income groups) and particular enterprises who are responsible for most such costs.

In addition, the inherent advantages that cities have or can have for combining high quality living conditions with low levels of resource use, waste and greenhouse gas emissions per person should not be forgotten (Mitlin and Satterthwaite 1996, UNCHS 1996). Nor, too, must the fact that wealthy rural or suburban households generally have higher levels of resource use and waste generation than their counter-parts living in cities as they own more automobiles, use them more often and have higher levels of energy use within their homes (ibid). What this paper has sought to stress is the areas where improved environmental performance is needed in cities and how these should also be integrated with the social, economic and political goals of sustainable development. This is not achieved by focusing on sustainable cities but on how city consumers, enterprises and governments can contribute more to sustainable development.

ACKNOWLEDGEMENTS

This paper draws on the work that the author has undertaken with the World Health Organization in preparing two documents whose findings are used in this paper – WHO 1992 and WHO 1996 – and on the work he undertook in preparing UNCHS 1996. He is particularly grateful to Sam Ozolins, Greg Goldstein and Wilfrid Kreisel at WHO and Donatus Okpala at UNCHS for their help. Thanks are also due to Cedric Pugh, Diana Mitlin, Nick Robins and Koy Thomson for their comments on an earlier draft.

NOTES

1   IIED monitors the priority given by international agencies to addressing basic needs and to urban development. A summary of the findings of its work in this regard was published in UNCHS 1996
2   The calculation for London was based on an area of 1,580 square kilometres (virtually all of which is built up area) with a population of seven million. The calculation for the lower Fraser Valley was for an urban-agricultural region of 4,000 square kilometres with 1.8 million inhabitants
3   These were published in a quarterly publication *Conserver Society Notes* by the Science Council of Canada in Ottawa
4. The social, economic and political aspects are described in more detail in Mitlin and Satterthwaite 1996
5   This association masks the many factors that influence fertility. It also obscures the fact that rapidly increasing or high per capita incomes are not necessary to bring down population growth rates or to have low population growth rates, as can be seen in, for instance, the state of Kerala in India where high priority to education and health care helped to achieve low population growth rates at a low per capita income and without coercive population control policies (Sen 1994). See also Sen et al 1994
6   The justification for avoiding this is discussed in more detail in Mitlin and Satterthwaite 1996
7   See, for instance, the lack of attention given to urban issues and urban policies in Carew-Reid et al 1994 and Dalal-Clayton 1996
8   The kinds of shifts in employment structure were summarized in Mitlin and Satterthwaite 1996; they are covered in more detail for Europe in Wikima 1993
9   Para 4, Istanbul Declaration
10 See paragraph 3 of the Istanbul Declaration; also paragraph 4 and paragraph 43b of the Habitat Agenda. Paragraph 29 talks of sustainable human settlements development ensuring 'economic development, employment opportunities and social progress, in harmony with the environment'
11 Paragraph 3 of the Istanbul Declaration; this is also repeated in paragraph 1 of the HabitatAgenda, then again in paragraph 8 and paragraph 43b; paragraph 21 talks of 'economic development, social development and environmental protection' being 'indispensable and mutually reinforcing components of sustainable development'.
12 Sivaramakrishnan 1997

REFERENCES

Bairoch, Paul (1988) *Cities and Economic Development: From the Dawn of History to the Present*, London: Mansell

Bartone, Carl, Janis Bernstein, Josef Leitmann and Jochen Eigen (1994) *Towards Environmental Strategies for Cities; Policy Considerations for Urban Environmental Management in Developing Countries*, UNDP/UNCHS/World Bank Urban Management Program No 18, Washington DC: World Bank

Blowers, Andrew (ed) (1993) *Planning for a Sustainable Environment*, London: Earthscan Publications

Breheny, M J (ed) (1992) *Sustainable Development and Urban Form*, European Research in Regional Science 2, London: Pion

Cairncross, Sandy, Jorge E Hardoy and David Satterthwaite (1990) 'The urban context' in Jorge E Hardoy, Sandy Cairncross and David Satterthwaite (eds), *The Poor Die Young: Housing and Health in Third World Cities*, London: Earthscan, pp 1–24

Carew-Read, Jeremy, Robert Prescott-Allen, Stephen Bass and Barry Dalal-Clayton (1994) *Strategies for National Sustainable Development: a Handbook for their Planning and Implementation*, London: Earthscan Publications

Cohen, Michael (1996) Reflections on Habitat II, Working Group on Habitat II of the Woodrow Wilson Center in Washington DC

Conway, Gordon R and Jules N Pretty (1991) *Unwelcome Harvest*, London: Earthscan

Dalal-Clayton, Barry (1996) *Getting to Grips with Green Plans: National-level Experiences in Industrial Countries*, London: Earthscan Publications

Díaz, Doris Balvin, José Luis López Follegatti and Micky Hordijk (1996) 'Innovative urban environmental management in Ilo, Peru', *Environment and Urbanization*, 8(1): pp 21–34

Douglas, Ian (1983) *The Urban Environment*, London: Edward Arnold

Douglas, Ian (1986) 'Urban Geomorphology', in P G Fookes and P R Vaughan (eds), *A Handbook of Engineering Geomorphology*, Glasgow: Blackie & Son, pp 270–283

Drakakis-Smith, David (1996) 'Third world cities: sustainable urban development, II – population, labour and poverty', *Urban Studies* 33(4–5), pp 673–701

European Commission – Expert Group on the Urban Environment (1994), *European Sustainable Cities* Part 1, Brussels: European Commission, X1/95/502-en, October

Goodland, Robert (1995) 'The concept of environmental sustainability', *Annual Review of Ecological Systems* 26, pp 1–24

Gore, Charles (1991) *Policies and Mechanisms for Sustainable Development: the Transport Sector*, mimeo

Hardoy, Jorge E, Diana Mitlin and David Satterthwaite (1992) *Environmental Problems in Third World Cities*, London: Earthscan

Harrison, Rob (1997) 'Ethical consumption: bare faced cheek', *New Internationalist* 289, April, pp 26–27

Hart, Roger (1997) *Children's Participation: The Theory and Practice of Involving Young Citizens in Community Development and Environmental Care*, London: Earthscan Publications

Haughton, Graham and Colin Hunter (1994) *Sustainable Cities*, Regional Policy and Development series, London: Jessica Kingsley

Jopling, John and Herbert Giradet (1996) *Creating a Sustainable London*, London: Sustainable London Trust

Kakakhel, B Shafqat (1996) 'To bracket or not to bracket: negotiating the Habitat Agenda', *Habitat Debate* 2(3/4): p 15

Leach, Gerald, Christopher Lewis, Frederic Romig, Ariane van Buren and Gerald Foley (1979) *A Low Energy Strategy for the United Kingdom*, London: Science Reviews Ltd

Leduc, James W and Eugene Tikhomirov (1994) 'Global surveillance for recognition and response to emerging diseases', *Annals of the New York Academy of Sciences* December, pp 341–345

Lovins, Amory B and L Hunter Lovins (1991) 'Least-cost climatic stabilization', *Annual Review of Energy and Environment*, 16, pp 433–531

McGranahan, Gordon, Jacob Songsore and Marianne Kjellén (1996) 'Sustainability, poverty and urban environmental transitions', in Cedric Pugh (ed), *Sustainability, the Environment and Urbanization*, London: Earthscan, pp 103–133

Mega, Voula (1996a) 'Our city, our future: Towards sustainable development in European cities', *Environment and Urbanization* 8 (1) April, pp 133–154

Mega, Voula (1996b) *Innovations for the Improvement of the Urban Environment: Austria, Finland, Sweden*, European Foundation for the Improvement of Living and Working Conditions Office for Official Publications of the European Communities, Luxembourg

Mitlin, Diana (1992) 'Sustainable development: a guide to the literature', *Environment and Urbanization* 4(1), pp 111–124

Mitlin, Diana and David Satterthwaite (1994) *Cities and Sustainable Development*, background paper for Global Forum '94, Manchester: Manchester City Council

Mitlin, Diana and David Satterthwaite (1996) 'Sustainable development and cities', in Cedric Pugh (ed), *Sustainability, the Environment and Urbanization*, London: Earthscan Publications, pp 23–61

O'Riordan, T (1989) 'The challenge of environmentalism' in R Peet and N Thrift (eds), *New Models of Geography*, Vol 1

Pearce, Fred (1997) 'Chill winds at the summit', *New Scientist* No 2071, 1 March, pp 12–13

Pretty, Jules, Irene Guijt, Ian Scoones and John Thompson (1992) 'Regenerating agriculture; the agroecology of low-external input and community-based development', in Johan Holmberg (ed), *Policies for a Small Planet*, London: Earthscan Publications, pp 91–123

Pugh, Cedric (1996) 'Conclusions' in Cedric Pugh (ed), *Sustainability, the Environment and Urbanization*, London: Earthscan, pp 229–243

Rabinovitch, Jonas (1992) 'Curitiba: towards sustainable urban development', *Environment and Urbanization* 4(2): pp 62–77

Rees, William E (1992) 'Ecological footprints and appropriated carrying capacity', *Environment and Urbanization* 4 (2): pp 121–130

Redclift, Michael (1996) *Wasted: Counting the Costs of Global Consumption*, London: Earthscan

Robins, Nick and Sarah Roberts (1996) *Sustainable Consumption, Inequality and Poverty*, London: IIED, mimeo

Robins, Nick and Alex Trisoglio (1992) 'Restructuring industry for sustainable development', in Johan Holmberg (ed), *Policies for a Small Planet*, London: Earthscan, pp 157–194

Sargent, Caroline and Stephen Bass (1992) 'The future shape of forests', in Johan Holmberg (ed), *Policies for a Small Planet*, London: Earthscan, pp 195–224

Satterthwaite, David (1997) 'Environmental transformations in cities as they get larger, wealthier and better managed', *The Geographic Journal* 163 (2), July, pp 216–224

Satterthwaite, David, Roger Hart, Caren Levy, Diana Mitlin, David Ross, Jac Smit and Carolyn Stephens (1996) *The Environment for Children*, London: Earthscan and UNICEF

Schmidt-Bleek, F (1993) 'MIPS revisited', *Fresenius Environmental Bulletin* 2 (8), pp 407–412

Sen, Amartya (1994) *Beyond Liberalization: Social Opportunity and Human Capability*, Development Economics Research Programme DEP No 58, London: London School of Economics

Sen, Gita, Adrienne Germain and Lincoln C Chen (eds) (1994), *Population Policies Reconsidered*, Boston: Harvard University Press

Sivaramakhrishnan, K C (1997) 'The legacy of Habitat II: issues of governance', Paper presented at the meeting of the Woodrow Wilson Center, February

Smit, Jac, Annu Ratta and Joe Nasr (1996) *Urban Agriculture: Food, Jobs and Sustainable Cities*, Publication Series for Habitat II, Volume One, New York: UNDP

Tischner, Ursula and Friedrich Schmidt-Bleek (1993) 'Designing goods with MIPS', *Fresenius Environmental Bulletin* 2 (8), pp 479–484

UNCHS (1996) *An Urbanizing World: Global Report on Human Settlements 1996*, Oxford: Oxford University Press

Wackernagel, Mathis and William Rees (1996) *Our Ecological Footprint: Reducing Human Impact on the Earth*, Gabriola (Canada): New Society Publishers

Ward, Barbara (1976) 'The Inner and the Outer Limits', The Clifford Clark Memorial Lectures 1976, *Canadian Public Administration* 19 (3), Autumn, pp 385–416

WHO (1992) *Our Planet, Our Health*, Report of the Commission on Health and the Environment, Geneva: WHO

WHO (1996) *Creating Healthy Cities in the 21st Century*, background Paper prepared for the Dialogue on Health in Human Settlements for Habitat II, Geneva: World Health Organization

Wikima Consulting (1993) *The Employment Implications of Environmental Action*, Report prepared for the Commission of the European Communities, Directorate-General on Employment, Industrial Relations and Social Affairs, London

Wohl, Anthony S (1983) *Endangered Lives: Public Health in Victorian Britain*, London: Methuen

World Commission on Environment and Development (1987) *Our Common Future*, Oxford: Oxford University Press

Chapter 6

Sustainability, Poverty and Urban Environmental Transitions

Gordon McGranahan, Jacob Songsore and Marianne Kjellén

(Reprinted from Cedric Pugh (editor), *Sustainability, the Environment and Urbanization*, Earthscan Publications, London, 1996, pp 103–34)

INTRODUCTION

The relationship between sustainability, poverty and the environment is complex and at times confusing. The problem is not just that it can be hard to discern where the sustainability arrow is pointing. The very status of sustainability remains unclear. Is sustainability 'a good thing' by definition or by implication? If, especially at certain times and in certain places, the single-minded pursuit of sustainability seems to be 'a bad thing', does this indicate that the definition needs to be reworked, or that sustainability should be only one objective, or constraint, among many? In this paper, it is argued that the primary environmental concerns of the more disadvantaged urban dwellers are not issues of sustainability, narrowly defined. Should a broader definition of sustainability be adopted, or should the pre-eminence of sustainability concerns be rejected?

Given the current popularity of sustainability, it is tempting to stretch the concept to fit one's preoccupations. Since poverty alleviation and the elimination of severe environmental health hazards are clearly of critical importance, doesn't this imply that they ought to be central to sustainability? Munasinghe follows a common trend when he justifies poverty alleviation as a means of addressing a social dimension of sustainability:

> The socio-cultural concept of sustainability seeks to maintain the stability of social and cultural systems, including the reduction of destructive conflicts. Both intragenerational equity (especially elimination of poverty), and intergenerational equity (involving the rights of future generations) are important aspects of this approach. (Munasinghe, 1993, p 3)

In common with many other attempts to incorporate poverty-related concerns under the rubric of sustainability, there are some serious problems with the manner in which a concern with poverty is being justified here. The underlying logic is that sustainability entails social stability, that poverty leads to conflict which undermines social stability, and hence that poverty is unsustainable. But the legitimate objection to poverty is surely the misery it entails, not the disruptions that occur when the immiserated protest. If this is the sort of means through which poverty alleviation can gain a place on the sustainability bandwagon, then it is probably better not to have a place there at all, but to plod along independently, or to latch on to alternative concepts wherein sustainability qualifies rather than incorporates alternative goals (as in sustainable development or sustainable poverty alleviation).

Somewhat surprisingly, there are also many serious urban environmental problems that are not easily portrayed as threats to sustainability, narrowly defined. Faecal matter is probably the most hazardous pollutant in many low-income cities. To say that the sanitation systems in these cities are unsustainable suggests quite a different set of issues, however. It could mean that the infrastructure or facilities cannot be maintained: a very real problem in many cities, but not of great relevance in areas with no facilities at all. Taking a more ecological perspective, it could mean that nutrient cycles are being disrupted – again, not a priority problem in areas where, say, open defecation is practised. It could even mean that sanitation is so bad that the cities are under threat from devastating epidemics or pandemics. But in the late 20th century, faecal pollution is primarily causing endemic health problems, which harm many urban dwellers, but not to the point of threatening to depopulate cities.

The most serious problem with broad definitions of sustainability is that they tend to marginalize the primary environmental concerns of the poor, even as they claim to incorporate them. As described below, increasing urban affluence changes the nature of the environmental challenge. The environmental priorities of the affluent clearly relate to sustainability: it is not so much the present as the future of the world's affluent minority that is at risk. Many of the environmental priorities of the urban poor, on the other hand, must be manipulated to be portrayed as sustainability issues: it is in the here and now that many of their most serious problems have their effects, and their burden on resources and global sinks is comparatively minor. Since the international environmental agenda in any case tends to be dominated by the concerns of the more vocal and powerful, adopting sustainability as an overarching principle reinforces existing tendencies to ignore the priorities of low-income groups.

On the other hand, it is important not to exaggerate the difference between those environmental problems which threaten sustainability, narrowly defined, and those which do not. There are many similarities, both physically and in terms of the collective action problems they pose, between the primarily local problems of the urban poor and the more extensive and long-term problems of more concern to the affluent. Moreover, if the poor majority can gain effective control over their local environments and successfully reduce the hazards which are now such a burden, they are far more likely to become active participants in efforts to prevent the global scale environmental abuse which threatens the future of both the poor and the affluent. Similarly, if the environmental nature of many water, sanitation and housing problems in Southern settlements is recognized, the poor are more likely to be able to take advantage of the global environmental movement to help address their short-term problems. Thus, the goal of creating a common platform for environmental improvement is laudable, even if concepts such as sustainability are not up to the task.

In the remainder of this chapter we attempt to situate the environmental problems of the urban poor in their international context and draw some action-oriented conclusions. In the section entitled Urban Environmental Transition, we provide the rough outlines of such a transition and link affluence to the scale and timing of environmental burdens. We argue that, with increasing affluence, environmental burdens tend to become spatially more diffuse, temporally more delayed and causally less directly threatening (ie environmental degradation is relatively more likely to undermine life-support systems and relatively less likely to threaten health directly). The next section continues with a presentation of selected results from a study of Accra, Jakarta and São Paulo, illustrating elements of this transition. Accra, the poorest of these three cities, faces the worst household level environmental problems, while São Paulo, the largest and most affluent, has some of the worst city-level problems and contributes the most (even per capita) to global problems. In the final section we focus on the local environmental problems of disadvantaged neighbourhoods and link their physical and institutional character with the qualities improvement efforts must have if they are to succeed.

URBAN ENVIRONMENTAL TRANSITIONS[1]

In the urban context, affluence is neither unambiguously harmful nor unambiguously beneficial to the physical environment. Under existing patterns of economic development, however, affluence does change the locus of the urban environmental challenge. Where one perceives the worst problems to be will vary depending upon whether one is concerned with very localized problems such as bad household water and sanitation and indoor air pollution, city-level problems such as ambient air and water pollution, or global problems such as global warming and ozone depletion. Generally:

- The urban environmental hazards causing the most ill health are those found in poor homes, neighbourhoods and workplaces, principally located in the South.
- The most extreme examples of city-level environmental distress are found in and around middle-income mega-cities and the industrial cities of the formerly planned economies.
- The largest urban contributors to global environmental problems are the affluent, living preponderantly in the urban areas of the North.

Whether one looks across cities, at the history of affluent cities, or even across different groups within a city, it is possible to discern the outlines of an environmental transition relating to affluence. As affluence increases, there tends to be a spatial shifting of environmental problems from the local to the regional and global. There also tends to be a temporal shifting from immediate health problems to, in the case of global warming, intergenerational impacts. These tendencies only reflect dispositions: policies, as well as demography and geography, can make an enormous difference, and vastly different environmental conditions can be found both within and among cities of comparable affluence. Generally, however, the poor create environmental problems for themselves and their neighbours, while the affluent distribute their environmental burdens over an expanding public.[2]

Thus, in poor cities and particularly their poor neighbourhoods, the most threatening environmental problems are usually those close to home (McGranahan 1993). The dangers of exposure are high, especially for women and children. Inadequate household water supplies and sanitation are typically more crucial to people's wellbeing than polluted waterways (Cairncross and Feachem 1993). There is often more exposure to air pollution in smoky kitchens than outdoors (Smith 1993). Waste accumulating, uncollected, in the neighbourhood often poses more serious problems than the waste at the city dumps. Flies breeding in the waste and mosquitoes breeding in water sites can add considerably to the local health risks (Chavasse et al 1994;

Schofield et al 1990). In the most disadvantaged neighbourhoods, these problems combine to create a complex of environmental health problems whose most evident burdens are high prevalences of diarrhoeal diseases (Bradley et al 1991; Cairncross and Feachem 1993; Huttly 1990) and acute respiratory infections (Berman 1991; Chen et al 1990; Graham 1990) among young children, but also extend to numerous other health problems (Hardoy et al 1990; Satterthwaite 1993).

A more affluent urban lifestyle employs more resources and creates more waste, but the rich devote part of their wealth to measures which protect themselves from environmental hazards. The problems close to home are the first to improve as affluence increases because they are the most clearly threatening and are institutionally the easiest to address. Moreover, the physical displacement of environmental problems is at once a means of avoiding personal exposure and a possible route to larger scale environmental problems. Water-borne sewerage systems, for example, reduce personal exposure to faecal material, but can lower the quality of the cities' waterways and strain the cities' water supplies. Electricity is a clean fuel where it is used, but electric power plants can be an important source of ambient air pollution. Industries may provide the incomes which allow people to take better care of their home and neighbourhood environments, but they can also bring pollution which degrades the ambient environment.

Thus, even as household and neighbourhood-level environmental problems recede from prominence for a growing segment of a city's population, there are pressures to increase ambient air pollution, hazardous waste problems, pollution of the waterways, and more generally the regional environmental burden of the city. If the broader environmental problems are not on the political agenda (and in most industrializing countries they have not been) these pressures will tend to lead to a general worsening of the ambient urban environment. The fact that interest in environmental protection has no strong power base within a city probably contributes to delays in implementing even relatively uncontroversial environmental controls.

Affluent cities, like affluent households and neighbourhoods, can and often do take measures to protect themselves. Over the past few decades, many cities in the North, and a growing number in the South, have improved the quality of their ambient air (United Nations Environment Programme and World Health Organization 1988) and to a lesser extent water (World Bank 1992). Remedial measures to cope with many of the worst excesses are well known (Douglas 1983), if not always applied. An affluent city can more easily afford the public finance and administration needed to regulate the more perceptible forms of pollution, and in any case affluent cities are more likely to be economically dependent on their services and commercial sector rather than on highly polluting heavy industry. Moreover, the emissions or concentrations of a range of water and air pollutants are not only observed to rise and then fall with increasing national income (Grossman and Krueger 1995; Shafik 1995), but economic analysis suggests that one might expect such a pattern given economically efficient abatement strategies (Selden and Song 1995).

Attempts to address citywide environmental problems do not, however, prevent economic growth from increasing contributions to global environmental problems. The resources consumed and greenhouse gases emitted to support even the cleanest of Northern cities are, on a per capita basis, far larger than those associated with the poorer cities of the South. Recent research confirms a general tendency for carbon dioxide emissions per capita to rise continuously with economic growth (Holtz-Eakin and Selden 1995; Shafik 1995). Relatively little progress has yet been made in introducing 'clean' production in the broadest sense of the term (Jackson 1993), or in shifting from the linear material flows which characterize most modern technologies to the closed cycles which some environmentalists argue ought to characterize post-modern technology (Wallgren 1994). The image of an 'ecological city' remains as utopian in the North as in the South, and it would require radical changes to even begin to approach what could be legitimately termed sustainable cities (White 1994). Since the institutional basis for negotiated restrictions on global environmental burdens are still rudimentary, the economic incentive for affluent countries to take effective measures remains negligible.

Accompanying the shift in the scale of environmental problems, from household and neighbourhood, to city and regional, to global, is a shift from issues of health to those of ecology and sustainability. Threats from intense environmental insults in and around people's homes usually affect the health of the inhabitants directly. Threats from the broader environmental burdens are typically more indirect, affect life-support systems in often subtle ways and take more time to manifest themselves. The environmental health problems which are more critical in affluent cities are typically those which are very poorly or only recently understood, involve delayed effects or cumulative low-level exposures, or are particular aspects of large-scale environmental change (Chivian et al 1993). Whether the broader environmental burdens are sustainable, even in the narrow sense, can be a very pertinent question. The burdens themselves are often the long-term side-effects of the creation of wealth. On the other hand, the sustainability of the more local burdens, such as inadequate household water and sanitation or indoor air pollution, is not really an issue. Such problems derive from practices people do not sustain by choice, and the burdens have already shown themselves all too able to persist.

In its broad outlines, the transition summarized above applies to cities. It suggests an association between a city's affluence, its environment and the health of its citizens. However, there are both poor and affluent people in almost every city. The average income of a city makes a difference, but environmental burdens are borne unevenly. People living in poor neighbourhoods are not only likely to face more household and neighbourhood-level environmental problems, but more than their share of the broader problems as well. For a variety of reasons, low-income settlements are more likely to be located near polluting industrial establishments, waste dump sites and heavily polluted waterways. Indeed, there is a sense in which the poor in rapidly industrializing cities face the worst of two worlds (Harpham et al 1988), and in some cases the environmental risks of poverty and industrialization can overlap and create destructive interactions (Smith and Lee 1993).

While the local character of many of the environmental problems of poverty means that it is necessary to look closely at intra-urban differences in environmental health, there is an inherently public aspect to the environmental problems of almost every level. Acting independently and selfishly, cities and nations would not contribute significantly to solve global environmental problems; industries, transporters and neighbourhoods would not contribute to solving citywide problems; and individuals and households would not contribute to solving neighbourhood problems. At every level, institutional mechanisms are needed to ensure that people are acting in the collective interest. And at every level, social movements have played, and will probably continue to play, an important part in ensuring that institutional as well as technical innovations are forthcoming. This holds despite the enormous differences in both the physical nature of the problems and their institutional contexts.

Alternatively, rapid population growth can act as a compounding factor at every level. Local environmental problems are often most severe where the urban population is growing rapidly, and migrants are particularly exposed to environmental health hazards. Citywide problems are typically more severe in larger cities. And more people, particularly more affluent people, generally mean a greater global burden.

Looking at environmental priorities in this manner, it seems reasonable to ascribe the disproportionate attention given to sustainability issues in the international environmental movement to the fact that the movement is dominated by the concerns of the affluent. It might seem fanciful, however, to suggest that when the now affluent cities were dominated by more localized environmental problems, the international agenda was too. But this would indeed seem to be the case.

A 19th century precursor to the modern environmental movement was the sanitary movement and, at that time, sanitation was very much an environmental concern. Average urban mortality rates in European cities were far higher than in their rural surroundings (Bairoch 1988). Bad sanitation, which then referred to a range of poorly understood environmental hazards rather than just excreta disposal, was increasingly seen as responsible for this urban disadvantage (Wohl 1983). Prominent scientists studied water, sanitary conditions and health, and reformers in urban centres around the world discussed both the technical and moral aspects of urban sanitary reform (Hamlin 1990; Ladd 1990; Luckin 1986). The topic was even of popular interest in many countries. The General German Exhibition of Hygiene and Lifesaving in 1883 attracted 900,000 visitors over a period of five months (Ladd 1990). As in environmental discussions today, one of the most heated debates was about the appropriate role for government, and whether attempts to impose sanitary improvements constituted an infringement on what we would now call the private sector. Eventually, the reformers won out. While the health problems were far worse in poor areas, the affluent were also at risk. Moreover, the ill health of the poor was itself felt to be a burden on the whole society. Politicians were even concerned that the military strength of their nations was being undermined (Shapiro 1985). It was gradually accepted by the politically powerful that the threat was indeed public and required a public response.

The environmental concerns of the world's affluent have moved on and international attention has followed suit. Now, comparisons of average urban and rural mortality rates do not display the same urban disadvantage, even in countries where urban sanitation is poor (Mosley et al 1993). However, averages hide gross disparities in the health status of urban dwellers (Harpham et al 1988; Schell et al 1993). Much the same applies to sanitary conditions and other localized environmental hazards. Many urban dwellers currently face environmental conditions roughly comparable to those which shocked the bourgeoisie in the 19th century. Even for the urban poor (now located primarily in the South), the environmental health burden may not be as high as it once was. Nevertheless, local environmental inadequacies in disadvantaged neighbourhoods probably remain the most important avoidable environmental causes of ill health. Indeed, the 1993 World Development Report, which focused on health, estimated that improving household environments could avert the annual loss of almost 80 million 'disability free' years of human life – more than the feasible improvement attributed to all other identified environmental measures combined (World Bank 1993b).

While the health risks of bad water, poor sanitation and the like have not been forgotten, it is no longer conventional to treat them as complex environmental problems requiring better science, innovative responses and social mobilization. Rather, by and large they are viewed as problems whose solution is known, but for which the requisite finances are not always available, to which insufficient priority is given, or which require a somewhat different mix of private and public sector involvement. This view has been reinforced by efforts to promote price reform in environmental service delivery, which have led the World Bank and other development agencies to emphasize the extent to which water, and to a lesser extent sanitation and other household environmental services, are like normal commodities whose supply ought to be determined through efficient market mechanisms, with full costs recovered from user fees whenever possible (Briscoe and Garn 1995; World Bank 1993a). In some cities, efficient provision on a commercial basis would indeed be an improvement over existing provisions through underfinanced public utilities.[3] But the complex of household and neighbourhood environmental problems which burden so many of the world's more disadvantaged neighbourhoods deserves far more in the way of response than yet another shift along the private-public axis, this time in the private direction.

From Environmental Health to Environmental Sustainability: Evidence from a Three-City Study

As indicated above, the most severe urban environmental health problems are concentrated in the South (Hardoy et al 1992; McGranahan 1993), where contributions to global environmental problems are comparatively small. There is, however, enormous variation within and between urban centres in the South. The cities which receive the most publicity are the mega-cities, where only a relatively small share of urban dwellers live. Often, these Southern mega-cities are portrayed as the epitome of environmental distress. The concentrated environmental burdens of these cities, as indicated by their ambient air pollution, water requirements, release of water pollutants, solid waste generation and local resource degradation, are often immense. However, in the light of the environmental transition described above, there is no reason to assume that city-level and household-level problems go hand-in-hand. Indeed, the results of a recent study of Accra (Benneh et al 1993), Jakarta (Surjadi et al 1994) and São Paulo (Jacobi 1995) suggest that the opposite is more likely to be true. Many of the worst environmental health problems are probably most severe in smaller, poorer settlements.

The three cities – Accra in Ghana, Jakarta in Indonesia and São Paulo in Brazil – span three continents and have no obvious cultural similarities. Table 6.1 provides summary statistics on the three cities.

Jakarta and São Paulo are both mega-cities, while Accra is considerably smaller and poorer. However, even Accra is larger and more affluent than the settlements most Southern urban dwellers live in. More than half of urban dwellers in the South live in cities of less than half a million people (UN 1995), and Ghana has one of the highest per capita incomes of the 47 countries ranked low on the Human Development Index (UNDP 1995).

In all three countries, the average income in the cities selected is higher than that of the country as a whole. At about the time of the survey, the estimated per capita expenditure in Accra was 50 per cent higher than the national average and that of Jakarta was 130 per cent higher. Alternatively, the São Paulo Metropolitan Region, with less than 12 per cent of Brazil's population in 1990, accounted for an estimated 18 per cent of the GDP of Brazil (Oliveira and Leitmann 1994).

Table 6.1 *Selected indicators of city affluence and size for Accra, Jakarta and São Paulo*

Selected indicators of city size and affluence	Accra (Ghana)	Jakarta (Indonesia)	São Paulo (Brazil)
1 Total area	935 sq km[a]	660 sq km[b]	1,577 sq km[c]
2 Population	1.6 m[a]	8.2 m[b]	9.5m[c]
3 Average annual population growth 1970 – 1990	3.8%[a]	3.1%[b]	1%[d]
4 National GDP per capita (measured at PPP[e]) 1992	$2,100	$3,000	$5,200

Notes

[a] Greater Accra Metropolitan Area which includes Accra, Ga and Tema Districts

[b] Jakarta DKI. The metropolitan area, often referred to as Jabotabek (including the districts of Jakarta DKI, Bogor, Tanggerang and Bekasi) had an estimated population of 16.8 million in 1990. Much of Greater Jakarta's recent growth is taking place in the periphery outside of Jakarta DKI and Jabotabek. Previously low-density areas such as Depok and Cibinong have population growth rates of 10% per year (Douglass, 1989)

[c] Refers to the City of São Paulo. The São Paulo Metropolitan Region had a population of 15.2 million according to the 1991 census

[d] Refers only to the 1980s for the City of São Paulo. Excluding the capital and considering the 37 municipalities of the São Paulo Region, the average annual growth rate jumps to 3.1 per cent

[e] Purchasing Power Parity

Sources

1 Leitmann 1993; 2 Benneh et al 1993; Surjadi et al 1994; Jacobi 1995; 3 Benneh et al 1993; Leitmann 1993; Jacobi 1995; 4 UNDP 1995

As described above, many of the most severe urban environmental hazards are found in and around poor people's homes and workplaces. Table 6.2 below summarizes some of the indicators of household-level environmental problems derived from representative surveys administered as part of the three-city study. While individually the comparability of such indicators is often doubtful, the overall picture is clear.

All of these indicators involve health risks for either diarrhoeal diseases or respiratory infections, two of the most significant causes of childhood morbidity and mortality.[4] Not having a water source at home is not only burdensome for women, but restricts hygiene practices. High levels of toilet sharing often lead to poor sanitary conditions in the toilets themselves, create more opportunities for faecal-oral diseases to be transmitted between households, and can lead to open defecation and faeces being mixed with solid waste. Without household garbage collection, waste often accumulates in the neighbourhood, providing ideal habitats for flies and rats. Where biofuels are used without proper ventilation, indoor air pollution may be severe and contribute to respiratory diseases. Flies in a kitchen, apart from providing a general indication of the sanitary state of the household, can facilitate the faecal-oral route of many diarrhoeal diseases.

Table 6.2 *Household environment indicators in Accra, Jakarta and São Paulo, 1991–1992*

Environment indicator	Accra % of sample (N=1000)	Jakarta % of sample (N=1055)	São Paulo % of sample (N=1000)
Water			
No water source at residence	46	13	5
Sanitation			
Share toilets with > 10 households	48	14-20	<3
Solid waste			
No home garbage collection	89	37	5
Indoor air			
Main cooking fuel wood or charcoal	76	2	0
Pests			
Flies observed in kitchen	82	38	17

Source: McGranahan and Songsore 1994

Table 6.3 *Household environment indicators in poor, middle-class and affluent neighbourhoods of the Greater Accra Metropolitan Area, 1991–1992*

Environment indicator	Poor % of sample (N=790)	Middle class % of sample (N=160)	Affluent % of sample (N=50)
Water			
No water source at residence	55	14	4
Sanitation			
Share toilets with > 10 households	60	17	2
Solid waste			
No home garbage collection	94	77	55
Indoor air			
Main cooking fuel wood or charcoal	85	44	30
Pests			
Flies observed in kitchen	91	56	18

Note: The three classes of neighbourhood are a grouping of the eight socio-ecological strata presented in Benneh et al 1993, *Environmental Problems and the Urban Household in the Greater Accra Metropolitan Area (GAMA) – Ghana*, Stockholm Environment Institute (Stockholm)

Source: Stockholm Environment Institute/University of Ghana household survey

In every case, the indicator improves between Accra and Jakarta and improves further between Jakarta and São Paulo. The more detailed household statistics confirm this trend. The most obvious explanation for the tendencies observed is the relative affluence of the three cities. Indeed, as indicated in Table 6.3, similar patterns are observed looking across different neighbourhoods of Accra.

The affluent neighbourhoods of Accra would seem to have roughly the same access to water and sanitation as the São Paulo averages, while the middle-class neighbourhoods are roughly comparable to the Jakarta averages. While affluent Accra dwellers are more likely to use a smoky cooking fuel than citizens of Jakarta and São Paulo – a fact that probably reflects Accra's smaller size – they use smoky fuels far less frequently than the poorer Accra dwellers, and among the most affluent households in Accra the cook exposed to the smoke may actually be a servant or poor relative.

These indicators reflect the health risks and inconvenience that households, and particularly women and children, face securing the necessities of daily life. The relevant environmental processes are predominantly local and such indicators say little about the level of strain on the city's resource base.

It was argued in the previous section that the strain placed on a city's resources tends to be less where many people are poor and consumption levels low. A selection of indicators related to city-level environmental burdens is provided in Table 6.4. These indicators are taken from a variety of sources and some are less comparable than the household-level indicators. Most reflect the size of the burden rather than the damage done, partly because the damage depends heavily on local geography and tends to be even less comparable.

While the differences are less clear-cut than with the household-level indicators, they do confirm the general tendency suggested, and illustrate the extent and manner in which some of the local environmental problems are displaced to the city-level. Both aggregate and per capita indicators are presented, although the scale of environmental burdens depends heavily on the size of the city.

Regional water scarcities are an increasing problem globally and can be particularly acute in the vicinity of large cities where they can lead to sharp increases in the cost of supplying water (Anton 1993; World Bank 1993a). As shown in Table 6.4, water consumption per capita is about 70 per cent higher in Jakarta than in Accra, and about 60 per cent higher again in São Paulo. Because of their relative sizes, these differences are magnified in the citywide figures. Water consumption increases with affluence both because it becomes more convenient and affordable to use and because new demands for water, such as for washing cars, develop. As noted above, the share of households with water sources in their homes increases from about half in Accra to 95 per cent in São Paulo and, as indicated in Table 6.4, the share of households with cars doubles. Many other measures of convenience and water-using devices would show similar patterns.

The principal water sources for Accra are the Densu river and the Black Volta which have the capacity to provide far more water than the current demand. The citywide impacts of Jakarta's water demands are somewhat difficult to determine. The majority of households in Jakarta use shallow wells, at least for washing (Surjadi et al 1994). Ground-water salination affects some 40 per cent of Jakarta's residents (Surjadi et al 1994) and this is often attributed to excess abstraction (Douglass 1989). However, the salination of the shallow aquifer used by households may be a long-standing natural phenomenon (Rismianto and Mak 1993), and it is possible that the

Table 6.4 *Indicators of city-level environmental burdens in Accra, Jakarta and São Paulo 1990,1991,1992*

Environment Indicator	Accra (metro)	Jakarta (city)	São Paulo (city)
Water			
1 Household water consumption (litres per capita per day)	82	138	215
2 Total water consumption (thousand cubic metres per day)	263	1,469	5,017 (metro)
Sanitation			
3 Sewage flow (thousand cubic metres per day)	46	35	2,400 (metro)
4 Sewage treatment (% treated)	20	1	26
Solid Waste			
5 Household solid waste generation (kg per capita per day)	0.5–0.6	0.6[a]	1–1.2
6 Municipal solid waste generation (tons per day)	1,000	5,000[a]	11,000
7 Waste collected (%)	75	79	90
Outdoor Air			
8 Automobile ownership (% of households)	16	26	33
9 Suspended particulate matter ($\mu g/m^3$ air – mid-1980s)	107–109	204–271	98

Notes: a Includes industrial waste; b metropolitan area
Sources: 1 Stockholm Environment Institute/University of Ghana/Atma Jaya Catholic University household surveys; Leitmann 1993; 2, 3 and 4 Leitmann 1993; 5, 6 and 7 Amuzu and Leitmann 1994; Leitmann 1993; Oliveira and Leitmann 1994; 8 Stockholm Environment Institute/University of Ghana/Atma Jaya Catholic University/Centro de Estudos de Cultura Contemporânea household surveys; 9 World Bank 1992

more serious long-term supply problems lie in the piped water system. The high consumption levels in São Paulo are all met through the piped water system, which is severely straining the city's water supplies (Anton 1993). Water scarcity is exacerbated during the dry winter and rationing is applied (Jacobi 1995).

Pollution of the waterways is a serious problem in the vicinity of all three cities. Many of São Paulo's and Jakarta's water quality problems are related to industrial activity, which is particularly intensive in and around São Paulo. Even faecal water pollution is more of a city-level problem in São Paulo, where the sewerage system reaches some three quarters of the residents, but 75 per cent of the sewerage is released untreated (Jacobi 1995). Forty cubic metres per second of raw sewage and industrial effluent are discharged into the Tietê River which has become almost entirely devoid of oxygen (Leitmann 1993). In Accra and Jakarta, where the sewerage systems are negligible, a larger share of the faecal material degrades in the neighbourhoods where it poses its main risks. This does not prevent the waterways of Accra and Jakarta from being very severely polluted with faecal material, however.

As shown in Table 6.4, solid waste generation is somewhat higher in São Paulo than in Accra or Jakarta. Most solid waste in the three cities is eventually collected by the city authorities, with a somewhat higher share in São Paulo. Overall it is the authorities of São Paulo, with its large size, high waste generation and high collection share, which copes with by far the largest solid waste burden. On the other hand, as depicted in Table 6.2, only 11 per cent of the households in Accra and 63 per cent in Jakarta have their refuse collected from the house. Households without home collection dump their wastes at collection points, official dump sites or other, often illegal, sites. While the garbage that is brought to the collection or dumping sites officially becomes the responsibility of the city authorities, when collection is intermittent, much of the environmental burden is carried by the nearby residents.

São Paulo is famed for its poor air quality. Indeed, during 1989 health warnings due to air pollution from carbon monoxide were issued for a total of 250 days, ozone for 108 days and particulates for 54 days. However, lead and sulphur dioxide levels have declined[5] with the increasing use of alcohol fuel (Hardoy et al 1992). The lowering of sulphur dioxide and lead pollution is a trend which São Paulo shares with most cities in the North. As depicted in Table 6.4, both Jakarta and Accra show measurements for suspended particulate matter well beyond the WHO guidelines (60–90 μg/cbm). According to these measurements, São Paulo's air pollution is considerably less, despite the large number of cars and the greater industrial activity. However, in Accra, air pollution problems are mainly concentrated to the industrial areas. Sites with traffic congestion also bring localized problems of airborne lead (ROG/UNDP/UNCHS 1989). Overall, outdoor air pollution is not a significant problem for Accra (Amuzu and Leitmann 1994). Actually, the high levels of indoor air pollution among wood and charcoal users (Benneh et al 1993) are more alarming, indicating that the main concerns for Accra remain in the home sphere.

As with the household level indicators, the attempt to find quantifiable indicators diverts attention from many of the more unique environmental problems characteristic of these cities. All of these cities face problems with watershed management, urban-led deforestation and land degradation, and a wide range of other environmental resources. Moreover, just as the household environmental problems were shown to vary significantly in Accra, as well as between the cities, so not all residents within a city place the same strain on the city-level environment.

Table 6.5 provides two of the indicators for city level burdens for the same types of neighbourhoods in Accra that were depicted in Table 6.3. Again, the figures for the middle class and affluent neighbourhoods of Accra are closer to the averages for Jakarta and São Paulo than they are to the figures for the poor neighbourhoods of Accra.

In summary, the household environment appears far better in São Paulo than in the other two cities, reflecting higher levels of private affluence as well as organised efforts to provide infrastructural facilities for the bulk of the population. On the other hand, even on a per capita basis, the levels of activities creating city-level environmental problems are highest in São Paulo, although the effects have been mitigated by more vigorous pollution control efforts in some areas, such as air pollution.

Jakarta appears, at least superficially, to have the worst of two worlds environmentally; it faces severe city-level problems, affecting fishing, agriculture and its watersheds (Douglass 1989; Hardoy et al 1992), but, due to poorly developed environmental infrastructure, has made little headway towards solving the unhealthy

Table 6.5 *Indicators of city-level environmental burdens in poor, middle-class and affluent neighbourhoods of the Greater Accra Metropolitan Area, 1991–1992*

Environment indicator	Poor	Middle class	Affluent
	% of Sample	% of Sample	% of Sample
	(N=790)	(N=160)	(N=50)
Water			
Consumption (litres per capita and day)	61	153	173
Outdoor air			
Automobile ownership (% of households)	9%	34%	58%

Note: The three classes of neighbourhood are a grouping of the eight socio-ecological strata presented in Benneh et al 1993, *Environmental Problems and the Urban Household in the Greater Accra Metropolitan Area (GAMA) – Ghana*, Stockholm Environment Institute (Stockholm)
Source: Stockholm Environment Institute/University of Ghana household survey

environment in many neighbourhoods. Still, most households are far more affluent than those in Accra, which is reflected in the many private solutions towards improving the household environment (Surjadi et al 1994).

Accra's residents face the most pervasive environmental health problems, related mainly to the low development of infrastructure to displace the environmental burdens away from the household sphere. Except for localized air and water pollution problems in areas of traffic congestion, industrial sites and lagoons, fishing and agriculture have not (yet) been adversely affected by city activities (Amuzu and Leitmann 1994).

The Environmental Problems of Unserviced Households and their Neighbourhoods

The foregoing empirical generalizations do not imply fixed relationships between affluence and environmental distress. It would be a mistake to think that low-income neighbourhoods are all insanitary, smoky, waste strewn and pest infested (Bapat and Crook 1984), that the open air and waterways of middle-income cities are always heavily polluted, or that affluence has to create a global environmental crisis. Similarly, there are circumstances when the homes of the affluent become environmentally hazardous and other circumstances when the poor contribute significantly to global environmental problems. Indeed, part of what makes environmental management such a challenge is that the connections between human activity and the environment cannot be reduced to a few simple relationships, and problems at different scales interrelate.[6] The generalizations described in the previous sections do, however, locate what appear to be the weakest links: the levels at which the most serious problems are likely to surface in the absence of good environmental management.

The remainder of this chapter focuses on local environmental problems in low-income settlements, again using examples from Accra, Jakarta and São Paulo. The level of poverty is taken to be such that most households in the settlements are not offered environmental amenities such as in-house piped water, sewers and door-to-door waste collection, and would not be willing to pay for such services if they were offered.[7] It is argued that in the absence of such services, local environmental management is both physically and socially extremely complex and must be tailored to local conditions. Partly as a result, the most effective strategies are likely to be in large part locally driven, not in the sense of individualistic private initiatives, but of concerted efforts to achieve locally defined goals. Simultaneously, effective local environmental management must be multifaceted, not only taking local environmental interconnections into account, but combining government programmes with contributions from NGOs and CBOs, combining scientific research with public participation and combining education with public debate and mechanisms for applying popular pressure to governments. In short, attempting simply to emulate the engineering solutions applied in affluent areas, but using less expensive technologies, is likely to fail.

In Accra, Jakarta or São Paulo, and indeed in virtually any city, the local environmental problems of disadvantaged neighbourhoods would undoubtedly be transformed if residents became appreciably more affluent, or if large sums of public funds were devoted to improving local infrastructure and providing environmental services. It is important, however, not to make the mistake of assuming that little can be done until it is possible to afford the standard 'modern' solutions. Indeed, the notion that everyone knows what needs to be done and the only problem is to find the resources to do it, can be very pernicious.

Poverty elimination is a more comprehensive and ultimately far more important goal, intimately linked to international as well as national economic relations, but it could be greatly assisted by local environmental improvement. Much recent work emphasizes that a lack of economic opportunity is only one aspect of urban poverty (Amis 1995a; Amis 1995b; Moser 1995; Rakodi 1995; Wratten 1995). For a variety of reasons, local environmental conditions, especially in unserved neighbourhoods, can easily become worse than income-poverty alone would dictate (McGranahan 1993). Growing private affluence is not always accompanied by commensurate improvements in local environmental conditions. Alternatively, where poverty persists, local environmental conditions can contribute to a vicious cycle of ill health and economic decline. To make matters worse, the poor often pay higher prices than the affluent for less convenient water, the use of less sanitary toilet facilities and smokier fuels (Cairncross and Kinnear 1992; Hardoy et al 1992; Soussan et al 1990). In many disadvantaged neighbourhoods, environmental improvement is itself a critical aspect of poverty alleviation.

It may be tempting to diagnose these environmental problems in disadvantaged settlements as simply reflecting the lack of infrastructure and household services. Defining the problem in terms of a solution which many cannot afford is inappropriate, however, unless public funds can make up for the private shortfall. While an emphasis on piped water connections and sewerage systems may be a useful means of drawing a small unserved minority up to standard, when the majority is unserved the same emphasis is likely to concentrate resources on the relatively well-off. This can again be illustrated with the examples of Accra, Jakarta and São Paulo.

In São Paulo, the expansion of water supplies and sewers to *favelas* (informal settlements) and other low-income settlements has had a major impact on some of the poorest São Paulo dwellers (Briscoe and Steer 1993; Munasinghe 1992). During the 1980s, the share of *favelas* with piped water supplies increased from 32 per cent to 99 per cent, and the share with sewerage systems increased from 1 per cent to 15 per cent (Briscoe and Garn 1995). While this expansion was predicated on political and economic change and a broader attempt to formalize low-income settlements, the fact that providing water and sewers is a relatively clear goal helped give it political potency, and the fact that the majority already had these services ensured that the expansion did reach the poor. Even in São Paulo, however, sewers built to what could be termed the industry standard would have been too costly to expand so rapidly, and the standard means of offering services would have been inappropriate in low-income areas. The 'condominial' system, which involved both technical and organizational adaptations, provided a cheaper alternative which was offered in a manner more responsive to the needs of low-income areas (Briscoe and Steer 1993). While the technical aspects of the condominial system did not involve new engineering principles, the deviation from the industrial standard and the political process through which it gained support, were both critical to its expansion.

In Jakarta, the expansion of piped water and sewers is less central, partly because Jakarta is poorer and partly because even relatively affluent households are likely to rely on wells and aqua privies rather than piped water and sewers (Surjadi et al 1994). The sanitation system operates with relatively little direct involvement by the government. The piped water situation depends on the salination of the ground water.[8] In the unsalinated areas, four out of five households use well water even for drinking and any effort to expand household connections will almost certainly affect primarily the well-off. In the salinated areas, on the other hand, almost everyone depends, either directly or indirectly, on piped water at least for drinking. Only 31 per cent have household connections, however, and even if expansion is rapid, the beneficiaries of new household connections will be primarily the well-off for some years to come. For the poorer majority, a more important issue with regard to the piped water system is how to increase the available supply of piped water in such a manner as to limit rent dissipation (or abnormal profits) in the water resale market.[9] Currently, vendors charge up to ten times the utility price for water and those who control sales from public hydrants make excess profits (Lovei and Whittington 1993). Attempts to increase competition have not been very successful (Crane 1994), and it is not clear whether the high prices are really the result of monopoly pricing, of more technical limits on the water supply which would also drive the price up in a competitive market, or of some combination of the two. What is clear is that a narrow emphasis on household water connections will not address the problems of the poor, and crude attempts to punish vendors are likely to decrease water supplies and raise the market price of water for low-income households still further.

In Accra, increasing centralized household service provision is also unlikely to reach those that need it most. As in Jakarta, articulated sewers are virtually insignificant. The government and the local communities are involved in supplying sanitary facilities and the utility plays an important role removing human waste, but most of the toilets in low-income areas are communal or at least widely shared. As in the salinated parts of Jakarta, everyone depends upon the piped water system, but only about 35 per cent of the surveyed households had indoor piping. About 24 per cent had private standpipes, 8 per cent used communal standpipes and 28 per cent obtained their drinking water primarily from vendors (Benneh et al 1993). While indoor piping is only slightly more common than in the salinated areas of Jakarta, the alternative supplies of piped water are more prevalent, and the mark-up for vendor water is far less, even taking account of the higher delivery costs in Jakarta.

As these examples illustrate, centralized household water and sanitation services are less relevant in poor neighbourhoods, and especially in the poor neighbourhoods of poor cities. Much the same applies to other household environmental services, such as door-to-door waste collection and the provision of clean fuels. For example, the enormous sums that have been spent in the past on subsidizing electricity have had at best a marginal impact on the cooking fuel patterns of poor urban households (McGranahan and Kaijser 1993). In any case, in many countries around the world the public sector is under pressure to retrench rather than expand. Especially in Africa, where cities have been growing rapidly and the economic plight of the public sector is often most severe, a general crisis in urban services developed in the 1970s and is still being felt (Stren and White 1989). Financially strapped central governments and local municipalities are not in a position to decide to expand public services to individual households in disadvantaged areas.

Not only have the state-run utilities received considerable criticism in recent years for failing to deliver local environmental services effectively (Briscoe and Garn 1995), but many environmentalists have noted that most centralized environmental service systems are themselves environmentally destructive at a broader level (Niemczynowicz 1993). In considering alternatives, however, it is important to keep in mind that the attraction of these systems in the past was not that they were considered technically optimal, but that they transformed an extremely complex network of interconnected environmental problems into a set of largely independent, centrally manageable, systems which could be technically controlled. Clean water is piped into homes, and waste water is piped out. Faeces are immediately sealed off from air and insects, and flushed away with the waste water. Solid waste is bagged, placed in closed containers and then carted away. Wires carry electricity into every room where it can be cleanly converted into heat, light or mechanical drive. Utilities and municipalities are left to manage the potentially polluting energy conversions, dispose of large quantities of liquid and solid waste, and find new water supplies. In affluent people's homes and neighbourhoods, however, it can seem as if environmental amenities are like any other commodities: goods purchased in the pursuit of the buyers' own well-being.[10]

In poor neighbourhoods where centralized household services are largely absent, households are more likely to have to share water sources, share sanitary facilities and share waste-disposal services. Local environmental problems are not only more severe but also tend to reinforce each other to create a complex of interrelated environmental hazards. Bad sanitation can lead to contaminated ground water, faeces finding its way into the solid waste, on to the open land, into the drainage ditches and generally into contact with other people. Flies breed in the human and solid waste, and can contaminate the food. Solid waste finds its way into the drains, causing accumulations of water where mosquitoes breed. Microbial food contamination makes thorough cooking important, but cooking with smoky fuels exposes women and children especially to hazardous pollutants. The mosquito coils and pesticides used to combat mosquitoes add to the air pollution and chemical hazards.

Under such circumstances, it is clear that individuals and households cannot choose a cleaner home and neighbourhood environment as they might choose a normal 'good' (McGranahan 1993). Their environmental problems arise mostly from other people's choices and actions. By and large, it is other people's faeces that are a threat, other people's waste that clogs the drains, other people's water where the mosquitoes are breeding, and so on. Children, who are those most affected by faecal-oral diseases, often move freely from house to house in the course of their play, reducing the importance of the child's own home environment still further (Pickering 1985). In crowded settlements, even smoke from wood and coal, typically fuels of the relatively poor, can easily become a neighbourhood problem that residents cannot avoid (Terblanche et al 1993). Problems relating to water supplies,[11] sanitation, food contamination and insect infestation are even more clearly intertwined, and people's actions are even more clearly interdependent.

Economists have long been aware that anonymous markets are not efficient institutions for handling such problems, which involve public goods, externalities and common property (Dasgupta provides a discussion of these and related concepts in the context of poverty (Dasgupta 1993, p 143)). In poor neighbourhoods, pest control is usually an example of a spatially delimited *public good*. A lower pest population typically benefits all local residents, regardless of whether they contributed to the control efforts. Thus, in an anonymous free market, people would not have sufficient incentive to contribute to pest control. An *externality* arises when, for example, one household's pit latrine contaminates someone else's well water and the polluting household does not take this damage into account. In this case, the market does not provide the polluter with sufficient incentive to desist. *Common property* problems can arise on marginal lands and in the waterways of a neighbourhood, when they are used without restraint and allowed to degrade. The common feature of all these examples is that individuals acting independently do not have the incentive to manage the environment properly.

These somewhat overlapping concepts of public goods, externalities and common property are frequently applied to large-scale environmental problems, often to justify government interventions, including taxes and subsidies. However, numerous institutions and organizations other than the government and private enterprises can and do play a role in environmental management, especially at the local level.[12] Ranging from nuclear households to extensive kinship networks, from community based organizations (CBOs) to international non-governmental organizations (NGOs), from recreational clubs to political parties, and from environmental associations and women's groups to orthodox religious organizations, the significance of these institutions in environmental management is increasingly being recognized. Where centralized household services are absent, such institutions are especially critical. Indeed, a good part of the variation in local environmental conditions across poor neighbourhoods probably reflects their different configurations of local institutions.

Large variations in both environmental conditions and institutional configurations are themselves characteristic of unserved neighbourhoods. The much debated differences in the quality of service provided by private versus public sector utilities pales into insignificance compared to environmental and institutional differences which can be encountered even within a single low-income neighbourhood. In a recent participatory assessment of local environmental conditions in a *kampung* in Jakarta, for example, residents could compare the extent to which different waters smelled, were sticky or irritated the skin, and contrasted, for example, the yellowish well water near an old swamp, the blackish, oily well water in another part of the neighbourhood, and the 'good' quality water from a deeper well sunk by the manager of a public toilet and bathhouse. Similarly, sanitary facilities ranged from pour flush aqua privies, to drop toilets, to no toilets, and from single household facilities, to shared facilities, to pay toilets owned by a local entrepreneur.[13] The residents' local environmental and health problems are closely interrelated, but are by no means homogeneous.

The prevalence of local externalities and public goods, the importance of local institutions, and the high level of diversity: all of these considerations underscore the importance of local participation in designing and implementing improvements, once the possibility of providing standard household level services is ruled out. At the same time, how such institutions operate locally depends very much on how the state functions at higher levels, and the services centralized utilities do provide to the more disadvantaged neighbourhoods. The problems of these neighbourhoods are often compounded by the fact that standard utility services are oriented towards providing services to well-defined households, rather than negotiating with and serving ill-defined groups of households and communities.[14] Moreover, the engineers who dominate utilities are naturally loath to treat the manner in which their services are employed and consequences they cannot directly control, as reflecting on their own performance. For almost a century, since household services became the norm in affluent cities, the professionalism of environmental engineers has been based on the premise that providing environmental amenities is a technical matter, best undertaken at a remove from politics and public negotiation. Changing this attitude is difficult and in some circumstances could have unfortunate consequences. Means must be found to make utilities more responsive to the complex needs of low-income communities.[15] How this is best achieved, however, is likely to vary from place to place. Often it may be more appropriate to support intermediary institutions which can articulate local demands, rather than expecting the utilities themselves to foster participation.

Just as unserved neighbourhoods are likely to face local externalities and public goods problems analogous to those of the larger-scale environmental problems, so also the need to understand environmental processes, so evident with respect to the large-scale environmental problems, is heightened at the local level by the absence of public services. Knowledge of both scientific principles and local specificities is important. Perhaps the most obvious gaps are more in communication than in knowledge per se. Local residents are often unfamiliar with basic environmental health and ecological principles which, while they may not be important to someone living in a fully serviced home, can be critical to someone who must fetch and carry water, build their own latrine, cook over smoky fires and implement their own pest control. Similarly, government officials are often woefully ignorant of conditions and practices in low-income settlements which, while they may not be important if the government is simply providing standard services, can be critical if the government is to play an enabling role.

In addition to these communication gaps, both scientists and local residents face considerable uncertainty in their own areas of relative strength. For example, scientists know a great deal more than laymen about the processes through which faecal oral diseases are transmitted, but leading experts can only guess that food contamination accounts for somewhere between 15 per cent and 70 per cent of diarrhoeas (Esrey and Feachem 1989), and do not know whether flies are a major transmission mechanism or relatively insignificant (Chavasse et al 1994). This uncertainty reflects both the inherent complexity of the subject, but also the dearth of serious and well-funded research efforts attempting to break new ground in this field. Alternatively, local residents can learn a great deal about their own local environment in a relatively short time through participatory research efforts (Mitlin and Thompson 1995). As regards more formal local knowledge, traditional schooling provides very little in the way of education on local environmental problems and could cover such issues far more thoroughly even using existing teaching techniques.

For far too long household environmental problems, such as inadequate water and sanitation, were portrayed as part of an old agenda which had simply not been completed. Now, the development establishment is actively constructing new approaches for addressing water supply, sanitation and environmental sustainability in the South (Serageldin 1994). However, it is still common to portray the local environmental problems of the poor as part of a relatively 'easy' agenda, the more serious challenge arising from the broader sustainability issues (Serageldin 1994, p 25). It would be more accurate to say the local environmental problems of the poor are relatively 'easy' to misdiagnose or ignore.

For many years it was received wisdom that problems of household water and sanitation were public health issues which the private sector with its commercial orientation could not be expected to address. While the critique of the private sector was based on experience, the implicit assumption that the public sector could be relied on to address these problems has proved presumptuous. Now, it is common to argue that a more commercial orientation to the pricing and delivery of environmental services, and more generally shifts back along the public-private axis, will help to provide the poor with better environmental services. In the words of a recent paper on water supply, sanitation and Agenda 21 by two senior World Bank officials:

> If financing policies can be 'got right', all of the other key sector issues – involvement of users, the assignment of responsibility for different actions to 'the appropriate level', the development of accountable institutions, appropriate standards, technology and service selection – will more readily fall into place. (Briscoe and Garn 1995)

There are three major problems with this view once one moves away from the simple world of household services and into neighbourhoods where services are shared, and water and sanitation conditions are closely intertwined with a wide range of other local environmental problems. First, it is far from clear how financing policies are to be 'got right,' despite a multitude of examples of how they can be 'got wrong'. It is particularly difficult to see how local finances are to be generated without having first determined, for example, how the users who share the environmental amenities will be involved and how responsibilities will be assigned. Second, neither water nor sanitation form coherent sectors whose key issues can be defined. It is the expensive, and in many cases unaffordable, infrastructure which allows water and sanitation to be sectoralized. Third, even accepting that the financing could be solved and the other sector issues defined, the problems of participation, accountability and the like are not going to fall into place. Indeed, the financial crisis of Southern utilities is more symptom than cause of a lack of participation and accountability.

CONCLUSION

A focus on sustainability implies a concern to avoid practices which, while perhaps superficially acceptable in the short term, undermine future possibilities. As such, sustainability is not as central to the environmental problems of the urban poor as it is to those of the affluent. In the more disadvantaged neighbourhoods, the environmental burdens are more local, more immediate and a more direct threat to health: the problem is not so much that these burdens cannot be sustained as that they ought not be sustained. There are systematic tendencies for sustainability to become more of an issue with respect to the more diffuse, delayed and indirect environmental burdens of affluence. Even within what is conventionally designated as the South, these tendencies are evident. Thus, the results of recent case studies indicate that regional sustainability issues are more pressing in Jakarta and São Paulo than in Accra, and within Accra the household-level problems are clearly worse in low-income neighbourhoods, while citywide burdens are more evident in the lifestyles of the affluent. São Paulo, the most affluent and largest of the three cities, has a greater concentration of polluting activities, but has also made more progress in controlling city-level pollution.

While environmental sustainability may not be a priority concern, poor urban neighbourhoods do often face complexes of environmental hazards which, far from being simple problems to be overcome with technology transfer or more efficient markets, require political mobilization and scientific and institutional innovation. These environmental hazards can include, for example, insufficient and poor quality water, poor sanitation, microbial food contamination, local accumulations of solid waste, insect infestation and smoky kitchens. In the absence of household-level environmental services, such hazards become closely interconnected and create externalities, public goods, common property problems, problems of decision-making under severe uncertainty, and other problems more commonly associated with large-scale environmental burdens.

History has shown that under normal circumstances commercial pressures do not motivate the private sector to provide adequate environmental amenities in low-income areas. It has also shown that under normal circumstances political pressures do not motivate the public sector to provide low-income neighbourhoods with adequate environmental amenities. Substantial improvements are likely to come not from shifting responsibilities back and forth between public and private sectors, but from measures which make actors in both sectors more responsive to environmental concerns, and especially local concerns.

NOTES

1   This section develops ideas presented in McGranahan and Songsore 1994
2   When epidemics and pandemics were a common cause of death, the environmental problems of the poor were a serious threat to the health of the affluent. Indeed, the sanitary reforms of the 19th century were predicated on an awareness of this interdependence. Responses to recent outbreaks of cholera and the plague indicate that current efforts to improve sanitary conditions in poor neighbourhoods would also proceed very differently if there was felt to be a serious threat to the well-off
3   It is important not to make too much of this comparison: there is little reason to assume that the more commercially oriented utilities will resemble the market ideal any more than public utilities resemble the ideal public service provider
4   For a statistical analysis of the relation between these or similar indicators and selected health problems in Accra, see the city report (Benneh et al 1993)
5   In the 1980s sulphur dioxide concentrations decreased by over 10 per cent per year and the annual lead average was below the WHO guideline range UNEP/WHO 1988: Assessment of Urban Air Quality
6   For example, local environmental changes which alter the manner in which infections spread and develop can lead to very different health risks in broader populations, including, for example, the emergence of more or less virulent disease strains (Ewald 1993, 1994)
7   It is sometimes argued that, since the urban poor already pay high prices for vendor water, a large share would be willing to pay for water piped into their homes if they were offered it at cost. However, the fact that if absolutely necessary low-income households are willing to pay high prices for

water does not mean that, if all options were made available at cost-price, they would choose in-house connections

8   In international literature, the salination of the shallow wells in Jakarta is often referred to as an example of the effects of excessive abstraction. However, the water may have been saline prior to the high levels of abstraction

9   Rent dissipation can occur when, for example, users or vendors expend resources queuing for water or otherwise attempting to achieve sectional preferment

10 The distinction between individual and household priorities and decisions can be critical (Rakodi 1991), but is not explored in this chapter

11 The benefits of water are closer to those of 'normal' commodities than those of sanitation and waste disposal, and a more commercial orientation is sometimes promoted on the grounds that household water supplies provide predominantly private benefits (Briscoe and Garn 1995). This does not apply to the disadvantaged neighbourhoods being discussed here, although it may apply to more affluent neighbourhoods who should indeed benefit from a more commercial approach

12 Non-governmental institutions and extra-market negotiations are central to institutional economics, as well as to anthropologists, sociologists and political scientists

13 The participatory appraisal was carried out by Save the Children, Jakarta, as part of a study of methods of household and community level environmental assessment. These examples are taken from a summary in a report to the UNCHS-World Bank-UNDP Urban Management Programme by Charles Surjadi and Rahmadi Purwana

14 Many poor urban households live in informal settlements that do not have a secure legal basis. Utilities are understandably apprehensive about investing in infrastructure within such settlements, and in some cases are expressly forbidden from providing any services directly

15 Some utilities in Northern countries are making significant efforts to adapt their services to the needs of lower income households, which is a positive sign even if these needs are far less complex since individualized household services are maintained (Beecher 1994)

REFERENCES

Amis, P (1995a) Employment creation or environmental improvements: A literature review of urban poverty and policy in India, *Habitat International,* 19(4):485–497

Amis, P (1995b) Making sense of urban poverty, *Environment and Urbanization,* 7(1):145–157

Amuzu, A T and Leitmann, J (1994) Accra, *Cities,* 11(1):5–9

Anton, D J (1993) *Thirsty Cities: Urban Environments and Water Supply in Latin America,* Ottawa, International Development Research Centre

Bairoch, P (1988) *Cities and Economic Development: From the Dawn of History to the Present,* London, Mansell Publishing

Bapat, M and Crook, N (1984) The environment, health, and nutrition: An analysis of interrelationships from a case-study of hutment settlements in the city of Poona, *Habitat International,* 8(3/4):115–126

Beecher, J A (1994) Water affordability and alternatives to service disconnection, *Journal of the American Water Works Association,* 86(10):61–72

Benneh, G, Songsore, J, Nabila, J S, Amuzu, A T, Tutu, K A, Yangyuoru, Y and McGranahan, G (1993) *Environmental Problems and the Urban Household in the Greater Accra Metropolitan Area (GAMA) – Ghana,* Stockholm Environment Institute (Stockholm)

Berman, S (1991) Epidemiology of acute respiratory infections in children of developing countries, *Reviews of Infectious Diseases,* 13 (Suppl. 6):455–462

Bradley, D, Cairncross, S, Harpham, T and Stephens, C (1991) *A Review of Environmental Health Impacts in Developing Country Cities,* Urban Management Program Discussion Paper No 6, World Bank/UNDP/UNCHS (Washington, DC)

Briscoe, J and Garn, H A (1995) Financing water supply and sanitation under Agenda 21, *Natural Resources Forum,* 19(1):59–70

Briscoe, J and Steer, A (1993) New approaches to sanitation – a process of structural learning, *Ambio,* 22(7):456–459

Cairncross, S and Feachem, R G (1993) *Environmental Health Engineering in the Tropics: An Introductory Text,* Chichester, John Wiley & Sons

Cairncross, S and Kinnear, J (1992) Elasticity of demand for water in Khartoum, Sudan, *Social Science and Medicine*, 2:183–189

Chavasse, D C, Blumenthal, U and Kolsky, P (1994) Fly control in prevention of diarrhoeal disease (Letter to editor), *The Lancet*, 344:1231

Chen, B H, Hong, C J, Pandey, M R and Smith, K R (1990) Indoor air pollution in developing countries, *World Health Statistics Quarterly*, 43:127–138

Chivian, E, McCally, M, Hu, H and Haines, A (eds) (1993) *Critical Condition: Human Health and the Environment*, Cambridge, Massachussetts, The MIT Press

Crane, R (1994) Water markets, market reform and the urban poor: Results from Jakarta, Indonesia, *World Development*, 22(1):71–83

Dasgupta, P (1993) *An Inquiry into Well-Being and Destitution*, Oxford, Oxford University Press

Douglas, I (1983) *The Urban Environment*, London, Edward Arnold

Douglass, M (1989) The environmental sustainability of development, *Third World Planning Review*, 11(2):211–238

Esrey, S A and Feachem, R G (1989) *Interventions for the Control of Diarrhoeal Diseases among Young Children: Promotion of Food Hygiene*, WHO/CDD No 89.30, World Health Organization (Geneva)

Ewald, P W (1993) The evolution of virulence, *Scientific American*, April:56–62

Ewald, P W (1994) *Evolution of Infectious Disease*, New York, Oxford University Press

Graham, N M H (1990) The epidemiology of acute respiratory infections in children and adults: A global perspective, *Epidemiologic Reviews*, 12:149–178

Grossman, G M and Krueger, A B (1995) Economic growth and the environment, *Quarterly Journal of Economics*, 110:353–378

Hamlin, C (1990) *A Science of Impurity: Water Analysis in Nineteenth Century Britain*, Bristol, Adam Hilger

Hardoy, J E, Cairncross, S and Satterthwaite, D (eds) (1990) *The Poor Die Young: Housing and Health in Third World Cities*, London, Earthscan

Hardoy, J E, Mitlin, D and Satterthwaite, D (1992) *Environmental Problems in Third World Cities*, London, Earthscan

Harpham, T, Lusty, T and Vaughan, P (eds) (1988) *In the Shadow of the City: Community Health and the Urban Poor*, Oxford, Oxford University Press

Holtz-Eakin, D and Selden, T M (1995) Stoking the fires? CO_2 emissions and economic growth, *Journal of Public Economics*, 57:85–101

Huttly, S R A (1990) The impact of inadequate sanitary conditions on health in developing countries, *World Health Statistics Quarterly*, 43(3):118–126

Jackson, T (ed) (1993) *Clean Production Strategies*, Boca Raton, Florida, Lewis Publishers

Jacobi, P (1995) *Environmental Problems Facing the Urban Household in the City of São Paulo, Brazil*, Stockholm Environment Institute (Stockholm)

Ladd, B (1990) *Urban Planning and Civic Order in Germany, 1860–1914*, Cambridge, MA, Harvard University Press

Leitmann, J (1993) *Rapid Urban Environmental Assessment: Lessons from Cities in the Developing World (Volume 2: Tools and Outputs)*, Urban Management and the Environment No 15, World Bank (Washington, DC)

Lovei, L and Whittington, D (1993) Rent-extracting behavior by multiple agents in the provision of municipal water supply: A study of Jakarta, Indonesia, *Water Resources Research*, 29(7):1965–1974

Luckin, B (1986) *Pollution and Control: A Social History of the Thames in the Nineteenth Century*, Bristol, Adam Hilger

McGranahan, G (1993) Household environmental problems in low-income cities: An overview of problems and prospects for improvement, *Habitat International*, 17(2):105–121

McGranahan, G and Kaijser, A (1993) *Household Energy: Problems, Policies and Prospects*, EED Report No 19, Stockholm Environment Institute (Stockholm)

McGranahan, G and Songsore, J (1994) Wealth, health, and the urban household: Weighing environmental burdens in Accra, Jakarta, and São Paulo, *Environment*, 36(6):4–11, 40–45

Mitlin, D and Thompson, J (1995) Participatory approaches in urban areas: Strengthening civil society or reinforcing the status quo?, *Environment and Urbanization*, 7(1):231–250

Moser, C O N (1995) Urban social policy and poverty reduction, *Environment and Urbanization*, 7(1):159–171

Mosley, W H, Bobadilla, J L and Jamison, D T (1993) The Health Transition: Implications for Health Policy in Developing Countries, in: Jamison D T, Mosley W H, Measham A R, Bobadilla J L (eds), *Disease Control Priorities in Developing Countries*, Oxford, Oxford University Press for the World Bank, 673–699

Munasinghe, M (1992) *Water Supply and Environmental Management: Developing World Applications*, Howe C W (ed) Boulder, Colorado, Westview Press

Munasinghe, M (1993) *Environmental Economics and Sustainable Development*, World Bank Environment Paper No 3, World Bank (Washington, DC)

Niemczynowicz, J (1993) New aspects of sewerage and water technology, *Ambio*, 22(7):449–455

Oliveira, C N E and Leitmann, J (1994) São Paulo, *Cities*, 11(1):10–14

Pickering, H (1985) Social and environmental factors associated with diarrhoea and growth in young children: Child health in urban Africa, *Social Science and Medicine*, 21(2):121–127

Rakodi, C (1991) Women's work or household strategies?, *Environment and Urbanization*, 3(2):39–45

Rakodi, C (1995) Poverty lines or household strategies? A review of conceptual issues in the study of urban poverty, *Habitat International*, 19(4):407–426

Rismianto, D and Mak, W (1993) *Environmental Aspects of Groundwater Abstraction in Dki Jakarta: Changing Views*, Report (Jakarta)

ROG/UNDP/UNCHS (1989) *Environmental Study of Accra Metropolitan Area*, Final Report, Town and Country Planning Department, Accra Planning and Development Programme (Accra)

Satterthwaite, D (1993) The impact on health of urban environments, *Environment and Urbanization*, 5(2):87–111

Schell, L M, Smith, M T and Bilsborough, A (eds) (1993) *Urban Ecology and Health in the Third World*, Cambridge, Cambridge University Press

Schofield, C J, Briceno-Leon, R, Kolstrup, N, Webb, D J T and White, G B (1990) The Role of House Design in Limiting Vector-Borne Disease, in Hardoy J E, Cairncross S, Satterthwaite D (eds)*The Poor Die Young*, London, Earthscan Publications

Selden, T M and Song, D (1995) Neoclassical growth, the J curve for abatement, and the inverted U curve for pollution, *Journal of Environmental Economics and Management*, 29(2):162–168

Serageldin, I (1994) *Water Supply, Sanitation, and Environmental Sustainability: TheFinancing Challenge*, World Bank (Washington, DC)

Shafik, N T (1995) Economic development and environmental quality: An econometric analysis, *Oxford Economic Papers*, 46:757–773

Shapiro, A L (1985) *Housing the Poor of Paris, 1850–1902*, Madison, University of Wisconsin Press

Smith, K R (1993) Fuel combustion, air pollution exposure, and health: The situation in developing countries, *Annual Review of Energy and the Environment*,(18):529–566

Smith, K R and Lee, Y-S F (1993) Urbanization and the Environmental Risk Transition, in Kasarda J D, Parnell A M (eds) *Third World Cities: Problems, Policies, and Prospects*, London, SAGE Publications: 161–179

Soussan, J, O'Keefe, P and Munslow, B (1990) Urban fuelwood: Challenges and dilemmas, *Energy Policy* (July/August 1990):572–582

Stren, R E and White, R R (eds) (1989) *African Cities in Crisis: Managing Rapid Urban Growth*, Boulder, Colorado, Westview Press

Surjadi, C, Padhmasutra, L, Wahyuningsih, D, McGranahan, G and Kjellén, M (1994)*Household Environmental Problems in Jakarta*, Stockholm Environment Institute (Stockholm)

Terblanche, A P S, Danford, I R and Nel, C M E (1993) Household energy use in South Africa, air pollution and human health, *Journal of Energy in Southern Africa* (May):54–57

UN (1995) *World Urbanization Prospects: The 1994 Revision: Estimates and Projections of Urban and Rural Populations and of Urban Agglomerations*, Report No ST/ESA/SER.A/150, United Nations (New York)

UNDP (1995) *Human Development Report 1995*, UNDP (New York)

UNEP/WHO (1988) *Assessment of Urban Air Quality*, Report, World Health Organization (Geneva)

Wallgren, B (1994) The Principles of the Ecocycle Society, in Council S E A (ed) *On the General Principles of Environmental Protection*, Stockholm, Ministry of Environment and Natural Resources

White, R R (1994) *Urban Environmental Management: Environmental Change and Urban Design*, Chichester, John Wiley & Sons

Wohl, A S (1983) *Endangered Lives: Public Health in Victorian Britain*, London, Methuen

Gordon McGranahan, Jacob Songsore and Marianne Kjellén

World Bank (1992) *World Development Report 1992: Development and the Environment,* New York, Oxford University Press

World Bank (1993a) *Water Resources Management,* A World Bank Policy Paper, World Bank (Washington, DC)

World Bank (1993b) *World Development Report 1993: Investing in Health,* New York, Oxford University Press

Wratten, E (1995) Conceptualizing urban poverty, *Environment and Urbanization,* 7(1):11–36

Further Reading

On Sustainable Cities in General

Sustainable Cities, Graham Haughton and Colin Hunter, Regional Policy and Development Series 7, Jessica Kingsley Publishers, London, 1994. A comprehensive and accessible overview of the subject

Sustainability, the Environment and Urbanization, Cedric Pugh (ed), Earthscan, London, 1996. (The paper by Gordon McGranahan, Jacob Songsore and Marianne Kjellén in this Reader is drawn from this edited volume)

Greening Cities: Building Just and Sustainable Communities, Joan Roelofs, the Bootstrap Press, New York 1996. Chapter 12 in this Reader is taken from one chapter of this book. Wide coverage of subjects, although primarily from a North American focus. For orders in Europe, available from Jon Carpenter Publishing, the Spendlove Centre, Charlbury, Oxfordshire OX7 3PQ, UK

Eco-City Dimensions, Mark Roseland (ed) New Society Publishers, Gabriola Island, 1997

The Challenge of Sustainable Cities: Neoliberalism and Urban Strategies in Developing Countries, Rod Burgess, Marisa Carmona and Theo Kolstee (eds), Zed Books, London and New Jersey, 1997

Three issues of the journal *Environment and Urbanization* (see details below) have been on sustainable cities

Sustainable Cities, Vol 4, No 2, 1992, includes the paper on urban agriculture in this Reader; also papers on: innovative environmental practice in Curitiba and Surabaya; cities' ecological footprints; the political economy of environmental management in Asia; environmental management and urban development; and waste management in various cities

Sustainable Cities Revisited, Vol 10, No 2, 1998, includes the case studies of Manizales (Chapter 14) and of the National Forum in Peru (Chapter 15) in this Reader. It also includes papers on: Chimbote's Local Agenda 21; 'localizing agenda 21' programmes in Nakuru (Kenya), Essaouira (Morocco) and Vinh City (Vietnam); avoiding anti-poor solutions to Mumbai's transport problems; how urban agriculture has changed over time in and around Mexico City; the environmental impact of the city of Bamenda's rapid growth; waste management in Manila (working with the waste-pickers) and in Cotonou (Benin); the concept of 'sustainability'; and how the military and the 'population control' lobby misrepresent the causes of environmental degradation to justify their roles

Sustainable Cities Revisited II, Vol 11, No 2, 1999. This includes case studies of local agenda 21s or other forms of environmental management in Surabaya, Porto Alegre and Leicester, and case studies of community-level agenda 21s from within Manizales and Lima

For a discussion of the issues regarding sustainable development and cities within a citywide and a community-level context, see *Human Settlements and Planning for Ecological Sustainability: The Case of Mexico City*, Keith Pezzoli, MIT Press, Boston and London, 1998

The International Council for Local Environmental Initiatives (ICLEI) has various general publications of relevance to sustainable development and cities, as well as many case studies of innovative local government action and guides to local government action. See ICLEI's web page http://www.iclei.org or write to ICLEI at City Hall, East Tower, 8th Floor, Toronto, Ontario M5H 2N2, Canada

For a stimulating discussion about 'sustainability' and its role within sustainable development, see Peter Marcuse, 'Sustainability is not enough', *Environment and Urbanization*, Vol 10, No 2, 1998, pp 103–111

See also Goodland, Robert, 'The concept of environmental sustainability', *Annual Review of Ecological Systems*, Vol 26, 1995, pp 1–24; and *The Ecologist*, 'Whose common future? Reclaiming the commons', *Environment and Urbanization*, Vol 6, No 1, April 1994, pp 106–130

Sustainable Development and Cities in Europe

From the Earth Summit to Local Agenda 21: Working Towards Sustainable Development, William M Lafferty and Katarina Eckerberg (eds), Earthscan, London, 1998. This is particularly interesting with its descriptions and discussion of progress towards the development of local agenda 21s in eight different European countries

Voula Mega's paper 'Our city, our future' in *Environment and Urbanization,* Vol 8, No 1, April 1996, pp 133–154 is a valuable review of new policies and innovations in Europe. She also wrote or edited a series of books on different European countries' or cities' experience with the environment and sustainable development for the European Foundation for the Improvement of Living and Working Conditions (Loughlinstown House, Shankill C Dublin, Ireland) and published by the Office for Official Publications of the European Communities (most European countries have sales outlets for these publications)

See also *European Sustainable Cities Part 1,* Expert Group on the Urban Environment, European Commission, X1/95/502-en, October 1994, Brussels

Four Journals Provide Regular Coverage of Sustainable City Issues

Local Environment, published by Carfax Publishing Company, PO Box 25, Abingdon, Oxfordshire OX14, 3UE, UK, e-mail: sales@carfax.co.uk. Three issues a year. Annual subscription: £90 (institution) or £26 (individual). For more details, see its web page on http://www.carfax.co.uk/Loe-ad.htm

Environment and Urbanization, published by the Human Settlements Programme, IIED, 3 Endsleigh Street, London WC1H ODD, UK, e-mail: humans@iied.org. A twice-yearly journal. Rates – one year: institutions £36 or US$62; individuals £22 or US$38; two year: institutions £62 or US$106; individuals £37 or US$63; three year: institutions £88 or US$150; individuals £52 or US$88. Half price for students or subscribers from Africa, Latin America and Asia (except Japan, Hong Kong and Singapore). Vol 4, No 2 (1992) was on 'Sustainable Cities' with Vol 10, No 2 (1998) on 'Sustainable Cities Revisited' and Vol 11, No 2 (1999) on 'Sustainable Cities Revisited II'. For more details, see http://www.iied.org/eandu

The Urban Ecologist. Address: 405 14th Street, Suite 900, Oakland, California 94612, USA, e-mail: urbanecology@igc.apc.org. A quarterly journal, this concentrates mainly on the US. Annual subscription is US$35 with an additional $5 for subscriptions from Mexico and Canada and $10 from elsewhere

The fortnightly international journal *Down to Earth* published by the Society for Environmental Communications in India has a wide and lively coverage of sustainable development issues and often includes papers or articles on sustainable city issues. Available from *Down to Earth,* 41 Tughlakabad International Area, New Delhi 110 062, India. For more details, see its web page on http//www.oneworld.org/cse

Journals such as *Urban Studies* and *Third World Planning Review* also publish papers of relevance to the theme of sustainable cities

Books that are Useful for their Coverage of Urban Environmental Problems

World Resources 1996–1997: The Urban Environment, The World Resources Institute, in collaboration with the United Nations Development Programme, the United Nations Environmental Programme and the World Bank, Oxford University Press, Oxford and New York, 1996

Towards Environmental Strategies for Cities; Policy Considerations for Urban Environmental Management in Developing Countries – Carl Bartone, Janis Bernstein, Josef Leitmann and Jochen Eigen, 1994. Published by and available from the UNDP/UNCHS/World Bank Urban Management Program, 1818 H Street NW, Washington DC, 20433, USA

During 2000, Earthscan will also be publishing a revised and much updated edition of*Environmental Problems in Third World Cities* – Jorge E Hardoy, Diana Mitlin and David Satterthwaite, Earthscan Publications, London, which was originally published in 1992. This describes the scale and range of environmental problems in cities in Africa, Asia and Latin America and how they affect human health, local ecosystems and global cycles

For a broad overview of urban change and the links with economic, social, political and environmental changes, see *An Urbanizing World: Global Report on Human Settlements 1996*, UNCHS (Habitat), Oxford University Press, Oxford and New York, 1996. This also looks at housing conditions, including provision for infrastructure and services and how the policies of governments and international agencies are changing towards housing and urban development

Part III
Different Sectoral Programmes that Contribute to the Achievement of Sustainable Development Goals in Cities

Chapter 7

Health: Creating Healthy Cities in the 21st Century

World Health Organization

(Reprinted from a World Health Organization Report of this same name which was prepared for a Dialogue on Health within the Second United Nations Conference on Human Settlements (Habitat II), held in Istanbul in 1996. This retains the text of the original, except for the removal of a short section outlining the scale and nature of urban change). This document is not a formal publication of the World Health Organization (WHO) and all rights are reserved by the Organization. The document may, however, be freely reviewed, abstracted, reproduced and translated, in part or whole, but not for sale or for use in conjuction with commercial purposes. The views expressed in documents by named authors are solely the responsibility of those authors.

INTRODUCTION

A Healthy Urban Future?

When considering what cities will be like as we move into the next century, there are two very different possible futures. The first is one in which the knowledge of how to create and sustain healthy cities is applied in both the North and the South. This is not an unrealistic urban future since there are examples of cities or city districts that have done so – making maximum use of local resources, involving all sectors of society and addressing the full range of health problems from infectious diseases and air pollution to unhealthy lifestyles, drug abuse and violence. Some of these cities are among the most healthy and valued living environments in the world; most but not all are in the North. The other examples are the cities or city-districts in which remarkable improvements have been made in health in recent decades, despite relatively low per capita incomes – and most of these are in the South.

Perhaps the main reason for their success is that promoting health and preventing disease and injury was recognized as being in everyone's interest and as everyone's responsibility. This meant a great range of initiatives not only by health professionals and public authorities but also by households, community organizations, schools, private enterprises and NGOs, and other voluntary sector organizations. Each contributed within their sphere and sector to the identification of health problems and their underlying causes and to acting on them. Although most initiatives were undertaken by people with no medical training, the health professionals and public authorities had a critical role in advising and supporting their efforts.

Healthy cities are based on models of city governance in which public authorities recognize the need to work with and support this great range of actors – a community-based coalition committed to violence prevention, a water, sanitation and health care programme for illegal settlements which combines government, community and external funding sources, a credit programme that allows low-income households to pay for the costs of connecting their homes to piped water systems, a neighbourhood-level scheme to ensure that each residential neighbourhood has play areas for children that are safe, clean and stimulating .... Achieving healthy cities means building on each city's own resources and on the skills and managerial capacities of its people and formal and informal institutions.

These programmes for healthy cities also build on the many potential advantages that cities have – for instance, the concentration of population that allows much lower costs for supplying each household with piped, treated water supplies and most forms of health, educational and emergency services. Sanitation and drainage may be costly in cities, as complex systems are needed to cope with high densities and large population concentrations but city households can generally afford to pay more – and are prepared to do so if they get a good service. In addition, as a later section will describe, there are sanitation systems that are far less costly than sewers that can be applied in many cities or city-districts. Health services (and referral systems for hospital care) may operate more efficiently in urban areas, and solutions may be easier for such key issues as:

- development of inputs from the user community to the decision-making processes and management of the health services;
- development and promotion of preventive services alongside curative services; and
- greater equity in provision of primary care services.

There is the worry that an increasingly urbanized world will also mean increasing pressure on the world's finite resource base and its global capacity to absorb or break down wastes. Urban households usually generate more waste than rural households, while their consumption patterns generally imply larger levels of greenhouse gas emissions per person. However, cities can combine healthy environments with an efficient use of resources, minimum wastes and extensive reuse or recycling of whatever wastes cannot be eliminated. For instance, the close proximity of so many water consumers gives greater scope for recycling or directly reusing waste waters, and the techniques for greatly reducing the use of fresh water in city homes and enterprises are well known where freshwater resources are scarce.[1] Cities also concentrate populations in ways which usually reduce the demand for land relative to population, especially if they have high-quality public transport and avoid the low-density automobile-dependent sprawl that is so common in North America and becoming more common around cities in other regions.[2]

An Unhealthy Urban Future

There is a second urban future which at present is more probable, since in most countries it is a continuation of existing trends. This is an urban future in which health problems and their underlying causes are not given adequate attention, where much of the urban population will suffer from diseases and injuries that are easily prevented, as is the case today in much of the South. The rapid rise in violence will continue – as is the case today in many cities in both the North and the South – as little attention is directed to such underlying causes as increasing inequality, discrimination, the easy availability of guns and poor quality living environments.

This is an urban future that shows the disadvantages that cities can bring for health, if their potential advantages for promoting health and preventing disease and injury outlined above are ignored. Cities, by concentrating people, increase the possibilities for the transmission of infectious diseases. Where there is inadequate provision for water, sanitation, drainage and garbage collection, the disease-causing agents or the vectors or animal hosts on which many rely proliferate. As the section on Emerging and Re-emerging Diseases describes, achieving healthy cities is made all the more difficult because of the emergence of new infectious diseases and the resurgence of other infectious diseases – for instance, as health-care systems prove unable to cope or as the disease-causing agents or the vectors that spread them develop a resistance to the public health measures taken to eliminate them.[3]

Cities also concentrate manufacturing enterprises with the most dangerous occupational health hazards, if these are not strictly controlled. Cities generally have the most serious problems with ambient air pollution, if environmental controls are not enforced. They also concentrate motor vehicles and without good management, the deaths and injuries from motor vehicle accidents mount. Without good management, cities become dangerous and unhealthy places.

If the urban future for much of the world is a continuation of what exists today, it is one in which millions of infants or children will die each year and tens of millions will have their physical and mental development impaired by avoidable or preventable diseases. This is an urban future where a high proportion of the adult population living in urban areas will constantly suffer from serious injuries or illnesses that should have been avoided. Today, more than a third of the urban population in Africa, Asia and Latin America live in housing of such poor quality with such inadequate provision for water, sanitation, drainage, garbage collection and health care that their lives and their health are constantly under threat. In such circumstances, it is common for one child in three to die before the age of five and for virtually all infants, children and adults who survive to have disease burdens many times higher than they should. For instance, the health burden per person from diarrhoeal diseases caught in 1990 was around 200 times higher in sub-Saharan Africa than in the North[4] and less overcrowded housing with adequate provision for water, sanitation and the safe preparation and storage of food would enormously decrease this health burden. Disease burdens from tuberculosis and acute respiratory infections (each, along with diarrhoeal diseases, among the largest causes of death worldwide) are generally much increased by overcrowding. Many accidental injuries happen when there are three or more persons living in each small room in shelters made of flammable materials and there is little chance of providing occupants (especially children) with protection from open fires or stoves.

There are also many serious health problems in many of the wealthiest cities in the North. For instance, there are low-income districts with average life expectancies that are 10 to 20 years below the national average and infant mortality rates that are three to four times what can be achieved by good practice in health promotion and health care.[5] There are also particular groups within city populations who face serious health problems – for instance, people living in overcrowded conditions or in shelters without basic services; even in countries in the European Union, there are millions of people living in dwellings without toilets, bathrooms or showers.[6] There are also millions of homeless people in both Europe and North America who face many additional health risks and usually great difficulties in obtaining health care. In the early 1990s, around 18 million citizens within the European Union were homeless or extremely badly housed, including 1.8 million people who in the course of a year depended on public or voluntary services for temporary shelter or who squat or sleep rough.[7] Changes in labour markets (especially the growth in the number of long-term unemployed) and welfare systems have also meant that adolescents and young adults make up a growing proportion of the homeless population in many countries.[8]

Problems of crime and violence have become increasingly serious in most cities in the North and the South. For instance, a recent report commented that:

> ... violence is among the biggest health threats in the United States. Interpersonal violence has invaded homes, schools, and streets everywhere, reaching what public health experts now conclude is epidemic proportions.[9]

More than half the world's population living in cities with 100,000 or more inhabitants are victims of a crime of some kind at least once every five years.[10] Crime rates are particularly high in the cities of Africa and North and South America.[11] Violent crime has increased in most cities in recent years; it usually accounts for between 25 and 30 per cent of all urban crimes.[12] It includes murder (or homicide), infanticide, assault, rape and sexual abuse and domestic violence. Domestic violence is a particularly serious problem, as will be described in the section on women. Murder rates have reached very high levels in many cities. Murder rates should be kept below 1 per 100,000 inhabitants per year as they are in some of the world's healthiest nations – but there are cities in the North and the South where the murder rate is over 70 per 100,000 inhabitants per year.

High levels of crime, especially of violent crime, are changing the spatial form of cities as middle- and upper-income groups increasingly live, work, shop and take their leisure in what are essentially fortified enclaves, each with sophisticated security systems and, increasingly, their own secure car park.[13] Since the journeys between them take place in private cars, there is little or no necessity to walk on the streets or to use open spaces. High levels of crime and fear of violence are also pushing shopping malls, office complexes and leisure activities outside central cities to the point where few middle- and upper-income groups visit the city centre.

The choices made today by governments and development assistance agencies will be a main influence on which of these two possible urban futures becomes the reality in the next century. This background document for the Dialogue on Health for Habitat II describes some of the most serious health problems evident in cities today and approaches by which they can be addressed. These approaches are all based on successful experiences.

They concentrate on five themes:

- Building healthy cities.
- Addressing emerging and re-emerging diseases.
- Environmental pollution and health (with a special focus on lead and on water and sanitation).
- Child health.
- Women's health (with a special focus on reproductive health).

HEALTHY CITIES

Cities Built from the Bottom Up

All cities are the result of an enormous range of investments of capital, expertise and time by individuals, households, communities, voluntary organizations and NGOs, as well as by private enterprises, investors and government agencies. Yet until recently, in many countries, city problems were assumed to be the responsibility of national or provincial/state agencies. One of the critical changes between Habitat I, the first UN Conference on Human Settlements in 1976 and Habitat II in 1996 is the change in emphasis away from what national governments should do to how national and provincial governments should support the efforts and initiatives of those living and working in cities. This includes supporting the efforts of city and municipal authorities and of individual households, community organizations, NGOs and private sector institutions. City authorities have a particularly critical role – not only in investment, planning and management but also in encouraging and supporting the initiatives and innovations of the other groups within their city. In most cities in the South, city and municipal authorities have limited power and resources, and limited capacity to raise revenues. Although decentralization programmes in many countries are permitting them a greater role, their effectiveness in promoting health and preventing or curing disease still depends on their skills in working with the resources and skills of other groups in the city.

A second critical change since Habitat 1 in 1976 is the recognition by city authorities that a person's health can be as much the result of conditions in the home, at school or at work as the quality of health care available to them.[14] Healthy cities need commitment and action to health promotion and disease or accident prevention within all sectors, not just from medical professionals.

These two changes in understanding are central to the Healthy Cities movement. The core of WHO's Healthy Cities programme is to support city and municipal authorities in working with NGOs, community organizations and other groups within each city to identify and act on the most serious health and environmental problems. The fact that these work in many sectors can be seen in the sub-programmes that many have for healthy schools, healthy workplaces or healthy hospitals. The Healthy Cities programme is not a blueprint that is given to city authorities that they have to follow but a process that permits the main health problems in a city and their causes to be identified and responses developed by all key actors within a city. Thus, it avoids the problem of promoting a standard set of solutions that can never fit the unique range of problems and possibilities for their resolution that exists in each city. It promotes co-operation between sectors and between different interest groups.

The Healthy Cities programme supports two aspects of governance at the local level:

(a) technical aspects, involving local level resource mobilization, plan formulation, technology application and resource allocation; and
(b) representational and participatory aspects, including participation, channels for popular representation and increased transparency and accountability in the workings of local authorities. Thus, the analysis of needs and the priority setting process in a Healthy Cities project involves both:

- the views of the communities involved in terms of their needs and priorities, that expresses fully the local perception of the problems and issues; and
- a technical assessment based on available health statistics and known epidemiological linkages between the health status and environmental and social conditions.

Both of these assessments must be combined in the course of developing the city health plan.

The consultation process with the community and many different agencies and groups seeks to develop a 'vision' of the future directions of the city and to understand its current (and past) strengths and weaknesses. This often includes a 'Vision workshop' that can start with the question: 'why is the city or town a fine place to live?' In all parts of the world, an appreciation of each city's cultural heritage and the cultivation of a 'sense of place' to celebrate its unique characteristics and history is proving important in mobilizing people to improve living conditions and address health and environmental problems.

The 'healthy cities week' in the city of Kuching in Malaysia provides an example of a wide-ranging consultation process. Questionnaires were circulated widely, asking people to list the five things they hated most and liked most in their city and wished for most. Other healthy cities programmes have used similar consultation processes, including school programmes which involved children in identifying the positive and negative aspects of the city and how the negative aspects could be tackled. The healthy city consultation process usually leads to a long-range city health plan in which priorities are set and the actions of different groups and sectors are integrated.

Many healthy city programmes include the setting up of special task forces to address particularly pressing problems. Task forces are generally city-wide and are based on:

- *specific settings* (eg healthy schools, food-markets, housing, settlements or neighbourhoods, industries) and
- *specific issues* such as safety, women's health, water and sanitation, priority diseases (for instance, malaria or HIV) or improved health clinics.

Task forces draw together people from different disciplines and combine staff from local authorities, other government agencies, NGOs and representatives of community organizations.

To date, over 1,000 cities around the world have initiated Healthy City programmes. Box 7.1 gives examples from Europe, North America, Asia and Africa.

City Leadership in Healthy City Projects

Among the global UN Conferences of the last 25 years, Habitat II is unusual in that it has involved local authorities from the outset and many of its recommendations are aimed at local authorities or at what higher levels of government should do to support local authorities. A growing number of case studies show how city authorities have undertaken innovative and successful approaches to addressing health and environmental problems. Many did not require large capital sums. In Latin America in particular, there seems to be a new generation of mayors that are associated with the return to or reinforcement of local democracy during the 1980s – many with

---

Box 7.1 *Examples of Healthy Cities Programmes*

Nabeul (Tunisia): This is a small city some 80 miles south of Tunis with international tourism and a ceramics industry as the main economic base. Great efforts have been made to improve sewerage, drainage and waste disposal. A Healthy Cities project also initiated a programme to control emissions of toxic chemicals and reduce air pollution from the ceramics industry by relocating some workshops, changing the technologies used and improving the management of liquid and solid wastes. Air pollution was reduced through the use of cleaner fuel and improvements in the traditional ovens. The city also organized the collection and safe disposal of medical wastes.[15]

Sherbrooke (Canada): Sherbrooke is one among a large network of cities and villages in the province of Quebec that have healthy cities or villages programmes. Up to the 1980s, Sherbrooke had thrived on textile, metalwork, timber and brewery industries and a large public sector but more recently, many jobs were lost and social and economic problems increased. The 'Healthy City Sherbrooke' movement initiated in 1988 with support and a budget from the city council has undertaken a number of initiatives including: a Young People's Square as a meeting place for 14–17-year-olds with a range of leisure activities; a housing programme for senior citizens that included training for architects and real estate developers in the needs of the elderly; a much improved collection of dangerous domestic rubbish; community-based projects to deal with vandalism, reduce the use of pesticides, lower water consumption and create smoke-free areas in restaurants; and an initiative that gave children aged 8 to 11 the chance to express their needs and vision of an ideal city which was then followed up by a series of church–park–school projects.[16]

Glasgow (United Kingdom): The largest city in Scotland and also its commercial and industrial centre with an unenviable health record, linked partly to the city's economic difficulties and decline as a centre of shipbuilding and heavy industry. Its Healthy Cities project recognized that health problems were not going to be solved by a medical approach since people's health was influenced by their personal behaviour, access to services, the quality of their homes (and the costs of keeping them warm) and the quality of their employment and the social and physical environments. Many local initiatives have promoted health for all, especially through community health workers.[17]

Chittagong (Bangladesh): The second largest city in Bangladesh with around 2 million inhabitants, the provision of services has not kept pace with the city's rapid growth and expansion in recent decades. The Healthy City project is guided by a steering committee chaired by the mayor and including representatives from different sectors and groups. This is supported by a project office within the city corporation, zonal task forces for specific plans and actions in particular areas (for instance, one of Chittagong's 41 wards has developed a pilot 'healthy ward' programme) and sectoral task forces responsible for specific plans and actions in, for instance, housing, water and sanitation.[18]

---

medical backgrounds. They are trying new approaches, showing a much greater concern for low-income groups and for a more open and accountable form of governance, avoiding long-established paternalist or patron-client approaches. For instance, several cities in Brazil including Porto Alegre and Belo Horizonte, have developed what is termed 'participative budgeting' which allows citizens a much greater involvement in setting priorities for municipal investments and a greater openness about how municipal revenues are acquired and spent.[19] Among the smaller cities,

Box 7.2 *Addressing housing and health problems in Cali, Colombia*

Under Mayor Rodrigo Guerrero, a wide range of responses were developed to address health problems in the city of Cali. These combined measures to generate employment and improve income as well as to improve housing and health and tackle problems of violence, since it was recognized that inadequate incomes were a major underpinning of poor health. These interventions also recognized that they had to build on the knowledge and resources of low-income groups themselves.

In regard to employment, a small business development programme was developed based on training, counselling and credit. More than 100,000 micro-enterprises went through this programme and more than $30 million has been made available in loans. The default rate is less than 1 per cent and each $1,000 in loans created another stable job opening. There was also a special programme for small merchants or corner food stores which included a course in business administration, access to credit and access to wholesale prices at special food distribution warehouses.

In regard to basic services, there was a large expansion in the proportion of the city population reached with water, sewers and electricity and universal provision of primary education. In addition, with support from the private sector and the Catholic Church, health-care provision was much improved in Aguablanca, an illegal settlement with some 300,000 inhabitants.

A recycling programme was started in low-income neighbourhoods that suffered from poor quality garbage collection services. Recycling centres were established with payment for recycled materials in the form of credits that could be used to improve their houses, pay for health care, purchase goods in the food warehouses noted above, or to purchase cobblestones for paving the streets. Materials brought to recycling centres could also be exchanged for bus tokens. Former street toughs were among those hired as garbage collectors and cleaners of parks, streets and marketplaces and they also received training as micro entrepreneurs.

A serviced site programme was set up which developed 25,000 lots with basic services. These could be afforded by low-income groups, unlike the public housing built by previous city administrations.

A violence prevention programme was initiated which included a ban on the carrying of handguns and knives, restrictions on the sale of alcohol in public places and mass campaigns to promote mutual tolerance. A municipal security council brings together the relevant players and studies the epidemiology of crime, neighbourhood by neighbourhood. Each week, a meeting is held in one of the city's 20 districts to discuss all matters related to crime and public security and to agree on actions to be taken. This is attended by the mayor and community leaders and is also open to the public. Peace-promoting groups have also been formed by young volunteers who act as legal counsellors and educators. They provide human rights education and suggest ways for people to resolve disputes and, if necessary, refer them to conciliation centres.

Sources: Guerrero, Rodrigo V, 'Innovative programs for the urban poor in Cali, Colombia' in Bonnie Bradford and Margaret A. Gwynne (eds), *Down to Earth: Community Perspectives on Health, Development and the Environment,* Kumarian Press, West Hartford, 1995, pp 17–22; Guerrero, Rodrigo, 'Cali: the right priorities', *World Health* issue on Healthy Cities, 49th Year, No 1, January–February 1996, p 10; Concha, Albert, Fernando Carrion and German Cobo (eds), *Ciudad y Violencias en America Latina,* UMP Serie Gestión Urbana, Quito, 1993

Manizales in Colombia and Ilo in Peru are noted for their innovation in developing long-range plans to improve environmental quality.[20] One of the best known examples comes from the city of Cali in Colombia where there have been some remarkable municipal programmes to improve housing conditions, reduce poverty and improve environmental conditions – with municipal authorities working with the private sector, the long-established *Carvajal* Foundation,[21] community organizations, NGOs and the Catholic Church – see Box 7.2. What is also noticeable in Box 7.2 is the range of actions that go beyond health care by including programmes to improve low-income groups' incomes, improve housing and basic services, and promote violence prevention.

City Networking for Health

One important aspect of the growing Healthy Cities movement has been the growth in city-to-city exchanges. City-twinning has been common for decades where a closer relationship is established between cities that have particular ties based on culture, language, a shared historical event or other bonds. But networks of cities built around health issues are more recent. Important networks have developed by language – for example, there are the Francophone, Spanish, Portuguese and Arabic speaking networks of Healthy Cities.

The types of networking that has developed includes:

(a) Established Healthy Cities assisting other cities in developing new projects, during the start-up phase.
(b) Multi-city Action Plans: this approach has become very popular in some regions, especially in Europe and involves a number of Healthy Cities network cities that decide to simultaneously address a particular health issue such as alcohol, nutrition, AIDS, diabetes or women's health. Cities agree to share their analyses, approaches and strategies, programmes and monitoring data so each learns from each other and the resources of many cities are brought to bear on the chosen health issue.
(c) Exchanges of experience of Healthy City programmes through conferences, seminars, newsletters and other means at national, regional and global levels.

EMERGING AND RE-EMERGING DISEASES

Introduction

Earlier sections have stressed how with good management in public health and environmental health and with all sectors of a city's society contributing to health, cities can be among the most healthy places to live in, work and visit. But without this, cities usually become among the most health-threatening of all human environments – as disease-causing agents and disease vectors multiply, as the large concentration of people living in close proximity to each other enormously increases the risk of disease transmission, and as health-care systems become unable to respond rapidly and effectively. If provision for sanitation, drainage and garbage collection breaks down or fails to keep up with a city's expanding population, this greatly increases health hazards, especially from human excreta and from diseases spread by vectors who breed in standing water (for instance, malaria and dengue), or breed in or feed on uncollected garbage. If health-care systems break down, or fail to keep up with the growth in population, the health problems of those who catch diseases are much magnified – for instance, acute respiratory infections quickly become major causes of infant and child death, although they are easily cured if treated appropriately. In addition, the key immunization programmes no longer work and diseases such as measles and diphtheria reappear as major causes of death. There are so many infectious and parasitic diseases that thrive when provision for water, sanitation, drainage, garbage collection and health care is inadequate or where it breaks down.

Emerging and Re-emerging Diseases

Twenty years ago, many health specialists thought that public health measures could soon stop infectious diseases being a common cause of death,[22] yet infectious diseases remain the world's leading cause of death, killing at least 17 million people a year.[23] There are two particular problems. The first is the emergence of new infectious diseases: at least 29 previously unknown diseases have emerged since 1973.[24] AIDS is the best known and one of the most widespread; by December 1995, there were 6 million AIDS cases and 17 million people who were HIV positive. Virtually all these 'new' diseases existed previously, either in nature – for instance, as infections of monkeys, as in the case of the Ebola virus – or in isolated communities; what is new is their emergence as significant public health problems as their incidence and geographic range suddenly increases.

The second problem is the re-emergence of well-known infectious diseases that were considered as being under control. For instance, cholera and yellow fever are now striking in regions that were once thought to be safe from them. Epidemic cholera was again reported in the Americas in January 1991, after being absent for many decades. Between 1991 and December 1995, over 1.3 million cases were reported, with over 11,000 deaths.[25] Yellow fever has for nearly half a century been considered a rural disease but many cities are at risk from it, especially in the Americas, because they are or have become infested with the *Aedes aegypti* mosquitoes that can transmit the disease. Others diseases are re-emerging because the pathogen or the vector which transmits it have become resistant to control measures – for instance, malaria where the *Anopheles* mosquito can no longer be killed by many insecticides and where the drugs used to provide immunity or to treat malaria are no longer effective. Malaria is still one of the world's most serious health problems as it kills more than a million people each year (mostly children) with a total of 250–450 million clinical cases each year.[26] Although malaria has long been considered mainly a rural disease, it has become one of the most serious health problems in many urban centres or districts within centres where the Anopheline mosquito can find standing water in which to breed.

Dengue and dengue haemorrhagic fever that are also spread by mosquitoes are growing problems as the number of outbreaks and epidemics has increased significantly in the last decade. There are some 3 million cases each year with more than 20,000 deaths and with some 2 billion people at risk, most of them in urban areas. In recent years, epidemics of dengue fever have swept Brazil, India and Australia for the first time ever.[27] There has also been a rapid rise in the number of cases of the more severe forms of the disease, dengue haemorrhagic fever and dengue shock syndrome.

Underlying Causes

A great range of economic, social and ecological changes help to explain why emerging and re-emerging diseases have become such a serious problem. These diseases must be understood as one component of a complex and changing global ecology which is shaped (and buffeted) by economic, social, environmental, demographic and technological changes – and, of course, microbial change and adaptation.[28]

Perhaps the main reason why such diseases take a large toll on human health is the low priority given by most governments and international agencies to public health and health care. One illustration is the failure to meet the commitment made by governments at Habitat I in 1976 to ensure a rapid expansion in the percentage of people with adequate provision for water and sanitation (see the section on Environmental Health for more details). In addition, during the 1980s, support for health services declined in many nations in both the North and the South, the decline being particularly serious in many African and Latin American nations that also faced economic decline and large cuts in public expenditures.

But other factors also underlie the emerging or re-emerging diseases, including the greater difficulties in preventing and controlling infectious diseases as societies urbanize, as population movements increase, and as disease-causing agents develop resistance to public health measures or adapt to changing ecological circumstances in ways which increase the risks of infection for human populations. The size and complexity of most urban settings also make it increasingly difficult to keep up adequate services.

Urbanization with the increasing concentrations of people in urban areas (and usually in larger cities) obviously increases the possibilities for the transmission of infectious diseases, because it concentrates those with infectious diseases and those who are susceptible to infection. Most cities also concentrate large numbers of people who are particularly vulnerable to infection – for instance, the many cities in the South with large numbers of infants and young children and people with their immune system compromised by undernutrition and worm infections. In many cities in both the North and the South, there is also the rapid rise in the number of people with HIV which also makes them particularly vulnerable to other infectious diseases. Many cities in the North and some in the South also have a high concentration of older people who are more vulnerable to many infectious diseases. The millions living in refugee camps are also vulnerable, with their high concentration of people living under stress, perhaps with inadequate nutrition, often with a high proportion of children and generally with rudimentary provision for water, sanitation, drainage and health care. The growth in the number of refugees has been dramatic; by 1994, 23 million people qualified as refugees compared to about 2.5 million 20 years previously.[29]

One defining characteristic of a city is the constant movement of people in and out of it. This can mean the arrival in the city of newcomers who bring new infections to which the city population has no immunity. Emerging or re-emerging diseases such as cholera, HIV and dengue are among the diseases that have become established in cities as infected people move there and public health measures were too slow or inadequate to contain them, with the city then becoming a gateway for the further dissemination of the infection.[30]

The rapid increases in travel and trade over the last few decades have greatly increased the opportunities for pathogens and vectors to spread to new areas. Every day, one million people cross an international border[31] while many times this number move within national boundaries. From 1950 to 1990, the number of passengers aboard international commercial flights increased 140-fold from 2 million to 280 million.[32] The pathogens can travel within humans and the speed of travel by air also means that travellers can enter or return to a city while incubating a disease that does not become apparent for some days or weeks.[33] There are many historic examples of travellers introducing new diseases into populations with no immunity with devastating consequences; the rapid growth in the number of people travelling and in the range and speed of their travel over the last few decades has greatly increased the problem.

There are also examples of disease vectors which spread with travel or trade – for instance, the mosquito responsible for transmitting dengue fever in Asia has become established in the United States, Brazil and parts of Africa, probably through the trade in rubber tyres.[34] It was probably contaminated bilge water from an Asian freighter that initiated the cholera epidemic in Peru that then spread around Latin America,[35] although it was the inadequate provision for piped water supplies and provision for sanitation in most cities in the continent that helped the spread of the infection.

Urban changes also create foci for disease vectors and new ecological niches for animals which harbour a disease agent or vector. This may be the result of the expansion of built-up areas, the construction of roads, water reservoirs and drains, and land clearance and deforestation,[36] or the result of increased volumes of human excreta, garbage or waste water that are not cleared away. In addition, as cities expand, it is common for low-income groups to develop settlements on land subject to flooding or on or beside wetlands, as this land has less commercial value and the inhabitants have more chance of being permitted to stay there. But this also means close proximity to places where various insect vectors can breed. *Anopheles stephensi*, the principal vector for urban malaria, is reported in India and the Eastern Mediterranean region to have adapted to survive in the urban environment and other species of anophelines have also adapted to breed in swamps and ditches surrounding urban areas in Nigeria and Turkey.[37] *Aedes aegypti*, the vector of dengue and urban yellow fever proliferates in tropical urban areas where provision for sanitation, garbage collection and drainage is inadequate – it often breeds in water sources such as soak-away pits and septic tanks. It also breeds in any container that catches or stores water – for instance, in water-storage tanks that urban populations use when piped water systems are unreliable or non-existent.

Global warming will also bring changes in the distribution of infectious diseases. Warmer average temperatures permit an expansion in the area in which 'tropical diseases' can occur. This is likely to be the case for many diseases spread by insect vectors – for instance, global warming is likely to permit an expansion of the area in which mosquitoes that are the vectors for malaria, dengue fever and filariasis can survive and breed.[38]

Another underlying cause of the emergence or re-emergence of certain diseases is that the disease-causing agents, including bacteria and viruses, and the insects or other vectors who spread them, have demonstrated a remarkable ability to survive public health measures.[39] Public health specialists did not foresee the ability of many agents of infectious diseases to rapidly develop resistance to the drugs or chemicals that had previously killed them. For instance, many bacterial disease-causing agents, including those that cause pneumonia, tuberculosis and typhoid fever, and some diarrhoeal diseases and forms of food poisoning have become resistant to many antibiotic drugs. This is not a new phenomenon and as early as the 1930s, the development of drug-resistant disease-causing agents was noted. However, the control of diseases in both human and in animal populations has come to rely heavily on antibiotics, while antibiotics are also widely used in animals to speed up their growth. The development and distribution of new antibiotics cannot keep up with the speed at which many disease-causing agents develop a resistance to them. The problem has been exacerbated in countries where antibiotic use is not controlled through their overuse and misuse. This is a hazardous and costly problem in all countries but in the poorer countries in the South, it is increasingly life-threatening as routine susceptibility testing and costly new antibiotics are not readily available.[40]

Tuberculosis is one example of a disease which in many parts of the world has developed resistance to drugs. It is responsible for some 3 million deaths each year and is the single largest cause of adult death in the world, accounting for a quarter of all adult deaths.[41] It mainly occurs among populations living in the poorest areas, with high levels of overcrowding and high numbers of social contacts. In urban areas, a combination of overcrowding and poor ventilation often means that one person with TB will transmit the disease to more than half their family members.[42] TB incidence has been increasing rapidly over the past decade or so, partly linked to the spread of HIV/AIDS. Although most deaths from TB are in the South, its incidence in many of the world's wealthiest nations has also increased during the 1980s and early 1990s, after decades of steady decline.[43] For instance, during the 1980s, TB re-emerged after decades of decline as a serious public health problem in the United States, partly because of a breakdown in public health,[44] partly because drug-resistant strains made its control more difficult.

Finally, we should remember that measures to control infectious diseases broke down or declined during the 1980s and early 1990s in many countries. The combination of public health measures and measures to ensure adequate provision for water, sanitation, drainage and health care tend to minimize human exposure to many pathogens. But the pathogens often remain in reduced numbers in reservoir hosts or in the environment or in small pockets of infection, and can take advantage of the opportunity to re-emerge, if there are breakdowns in preventive measures.[45] Diphtheria, which should have been kept in check by immunization, re-emerged as a major cause of death in many of the republics that formerly made up the Soviet Union. For instance, the number of cases in the Ukraine increased 100-fold when comparing 1980 to 1993 and this mostly affected the urban population.[46] As noted above, a breakdown in public health measures is one reason for the resurgence of tuberculosis in the United States. The impact of cholera in Latin America would have been much reduced if urban populations had been better served by well-functioning water supply, sanitation and health-care systems. One reason why HIV spread so rapidly in many countries (in both urban and rural areas) was the failure of public health systems to respond rapidly and to focus attention on prevention for groups who were particularly at risk. Part of the reason was the tendency of many governments to deny the presence of HIV-infected people within their borders or to downplay the number of people infected; this is one of many possible examples of the reluctance of governments to be honest about the danger of infectious diseases within their borders if they fear it will discourage tourism and foreign investment.[47]

A Framework for Solving the Problem

The centre of any initiative to address the problem of emerging and re-emerging diseases in cities is the healthy cities model that has already been described, with good management in public and environmental health and with all sectors of a city's society supported in contributing to health. The better the quality and the more universal the coverage of systems providing piped water, sanitation, drainage, the collection and safe disposal of garbage and primary health care, the less the risk of emerging or re-emerging diseases. Good practice in health promotion and prevention in hospitals, health-care clinics, schools and day-care centres, and a control over the use of drugs to avoid the emergence of drug-resistant organisms are also important. So, too, is enhancing the capacity of institutions within the city and nation for disease surveillance and monitoring. More support is also needed for primary health-care workers and community-based health promoters who are the front-line in disease prevention and generally the first to detect emerging or re-emerging diseases. In urban areas, these front-line health workers often have to face competition from senior health practitioners working either in public or in private settings, and the problems of the urban front-line health workers have rarely been tackled adequately. But taking action on all of these fronts may depend on a recognition within each society of the great benefits of giving greater attention to health and to addressing the underlying causes of ill health and injury. The individual and societal benefits from a focus on disease and injury prevention and health promotion have long been evident; however, most governments have paid too little attention to prevention and most development assistance agencies have given it a low priority.[48]

ENVIRONMENTAL HEALTH

Introduction

In every city, there is a considerable range of biological and chemical pollutants that cause or contribute to disease. Some pose health risks for the entire city population, others for particular groups. Some pollutants have health impacts concentrated in particular periods – for instance, when particular weather conditions inhibit the dispersal of air pollutants away from a city or during periods of high rainfall when flooding spreads faecal matter all over the flooded areas and pollutes water sources in cities ill-equipped to deal with flooding. The range of these pollutants and the extent of the risk they pose to city populations varies enormously from city to city.

This section will concentrate on the pollutants associated with inadequate provision for water and sanitation and with inadequate control of air pollution. The first is, arguably, the single most serious environmental problem in cities in terms of its health impact, although the problem is concentrated in urban areas in Africa, Asia and Latin America. The second is a problem in cities all over the world, affects a high proportion of the world's urban population and has health implications which have been underestimated.

Water and Sanitation[49]

Introduction: Every year, more than 5 million people die from illnesses linked to un-safe drinking water, improper excreta disposal and unclean domestic environments, virtually all of them in the South.[50] At any given time, perhaps half of the urban and the rural population of the South are suffering from one or more of the main diseases associated with water supply and sanitation. Diarrhoeal diseases remain among the most prominent causes of premature death and illness in many urban areas, and these diseases are strongly related to unsanitary excreta disposal, poor personal and domestic hygiene and unsafe drinking water. These conditions are also linked to infection with intestinal worms which affect a large proportion of the population living in urban areas. Trachoma is one among several diseases associated with a lack of water for regular washing; it causes serious health problems for tens of mil-lions of urban dwellers with millions also suffering from blindness or severe com-plications. And, as the section on Emerging and Re-emerging Diseases described, malaria and dengue fever are also associated with water but in this instance through the disease vector (mosquito) breeding in standing water; both these diseases are increasingly serious urban problems.

Water and sanitation coverage: The proportion of urban dwellers with provision for piped water and sanitation has improved considerably since Habitat 1, the first UN Conference on Human Settlements, 20 years ago. *However, with the rapid increase in urban populations in the South over the last 20 years, the number of people not served by water supplies and sanitation has increased, not declined.* In 1994, close to 300 million urban dwellers were still not served by water supplies and close to 600 mil-lion were without sanitation. Thus, most governments failed to meet the commit-ments they made at Habitat 1 to give a much higher priority to water and sanita-tion and to ensure that by 1990 virtually all urban (and rural) dwellers would be adequately served. There is also less development assistance as many international agencies have reduced their budgets for water supply and sanitation since the end of the International Drinking Water Supply and Sanitation Decade (1981–1990).[51]

In addition, the number of urban dwellers lacking safe, sufficient and conve-nient supplies of water is substantially higher than the figures noted above.[52] Much more than 300 million urban dwellers lack a water supply that is regular and piped into their home or yard. Many governments include in their official statistics of people 'adequately' served with water all households with public standpipes nearby, even when there is only one tap for dozens or even hundreds of households. In addition, many public standpipes are poorly maintained or connected to water-supply sys-tems that function intermittently. Thus, tens of millions of urban dwellers judged by official statistics to have adequate water supply still face great difficulties in ob-taining sufficient water for good health. Most of those affected are low-income house-holds living in ever-expanding peri-urban settlements which are such common fea-tures in most cities in the South.

Similarly, more than 600 million urban dwellers lack provision for sanitation that is easily accessible, that minimizes the possibility of human contact with hu-man excreta and that is easy to maintain. Many government statistics consider all households that in theory have access to a communal pit latrine as having adequate sanitation. It is rare for such latrines to be kept clean and well maintained when shared by dozens of households.[53]

Alternative approaches to improving water and sanitation: The capital costs of im-proving water supplies and sanitation can appear daunting. Many cities are facing

Table 7.1 *Coverage of water supply and sanitation for urban areas, 1994*

Region	Urban population served by water supply		Urban population with sanitation coverage	
	Millions of inhabitants	Per cent	Millions of inhabitants	Per cent
Africa	153	64	131	55
Central and South America and the Caribbean	306	88	254	73
Asia and the Pacific	805	84	584	61
Western Asia	51	98	36	69
Total	1,315	82	1,005	63

Source: WHO/UNICEF Joint Monitoring Programme

high costs in increasing water supplies as all easily tapped local sources have been used up (and/or polluted) and as tapping new sources involves expensive capital projects with the cost of water per unit volume being several times higher than from existing sources.[54] In addition, a conventional sewage system can cost $1,000 or more per household, so the cost of installing sewers for, say, half the population of a city of 2 million people implies a total cost of $200 million.[55] In most cities in the South, the local authorities lack the capacity to finance this. National authorities and international agencies are reluctant to fund it, partly because costs cannot be recovered from user-charges, especially if the sewerage system reached the low-income areas. There are also serious technical constraints to the installation of sewer networks in established, congested urban environments.

However, there is an alternative approach to the conventional, externally funded contractor-built water and sanitation project based on Northern models and technologies. This is to consider what can be done to improve conditions, building on systems that are already present in any city and making maximum use of local resources, skills and managerial capacities.[56] For instance, in many cities or particular city districts in low-income countries where residential areas are not too dense, Ventilated Improved Pit latrines within each housing plot may be the most appropriate solution, and they can later be converted into pour-flush latrines which in turn are later connected to a low-cost sewage system, as resources permit and households' capacity to afford them increases.[57] It is also possible to develop sewer systems incrementally rather than having to finance a citywide system, as can be seen in the many districts that have developed their own sewer system linked to a community septic tank, rather than waiting for a citywide system to reach them.

Cities facing escalating costs for increasing water supplies can usually substitute 'good local management' for capital investment. As much as 50–60 per cent of the water entering a water distribution system can be lost or unaccounted for – for instance, this was the case in Cairo, Mexico City, Baranquilla, Lima and Jakarta – compared to 10–15 per cent in well-managed public water supply systems.[58] Here, investment in better leak detection and in overall maintenance and repair of the water system can greatly increase the available supply of fresh water, and usually much more cheaply than any project to increase the volume of water available for distribution. Promoting efficient water use by households and industries can also have the same effect of increasing available water supplies – for instance, through higher prices and, for the largest water users, incentives to reduce use.

There are many examples of initiatives in different cities that show that these alternative approaches can work. These brought great improvements in water supply and sanitation at relatively low cost, including some in which much of the cost was recovered, even in low-income areas. These include:

- initiatives to provide water piped into the homes of low-income households where the households concerned repaid the cost and still paid less per month than they previously paid to water vendors, as in the UNICEF supported health, water and sanitation programme in El Mesquital in Guatemala City;[59]
- community installed and managed sewers such as in Orangi in Karachi that reduced costs so much (to between a fifth and a sixth of the cost that the municipal authority would have charged them for doing this work) that the low-income households could afford to pay the costs;[60] and
- credit programmes for low-income households that allowed them to pay for the costs of improving their homes and for the costs of piped water connections and improved provision for sanitation and drainage, with virtually all of those who took on loans fully meeting the loan-repayment schedules.[61]

Although very diverse in what was done, these initiatives share certain characteristics which kept down capital costs. Most made maximum use of local resources, including the knowledge, management capacity and labour of the low-income groups themselves. In many, individuals and representative community organizations took on some or most of the work that would normally be undertaken by external contractors which greatly reduced costs. Many used technologies that were cheaper than conventional contractor-built or public works-built projects – for instance, integrating drains into schemes to improve roads, installing simplified sewer systems or using on-site sanitation – for instance, Ventilated Improved Pit Latrines.

On the cost recovery side, as capital costs were kept down, so the gap between costs per household and households' capacity to pay was much reduced and the possibility of low-income households being able to afford to repay the costs was much increased. There are also examples of loan programmes for urban sanitation that achieved high levels of repayment.[62] Low-income households are often prepared to pay more for a water supply piped into their home than for a shared water standpipe because of the large savings in time and effort that this brings to them.

The examples of low-cost water and sanitation projects, including those that achieved cost recovery, are generally projects considered by the low-income households who benefited from them as *their* projects. These households also recognized that external funding was limited. No household will accept low-cost solutions that also involve them in providing a lot of the management and labour input if they believe they can negotiate a much more expensive, contractor-implemented solution from governments or international agencies. In addition, alternative solutions to conventional piped water and sewer systems must be developed in full consultation with the beneficiaries and with considerable care taken not to make unrealistic assumptions about the extent to which individual households and community organizations can contribute to construction, maintenance and repair. For instance, external agencies have often assumed that low-income households have time to contribute labour free to install and maintain new systems as they are 'underemployed', when virtually all adult household members work long hours; they only appear underemployed because the work they do is informal and unregistered.

There have also been problems with the maintenance of some of the cheaper on-site sanitation systems – for instance, where pit latrines were constructed with an unrealistic assumption about the capacity of municipal latrine-emptying services to expand their coverage.

Urban Air Pollution

Introduction: Polluted air has become an almost inescapable part of urban life throughout the world. In hundreds of cities, WHO guidelines or national air quality standards are often exceeded for many pollutants such as sulphur dioxide, nitrogen oxides, suspended particulate matter, ozone and lead. More than 1.5 billion urban dwellers are exposed to levels of ambient air pollution that are above the recommended maximum levels. Estimates by WHO suggest that worldwide, about 400,000 additional deaths annually are to be attributed to ambient air pollution. Given the rate at which many cities and polluting activities are growing, perhaps most especially the rapid growth in the number of motor vehicles, air pollution will worsen unless forceful control measures are being implemented.

There has been progress in controlling some air pollutants. While great successes in reducing sulphur dioxide, suspended particulate matter and lead have been achieved in the wealthier countries, the management of nitrogen oxides and ozone still awaits a satisfactory solution. There has been much less progress in most cities in developing countries where the control of air pollution is only at its very beginning, and it is generally in the largest cities or the largest industrial complexes where most remains to be done.

Sources of air pollution: Most urban air pollution comes from the combustion of fossil fuels for domestic heating or power generation, or from motor vehicles, industrial processes and the disposal of solid wastes by incineration, although the relative importance of these different sources varies greatly from city to city. Initially, pollution control and monitoring concentrated on sulphur dioxideand suspended particulate coming from fixed sources – for instance, factories, power stations and domestic heaters. But increasingly, the traffic-related air pollutants, nitrogen oxides, carbon monoxide and lead, and, as a secondary pollutant, ozone, have become incorporated into air quality considerations. Furthermore, greater attention is being paid to particular chemicals and particular size particles within suspended particulate matter which pose higher health risks.

Health effects of air pollution: Air pollution can adversely affect human health, not only by direct inhalation, but also indirectly by other exposure routes, such as drinking water contamination, food contamination and skin transfer. Most of the traditional air pollutants directly affect the respiratory systems. Increased mortality, morbidity and impaired pulmonary function have been associated with elevated levels of air pollutants. The uptake of carbon monoxide can lead to cardiovascular and neurobehavioural effects while the uptake of lead by children can impair their learning ability (see Box 7.3).

Approaches to air quality management: The aim of a health-oriented air pollution control programme is to promote a better quality of life by reducing air pollution to the lowest level possible. Air pollution control programmes and policies, whose implications and priorities vary from country to country, cover all aspects of pollution (air, water, etc) and involve co-ordination among areas such as industrial development, city planning, water resources development and transport policies. Air quality management aims to preserve air quality by prescribing the tolerated degree of pollution, leaving it to the local authorities and polluters to devise and implement actions which will ensure that this degree of pollution will not be exceeded.

Typical measures in air quality management include enactment of an extended public mass transport system, land-use planning measures, new technologies, reduction of traffic and 'shut-down' of factories during unfavourable weather conditions, or of reduction measures at sources.

Box 7.3 *Lead and children's health*

The impact on health of lead has been underestimated, especially for children.[63] In many cities in developed and developing countries, there are particular groups of children with a very high exposure to lead. In some of them, it has been shown (by epidemiology) that a considerable proportion of the child population is suffering from impairment of learning ability, intelligence (including their IQ lowered by several points) and fine motor co-ordination and behavioural problems because of exposure to lead. This situation is also to be expected in those cities with high lead exposure where similar studies have not been performed. The impact of lead on child health continues to affect them into adulthood; a study of young adults that had been exposed to higher levels of lead in their infancy found that they tended to be under-achievers: they had a lower standing in school, increased absenteeism, less vocabulary and lower grammatical reasoning scores, poorer eye-hand co-ordination and longer reaction times.[64]

There has been an enormous increase in the use of lead during the 20th century, although patterns of lead emission to the atmosphere have changed. The initial increase due to smelting and coal-burning that started with the Industrial Revolution has been checked by improved industrial controls, but the decrease in those emissions has been more than offset by emissions from motor vehicle exhaust fumes. Today, about 80–90 per cent of airborne lead that can be traced to its source comes from motor vehicles that use gasoline with a lead additive. The degree of pollution from this source differs from country to country, depending on motor vehicle density and the extent of efforts to reduce the lead content of petrol and to promote the use of lead-free gasoline.

The use of a lead additive in gasoline has been declining in most countries in the North and this has meant a substantial decrease of blood lead levels in the general population. However, leaded fuel is still widely used in many countries, especially in the South. Given that in these countries poor nutritional status and a poor home environment may potentiate the effect of lead exposure in a great proportion of children, there is an urgent need for regulation and the replacement of leaded fuels.

Reducing children's exposure to lead is important not only for the obvious ethical reasons – what right does any society have to put into children's environments a toxic substance that causes loss of intelligence and behavioural difficulties? – but also for the cost-savings it brings in having fewer children needing special care and the economic benefits of children reaching higher educational standards. For instance, an estimate in the USA suggests that the average benefits of preventing blood lead levels from rising above 24 ug/dl is $1,300 in medical costs avoided and $3,331 in special education costs avoided.

CHILDREN

Introduction

The health status of children in any urban area is one of the most sensitive indicators of the quality of housing and basic services. It is also an indicator of the extent to which there is a 'healthy city' spirit and awareness within the city which can identify and act on serious hazards for children. This is because children are particularly vulnerable to most infectious and parasitic diseases, chemical pollutants and physical hazards. Their immune systems take time to develop the capacity to protect them from common infectious diseases. They remain particularly vulnerable to diarrhoea, pneumonia and malaria which are among the major causes of child death worldwide, yet children should not die from these diseases since all three are generally easily cured, if diagnosed in time and treated appropriately. Unless immunized, they also remain particularly vulnerable to diseases such as measles, polio, tuberculosis, tetanus and whooping cough (pertussis); measles also remains among the most prominent causes of child death. Children are also particularly susceptible to many chemical pollutants, as in the case of lead, as described in Box 7.3 (above).

The quality of the environment into which an infant is born exerts a powerful influence on whether she or he will survive their first birthday and, if they do, their subsequent physical and mental development. In families and societies with the knowledge and resources to ensure that households have a safe and secure home within a well-managed city, less than one infant in 100 dies before their first birthday; and most such deaths are not linked to the quality of the home and its surrounds or to health care provision but to conditions the infants had at birth – for instance, a congenital deformity, a genetic disease, a birth injury or physical immaturity.

A good quality shelter minimizes or reduces most of the hazards that can threaten the life or health of a child at all stages in their development. A commitment to child health means that hazards are minimized in other places where children spend significant parts of their day – for instance, play groups, day-care centres and all forms of schools, and in the places where they play. The paths, roads and forms of transport they use to get to and from these places must also be safe. Within societies with sufficient resources and a commitment to child health, individual, household, community and state actions combine to ensure that hazards for children are minimized. They also ensure that the health impact of injuries or illnesses are minimized and that parents (or carers) can cope with the cost of their child's illness or injury. Emergency services can ensure rapid and effective response when children become seriously ill or are injured. Parents are also able to take time off work to look after a sick or injured child without a loss of income that threatens the health or survival of the household.

However, a large part of the world's children do not live in societies with such provisions for child health. For instance, in the South, hundreds of millions of children live in overcrowded, poor quality shelters in urban areas where these basic supports for child health are not present. They live, several persons to each room, in shelters with no piped water and inadequate or no provision for sanitation. They often live in illegal settlements where the household in which they live is under a constant threat of eviction. In most such settlements, accidental fires are commonplace as many shelters are made of temporary and flammable materials. But there are no emergency services that will react rapidly to help put out fires, treat those injured and transport those needing hospital treatment to a hospital. There is often no health service to which people can turn when their children are sick or injured. In circumstances such as these, it is common for one child in ten to die before their fifth birthday; among the poorest families living within urban areas with the least provision to protect the infant from infectious and parasitic diseases and where health services are most inadequate or non-existent for both mothers and infants, one child in two may die before their fifth birthday. *The proportion of infants who die from infectious and parasitic diseases among households living in the poorest quality housing in Africa, Asia and Latin America is several hundred times higher than for households in West Europe or North America.* Of the 12.2 million children under the age of five who die each year in the South, 97 per cent of these deaths would not have occurred if these children had been born and lived in the developed countries with the best health and social conditions.[65]

The Preventable Causes of Death, Illness and Injury

Where reliable data are available on the causes of death among children living in urban areas or particular districts within urban areas that have poor quality housing and a lack of basic services, what is noticeable is not only the large number of children who die but also the extent to which they die from diseases that are easily prevented or cured. The best examples are diarrhoea and acute respiratory infections. Diarrhoeal diseases remain among the major causes of infant and child death in many urban areas in the South, but with good housing conditions and health care, they should not. They are usually caused by one of a number of food or waterborne pathogens. The risk of dying from diarrhoea is greatly increased in malnourished children.[66] However, many of the deaths from diarrhoea could be avoided by giving the sick child increased fluids to drink and by continuing to feed them.

Acute respiratory infections, mostly pneumonia, remain the largest cause of death in many urban areas,[67] yet such infections are easily cured, if diagnosed quickly and treated properly. Children are more vulnerable to respiratory disease and a child who is weakened by frequent illness and poor nutrition is still more vulnerable. A child who contracts bronchitis or pneumonia in the South is 50 times more likely to die than a child in Europe or North America.[68] For those who survive, growth is often set back; a severe respiratory infection will weaken a child's body, making her or him more susceptible to further infection and further malnutrition.

Measles and tetanus also remain major causes of child death yet both are preventable by immunization. However, immunization programmes have led to a large decrease in the deaths of children under five from measles and of newborn infants from tetanus between 1983 and 1993, largely because of immunization of children under one against measles and tetanus immunization of pregnant women.

Tens of millions of urban households use coal or biomass fuels on open fires or inadequately vented stoves for cooking and, where needed, heating. Infants and young children may be heavily exposed because they remain with their mothers – for instance, strapped to their backs while fires are tended and cooking done. Exposure to pollutants may retard growth and lead to increased numbers of acute respiratory infections, including pneumonia and, in adulthood, the development of chronic obstructive lung disease.[69] Reducing indoor air pollution from very high to low levels may reduce the incidence of childhood pneumonia and the number of deaths it causes. This will require intervention studies.

It is also common for a high proportion of all children in poor urban settlements in Africa, Asia and Latin America to have intestinal worm infections. For instance, a study in one subdistrict in East Jakarta in 1985 showed that 69 per cent of the under-five population were infected with *Ascaris* (round worm) and 11 per cent with *Trichuris* (whip worm) while 43 per cent were infected with both.[70] Many other studies in low-income settlements lacking basic services have found a high proportion of young children with intestinal worm infections and often with both round worm and whip worm.[71]

Where progress has been made in reducing the incidence or health impact of infectious and parasitic diseases, accidents are often found to be a major cause of injury or death among children. Even in homes in the wealthy nations of the North, injuries occurring within the home are among the major causes of hospital admissions for young children. In the South, injuries account for more than a fifth of deaths among boys and a seventh of deaths of girls.[72] An analysis of accidents in children in ten nations in the South in 1982 found they were the main cause of death for 5–9-year-olds and 10–14-year-olds.[73] Injuries from falls are common in substandard housing and in settlements with no all-weather paths or roads and on sites on steep slopes and children are particularly at risk. A survey of 599 'slum' children of under five in Rio de Janeiro found that accidents accounted for 19 per cent of all health problems; most reported accidents were falls (66 per cent), cuts (17 per cent) and burns (10 per cent).[74]

How Health Risks Change with Age

As children grow and develop, certain risks diminish – for instance, as the immune system of an infant or young child develops to protect them from various communicable diseases or as they are immunized. The transfer of infants and young children from exclusive reliance on breast milk to powdered milk and to semi-solid and solid foods is also hazardous, unless the food and bottled milk can be prepared and stored, free from pathogens. Housing where food and milk can be prepared hygienically (and, where necessary, with water that has been boiled) and stored in fridges and where children's bottles, bowls, mugs and feeding utensils can be easily washed and, where necessary, sterilized, greatly reduces this risk.

The increasing mobility of the infant and young child as they learn to crawl and then walk, and the natural curiosity of a healthy child also means a much increased level of risk in poor quality housing and living environments. For instance, a home with inadequate provision for washing and sanitation increases greatly the risk of the child ingesting faecal pathogens. Objects with faecal matter on them may be found on the floor or around the house and put by the child in its mouth. Or a young child's hands may be contaminated with faecal matter as it plays in the area around the house. Infants and children are particularly at risk from serious injuries from falls down steps or slopes or coming into contact with fires, stoves or hot water. Burns and scalds are particularly common in crowded, cramped conditions where families of five or more share one small room and where it is almost impossible to protect infants and children from open fires or stoves. Accidental poisonings are also common since, in such circumstances, it is difficult to keep items such as household bleach, kerosene and other poisons away from children's reach. The health impact of accidents is also compounded by the lack of a health service which can rapidly provide emergency treatment, followed by longer term treatment and care.[75]

As children grow older, so they learn to avoid some of the most serious hazards. For instance, as children learn about the importance of handwashing after defecation and of personal hygiene in general, so may the risk of contracting various water-borne or water-washed diseases diminish. Although children can learn to avoid hazards from a relatively early age, their natural curiosity, increased mobility and learning through risk-taking exposes them to new hazards in the places where they play. Where garbage is uncollected, sanitation inadequate (so sites around the house are contaminated with faecal matter) and drainage inadequate, their play with soil, water and waste materials in the areas around the house can be particularly hazardous. For older children, accidents outside the home are often a major cause of injury or premature death. For instance, motor accidents were found to be the leading cause of death for 5–14-year-olds in the state capitals of Brazil.[76] In cities in both the North and the South with high levels of violence, homicides can also figure as among the most common causes of death for older children.[77]

Low-income families are obviously less able to afford the kind of housing that provides children with a safe and stimulating environment. Adults in low-income households are generally more constrained in the time that they can spend with their children, because all adult members have to work (often long hours) to maximize income. This may not pose problems where extended kinship networks, preschool playgroups or child-care centres can provide the supervision and stimulation that infants and young children need. But many poor households lack such support. Young children often remain for several hours each day with little or no adult supervision, or the supervision is entrusted to older siblings who are less able to anticipate and prevent household injuries and have little capacity to act swiftly if the children become sick or injured. Without adult supervision, it is also much more difficult to teach them health-enhancing behaviours – for instance, in regard to defecation and washing habits. Mothers who have to return to work soon after the birth of a child are also less able to continue breastfeeding, except in the very rare instances where employers make special provision to help them do so.

But children need more than 'safe open play spaces' and school yards. They need places that are exciting and diverse, where they can direct their own play. This is also important for learning about social co-operation; children need time alone with their peers and with different age groups.[78] The influence of play on child development includes the development of motor skills, communication, creativity, logical thinking, emotional development, and social and socialized behaviour.[79] Much of children's play is a training ground for their later participation with adults in work; it is also a central part of learning about the properties of materials and developing physical skills.[80] The need for special provision for children's play is particularly important in places where there is little open space – for instance, densely populated urban areas. It becomes all the more urgent where there is also a need to keep children away from roads and other hazardous places.

Children Particularly at Risk

It is not only certain age groups among 'children' who are particularly at risk. There are also differentials by gender and particular risks faced by children who begin work early or who are street children.

In many societies, girls' nutritional and health needs receive a lower priority than boys within the household. Girls' health problems may also receive less attention than boys', with proportionately more male children being treated sooner in health services and with more financial resources allocated to their health. These discriminatory practices have serious implications as to how girl infants and young children can cope with disease and the impact of environmental hazards. Some societies also practice female infanticide in order to save scarce resources for a desired future male child.[81]

UNICEF have a term 'children in especially difficult circumstances' to include working children, street children, abused, neglected and abandoned children, children caught in armed conflict and children affected by disasters.[82] It is obvious that these usually face particularly serious health problems.

In regard to street children, most are 'children on the street' who have strong family connections, may attend school and in most cases return home at the end of the day. Here the additional health problems associated with being street children centre on the hazards to which they are exposed during their work – for instance, traffic accidents, especially for those selling goods to passing motorists on roads or highways. For 'children of the street' (with family ties but who visit their families only infrequently) and 'abandoned children', who see the street as their home and seek shelter, food and a sense of community among their companions there, the hazards to health are obviously much greater. For instance, the work they undertake may be particularly hazardous and they often have no adult to whom to turn when sick or injured. They generally have very poor quality accommodation (often sleeping in the open or in public places) and great difficulties in getting access to places to wash, obtain drinking water, latrines and health services. They are also exposed to child abuse, not least when child prostitution turns out to be one of the more dependable ways of ensuring sufficient income for survival.

There are also other children in especially difficult circumstances who face particular risks. For instance, a study in Bombay identified children of pavement dwellers and construction workers and 'hotel boys' as particularly vulnerable, along with street children.[83] For instance, the children of construction workers who live on site lack access to schools, day care, health facilities, water and sanitation, and life on construction sites also poses particular hazards for children.[84]

Tens of millions of children are exposed to serious health hazards at work. It is difficult to specify at what point children's work ceases to be a natural apprenticeship to the responsibilities of adulthood and becomes excessive and exploitative. But certainly, for millions of children, their work burden reaches the point where it impedes their development. An estimated 80 million children between the ages of 10 and 14 undertake work that is either so long or so onerous that it interferes with their normal physical and mental development.[85]

For children working in industry, there are many environmental hazards.

> ...children are more susceptible than adults to accident, injury and industrial disease. Small, weak and inexperienced workers are more at risk from dangerous machinery and materials, heavy weights and the heat of industrial processes; and more prone to chemical poisoning and respiratory complaints caused by the many air-borne hazards.[86]

Excessive work usually means not only exposure to physical and often chemical hazards but also limited school attendance or early drop out from school.

Cities Should be Safe for Children

Infectious and parasitic diseases should not figure as major causes of infant and child deaths. The toll that injuries take on infant and child health in the home, neighbourhoods and other places where children spend part of their day can often be considerably cut. Many of the interventions that reduce the toll that such diseases and injuries take on children are not costly. Indeed, the integrated management of childhood illness is considered to be among the most cost-effective interventions in reducing the global burden of disease in both low-income and middle-income countries.[87] Obviously, the greatest difficulties in funding such interventions come in the nations with the lowest incomes and the least prosperous economies and in the urban districts with the lowest income inhabitants who have the least possibility of repaying the cost of the needed interventions. But there are many examples of successful interventions to prevent disease and reduce disease and injury burdens for children which required modest levels of external funding, including numerous examples of community-based initiatives which received some support from local NGOs or Foundations (and sometimes from municipalities, government agencies or international agencies). Many also recovered most of their costs. There is also the fact that much child illness and death is preventable at low cost as in the vaccine preventable diseases and in addressing micronutrient deficiencies such as iodine, vitamin A, iron and zinc. The cost of curing or controlling many of the infectious and parasitic diseases associated with poor quality living environments is also very low.[88] But what is needed is the political will to make child health and development a priority backed up with increased support for the most effective interventions and for the social and health workers who are critical to the effectiveness of many of these interventions.

WOMEN

Introduction

Since any person's health is so influenced by their income level, the assets they own and their level of education, the discrimination that most women face in labour markets, in the right to own or purchase assets and in access to education also means worse health. In most countries, women's average incomes are substantially lower than men's and women own only a small proportion of all capital assets.[89] Two-thirds of the world's illiterate adult population are women.[90]

In most urban centres, women face five particular disadvantages for health. The first is that bearing and giving birth to children is very hazardous to both mother and child without a healthy, secure home and good quality health services. Second, not only are health care services often inadequate but they are also inappropriate to women's health needs. Third, managing the household and rearing children – tasks usually undertaken by women – are arduous and often dangerous where housing conditions are poor and there is inadequate provision for water supply, sanitation, drainage and health care. Fourth, there is the discrimination that women face in access to education, labour markets and in resource allocations within households, each with obvious implications for health. Finally, a large and probably growing proportion of women in urban areas are killed or injured by violence, including domestic violence. More details of each of these are given below.

Reproductive Health

Women are at risk not only from complications from pregnancy and childbirth. They must also deal with unwanted pregnancy, suffer the complications of unsafe abortion, bear most of the burden of contraception and are more exposed to contracting and suffering the complications of reproductive tract infections, particularly sexually transmitted diseases.

Every year, more than half a million women die of causes related to pregnancy and childbirth[91] while 23 million suffer serious complications with childbirth and 15 million suffer long-term morbidity.[92] Virtually all those who die are in Africa, Asia and Latin America. Inadequate contraception, unsafe abortion, lack of sanitation and inferior health care are some of the reasons why the risk of dying in childbirth is over 100 times greater among poor women in the South than among women in the North.[93] Services for childbearing women remain woefully inadequate in preventing death and treating morbidity.[94] In many instances, the problem for maternal health is not the absence of health services but their poor quality, with inadequate management of complications being responsible for many maternal deaths.[95]

The risk for a mother of dying during pregnancy or childbirth in a poor urban district can be 1000 times or more than for a mother from a wealthy household living in a healthy environment with good quality health services and antenatal and post-natal care. Women's reproductive system is particularly sensitive to adverse environmental conditions; every stage of the multi-step process of reproduction can be disrupted by external environmental agents, leading to increased risk of abortion, birth defects, fetal growth retardation and perinatal death.[96]

In addition, a woman's health and nutritional status substantially affect her capacity to cope with difficulties during pregnancy, childbirth and the post-partum period, to produce a strong healthy baby and to breastfeed and care for it.[97] In some countries, gender-based discrimination in the quantity and quality of food available to women compared to men and thus in women's nutritional status from infancy to adulthood, put pregnant women at even higher risk.[98] A combination of poverty and of the discrimination against women mean that over half of all pregnant women in the South are anaemic and this is one of the causes of high maternal morbidity and mortality. Hookworm infections are a further problem as millions of pregnant women in urban (and rural) areas are infected with resulting chronic blood loss and gradual depletion of the body's iron stores.

Reproductive health implies much more than better health services for pregnant women and for women with young children. It implies equity and respect for the rights of women at all ages. It implies sexual and reproductive health programmes for young people to lessen the health risks that female children and adolescents face in terms of unwanted pregnancies (and all the life-threatening dangers that this can bring such as unsafe abortions) and pressure from older men to have sex with them. Health services for younger women are also important because without them, many are severely anaemic, malnourished and stunted, pregnant or infected with sexually transmitted diseases when they use family planning and maternal and child health services for the first time.[99]

Reproductive health programmes should also promote responsible sexual behaviour among men.[100] Worldwide, the disease burden of sexually transmitted diseases in women is more than five times that in men. Most sexually transmitted diseases are transmitted more readily from men to women than from women to men. For instance, the transmission of HIV from men to women is 2–4 times more efficient than from women to men. By the year 2000, over 13 million women are likely to be infected with HIV. Women with sexually transmitted diseases are more likely than men to have no obvious symptoms of disease and are less likely to seek treatment, resulting in chronic infections with more long-term complications. Women usually face more difficulties than men in getting access to appropriate treatment for sexually transmitted diseases and have to face societal attitudes that stigmatize women but not men when they seek treatment. Women are also put at risk by the irresponsible sexual behaviour of their partners; studies in some countries have shown that up to 30 per cent of HIV infections are occurring in women whose only risk behaviour was sexual intercourse with a single male partner who had had unprotected sex with other partners.

Health Care

The inadequacies in health care exist not only for reproductive health but for other aspects of women's health. For instance, child health programmes have invested little in ending the discriminatory and abusive treatment of girls by families, communities and health services.[101] Preventive health services generally have no interest in women who are sterile or beyond reproductive age, as can be seen by the amount of preventable cancers and sexually transmitted diseases that women have. In general, health-care systems have been slow to recognize the nutritional and health problems that are faced by elderly women. Most health-care services have failed to recognize the extent of violence suffered by women and even where they do, they have often found it difficult to develop appropriate responses.

Even where health services are provided, the women for whom they are intended are rarely consulted about the most appropriate designs and services – for instance, about the most appropriate locations and about opening hours.[102] Working women often have difficulty using health services, as they are only open during working hours.

Many women accept ill health, ignoring painful and debilitating symptoms, because in their culture a woman is expected to endure without complaint or perhaps because they have no alternative.[103] Women are often found to underuse health services. Although they suffer from levels of disease comparable to those of men – and even higher in the area of reproductive health – they wait longer than men before seeking treatment and have difficulty leaving their families and household duties behind if long hospitalization is required. For instance, one study found that only 16 per cent of the people attending malaria clinics were women, yet surveys showed no significant difference between men and women in susceptibility to malaria.[104]

Managing Households and Child Rearing

Women are generally far more severely affected than men by poor and overcrowded housing conditions, inadequate provision of water, sanitation, health care, schools and nurseries because they take most responsibility for looking after infants and children, caring for sick family members and managing the household.[105] It is generally women who are responsible for the disposal of human wastes when provision for sanitation is inadequate and this exposes them to diseases associated with human excreta. The fact that women take most responsibility for child care means that they also have to cope with most of the illnesses and injuries from which infants and children suffer. Caring for the sick and handling and laundering soiled clothes are particularly hazardous tasks when water supplies and sanitation and washing facilities are inadequate.[106] The people within a household who are responsible for water collection and its use for laundry, cooking and domestic hygiene also suffer most if supplies are contaminated and difficult to obtain, and these people are generally women or girls. Women often suffer more than men from chronic back pain because they have to collect water from wells or public standpipes; policy-makers almost always have piped water systems in their homes and they forget just how heavy water is and the immense physical effort needed to fetch and carry enough water for a household's needs even from standpipes 20–30 metres from a house. As noted earlier, tuberculosis is a particularly serious problem among low-income urban dwellers living in overcrowded conditions and suffering from undernutrition. Women seem to be most vulnerable to tuberculosis in their early and reproductive years and the biological changes that occur in those years may make women more likely to progress to tuberculosis once infected. Tuberculosis is also an indirect or contributory cause to many maternal deaths.

A large proportion of urban households in the South use coal, wood or other smoky fuels for cooking and, where needed, heating in open fires or poorly vented stoves. It is generally women (or girls) who take responsibility for tending the fire and doing the cooking and who inhale larger concentrations of pollutants over longer periods.[107] It is usually women who take responsibility for firewood gathering and subsistence crop and livestock production in the millions of urban households where these are important components of households' livelihoods; rarely, if ever, do urban housing schemes make allowances for these activities and urban land use and zoning regulations usually discriminate against such tasks.[108]

As Crewe notes:

> The main reason why household energy management, indoor air pollution and other health consequences of unsafe kitchens are receiving so little attention is that the managers of energy resources in households are almost always women. In all cultures women's status tends to be lower than men's, which often means that neither women's household problems nor the technical expertise they can bring to bear on these problems are taken seriously enough. Moreover, household work everywhere is unpaid, invisible, low-status work which is not included in national economic statistics. Yet the enormous amount of time it takes a woman to do this work has significant implications for the health of her entire family.[109]

The fact that both governments and development assistance agencies have been slow to recognize and act on women's needs and priorities is reflected in government-provided services or housing programmes: the practical needs of those responsible for child care and household management (overwhelmingly women) are rarely given the priority they deserve. For instance, there is an urgent need in many low-income urban settlements for good quality day-care facilities that combine a commitment to child health and to providing children with a stimulating, healthy and enjoyable environment with providing greater possibilities for women to work.

Such day-care facilities are of particular importance where women's incomes are important components of household incomes. Obviously, they have even greater importance for single-parent households (most of them headed by women). In many low-income urban settlements 30 or more per cent of households are headed by women either because a male partner is temporarily absent or because of separation or death.[110] The woman is often the only income-earner in the household and has to combine income-earning with child-rearing and household management. Thus, she faces all the problems noted already concerning the inadequacies in provision for infrastructure and services and the discrimination that prohibits the kinds of income-earning activities in which women commonly engage. In addition, in many urban areas, the safety net of kinship or the extended family which can make it easier for mothers with the triple responsibility of household management, child rearing and earning an income to manage either does not exist or has been eroded.

In general, the lower the income of a household, the poorer the quality and size of the home with both the children and the parents subject to a higher level of stressors such as higher and more continuous noise levels, overcrowding, air, soil or water pollution, inappropriate design, inadequate maintenance of the physical structure and inadequate services. Such housing environments tend to ensure a higher incidence of mental disorders and social pathologies, and, obviously, the adults that spend most of their time in the home looking after children (generally women) are most at risk.[111] Community surveys in the South usually find more women than men suffering from some form of mental illness but more men getting treatment. Depression and anxiety are mainly a problem in adults and women suffer from these disorders at approximately double the rate of men.[112] Worldwide, it seems that women are disproportionately affected by problems of mental health, but this is linked to situations of alienation, powerlessness and poverty and to such problems as domestic violence and sexual abuse and not to any innate inability to cope.[113]

Gender Inequality

Improving women's health depends not only on improved health services, housing and basic services – what are often termed their practical needs – but also on meeting their strategic needs such as increased access to resources, education and employment, and to the promotion of their human rights and fundamental freedoms. Illiteracy among women means not only the inability to read and write but also the denial of information that is central to their understanding of how their body functions and how they can prevent diseases and protect themselves – and, for those with families, also protect their children.

Gender inequality is even a serious problems for unborn girls in many societies as the high value placed on sons also means discrimination with serious health consequences for women. In extreme cases, it may lead to prenatal sex selection in favour of boys or female infanticide. Men and boys often receive preference in food within households and with expenditure on medicines and health care when sick or injured.

In many societies, women face discrimination in obtaining accommodation in urban areas – for instance, that prevent or inhibit them from owning or purchasing land for housing or obtaining a credit to purchase or build a house or getting access to a public programme or to renting private sector accommodation.[114] Although this discrimination affects single women, it usually affects women-headed households more in their search for an adequate shelter and basic services for their household. For instance, women-headed households often cannot successfully apply for housing credit or for a place in a public housing or serviced site programme. In some programmes, only men could apply on behalf of a household. In others, proof of formal, stable, full-time employment is required but women-headed households are rarely able to find a formal job, given both the discrimination against women in the job market and the fact that a formal job is very difficult to combine with rearing and caring for infants and children.[115] Discrimination against women in access to employment and in wage levels also means they have less income and thus less to spend on housing, and less choice within housing markets.

One consequence of the discrimination that women face in urban labour markets is their concentration in the informal sector, including small, under-regulated enterprises. These are enterprises that usually avoid meeting occupational health and safety regulations, so many entail exposure to carcinogenic chemicals, excessive noise, health and humidity, physical strain and eye fatigue. Women are often preferred to men in labour-intensive assembly plants because lower wages can be paid, usually justified by the claim that they are secondary income earners when many are their household's main or only income earner. In many cities, prostitution becomes a common means of livelihood for low-income women, underpinned by the lack of less dangerous income-earning opportunities and often by coercive social structures.

Violence

Violence against women is reaching alarming proportions in many cities in both the North and the South. Such violence is not confined to particular income groups, cultures or ages, and is now understood to be embedded in the unequal power relationships between men and women.[116] Only recently has the significance of violence within public health been recognized – for instance, as domestic violence and rape were found to be significant causes of female morbidity and mortality. The 1993 World Development Report suggests that women aged 15–44 face a heavier health burden from rape and domestic violence than they do to breast cancer, cervical cancer, obstructed labour, heart disease, respiratory infections, motor vehicle accidents or war.[117] In the North, rape and domestic violence account for almost a fifth of the health burden suffered by women aged between 15 and 44.[118] In some countries, domestic violence has become the leading cause of injury for women within this age group. For instance, in the United States battering is the leading cause of injury to women and accounts for nearly one-third of all emergency room visits by women.[119] Surveys in various countries in the South found that between a third and half (or more) of women surveyed report being beaten by their partner.[120]

Both men and women experience violence in many forms and both suffer considerable damage to their health because of it. But the nature of the violence to which they are exposed is almost always different. Although in the North and in much of the South, murder rates are higher among men than women, there are also societies where men murdering their wives or burning them for not bringing enough dowry remain among the principal causes of murder.[121] The causes of violence also differ, as do the impacts on their lives. Women are generally exposed to violence at all levels, from domestic violence within the home, intimidation and sexual harassment in the workplace, and settings outside the home and workplace where women are subject to random violence. There is also the large-scale, systematic violence against women so often found in situations of conflict and mass movement of people. In urban areas where women are at risk from violence, this greatly restricts their mobility, which further weakens their position within the labour market and restricts their opportunities for visiting family and friends and for leisure.[122] In virtually all urban centres, the threat of violence places more restrictions on women than men.

Ways Forward

What is sought for women in urban areas (and rural areas) is health security which includes not only accessible and affordable health care that addresses women's reproductive, sexual and other health needs but also adequate nutrition, access to information and education, freedom from violence and the right to work in safe environments. This requires action to tackle the underlying causes – for instance, the rising incidence of poverty and homelessness in many urban areas and the underlying causes of the growth in violence which include growing inequality, the easy availability of guns, substance abuse and the witnessing of acts of violence.[123]

The basis for this is women's right to health and to freedom from discrimination. But there are also important advantages for other groups when these rights are respected. For instance, healthy and adequately fed mothers produce healthier children; malnutrition and ill health in mothers can initiate a cycle of ill health in their children, as many of these women will bear low birth-weight babies whose future growth and development will be jeopardized from the start. The half a million women who die of causes related to pregnancy and childbirth each year leave some 1 million children without mothers.[124] Box 7.4 below points to the steps needed in moving towards a gender-aware city.

If women's health needs are to be addressed, the professionals responsible for health care and for other aspects of the urban environment must utilize more par-

---

Box 7.4 *Moving towards a gender-aware city*

Women and men have different roles and responsibilities – within households, communities and the labour market. In these different roles, women and men have different access to and control over resources. Urban policies, planning and management must contribute to a reduction in gender-based inequities and ensure that women and men get equal access to credit (for housing or small-scale enterprises), vocational training and government housing schemes. But they must also respond to the fact that women and men have different needs and priorities. Programmes or projects that target 'the household', 'the community', 'the neighbourhood' or 'low-income groups' must recognize that the needs and priorities of women within each household, community or neighbourhood or within low-income groups will differ from those of men.

Integrating gender issues into urban policy, planning and management will make urban development more effective. First, it helps ensure that limited resources are used more effectively, as both women's and men's needs and priorities are addressed. Second, it facilitates the active involvement of both women and men in all stages of development which will reduce project failures and wasteful expenditure.

Source: UNCHS, *An Urbanizing World: Global Report on Human Settlements 1996,* Oxford University Press, 1996, drawing from Jo Beall and Caren Levy, *Moving Towards the Gendered City,* Overview paper prepared for the Preparatory Committee for Habitat II, Geneva, 11–22 April 1994

---

ticipatory and qualitative methods of information gathering that allow a more accurate understanding of women's needs and priorities. They need to develop new approaches, especially working with women in low-income settlements, as in the range of innovations developed in Guatemala City within illegal settlements that included women chosen by their surrounding households to be trained as health promoters and new models of community-based day care.[125] There also needs to be more collaboration between the different sectoral programmes such as programmes for family planning, maternal and child health and the control of sexually transmitted diseases and good liaison between the police, legal services, NGOs and community organizations, if domestic violence and sexual abuse is to be addressed.

NOTES AND REFERENCES

1   See, for instance, The Water Program, *Water Efficiency: A Resource for Utility Managers, Community Planners and other Decision Makers*, Rocky Mountain Institute, Snowmass, 1991

2   See, for instance, Chapters 8 and 9 of UNCHS (Habitat), *An Urbanizing World: Global Report on Human Settlements, 1996*, Oxford University Press, Oxford and New York, 1996

3   The Harvard Working Group on New and Resurgent Diseases, 'New and resurgent diseases: a failure of attempted eradication', *The Ecologist*, Vol 25, No 1 January 1995 pp 21–26

4   World Bank, *World Development Report 1993; Investing in Health*, published for the World Bank by Oxford University Press, Oxford, 1993

5   UNCHS (Habitat) 1996, op cit

6   Avramov, Dragana, *Homelessness in the European Union: Social and Legal Context for Housing Exclusion in the 1990s*, FEANTSA (European Federation of National Organizations Working with the Homeless), Brussels, 1995

7   Avramov 1995, op cit

8   UNCHS (Habitat) 1996, op cit

9   Cohen, Larry and Susan Swift, 'A public health approach to the violence epidemic in the United States', *Environment and Urbanization*, Vol 5, No 2, October 1993, pp 50–66

10 UNICRI (United Nations International Crime and Justice Research Institute) (1995), *Criminal victimisation of the developing world*, Rome, drawing from UNICRI and Ministry of Justice of the Netherlands, international survey of victims of crime (1988–1994), based on a sample of 74,000 persons in 39 countries

11 UNICRI 1995, op cit

12 UNICRI 1995, op cit

13 See, for instance, Caldeira, Teresa, 'Building up walls: the new pattern of spatial segregation in São Paulo', *International Social Science Journal*, No 147, March 1996

14 WHO, *Healthy Cities for Better Life*, Information Pack for World Health Day – 7 April 1996, Geneva

15 Giroult, Eric R J, 'Innovations in West and North Africa', *World Health* issue on Healthy Cities, 49th Year, No 1, January–February 1996, pp 11

16 Dupriez, Agnèz, 'The Quebec Network', *World Health* issue on Healthy Cities, 49th Year, No 1, January–February 1996 , pp 18–19; WHO, *Healthy Cities for Better Life*, Information Kit prepared for World Health Day 1996, WHO, Geneva, 1996

17 Black, David, 'Glasgow: working together to make a healthier city', *World Health* issue on Healthy Cities, 49th Year, No 1, January–February 1996, pp 22–23

18 Werna, Edmundo and Trudy Harpham, 'The Chittagong Healthy City project', *World Health* issue on Healthy Cities, 49th Year, No 1, January–February 1996, pp 24–25

19 Paixao Bretas, Paulo Roberto,'Participative budgeting in Belo Horizonte: democratization and citizenship', *Environment and Urbanization*, Vol 8, No 1, April 1996

20 Doris Balvin Diaz, José Luiz Lopez Follegatti and Micky Hordijk, 'Innovative environmental management in Ilo, Peru', *Environment and Urbanization*, Vol 8, No 1, April 1996

21 This is a private foundation established by a successful printing firm in Cali which pioneered programmes to support the development of micro-enterprises and which has also supported many other social programmes

22   The Harvard Working Group on New and Resurgent Diseases, 'New and resurgent diseases: a failure of attempted eradication', *The Ecologist*, Vol 25, No 1, January 1995, pp 21–26

23   WHO, 'The World Health Report 1996: fighting disease, fostering development', Document prepared for the 49th World Health Assembly. A49/3, 1996

24   Garrett, Laurie, 'The return of infectious disease', *Foreign Affairs*, January/February 1996, pp 65–79

25   WHO unpublished data. See also PAHO, *El colera en las Americas*, Informe No 10, Washington DC, June 1994 quoted in Satcher, David, 'Emerging infectious: getting ahead of the curve', *Emerging Infectious Diseases*, Vol 1, No 1, January 1995, pp 1–6

26   WHO, *A Global Strategy for Malaria Control*, World Health Organization, Geneva, 1993

27   The Harvard Working Group on New and Resurgent Diseases 1995, op cit

28   Institute of Medicine, *Emerging Infectious: Microbial Threats to Health in the United States*, National Academy Press, Washington DC, 1992, quoted in Satcher 1995, op cit

29   Kane, Hal, *The Hour of Departure: Forces that create Refugees and Migrants*, Worldwatch Paper 125, Worldwatch Institute, Washington DC, 1995. Note that this source also estimated that there were 27 million 'internal' refugees who have fled from persecution but have not crossed international boundaries

30   Morse, Stephen S, 'Factors in the emergence of infectious diseases', *Emerging Infectious Diseases*, Vol 1, No 1, January–March 1995, pp 7–14

31   Garrett 1996, op cit

32   National Health Policy Forum, *Emerging and Reemerging Infectious Diseases: A Major Public Health Challenge*, Issue Brief No 686, The George Washington University, Washington DC, 1996

33   The Harvard Working Group on New and Resurgent Diseases 1994, op cit

34   Morse, S S, 'Examining the origins of emerging viruses', in S S Morse (ed), *Emerging Viruses*, Oxford University Press, Oxford, 1993, quoted in The Harvard Group on New and Resurgent Diseases, 1995, op cit

35   Anderson, C, 'Cholera epidemic traced to risk miscalculation', *Nature*, Vol 354, 1991 quoted in Morse, Stephen S, 'Factors in the emergence of infectious diseases', *Emerging Infectious Diseases*, Vol 1, No 1, January–March 1995, pp 7–14

36   WHO, *Our Planet, Our Health*, Geneva, 1992

37   WHO 1992, op cit

38   WHO 1992, op cit

39   The Harvard Working Group on New and Resurgent Diseases 1995, op cit

40   Leduc, James W and Eugene Tikhomirov, 'Global surveillance for recognition and response to emerging diseases', *Annals of the New York Academy of Sciences*, December 1994, pp 341–345

41   WHO, *The World Health Report 1995: Bridging the Gaps*, World Health Organization, Geneva, 1995

42   Cauthen, G M , A Pio and H G ten Dam (1988), *Annual Risk of Tuberculosis Infection*, World Health Organization, Geneva; WHO (1990), *Environmental Health in Urban Development*, Report of a WHO Expert Committee, World Health Organization, Geneva

43   The Harvard Working Group on New and Resurgent Diseases 1995, op cit

44   Morse 1995, op cit

45   Ibid

46   WHO, *Weekly Epidemiological Record* No 34, 26 August 1994

47   Garrett 1996, op cit

48   UNCHS 1996, op cit

49   This draws heavily on Warner, Dennis B, 'Water needs and demands: trends and opportunities from a domestic water supply, sanitation and health perspective', paper presented at the Workshop on 'Scenarios and Water Futures', Stockholm Environment Institute, Boston, 1995

50   WHO, *Community Water Supply and Sanitation: Needs, Challenges and Health Objectives*, A48/INF.DOC./2, 28 April 1995

51   WHO 1995, op cit

52   See, for instance, Warner 1995, op cit and WHO/UNICEF, *Water Supply and Sanitation Sector Monitoring Report 1993*, WHO/UNICEF Joint Monitoring Programme, Geneva, 1993

53   There are exceptions to this, as in public toilets and washing facilities that are run by local NGOs that fully cover operation and maintenance costs through low user charges

54   World Bank, *World Development Report 1994 – Infrastructure for Development*, Oxford University Press, 1994; Bhatia, Ramesh and Malin Falkenmark, 'Water resource policies and the urban poor:

innovative approaches and policy imperatives', a background paper for the Working Group on 'Water and Sustainable Urban Development', International Conference on Water and the Environment: Development Issues, Dublin, 1992

55   Assuming five persons per household, the one million people would live in 200,000 households, with a $1,000 a household cost

56   See, for instance, the discussion of the 'alternative project cycle' in UNDP/World Bank Water and Sanitation Programme, *Proceedings of Workshop on Sanitation for Poor People in Urban Areas*, mimeo, London, 1996

57   For more details, see Mara, Duncan, *Low-Cost Urban Sanitation*, John Wiley & Sons, Chichester, 1996

58   Bhatia and Falkenmark 1992, op cit

59   Espinosa, Lair and Oscar A López Rivera, 'UNICEF's urban basic services programme in illegal settlements in Guatemala City', *Environment and Urbanization*, Vol 6, No 2, October 1994, pp 9-29

60   See, for instance, Orangi Pilot Project, 'NGO Profile: Orangi Pilot Project', *Environment and Urbanization*, Vol 7, No 2, October 1995

61   See, for instance, Mitlin, Diana (1998), *Reaching Low-income Groups with Housing Finance*, IIED, London

62   See, for instance, the Urban Sanitation Improvement Team's programme in Lesotho – Mara 1996, op cit. A study of sanitation options for Kumasi in Ghana also found that providing VIP latrines would require some subsidy, but not if loans were available at a real interest rate of 10 per cent a year over a 20-year period – Whittington, Dale, Donald T Lauria, Albert M Wright, Kyeongae Choe, Jeffrey A Hughes and Venkateswarlu Swarna, *Household Demand for Improved Sanitation Services: a Case Study of Kumasi, Ghana*, UNDP-World Bank Water and Sanitation Program, Washington DC, 1992

63   WHO, *Lead and Health*, one of a special series of reports for local authorities, WHO Regional Office for Europe, Copenhagen, 1996; also WHO, *Our Planet, Our Health*, Report of the WHO Commission on Health and Environment, World Health Organization, Geneva, 1992

64   Needleman, Herbert L, Alan Schell, David Bellinger, Alan Leviton and Elizabeth N Allred, 'The long-term effects of exposure to low doses of lead in childhood: an eleven year follow up report' *The New England Journal of Medicine*, Vol 322, No 2, 1991, pp 83–88

65   WHO, *The World Health Report 1995: Bridging the Gaps*, World Health Organization, Geneva, 1995

66   WHO, *Our Planet, Our Health*, Report of the Commission on Health and Environment, Geneva, 1992

67   WHO, *Programme Report 1988*, Programme for the Control of Acute Respiratory Infections, WHO Document WHO/ARI/89.3, Geneva, 1989; WHO 1992, op cit

68   Pio, A, 'Acute respiratory infections in children in developing countries: an international point of view', *Pediatric Infectious Disease Journal*, Vol 5, No 2, 1986, pp 179–183

69   WHO 1992, op cit

70   Budiman, Gani and others, 'The nutritional and health status of children under five in the sub-district of West Padmangan, Metropolitan Jakarta', paper presented at a workshop on 'Population Health Systems' Interaction in Selected Urban Depressed Communities', March 1988

71   See the many studies cited in Bradley, David, Carolyn Stephens, Sandy Cairncross and Trudy Harpham, *A Review of Environmental Health Impacts in Developing Country Cities*, Urban Management Program Discussion Paper No 6, The World Bank, UNDP and UNCHS (Habitat) Washington DC, 1991

72   WHO 1995, op cit

73   Manciaux, M and C J Romer, 'Accidents in children, adolescents and young adults: a major public health problem' *World Health Statistical Quarterly*, Vol 39, No 3, 1986, pp 227–231

74   Reichenheim, M and T Harpham, 'Child accidents and associated risk factors in a Brazilian squatter settlement' *Health Policy and Planning*, Vol 4, No 2, 1989, pp 162–167

75   Goldstein, Greg, 'Access to life saving services in urban areas' in Hardoy, Jorge E et al (eds) *The Poor Die Young: Housing and Health in Third World Cities*, Earthscan Publications, London, 1990

76   PAHO, 'Research on Health Profiles: Brazil 1984', *Epidemiological Bulletin of the Pan American Health Organization*, Vol 9, No 2, 1988, pp 6–13, quoted in Bradley and others 1991, op cit

77   See, for instance, Stephens, Carolyn, Ian Timaeus, Marco Akerman, Sebastian Avle, Paulo Borlina Maia, Paulo Campanerio, Ben Doe, Luisiana Lush, Doris Tetteh and Trudy Harpham, *Environ-*

ment and Health in Development Countries: an Analysis of Intra-urban Differentials Using Existing Data, London School of Hygiene and Tropical Medicine, London, 1994

78 Hart, Roger A, *Children's Participation; from Tokenism to Citizenship*, Innocenti Essays No 4, UNICEF International Child Development Centre, Florence, 1992

79 Hughes, Bob, 'Children's play – a forgotten right' *Environment and Urbanization*, Vol 2, No 2, October, 1990, pp 58–64

80 Hart 1992, op cit

81 Ennew, Judith and Brian Milne, *The Next Generation; Lives of Third World Children*, Zed Books, London, 1989; see also Allsebrook, Annie and Anthony Swift, *Broken Promise: The World of Endangered Children*, Hodder & Stoughton, 1989

82 UNICEF, 'Children in especially difficult circumstances', document based on the Executive Board Resolutions E/ICEF/1986/CRP 33 and 37 and distributed as CF/PD/PRO-1986-004, New York, 1986

83 Patel, Sheela, 'Street children, hotels boys and children of pavement dwellers and construction workers in Bombay: how they meet their daily needs', *Environment and Urbanization*, Vol 2, No 2, October 1990, pp 9–26

84 ibid

85 UNICEF, *The State of the World's Children 1991*, Oxford University Press, Oxford, 1991

86 Lee-Wright, Peter, *Child Slaves*, Earthscan Publications, London, 1990

87 World Bank, *World Development Report 1993; Investing in Health*, published for the World Bank by Oxford University Press, Oxford, 1993

88 See WHO 1995, op cit for many examples

89 At the outset of the United Nations Decade for Women in 1975, it was noted that women constitute half the world's population but own only 1 per cent of its property – see UNCHS (Habitat), *Women in Human Settlements Development: Getting the Issues Right*, UNCHS (Habitat), Nairobi, 1995. No more recent statistic was found

90 WHO, *Women's Health: Improve our Health, Improve the World*, WHO Position Paper for the Fourth World Conference on Women, Beijing, China, WHO, Geneva, 1995

91 UNICEF, *The State of the World's Children 1991*, Oxford University Press, Oxford, 1991

92 WHO, *Facts and Figures on Women's Health*, Fact Sheet prepared for the United Nations Fourth Conference on Women, WHO, Geneva, 1994

93 WHO 1995, op cit

94 Germain, Adrienne, Sia Nowrojee and Hnin Hnin Pyne, 'Setting a new agenda: sexual and reproductive health and rights', *Environment and Urbanization*, Vol 6, No 2, October 1994, pp 133–154

95 WHO, 'Women and children continue to suffer ill-health', press release drawing on Executive Board Documents: EB/18 – *Maternal and Child Health and Family Planning* and EB93/INF.COD./3 – *Maternal and Child Health and Family Planning*, WHO, Geneva, 1994

96 WHO, *Reproductive Health: a Key to a Brighter Future*, WHO Special Programme of Research Development and Research Training in Human Reproduction, Geneva, 1992

97 World Bank, *World Development Report – 1990; Poverty*, Oxford University Press, Oxford, 1990

98 Mason, John B and S R Gillespie, 'Policies to improve nutrition: what was done in the 1980s', *SCN News*, No 6, United Nations ACC/SCN, Geneva, 1990, pp 7–20

99 Germain and others 1995, op cit

100 See, for instance, Germain and others 1995

101 Germain and others 1995, op cit

102 Moser, Caroline O N, 'Women, human settlements and housing: a conceptual framework for analysis and policy-making', in Caroline O N Moser and Linda Peake (eds), *Women, Housing and Human Settlements*, Tavistock Publications, London and New York, 1987, pp 12–32

103 WHO 1995, op cit

104 WHO, *Facts and Figures on Women's Health*, Fact Sheet prepared for the United Nations Fourth Conference on Women, WHO, Geneva, 1994

105 Beall, Jo and Caren Levy, *Moving Towards the Gendered City*, overview paper prepared for the Preparatory Committee for Habitat II, Geneva, 11–22 April 1994; Moser 1987, op cit; Lee-Smith, Diana and Catalina Hinchey Trujillo, 'The struggle to legitimize subsistence: Women and sustainable development' *Environment and Urbanization*, Vol 4, No 1, April 1992, pp 77–84

106 Sapir, D, *Infectious Disease Epidemics and Urbanization: a Critical Review of the Issues*, paper prepared for the WHO Commission on Health and Environment, Division of Environmental Health, WHO, Geneva, 1990

107 WHO, *Our Planet, Our Health*, Report of the Commission on Health and Environment, Geneva, 1992

108 Lee-Smith and Trujillo 1992, op cit

109 Crewe, Emma, 'Indoor air pollution, household health and appropriate technology; women and the indoor environment in Sri Lanka', in Bonnie Bradford and Margaret A Gwynne (eds), *Down to Earth: Community Perspectives on Health, Development and the Environment*, Kumarian Press, West Hartford, 1995, pp 94–95

110 Moser 1987, op cit

111 WHO 1992, op cit

112 Blue, Ilona and Trudy Harpham, 'The World Bank World Development Report: Investing in Health', reveals the burden of common mental disorders but ignores its implications, *British Journal of Psychiatry* Editorial, Vol 165, 1994, pp 9–12

113 Reported in a WHO Press Release, 7 March 1994, drawing from Dennerstein, L, J Astbury and C Morse, *Psychosocial and Mental Health Aspects of Women's Health*, WHO/FHE/MNH/93.1, WHO, Geneva, 1993

114 UNCHS (Habitat), *An Urbanizing World: Global Report on Human Settlements, 1996*, Oxford University Press, Oxford and New York, 1996

115 Moser 1987, op cit

116 See, for instance, Miranda Davies (ed), *Women and Violence*, Zed Press, London, 1994

117 World Bank, *World Development Report 1993; Investing in Health*, published for the World Bank by Oxford University Press, Oxford, 1993

118 WHO, *Health in Social Development*, WHO Position Paper for the UN Social Summit, WHO, Geneva, 1995

119 Cohen, Larry and Susan Swift, 'A public health approach to the violence epidemic in the United States', *Environment and Urbanization*, Vol 5, No 2, 1993

120 See Heise, Lori, 'Violence against women: the hidden health burden', *World Health Statistics Quarterly*, Vol 46, No 1, 1993, pp 78–85 for a summary of the findings from many different studies

121 UNCHS 1996, op cit

122 Davies 1994, op cit

123 Cohen and Swift 1993, op cit

124 UNICEF 1991, op cit

125 Espinoza and Lopez Rivera 1994, op cit

Chapter 8

Transport: Reducing Automobile Dependence

Peter Newman

(Reprinted from *Environment and Urbanization*, Vol 8, No 1, April 1996, pp 67–92)

Summary: Successful and wealthy cities are usually associated with high levels of automobile use and are struggling to cope with the large economic, social and environmental costs this brings. This paper shows how such cities do not need to depend on high levels of private automobile use and describes how automobile dependence has been reduced in many of the most successful cities in the North and kept relatively low in some of the wealthiest cities in the South.

INTRODUCTION

In the post-war era, falling energy prices and rising car ownership have transformed cities, allowing the increased physical separation of activities and the progressive spread of urban hinterland at lower densities. The dispersal of employment, retailing and service facilities creates an equivalently dispersed pattern of trips that is anathema to public transport operation. Lower average densities mean a decline in pedestrian accessibility, longer trip lengths and reduced catchment populations for public transport routes. The result is increased car dependence, profligate energy use and global pollution.[1]

The extent to which a city's population has become dependent on the use of private automobiles varies greatly, even for cities where the inhabitants have comparable levels of income. A detailed study of 32 major cities in North America, Europe, Australia and Asia found that the cities could be divided into five categories of automobile dependence.[2] Most US and Australian cities were within categories one and two which have a high or very high automobile dependence and, at most, a minor role for public transport, walking and cycling. Most European cities fell into categories three and four which had moderate or low automobile dependence and an important role for public transport. However, Munich and Paris, both among the most prosperous cities in Europe, along with three of the most prosperous Asian cities (Tokyo, Singapore, Hong Kong) had a very low automobile dependence with public transport, walking and cycling more important than cars.

Figure 8.1 plots fuel consumption per person in these 32 cities against urban density (persons per hectare). It shows not only the very great differences in fuel

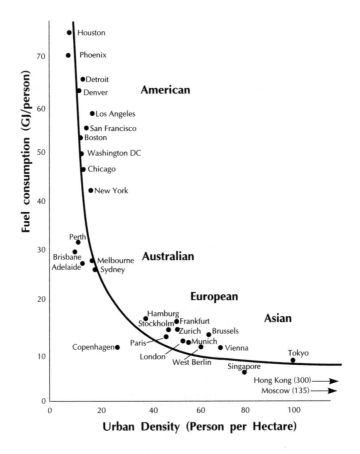

Source: Newman, Peter W G and Jeffrey R Kenworthy (1989),
Cities and Automobile Dependence: an International Sourcebook,
Gower Technical, Aldershot

Figure 8.1 *Population density against gasoline consumption per person for 32 cities (data for 1980)*

consumption per person between cities but emphasizes the fact that wealthy, prosperous and desirable cities can have relatively low levels of fuel consumption per person. For instance, cities such as Vienna, Copenhagen and Stockholm are among the most wealthy and desirable cities in which to live, yet they have one-fifth to one-tenth the level of fuel consumption of US cities. Many European cities have per capita incomes higher than Australian cities and yet have two to three times less use of automobiles.

Table 8.1 below sets out the key data on levels of automobile dependence in the 32 cities. The relatively low levels of automobile dependence in the Asian and some of the European cities are associated with higher population densities, a more efficient public transport system and effective demand management measures. In the three Asian cities in Table 8.1, nearly two-thirds of all travelling in terms of passenger

Table 8.1 *Comparing cities in terms of use of cars and public transport (all statistics for 1980)*

	Wealthy Asian cities	European cities	Australian cities	US cities
Cars per 1000 people	88	328	453	533
Gasoline use per person	5,493	13,820	29,829	58,541
Car vehicle kilometres per person	1,067	3,485	5,794	8,715
The share of public transit in total passenger kilometres	64	25	8	4
Public transport vehicle kilometres of service per person	103	79	56	30
Proportion of workers walking or cycling	25	21	5	5
Metropolitan population density	160	54	14	14
Inner area population density	464	91	24	45
Outer area population density	115	43	13	11

Source: Sustainable Urban Transport Systems Project, ISTP. The Asian cities were Tokyo, Singapore and Hong Kong

kilometres was undertaken on public transport. Many other large cities in Asia also have most passenger movement by public transport – for instance, in the mid-1980s, over two-thirds of all motorized trips in Seoul, Bombay, Shanghai, Manila[3] and Calcutta, as well as Tokyo and Hong Kong were made by bus, rail or subway.[4]

Table 8.1 also shows great contrasts between the cities in terms of the proportion of workers walking or cycling. Cities in China such as Shanghai and Tianjin have among the highest rates of bicycle use in the world,[5] although in both, these rates may be declining rapidly with the rapid growth in the number of automobiles and with transport plans oriented towards increasing automobile use. Most cities in the South also have a high proportion of trips made on foot. But it is not only cities in relatively low-income countries that have a high proportion of trips made by walking or bicycling. For instance, in cities in West Germany in 1989, 27 per cent of trips were made by walking with 10 per cent by bicycle.[6] In many cities in Denmark, France, Sweden, Germany and the Netherlands, a high proportion of all trips are made by bicycle; in Delft (the Netherlands) where special attention has been given to encouraging bicycle use, 43 per cent of trips are made by bicycle and 26 per cent by walking.[7]

The differences in the average population densities of inner and outer areas and in the overall metropolitan densities in Table 8.1 are particularly notable. Many cities or their inner areas – for instance, the historic city and the central business district – have remained what can be termed traditional 'walking cities' with high densities (generally between 100 and 200 persons per hectare) and a mix of land uses which allows a high proportion of all trips to be made on foot. 'Transit cities', which generally have between 70 and 100 persons per hectare, developed as train or tramlines greatly extended the area of cities, although with high-density pockets generally developing around each suburban railway station. 'Automobile-dependent cities' only became possible with high levels of private automobile ownership

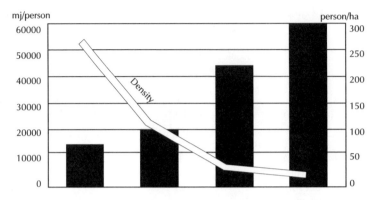

Source: Based on data drawn from Newman, Peter W G and Jeffrey R Kenworthy (1989), *Cities and Automobile Dependence: an International Sourcebook*, Gower Technical, Aldershot

Figure 8.2 *Gasoline use and urban density in New York's centre and its inner and outer area*

and these are characterized by much lower densities (generally between 10 to 20 persons per hectare) and extended, low-density suburbs.

Many cities have a small 'walking city' centre, a distinctive 'transit city' with higher densities and very different transport patterns, surrounded by an 'automobile-dependent city' with uniformly low-density suburbs and high car use.[8] Figure 8.2 shows how gasoline use per person remains relatively low for those in central New York but is nearly twice as high for those in the inner-city area and some five times higher for those in the outer areas. Comparable contrasts were found in a study in Toronto in 1986 where those living in the dense city core travelled on average 9.4 kilometres a day by automobile compared to 13.4 by those in less dense inner suburbs and 21.7 for those in low-density outer suburbs.[9] In most cities, there are also large variations in rates of car ownership and use between high-, middle- and low-income areas.

Although the general trend has been for increasing car dependence and decreasing density, as cities become more prosperous there are many instances of wealthy cities where densities have increased in recent years – for instance, in many historic urban cores or in new urban villages in Europe – and in which public transport and walking or cycling have grown at the expense of car travel.[10] The final section of this paper, on responses to transport problems, has several examples of cities where high quality public transport and other measures to support inner-city development have encouraged more people to live in central areas.

THE COSTS AND BENEFITS OF AUTOMOBILE DEPENDENCE

Few cities have been successful in coping with the rapid growth in the number of road vehicles. The economic costs of congestion in many major cities are estimated in terms of billions of US dollars and any city with serious congestion is likely to lose new investments to other, less congested areas. Congested roads and a lack of an efficient public transit system also mean high costs for low-income households. In large cities lacking effective public transport systems, it is common for low-income households to spend 20 per cent or more of their income on transport and for those living in peripheral areas to spend three to four hours a day travelling to and from work.[11]

Those who own and use road vehicles rarely pay for the full range of social and environmental costs they directly or indirectly generate.[12] For instance, there are the very considerable health costs associated with road vehicles, much of which are borne by those not using motor vehicles. Globally, road traffic accidents are thought to be the leading cause of death among adolescents and young adults.[13] One recent estimate suggested that some 885,000 people die each year from traffic accidents[14] and many times this number are seriously injured.[15] More than a million people have died from traffic accidents within the European Union over the last 20 years and more than 30 million have been injured and/or permanently handicapped.[16] In the United States, more than 40,000 people are killed each year through road accidents and over 3 million injured.[17] However, around three-quarters of all traffic accidents now occur in the South, even though there are still many more road vehicles in the North. There are enormous variations between countries in the rate of road deaths per 100,000 vehicles. For instance, in Japan and among countries in Europe with the lowest road death rates, in 1990 or 1991 there were between 18 and 22 road deaths per 100,000 motor vehicles. The European countries with rates below 22 included the Netherlands, Norway, Sweden, Switzerland and the UK.[18] In some European countries, the rate is three to four times as high. In many countries in the South, the rate is 15–30 times higher. For instance, in Kenya, the rate is some 30 times as high (in 1991 there were 580 road fatalities per 100,000 vehicles).[19] Kenya also has a rate of road deaths per person comparable to that in several European nations despite having far fewer road vehicles per person. In India, there are more fatalities each year from road accidents than in the United States, yet it has fewer than one-twentieth the number of the road vehicles.[20] One estimate for Thailand suggested that around half of the 20,000 lives that are lost each year to accidents are a result of traffic accidents,[21] which would give Thailand a higher fatality rate per person from traffic accidents than most European countries despite having far fewer road vehicles per person. Kuwait and Venezuela have two to three times more people dying from motor vehicle accidents per 100,000 inhabitants than most countries in Europe.[22]

In some of the world's largest cities, thousands of people are killed each year through automobile accidents.[23] Even in cities with very low levels of automobile ownership, such as Delhi and Beijing, several hundred fatalities per year from traffic accidents were being reported in the early 1980s[24] and the number of fatalities has probably risen considerably since then. It is pedestrians or cyclists who are most often killed or injured – and children who are particularly vulnerable.[25] Since it is generally low-income groups who walk or bicycle most, there is also a transfer of costs from the wealthier car owners and car users to the poorer pedestrians and cyclists.

In most cities, road vehicles are a major source of air pollution, particularly in the North. They are also a major source of noise while road and highway construction programmes are among the most disruptive construction projects within cities, and they are often a major cause of forced evictions.[26] Private automobiles are also a major and rapidly growing source of greenhouse gases, as their share in total fossil fuel consumption grows in most countries. And as city transport systems and spatial structures become increasingly automobile oriented, so those who cannot drive or cannot afford motor vehicles become increasingly disadvantaged. This affects in particular the poor, the elderly who do not drive or can no longer drive, and children and youth. There are often particular gender biases as public transport services decline, especially as they become more infrequent outside the 'rush hours' when most people go to and from work. This affects those who use them at other times – for instance, the people who are responsible for looking after the household and children (usually women) or those who combine domestic responsibilities with part-time work (usually women) whose journeys to and from work are outside the conventional rush hours.

It has also become clear that building ever more highways and freeways is no solution. Even if traffic congestion is reduced (which is rarely the case), the level of resource use and greenhouse gas emissions increases greatly. One of the most dramatic differences when comparing national statistics is the scale of the differences in passenger vehicles per 1000 inhabitants. Most of the more populous Asian and African countries have less than one-hundredth of the passenger cars per person of the world's wealthiest nations. Even with major advances in the fuel efficiency of automobiles and in resource conservation – for instance, through high levels of recycling for automobile parts and through automobiles that last longer – the increase in fossil fuel use and resource use, if these countries sought to reach levels of private automobile use comparable to those that are now common in the wealthiest countries, would place enormous strains on the world's finite resource base and finite capacity to absorb greenhouse gases without major climatic change.

TRANSPORT AND CITIES IN THE SOUTH[27]

Most city and municipal authorities in the South face great difficulties in improving what are currently grossly inadequate public transport systems to a level where they not only meet the needs of low-income groups but also encourage many middle- and upper-income groups to use them instead of private automobiles. Many major cities in the South face comparable problems to Northern cities with regard to traffic congestion and air pollution arising from road vehicles.[28] Within the richer cities, rates of automobile ownership per capita can be as high as in cities in the North. Even where they are much lower, less provision for roads in cities, poor road maintenance and poorly functioning traffic management systems often ensure high levels of congestion. Congestion combined with less efficient and poorly maintained engines and higher levels of lead-based additives in gasoline can also mean comparable or higher levels of automobile-related air pollution, even when the number of road vehicles in use is substantially smaller.[29]

In many, if not most cities in the South, the quality of public transport is poor and, in recent years, has been falling further and further behind demand. In most cities in Africa, Asia and Latin America, growth in the supply of public transport by the formal sector is slower than the population growth, and the deficit in the supply of services is further widened because the larger the city grows, the greater the average length of travel. In several sub-Saharan African cities, there has even been a major decline in the supply of public transport, despite growing populations. In others, such as Nairobi and Abidjan, the main public transport operators increased the number of vehicle kilometres during the 1980s but at a rate that was much slower than population growth. In India, the supply of public transport services stagnated in Bombay, did not match population growth in Bangalore and only in Madras did it increase faster than the population. There are usually too few vehicles relative to demand and a serious problem of maintenance as existing vehicles are overused and too little attention is given to maintenance. For many nations, there is also the problem of the high import costs of oil and public transport vehicles (and of all spare parts); only a minority of nations produce automobiles, buses and trucks, and most that do simply assemble imported components.

In many cities, a high proportion of all trips on public transport are provided by informal private sector services. By the end of the 1980s, the informal sector had between a 40 and 80 per cent share in public transport in most capital cities of sub-Saharan Africa. It also dominated public transport in many cities in South Asia, except the large ones where institutionalized transport usually had the lead. Where routes and timetables are not defined, informal transport is more expensive than regular transport, is often hardly affordable by the urban poor and may be dangerous.

One other common problem is the fact that revenues for most publicly owned bus, railway and metro systems do not cover costs, so there are no revenues on which to draw to improve maintenance and the quality of the service and to invest in expanding the service. Politicians are reluctant to raise prices because of the political protests this would cause, not least because many low-income households would be seriously affected. But a failure to address this simply means a continuing deterioration in the quality of the service while unmet demands continue to grow.

There is also the problem of the spatial incoherence of the built-up area within and around the city. In most cities, there are many districts where no buses can go. These include historic city centres where roads and lanes are too narrow for buses, and most illegal or informal settlements which are usually on sites often flooded or waterlogged or on steep slopes with no motorable roads. In the absence of land-use planning and where illegal settlements become the only viable source of housing for most low-income groups, cities expand in a haphazard manner, with very densely populated settlements of different sizes interspersed with large areas with little or no development and often low-density suburban developments for middle- and upper-income groups.[30] This pattern greatly increases the difficulty of providing cost-effective public transport.

TRENDS IN AUTOMOBILE DEPENDENCE

The global cities study mentioned earlier is being updated to include data for 1990. The 1980s was the first decade where it would be possible to judge the impact of the global sustainability agenda on cities in terms of their transportation. The early data are summarized in Table 8.2, showing trends.

Car Use Trends

US cities have continued to accelerate in car use per capita (2.3 per cent in the 1980s compared to 2.2 per cent in the 1970s); their 2,400 kilometres of growth per capita in the ten years to 1990 is equal to the total vehicle kilometres travelled (VKT) per capita in Paris or London in the 1980s. European and Asian cities starting from a

Table 8.2 *Trends in the use per person of automobiles and public transport in world cities, by region*

	Year	US cities	Australian cities	Toronto	European cities	Asian cities
Car use	1970	7,334	4,628	n/a	2,750	913
(vehicle kilometres	1980	9,168	5,850	4,807	3,798	1,067
travelled per person)	1990	11,559	6,589	5,680	4,754	1,487
Public	1970	48	118	154	249	454
transportation	1980	57	93	202	290	430
(trips per person)	1990	64	91	210	359	496

Sources: ESCAP, *State of Urbanization in Asia and the Pacific 1993*, Economic and Social Commission for Asia and the Pacific, ST/ESCAP/1300, United Nations, New York, 1993; Kenworthy, Jeff, Paul Barter, Peter Newman and Chamlong Poboon (1994), 'Resisting automobile dependence in booming economies; a case study of Singapore, Tokyo and Hong Kong within a global sample of cities', paper presented at the Asian Studies Association of Australia Biennial Conference 1994, Murdoch University, Perth; and Urban Redevelopment Authority (1991), *Living the Next Lap: Towards a Tropical City of Excellence*, Singapore.

much lower base grew only 950 kilometres and 420 kilometres per capita, though this 2.2 per cent and 3.3 per cent per annum growth is still a real concern for a sustainable future.

The Australian and Canadian cities are showing an interesting trend towards reduced growth in VKT. In the 1960s, Australian cities' VKT grew by 4.5 per cent, by 2.3 per cent in the 1970s and by 1.2 per cent in the 1980s. If projected, this leads to zero growth in the 1990s (see Figure 8.3).

Toronto is similar (along with other Canadian cities in prelimary data) with just 1.6 per cent growth in the 1980s (873 kilometres of growth per capita). Figure 8.4 shows the differences between the US and other cities in terms of the growth in vehicle kilometres travelled in cars per person during the 1980s.

The reduced growth in car use in Australian and Canadian cities (especially compared to US cities) may be due to:

- Reurbanization of older suburbs which leads to reduced travel: reurbanization in Australian cities is now more than 30 per cent and up to 50 per cent of all development;[31] it is also very strong in Canadian cities.
- Development of nodal subcentres in outer suburbs that also reduce the need for travel and make transit more viable; signs of these emerging subcentres are apparent in Australia but not as much as in Canadian cities.[32]
- Better urban environments which encourage both the reduction in the need for car journeys to 'leapfrog' unsafe urban areas (as in US cities), and more walking and cycling.
- Less dispersion and development of highly car-dependent 'edge cities' which have been characteristic of US urban growth patterns.[33]

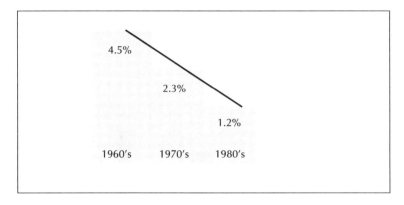

Figure 8.3 *Average increase in car use (vehicle kilometres travelled per capita) in Australian cities*

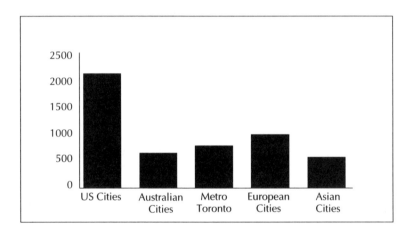

Figure 8.4 *Increases in car use (vehicle kilometres travelled per capita) in cars in global cities, 1980–1990*

Public Transport Use

Despite predictions by Lave[34] that transit can never compete with the car and that it is in a terminal state of decline everywhere, the actual data from most cities is quite positive (see Figure 8.5).

Transit in US cities is still low but is growing again. In Australian cities it has stabilized and indeed may have started growing again in the 1990s.[35] It grew in Toronto, the European cities and the Asian cities. The average transit trips per capita growth in European cities is more than the total per capita use in US cities. In Asian cities the growth was much more again. Growth in transit in European cities is accelerating (2.1 per cent in the 1980s compared to 1.5 per cent in the 1970s). Such trends are a positive sign of sustainability.

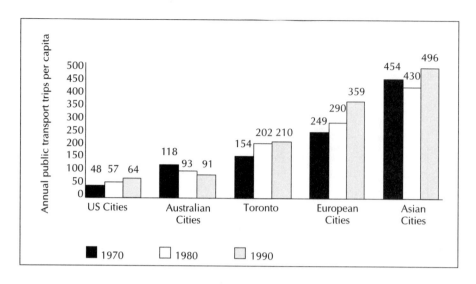

Figure 8.5 *Trends in per capita public transport use in world cities by region, 1970–1990*

Some of the world's wealthiest and most successful cities have been reducing their citizens' dependence on private automobiles. This can be seen in a comparison between Los Angeles, Zurich and Singapore on how their car use and transit use changed between 1980 and 1990. In Los Angeles, car use continued to grow rapidly, with a decline in the use of public transit, whereas in Zurich and Singapore there was far less growth in car use and a considerable increase in the use of public transit. Thus, the substantial increases in income which have occurred in the past ten years in Zurich and Singapore have gone mostly into public transit use and not into private car use and this reflects their cities' overall plans and priorities to achieve this. Los Angeles, on the other hand, has not attempted to control automobile dependence; here, it is accepted that there is a culture which has little belief in planning other than the facilitation of individual mobility. The use of private automobiles has almost inevitably grown as a result.

The Asian Cities Study

We are conducting a more detailed study of the sustainability of seven Asian cities. This is being done partly for the World Bank to highlight further the question of transportation priorities and their link to land use and infrastructure as well as the role of personal income in shaping these patterns. Table 8.3 contains the preliminary data.

The data indicate the following:

- There is little obvious relationship between automobile travel patterns and income. Hong Kong, Singapore and Tokyo average 13 per cent of the car use of US cities despite having much higher wealth levels (average of 44 per cent, with

Table 8.3 *Transportation infrastructure and land use in seven Asian cities, 1990*

	Tokyo	Singapore	Hong Kong	Manila	Bangkok	Kuala Lumpur	Jakarta	Surabaya
City median income (US$ 1990) and	38,229	12,860	15,077	3,058	4,132	6,539	1,975	1,975
% of US	77	26	30	6	8	13	4	4
Car use per person km and	2,103	1,864	493	860	1,562	2,687	383	237
% of US car use	19	17	4	8	14	24	3	2
Public transport use per capita (trips per year)	461	457	570	727	340	337	206	122
% of motorized trips by public transport	62	72	89	73	31	30	47	29
% of all trips by walking & cycling	45	n/a	n/a	30	14	20	43	25
Length of road (metres per person)	19	1.0	0.3	0.6	0.6	1.5	0.5	0.3
Density (persons per hectare)	104	87	300	198	144	69	195	186

Source: Kenworthy, Jeff, Paul Barter, Peter Newman and Chamlong Poboon (1994), 'Resisting automobile dependence in booming economies; a case study of Singapore, Tokyo and Hong Kong within a global sample of cities', paper presented at the Asian Studies Association of Australia Biennial Conference 1994, Murdoch University, Perth; and Urban Redevelopment Authority (1991), *Living the Next Lap: Towards a Tropical City of Excellence*, Singapore

Tokyo being 77 per cent of US cities). Their wealth is much more directed into transit which is on average eight times US levels.

• Bangkok, Kuala Lumpur, Jakarta and Surabaya have only 10 per cent of US incomes and are thus much poorer than Tokyo, Singapore and Hong Kong. On the other hand, transit use is generally underdeveloped compared to the richer Asian cities (about half of Manila is not considered – see below). These are the cities (especially Bangkok) where traffic levels are major economic and environmental issues. Thus, it appears that their wealth is being converted into automobile use on the American model in these cities rather than into transit as found in the Singapore, Tokyo and Hong Kong model.

• Manila has a very high transit use with its *jitney* system, though its 727 trips per capita is not as impressive when compared on a passenger kilometre basis, as most trips are very short. As car use grows it is increasingly difficult for transit to remain competitive, thus Manila is preparing to build more segregated electric rail services.

• Jakarta and Surabaya have comparatively very little car use but also the lowest level of transit use. Traffic issues are generally leading to higher automobile infrastructure rather than to more transit. These Indonesian cities are faced with a future like Bangkok's if they continue down that path.

- In peak periods, when road space is at a premium, cities such as Tokyo, Hong Kong, Singapore and Manila average 74 per cent of motorized work trips on transit. On the other hand, Bangkok, Kuala Lumpur and Surabaya have a mere 30 per cent, highlighting a growing difference in transportation priorities in these cities. Jakarta is between these two groups with 47 per cent.
- Modal split patterns also vary in interesting ways. Wealthy Tokyo has a very large 45 per cent of all trips on foot and by bicycle, while much poorer Bangkok and Kuala Lumpur have only 14 per cent and 20 per cent respectively. Traffic in Bangkok is now so bad it makes any walking or cycling almost impossible. Private transportation accounts for over 50 per cent of total trips in Bangkok and Kuala Lumpur, while in Tokyo it is only 27 per cent. In Surabaya, the least wealthy of all the cities, 47 per cent of trips are now by private transportation (particularly motor-cycles) and walking and cycling has fallen to 35 per cent, down from 53 per cent in 1980.
- All these Asian cities have land-use structures that are built for transit and walking rather than for automobiles. Those cities opting to facilitate automobile use rather than transit are showing all the signs of an inherently dysfunctional system. They also have a much better chance of coping with a world where automobile dependence must be overcome (including the sustainability agenda to reduce fuel use and greenhouse gas production) than US and Australian cities. They just need to invest in the transit/cycling/walking infrastructure. US and Australian cities must also restructure their urban form.

SOLUTIONS TO AUTOMOBILE DEPENDENCE

National and city governments in both the North and the South are questioning the future of cities and urban systems in which private automobiles have the central role in the transport of people. This stems from a greater recognition of the economic, social and environmental costs of 'automobile-dependent' cities that were described above. Solutions to automobile dependence are thus being sought across the globe.

Automobiles and trucks can be 'civilized' through technological advances that greatly reduce fuel use and polluting emissions and increase safety both for the vehicle users and for other road users.[36] Sophisticated traffic management systems can increase efficiency in the use of road spaces and the number of vehicles using road systems without congestion. But, increasingly, even if the incorporation of these advances was accelerated, it is seen as insufficient as the sheer volume of cars, trucks and other motorized road vehicles overwhelms cities. This is especially so in high-density cities that have a low proportion of their total area devoted to roads, as in many cities in Europe and in the South. Seeking to expand road systems to cope with projections of increased automobile use in high-density cities also disrupts the urban fabric and displaces large numbers of people. It was the scale of this disruption in cities in the North that helped to generate a re-evaluation of the priority that was being given to private automobile users. For many of the major cities in the South, the number of automobiles is growing much more rapidly than the number of people, and building the roads and highways to cope with projections for increased automobile use will mean the displacement of tens of thousands (or more) people in each such city. There is also the more recent recognition that people who do not have access to a car are significantly disadvantaged as automobile dependence within a city or region increases since this also leads to a deterioration in public transit and a city in which access to workplaces, schools, shops and services is increasingly difficult without a car.

Despite the doubts as to whether the use of private cars can be controlled, not least because of the power of the economic interests behind the automobile-dependent model, there is a growing awareness of the need to plan to reduce automobile-dependence within cities.[37] Many cities have pedestrianized their central districts; for most, this was easily done as these were historic city centres that originally developed as 'walking cities' before the advent of motorized transport. But there are also many examples of cities which have reduced automobile dependence through innovations in public transit and controls on automobile use in both the North and the South. They include Hong Kong, Singapore and Surabaya in Asia, Curitiba in Latin America, Zurich, Copenhagen and Freiburg in Europe, Toronto and Portland in North America and Perth in Australia, and the means by which they achieved this are outlined below. The fact that this list includes some of the wealthiest cities in both the North and South shows that reducing automobile dependence is possible even in societies with high levels of automobile ownership.

There is also much discussion about the need for public transit-oriented development as the basis for any sustainable city.[38] The link with sustainable development comes from the fact that there is a rapid growth in the number of automobile-dependent cities and in most of these cities, automobile dependence is still increasing. The world's consumption of fossil fuels and total emissions of greenhouse gases would increase dramatically if the whole world's population came to be as automobile dependent as North America, Western Europe or Australia. The OECD and the World Bank have begun to recognize this and are stressing how transport funding needs to be more critically evaluated.[39] But, in a globally connected world, the reduction of automobile dependence (and its associated energy use, resource use, air pollution and greenhouse gas emissions) should be directed both to cities where automobile dependence is highest and to cities in the South where short-term and long-term measures can reduce their automobile dependence while also enhancing their prosperity and quality of life.

KEY POLICY CONCLUSIONS

Four key conclusions of relevance to public policy can be drawn from the data on cities around the world as to how automobile dependence can be reduced:

- *Public transport infrastructure* – investment in transit infrastructure can help to shape the city as well as ease traffic problems – for instance, encouraging 'walking cities' to develop around light railway or rapid busway stations. There is a considerable range of technological options too, varying in price, capacity and speed and these include options such as express busways that do not require heavy investments. It is also possible to 'upgrade' as demand rises and as cities grow in size and wealth – for instance, as light railways or trams replace express busways. It is also possible to draw on private sector resources – for instance, through city authorities providing the framework within which private bus companies bid for particular routes or areas. But this can only be achieved if public transit is part of a broader policy that discourages low-density developments and unnecessary automobile use. If public transit is left as a supplementary process in streets designed for the automobile, there will be no resolution of the transport dilemma.

- *Pedestrian/cycle orientation* – if the goal is to provide for the most efficient, equitable and human form of transport, this means a city with provision for cycling, good walking space on streets and in public squares, and traffic-free shopping streets. Any city that neglects this dimension will find social and economic problems as well as the obvious environmental ones.
- *Density* – the need to maintain land-use efficiency is linked closely to transport. Dispersing land uses at low density creates automobile dependence. Dense urban villages linked by public transit creates the opportunity for 'walking city' and 'transit city' characteristics to be introduced into the automobile-dependent city (see Figure 8.5 which should be compared to Figure 8.2). Similarly, introducing new and efficient public transit lines into rapidly growing cities can encourage the development of such dense urban settlements and limit low-density sprawl, especially if land-use planning helps to encourage such developments.
- *Planning and control* – all three of the above policies have strong market pressures behind them. But they also require planning to facilitate them. This planning is not heavy-handed bureaucracy but an expression of any city's cultural values, and also of the needs and priorities of pedestrians and cyclists and of children, youth and all other citizens who cannot or do not use cars. It highlights the priority on the urban and on access to city services for all people. All cities have some commitment to this social value. If automobile dependence is not resisted through conscious planning, it will erode or help to destroy most attempts to maintain community life in an urban setting. For all cities, but particularly those in the South, strong neighbourhoods need to be protected from the dispersing and disruptive aspects of the automobile, while in many cities in the wealthiest market economies of the world, the policy of reducing automobile dependence is part of a process to reclaim residential neighbourhoods.

CASE STUDIES IN RESOLVING OR LIMITING PRIVATE AUTOMOBILE DEPENDENCE

Apart from general principle, it is important to learn from individual cities how they have been able to overcome automobile dependence. It is also important to learn of the challenges that need to be faced by cities that are seeking to address problems of increasing traffic congestion and rising levels of private automobile ownership and/ or use. Below are short notes on the measures taken to reduce automobile dependence in a range of cities.

Singapore and Hong Kong

Both Singapore and Hong Kong have remarkably successful transit systems and very low car usage. They have not always been so well balanced but faced the dilemma of the automobile and constantly opted to provide more for public transit than for the car. In order to achieve this, Singapore and Hong Kong have made citywide planning a very high priority.[40] The transit system in both cities is fixed, rapid and comfortable (electric rail) and is also flexible and local (minibus). This is supplemented by non-motorized means such as walking and cycling. Central to the success of this model is high-density urban development that is closely integrated around the transit system. Such densities seem excessive to Anglo-Saxon perceptions but are not so culturally unacceptable, particularly when they are associated with good planning that results in high levels of health and other quality of life indicators.[41] In Singapore, high quality provision of public transit was also supplemented by heavy taxes on car ownership and an 'area licensing scheme' that charges cars entering the central city, although car pools of four or more riders are allowed to enter free.[42] Many other measures are being taken to encourage walking and cycling – for instance, separated bikeways along roads and in the new towns to facilitate access to the mass rapid transit stations and extensive pedestrian precincts and malls.[43]

Many of the larger cities in Africa, Asia and Latin America already have high levels of automobile ownership, and many more have a much more rapid growth in car ownership than in population. Most are seeking to address this with transport priorities dominated by new roads and highways and increased provision for car parking. Many such cities already have huge traffic problems as well as associated environmental and social problems. For them there is the obvious solution – to implement public transport systems similar to those of Hong Kong, Singapore or Curitiba. The density of development in most cities in these regions is more than adequate to enable good transit systems to be built. And for rapidly growing cities, decisions made now about good public transit can ensure that the city's physical growth in the future avoids the problems of automobile-dependent, low-density sprawl. Many proposals and plans for transit systems exist in cities like Bangkok which are becoming overwhelmed by automobiles, usually with a mixture of finance from private and public sources.

Curitiba

The problem for most cities whether in the North or the South is how to minimize the cost of public transit whilst putting in sufficient investment to make it a viable alternative to increasing private automobile use. Curitiba in Brazil is a city which has shown how to do this by channelling investment of scarce urban resources into a coherent, city-wide transit service that is closely integrated to land use policy and other social policies in the city. Box 8.1 describes its public transport system.

Three other aspects of Curitiba's transport policy are also worth noting:[44]

- it has one of the lowest accident rates per vehicle in Brazil;
- there are considerable savings for inhabitants on expenditure on transport (on average, residents spend only about 10 per cent of their income on transport which is relatively low for Brazil); and
- social policies have been integrated into the system through insistence on low-cost fares across the city, and on access to the system for those with disabilities (wheelchairs can enter the bus directly once in the bus boarding tube and old buses are used to provide special services for the heavily disabled).

The next phase of Curitiba's growth is to develop higher capacity rail services along the main axes which can now be done as the city develops, based on its original low-cost buses.

Box 8.1 *Public transport and other environmental initiatives in Curitiba, Brazil*

The public transport system which has been developed over the last 20 years began with the use of express buses on exclusive busways on axes radiating from the city centre. These proved much cheaper and less disruptive than conventional metro or light railway systems. Over the years, these axes have been further developed and new urban developments have been encouraged to concentrate along them. There are five main axes, each with a 'trinary' road system. The central road has two exclusive bus lanes in the centre for express buses and is flanked by two local roads. Each side of this central road, one block away, are high-capacity, free-flowing, one-way roads – one for traffic flowing into the city, the other for traffic flowing out of the city. In the areas adjacent to each axis, land-use legislation has encouraged high-density residential developments along with services and commerce. The express buses running along these axes are served by inter-district and conventional feeder buses with connections between them organized in a series of bus terminals.

With a more deconcentrated pattern of employment, the central city areas could be pedestrianized and the historic buildings protected from redevelopment. Several main thoroughfares have been closed to traffic and converted into tree-lined walkways. One important complementary action was the municipal government's acquisition of land along or close to the new transport axes, prior to their construction. This allowed the government to organize high-density housing programmes close to the transport axes; in all, some 17,000 lower-income families were located close to them.

At present, there are 53 kilometres of express lines, 294 kilometres of feeder lines and 167 kilometres of inter-district lines. Buses are colour coded: the express buses are red, inter-district buses are green and the conventional (feeder) buses are yellow, and there is full integration between all buses. Large bus terminals at the end of each of the five express busways allow people to transfer to inter-district or feeder buses and one single fare is valid for all buses. Along each express route, smaller bus terminals are located approximately every 1400 metres, equipped with newspaper stands, public telephones and post office facilities. Here passengers arrive on feeder buses and transfer to the express buses. The latest innovation is the introduction of the 'direct' express buses with fewer stops and where passengers pay before boarding from special raised tubular stations. These new stations (with platforms at the same height as bus floors) cut boarding and deboarding times. This rapid bus system with 'boarding tubes' can take twice as many passengers per hour as the other express buses and three times as many passengers per hour when compared to a conventional bus operating in a normal street. The boarding tubes also eliminate the need for a crew on board to collect fares, which frees up space for more passengers.

Curitiba's public transport system is used by more than 1.3 million passengers daily. Twenty-eight per cent of express-bus users previously travelled by car. This has meant savings of up to 25 per cent in fuel consumption city-wide. Curitiba's public transportation system is a major reason for the city having one of the lowest levels of ambient air pollution in Brazil.

Source: Rabinovitch, Jonas (1992), 'Curitiba: towards sustainable urban development', *Environment and Urbanization,* Vol 4, No 2, October

Surabaya

Cities without the funding potential for major transit systems must try other ways of managing the automobile or it will quickly destroy their cities. In the South, what is termed the 'non-motorized transport sector', which includes bicycles and walking, is largely neglected and is seen as an expression of older, less fashionable values – ironically, at a time when it is seen once again as fashionable and modern in Europe. In both the North and the South, it has huge potential if it is properly facilitated.[45]

Surabaya provides an excellent example of support for non-motorized transport. Surabaya is a dense, walking oriented city with little motorized transport. The goal of Surabaya was how to build on this strength whilst providing improved quality of life for its residents. The city developed an extensive programme to improve housing, infrastructure and services in the traditional *kampungs*. But the upgrading also retained narrow alleys and these were made attractive with planting and a strong emphasis on pedestrians.[46] This is a demonstration of how planning can work in cities in less urbanized and industrialized economies. It also shows how an emphasis on participation and grassroots involvement can work in such a city environment.

Zürich, Copenhagen and Freiburg

Each of these is an example of cities that have made concerted efforts to contain the automobile whilst improving the quality of life of their citizens. In Zürich, there has been a spectacular increase in the use of public transit and a containment in the growth in car use. This has occurred despite substantial growth in per capita incomes in Zürich. How has Zürich managed to channel its wealth into such positive city-building processes rather than the city-destroying processes of dispersal, pollution and community disturbance associated with automobile dependence? In the 1970s, Zürich had to make a decision about its trams. Instead of bowing to the car lobby and scrapping the tram system (as most European cities had done), it expanded its old tram system and upgraded the services so tram-users never had to wait more than six minutes and had total right of way at traffic lights.

As trams became fashionable, public attention was directed to other amenities – pedestrian malls and outdoor cafés – that were allowed to take up road space and parking lots. The strategy was 'to point out other better possibilities of use'. People began to respond to the attractions of the public realm and made private sacrifices to be part of that. This is the key to resolving the dilemma of the automobile: a city should provide something more appealing to its citizens than automobile-based decisions can provide.

Copenhagen is an example of a city that has sought to resolve the dilemma of the automobile using innovative social planning. The city has a transit-oriented urban form, but it was not enough in itself as the use of private automobiles was growing and there was a need to resist this.

> By the 1960s, American values had begun to catch on – separate isolated homes and everyone driving. The city was suffering so how could we reverse these patterns? We decided to make the public realm so attractive it would drag people back into the streets, whilst making it simultaneously difficult to go there by car.[47]

Table 8.4 *Transport trends in Freiburg, Germany, 1976–1991*

Transport factor	1976	1991	% increase 1976–1991
Total daily trips	385,000	502,000	+ 30.4%
Total daily auto trips	231,000	234,000	+ 1.2%
Auto's share of non-pedestrian trips	60%	47%	na
Bicycle's share of non-pedestrian trips	18%	27%	na
Public transit's share of non-pedestrian trips	22%	26%	na

Source: Pucher, S and J Clorer (1992), 'Taming the automobile in Germany', *Transportation Quarterly*, Vol 46, No 3, pp 383–395

Each year, the amount of space for car parking was reduced by 3 per cent and more streets were pedestrianized. Each year, city housing was built or refurbished and streets were made more attractive to pedestrians and to street life in general through landscaping, sculptures and seating (including 3000 seats in sidewalk cafés). Each year they introduced more street musicians, markets and other street life and street festivals that became increasingly popular. 'The city became like a good party.'[48] The result has been not only a reduction in the traffic but growth in the vitality of the city area. Social and recreational activity has tripled in Copenhagen's major streets and this was despite the conventional wisdom that:

- 'Denmark has never had a strong urban culture.'
- 'Danes will never get out of their cars.'
- 'Danes do not promenade like Italians.'

This turnaround from what had appeared to be a strong trend towards increasing automobile dependence took only 20 years. The newly invigorated public realm of the city is so attractive that there is a declining market for single detached homes on the urban fringe; they are apparently 'too far away' and 'too private'.

Freiburg in Germany is another city that has shown how it is possible to virtually stop the growth of car use, even when car ownership is growing. Freiburg's car ownership rose from 113 per 1000 people in 1960 to 422 per 1000 in 1990, only a little under the average for the Zürich agglomeration and only 12 per cent less than the national average for West Germany (481 per 1000).[49] Table 8.4 shows how, despite this growth in the availability of cars, car use has remained virtually constant since 1976. Public transport passengers have increased by 53 per cent and bicycle trips have risen by 96 per cent between 1976 and 1991.

The growth in car trips in Freiburg over 15 years was only 1.3 per cent, yet total trips increased 30 per cent. The growth in mobility was supplied principally by increased public transport and bicycling. In fact, the share of trips by car *declined* over the 15 years from 60 per cent to 47 per cent. The growth in car ownership has also begun to slow down;[50] Freiburg had previously had higher than average car ownership within what was West Germany as a whole, whereas now it has below average car ownership.

Freiburg's success in 'taming the automobile' was the result of a combination of transportation and physical planning strategies:

First, it has sharply restricted auto use in the city. Second, it has provided affordable, convenient, and safe alternatives to auto use. Finally, it has strictly regulated development to ensure a compact land use pattern that is conducive to public transport, bicycling and walking.[51]

Restricted automobile use has been achieved through mechanisms such as pedestrianization of the city centre, area-wide traffic-calming schemes (including a citywide speed limit of 30 kilometres per hour in residential areas) and more difficult, expensive parking. Freiburg's improvements to public transit have focused on extending and upgrading its light rail system rather than buses. Buses are used as feeders to the light rail system. Land-use regulations are similar to those in many other parts of Europe and have involved limiting the overall amount of land available to development and strictly zoning land for agriculture, forests, wildlife reserves or undeveloped open space.

The important savings in automobile use arising from the more compact urban patterns that have resulted from these latter policies should also be noted.[52]

Toronto and Portland

North America has been the area most associated with high levels of automobile ownership and use. Toronto and Portland are now, however, among the cities that have overcome the dominant paradigm of automobile-based planning. Central to both stories is how community organizations forced planners to think again about freeway proposals.

Toronto has made a deliberate policy of transit-oriented development for a number of decades. Whilst not always consistently applied, it has been more successful than in any other North American city.

Toronto is far less dominated by cars and indeed is the best North American example of transit-oriented development. From 1960 to 1980, use of Toronto's public transport grew by 48 per cent. The central city of Toronto grew and the overall density increased by 8 per cent (particularly along its transit lines). The Mayor of Toronto from that period tells the story of how it happened. The authorities in Toronto were very influenced by the book *The Death and Life of Great American Cities*[53] which stressed the need for people to go back to a more urban character and to rediscover public spaces. The author, Jane Jacobs, went to live in Toronto and was very influential in a movement there that was designed to stop the building of a major freeway called the Spadina Expressway. This initiated a public community-based move for a different kind of city.

Once the halting of the freeway had defined the city's direction, the decision was made to emphasize transit-oriented development. Toronto changed in 20 years from a city that was very car based to one that is substantially based around public transport. As a result, it has been able to revitalize the downtown area and develop a series of transit-centred subcities.

The overall process was something that the Mayor said they were never confident about; they were not sure that they would be able to achieve a city that was moving away from the automobile but were surprised by how well it worked. It is now a very vibrant city. It is a city that planned its development around public transit. It has even built 30,000 houses in the city centre over the past 10 years and this has reduced the morning peak by 100 cars for every 120 units built.[54] There are families living in the city centre in the European tradition which contributes much to the vitality and safety of the public spaces.

Portland, in the United States, has shown that an increasingly automobile-dominated city is not inevitable. During the 1970s, there were plans to build the Mount Hood Expressway through the city. When it was decided by the community not to build it but instead to go for a light rail system (MAX), the majority of transport experts laughed, and the new system planned was even dubbed the 'streetcar named expire' as the experts claimed that in a modern city you cannot get people out of their cars.

The new system proved to be a transport success story with a doubling of the patronage over the bus system it replaced and a large off-peak usage by families going into the city. The only political problem with the decision to go for light rail instead of a freeway is that many other corridors want the MAX system extended along them, so plans are being developed to extend it. There have also been several other important side effects. One is that the city centre has come alive after the business community recognized the opportunity provided by MAX and took the initiative to help repave the city streets and install lots of seats, flower planters and other elements of good urban design at the street level. The city centre is among the most attractive in the USA. The downtown area went from 5 per cent to 30 per cent of the city's total retailing because of the light rail and added housing rather than parking. There was even a central city car park that was replaced with a public meeting place and a downtown freeway that was replaced with a riverfront park.[55] Another development has occurred in the suburbs where citizens, encouraged by their victory over the freeway, have started to push for traffic calming. In response to this, the city government began a 'Reclaim Your Street' project where residents and the government architect plan together how to slow down traffic and make it easier for pedestrians and cyclists (see Box 8.2 for an example of the benefits of traffic calming). Finally, the city has now recognized that MAX provides the opportunity to develop an integrated approach to land development. They have now developed a plan to curtail outer-area growth and redirect it to urban redevelopment around transit stops so that 85 per cent of all new growth must be within five minutes walk of a designated transit stop.[56]

Perth

For over 50 years new suburbs have been built in Australia on the assumption that the majority of people will not need a public transit service. Suburbs were built at uniformly low densities of 10–12 dwellings per hectare and without access to rail services. This left suburbs with a subsidized bus service that rarely came more than hourly at off-peak times. It is not surprising that the Australian suburban lifestyle rapidly became highly automobile-dependent.

One such corridor in Perth was the city's Northern suburbs which grew rapidly in the 1960s and 1970s along low-density, car-dependent lines. Two original rail reserves were removed in the 1960s as planners saw no future for transit other than back-up bus services. However, by the 1980s, the freeway serving the corridor was highly congested at peak hours and the community was dissatisfied with the bus service. A strong political push for a rail service resulted in the Northern Suburbs Rapid Transit System.[59] The 33-kilometre electric rail service has only seven stations which allows a very rapid service. It also features trains that are linked by bus

---

Box 8.2 *Traffic-calming: the European experience*

There are many examples of traffic-calming schemes in Europe that have greatly reduced accidents. One is run by the German federal government which has sponsored area-wide traffic-calming schemes in cities of different sizes from Berlin down to a village of 2300 inhabitants. In the Netherlands, the federal government has also sponsored a wide range of traffic-calming initiatives since 1977, including area-wide traffic-calming demonstration projects in Eindhoven and Rijswijk. Both the number and severity of accidents is usually significantly reduced, as reducing speed greatly reduces the risk of serious injury and the danger to pedestrians and cyclists. Berlin's area-wide scheme resulted in the following reductions in accidents:

Type of traffic	Measure	% Reduction in accidents
All traffic	Fatal accidents	57
	Serious accidents	45
	Slight accidents	40
	Accident costs	16
Non-motorized	Pedestrians	43
	Cyclists	16
	Children	66

Most other schemes report similar results – for instance, in Heidelberg accidents fell by an average 31 per cent with casualties falling by 44 per cent after a residential speed limit of 30 kilometres per hour and other traffic-calming measures were introduced.[57] Area-wide schemes in the Netherlands have reduced accidents in residential areas by 20 per cent overall and accidents involving injury by 50 per cent (measured per million vehicle kilometre) and there was no increase in accidents in surrounding areas.[58]

Source: Newman, Peter and Jeff Kenworthy with Les Robinson (1992), *Winning Back the Cities*, Australian Consumers' Association, Pluto Press, Australia. The table on Berlin is drawn from Pharoah, T and J Russell (1989), *Traffic calming: Policy Evaluation in Three European Countries*, Occasional Paper 2/89, Department of Planning, Housing and Development, Southbank Polytechnic, London

---

services interchanging passengers directly on to the stations. This allows cross-suburban bus services to be provided once the station nodes became the focus for bus routes rather than the Central Business District.

The new service has been successful but it reveals the problem of transport planners not believing that good public transit can succeed in modern cities. Three predictions were made about the rapid transit system which were proved wrong:

Prediction 1: Rail will lose patronage over buses as people don't like transferring.
Result: 40 per cent *increase* with rail-bus over bus-only in the corridor.
Conclusion: People will transfer if they can move to a superior form of service.

Prediction 2: You will never get people out of their cars as the freeway is so good and parking so easy in Perth.

Result: 25 per cent of the patrons on the northern line gave up using their cars.
Conclusion: Even in an automobile-dependent city, people can give up their cars.

Prediction 3: It will be a financial disaster.
Result: It was completed on budget and on time, winning many awards for engineering and architecture. It is almost breaking even in running costs.
Conclusion: If people are given a good option then rail infrastructure can be viable in modern cities.

Perth still has a long way to go before it overcomes its automobile dependence. One of the positive trends has been the growth in transit-oriented urban villages around the new electric rail service stations. These urban villages provide not only a good, close, rail option for residents and employees in the villages but much of the need for a car is replaced by a short walk to local services. This process can continue as more people discover the value of a less automobile-dependent lifestyle.

Alternative Planning Models in New Cities

Two new cities, Milton Keynes in the United Kingdom and Almere in the Netherlands, illustrate the differences between a new city developed on the assumption

Table 8.5 *A comparison of travel and land use in two New Towns: Milton Keynes (UK) and Almere (Netherlands)*

	Milton Keynes	Almere
Modal split (%)		
Car	59	35
Public transport	17	17
Bicycle	6	28
Walk	18	20
Land use		
Average travel distance	7.2 km	6.9 km (much less for non-work)
% of trips more than 3 km	45	85
Density (dwellings per hectare)	20	35–40
Form	scattered, separated use	organic, mixed use
Automobile dependence		
Proportion who see a car as 'essential'	70	50
% households with children under 12 years who are always supervised outside the home	52	16
% who are never supervised outside the home	8	48

Source: Roberts, J (1992), *Changed Travel – Better World? A Study of Travel Patterns in Milton Keynes and Almere*, TEST, London

that most people would travel by private automobile and a new city developed at a density similar to traditional settlements – ie to a settlement pattern that predated the automobile. The Garden City concept developed by Ebenezer Howard was first proposed 100 years ago in response to the smoky, overcrowded industrial cities of Britain. The concept has been the inspiration for many new towns since. However, not all have kept to the key concepts as developed by Howard. In particular, densities in residential areas have been lowered considerably on the basis of 'nothing gained by overcrowding', the slogan of the Town and Country Planning Association for most of this century. This dislike of high density seems to be an Anglo-Saxon characteristic that has been exported to most English-speaking cities.[60]

What is lost by lowering densities below 35 to 40 dwellings per hectare is the walking scale of cities and its viability for public transit. What is left is an automobile dependence that creates so many problems. This can be seen most clearly in the difference between Milton Keynes, a UK New Town and Almere a similarly sized Dutch New Town. Both were inspired by Garden City concepts but Milton Keynes reduced its densities to 20 dwellings per hectare and also separated its housing from employment and shopping zones by large distances. Almere was denser and more mixed as in traditional Dutch settlements.

Perhaps the most marked difference is in the degree of automobile dependence which is expressed by the proportion of people who see a car as 'essential' and the related difference in confidence in allowing children to be unsupervised on streets. This difference is about confidence in the public realm. It is obviously related to many social factors, but its link to the structure and form of the city cannot be underestimated. A walking environment is not created by scattering land uses at densities which demand the use of an automobile.

CONCLUSIONS

The private automobile poses a dilemma in all cities. It raises significant questions about the economic, social and environmental impact of technology, whether as part of the planning process in cities in the North or South or as part of development assistance. Many development assistance agencies explicitly or implicitly favour the automobile-dependent city in the transport and infrastructure projects they support.

The inappropriateness of such a model can be seen in the scale of the problems with traffic congestion and pollution related to internal combustion engines in cities in the South and the very high rates of accidental deaths and injuries, even though most cities have much lower levels of private automobile ownership per person than cities in the North. Much of the advice on solving the problem is still within the automobile-dependent model in the form of plans that spread cities outwards in reduced densities and in the building of freeways that usually bring an enormous displacement of people. These just create further automobile dependence.

Examples given in this paper suggest that the problem can be resolved, as most cities have not developed to the scale and low density that make public transit options unfeasible. But the difficulties in doing so should not be underestimated. First, very rarely is there an agency in a city or metropolitan area that has the authority to promote comprehensive solutions, and different agencies or ministries have their own objectives, priorities and resources.[61] Second, ministries or agencies concerned with roads are often more powerful than agencies concerned with public transit, and are also backed by powerful lobbies that represent automobile owners, automobile manufacturers and construction companies.

However, the case studies in this section do show that these constraints can be overcome. Ironically, it may be the increasing realization that all major cities must remain competitive in a world market to attract productive investment that will, once again, legitimize substantial government intervention in limiting automobile dependence, and the economic, social and environmental costs this implies. The case studies also show how automobile dependence in cities in the North can be slowed and even reversed through planning that puts greater emphasis on public transit and non-motorized travel. The case studies offer some hope although few cities have integrated, coherent plans to overcome automobile dependence and most rely too much on technological advances to resolve more fundamental problems in the planning of their cities. Solutions in cities in the South are also being found either through an emphasis on public transport or non-motorized travel. Both require a commitment to planning that is in essence the recognition that social aspects of development are essential for sustainable and civilized cities.

NOTES AND REFERENCES

1   Barton, H (1992) 'City transport: strategies for sustainability' in M J Breheny (ed), *Sustainable Development and Urban Form*, European Research in Regional Science 2, Pion, London, pp 197–216

2   Newman, Peter W G and Jeffrey R Kenworthy (1989) *Cities and Automobile Dependence: an International Sourcebook*, Gower Technical, Aldershot

3   Including *jitneys* and other forms of paratransit

4   ESCAP, *State of Urbanization in Asia and the Pacific 1993*, Economic and Social Commission for Asia and the Pacific, ST/ESCAP/1300, United Nations, New York

5   Ibid

6   World Resources Institute (WRI) in collaboration with the United Nations Development Programme, the United Nations Environment Programme and the World Bank (1996), *World Resources 1996–97*, Oxford University Press, Oxford and New York

7   European Environment Agency, *Europe's Environment: the Dobris Assessment*, Copenhagen, 1995

8   Newman, Peter, Jeff Kenworthy and Peter Vintila (1992), *Housing Transport and Urban Form*, National Housing Strategy Paper 15, Dept of Health, Housing and Community Services, Canberra

9   Gilbert, Richard (1992), 'Cities and Global Warming' in James McCulloch (ed), *Cities and Global Change*, Climate Institute, Washington DC

10 Newman, Peter and Jeff Kenworthy with Les Robinson (1992), *Winning Back the Cities*, Australian Consumers' Association, Pluto Press, Australia

11 UNCHS (Habitat) (1994), *Urban Public Transport in Developing Countries*, UNCHS (Habitat), Nairobi

12 World Resources Institute (WRI) (1996) op cit

13 Mohan, D and C J Romer (1991), 'Accident mortality and morbidity in developing countries' in M Manciaux and C J Romer (eds), *Accidents in Childhood and Adolescence; the Role of Research*, World Health Organization, Geneva, 1991, pp 31–38 quoted in W Odero (1994), 'Road traffic accidents in Kenya', paper presented at the Urban Health Conference, London School of Hygiene and Tropical Medicine, 6–8 December 1994

14 WHO (1995), *The World Health Report 1995: Bridging the Gaps*, World Health Organization, Geneva

15 WHO (1992), *Our Planet, Our Health*, the Report of the World Commission on Health and Environment, Geneva

16 European Environment Agency (1995) op cit

17 OECD (1995), *OECD in Figures: Statistics on the Member Countries*, 1995 edition, Paris

18 Department of Transport, UK, quoted in Central Statistical Office, *Social Trends*, 1994 Edition, HMSO, London

19 Odero, W (1994), 'Road traffic accidents in Kenya', paper presented at the Urban Health Conference, London School of Hygiene and Tropical Medicine, 6–8 December 1994

20 India was reported to have 60,000 fatalities a year from road accidents. World Resources Institute (WRI) (1996) op cit

21 Centre for Health Economics (1994), 'Economic costs of traffic accidents' in *Health Economics Issues*, Vol 1, No 1, Chulalongkom University, Bangkok, pp 2–5

22 See tables 4a, 4b, 5a and 5b in Bourbeau, Robert (1993), '*Analyse comparative de la mortalité violente dans les pays développés en dans quelques pays en développement durant la période 1985–89*' in *World Health Statistics Quarterly*, Vol 46, No 1, pp 4–33

23 For instance, in 1991, there were 8863 deaths from traffic accidents in São Paulo and 1365 in Seoul; in Buenos Aires, there were 3750 in 1988. Figures taken from the Governor of Tokyo and Summit Conference of the Major Cities of the World, *Major Cities of the World*, Tokyo Metropolitan Government, Tokyo, 1991, quoted in Sassen, Saskia (1994), *Cities in a World Economy*, Pine Forge Press, Thousand Oaks, London, New Delhi

24 ESCAP (1993) op cit

25 European Environment Agency (1995) op cit

26 See the papers in *Environment and Urbanization*, Vol 6, No 1, April 1994 on evictions

27 This section draws on UNCHS (Habitat) (1994), op cit

28 European Environment Agency (1995) op cit

29 Hardoy, Jorge E, Diana Mitlin and David Satterthwaite (1992), *Environmental Problems in Third World Cities*, Earthscan Publications, London

30 Hardoy, Jorge E and David Satterthwaite (1989), *Squatter Citizen: Life in the Urban Third World*, Earthscan Publications, London

31 Newman, Peter (1993), 'Cities and development – an emerging Asian model' in *Development Bulletin*, Vol 27, pp 20–22

32 Kenworthy, Jeff, Paul Barter, Peter Newman and Chamlong Poboon (1994), 'Resisting automobile dependence in booming economies; a case study of Singapore, Tokyo and Hong Kong within a global sample of cities', paper presented at the Asian Studies Association of Australia Biennial Conference, Murdoch University, Perth

33 Urban Redevelopment Authority (1991), *Living the Next Lap: Towards a Tropical City of Excellence*, Singapore, quoted in Kenworthy et al 1994 (ibid)

34 Rabinovitch, Jonas (1992), 'Curitiba: towards sustainable urban development' in *Environment and Urbanization*, Vol 4, No 2, October

35 Urban Redevelopment Authority (1991) op cit

36 Lovins, Amory B and L Hunter Lovins (1991), 'Least-cost climatic stabilization' in *Annual Review of Energy and Environment*, Vol 16, pp 433–531

37 Newman, Peter, Jeff Kenworthy and Peter Vintila (1995), 'Can we overcome automobile dependence? Physical planning in an age of urban cynicism' in *Cities*, Vol 12, No 1, February, pp 53–65; also Laquian A A (1993), *Planning and Development of Metropolitan Regions*, Proceedings of Conference, Bangkok, June/July, Asian Urban Research Network, Centre for Human Settlements, School of Community & Regional Planning, UBC, Canada, 1993; and Mitlin, Diana and David Satterthwaite (1994), 'Cities and sustainable development', background paper for Global Forum '94, Manchester City Council, Manchester

38 Hope, C and S Owens (1994), *Moving Forward: Overcoming the Obstacles to a Sustainable Transport Policy*, Cambridge University, White Horse Press, Cambridge; also Calthorpe, P (1993), *The Next American Metropolis: Ecology and Urban Form*, Princeton

39 Kreimer, A, T Lobo, B Menezes, M Munasinghe and R Parker (1993), *Towards a Sustainable Urban Environment: the Rio de Janeiro Study*, World Bank Discussion Papers 195, Washington DC; also Serageldin, I and R Barrett(1993), *Environmentally Sustainable Urban Transport: Defining a Global Policy*, World Bank, Washington DC

40 Wang, L H and A G O Yeh (eds) (1993), *Keep a City Moving: Urban Transportation Management in Hong Kong*, Asian Productivity Organization, Tokyo

41 Newman (1993) op cit

42 Kenworthy et al (1994) op cit

43 Urban Redevelopment Authority (1991), *Living the Next Lap: Towards a Tropical City of Excellence*, Singapore

44 Rabinovitch (1992) op cit
45 Replogle, M (1992), *Non-Motorised Vehicles in Asian Cities*, World Bank Technical Paper No 162, World Bank, Washington DC; also Replogle, M, 'Bicycles and cycle rickshaws in Asian cities: issues and strategies', *Transport Research Record* No 1372 on non-motorized transportation
46 Silas, Johan (1989), *Surabaya – the Fast Growing City of Indonesia – the Housing Experience*, Municipal Government of Surabaya
47 Gehl, J (1992), 'The challenge of making a human quality in the city' in *Perth Beyond 2000: a Challenge for a City*, Proceedings of the City Challenge Conference, Perth, September 1992
48 Ibid
49 Pucher, S and J Clorer (1992), 'Taming the automobile in Germany' in *Transportation Quarterly*, Vol 46, No 3, pp 383–395
50 Ibid
51 Pucher and Clorer (1992) op cit
52 Ibid
53 Jacobs, Jane (1965), *The Death and Life of Great American Cities*, Pelican, London
54 Nowlan, D M and G Stewart (1992), 'The effect of downtown population growth on commuting trips: some recent Toronto experience' in *Journal of the American Planning Association*, Vol 57, No 2, pp 165–182
55 Arrington, M (1993) 'Portland: transportation and land use – a shared vision' in *Passenger Transport*, Vol 2, No 3, pp 4–14
56 Ibid
57 Hass-Klau, C (1990), *An Illustrated Guide to Traffic Calming: the Future Way of Managing Traffic*, Friends of the Earth, London
58 Hass-Klau, C (1986) (ed), 'New ways of managing traffic', Special issue of *Built Environment*, Vol 12, No 1/2
59 Newman (1993) op cit
60 Newman P W G and T L F Hogan (1981), 'A review of urban density models: towards a resolution of the conflict between populace and planner' in *Human Ecology*, Vol 9, No 3, pp 269–303
61 UNCHS (Habitat) (1994) op cit

Chapter 9

Production: Producing, Providing, Trading: Manufacturing Industry and Sustainable Cities

Nick Robins and Ritu Kumar

(Reprinted from *Environment and Urbanization* Vol 11, No 2, October 1999).

Summary: This paper describes the innovations required from companies, local authorities and national governments to make manufacturing industry contribute to sustainable development in cities. It argues that the urban dimension has often been overlooked in discussions on industry and sustainable development, with most attention focusing on the roles of the individual firm and/or national policy in achieving change. The paper then presents a series of examples to demonstrate how industry will need to become responsible not only for the social and environmental performance of its own production activities, but also for the sourcing of raw material inputs 'upstream' and for the emissions and wastes that its products generate 'downstream'.

Key Terms

Dematerialization: The tendency for economies to use less material and energy inputs per unit of output as they develop.

Eco-efficiency: A business strategy to provide goods and services while continuously reducing ecological impacts ('more with less').

Industrial ecology: A vision of industrial organization that applies the lessons of natural ecosystems to environmental management, particularly in terms of ensuring that wastes from one process become inputs for another.

Sustainable production: A production process that provides goods and services that meet needs and enhance quality of life, respects environmental limits in terms of resource use and pollution and leads to a reduction of inequality and poverty among employees and the wider community.

CONFRONTING THE INDUSTRIAL DILEMMA

For over a century, manufacturing industry has frequently been seen as a villain of urban development, driving economic growth and technological innovation at high costs to both society and the environment.[1] As Britain's Royal Commission on Noxious Vapours reported back in 1878 'it is not a question of a few manufactories, but of industries all over the country, which in relation to man are causing pollution of the air in degrees sufficient to make them common law nuisances'.[2] But a thriving manufacturing sector can also provide the economic base for achieving sustainable development in many urban centres, generating wealth and employment and producing goods and services that meet needs and improve quality of life.

The hundredfold expansion in global industrial output since 1750 has often been bought at the cost of exploitative working practices, threats to occupational and community health and safety, profligate energy and material use, extensive air and water pollution and the generation of hazardous waste and toxic chemicals.[3] Not only have the bulk of these impacts been concentrated in the world's growing urban areas, but the burden has been unevenly distributed both within the city and its hinterland. The costs of industrial growth have thus pressed hardest upon the poor, the marginalized and the racial and ethnic minorities in urban areas, who have neither the resources nor the influence to avoid or control industrial hazards either in the community or in the workplace. Beyond the factory gate, industry has also supported public policies and consumer lifestyles that have produced a highly material-intensive urban landscape, dominated by the private car, the archetypal industrial product. In perhaps the most disturbing case, the General Motors' subsidiary, National City Lines, bought and then closed the networks of street cars and trolley buses in 45 cities in the USA during the 1930s and 1940s, paving the way for the predominance of the automobile.[4] Finally, globalization means that the social and environmental impacts of industry can no longer be confined to particular locations. Through international trade and investment, companies can draw on the natural capital of distant places, creating 'ecological footprints' in the process for which they have no direct responsibility.[5]

Yet this dark side to the industrial revolution has generated its own response in the form of citizen and community initiatives, local and national policy and law making, as well as corporate responsibility programmes to contain and channel the energies of industry into more sustainable directions.[6] Rising public expectations, the slow squeeze of regulation, market pressures from consumers and investors as well as the structural shift away from heavy industries have all served in most affluent countries to control many of the traditional problems associated with industrial production. The pollution load in the rivers flowing into Mersey Basin in North West England, for example, has fallen by 80 per cent over the last 25 years. These pressures have contributed to a slow, but significant 'dematerialization' of industrial output.[7] Thus, between 1970 and 1990, the output of the chemicals industry in the industrialized world more than doubled, while energy consumption per unit of output fell by 57 per cent.[8]

However, in much of Latin America and Asia and some of Africa, domestic expansion and globalization have combined to produce a rapid increase in the urban environmental problems generated by industry. According to the most recent World Resources report, 'industrial wastes are growing in quantity and becoming more varied, more toxic and more difficult to dispose of or degrade'. This is placing special stress on urban regions because the 'densities in cities where much of the industrial production is located far surpass those in developed countries, so the number of people exposed to pollutants is potentially much greater'.[9] These problems are unlikely to abate without substantial changes to the policy framework, urban management and corporate practice.

SIGNS OF HOPE

From the business perspective, there are signs of hope that the importance of sustainable development is now being accepted. Over the last decade, the focus of attention has moved from controlling environmental hazards to stimulating sustainable industrial development throughout the entire product life-cycle. Indeed, the 1990s have witnessed a significant shift among the enlightened sections of the global business community away from denial and resistance to change towards a more proactive approach, seeking to go 'beyond compliance' and using the sustainability imperative as a driver for innovation. As the World Business Council for Sustainable Development declared at the 1992 Earth Summit in Rio de Janeiro, 'progress towards sustainable development makes good business sense because it can create competitive advantages and new opportunities'.[10] At Rio, the Business Council launched the term 'eco-efficiency' to describe a new industrial vision combining prosperity with radically reduced resource use and environmental damage, recognizing that this will only happen with 'a break with business-as-usual mentalities and conventional wisdom that sidelines environmental and human concerns'. Six main strategies for implementing eco-efficiency have been identified: [11]

- reducing the material intensity of goods and services;
- reducing the energy intensity of goods and services;
- reducing the dispersion of toxic wastes and by-products;
- maximizing sustainable use of renewable resources;
- extending product durability; and
- increasing the service intensity of goods and services.

Business guru Michael Porter now supports the eco-efficiency hypothesis, arguing that 'properly designed environmental standards can trigger innovations that lower the total cost of a product or improve its value – ultimately, this enhanced *resource productivity* makes companies more competitive not less'.[12]

Leading companies are taking up the challenge, both to revitalize the material intensive and polluting industries of the past – iron and steel, chemicals, oil refining, pulp and paper and cement – and also to press ahead with the potentially eco-efficient sectors of the future, notably information and telecommunications. The health, safety and environment goals at British Petroleum, one of the world's largest oil corporations, are now to ensure 'no accidents, no harm to people and no damage to the environment'. This is a daunting prospect for a company dealing in fossil fuels, whose processes and products currently produce about 1 per cent of global carbon dioxide emissions, the major greenhouse gas. In the information sector, the Xerox Corporation, a provider of office products, has set itself the triple goal of waste-free manufacturing producing waste-free products operating in waste-free offices. Zero landfill is now the product design goal and everything that the company delivers to the customer is returnable, enabling Xerox to reuse 98 per cent of the parts from old copiers. All this brings financial savings, increased productivity and a more comfortable workplace for its customers.

The question now facing policy-makers, business executives and communities across the world is how to accelerate this shift and ensure that manufacturing industry makes a positive contribution to sustainable development in cities. The challenge for the next industrial revolution is twofold:

First, the post-industrial countries of North America, Western Europe and East Asia need to move to sustainable patterns of production and consumption. Pioneering work at the Wuppertal Institut has calculated that 'western style processes, products, infrastructures and services need to be dematerialized by an average factor of 10 compared to present conditions on a cradle to grave basis' over the next 50 years.[13] Much of this will have to come from radical improvements in the production processes and products of manufacturing industry. According to Ernst von Weiszaecker and Amory Lovins, many cost- and resource-saving options already exist for 'doubling wealth and halving resource use'.[14]

Second, countries which are industrializing will need to 'leapfrog' to sustainable industrial development if they arc not to repeat the mistakes of the affluent world by adopting patterns of production and consumption which prove costly and difficult to reform. Following an exhaustive assessment of India's environmental performance in the 50 years since Independence and looking ahead another half-century to 2047, the Tata Energy Research Institute has concluded that 'it is vital that we are not locked onto paths that lead to suboptimal dependence on a particular technology', citing the industrialized world's reliance on the automobile as the archetype.[15] Despite the massive obstacles that many countries face in making such a shift, a look at past trends in industrialization suggest that new paths are always pioneered outside the dominant regions: mass production developed in the USA not Britain and lean production emerged in Japan not the USA. As a result, David Wallace of the London-based Royal Institute for International Relations argues that 'those developing countries where rapid industrialisation is now beginning are the natural location for new principles of sustainable production to take root and evolve'.[16]

INDUSTRY AND SUSTAINABLE CITIES – THE MISSING LINKAGE

To date, however, there have been few explicit linkages between this new, more positive agenda for industry and sustainable development and the pressing issues of urban growth and renewal. A brief review of the landmark reports on business and sustainable development published during the 1990s reveals few references to the dynamic between industrial performance and the urban environment.[17] Most focus on generic issues for national policy making and/or the management of individual firms, ignoring the specific spatial issues facing particular towns and cities. It is as if sustainable industrial development can be pursued free of context and location.

But industrial development is not geographically neutral. It is concentrated in particular towns and cities for a complex package of reasons, with critical consequences for the management of local carrying capacity and community health. As Lewis Mumford wrote of industrial development in Victorian cities: 'note the environmental effect of the *massing* of industries that the new regime tended to make universal. A single factory chimney, a single blast furnace, a single dye works may easily have its effluvia absorbed by the surrounding landscape: twenty of them in a narrow area effectively pollute the air or water beyond remedy'.[18]

Looking ahead, the much-needed shift from a linear to a closed loop manufacturing system will require far greater attention to local flows of materials within city regions – the critical insight of the 'industrial ecology' movement. Furthermore, it is also in cities, in sectoral and economic clusters that industry learns and where the exchange of new ideas and techniques will occur. If manufacturing industry is to be a driver of sustainable development in cities, then action will need to be taken at three levels simultaneously:

- *Industry:* Individual companies and business sectors will need to develop and implement comprehensive management systems that make positive social, economic and environmental contributions to urban development. This will involve action to change manufacturing processes to take account of the impacts of production on immediate city surroundings, integrate social and environmental factors into supply chain policies for material inputs and to extend responsibility to the life-cycle performance of the goods and services it produces.
- *City:* Local authorities and other public agencies charged with urban management will need to put in place strategies that drive industrial production in urban areas according to clear targets for sustaining local carrying-capacity and ensuring community benefit. This will mean changes to traditional spatial planning, assessment and zoning procedures, targeting investments at collective infrastructure services that support this integrated approach, stimulating the sharing of experience within industry, particularly among small and medium-sized enterprises and providing mechanisms to ensure the public accountability of industry to citizens and the wider community.
- *National policy:* National governments in co-operation with international agencies will need to establish the broad policy framework of regulatory controls, economic incentives and public investments to ensure positive social, economic and environmental benefits from industrial production and consumption. This means integrating sustainable development targets into core government policies, such as finance and tax, trade, technology, industry, energy, transport, as well as environmental protection and development co-operation.

Few industries or cities meet these still ambitious requirements. The rest of this paper examines the main challenges involved in making the transition to sustainable manufacturing operations in cities, drawing material from international experience, notably from Britain and India.

PRODUCING SUSTAINABLY IN CITIES

Industrial production in cities has long been associated with a range of human and environmental hazards, now seared into the collective memory through a set of emblematic incidents, notably Love Canal (hazardous waste), Minimata (mercury effluent) and Bhopal (explosion) – all three the product of the chemical industry (see Box 9.1). Indeed, only a few key industrial sectors are responsible for the bulk of energy and material consumption along with pollution and waste generation, notably agro-foodstuffs, metals extraction and processing, cement works, the pulp and paper industry, oil refining and the chemicals industry. In the USA, just four primary production industries – paper, plastics, chemicals and metals – account for 71 per cent of toxic emissions from all manufacturing, while iron and steel, chemicals, refining and pulp and paper and cement, are responsible for 45 per cent of total industrial energy consumption.[19] Similarly, in India, petroleum refineries, textiles pulp and paper and industrial chemicals produce 27 per cent of the industrial output, but contribute 87 per cent of sulphur dioxide emissions and 70 per cent of nitrogen emissions from the entire industrial sector.[20]

Box 9.1 *Responsible care in the chemical industry*

Responding to public pressure to demonstrate improved performance, a growing number of codes of conduct have been issued by industry at the sectoral and national levels. One of the leading examples is the Responsible Care programme initiated in the Canadian chemical industry in the 1980s to raise its environmental, health and safety performance and improve its public image. Responsible Care now extends to 40 countries, covering 86 per cent of global chemical production. Led by the chemical industry association in each country, the aim is to develop a collective response to shared problems for the industry as a whole, encouraging learning and using peer pressure to drive up standards. In the UK, member companies have cut discharges of critical pollutants to water by 89 per cent since 1990, while in the Netherlands, members of the VNCI had by 1994 reduced emission levels by 50 per cent against a 1985 baseline, more than five years ahead of schedule.[21] In Germany, the chemical industry has signed 30 'self-commitments' since the late 1980s on a range of environmental problems, which it claims are quick, cheap and flexible, since they allow companies to choose the most efficient way to achieve the environmental goal.

But environmental groups and trade unions have had reservations about both the motivations for and performance of voluntary initiatives, such as Responsible Care. Workers in the chemical industry lack the necessary bargaining power, access to information, expertise and confidence to be able to meet, discuss and bargain as equals with management on issues of health, safety and the environment. They also have not been involved in the design and implementation of the programme. An international survey of trade unions in the chemical sector in 1997 showed that trade union representatives were neither widely involved in, nor well informed about the programme. As a result, there is a basic lack of trust with Responsible Care widely perceived as a public relations exercise designed to avoid regulation. Many claims – often untested and untestable – have also been made about the programme by participating companies. According to Reg Green, Health, Safety and Environment Officer at the International Federation of Chemical, Energy, Mine and General Workers' Unions (ICEM), 'the only way that the Responsible Care programme and other voluntary industry initiatives can have a credible future is if workers, their representatives and the broader community are meaningfully involved'.[22] ICEM is now pressing for education and training programmes to enable workers and trade union representatives to play an active part in Responsible Care, and exploring opportunities for signing formal agreements between Responsible Care companies and trade unions.

Within each industrial sector, environmental impacts can vary considerably between the best and worst performers, driven by factors such as company size, location, profitability and availability of clean technologies. As part of IIED's Sustainable Paper Cycle report, a global assessment was carried out into the regional distribution of production and pollution.[23] This concluded that Asia is responsible for about 24 per cent of pulp and paper capacity, but generates over 60 per cent of water effluent measured as total suspended solids (TSS). North America, by contrast, produces more than 37 per cent of world output with only 10 per cent of global TSS emissions. As a result, the investment costs to meet 'good' environmental standards have been estimated at US$95 per tonne of pulp in Asia and US$60 in North America. The figures

Table 9.1 *Environmental impacts of selected industries*

Sector	Air	Water	Soil/Land
Chemicals (industrial organic inorganic and compounds, excluding petroleum products)	Many and varied emissions depending on processes used and chemicals manufactured Emissions of particulate matter, SO_2, NO_X, CO, CFCs, VOCs and other organic chemicals, odours Risk of explosions and fires	Use of process water and cooling water Emissions of organic chemicals, heavy metals (cadmium, mercury), suspended solids, organic matter, PCBs Risk of spills	Chemical process wastes disposal problems Sludges from air and water pollution treatment disposal problems
Paper and pulp	Emissions of SO_2, NO_X, CH_4, CO_2, CO, hydrogen sulphide, mercaptans, chlorine compounds, dioxins	Use of process water Emissions of suspended solids, organic matter, chlorinated organic substances, toxins (dioxins)	
Cement, glass, ceramics	Cement emissions of dust, NO_X, CO_2, chromium, lead, CO Glass emissions of lead, arsenic, SO_2, vanadium, CO, hydrofluoric acid, soda ash, potash, specialty constituents (eg chromium) Ceramics emissions of silica, SO_2, NO_X, fluorine compounds	Emissions of process water contaminated by oils and heavy metals	Extraction of raw materials Soil contamination with metals and waste-disposal problems
Mining of metals and minerals	Emissions of dust from extraction, storage and transport of ore and concentrate Emissions of metals (eg mercury) from drying of ore concentrate	Contamination of surface water and groundwater by highly acidic mine water containing toxic metals (eg arsenic, lead, cadmium) Contamination by chemicals used in metal extraction (eg cyanide)	Major surface disturbance and erosion Land degradation by large slag heaps
Iron and steel	Emissions of SO_2, NO_X, hydrogen sulphide, PAHs, lead, arsenic, cadmium, chromium, copper, mercury, nickel, selenium, zinc, organic compounds, PCDDs/PCDFs, PCBs, dust, particulate matter, hydrocarbons, acid mists Exposure to ultraviolet and	Use of process water Emissions of organic matter, tars and oil, suspended solids, metals, benzene, phenols, acids, sulphides, sulphates, ammonia, cyanides, thiocyanates, thiosulphates,	Slag, sludges, oil and grease residues, hydrocarbons, salts, sulphur compounds, heavy metals, soil contamination and waste-disposal problems

Table 9.1 *Continued*

	infrared radiation, ionizing radiation	fluorides, lead, zinc (scrubber effluent)	
	Risks of explosions and fires		
Non-ferrous metals	Emissions of particulate matter, SO_2, NO_X, CO, hydrogen sulphide, hydrogen chloride, hydrogen fluoride, chlorine, aluminium, arsenic, cadmium, chromium, copper, zinc, mercury, nickel, lead, magnesium, PAHs, fluorides, silica, manganese, carbon black, hydrocarbons, aerosols	Scrubber water containing metals Gas-scrubber effluents containing solids, fluorine, hydrocarbons	Sludges from effluent treatment, coatings from electrolysis cells (containing carbon and fluorine), soil contamination and waste-disposal problems
Coal mining and production	Emissions of dust from extraction, storage and transport of coal Emissions of CO and SO_2 from burning slag heaps CH_4 emissions from underground formations Risk of explosions and fires	Contamination of surface water and groundwater by highly saline or acidic mine water	Major surface disturbance and erosion Subsidence of ground above mines Land degradation by large slag heaps
Refineries, petroleum products	Emissions of SO_2, NO_X, hydrogen sulphide, HCs, benzene, CO, CO_2, particulate matter, PAHs, mercaptans, toxic organic compounds, odours Risk of explosions and fires	Use of cooling water Emissions of HCs mercaptans, caustics, oil, phenols, chromium, effluent from gas scrubbers	Hazardous waste, sludges from effluent treatment, spent catalysts, tars
Leather and tanning	Emissions including leather dust, hydrogen sulphide, CO_2, chromium compounds	Use of process water Effluents from the many toxic solutions used, containing suspended solids, sulphates, chromium	Chromium sludges

Source: Drawn from Table 2.3 from *World Resources 1998–99* which had adapted it from World Health Organization (WHO), *Health and Environment in Sustainable Development: Five Years after the Earth Summit* (WHO, Geneva, 1997), Table 3.10, p 64.

for Asia underestimate the full cost as they exclude all China's 8000 pulp mills and 10,000 paper mills which produce less than 1000 tonnes per annum. For these factories, it might be less expensive to build entirely new larger mills than to try to upgrade existing small units, although this could have other costs, such as loss of employment and increased industrial concentration.

SUSTAINABLE PRODUCTION AND SOCIAL JUSTICE

For sustainable production in cities to become a reality, a strong social justice element is necessary. The issue is not just to reduce environmental hazards from industry in cities, but to give priority to those social groups facing greatest risk. In the USA a 1987 study showed that race is the most significant factor determining the location of commercial hazardous waste facilities and that three out of every five African–American and Hispanic–American citizens lived in communities with uncontrolled waste sites.[24] Indeed, people of colour communities have often been deliberately targeted for toxic and hazardous waste facilities.

These disparities in the distribution of environmental hazards has given birth to the environmental justice movement in the USA and elsewhere. In Los Angeles, for example, 'maps of pollutants' concentration unfailingly show the hot spots near industrial agglomerates, the areas where people of lower social class – Latino, black, recent immigrants from Asia – tend to live'.[25] The Labor/Community Strategy Center has formed the WATCHDOG coalition to ensure that public agencies in LA fulfil their legal obligation to improve the quality of the air that all citizens breathe and not become captured by the industrial polluters they are supposed to regulate. The trade union roots of the Center also ensure that it is committed to protecting jobs and ensuring that workers and the community have a voice in the inevitable trade-offs that need to be made. More recently, plans to establish a $700 million polyvinyl chloride (PVC) factory in the mainly black community of Convent, Louisiana, were withdrawn after strong local opposition. The community was supported by the US Environmental Protection Agency, which established an Office of Environmental Justice in 1992, and following a Presidential Executive Order in 1994 has been examining a number of cases where the civil rights of people of colour are being denied through disproportionate environmental damage.[26]

Local Agenda 21 exercises can provide a forum in which the concerns of marginalized communities about industrial pollution can be voiced. Since the end of apartheid in South Africa, communities in Durban have become more vocal in their opposition to current industrial practices, notably against local oil refineries. As part of the city's Local Agenda 21 exercise, citizens gained the opportunity to identify community-based indicators of industrial performance and integrate these into a wider strategic environmental assessment.[27] In the coastal town of Chimbote in Peru, pollution from the fishmeal industry and a steel-processing firm contaminates the surrounding air, water and soil and poses a serious threat to the town's inhabitants. Driven by a local NGO, the Association for the Defense and Conservation of the Environment of the Province of La Santa (ADECOMAPS), the Local Agenda 21 process has enabled citizens and community groups to design a shared vision of the future – with strong participation from women and children – and develop an urban environmental management project by consensus. But there are weaknesses. The provincial mayor has resisted the process and the fish industry has still to engage with the local population, with about 80 per cent of businesses doing nothing to control their environmental hazards.[28] Local NGOs are now seeking to link up with environmental groups in the major export markets for the fishmeal industry in order to place pressure on retailers and consumers to raise standards of the Peruvian companies.

'Right to know' legislation, which requires companies to report publicly their annual emissions of toxic chemicals, also offers a powerful counterweight for communities suffering industrial pollution. In the USA, companies have to report annually their emissions of over 600 toxic chemicals as part of the Toxic Release Inventory (TRI). For many companies, the need to account for these substances for the first time provided a major prompt to waste minimization efforts. It also gave communities the information required to press for risk-reduction efforts. The Right to Know Network, funded with the assistance of the US EPA, provides TRI data and further support to communities. The Netherlands and the UK have now installed similar systems, and the OECD has developed a model for other countries to develop a Pollution Release and Transfer Register.[29] Registers of contaminated land have also been used for some time in the USA, Germany and the Netherlands. But there remains strong industrial resistance to full public disclosure of their past and present risks and liabilities.

STORING UP PROBLEMS FOR THE FUTURE

Beyond the pressing environmental hazards that industrial production can impose on today's generation, it can also store up problems for the future. Industrial emissions of carbon dioxide lead to concentrations in the upper atmosphere that contribute to long-lasting climate change. Poor waste management results in contaminated land, blighting development and incurring extensive clean-up costs, which the original polluters still rarely pay for, despite the extension of liability laws. In Britain, the birthplace of the Industrial Revolution, there are over 200,000 hectares of contaminated land, with potential clean-up costs in the region of £10–30 billion.[30]

Inadequate effluent control can also generate a build-up of toxic materials in rivers and seas, which can remain long after emissions have been reduced. On the Mersey, for example, ICI's Runcorn plant has manufactured chlorine by the electrolysis of brine for many decades. The plant uses the flowing mercury cathode cell process, which historically produced considerable amounts of mercury effluent with potentially severe consequences for human and other life. Regulatory controls and industrial investment has cut discharges of mercury from the Runcorn site from 60 tonnes a year in the mid-1970s to less than half a tonne in 1997.[31] Despite these substantial discharge reductions, there remains an accumulated reservoir of mercury in the sediments of the Mersey Estuary, although recent research suggests that levels of mercury in fish are starting to decline too.[32]

FOUR STEPS TO SUSTAINABLE PRODUCTION

Within the conventional model of industrial production, the environment is viewed simply as a source of raw material inputs and a sink for the inevitable wastes generated by production and product use. When environmental problems have arisen, the first response was often to control pollution through measures to 'dilute and disperse' emissions. Now, industrial pioneers are focusing on eliminating pollution and waste in the production process first through steps to improve efficiency, then to institutionalize environmental factors into mainstream manufacturing and finally to restructure production to make zero emissions the norm. For sustainable cities, this four-step process is presented in Table 9.2.

Table 9.2 *Four steps to sustainable industrial production in cities*

	Firm	City	Nation
Step 1: Control	End of pipe technology	Relocation	End of pipe regulation
Step 2: Efficiency	Cleaner production	Collective environmental services	Environmental assessment
Step 3: Institutionalize	Life-cycle environmental management	Eco-industrial estates	Integrated pollution control
Step 4: Restructure	Zero emissions	Carrying capacity planning	Extended producer responsibility

THE NEED FOR PLANNING

Perhaps the most basic requirement in ensuring the sustainable growth of industrial cities and urban areas is a sound regional plan based on estimates of its carrying capacity, including detailed information and recommendations on the zoning and siting of industry. Unfortunately many cities in the North and the South have not been planned with foresight, but have grown instead almost haphazardly. The consequences are clear: declining air and water quality, water shortages, congestion, noise and, increasingly, industrial closures (see Box 9.2).

Box 9.2 *Constraints to industrial pollution control in Indian cities*

- Land-use patterns are poorly regulated.
- Industrial areas are often located amidst residential areas.
- Large numbers of small-scale industries, located in clusters, lack pollution control and treatment facilities.
- Many facilities use obsolete and/or inefficient production processes that generate high volumes of wastes.
- An absence of clear responsibility for the safe collection, transportation and disposal of industrial waste.

Source: TERI, *Looking Back to Think Ahead,* Tata Energy Research Institute, New Delhi (1998)

In India, public pressure in response to the deteriorating urban environment is forcing governments to pass new legislation resulting in the closure and relocation of industry. The case of the petroleum refinery and small iron foundries around the Taj Mahal in India is one of the better known examples where industries have been threatened with closure if they fail to install pollution-control measures and/or relocate. Other cases in India include the textile industry in Tirupur where 460 units were closed by order of the Supreme Court in May 1998 for failing to install effluent treatment plants. The court ruling came after a lengthy legal battle on a petition filed by local farmers who claimed that the discharge of untreated waste water by textile manufacturers had polluted irrigation water and was affecting agricultural produce. This and similar incidents have prompted the Ministry of Environment and Forests (MOEF) of India to come up with new national legislation requiring highly polluting industries to be located 25 kilometres outside of cities with a population of 1 million and 7 kilometres away from biosphere reserves, national parks and wetlands. The ruling will also ban industrial units from locating near archaeological monuments.

Relocating industry is clearly an option of last resort, often bringing severe socioeconomic costs in terms of local livelihoods. Such actions point to the need for proactive regional planning based on an environmental assessment of local and regional carrying capacity. Although many industrial cities in India are well established, it is still possible to elaborate rigorous regional plans for existing and new industries. One such example is the Jamshedpur region in the eastern state of Bihar. The concentration and rapid growth of heavy industry, based around the Tata Iron and Steel Company (TISCO), has put immense pressure on the natural resources of the region. The Subranekha river, the main source of domestic and industrial water supply, is polluted and depleted, causing conflict with other water users downstream. Air quality also fails to meet national ambient standards and solid wastes are not properly managed.

The National Environmental Engineering Research Institute has now been commissioned by local industries to carry out a regional environmental impact assess-

---

Box 9.3 *Environmental management of industrial estates*

Since 1970, the number of industrial estates has increased dramatically, especially in the rapidly industrializing countries of Asia, and now stands at over 12,000. More than 500 of these are categorized as export processing zones. Although many of today's industrial estates pose a substantial threat to the environment, the UN Environment Programme argues that systematic and continuous environmental improvement could raise the overall performance of industrial estates, citing good practice around the globe. For example, the Industrial Estate Authority of Thailand has adopted an environmental policy that includes joint implementation with the community and business partners, and support for waste minimization. In India, the range of companies operating in and around the Jeedimetia Industrial Estate near Hyderabad set up an independent effluent company to treat their waste water efficiently, while the Penang Development Corporation in Malaysia provides incentives to encourage the establishment of proper facilities for hazardous wastes. Improvements in environmental management have often brought financial benefits. UNEP has recently developed environmental management guidelines for new and existing estates along with worksheets for estate managers .[33]

ment study. The study is the largest such exercise in India and although it is still to be finalized, interim conclusions highlight the importance of an integrated and collective approach by both business and municipal authorities to environmental management. Industrial estates can offer opportunities for such an approach (see Box 9.3).

MINIMIZING INDUSTRIAL WASTE

Cleaner production, pollution prevention, waste minimization and eco-efficiency – largely interchangeable phrases to describe efforts to cut environmental impacts and improve resource efficiencies – are now entering the industrial mainstream. Many large manufacturers have adopted corporate wide programmes, such as 3M's Pollution Prevention Pays (3P) scheme, which has now saved more than $750 million and cut environmental impacts dramatically. The Dow chemical company has introduced its own Waste Reduction Always Pays Programme (WRAP), and each of Dow's manufacturing divisions are responsible for the development and implementation of its own WRAP projects. Dow has calculated that WRAP has led to substantial reductions in emissions and inputs, such as a 50 per cent reduction in spills at a polyurethane plant; an 80 per cent reduction in consumption of a reactant in an agricultural products plant; and a 93 per cent reduction in air emissions and 48 per cent increase in production capacity at a latex plant. WRAP projects also save money and are expected to continue yielding 30–40 per cent returns on capital for the foreseeable future.

A persistent problem has been the failure to stimulate waste minimization among smaller companies, who often lack the awareness, managerial and financial resources, regulatory scrutiny or public reputation, that drive programmes in large international firms. One approach has been to establish demonstration projects in particular towns and cities to encourage take-up (see Box 9.4).

In Britain, one of the leading examples is the Aire and Calder project in Yorkshire, which brought together 11 companies on the Aire and Calder river valleys to assess the benefits of a systematic approach to emissions reduction. The project had three major features: first, it took a river catchment rather than a sector focus in order to provide a common interest for participants and provide a link to the local community; second, it required companies to make a financial contribution to stimulate a greater sense of ownership and commitment; and third, the project made use of a club approach, bringing the project champions together with local regulators in a continuous learning exercise to review progress and exchange information.

Waste minimization audits were carried out within each company, generating an initial list of 900 measures which could reduce waste, improve efficiency and save money. More than two-thirds of the savings came from reductions in the use of inputs, such as raw materials, energy and water, achieved through relatively simple 'good housekeeping' and technology modifications, highlighting the importance of viewing waste as a symptom of inefficient resource use rather than as an inevitable by-product to be managed.[34] Within two years, 60 per cent of measures had been implemented, generating financial savings of £3.35 million; just under 90 per cent of these measures had pay-back periods of less than two years. Following the success of Aire and Calder and similar initiatives, about 16 regional waste minimization clubs have been established across Britain to provide a framework of mutual encouragement and peer pressure.

But, despite these impressive financial and environmental savings, the resource efficiency ethic has still to be institutionalized within business, despite regulatory and supply chain pressures and the examples of good practice from a host of pilot projects. One recent study suggests that almost half of UK companies still have no plans for waste minimization and do not even keep track of the costs of waste generation, and so generally underestimate the costs of waste management and overestimate the costs of minimization.[35] This points to the continuing inability of the regulatory framework to make polluters pay the full costs of their impacts on the environment. The need for co-ordinated action bringing together industry

---

Box 9.4 *Collective action for waste minimization in Surat*

Surat is one of the largest industrial centres in the western Indian state of Gujarat, based around the production of synthetic textiles. Its 220 synthetic textile processing units and 15 dyestuff manufacturers between them consume 10 million gallons of water per day and release more than 7 million gallons of largely untreated effluents into Surat's drains and creeks every day. Most of these units are small or medium in scale and have either none or at best very basic effluent treatment facilities. As a result of the excessive extraction of ground water, the water table has fallen from 18 metres to 55 metres. Unchecked industrialization has also had an adverse impact on Surat's air quality, with particular problems faced by residents in neighbouring domestic areas. Finally, the poor state of Surat's water, sanitation and waste-management facilities aggravated the effects of the plague which struck the city in 1994. In the aftermath of the plague, state and city authorities came under intense pressure to enforce municipal legislation and stringent pollution control norms.

According to a recent study, 'Surat is a prime example of how effective enforcement of laws could miraculously transform the "plague city" to the "second cleanest city" in India'.[37] Proper enforcement along with pressures of depleting natural resources and cost-efficiency considerations prompted the textile industry in Surat to initiate voluntary action to promote waste minimization. In 1994, a Waste Management Group (WMG) was set up by textile processors, dyestuff manufacturers and academics. The group's objective is to minimize waste generation and create awareness about the benefits of pollution prevention and control within the textile industry. Waste minimization in the textile industry is achieved through reusing and recycling water and chemicals, and through chemical substitution. The WMG disseminated information on the benefits and costs of environmental audits and waste minimization, as well as preparing Safety Data Sheets for 200 chemicals and dyes commonly used by the textile manufacturers in Surat. The Group carried out environmental impact studies for the textile industry, prepared manuals on energy and water conservation and launched waste minimization demonstration projects.

The activities of the WMG have brought financial savings as well as water and energy conservation. For example, Garden Vareli Mills spent 20 million rupees (approximately £295,000) on installing effluent water reuse plants and is now reaping the benefit by reusing up to 80 per cent of the effluents discharged every hour. It also recycles the water used to cool jet dying machines. By automating the printing machines to stop overflow of water, Paradise Prints saves 1.1 million litres of water every month. Reusing dyebath water conserves another 70,000 litres each month, reducing the pollution load by 90 per cent. Energy consumption is down by 40 per cent and chemical use by 85 per cent.

---

and government to reduce pollution loads is further highlighted in the case of small-scale lead smelters in Calcutta.[36] A recent study concludes that the most efficient way to improve the environmental performance of these units is for government and industry to adopt an interactive approach combining technical, economic and policy measures. Purely technical solutions adopted by the industry on its own are unlikely to solve the problem since very often these solutions are not the most cost effective.

Institutionalizing Environmental Responsibility

Environmental management systems (EMS) are now growing in importance as a voluntary tool for corporations to institutionalize environmental responsibility throughout their operations. The two main initiatives for certifying EMS are the EU's Eco-Management and Audit Scheme (EMAS) and the International Organization for Standardization's ISO14001 system. Internationally, ISO14001 is more likely to become the benchmark, given its privileged status within the World Trade Organization (WTO) framework. The ISO14001 standard lays down the requirements which companies need to meet achieve third-party certification. Companies need to have an environmental policy, assess their environmental aspects and legal obligations, install a management system, carry out periodic internal audits and make a public declaration that ISO14001 is being implemented. ISO14001 is very much an internal management tool and it is left up to companies themselves to define their environmental policy and the scope of the system (eg whether it applies to their entire operations or only to particular sites). Companies applying for ISO14001 have to commit to continuous improvement of the environmental management system, not to improve environmental performance itself.

By the end of 1998, more than 5,000 certificates had been awarded worldwide, with Japan, Germany and the UK dominating so far; the uptake in Asia remains strong, with growing numbers of companies in China, India, Korea, Malaysia and Thailand getting certified. Further growth is expected as companies start to use ISO14001 as part of supply chain management, making it crucial for access to the global marketplace, according to its advocates. Leading companies such as IBM and Daimler-Benz are now asking their suppliers to seek certification.

But others view the current ISO14001 standard as 'a missed opportunity to contribute to global sustainable industrial development'.[38] Countries from the South have been poorly represented in the design of ISO14001 and are concerned at the extra costs it could bring, particularly for small and medium-sized producers. In addition, the ISO scheme does not provide any guarantee of higher environmental performance or ensure that companies commit to pollution prevention. It also marks a step backwards in terms of employee and public participation from the agreements signed at Rio and does not require companies to report publicly on their environmental performance, although many large firms do now issue corporate environmental reports.[39] In the forthcoming round of revisions to the ISO system, considerable efforts will be needed to turn the scheme from a relatively closed business-to-business tool to one which can stimulate progress towards sustainable production and greater corporate accountability.

BEYOND ECO-EFFICIENCY: MOVING TO INDUSTRIAL ECOLOGY

Despite the gains made by waste minimization and pollution-prevention initiatives, there is a growing recognition that cleaner, more efficient production in itself may not deliver sustainability. As William McDonagh and Michael Braungart have suggested recently, 'relying on eco-efficiency to save the environment will in fact achieve the opposite – it will let industry finish off everything quietly, persistently and completely'.[40] The problem as they see it is one of design and the need to move from the traditional linear industrial approach to one that draws inspiration from natural systems so that 'all products and materials manufactured by industry must after each useful life provide nourishment for something new'. Eco-efficiency only slows down the rates of contamination and depletion, but does not eliminate the design flaw itself. These principles were applied to the development of a new type of 'ecologically intelligent' textile. After exhaustive investigation, the end result produced water effluent as clean leaving the factory as entering it.

A similar ethic guides the UN Zero Emissions Research Initiative which defines the concept of zero emissions as 'No liquid waste. No gaseous waste. No solid waste. All inputs are used in production. When waste occurs, it is used to create value by other industries'.[41] ZERI thus aims to go beyond minimizing downstream effects within existing industrial processes – the focus of most cleaner production initiatives – and search for new industries upstream in the process and find value-added use for the residues which have no value in the main production. The first zero emissions sorghum brewery has been launched in Namibia. Its by-products, such as spent grains, yeast sediment and waste water, are used to raise livestock and fish, fertilize crops, produce biogas and substrate for growing mushrooms, proving it is possible to have 'good beer, no chemicals, no pollution, more sales and more jobs'. The first 'zero emission' industrial park is also under development in Chattanooga.[42]

Underlying these pioneering efforts is the philosophy of industrial ecology.[43] In place of the traditional model of industry in which individual manufacturing units take in raw materials and generate products to be sold and waste to be disposed of, the consumption of energy and materials is brought to sustainable levels and the effluents of one process serve as the raw material for another. Industrial ecology is critical to the development of sustainable cities as it goes beyond the conventional focus on the individual firm to place industrial production within a wider ecosystem view. Applying industrial ecology to manufacturing in cities could result in less use of virgin materials, a cut in pollution, increased energy efficiency and a reduction in waste volumes requiring disposal.

At the most basic level, industrial ecology can be applied through the exchange of by-products between different companies and sectors. The industrial district of Kalundborg in Denmark is now the most famous example of an industrial ecosystem, where for 15 years a refinery, coal-fired power plant and a pharmaceutical plant have exchanged surplus energy, waste heat and other materials. Although these exchanges developed incrementally, financial savings of $120 million have been realized from investments of about $60 million. The Kalundborg industrial symbiosis system is now globally known and other examples are starting to emerge. In Texas, a range of by-product synergies have been developed by a cluster of cement, steel and auto-shredding operations. The Chapparral Steel Company has increased profits and reduced pollution by using electric arc furnace slag as an input for cement making. Other possibilities exist for retrofitting existing industrial areas and designing new 'eco-industrial parks' based on a complex interlocking of different companies and sectors using the principles of industrial ecology right from the start.

But while these examples of industrial ecology certainly offer considerable financial and environmental savings by taking a systems approach to managing local material flows, they are by no means sustainable. For example, the Kalundborg system relies on material exchange from fossil fuel-based producers. A more thorough restructuring is required, moving away from dependence on extractive resources.

INDUSTRIAL RESTRUCTURING FOR SUSTAINABLE CONSUMPTION

While the social and environmental problems generated by industrial production remain acute in many cities, the link between urban development and industrialization has now been broken in the highest income countries. As a result, 'the wastes associated with dissipative consumption now exceed waste emissions from manufacturing processes per se by a considerable margin in the most advanced economies'.[44] In the contemporary post-industrial city, the environmental costs associated with manufacturing occur beyond the factory gate, generated during the sourcing, consumption and disposal of industrial products in urban regions. As Lee Schipper has described the sustainability challenge for energy use, the problem has shifted 'from production to pleasure'. Thus, growth in individual mobility and household comfort alone since 1973 raised energy use in high-income countries almost as much as improved efficiency reduced energy use.[45]

Increasing attention is being focused on sustainable consumption strategies in the urban regions of the North: improving the efficiency of product use, changing land use policies to enable less material intensive lifestyles; extending producer responsibility for the wastes generated by industrial products at the end of their useful life; and delinking quality of life improvements from consumption growth. This agenda goes beyond the old 'green consumer' phenomenon, which relied on the purchasing power of an informed and affluent minority to drive demand for sustainable goods and services. The emerging vision is of a new service economy, in which manufacturing companies provide services rather than sell products, delivering more function and less 'stuff': selling light not energy, cleaning not solvents, pest control not pesticides, comfort not carpets, mobility not cars.[46] One result is a possible shift to leasing rather than purchasing consumer durables, such as electronics. For example, in the USA, Interface, a commercial floor covering company has launched an innovative programme selling its customers 'comfort' rather than carpets. The customer leases the floor covering and once it comes to the end of its useful life a new version is provided and the old material is recovered and reused.[47]

Pressure is also coming to rethink consumption from a shift in responsibility for waste management from public authorities to producers. In Germany, the 1996 Closed Substance Cycle and Waste Management Act means that whoever produces, markets and consumes goods is responsible for the avoidance, recycling, reuse and environmentally sound disposal of waste. Starting with packaging, this has resulted in about a 10 per cent reduction since 1991. An extended producer responsibility approach is now being applied to the electronics and automobile sectors.

TAKING RESPONSIBILITY FOR TRADE

The move to make producers responsible for the end of life waste generated by their products is matched by growing pressures to ensure that the sourcing of products sold in post-industrial cities is carried out on an ethical and sustainable basis. Trade liberalization, the increasing dominance of multinational corporations, information technology and historically low energy prices have enabled manufacturers to relocate and contract out production into developing economies and reimport the semi-finished products for final assembly. However, this process has often been accompanied by a parallel relocation of environmental hazards.

Rising concern about the environmental and social impacts along the supply chain production is now prompting change, however.[48] A growing number of North American and European companies, including retailers, are integrating social and environmental requirements into their supplier requirements, particularly for food, forest products, electronics and textiles (see Box 9.5). But it is not yet clear how the risks and rewards of these schemes will be distributed along the supply chain and there is concern that ill-thought out initiatives could disadvantage the less powerful members of the suppliers. As some Indian industrialists commented recently, 'If we are slow in responding to the demands of the times and are weak in our commitments it will only strengthen the belief in the North that trade restrictions on a multilateral level are adequate instruments for achieving improvements. Are we, the developing countries, ready to face this challenge?'[49]

Fashion-conscious and alert to consumer trends, the textiles industry has been sensitive to intensifying international scrutiny of the life-cycle social and environmental impacts of growing, processing and using clothes. All this has had implications for trade, where many countries in the South have a critical role. Key initiatives include efforts to shift cotton production on to a more sustainable basis using organic and integrated pest-management techniques and bans on the use of potentially harmful dyes in the manufacturing stage.

Responding to consumer and citizen pressures, retailers are increasingly a driving force for change, introducing codes of conduct to implement social and environmental standards along the chain. One of the leaders is Otto Versand, a German

---

Box 9.5 *Towards a sustainable timber trade*

Established in the early 1990s by citizen groups concerned about the failure of government policy to regulate poor forest practice, the Forest Stewardship Council has established principles and criteria for sustainable forest management which are used to certify the performance of forest operators; successful companies can use the FSC logo on their products, provided that the chain of custody is certified. Right from the beginning, the FSC has worked to develop markets for certified timber. In the UK, the Worldwide Fund for Nature (WWF) has established a buyers' group for FSC certified products, which now has 85 members, including major DIY stores, supermarkets and magazine and paper products manufacturers and retailers, which together account for 14 per cent of the UK's consumption of forest products. Since November 1996, the area of certified forest has more than doubled to 6.3 million hectares in 20 countries and it is expected that 10 million hectares will be certified by the end of 1998.

family owned company which is now the world's largest mail order firm, with 1996–1997 turnover of DM25.9 billion. About half of its products are sourced from overseas. Environmental standards have played an important role in supplier policies for a number of years and have been promoted in co-operation with supplier companies. Otto Versand is now beginning to address social issues. In their 1996 annual report the firm states: 'In order to guarantee sustainable production, suppliers are requested to implement social minimum standards next to ecological ones. Otto Versand also in the future will exploit all possibilities in order to promote a justifiable environmental, social and thereby sustainable trade policy'.[50]

But beyond screening the social and environmental performance of products, a further challenge for sustainable trade is to cut the environmental costs of freight transport and thereby increase the proximity of production and consumption. 'A new equilibrium will have to emerge between economies of scale and resource efficiency', according to Ernst von Weizsäcker. This could bring many benefits for city economies, as 'the depth of manufacture will increase again as the supply of parts from very distant places becomes an apparent absurdity'.[51]

VISIONS FOR THE FUTURE

If cities are to prosper in a fair and sustainable way, then a new role will have to be found for manufacturing industry. It has taken over a hundred years to realize that industrial production needs to be firmly rooted within the constraints implied by local carrying capacity and social need. But the challenge goes far beyond the factory gate and extends to the materials that industry sources and the products it sells in urban areas. From the review of international practice, the following elements appear to be essential for making the transition:

1   *Market transformation:* Sustainable industrial production and consumption in cities requires a market transformation on both the supply and demand sides. Making this happen will require public policies at the city and national level to steer industrial development markets through regulation, economic instruments and planning (including strategic environmental assessment) to deal with persistent 'market failures'.
2   *Environmental regeneration:* The goals for manufacturing in sustainable cities go beyond reactive environmental protection; ultimately, industry must ensure that the processes it uses and the products it provides cause no net loss of local and global carrying capacity – and indeed, lead to the regeneration of environmental capacities for future generations.
3   *Social justice:* Historically, the costs of industrial development in cities have fallen mostly on the poor and excluded. A critical element for sustainable cities is social justice and for the manufacturing sector, this implies effective measures both to control environmental hazards for employees and the surrounding community and to give access to critical decision-making that affects the distribution of costs and benefits from industrial production.
4   *Extended responsibility:* Taking a life-cycle approach to sustainable development requires producers and retailers to adopt an extended sense of responsibility for the social and environmental impacts of their products from cradle to grave, assuring raw materials are sustainably sourced, zero pollution during manufacture and programmes for efficient consumption and recycling after use.

5   *Resource productivity:* The scale of the sustainability imperative for manufactur-
    ing industry requires a concerted focus on boosting resource productivity, go-
    ing beyond the relatively simple savings that can be made through 'good house-
    keeping' measures to the process optimization and re-engineering steps that
    can deliver 'factor 4' and 'factor 10' improvements.

6   *Infrastructure investment:* Many of the problems facing industrial development
    in cities go beyond market failures and are to do with misconceived public poli-
    cies which subsidize pollution and waste through long-term investments in ma-
    terial-intensive land-use patterns. Instead, significant public investments will be
    required in collective effluent and waste treatment, energy-efficiency programmes
    and mass freight and transit systems.

7   *Planning and precaution:* Sustainable development is by definition focused on
    the long term and for manufacturing this means adopting a precautionary ap-
    proach to future developments to avoid the build-up of potential liabilities, such
    as contaminated land and also to ensure that technological innovation is geared
    to sustainability requirements.

8   *Community empowerment:* Achieving sustainable development involves trade-
    offs and the resolution of competing interests. Industry needs to continually
    earn its 'licence to operate' from the wide group of stakeholders that are affected
    by its operations: employees, consumers, the community. Ensuring that these
    often under-represented groups have an impact on industrial development will
    require community empowerment through consultation, participation and pub-
    lic reporting.

9   *Local partnerships:* The complexities of sustainable industrial development re-
    quire new types of partnership within industry, between industry and the pub-
    lic sector and with its wider group of stakeholders. Such partnerships are par-
    ticularly important to build up peer and community pressure for action and to
    stimulate the more open sharing of experience and good practice.

10 *Global co-operation:* Globalization and the increasing ferocity of international
    competition means that individual companies, cities or countries cannot uni-
    laterally move to sustainable manufacturing systems. Global action is required
    to set the broad 'rules of the game' for industrial production and consumption,
    to encourage co-operation along international supply chains and drive the fi-
    nancial and technological transfers to countries in the South that are necessary
    for 'leap-frogging' to take place.

Some cities are already starting to explore the possibilities. In the City-Region 2020
project, analysts have investigated the prospects for long-term sustainable development in the British city of Manchester. As Joe Ravetz, the project leader, explains,
'Manchester, arguably the world's first industrial city, is a topical place to explore the
sustainable local economy'. Although the city faces a host of historical and present day
obstacles to sustainability, 'there is every possibility that its post-industrial economy
could be based on zero-emission ethical trade'.[52] The long-term social, economic and
environmental benefits are now becoming clear. The task is for citizens, communities and companies to push forward with industrial restructuring as part of the transition to sustainable cities.

NOTES AND REFERENCES

1   Nick Robins and Alex Trisoglio, 'Restructuring Industry for Sustainable Development' in Johan Holmberg (ed), *Policies for a Small Planet*, Earthscan (1992)
2   John Simon, Minutes of Evidence, Royal Commission on Noxious Vapours (1878) quoted in Anthony S Wohl, *Endangered Lives: Public Health in Victorian Britain*, Methuen, London (1983)
3   See A Grubler, 'Industrialisation as a Historical Phenomenon', in R Socolow et al (ed) *Industrial Ecology and Global Change*, Cambridge University Press (1994) for a review of long-term trends
4   H Stretton, *Urban Planning in Rich and Poor Countries*, Oxford University Press, Oxford (1978) quoted in Graham Haughton and Colin Hunter, *Sustainable Cities*, Jessica Kingsley Publishers, London and Bristol Pennsylvania, 1994
5   William Rees, 'Ecological footprints and appropriated carrying capacity' in *Environment and Urbanization*, Vol 4, No 2, October 1992
6   See Karl Polanyi, *The Great Transformation*, Victor Gollancz (1945) for the classic exposition of this double movement
7   See Barbara Ward, *Progress for a Small Planet*, Pelican Books, London 1979 and World Commission on Environment and Development, *Our Common Future*, Oxford University Press, Oxford (1987)
8   OECD, *State of the Environment*, Organization for Economic Cooperation and Development, Paris, 1991
9   World Resources Institute, *World Resources 1998–99*, Oxford University Press (1998)
10   Stefan Schmidheiny, *Changing Course*, MIT Press, Cambridge MA (1992)
11   Nick Robins, *Getting Eco-Efficient*, World Business Council for Sustainable Development, Geneva (1994)
12   Michael E Porter and Claas van der Linde, 'Green and Competitive: Ending the Stalemate', *Harvard Business Review*, September–October 1995
13   F Schmidt-Bleek, *The Factor 10*, UNEP Cleaner Production Conference, Oxford, September 1996
14   Ernst von Weizsaecker, Amory B Lovins and L Hunter Lovins, *Factor 4*, Earthscan, London (1998)
15   TERI, *Looking Back to Think Ahead*, Tata Energy Research Institute, New Delhi (1998)
16   David Wallace, *Sustainable Industrialization*, Earthscan/RIIA, London (1996)
17   Works reviewed included: Stefan Schmidheiny, *Changing Course*, MIT Press (1992); Tim Jackson (ed), *Clean Production Strategies*, Lewis (1993); Paul Hawken, *The Ecology of Commerce*, Harper (1993); Claude Fussler, *Driving Eco-Innovation*, Pitman (1996); John Elkington, *Cannibals with Forks*, Capstone (1997); and Ernst von Weizsaecker, Amory B Lovins and L Hunter Lovins, *Factor 4*, Earthscan (1998)
18   Lewis Mumford, *The City in History*, Penguin, Harmondsworth (1974)
19   See OECD, *State of the Environment Report*, Paris (1991); WorldWatch Institute, *State of the World Report 1995*, Earthscan, London (1995)
20   TERI, op cit (1998)
21   International Council of Chemical Associations, *Responsible Care Status Report*, ICCA, Brussels (1996)
22   Green, Reg, 'The Chemical Industry's Responsible Care Programme: Viewed from an international trade union perspective' in *Industry and Environment*, Vol 21, No 1–2, January–June 1998
23   Maryanne Grieg-Gran et al, *Towards a Sustainable Paper Cycle*, IIED, London (1996)
24   Michael K Dorsey, 'Toward an Idea of International Environmental Justice', in *World Resources 1998–99*
25   Charlie Pye-Smith, Grazia Borrini Feyerabend and Richard Sandbrook, *The Wealth of Communities*, Earthscan, London (1994)
26   Chris Church, *A Disproportionate Impact ?*, UNED-UK, London (1998)
27   Robert Nurick and Victoria Johnson, 'Towards community-based indicators for monitoring quality of life and the impact of industry in south Durban', *Environment and Urbanization*, Vol 10, No 1, April 1998
28   Maria Elena Foronda F, 'Chimbote's Local Agenda 21: initiatives to support its development and implementation' in *Environment and Urbanization*, Vol 10, No 2, October 1998
29   Ewa Charkiewicz, PRTR – *A Right to Know Tool and an Incentive to Clean Up*, Tools for Change, Autumn 1997
30   Rupert Howes, Jim Skea and Bob Whelan, *Clean and Competitive ?*, Earthscan (1997)

31 National Rivers Authority, *The Mersey Estuary, A Report on Environmental Quality* (1995)

32 ICI, Environmental Issues, Runcorn Site (1998)

33 UNEP, *The Environmental Management of Industrial Estates*, UN Environment Programme, Industry and Environment Office, Paris (1997)

34 For more information on Aire and Calder, see Rupert Howes, op cit (1997)

35 Tim Jackson, *Material Concerns*, Routledge, London (1996)

36 Nandini Dasgupta, Greening small recycling firms: the case of lead smelting units in Calcutta, in *Environment and Urbanization*, Vol 9, No 2, October 1997

37 Prasad Modak, *Case Studies of Cleaner Production*, Environment Management Centre, Mumbai (1998)

38 Riva Krut and Harris Gleckman, *ISO14001: A Missed Opportunity for Sustainable Global Industrial Development*, Earthscan, London (1998)

39 See 'Sustainability and UNEP', *Engaging Stakeholders: The Benchmark Survey*, UNEP, Paris (1996) for a useful review of international practice

40 William McDonagh and Michael Braungart, The Next Industrial Revolution, The Atlantic Monthly, October 1998

41 ZERI, *A New Hope for Sustainable Development in Africa*, University of Namibia and United Nations University (1998)

42 Karen Schmidt, 'The zero option', *New Scientist*, 1 June 1996

43 For a useful historical overview of industrial ecology, see Suren Erkman, *Journal of Cleaner Production* (1997)

44 Robert Ayres, 'Industrial Metabolism' in Tim Jackson (ed) *Clean Production Strategies*, Lewis Publishers (1993)

45 Lee Schipper, *Energy Use and Human Activity: What's Wrong and What can be Done?*, in Symposium: Sustainable Consumption, Ministry of Environment, Norway, 1994

46 Tim Jackson, *Material Concerns*, Routledge (1996)

47 Nick Robins and Sarah Roberts, *Consumption in a Sustainable World*, Ministry of Environment, Oslo (1998)

48 Nick Robins and Sarah Roberts, *Unlocking Trade Opportunities*, IIED, London (1997)

49 Aloke Mookherjea, A K Ghose and Ranjana Ganguly, Synergy of Trade and Environment, in *Green Business Opportunities*, CII, New Delhi, January–March 1998

50 Nick Robins and Sarah Roberts, *Environmental Responsibility in World Trade*, British Council, London (1998)

51 Ernst Von Weiszaecker, 'How to achieve progress towards sustainability?' in *Report of the Symposium: Sustainable Consumption*, Ministry of Environment – Norway, Oslo (1994)

52 Joe Ravetz, *City-Region 2020*, Earthscan, London, forthcoming 1999

Chapter 10

Agriculture: Urban Agriculture for Sustainable Cities: Using Wastes and Idle Land and Water Bodies as Resources

Jac Smit and Joe Nasr

(Reprinted from *Environment and Urbanization*, Vol 4, No 2, October 1992, pp 141–152. For those seeking more information, see the book by these two authors and Annu Ratta – *Urban Agriculture: Food, Jobs and Sustainable Cities*, Jac Smit, Annu Ratta and Joe Nasr (1996). Publication series for Habitat II, Vol 1, UNDP, New York. A new updated edition will be published in 2000)

Summary: This paper describes how cities can be transformed from being only consumers of food and other agricultural products into important resource-conserving, health-improving, sustainable generators of these products. In particular, agriculture in towns, cities and metropolitan areas can convert urban wastes into resources, put vacant and under-utilized areas into productive use, and conserve natural resources outside cities while improving the environment for urban living. Agriculture within urban and peri-urban areas is defined as a common and beneficial land use. This paper also gives examples of urban agriculture programmes which help to alleviate poverty while creating these benefits.

THE SCALE AND SCOPE OF URBAN AGRICULTURE

This paper argues that sustainable cities require an economic process to close the open loop system where consumables are imported into the urban areas and their remainders and packaging dumped as waste into the bioregion and biosphere. Thus, the 'through-put' of resources by towns and cities needs to be reduced.

The urban agriculture referred to in this paper is food and fuel grown within the daily rhythm of the city or town, produced directly for the market and frequently processed and marketed by the farmers or their close associates. It includes:

- aquaculture in tanks, ponds, rivers and coastal bays;
- livestock (particularly micro-livestock) raised in backyards, along roadsides, within utility rights-of-way, in poultry sheds and piggeries;
- orchards, including vineyards, street trees, and backyard trees; and

- vegetables and other crops grown on roof-tops, in backyards, in vacant lots of industrial estates, along canals, on the grounds of institutions, on roadsides and in many suburban small farms.

Urban agriculture is presented as a large and growing industry that uses urban waste water and urban solid waste as inputs which close ecological loops when processed on idle land and water bodies. The positive impacts of this neglected industry include: improved nutrition and health, an improved environment for living, increased entrepreneurship and improved equity.

The scale of urban agriculture in the world is far above common perceptions. In Kenya and Tanzania, two out of three urban families are engaged in farming, some full-time as entrepreneurs or wage earners and more as a part-time household activity.[1] In Taiwan over half of all urban families are members of farming associations. Large Chinese cities produce 90 per cent and more of their vegetable requirement within their urban regions. In America one-third of the agricultural product (in dollar terms) is produced within metropolitan areas.[2] Japan, The Netherlands and Chile are other examples of countries where there are more urban than rural farmers.

The benefits of urban agriculture vary with time and place. It is often a first line of defence against hunger and malnutrition at times of particular stress, as in Kinshasa and Lima at the time of this writing. It is a major process of poverty alleviation during periods of economic recovery, as seen during recent visits to Lusaka and Dar-es-Salaam. It improves the quality of the urban environment through greening and a reduction in pollution, beginning in the low-income neighbourhoods (where the greatest needs lie). It strengthens the economic base of a city or town by adding an 'import substitution' industry that includes production, processing, packaging and marketing. It does this primarily through small enterprises, although medium and large operations are also involved. Finally, urban agriculture, by closing open loops and reducing the through-put of resources in cities and towns, makes a large contribution to balancing the global ecology.

The core of this paper will focus on the resource aspect of urban agriculture. The relationship between urban agriculture and resources can be described as being three-pronged. First, some urban by-products, such as waste water and organic solid waste, can be recycled and transformed into resources or opportunities for growing agricultural products within urban and peri-urban areas. Second, some areas of cities, such as idle lands and bodies of water, can be converted to intensive agricultural production. Third, some other natural resources, such as energy for transportation and cooling, can be conserved through urban agriculture.[3]

The primary evidence for this study was assembled during visits to cities in 18 countries in Asia, Africa and Latin America during the past year. Support has poured in from many sources, from farmers in the field to prestigious centres of learning.

URBAN WASTES AS RESOURCES

With the rapidly growing metropolitan areas in Third World countries comes a concomitant growth in a variety of by-products of urban life. One of the principal limits to the sustainability of towns and cities is the disposal of some of these by-products, namely waste water and solid waste. Simply put, mega-cities of both the Third and the First Worlds, as well as smaller cities everywhere, are having increasing difficulty dealing with the problems of solid and liquid wastes.

A paradigmatic change in the way wastes are viewed may be starting to emerge globally, and it is important for this change to continue and to be accelerated. Wastes (with exceptions) need to be seen not as a problem to be disposed of, but as a resource for sustainable development. A vision of metropolitan areas is evolving from primarily *open loop* systems with one-way flows of resources (in) and wastes (out), to primarily *closed loop systems* where the definition of wastes and resources becomes blurred. In other words, cities can become more *resourceful* in both the literal and the figurative senses. Urban agriculture is a clear and significant example of this possibility of converting the consume-dispose open loops into consume-process-reuse closed loops.

One of the most significant imports into urbanized areas is food. At the same time, cities export daily a vast volume of wastes to be disposed of in their bioregion or in adjacent regions, with low-income cities having a much higher share of total waste as organic and food wastes. Historically, these wastes have been inputs into the production of a city's food and they can again become so. Converting food waste into fresh food reduces food costs, improves the quality of food available, improves the environment for living, creates jobs and reduces municipal management costs.

The reuse of urban waste, particularly metal, glass and paper, is already an established practice in even the most wasteful cities in Europe, Japan and North America, as is the recycling of a wider variety of products in Third World countries. The recycling of organic wastes, particularly in Third World countries, may be more significant to the ecology of urban bioregions because nutrient and pathogen pollution of the ecology are damaging to the health of the population and reduce the capacity of the environment to sustain future generations.[4] Urban agriculture can play an especially significant role in the recycling of organic wastes. These wastes can be divided into two categories: waste water and solid waste.

Waste Water

In cities of the arid and semi-arid regions, the availability of water for household use is limited. Water for irrigation is even less available. Thus, nutrient-rich waste water provides a precious agricultural input. Its value increases with a decreasing income level, as the potential user has less capacity to pay for organic and chemical fertilizers. Its value is also enhanced as it is available close to markets.

Waste water can substitute for fresh water, which then increases the availability of fresh water for drinking, cooking and other uses. It is self-evident that the urban areas produce great amounts of waste water of human origin, in direct proportion to their population. It therefore makes special sense to use it for irrigation of land and aquatic crops within metropolitan areas and adjacent to towns.

A number of cities in Third World countries already use this resource wisely. It has been estimated that one-tenth or more of the world's population currently eats food produced on waste water.[5] Mexico City pumps over half of its sewage 50 miles and more to the north, where it is used to irrigate over 100,000 hectares for livestock feed. One hundred other cities in Mexico use similar systems. Calcutta produces one-third of its fish in sewage-fed lagoons and a similar share of its vegetables from waste-water irrigation.[6]

Cities from China to California convert waste water safely into food. However, for each city that does so safely, the formal and informal sectors in many more cities are allowed to operate without monitoring or are directly engaged in practices that spread disease through improper use.

Some obstacles confront the utilization of waste water in urban agriculture. First, the use of wastes as agricultural inputs is more feasible in the urban areas of Third World countries than in those of industrial ones, as their wastes contain less chemicals and toxic materials. Careful monitoring is clearly necessary for such usage, and some cities in the Third World have built up sizeable industries over the past few decades. Still, even areas of heavy industry can contribute to urban agriculture. A good illustration is the Camaçari petrochemical complex in eastern Brazil, where the sludge recovered from the factories is used to improve the soils of nearby agricultural areas.[7]

A more serious obstacle to the use of municipal effluent as an input to food production in Third World countries is the presence of pathogens and vectors. Fortunately, this problem is readily manageable. Pathogens can be removed using two approaches. First, the waste water can be biologically treated to remove the pathogens sufficiently so that it can be safely used for irrigation and as a medium for raising fish and other aquatic crops. Low-capital intensive processes for eliminating pathogens and vectors exist. These commonly use: sunlight, time and an intermediate plant or animal such as algae or duckweed which is then used as organic fertilizer or animal feed.[8]

The second approach to managing the problem of pathogens focuses on the crop that is grown using waste water as an input, rather than the waste water. The susceptibility of crops to contamination varies. Some plants or animals absorb, retain and transmit pathogens more than others. At the simplest, fruit at the end of a branch transmits fewer pathogens than a leaf crop such as lettuce. Crops that are used as feed or inputs in the production of further crops are an extra step removed from human consumption and therefore usually safer.[9] The Mexico City system is an inefficient but effective example. Finally, many cities use waste water to grow forest crops for fuel, construction materials and improvement of the environment, ie non-food crops.

The most subtle and challenging hurdle to cross in the use of urban waste water for human food consumption may be 'culture'. In a number of cultures, irrigation with 'soiled water' is taboo. The first reaction to the concept is often an immediate 'But, it is not safe!'. The idea of properly 'disposing of' waste water dates back to the 'microbe hunters' of the late 19th century. This view, deeply ingrained in the 'modern' psyche, is communicated to many newly modernizing cultures.

Fear of contamination by unclean water has, over time, become institutionalized in law and in a reluctance by many governments and bureaucracies to move beyond this black-and-white view of water. Professional city managers and planners are concerned traditionally with public health and infrastructural efficiency; until the 1990s, they have generally been little concerned with the efficient reuse of waste to achieve ecologically sustainable towns and cities. Rather, they have tended to act as the enforcers of cultural values rooted in history rather than on today's problems and the ecological discoveries of the post-World War II period.[10]

Western cultural attitudes are not the only cultural barriers. Obstacles also exist among traditional cultures. Some of these obstacles are religious. In Muslim countries, for example, there is usually particular reticence to using waste water for aquaculture and irrigating crops. As the Middle East runs out of fresh water, it may need to be in the front line of waste-water agricultural research.

Some choices have to be made in the implementation of waste water reuse in urban agriculture. Where and when is it appropriate? At what scale is it best introduced? What might be the process in new and established cities? Choice, which is perforce political, must give local weight to at least the following: the cultural acceptability (less efficient processes may be called for in some cities), the relative scarcity of water or reliability of the source, the current and projected condition of the environment for living and its sustainability, the health implications for the population (in cities without an efficient sewer system reuse may be more urgent), and the cost of water, especially to low-income groups.

The scale of the waste-water management system is technically and politically significant. While waste-water systems since the middle of the 19th century have been based on the principles of economies of scale, modern biological technology seems to favour smaller systems. Considering energy, infrastructure and ecological impacts, neighbourhood and community systems may be both more appropriate and more efficient. This suits urban agriculture, which clearly can benefit from relatively dispersed sources of waste water for irrigation and aquaculture.

The transformation of waste water from a pollutant to an input is, in most applications, likely to be gradual rather than abrupt. The conversion from the 19th-century 'disposal system' to the 21st-century 'reuse system' may take a generation, being phased in over the useful life of the old system or according to the capacity of urban agriculture to absorb it. It can often be introduced first with non-existent or newly developing sewerage systems in portions of cities and towns. The overarching aim of the waste-water management system may well include the minimization of through-put. Thus, less waste water leaving a city may indicate a better system.

One in ten of the human population currently consumes food produced by the direct use of waste water, most of it with no or incomplete treatment. Urban agriculture offers a solution to this vast health problem, when properly practised. Rural and urban wastes dumped and leached into rivers, lakes, bays/lagoons, seas and the oceans are one of the greatest degraders of our bioregions and the biosphere. Waste-water aquaculture, livestock and horticultural farming systems focused on Third World urban markets can be a major tool in arresting and, in time, reversing this devastation.

Solid Waste

Solid waste in most cities and towns is a significant and essential input to sustainable urban agriculture. The contributions of solid waste are best separated into the organic and inorganic. The latter's usefulness in agriculture is as a source of soil, supplies and raw materials for construction. Chemical by-products from manufacturing are useful in soil improvement. Construction debris provides the base for shaping fields and ponds. Planting containers are built from wood and plastics of all sorts, recycled and reprocessed. Tyres are used as containers. Barrels hold irrigation water. Cut plastic bottles are used to grow crops on walls and fences, and plastic bags and sheeting are used as a mulch to conserve water and retard weeds. The more significant inputs are the organic solid wastes. The leading sources of organic wastes vary from climate to climate and economy to economy. Food wastes are always near the top of the list. Some foods generate more wastes than others, eg cabbage and green coconuts in tropical climates. In temperate climates, street trees and grass clippings are a significant source of organic waste. Some manufacturing processes such as paper production generate high levels of organic wastes. With proper concern about the lead content of some coloured inks, paper is a good mulch and soil-enhancing agent.

Many of the benefits of, and the impediments to, the utilization of waste water detailed above apply somewhat to organic wastes. Thus, health and cultural considerations are applicable here also. However, the wide use of organic solid wastes is far more accepted, as the prejudices against them do not exist in the same way, and the widespread use of manure as a fertilizer has never disappeared. Composting is widely accepted as a beneficial activity and its use is expanding, albeit not always using efficient processes.

The hurdles to a wider and more efficient use of solid wastes in urban agriculture are different than for waste water. Much of the agriculture that exists within urban areas is small scale and quite dispersed. The solid waste that originates in households and businesses in many cities is collected as a large system and transported to some major dumping locations within or outside the city. This process is not very conducive to maximizing the utilization of solid waste in agriculture or regenerating the natural resources of the city. Furthermore, most solid-waste management systems do not separate organic and inorganic and toxic and non-toxic wastes. Many solid wastes are also disposed of through waste-water systems.

A goal for managing solid waste in urban areas should therefore be to minimize the through-put. Thus, a basic measure of the soundness of the system is the paucity of solid waste exiting the urban area or bioregion. Redesigning solid-waste management from the point of view of the urban farmer and future generations may suggest sorting waste at the home or business and at the farm within or at the edge of the community. Such a system would aim to transform waste to fertile soil, green plants and food within portions of a city. It would principally collect and sort what is suitable as agricultural and landscape inputs, including composting and other modifications, before reuse.

An example is a farm in Jakarta on the property of a racetrack. The farmers recycle the track's wastes and those of the high-income surrounding neighbourhood. The wastes are sorted at a station within the farm. Glass, metal and cloth go to a recycling centre and organic material is composted on site. Everything moves by handcart. Thus, what goes to suburban, metropolitan landfills is very limited, and jobs and fresh food are generated within the community.

In addition to the system considerations, the use of organic solid waste as fertilizer has implications at the farm, household and neighbourhood levels. Thus, the urban farm, whether animal, horticultural or other, can be organized to collect and process as much of its nutrient-providing wastes as possible. The household with a backyard or a rooftop garden can be set up to reuse its own organic waste. Consequently, this is partly a technical matter and partly a matter of extension specialists showing the farmer *how* solid waste can be an input in urban agriculture.

In most urban situations, urban farmers collaborate with neighbours. Support from the municipality and major institutions is less common, and there are some legal obstacles to the retention and reuse of solid waste, especially in the more industrialized countries. However, some universities and botanical gardens have good support programmes in the Philippines, the USA, India and other countries. In conclusion, the foremost hurdles to a wider use of solid waste in urban agriculture are organizational rather than technical, sanitary or cultural, as is the case with waste water.

UNDER-UTILIZED URBAN LAND AND WATER SURFACES AS RESOURCES

Not only should the waste by-products of the urban areas be perceived and utilized as resources to be input into agricultural production within the urban domain, but the urban setting itself should also be seen as a resource to be tapped for the same productive purposes.

Cities in Third World countries are widely perceived as solidly built up with no area to spare. The use of a land area inside or at the edge of a city is seen typically as being at most an interim activity. Agriculture and urbanization are commonly viewed as conflicting activities. A closer look reveals, however, that there are considerable land and water areas in the urbanized sphere that are available for agricultural use. Furthermore, the agricultural use of areas at the edge of cities should not be regarded as a marginal use, but rather as an integral part of that urban area's expanding productive system. As the city grows, agriculture can grow with it, as the periphery extends and infill construction takes over farm sites.

Our studies to date indicate that nutritional self-reliance, in the sense of an urban area producing half or more of its nutritional requirements, is possible in all but the harshest climates, after consideration of land and water needs. The 1980 census found that the 18 largest urban regions in China were self-sufficient in vegetables and some even exported some of their surplus produce to other regions. Hong Kong, one of the world's densest cities, produced 40 per cent of its fish requirements within its waters in the mid-1980s and continues to develop more efficient technologies.

Every city has a special history, economy, landscape and culture. Whether urban agriculture can be established or expanded as an industry will depend on a city's special circumstances. Non-availability of land and water surfaces tends not to be a constraint to urban agriculture. The limits are more likely to be labour costs, or returns to labour, legal restrictions and land rent considerations. Legal and economic access to land and water bodies is a common problem.

All cities and towns have a number of vacant and underutilized surfaces in urban areas that can be used for agriculture. These surfaces include those areas not suited for built-up uses, idle public and other lands, lands that can have an interim use, community lands and household areas. The following sections describe how these can be used for urban agriculture.

Areas Not Suited for Built-up Uses

The most important such areas are probably those which are not suitable for substantial building. These include steep slopes, wetlands and flood-plains. For environmental reasons, the settlement of these areas is not desirable. Even if feasible, it can be costly to service. These areas are best kept as permanent open space, including cultivation.

In the case of steep slopes, forestry or terraced horticulture may be the best use of the land, stabilizing the slopes, preventing erosion and absorbing air pollution. Mexico City, for example, is attempting to maintain, for ecological reasons, a 'green belt' on its surrounding mountains. Mexico City also provides one of the best-known examples of an appropriate use of wetlands in its centuries-old *chinampas* farming system which combines aquatic, tree, vegetable and flower production with recreation, tourism and the trading of other areas' produce.[11] The floating fish-farms of Hong Kong are an example of a marine urban farming system. Finally, it is clear that intensive agriculture may be one of the only suitable economic uses for fertile but flood-prone areas anywhere.

Idle Public and Other Lands

In addition to the areas whose best use is for agriculture, there are a number of land areas in cities that are reserved in the longer term for other uses but which incorporate vast underutilized or unutilized tracts of land. These areas have a great potential for food production, waste-processing and other uses that enhance the environment.

As with waste water, a change in thinking is often needed to achieve this on a wide scale. If every sizeable piece of land (both public and private) which is not fully developed is looked at with the question 'Why is this land idle?' in mind, it would be possible to identify many potential agricultural areas. Resistance from those holding the land is often encountered, usually due to fear of loss of control. Since the agricultural use does not *have to be* permanent, these fears can be assuaged.

The use of the legal system is crucial for institutionalizing farmers' access to idle land. The validity and enforceability of leases and contracts can determine whether arrangements for such uses will be practicable. An important legal principle here is that of usufruct, which is essentially that any citizens can use land which is idle as long as the utility of the land to the owner is not diminished. Usufruct is basic in Roman law and some of its derivatives, including Italian and Spanish law. Much tribal law in Asia and Africa includes usufruct principles.

Many idle lands in cities are public or quasi-public, making their utilization for productive purposes even more imperative to serve the common good. They include land surrounding airport runways, low-density university areas, military reservations, prisons, hospitals and parks. These frequently cover very large areas in the cities of many Third World countries.

A number of these open areas are already used for agricultural purposes. The public entities that have leases for urban agriculture in operation include an airport in Cameroon, the University of Manila, hospitals in Lima, the Presidio military base in San Francisco and the Palace grounds in Bangkok. The case of the Jakarta racetrack has been described already in the context of solid waste management.

A special case of farming on public lands is agriculture along roadsides and other rights-of-way. It is a special case for two reasons. First, the area of land and its distribution throughout the urbanized areas are usually on a far greater scale than with other idle public lands. Second, the nature of the public area has significantly different implications for the nature of the agriculture. The linearity of the land means that it can extend far outside the metropolis and still be part of its foodshed. However, it also exposes the products to particular hazards such as theft and lead poisoning from car exhausts; this means the need for a careful selection of what is grown.

The fact that such agricultural areas follow transportation lines makes them especially suitable for the most intensive and productive types of food cultivation, allowing far easier access to the market or even roadside sale. One can witness radial foodsheds outside most major cities in sub-Saharan Africa. São Paulo has intensive agriculture under high-voltage electrical lines. In Europe, such farming is more commonly found along 19th-century railroads and canals.

Interim Use of Land

The use of idle urban lands for agriculture does not have to be permanent or even long-term. It can be a very adequate interim use. In Durgapur, a large planned industrial city in West Bengal, the plant managers leased land that was not to be built on until later years and provided access to the water reservoir which is used for cooling the steel, to the workers' union. The industrial city thus started to become nutritionally self-reliant.[12]

As a city grows, its perimeter grows more rapidly than its area. Therefore, there is always new land available temporarily at the edge of the city. As it grows, it is also always tearing down and rebuilding older neighbourhoods. Consequently, one finds temporary sites for urban agriculture near the centre. It is even possible for old factory buildings to be converted into mushroom and greenhouse agriculture.

While the lack of a secure tenure is very detrimental to a farmer who does not know whether he or she will see the fruit of their effort, tenure that is assured for a minimum of one season can be sufficient (depending on the crop and the condition of the land) for a farmer to be willing to farm. This can be vividly illustrated by the case of Matahalib Gardens, a community garden created in an idle, rubble-strewn parcel between two shanty areas of Manila. This community garden was very successful during its first year. In the second year, however, as word spread that the parcel was to be reclaimed for development, the efforts of the gardeners dropped and the yield fell with it dramatically. Thus, the interim availability of land is sufficient for farming, as long as it is a *secure* interim use.[13]

Tenure can be secured informally or it can be formalized through a contract. Again, the idea of usufruct, fruitfully using others' land, is key in validating interim urban agriculture. A number of countries and local governments have begun to articulate this principle. Peru is urging public and private landowners to make 'free land' available to farmers' associations.[14] The government of Indonesia and the municipality of Jakarta have a policy and programme of persuading public and private landowners to make 'sleeping land' productive.[15] New York City has made over 1000 vacant city-owned lots available to groups of farmers, and another 11,000 at public housing estates or projects.

Community Lands

Community gardening, along with backyard gardening, is the farming system most immediately associated with the idea of urban food production. Its contribution is clearly not negligible. It is particularly common in cultures where a long tradition of urban multicrop gardening exists.[16]

However, urban community agriculture goes beyond the community garden. Two other variants are worth mentioning. First, school gardens aim specifically at improving the nutritional status and consequently the health of school children, as well as instilling in them the techniques and habits of growing what they eat. Elementary school gardens have been, in some cultures, particularly effective in introducing urban farming to the families of the students. Second, in Latin America in particular, some of the community kitchens (*comedores populares*) increasingly have adjacent gardens to grow part of what is cooked in the kitchen and served to the members.[17]

Household Surfaces

As with community lands, there are more surfaces in the household where food can be grown than the backyard. The potential for using rooftops, balconies and the like for growing vegetables and micro-livestock for consumption and sale is largely untapped. Field visits to some homes provides a real eye-opening experience as to how resourcefully home surfaces, even in apartments, can be used. The range of what is produced in homes also goes beyond just vegetables and fruit trees. For instance, medicinal herbs on rooftops in Santiago, silkworms on balconies in old Delhi, pigeons in downtown Cairo, rabbits in Mexico City's illegal settlements and orchids in houses throughout Bangkok.

The most vivid example is the very successful introduction of low-technology hydroponics into the homes, particularly the rooftops, of a dense squatter area of Bogotá called Jerusalem. This was achieved in containers placed on very light wooden structures in up to three layers and is a highly productive activity directed primarily at supplying metropolitan supermarkets. The women farmers typically earn as much as (or more than) their semi-skilled husbands.[18]

CONSERVATION OF RESOURCES THROUGH URBAN AGRICULTURE

So far, we have described idle resources of cities and towns that can be *utilized* for agricultural production, whether as inputs or as cultivable surfaces. Another way of looking at the relationship between urban agriculture and resources is that some other resources can be *conserved* through urban agriculture. The contribution of urban agriculture to the conservation and better use of energy, bioregional ecologies and human resources will be outlined next.

We will begin with the most straightforward cases of resource conservation. Simply put, urban agriculture saves *energy*. On average, the food in a supermarket in the United States travels an estimated 2000 kilometres (1300 miles) between its point of production and its point of consumption. With increased urban agriculture, this average distance can be cut significantly. In other countries, the distance saved may not be as great but the impact may be greater. The resulting savings in energy and transport costs are obvious. Not so obvious are the savings in storage, including cold storage, and the savings in product lost due to handling and transport.

Urban production of fuelwood (eg eucalyptus) can substitute for other, imported sources of energy or for fuelwood grown at greater distances. It may help to reduce the expansion into rainforests and other fragile ecosystems, while helping to clean the air in cities.

The concept of 'fungibility' is crucial to explaining further contributions of urban agriculture: some resources can be substituted for others, freeing them for alternate uses. This has relevance to urban agriculture, both at the macro and at the micro levels. An analogy here would be useful. Recycling a newspaper does not save the tree in the Amazon from which that paper came, but rather helps save another tree that would be cut to make another newspaper. Similarly, urban agriculture can be seen as allowing rural agriculture to become more focused on those methods and crops where there is a clear advantage for generating income, including export crops.

At the household level, this concept of 'fungibility' has even more important implications. In many large urban areas, lower-income households spend over half their incomes on food.[19] As the largest component of household expenditure, any saving on food expenditure translates into a significant portion of the income becoming available for other non-food expenditure. Similarly, if urban agriculture results in surpluses that are sold or is undertaken specifically for the market, the resulting addition to the income can be sizeable. Either way, the relationship between household income and the contribution of urban agriculture is clearly vital as household resources are either expanded or freed for reallocation. Cases of women in urban households earning more from food production than their government/worker husbands wages were not unusual.

The concept of 'fungibility' can be extended to the conservation of bioregions and their resources. Urban agriculture can reduce the pressure to convert deserts, mountain slopes and rainforests into cropland, as well as the pressure to cut woodlands for fuelwood. Likewise, aquaculture has been one of the fastest growing farming systems of the 1980s. As cities grow their own fish and other aquatic crops, the pressure on the oceans and other water bodies outside metropolitan areas can be reduced. The much higher yields from urban agriculture techniques when compared to those from rural agriculture can make these reductions in pressure particularly significant.

A final type of resource that can be conserved through urban agriculture is the human resource. Many of the residents of urban areas in Third World countries still have strong links to the rural realm. With those links come a knowledge and appreciation for working the land and the water. It would be a mistake to leap to the assumption that rural farming skills can be transferred without modification to urban agriculture. By and large, rural farming systems do not work in the city. Rather, rural roots establish a basis or context for action. Some of the body of knowledge and outlook is transmitted to the next generations. Thus, the urban migrants and refugees can be recognized as human *resources*. This is particularly the case in instances of 'underemployment', where not only is knowledge available, but also time.

Furthermore, urban agriculture offers opportunities to some groups in particular and thus has positive impacts on equity. In many cultures and places, urban agriculture is women's agriculture. Moreover, urban agriculture by its nature is a low-capital, high-labour industry and attracts small low-income entrepreneurs and employs part-time and temporary low-skilled workers.[20] Thus, the urban agriculture industry provides income to new arrivals in the city, teenagers, retired persons and child-carers.

CONCLUSIONS

It can be concluded that sustainable development is unthinkable without sustainable urbanization, as during the next generation we cross over the threshold where more than half the world's population will live in urban areas, and as urban per capita consumption (resource through-put) continues to increase its advance over rural per capita consumption.

Ecologically sustainable urbanization is also inconceivable without urban and peri-urban agriculture, as can be seen in the cases noted in this paper and in others which will be covered in a monograph now in the process of publication. Briefly, urban agriculture is the largest and most efficient tool available to transform urban wastes into food and jobs, with by-products of an improved living environment, better public health, energy savings, natural resources savings, land and water savings and urban management cost reductions. We have concluded that the place to begin urban agriculture as a programme towards ecologically sustainable cities is in the low-income neighbourhoods, for several reasons. First, these are the fastest growing portions of Third World cities. Second, these neighbourhoods have on average the worst environmental conditions, and the poor environmental conditions 'spill over' to the rest of the city and the bioregion.

Urban agriculture is the programme of choice because it is low capital and high labour (and thus well suited to low-income families). While improving the environment, it produces food and health (green city = healthy city). It produces jobs and enterprises and improves economic security. It contributes to social sustainability while increasing ecological sustainability.

Urban agriculture is truly a vast 'opportunity missed'. The opportunity is missed because much more can be accomplished with existing technology and because little effort has been put into optimizing the capacity of urban agriculture.

We hope that this article will be a challenge to stimulate:

- surveys of what urban agriculture is in many diverse places;
- analyses of the farming systems that make up urban agriculture;
- studies of the costs and benefits of urban agriculture;
- studies of the implications of urban agriculture on urban planning, environment and poverty;
- demonstration projects, particularly South–South technology transfer; and
- conferences to share information and, of course, publication.

NOTES AND REFERENCES

1   Mazingira Institute (1987) *Urban Food Production*, Nairobi. See in particular Part 3 – section 'Problems', pp 166–170 and Tables 3.95 to 3.97
2   Heimlich, Ralph E (1989) *Land Use Transition in Urbanizing Areas*, proceedings of a workshop, ERS/USDSA, Washington DC
3   Sachs, I and D Silk (1990) *Food and Energy*, (UNU-FEN) UNU Press, Paris. Chapter 5 summarizes the benefits and problems of Urban Agriculture
4   Obeng, Letitia, A and F W Wright (1987) *The Co-composting of Domestic Solid and Human Wastes*, World Bank Technical Paper No 57, Washington DC. Chapter 3 presents systems for control of pathogens. Chapter 6 covers economic feasibility
5   Lunven, Paul (1992) presentation at the Urban Nutrition Conference, Mexico City, February, unpublished
6   Ghosh, D (1990) 'Wastewater-fed aquaculture in the wetlands of Calcutta: an overview' in *Wastewater-fed Aquaculture*, AIT & ICLARM, Bangkok
7   Catao Aguiar, Sergio and Jaire José Farias (1986) 'Food and energy from industrial wastes', *UNU Work in Progress*, Vol 10, No 1, p 3
8   Shuval, H I et al (1986) *Wastewater Irrigation in Developing Countries*, World Bank Technical Paper No 51, Washington DC (Chapter 5 discusses treatment for pathogens); and US Environmen-

tal Protection Agency (1981) *Land Application of Municipal Sewage and Sludge for the Production of Fruits and Vegetables* EPA, Washington DC (this document sets up policy and guidance on procedures for pathogens, lead and PCB treatment and has an appendix on crop selection)

9   Bartone, Carl R, et al (1985) *Monitoring and Maintenance of Treated Water Quality in the San Juan Lagoons,* PAHO/WHO/CEPIS, Lima. The Introduction and Table 1 present an overview of the issue and its resolution

10   Jorge Hardoy defines this point as the critical barrier to urban agriculture achieving its full potential, in a personal communication in Argentina, March 1992. See also Meier, Richard, L (1988) *Ecological Planning and Design,* Working Paper, University of California at Berkeley, CEPR-WP-02-88, and Declan, Kennedy (1990) 'Urban Perma-culture' in Canfield, C (ed), *Eco-city Conference,* Urban Ecology, Berkeley, CA (Chapter 4 presents eco-city theory)

11   Grupo de Estudios Ambientales (1986) *Por la Regeneracion de Xochimilco,* GEA, Mexico City. This has a brief overview of the raised bed aqua/agriculture and a projection of its future

12   Smit, Jac (1968) *'Durgapur Structure Plan',* West Bengal Government, West Bengal, India

13   Yeung, Yue-Man (1986), 'Urban agriculture: three cities in Asia', *UNU Work in Progress,* Vol 10, No 1, p 7

14   HUFACAM, in the Ministry of Agriculture, was established in 1988 to promote urban agriculture in collaboration with local government and NGOs

15   Buku Panduan (1991) paper presented at the Urban Agriculture Seminar, Jakarta, 30–31 August

16   Wade, Isabel (1987) 'Community food production', *Food and Nutrition Bulletin,* Vol IX, No 2, p 29–36. This compares three community garden programmes in Asia, Africa and Latin America

17   School gardens have been supported in Asia and Africa by the Asian Vegetable Research and Development Centre (AVRDC), Taiwan, and in Asia and Latin America by the International Institute for Rural Reconstruction (IIRR), Philippines. *Comedores* gardens are being supported by CARE, Peru, and HUFACAM, Peru, and others

18   Zapp, Jorge (1991) *'Cultivos sin tierro: hidroponia popular',* UNFIE/PNUD, Bogotá

19   Population Crisis Committee (1990) *'Cities: Life in the World's 100 Largest Metropolitan Areas',* Washington, DC

20   Freeman, Donald B (1991) *A City of Farmers,* McGill/Queens University Press, Montreal. Part 3, pp 103–122, analyses the significance of urban agriculture to the community and to the nation

Chapter 11

Building and Designing with Nature: Urban Design

Joan Roelofs

This is drawn from Chapter 2 of Joan Roelofs' book on *Greening Cities: Building Just and Sustainable Communities*, The Bootstrap Press, New York (1996). The text is complete, although we could not include the photographs and some of the diagrams and boxes. The book from which this extract is drawn has many other chapters that will be of interest to anyone wanting further information on Sustainable Cities. The opening chapter discusses 'what are green cities' with subsequent chapters discussing energy, water, transport, food and agriculture, waste, health, economy, recreation, culture, democracy and eco-city institutions. There is also an appendix listing organizations concerned with Greening Cities and a selected bibliography.

URBAN DESIGN

What would a green city look like? It might be designed anew, but it is more likely to be one that has evolved over time. Certain features are important: diversity and vitality; respect for human health and the environment; resource conservation; human scale; accessibility for all groups; and a place for socializing, education and politics, as well as commerce. Cities may become greener using the powers they have over planning and redevelopment, in the creation of municipal infrastructure, through investments and by regulatory policies.

Several models, some utopian, influence green city advocates. Paradoxically, the layouts of monasteries and royal palaces can be detected in the fantasy villages of the hedonistic socialist Charles Fourier (1772–1837). Fourier believed that 1620 people should live in communities (called phalansteries) to share the work, the wealth, the fun, and the enormous variety of tastes and passions in the combined order. Growing food (in gardens and orchards), cooking and eating would be major activities in his new world. Sex, in all the non-violent varieties imaginable by this diverse crowd, was also an important feature. Manufacturing would be reduced to bare necessities, such as fine glassware for *le vin* and tureens for *potage*.

There are many amazing insights in his slightly mad vision; his compact scheme for a totally full life would conserve resources, reduce pollution and facilitate the utmost in conviviality. The imaginary phalanstery has been a potent image for later planners and dreamers. For example, Fourier's plan included 'street galleries' or covered walkways between houses and workshops so that bad weather would not discommode anyone or deter dallying at chance encounters. The inspiration for Fourier's architecture was probably the Palais-Royal of Paris, in his day a thriving quartier of shops, cafés, gardens, apartments, and dens of iniquity, with all-weather protection from colonnades and atria. The street galleries reappear in the influential utopian novel of 1888 by Edward Bellamy, *Looking Backward.*

A phalanstery is not a city. Utopian socialists and creators of intentional communities may indeed have turned their backs on the city. Nevertheless, almost all contemporary city reformers want to incorporate some communal aspects.

The 1960s protest movements – especially in Paris – found inspiration in Fourier, either directly, or via the philosopher Herbert Marcuse. Fourier's green, libertarian vision was reincarnated in Ernest Callenbach's 1975 novel, *Ecotopia*, which in turn influenced bioregionalism and the US Green political movement. Although the narrator, William Weston, may evoke Bellamy's Julian West, the ambience of *Ecotopia* is closer to William Morris' anti-Bellamy utopia, *News From Nowhere.*

Callenbach includes many now-common Green City features; his ideas are embodied in the theory and practice of the extensive California urban ecology movement. For example, in Ecotopia, buried urban creeks are restored; living downtown over shops is in vogue; public transportation replaces private cars, with free bicycles available; and all materials are recycled, including sewage sludge used as fertilizer. Towns are decentralized and built around public transit hubs. Energy production and the economy are bioregional, with only a tad of imports and exports.

As in the Fourierist vision, Callenbach provides for communal living and a materially simple yet emotionally rich life-style. The Ecotopians are light upon the earth with their steady-state economy. Their 20-hour work week is full of casual bantering and philandering, which makes material possessions small in quantity and importance.

Ebenezer Howard's Garden City was also a major influence on Green City advocates (Figure 11.1). Two Garden Cities were created in Great Britain in Howard's lifetime (he lived in them) and the many post-World War II British 'New Cities' reflected his model. He envisioned compact, self-contained cities, with everything within walking distance. Community facilities would be located in a circular city centre. A park would surround the centre, encircled by the 'Crystal Palace',' an enclosed 'shopping mall' and Winter Garden. Beyond this would be houses and gardens, some with co-operative kitchens. All along the perimeter were the workplaces: factories, farms, asylums, etc, linked by a circular railway connected to the intercity railroad system. Howard thought that his plan would combine the advantages of town and country, and provide for a lively community life as well as easy travel elsewhere.

TRANSPORT AND DESIGN

Today, green-oriented planners and the proponents of 'urban villages' believe reducing automobile dependence to be the most important urban design consideration. Private automobiles create manifold problems: their cost and fuel needs drain wealth from a community; they are the major source of urban pollution; commuting is time-consuming and often exasperating; and much urban space is devoted to cars, harming the ecology, economy and social life of cities. Furthermore, 'sprawl' results from

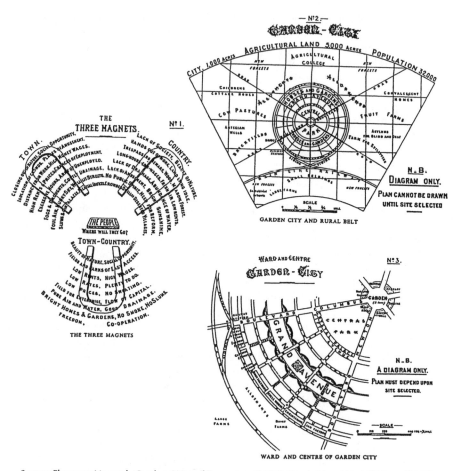

Source: Ebenezer Howard, *Garden Cities of To-morrow* (1898), Cambridge, MA: MIT Press (1965)

Figure 11.1 *Garden cities*

low-density, car-based development, which invades farmlands, wetlands and forests. The automobile also has social consequences. Those who do not drive become second-class citizens, and for everyone, cars and roads separate neighbours and prevent intermingling.

Two initiatives out of this wasteful configuration (especially prevalent in Australia and North America), are described by Peter Newman: 'One... [is] the "urban-commons" view and the other [is] the "rural-commons" view. What they share is a belief in the "commons" – that age-old concept of land which is held in common trust for the use and benefit of all.' The rural commons ideal seeks self-sufficiency:[1]

> Most of the food, ... could be produced locally, most of the work will be available locally, most of the educational and recreational opportunities will be available locally, and most of the friendships and social meanings will be found locally.... Co-operative ventures could be established to manage water and solar power or to establish and run urban forests, or to develop co-operative artisan and light industry workshops...

Newman prefers the 'urban-commons' approach (see Figure 11.2):

> This view is less concerned with local self-sufficiency and more with the city as a system. It suggests that the city should be contained from its sprawl and rebuilt from within.... It suggests that the public areas, public concerns, public transport, etc, should become the focus of an urban renewal based on a redesign and recommitment to the city and its public values. The public areas of high density urban villages would be car-free areas suitable for children to play in and adults to mix. Enough trees and gardens could be planted for a quality environment, with perhaps some agricultural production and urban forestry. The city in this view does not need to be a replacement for the country but it does need to be in sympathy with the environment, to use resources carefully and to be closely designed to fit in with the local water regime, the local terrain and the local habitat. But it is a city with all its specialisations, diversity and commerce.

Other terms for this vision are the 'transit city', and the 'pedestrian pockets' associated with the United States architect Peter Calthorpe. These provide for several city subcentres linked by light rail or other public transport. The subcentres would be villages of mixed use – housing, commercial, light industrial – with a diverse population in terms of race, income, sexual orientation, family structure or none, unlike the 'monoculture' of the typical suburb. This compact design would promote walking or cycling to shopping, recreation, workplaces and education facilities, and to public transport for those who must commute. Public squares, sidewalk cafés and buskers are part of this vision, and 'hanging out' a major avocation. Neighbourhoods would encourage commingling. 'Traffic calming' would make streets an extension of living spaces and front porches would connect residents with each other and with passers-by. (A proposed ordinance in one United States city required front porches

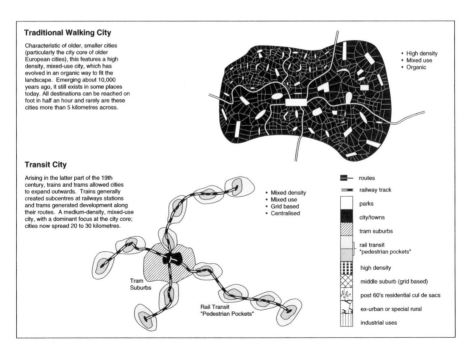

Figure 11.2 *Four different city types*

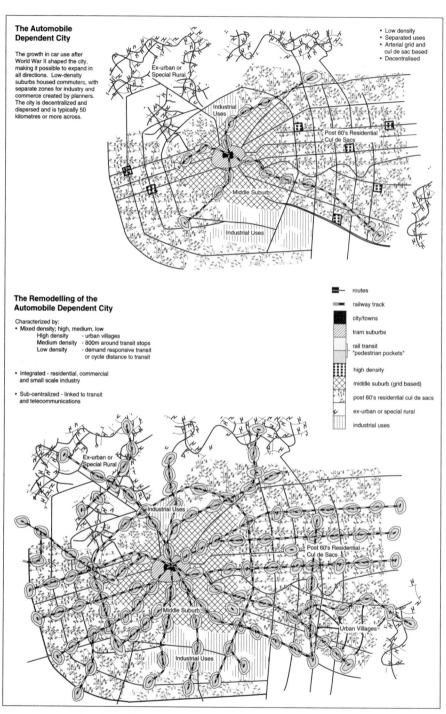

The Automobile Dependent City

The growth in car use after World War II shaped the city, making it possible to expand in all directions. Low-density suburbs housed commuters, with separate zones for industry and commerce created by planners. The city is decentralized and dispersed and is typically 50 kilometres or more across.

- Low density
- Separated uses
- Arterial grid and cul de sac based
- Decentralised

Ex-urban or Special Rural

Industrial Uses

Post 60's Residential Cul de Sacs

Middle Suburb

Industrial Uses

The Remodelling of the Automobile Dependent City

Characterized by:
- Mixed density; high, medium, low
  - High density – urban villages
  - Medium density – 800m around transit stops
  - Low density – demand responsive transit or cycle distance to transit

- Integrated – residential, commercial and small scale industry

- Sub-centralized – linked to transit and telecommunications

routes

railway track

city/towns

tram suburbs

rail transit "pedestrian pockets"

high density

middle suburb (grid based)

post 60's residential cul de sacs

ex-urban or special rural

industrial uses

Ex-urban or Special Rural

Industrial Uses

Post 60's Residential Cul de Sacs

Middle Suburb

Urban Villages

Industrial Uses

SOURCE: Peter Newman, Jeff Kenworthy and Peter Vintila (1993), *Housing Transport and Urban Form*, National Housing Strategy Background Paper 15, Dept. of Health, Housing and Community Services, Canberra

Figure 11.2 *Continued*

on all new houses.) Most people, in subcentres or the central city, would live right in the midst of things, including over shops, to make for a livelier, more affordable and safer city. Of course, there would be ample greenery and even urban agriculture. The current desertion of residential areas during the day and business areas at night, with arduous commuting in between, not only wastes resources and land, but it also destroys the city's cultural life. Today, the neighbourhood video store or the TV is more convenient than trekking back to the city for live theatre.

Urban villages have been created in various parts of the world – eg Vancouver, Canada; Munich, Germany; Davis, California, US; and many are in the planning stages. One innovative model is underway in Adelaide, Australia (see below).

ALTERNATIVE HOUSEHOLDS

In addition to the automobile, Green City critics indict typical housing patterns, especially 'suburban sprawl' created by single family homes on large lots. These don't reflect today's reality; households are increasingly composed of single persons, single parents, working couples, retired couples or friends. The 'housewife' tending the place and doing all the driving is practically extinct.[2] People seek co-operative arrangements, and easy access to shops, services and other people – in short, neighbourhoods.

A radical approach is the abandonment of the private household in favour of communal living. This is another legacy of Fourier, who believed that the economic, environmental and social costs of individual households were intolerable. Fourier's views are relevant today as families are getting smaller all the time and fulfilling fewer and fewer of their traditional functions. Divorce is the norm and reports from so-called 'intact' families are not cheerful. Families are now primarily consumption units; social pressure and public policy encourages the creation of these abundantly equipped units, which are lavish by material standards only. The consolidation, on a voluntary basis, of adults with or without children, into 'families' of seven or ten adults plus their children, would have many advantages in addition to saving energy, services and resources. Local government, which usually discourages such arrangements, could support such resource-saving alternatives.

In 19th-century United States, intentional communities were an important and respectable model of human settlement. Their proponents contrasted them with the usually isolated, violent and culturally impoverished frontier farmhouse. More than 100 existed, populated by the native-born and those who immigrated because of the favourable community-building opportunities. Some had a religious basis, such as the Hutterite and Shaker communities; others were attempts to follow the plans of Fourier and Robert Owen, such as New Harmony in Indiana. The Oneida community of New York State combined 'Perfectionist' Protestantism with Utopian socialist ideas, including equality of women and eroticization of work. Its experimental group marriage, while rejecting Fourier's orgiastic embellishments, lasted for the nearly 40-year life of the community. All property was shared as well; the community produced its own food and its enterprises provided a lucrative trade with the outside world. Despite its fundamentalist religious orientation, it was very receptive to scientific developments and avant-garde culture.

Except for some of the religious communities, most did not survive beyond the 19th century. However, they inspired early 20th-century feminists, who sought to eliminate the onerous caretaking role required by individual kitchens and laundries.[3]

The 1917 Russian Revolution also stirred hopes of communalism. One of its leaders was the Fourierist Alexandra Kollontai. However, Utopianism in all its forms (as well as the original meaning of 'Communist') was soon discarded in favour of a bureaucratic–industrial   state.

The 1960s counter-culture, in many countries, created another wave of intentional community building. Many of these communes have been cleaned up and are flourishing today.[4] While they are not themselves 'cities', they contribute to the Green City movement in two ways. First, they are models of self-sufficiency, compact living and conviviality, features to be incorporated in Green Cities. Second, Green City planners include communal households among the living arrangements within cities, as did Ebenezer Howard.

Buckminster Fuller and other 'technological' Utopians have inspired communities such as Arcosanti in Arizona. There architect Paolo Soleri is directing the construction of a self-contained three-dimensional city, with vast structures of concrete and glass. Greens may recoil at the 'unnatural' environment of these structures, but the Ecotopian model may be prophetic. There, 'high tech' and 'low tech' each had its place; modular stretchable plastic housing co-existed with wooden huts.

CO-HOUSING

A semi-communal model growing in popularity is co-housing, which can be situated in urban villages along with more conventional housing types.[5] Co-housing, pioneered in Denmark, provides for smallish individual apartments or houses and also shared space. This usually includes social areas, workrooms, laundries, guest rooms, child care and play areas, gardens, etc. A distinctive feature is a common kitchen and dining-room where dinners are prepared and eaten communally several days a week (Figure 11.3).

Many of the co-housing developments now in existence have been designed by their future residents over several years. They may consist of free-standing houses, town houses or a large building – for example, a recycled factory. They provide both public and private space, including small private yards. Some developments integrate low-income, government-subsidized housing and privately rented or owned limited equity units. The participatory process tends to exclude those who are unable to plan so far ahead, but when units become vacant, new members can join.

Primarily living units and not producers' co-operatives, they differ from intentional communities. However, members as individuals or groups may have cottage industries within the community. Thus, they might evolve into more of an Oneida-type community, especially as the traditional workplace and traditional family further erode.

HET GROENE DAK: THE GREEN ROOF

This ecological co-housing community occupies a square city block in the 'liberator's' neighbourhood of Utrecht, the Netherlands. Of the 66 attached houses, 40 are rented and 26 are owner-occupied. Like much housing in that country, it was publicly funded but built by a private non-profit housing corporation. Many tenants receive government subsidies towards their rent, as well as 'social wages' if they are unemployed. However, some perform socially useful work by demonstrating the ecologically sound

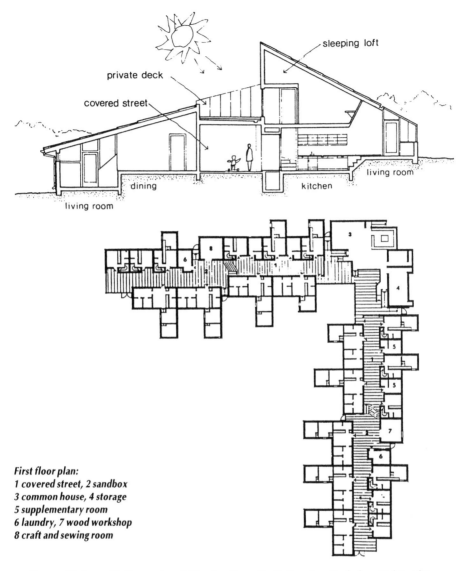

Source: Kathryn McCamant and Charles Durrett, *CoHousing,* Berkeley: Habitat/Ten Speed Press, Berkeley (1988, 1994). Reprinted by permission

Figure 11.3 *Design of covered street in Danish co-housing community*

living arrangements, presenting slide shows throughout the country and receiving curious visitors.[6]

There is a mix of families, couples, single people and groups, which may have both heterosexual and homosexual members and are considered 'non-traditional families'. Michel Post belongs to one such family of five people. They have a common room for music and share a shower, composting toilet, garden tool-shed, workshop, laundry and computer/copier room. Because there is a composting toilet, only grey water is discharged as waste, which is purified in a backyard reed bed and re-cycled for domestic uses, such as the solar heated washing-machine. The top-floor laundry room had clothes-lines for drying. The group maintains a small shop where ecological products and literature are sold.

Surprisingly, they did not share a kitchen or eat together, as in most co-housing communities. In a group so small, some members felt that cooking responsibili-ties would result in far too rigid a schedule. Where 50 units share meals five days a week, as in many Danish co-housing communities, two units work together and are responsible for the community meal only once every five weeks.

The community as a whole shared garden space, play areas and a common house. The house, within a block-enclosed yard, indeed had a 'green roof' with grass growing on it, which is considered most energy efficient. Its walls were built of local materials: straw, clay and chalk, and the interior furnishings were of domes-tic hardwoods. The house is used for ecological education, meetings, parties and twice-yearly dinners of the entire community. It is also rented to other organizations for income.

The Green Roof is impressive as a demonstration project and must be appreci-ated by the inhabitants since nobody had moved out in the first year and a half of its existence. Michel hoped that no one would have to leave because of retirement. He wanted the Green Roof to become a model, incorporating the necessary facilities into the community so that 'old folks' homes' would eventually disappear.

As its experimental features prove themselves, it is likely that they will be used in new housing projects. The Dutch are quick to adopt energy-efficient and non-toxic construction techniques in government-subsidized housing, which is 50 per cent of the total housing. For the founders of this experimental community and others, new frontiers may always beckon; innovators must be true to their natures. Michel thought that some day he would like to live 'on the land' in a community of about 20 people, producing all their own food. As he ate no animal protein, this would be an innova-tive project in a land where farms are thick with cows and pigs.

ECOVILLAGE AT ITHACA

In the United States the co-housing model, like many innovations, is moving east from California. As of 1994, 17 new co-housing developments, most with strong sustainable goals, have been completed in the US.[7] In Ithaca, New York, where a large university is situated in a rural area, a co-housing village is being planned for 500 residents. Ultimately there will be six neighbourhoods, each with a common house. One objective is to 'integrate design for human needs (shelter, food produc-tion, social interaction, energy, work) with land and water conservation and ecosys-tem preservation'.[8] The project has several notable features.

One is a commitment to local food production (even in a Northern climate). So that their operations may become economically viable, farmers will be assisted in developing outside markets. Furthermore, education for residents and others is designed to persuade people that it is worthwhile to pay the somewhat higher costs of producing food in ways non-exploitative to the environment and workers.

Second, Cornell University has provided support and technical assistance. Stu-dent projects (including PhD dissertations) in a variety of disciplines have been in-tegrated with EcoVillage planning. Cornell's strong professional schools such as City and Regional Planning, Landscape Architecture, Architecture, Engineering and Agriculture create a mutually beneficial arrangement.

Third, the Ithaca EcoVillage has a sister relationship with the Village of Yoff, in Senegal, where an ecovillage will be created based on traditional ways of sustainability. A Cornell PhD candidate, Serigne Mbaye Diene, who is a local government official in Yoff, provides liaison between the groups. The Third International EcoCity Conference was held in Yoff in January 1996; the Ithaca group provided major organizing resources.

SHOPPING

Most intentional communities were largely self-sufficient and required little shopping. Today, any form of collectivized living can centralize shopping and make it more efficient. Some might argue that it is not merely a waste of time and energy; that the activity expresses a human behavioural tendency left over from the hunter-gatherer days, which was most of human history. Assuming that there will be shopping in green cities, what forms might it take?

The corner 'general store' is one useful type. For many daily purchases it would save the shopper's time and avoid wasteful driving. Furthermore, it can be a place where neighbours meet informally and exchange gossip, post notices and discuss politics. In the 1930s, in Sweden, some apartment buildings were designed for working couples with children and included shops, cafeterias, day-care centres, etc – the 'corner store', in effect, may be downstairs. The British 'New Towns' have corner shops and pubs, for convenience and safety.

For greater variety, the street markets and covered markets found throughout the world are compelling, even to an anti-consumerist. Local organic food, freshly caught fish, crafts, used items, as well as mass-produced goods are available. Cafés and buskers encourage one to dally for hours, but it is also possible to find the necessary items quickly and leave. What particularly commends this form is that it is usually municipally owned and therefore can be regulated in the interests of health and honesty; it permits small producers to sell directly; and it is often outside or well ventilated. Processed foods are available, but do not dominate as in supermarkets.

This ambience may also be present in 'Main Street' or 'High Street' shopping. Yet that is becoming a rare option as automobile-oriented shopping plazas, drive-in liquor stores and so forth spring up everywhere. 'Main Street', on the other hand, is easily accessible by foot, bike or car, and parking lots can be placed behind shops. One way to keep this shopping system alive is to provide free delivery service (by city van) for those shopping downtown on foot or bike.

Delivery systems in general make sense. They replace many automobile trips with a few circulating trucks. While a convenience for all, they are essential for those who are ill, frail, stuck at home with sick children, totally tied up or otherwise homebound. Researchers who are gathering information may appreciate the groceries arriving on the doorstep. Mobile vendors, common in this author's childhood, might still be an economical and ecological method in medium-density neighbourhoods, enabling those who must view a purchase before they buy it to do so.

But what about shopping malls? They have many shortcomings from a green perspective. They promote long automobile trips and consequent energy consumption, pollution and traffic congestion. Huge areas are paved over for parking lots, with resulting climate modification; impeded drainage; and destruction of farmland, forest, wetlands and neighbourhoods. Their interiors are filled with recirculated air featuring out-gases from the plastics that comprise most of the 'goods' for sale, the construction, the carpeting and even the food. Unlike open market shopping or Main Street shops, which constantly admit outside air, shoppers and employees are in an enclosed area for many hours. That teenagers have no other place to hang out or older people to safely take walks indicates a civic lack that must be addressed.

The long distances travelled encourage 'making a day of it', and consequent over-consumption of trendy items. Shops devoted entirely to items with pig motifs have been sighted. Women's apparel predominates in malls, whereas most, including the poor, already have enough, although the quality may be low. Thrift shops are over-burdened with offerings. All this shopping requires additional landfill space for last year's impulse purchases.

The economic impact is also mostly negative. Shopping malls consisting of chain stores ultimately destroy the often locally owned 'Main Street' shops. Profits are thus siphoned out of the community, although a considerable amount of investment capital may have come from local banks. Local residents' savings enrich developers and chain-store owners. The merchandise, often from Third World factories and plantations, doesn't help local industry or, for that matter, the people or environment overseas. One chain-store giant lauds its 'cultural diversity' and cites as an example a Colombian-born supplier: 'Flowers are grown on the company's farms in Columbia [*sic*]. "Only 56 hours elapse from the time they're blooming on the farm until they're in the stores," says Lorenzo. "Wal-Mart customers get our very freshest flowers."'

It is almost inevitable that large malls destroy downtown shopping, weakening community interaction and eliminating local retailers who usually have an interest in the city's prosperity. They create hardship for children, the elderly, the other abled and the busy, who can't easily get to the mall. Furthermore, the 'choice' and 'competition' that free enterprise is supposed to provide disappears. The only competition that may arise is a new mall a few miles away. This will probably kill the 'old' mall (they age in about seven years), not because the new one has anything substantially different to offer, but because of its newness. Unfortunately, the technology for decommissioning a dead mall is lacking. A similar problem arises with 'competing' fast-food places, supermarkets and discount stores. Their hulks are eyesores, representing resource waste and environmental destruction.

Some claim that malls are inevitable and that we might as well make the most of them. Prof Brian Goodey of Great Britain:

> [S]aw the potential of the city centre as a place of learning and yearned to see a classroom in a shopping centre. The Southampton Institute has such a dream for its main campus focus, which is poised to take advantage of a shift in shopping habits from the northern part of the Above Bar retail area. Meanwhile, Southampton's Environment Centre is already offering a 'classroom' to students, shoppers and businesspeople in the Marlands Shopping Mall, close to the Civic Offices.[9]

In Minnesota, the Mall of America (which was financed by the college teachers' pension fund) includes a school: 'Tuesday nights, Sandy Zeiss takes a three-hour MBA class in retailing at the mall school's graduate division. "It's been a very useful, hands-on course," she said. "Of course, it's not quite the same prestige as going to a campus."'

> Already, there are the beginnings of a new academic discipline with its own language. For example, the mall school has an internship program that places students in mall busi-

nesses where they work with store managers. A 31-page scholarly paper in which Mall of America educators describe their school explains the internship program this way: 'Experiential learning activities will be tied to real-life experiences, with a career component for children to enjoy the hands-on experiences available.'[10]

As schools, city offices and public libraries locate in malls, consumerism may replace all other values of public life. Shopping, like other addictions, can be regulated in the interests of the community. It is a powerful and potentially destructive force to persons, communities and the environment. Zoning could be revised to restrict the general 'commercial' category which permits competing 'knockout' enterprises (eg fast food, supermarket, discount stores) in the same area. The community could decide which enterprises were welcome after a publicly financed study of the costs and benefits of different retailing options. Today the information comes from the well-financed side of the giant retailers and developers.

An approach which may appear radical, but is actually quite traditional, is Ebenezer Howard's idea that the city own and control retailing facilities. Public markets still exist throughout the world, and they foster the city's role as nurturer and educator, rather than dominating life with consumerism. In cold climates or anywhere, by all means have the 'Crystal Palace' glass enclosed, with winter gardens for strolling, playgrounds and attended child care. A downtown location can be accessible by foot for those with a most useful piece of appropriate technology, a folding shopping cart; by bicycle; by public transport (designed with level entrances to accommodate shopping carts, bicycles, carriages and wheelchairs); or by shuttlebus to parking lots for those who will or must drive. Furthermore, markets can provide delivery services for those who shop in person or those who order via phone, fax, e-mail, mail or friend. There would still be 'corner stores' for daily necessities.

Local economic self-sufficiency can be encouraged by allotting the best places at the lowest (or no) cost to local organic food producers, waste-based industries, craftspeople, small manufacturers, used goods dealers and the like. The community will still need to set standards for health, safety and environmental implications of products. Outside retailers or products can be given space in the market if the community agrees, after investigation of labour and environmental conditions in the production process. The market administration could develop workers' co-operatives to produce the locally missing urgent items, or deal directly with distant co-operatives which can supply the goods.

LANDSCAPING

While we might assume that the green parts of the city serve green values, often they do not.

> Traditionally, parks and open spaces have been seen as a nurtured high-maintenance horticultural landscape whose basis for form depends on high-energy inputs and horticultural technology. As a universal solution to urban landscapes, it offers little in diversity, sensory richness, or sense of place. There is a contradiction in values in the desire to nurture this 'pedigree' landscape but suppress the 'fortuitous' and diverse landscape of naturalizing waste spaces. But changing economic and social conditions are forcing us to re-evaluate conventional views of what open space is all about. Necessity generates new solutions. The naturalization of formally manicured landscapes is increasingly becoming an accepted alternative in many places – along road rights-of-way, in some parks and institutions... The

rehabilitation of once degraded landscapes with native forests, wetlands, and meadows minimizes costly maintenance and enriches the environment. It involves the transfer of biologically sound rural skills of forestry and land management to the city – namely, the concept of design over time. These processes are more economically viable, produce more useful and richer landscapes, and are environmentally more appropriate. If these benefits are the results of budget cutbacks, then we should support the concept of economy of means.[11]

Green belts and green corridors in cities often presuppose automobile transportation and although they provide some help for the environment, they may not be user friendly. For example, Canberra, capital city of Australia, has miles of grass and parks lining roadways. Imposing plazas and official buildings are surrounded by vast lawns. However, on a delightfully cool Sunday in midsummer, this author was the sole pedestrian on the magnificently landscaped mile between the city government and the national government centres. A fountain spewing from the small man-made lake was also not friendly to walkers.

Landscape that serves many functions is both economic and ecological. As well as recreational uses, natural landscape can absorb stormwater and pollution, keep built-up areas cool in summer and warm in winter, provide habitat for wildlife, assist in the purification of waste water and act as a prime educational resource. Schoolyards can employ the same principles. Using native plants will encourage wildlife. They also require less water and fertilizer and are more pest-resistant. The city of Chicago has decided that planting trees would save millions of dollars.[12] The restoration of buried creeks, filled-in marshes and natural shorelines can have historical as well as environmental significance.

Another perspective on urban landscaping is permaculture, which not only employs planting for windbreaks, habitats, etc, but also provides basic products – food, drink, clothing, rugs, furniture, rope, medicines, paper, decoration and so forth. Permaculture uses exotic species as well as native ones and requires vigilance to ensure that harvesters are on duty before fruits and nuts fall all over the city hall plaza. Much of the 'greenery' in a permaculture design would be in allotment gardens, rooftop gardens, and urban farms and forests. Hospitals, universities and other institutions, rather than sitting on acres of lawn, would rise from lush useful vegetation, cared for by their inmates, as in the mental hospital in Santiago, Cuba.

Public buildings in the green city would not be imposing isolated marble structures frequented only by bureaucrats. Although the old buildings could still be used, they would become accessible to everyone, removing not only architectural but also class and hierarchical barriers. New public buildings might include a research centre for urban technology and design, electronically linked to similar centres in other cities. Another facility could evaluate consumer products, both local and imported, checking not only the usual durability, safety and other standards, but also researching the environmental and labour conditions under which they were produced, and their disposal requirements. The worldwide network of such research centres could make videos of, for example, the conditions of Kurdish rugmakers or Australian opal miners, so citizens could decide if these goods might be sold in the 'Crystal Palace'. The videos, as well as others describing useful environmental technology, could be available to all via the network.

Some public buildings could be modelled on the 'casas del pueblo', which were neighbourhood coffee houses in pre-Civil War Spain where people could meet and read revolutionary literature – a green city should not be stagnant. Political talk and socializing could also occur in community centres for repairing furniture, mending clothes and re-evaluating failed programmes. Whether people are living communally or not, the sharing of resources promotes conservation as well as access to a varied and high standard of life. The more developed world needs to model frugal yet rich consumption. 'Telecottages' can allow everybody personal use of sophisticated computers, fax and other communications systems. Non-polluting vehicles and garden equipment can also be shared among neighbours. The variety of personal possessions can be extended by having a permanent 'swap shop' area, perhaps in the mending house.

The process of urban design must be green if the result is to be. This calls for democratic participation in planning the city, whether new construction, renovation or demolition. Participation cannot be limited to 'chamber of commerce' types, with designated social service personnel representing 'the poor'. The 'bourgeoisie' must now include those who are often disadvantaged by urban design: children, the other abled, the homeless, rainbow family, gypsies, lost souls, elders, buskers, etc. This will make for a more diverse and stimulating cityscape and one where all sorts of people, including visitors, will feel at home.

THE HALIFAX PROJECT

The Halifax EcoCity Project proposes to build a 'piece of ecocity' on a 2.4 hectare (c 5 acres) site in downtown Adelaide, Australia. The site, now owned by the city of Adelaide, became vacant when city public works facilities were moved elsewhere. The project, also called 'Ecopolis', is intended to be:

> ... [A] pilot project, demonstrating what is possible in re-thinking our cities and providing a fund of ideas and experience to be used elsewhere. Having far more than just a residential focus, it is about creating human settlement in which buildings, social structure and natural processes are integrated, to fit the satisfaction of human needs into the dynamic ecological balance of living systems. The way it will do this is by following the Ecopolis Development Principles for ecologically sustaining development...(Figure 11.4)[13]

The project was initiated by architects and planners Paul Downton, Cherie Hoyle and Emilis Prelguskas, and now has many supporters and affiliates. Some are volunteers, including future residents of the eco-city; other participants are businesses, unions and non-governmental organizations.

Unlike most urban villages, Ecopolis will be located right in the central business district, which already has town-house residential areas.

> The design proposes a community of 1,000 people with pedestrian streets, squares and courtyards, and energy efficient buildings of 3 to 5 stories with belvederes rising above them. The buildings use mud bricks, stabilised rammed earth, lightweight concrete and timber frame construction to create a variety of spaces and places which respond directly to the needs and creativity of the inhabitants as well as the imperatives of healthy environmental performance and ecological responsibility. There is no mindless repetition as the plan and detail design of every dwelling will be worked out through a 'barefoot architect' program which involves architects and urban ecologists in a direct consulting and educational role with all incoming members of the new community.[14]

The current design features solar cooling, heating and generation of electricity, with gas for back-up heating and power, as well as cooking. Permaculture and roof

•1   restore degraded land
by using appropriate building
processes and non-toxic
materials, by rebuilding a strong
sense of local community,
through education and co-
operation it is possible for
development to actually be good
for the land where it is situated.
Where the city in the past has
destroyed the environment,
ecological cities can, and must,
make good the damage.

•2   fit the bioregion
to be truly ecological you must
take account of the biological
area, or bioregion, around you,
with its own particular landscape,
climate, indigenous species and
local cultures.

•3   balance development
means balancing the intensity of
development with the ecological
carrying capacity of the land, and
protecting areas of ecological
importance.

•4   halt urban sprawl
when urban planning is based on
multiple centres for economic
and cultural activity, rather than
just one or two as we have at the
moment, it is possible to
eliminate the problems of urban
sprawl. Such centres have
medium to high density housing,
and allow for a network of green
belts and the development of
ecological corridors in between.
They also make public transport
and infrastructure planning more
efficient.

**•5   optimize energy
        performance**
by operating at low levels of
energy consumption, making
efficient use of renewable and
local energy resources, and using
local energy production and
techniques of resource reuse.

**•6   contribute to the
        economy**
supporting and promoting
appropriate economic activity,
creating and servicing new 'niche'
markets, focusing more on local
production, consumption and
exchange, restoring the
productive capacity of land,
providing education; such
measures can make a strong
economic contribution.

**•7   provide health and
        security**
employing appropriate materials
and careful planning to create
safe and healthy places for people
to live, work and play.

•8   encourage community
building community is a vital
part of ecological development.
In an atmosphere of mutual
support and trust many things are
made possible and many social
problems reduced. (A lot of older
people recognise that this is
something we have lost sight of
in more recent times.) Shared
facilities for work, play, education
and culture are a part of making
this a reality, starting at the level
of the local neighbourhood.

•9   promote social equity
by employing economic,
ownership and decision making
structures which follow principles
of social equity and local
democracy.

•10   respect history
all the valuable buildings and
other artifacts of our unique
heritage can be restored and
thoughtfully incorporated in
development which places
cultural and social values on an
equal footing with economic
benefit.

**•11   enrich the cultural
        landscape**
by supporting and promoting
cultural diversity and expression,
encouraging people to discover
their own creativity and
incorporating ecological
awareness into all aspects of
human settlement.

•12   heal the biosphere
contributing to the restoration of
the global ecosystem by paying
attention to:
☐ air
☐ water
☐ soil
☐ energy
☐ biomass
☐ food
☐ biodiversity
☐ habitat
☐ ecolinks
☐ waste

The project is about people, their
relationships with each other and
with the ecology of which they are a
part - evolving appropriate strategies
for creating ecological development is
an integral part of that process and
involves all of us in one way or
another. These principles summarise
what *The Halifax Project* is about (as
well as being applicable to any
development); they reflect many years
of thought and activity. Originally
put together by Paul Downton,
Chérie Hoyle and Emilis Prelgauskas,
the version here has been adapted for
The Catalyst by Matt Fisher.

Source: The Catalyst: Newsletter of the Halifax Project, No 1, April 1993

Figure 11.4 *Ecopolis development principles*

gardens will supply food. Stormwater will be collected and grey water reused. There will be at least one co-housing arrangement.

Another feature of the project is rural restoration:

> People living in cities demand materials for shelter, food and resources for energy which are 'extracted' from the environment located away from the city... Therefore an integral part of the Halifax EcoCity Project is to also treat that rural balance; the securing of 1 hectare of degraded rural land [for] each person who moves onto the inner city site. That secured rural land can then, as part of inner city project works, be stabilized, repaired, have its original ecology reintroduced, have portions set aside for useful purposes allied to the inner city development. This includes production of food, energy, (particularly in the form of woodlot) and use as passive and active recreation space... Land may be owned by the Project, by participants in the project, by persons with a sympathetic connection to the project; or be secured in the form of leases from unconnected sources.[15]

The cost of the Ecopolis is estimated at $60 million, and much has already been pledged by churches, non-governmental organizations and credit unions. The group prefers financing from such sources and does not want money from banks. The thousand residents will also be funders.

On 7 February 1994 the Halifax Project was the main agenda item at an Adelaide City Council meeting. The gallery was filled (including this author) and many enthusiasts were sitting or standing in the aisles. There had been extensive community discussion of the project for years, the councillors already had strong opinions about it and several of them passionately defended it. Some liked the idea of initiating environmentally sustainable development; others hoped that this would bring people back to city living. The more conservative supporters, including the Lord Mayor, argued that 'since we lost the Grand Prix [an automobile race] the Ecopolis might be another way of bringing tourists to Adelaide'. (I wondered whether these visitors would be the big spenders they expected. I, being one of those eco-researcher-tourists, was staying in an intentional community eating organic veggies.)

The opponents of the project believed that any developer should have a chance to bid on the property, and the City Planner supported this protocol. Some questioned the financial competence of the group, to which the supporters countered that commercial developers are not held to such high standards. A further consideration was that the land was somewhat contaminated and a few councillors wanted to postpone any decision until remediation had occurred. Supporters argued that the Ecopolis group would have a very high standard and that it would be better to let them arrange for the decontamination. Finally, the majority of the council agreed that the proposal was different from an ordinary commercial development and that it deserved special treatment. They voted eleven to three to grant the Halifax Project an option to purchase the site, with the following conditions:

1 In response to the request from Urban Ecology Australia, Council agree in principle to offer to them a one-year option to purchase 'the Halifax' site subject to:
   a) a staged development being possible;
   b) the site remaining as a single entity;
   c) a minimum of 25 per cent of low cost public housing;
   d) an economic feasibility being submitted to Council within three months.

2 A Working Party be formed consisting of three elected members and appropriate representatives of the administration.

3   The Working Party establish the current market value of the site, taking into account site remediation costs to the best possible practical standards.

4   The Working Party establish the option value.

5   The Working Party prepare Draft Heads of Agreement.

6   The Working Party report to the Council no later than Monday 7th March.[16]

The Halifax Project is underway and has attracted worldwide interest.

REFERENCES

1   Peter Newman, 'Sustainable Settlements', *Habitat Australia* (August 1991): 20
2   Dolores Hayden, *Redesigning the American Dream* W W Norton, New York (1984)
3   Dolores Hayden, *The Grand Domestic Revolution* MIT Press, Cambridge (1981)
4   *Communities Directory: A Guide to Cooperative Living*, Fellowship for International Community, Langley, Washington (1995)
5   Kathryn McCamant and Charles Durrett, *Co-housing* Habitat/Ten Speed Press, Berkeley (1988, 1994)
6   Interview with Michel Post, 9 August 1994, Utrecht, the Netherlands
7   McCamant and Durrett, op cit (1994)
8   *EcoVillage at Ithaca: Third Annual Report, July 1, 1993–December 31, 1994,* Ithaca, New York (1995)
9   Phil Turner, 'Reshaping Cities for the 21st Century?', *Streetwise* 14 (1993):10
10   Michael Winerup, 'All Under One Roof: Stores and Education' *The New York Times*, 2 May 1994, p 8B
11   Michael Hough, 'Formed by Natural Process – A Definition of the Green City' in David Gordon (ed) *Green Cities* (Montreal: Black Rose, 1990), pp 16–17
12   The original chapter included a 1994 article from the *New York Times* which described how the planting of 95,000 trees in metropolitan Chicago could result in a net benefit of US$38 million over 30 years – for instance, through making it less costly to heat and cool buildings, by absorbing air pollution and by conferring a range of other environmental benefits
13   *Catalyst*, April 1993: 3
14   op cit Reference 8
15   Emilis Prelgauskas, 'The rural balance to inner city living', *Urban Ecology Newsletter* 8, April 1994: 5
16   Draft distributed by Adelaide City Council Meeting, 7 February 1994

Chapter 12

Planning: Green Cities, Growing Cities, Just Cities? Urban Planning and the Contradictions of Sustainable Development

Scott Campbell

(Reprinted by permission of the Journal of the American Planning Association, Vol. 62, No. 3, Summer 1996, pp 296–312.)

Nothing inherent in the discipline steers planners either towards environmental protection or towards economic development – or toward a third goal of planning: social equity. Instead, planners work within the tension generated among these three fundamental aims, which, collectively, I call the 'planner's triangle' with sustainable development located at its centre. This centre cannot be reached directly, but only approximately and indirectly, through a sustained period of confronting and resolving the triangle's conflicts. To do so, planners have to redefine sustainability, since its current formulation romanticizes our sustainable past and is too vaguely holistic. Planners would benefit both from integrating social theory with environmental thinking and from combining their substantive skills with techniques for community conflict resolution, to confront economic and environmental injustice.

In the coming years planners face tough decisions about where they stand on protecting the green city, promoting the economically growing city and advocating social justice. Conflicts among these goals are not superficial ones arising simply from personal preferences. Nor are they merely conceptual, among the abstract notions of ecological, economic and political logic, nor a temporary problem caused by the untimely confluence of environmental awareness and economic recession. Rather, these conflicts go to the historic core of planning and are a leitmotif in the contemporary battles in both our cities and rural areas, whether over solid waste incinerators or growth controls, the spotted owls or nuclear power. And though sustainable development aspires to offer an alluring, holistic way of evading these conflicts, they cannot be shaken off so easily.

This paper uses a simple triangular model to understand the divergent priorities of planning. My argument is that although the differences are partly due to misunderstandings arising from the disparate languages of environmental, economic and political thought, translating across disciplines alone is not enough to eliminate these genuine clashes of interest. The socially constructed view of nature put forward here challenges the view of these conflicts as a classic battle of 'man versus nature' or its current variation, 'jobs versus the environment'. The triangular model is then used to question whether sustainable development, the current object of planning's fascination, is a useful model to guide planning practice. I argue that the current concept of sustainability, though a laudable holistic vision, is vulnerable to the same criticism of vague idealism made 30 years ago against comprehensive planning. In this case, the idealistic fascination often builds upon a romanticized view of pre-industrial, indigenous, sustainable cultures – inspiring visions, but also of limited modern applicability. Nevertheless, sustainability, if redefined and incorporated into a broader understanding of political conflicts in industrial society, can become a powerful and useful organizing principle for planning. In fact, the idea will be particularly effective if, instead of merely evoking a misty-eyed vision of a peaceful ecotopia, it acts as a lightning rod to focus conflicting economic, environmental and social interests. The more it stirs up conflict and sharpens the debate, the more effective the idea of sustainability will be in the long run.

The paper concludes by considering the implications of this viewpoint for planning. The triangle shows not only the conflicts, but also the potential complementarity of interests. The former are unavoidable and require planners to act as mediators, but the latter area is where planners can be especially creative in building coalitions between once-separated interest groups, such as labour and environmentalists, or community groups and business. To this end, planners need to combine both their procedural and their substantive skills and thus become central players in the battle over growth, the environment and social justice.

THE PLANNER'S TRIANGLE: THREE PRIORITIES, THREE CONFLICTS

The current environmental enthusiasm among planners and planning schools might suggest their innate predisposition to protect the natural environment. Unfortunately, the opposite is more likely to be true: our historic tendency has been to promote the development of cities at the cost of natural destruction: to build cities we have cleared forests, fouled rivers and the air, levelled mountains. That is not the complete picture, since planners also have often come to the defence of nature, through the work of conservationists, park planners, open space preservationists, the Regional Planning Association of America, green-belt planners and modern environmental planners. Yet along the economic-ecological spectrum, with Robert Moses and Dave Foreman (of *Earth First!*) standing at either pole, the planner has no natural home, but can slide from one end of the spectrum to the other; moreover, the midpoint has no special claims to legitimacy or fairness.

Similarly, though planners often see themselves as the defenders of the poor and of socio-economic equality, their actions over the profession's history have often belied that self-image (Harvey 1985). Planners' efforts with downtown redevelopment, freeway planning, public-private partnerships, enterprise zones, smoke-stack-chasing and other economic development strategies don't easily add up to equity planning. At best, the planner has taken an ambivalent stance between the goals of economic growth and economic justice.

In short, the planner must reconcile not two, but at least three conflicting interests: to 'grow' the economy, distribute this growth fairly and in the process not degrade the ecosystem. To classify contemporary battles over environmental racism, pollution-producing jobs, growth control, etc as simply clashes between economic growth and environmental protection misses the third issue, of social justice. The 'jobs versus environment' dichotomy (eg the spotted owl versus Pacific Northwest

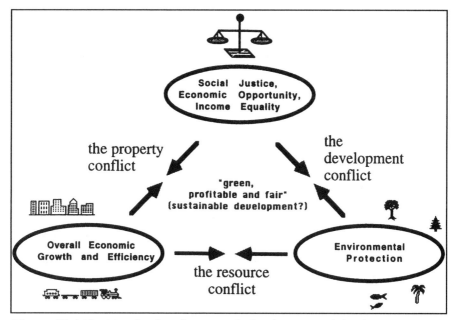

Figure 12.1 *The triangle of conflicting goals for planning and the three associated conflicts. Note*: Planners define themselves, implicitly, by where they stand on the triangle. The elusive ideal of sustainable development leads one to the centre*

timber jobs) crudely collapses under the 'economy' banner the often differing inter-ests of workers, corporations, community members and the national public. The intent of this paper's title is to focus planning not only for 'green cities and growing cities', but also for 'just cities'.

In an ideal world, planners would strive to achieve a balance of all three goals. In practice, however, professional and fiscal constraints drastically limit the leeway of most planners. Serving the broader public interest by holistically harmonizing growth, preservation and equality remains the ideal; the reality of practice restricts planners to serving the narrower interests of their clients, that is, authorities and bureaucracies (Marcuse 1976), despite efforts to work outside those limitations (Hoffman 1989). In the end, planners usually represent one particular goal – plan-ning perhaps for increased property tax revenues, or more open space preservation, or better housing for the poor – while neglecting the other two. Where each planner stands in the triangle depicted in Figure 12.1 defines such professional bias. One may see illustrated in the figure the gap between the call for integrative, sustainable development planning (the centre of the triangle) and the current fragmentation or professional practice (the edges). This point is developed later.

The Points (Corners) of the Triangle: the Economy, the Environment and Equity

The three types of priorities lead to three perspectives on the city: the economic de-velopment planner sees the city as a location where production, consumption, distribution and innovation take place. The city is in competition with other cities for markets and for new industries. Space is the economic space of highways, market areas and commuter zones.

The environmental planner sees the city as a consumer of resources and a producer of wastes. The city is in competition with nature for scarce resources and land, and always poses a threat to nature. Space is the ecological space of greenways, river basins and ecological niches.

The equity planner sees the city as a location of conflict over the distribution of resources, of services and of opportunities. The competition is within the city itself, among different social groups. Space is the social space of communities, neighbourhood organizations, labour unions: the space of access and segregation.

Certainly there are other important views of the city, including the architectural, the psychological, and the circulatory (transportation); and one could conceivably construct a planner's rectangle, pentagon or more complex polygon. The triangular shape itself is not propounded here as the underlying geometric structure of the planner's world. Rather, it is useful for its conceptual simplicity. More importantly, it emphasizes the point that a one-dimensional 'man versus environment' spectrum misses the social conflicts in contemporary environmental disputes, such as loggers versus the Sierra Club, farmers versus suburban developers or fishermen versus barge operators (Reisner 1987; Jacobs 1989; McPhee 1989; Tuason 1993).[1]

Triangle Axis 1: The Property Conflict

The three points on the triangle represent divergent interests and therefore lead to three fundamental conflicts. The first conflict – between economic growth and equity – arises from competing claims on and uses of property, such as between management and labour, landlords and tenants, or gentrifying professionals and long-time residents. This growth-equity conflict is further complicated because each side not only resists the other, but also needs the other for its own survival. The contradictory tendency for a capitalist, democratic society to define property (such as housing or land) as a private commodity, but at the same time to rely on government intervention (eg zoning or public housing for the working class) to ensure the beneficial social aspects of the same property, is what Richard Foglesong (1986) calls the 'property contradiction'. This tension is generated as the private sector simultaneously resists and needs social intervention, given the intrinsically contradictory nature of property. Indeed, the essence of property in our society is the tense pulling between these two forces. The conflict defines the boundary between private interest and the public good.

Triangle Axis 2: The Resource Conflict

Just as the private sector both resists regulation of property yet needs it to keep the economy flowing, so too is society in conflict about its priorities for natural resources. Business resists the regulation of its exploitation of nature, but at the same time needs regulation to conserve those resources for present and future demands. This can be called the 'resource conflict'. The conceptual essence of natural resources is therefore the tension between their economic utility in industrial society and their ecological utility in the natural environment. This conflict defines the boundary between the developed city and the undeveloped wilderness, which is symbolized by the 'city limits'. The boundary is not fixed; it is a dynamic and contested boundary between mutually dependent forces.

Is there a single, universal economic-ecological conflict underlying all such disputes faced by planners? I searched for this essential, Platonic notion, but the diversity of examples – water politics in California, timber versus the spotted owl in the Pacific Northwest, tropical deforestation in Brazil, park planning in the Adirondacks, green-belt planning in Britain, to name a few – suggests otherwise. Perhaps there is an *Ur-Konflikt*, rooted in the fundamental struggle between human civilization and the threatening wilderness around us, and expressed variously over the centuries. However, the decision must be left to anthropologists as to whether the essence of the spotted owl controversy can be traced back to neolithic times. A meta-theory tying all these multifarious conflicts to an essential battle of 'human versus nature' (and, once tools and weapons were developed and nature was controlled 'human versus human') – that invites scepticism. In this discussion, the triangle is used simply as a template to recognize and organize the common themes; to examine actual conflicts, individual case studies are used.[2]

The economic-ecological conflict has several instructive parallels with the growth-equity conflict. In the property conflict, industrialists must curb their profit-increasing tendency to reduce wages in order to provide labour with enough wages to feed, house and otherwise 'reproduce' itself – that is, the subsistence wage. In the resource conflict, the industrialists must curb their profit-increasing tendency to increase timber yields, so as to ensure that enough of the forest remains to 'reproduce' itself (Clawson 1975; Beltzer and Kroll 1986; Lee, Field and Burch 1990). This practice is called 'sustained yield', though timber companies and environmentalists disagree about how far the forest can be exploited and still be 'sustainable'. (Of course, other factors also affect wages, such as supply and demand, skill level, and discrimination, just as lumber demand, labour prices, transportation costs, tariffs and other factors affect how much timber is harvested.) In both cases, industry must leave enough of the exploited resource, be it human labour or nature, so that the resource will continue to deliver in the future. In both cases, how much is 'enough' is also contested.

Triangle Axis 3: The Development Conflict

The third axis on the triangle is the most elusive: the 'development conflict', lying between the poles of social equity and environmental preservation. If the property conflict is characterized by the economy's ambivalent interest in providing at least a subsistence existence for working people, and the resource conflict by the economy's ambivalent interest in providing sustainable conditions for the natural environment, the development conflict stems from the difficulty of doing both at once. Environment-equity disputes are coming to the fore to join the older dispute about economic growth versus equity (Paehlke 1994, pp 349–50). This may be the most challenging conundrum of sustainable development: how to increase social equity and protect the environment simultaneously, whether in a steady-state economy (Daly 1991) or not. How could those at the bottom of society find greater economic opportunity if environmental protection mandates diminished economic growth? On a global scale, efforts to protect the environment might lead to slowed economic growth in many countries, exacerbating the inequalities between rich and poor nations. In effect, the developed nations would be asking the poorer nations to forgo rapid development to save the world from the greenhouse effect and other global emergencies.

This development conflict also happens at the local level, as in resource-dependent communities, which commonly find themselves at the bottom of the economy's hierarchy of labour. Miners, lumberjacks and mill workers see a grim link between environmental preservation and poverty, and commonly mistrust environmentalists as elitists. Poor urban communities are often forced to make the no-win choice between economic survival and environmental quality, as when the only economic opportunities are offered by incinerators, toxic waste sites, landfills and other noxious land uses that most neighbourhoods can afford to oppose and do without (Bryant and Mohai 1992; Bullard 1990, 1993). If, as some argue, environmental protection is a luxury of the wealthy, then environmental racism lies at the heart of the development conflict. Economic segregation leads to environmental segregation: the former occurs in the transformation of natural resources into consumer products; the latter occurs as the spoils of production are returned to nature. Inequitable development takes place at all stages of the materials cycle.

Consider this conflict from the vantage of equity planning. Norman Krumholz, as the planning director in Cleveland, faced the choice of either building regional rail lines or improving local bus lines (Krumholz et al 1982). Regional rail lines would encourage the suburban middle class to switch from cars to mass transit; better local bus service would help the inner-city poor by reducing their travel and waiting time. One implication of this choice was the tension between reducing pollution and making transportation access more equitable, an example of how bias toward social inequity may be embedded in seemingly objective transit proposals.

IMPLICATIONS OF THE PLANNER'S TRIANGLE MODEL

Conflict and Complementarity in the Triangle

Though I use the image of the triangle to emphasize the strong conflicts among economic growth, environmental protection and social justice, no point can exist alone. The nature of the three axial conflicts is mutual dependence based not only on opposition, but also on collaboration.

Consider the argument that the best way to distribute wealth more fairly (ie to resolve the property conflict) is to increase the size of the economy so that society will have more to redistribute. Similarly, we can argue that the best way to improve environmental quality (ie to resolve the resource conflict) is to expand the economy, thereby having more money with which to buy environmental protection. The former is trickle-down economics; can we call the latter 'trickle-down environmentalism'? One sees this logic in the conclusion of the Brundtland Report: If large parts of the developing world are to avert economic, social, and environmental catastrophes, it is essential that global economic growth be revitalized' (World Commission on Environment and Development 1987). However, only if such economic growth is more fairly distributed will the poor be able to restore and protect their environment, whose devastation so immediately degrades their quality of life. In other words, the development conflict can be resolved only if the property conflict is resolved as well. Therefore, the challenge for planners is to deal with the conflicts between competing interests by discovering and implementing complementary uses.

The Triangle's Origins in a Social View of Nature

One of the more fruitful aspects of recent interdisciplinary thought may be its linking the traditionally separate intellectual traditions of critical social theory and environmental science/policy (eg Smith 1990; Wilson 1992; Ross 1994). This is also the purpose of the triangle figure presented here: to integrate the environmentalist's and social theorist's world views. On one side, an essentialist view of environmental conflicts ('man versus nature') emphasizes the resource conflict. On another side, a historical materialist view of social conflicts (eg capital versus labour) emphasizes the property conflict. By simultaneously considering both perspectives, one can see more clearly the social dimension of environmental conflicts – that is, the development conflict. Such a synthesis is not easy: it requires accepting the social construction of nature but avoiding the materialistic pitfall of arrogantly denying any aspects of nature beyond the labour theory of value.

Environmental conflict should not, therefore, be seen as simply one group representing the interests of nature and another group attacking nature (though it often appears that way).[3] Who is to say that the lumberjack, who spends all his or her days among trees (and whose livelihood depends on those trees), is any less close to nature than the environmentalist taking a weekend walk through the woods? Is the lumberjack able to cut down trees only because s/he is 'alienated' from the 'true' spirit of nature – the spirit that the hiker enjoys? In the absence of a forest mythology, neither the tree cutter nor the tree hugger – nor the third party, the owner/lessee of the forest – can claim an innate kinship to a tree. This is not to be an apologist for clear-cutting, but rather to say that the merits of cutting versus preserving trees cannot be decided according to which persons or groups have the 'truest' relationship to nature.

The crucial point is that all three groups have an interactive relationship with nature: the differences lie in their conflicting *conceptions* of nature, their conflicting *uses* of nature and how they incorporate nature into their systems of values (be they community, economic or spiritual values). This clash of human values reveals how much the ostensibly separate domains of community development and environmental protection overlap and suggests that planners should do better in combining social and environmental models. One sees this clash of values in many environmental battles: between the interests of urban residents and those of subsidized irrigation farmers in California water politics; between beach home-owners and coastal managers trying to control erosion; between rich and poor neighbourhoods, in the siting of incinerators; between farmers and environmentalists, in restrictions by open space zoning. Even then, President George Bush weighed into such disputes during his 1992 campaign when he commented to a group of loggers that finally people should be valued more than spotted owls (his own take on the interspecies equity issue). Inequity and the imbalance of political power are often issues at the heart of economic-environmental conflicts.

Recognition that the terrain of nature is contested need not, however, cast us adrift on a sea of socially constructed relativism where 'nature' appears as an arbitrary idea of no substance (Bird 1987; Soja 1989). Rather, we are made to rethink the idea and to see the appreciation of nature as an historically evolved sensibility. I suspect that radical environmentalists would criticize this perspective as anthropocentric environmentalism and argue instead for an ecocentric world view that puts the Earth first (Sessions 1992; Parton 1993). It is true that an anthropocentric view, if distorted, can lead to an arrogant optimism about civilization's ability to reprogramme nature through technologies ranging from huge hydroelectric and nuclear plants down to genetic engineering. A rigid belief in the anthropocentric labour theory of value, Marxist or otherwise, can produce a modern-day Narcissus as a social-constructionist who sees nature as merely reflecting the beauty of the human aesthetic and the value of human labour. In this light, a tree is devoid of value until it either becomes part of a scenic area or is transformed into lumber. On the other hand, even as radical, ecocentric environmentalists claim to see 'true nature' beyond the city limits, they are blind to how their own world view and their definition of nature itself are shaped by their socialization. The choice between an anthropocentric or an ecocentric world view is a false one. We are all unavoidably anthropocentric; the question is which anthropomorphic values and priorities we will apply to the natural and the social world around us.

SUSTAINABLE DEVELOPMENT: REACHING THE ELUSIVE CENTRE OF THE TRIANGLE

If the three corners of the triangle represent key goals in planning and the three axes represent the three resulting conflicts, then I will define the centre of the triangle as representing sustainable development: the balance of these three goals. Getting to the centre, however, will not be so easy. It is one thing to locate sustainability in the abstract, but quite another to reorganize society to get there.

At first glance, the widespread advocacy of sustainable development is astonishing, given its revolutionary implications for daily life (World Commission 1987; Daly and Cobb 1989; Rees 1989; World Bank 1989; Goodland 1990; Barrett and Bohlen 1991; Korten 1991; Van der Ryn and Calthorpe 1991). It is getting hard to refrain from sustainable development; arguments against it are inevitably attached to the strawman image of a greedy, myopic industrialist. Who would now dare to speak up in opposition? Two interpretations of the bandwagon for sustainable development suggest themselves. The pessimistic thought is that sustainable development has been stripped of its transformative power and reduced to its lowest common denominator. After all, if both the World Bank and radical ecologists now believe in sustainability, the concept can have no teeth: it is so malleable as to mean many things to many people without requiring commitment to any specific policies. Actions speak louder than words, and although all endorse sustainability, few will actually practise it. Furthermore, any concept fully endorsed by all parties must surely be bypassing the heart of the conflict. Set a goal far enough into the future, and even conflicting interests will seem to converge along parallel lines. The concept certainly appears to violate the Karl Popper's requirement that propositions be falsifiable, for to reject sustainability is to embrace non-sustainability – and who dares to sketch that future? (Ironically, the non-sustainable scenario is the easiest to define: merely the extrapolation of our current way of life.)

Yet there is also an optimistic interpretation of the broad embrace given sustainability: the idea has become hegemonic, an accepted meta-narrative, a given. It has shifted from being a variable to being the parameter of the debate, almost certain to be integrated into any future scenario of development. We should therefore neither be surprised that no definition has been agreed upon, nor fear that this reveals a fundamental flaw in the concept. In the battle of big public ideas, sustainability has won: the task of the coming years is simply to work out the details and to narrow the gap between its theory and practice.

Is Sustainable Development a Useful Concept?

Some environmentalists argue that if sustainable development is necessary, it therefore must be possible. Perhaps so, but if you are stranded at the bottom of a deep well, a ladder may be impossible even though necessary. The answer espoused may be as much an ideological as a scientific choice, depending on whether one's loyalty is to Malthus or Daly. The more practical question is whether sustainability is a useful concept for planners. The answer here is mixed. The goal may be too far away and holistic to be operational: that is, it may not easily break down into concrete, short-term steps. We also might be able to *define* sustainability yet be unable ever to actually measure it or even know, one day in the future, that we had achieved it. An old eastern proverb identifies the Western confusion of believing that to name something is to know it. That may be the danger in automatically embracing sustainable development: a facile confidence that by adding the term 'sustainable' to all our existing planning documents and tools (sustainable zoning, sustainable economic development, sustainable transportation planning), we are *doing* sustainable planning. Conversely, one can do much beneficial environmental work without ever devoting explicit attention to the concept of sustainability.

Yet sustainability can be a helpful concept in that it posits the long-term planning goal of a social-environmental system in balance. It is a unifying concept, enormously appealing to the imagination, that brings together many different environmental concerns under one overarching value. It defines a set of social priorities and articulates how society values the economy, the environment and equity (Paehlke 1994, p 360). In theory, it allows us not only to calculate whether we have attained sustainability, but also to determine how far away we are. (Actual measurement, though, is another, harder task.) Clearly, it can be argued that, though initially flawed and vague, the concept can be transformed and refined to be of use to planners.

History, Equity and Sustainable Development

One obstacle to an accurate, working definition of sustainability may well be the historical perspective that sees the practice as pre-existing, either in our past or as a Platonic concept. I believe instead that our sustainable future does not yet exist, either in reality or even in strategy. We do not yet know what it will look like; it is being socially constructed through a sustained period of conflict negotiation and resolution. This is a process of innovation, not of discovery and converting the non-believers.

This point brings us to the practice of looking for sustainable development in pre-industrial and non-Western cultures (a common though not universal practice). Searching for our future in our indigenous past is instructive at both the philosophical and the practical level (Turner 1983; Duerr 1985). Yet it is also problematical, tapping into a myth that our salvation lies in the pre-industrial sustainable culture. The international division of labour and trade, the movement of most people away from agriculture into cities and exponential population growth lead us irrevocably down a unidirectional, not a circular path: the transformation of pre-industrial, indigenous settlements into mass urban society is irreversible. Our modern path to sustainability lies forward, not behind us.

The key difference between those indigenous, sustainable communities and ours is that they had no choice but to be sustainable. Bluntly stated, if they cut down too many trees or ruined the soil, they would die out. Modern society has the options presented by trade, long-term storage and synthetic replacements; if we clear-cut a field, we have subsequent options that our ancestors didn't. In this situation, we must *voluntarily choose* sustainable practices, since there is no immediate survival or market imperative to do so. Although the long-term effects of a non-sustainable economy are certainly dangerous, the feedback mechanisms are too long-term to prod us in the right direction.

Why do we often romanticize the sustainable past? Some are attracted to the powerful spiritual link between humans and nature that has since been lost. Such romanticists tend, however, to overlook the more harsh and unforgiving aspects of being so dependent on the land. Two hundred years ago, Friedrich Schiller (1965, p 28) noted the tendency of utopian thinkers to take their dream for the future and posit it as their past, thus giving it legitimacy as a cyclical return to the past.[4] This habit is not unique to ecotopians (Kumar 1991); some religious fundamentalists also justify their utopian urgency by drawing on the myth of a paradise lost. Though Marxists don't glorify the past in the same way, they, too, manage to anticipate a *static* system of balance and harmony, which none the less will require a cataclysmic, revolutionary social transformation to reach. All three ideologies posit some basic flaw in society – be it Western materialism, original sin or capitalism – whose identification and cure will free us from conflict. Each ideology sees a fundamental alienation as the danger to overcome: alienation from nature, from god or from work. Each group is so critical of existing society that it would seem a wonder we have made it this far; but this persistence of human society despite the dire prognoses of utopians tells us something.

What is the fallout from such historical thinking? By neglecting the powerful momentum of modern industrial and post-industrial society, it both points us in the wrong direction and makes it easier to marginalize the proponents of sustainable development. It also carries an anti-urban sentiment that tends to neglect both the centrality and the plight of mega-cities. Modern humans are unique among species in their propensity to deal with nature's threats, not only through flight and burrowing and biological adaptation, nor simply through spiritual understanding, but also through massive population growth, complex social division of labour and the fundamental, external transformation of their once-natural environment (the building of cities). Certainly, the fixation on growth, industry and competition has degraded the environment. Yet one cannot undo urban-industrial society. Rather, one must continue to innovate through to the other side of industrialization, to reach a more sustainable economy.

The cyclical historical view of some environmentalists also hinders a critical understanding of equity, since that view attributes to the environment a natural state of equality rudely upset by modern society. Yet nature is inherently neither equal nor unequal, and at times can be downright brutal. The human observer projects a sense of social equity on to nature, through a confusion, noted by Schiller, of the idealized future with myths about our natural past. To gain a sense of historical legitimacy, we project our socially constructed sense of equality on to the past, creating revisionist history in which nature is fair and compassionate. Society's path to equality is perceived not as an uncertain progress from barbarism to justice, but rather as a return to an original state of harmony as laid out in nature. In this thinking, belief in an ecological balance and a social balance, entwined in the pre-industrial world, conjures up an eco-Garden of Eden 'lost' by modern society.[5]

It will be more useful to let go of this mythic belief in our involuntary diaspora from a pre-industrial, ecotopian Eden.[6] The conflation of ecological diasporas and utopias constrains our search for creative, urban solutions to social-environmental conflict. By relinquishing such mythic beliefs, we will understand that notions of equity were not lying patiently in wait in nature, to be first discovered by indigenous peoples, then lost by colonialists, and finely rediscovered by modern society in the late 20th century. This is certainly not to say that nature can teach us nothing. The laws of nature are not the same thing, however, as natural law, nor does ecological equilibrium necessarily generate normative principles of equity. Although we turn to nature to understand the context, dynamics and effects of the economic-environmental conflict, we must turn to social norms to decide what balance is fair and just.

How, then, do we define what is fair? I propose viewing social justice as the striving towards a more equal distribution of resources among social groups across the space of cities and of nations – definition of 'fair' distribution. It should be noted that societies view themselves as 'fair' if the *procedures* of allocation treat people equally, even if the *substantive* outcome is unbalanced. (One would hope that equal treatment is but the first step towards narrowing material inequality.) The environmental movement expands the space for this 'equity' in two ways: 1 intergenerationally (present versus future generations) and 2 across species (as in animal rights, deep ecology and legal standing for trees). The two added dimensions of equity remain essentially abstractions, however, since no one from the future or from other species can speak up for their 'fair share' of resources. Selfless advocates (or selfish ventriloquists) 'speak for them'.

This expansion of socio-spatial equity to include future generations and other species not only makes the concept more complex; it also creates the possibility for contradictions among the different calls for 'fairness'. Slowing worldwide industrial expansion may preserve more of the world's resources for the future (thereby increasing intergenerational equity), but it may also undermine the efforts of the underdeveloped world to approach the living standards of the West (thereby lowering international equity). Battles over Native American fishing practices, the spotted owl and restrictive farmland preservation each thrust together several divergent notions of 'fairness'. It is through resolving the three sorts of conflicts on the planner's triangle that society iteratively forms its definition of what is fair.

The Path Towards Sustainable Development

There are two final aspects of the fuzzy definition of sustainability: its path and its outcome. The basic premise of sustainable development is one that, like the long-term goal of a balanced US budget, is hard not to like. As with eliminating the national debt, however, two troubling questions about sustainable development remain: How are you going to get there? Once you get there, what are the negative consequences? Planners don't yet have adequate answers to these two questions; that is, as yet they have no concrete strategies to achieve sustainable development, nor do they know how to counter the political resistance to it.

On the *path* towards a sustainable future, the steps are often too vague, as with sweeping calls for a 'spiritual transformation' as the prerequisite for environmental transformation. Sometimes the call for sustainable development seems to serve as a vehicle for sermonizing about the moral and spiritual corruption of the industrial world (undeniable). Who would not want to believe in a holistic blending of economic and ecological values in each of our planners, who would then go out into the world and, on each project, internally and seamlessly merge the interests of jobs and nature, as well as of social justice? That is, the call to planners would be to stand at every moment at the centre of the triangle.

But this aim is too reminiscent of our naive belief during the 1950s and 1960s in comprehensive planning for a single 'public interest', before the incrementalists and advocacy planners pulled the rug out from under us (Lindblom 1959; Altshuler 1965; Davidoff 1965; Fainstein and Fainstein 1971). I suspect that planners' criticisms of the sustainable development movement in the coming years will parallel the critique of comprehensive planning 30 years ago: the incrementalists will argue that one cannot achieve a sustainable society in a single grand leap, for it requires too much social and ecological information and is too risky. The advocacy planners will argue that no common social interest in sustainable development exists, and that bureaucratic planners will invariably create a sustainable development scheme that neglects the interests both of the poor and of nature. To both groups of critics, the prospect of integrating economic, environmental and equity interests will seem forced and artificial. States will require communities to prepare 'Sustainable Development Master Plans', which will prove to be glib wish lists of goals and suspiciously vague implementation steps. To achieve consensus for the plan, language will be reduced to the lowest common denominator and the pleasing plans will gather dust.

An alternative is to let holistic sustainable development be a long-range goal; it is a worthy one, for planners do need a vision of a more sustainable urban society. But during the coming years, planners will confront deep-seated conflicts among economic, social and environmental interests that cannot be wished away through admittedly appealing images of a community in harmony with nature. One is no more likely to abolish the economic-environmental conflict completely by achieving sustainable bliss than one is to eliminate completely the boundaries between the city and the wilderness, between the public and private spheres, between the haves and have-nots. Nevertheless, one can diffuse the conflict and find ways to avert its more destructive fallout.

My concern about the *ramifications* of a sustainable future is one that is often expressed: steady-state, no-growth economics would be likely to relegate much of the developing world – and the poor within the industrialized world – to a state of persistent poverty. The advocates of sustainable development rightly reject as flawed the premise of conventional economics that only a growth economy can achieve social redistribution. And growth economics has, indeed, also exacerbated the environment's degradation. However, it is wishful thinking to assume that a sustainable economy will automatically ensure a socially just distribution of resources.[7] The vision of no-growth (commonly though not universally assumed to characterize sustainable development) raises powerful fears, and planners should be savvy to such fears. Otherwise, they will understand neither the potential dangers of steady-state economics nor the nature of the opposition to sustainable development.

Rethinking/Redefining Sustainable Development

Despite the shortcomings in the current formulation of sustainable development, the concept retains integrity and enormous potential. It simply needs to be redefined and made more precise. First, one should avoid a dichotomous, black-and-white view of sustainability. We should think of American society not as a corrupt, wholly unsustainable one that has to be made pure and wholly sustainable, but rather as a hybrid of both sorts of practices. Our purpose, then, should be to move further towards sustainable practices in an evolutionary progression.

Second, we should broaden the idea of 'sustainability'. If 'crisis' is defined as the inability of a system to reproduce itself, then sustainability is the opposite: the long-term ability of a system to reproduce. This criterion applies not only to natural eco-systems, but to economic and political systems as well. By this definition, Western society already does much to sustain itself: economic policy and corporate strate-gies (eg investment, training, monetary policy) strive to reproduce the macro- and micro-economies. Similarly, governments, parties, labour unions and other politi-cal agents strive to reproduce their institutions and interests. Society's shortcom-ing is that as it strives to sustain its political and economic systems, it often neglects to sustain the ecological system. The goal for planning is therefore a broader agenda: to sustain, simultaneously and in balance, these three sometimes competing, some-times complementary systems.[8]

Third, it will be helpful to distinguish initially between two levels of sustainability: specific versus general (or local versus global). One might fairly easily imagine and achieve sustainability in a single sector and/or locality – for example, converting a Pa-cific Northwest community to sustained-yield timber practices. Recycling, solar power, cogeneration and conservation can lower consumption of non-sustainable resources. To achieve complete sustainability across all sectors and/or all places, however, re-quires such complex restructuring and redistribution that the only feasible path to global sustainability is likely to be a long, incremental accumulation of local and industry-specific advances.

What this incremental, iterative approach means is that planners will find their vision of a sustainable city developed best at the conclusion of contested negotia-tions over land use, transportation, housing and economic development policies, not as the premise for beginning the effort. To first spend years in the hermetic iso-lation of universities and environmental groups, perfecting the theory of sustainable development, before testing it in community development is backwards. That ap-proach sees sustainable development as an ideal society outside the conflicts of the planner's triangle, or as the tranquil 'eye of the hurricane' at the triangle's centre. As with the ideal comprehensive plan, it is presumed that the objective, technocratic merits of a perfected sustainable development scheme will ensure society's accep-tance. But one cannot reach the sustainable centre of the planner's triangle in a single, holistic leap to a preordained balance.

THE TASK AHEAD FOR PLANNERS: SEEKING SUSTAINABLE DE-VELOPMENT WITHIN THE TRIANGLE OF PLANNING CONFLICTS

The role of planners is therefore to engage the current challenge of sustainable de-velopment with a dual, interactive strategy: (1) to manage and resolve conflict; and (2) to promote creative technical, architectural and institutional solutions. Planners must both negotiate the procedures of the conflict and promote a substantive vision of sustainable development.

Procedural Paths to Sustainable Development: Conflict Negotiation

In negotiation and conflict resolution (Bingham 1986; Susskind and Cruikshank 1987; Crowfoot and Wondolleck 1990), rather than pricing externalities, common ground is established at the negotiation table, where the conflicting economic, social and environmental interests can be brought together. The potential rewards are numerous: not only an outcome that balances all parties, but avoidance of heavy legal costs and long-lasting animosity. Negotiated conflict resolution can also lead to a better understanding of one's opponent's interests and values, and even of one's own interests. The very process of lengthy negotiation can be a powerful tool to mobilize community involvement around social and environmental issues. The greatest promise, of course, is a win-win outcome: finding innovative solutions that would not have come out of traditional, adversarial confrontation. Through skilfully led, back-and-forth discussion, the parties can separate their initial, clashing substantive demands from their underlying interests, which may be more compatible. For example, environmentalists and the timber industry could solve their initial dispute over building a logging road, through alternative road design and other mitigation measures (Crowfoot and Wondolleck 1990, pp 32–52).

However, conflict resolution is no panacea. Sometimes conflicting demands express fundamental conflicts of interest. The either-or nature of the technology or ecology may preclude a win-win outcome, as in an all-or-nothing dispute over a proposed hydroelectric project (Reisner 1987) – you either build it or you don't. An overwhelming imbalance of power between the opposing groups also can thwart resolution (Crowfoot and Wondolleck 1990, p 4). A powerful party can simply refuse to participate. It is also hard to negotiate a comprehensive resolution for a large number of parties.

Planners are likely to have the best success in using conflict resolution when there is a specific, concise dispute (rather than an amorphous ideological clash); all interested parties agree to participate (and don't bypass the process through the courts); each party feels on equal ground; there are a variety of possible compromises and innovative solutions; both parties prefer a solution to an impasse; and a skilled third-party negotiator facilitates. The best resolution strategies seem to include two areas of compromise and balance: the procedural (each party is represented and willing to compromise); and the substantive (the solution is a compromise, such as multiple land uses or a reduced development density).

Procedural Paths to Sustainable Development: Redefining the Language of the Conflict

A second strategy is to bridge the chasms between the languages of economics, environmentalism and social justice. Linguistic differences, which reflect separate value hierarchies, are a major obstacle to common solutions. All too often, the economists speak of incentives and marginal rates, the ecologists speak of carrying capacity and biodiversity, the advocate planners speak of housing rights, empowerment and discrimination, and each side accuses the others of being 'out of touch' (Campbell 1992).

The planner therefore needs to act as a translator, assisting each group to understand the priorities and reasoning of the others. Economic, ecological and social thought may at a certain level be incommensurable, yet a level may still be found where all three may be brought together. To offer an analogy, a Kenyan Gikuyu text cannot be fully converted into English without losing something in translation; a good translation, nevertheless, is the best possible way to bridge two systems of expression that will never be one, and it is preferable to incomprehension. The danger of translation is that one language will dominate the debate and thus define the terms of the solution. It is essential to exert equal effort to translate in each direction, to prevent one linguistic culture from dominating the other (as English has done in neocolonial Africa). Another lesson from the neocolonial linguistic experience is that it is crucial for each social group to express itself in its own language before any translation. The challenge for planners is to write the best translations among the languages of the economic, the ecological and the social views, and to avoid a quasi-colonial dominance by the economic *lingua franca,* by creating equal two-way translations.[9]

For example, planners need better tools to understand their cities and regions not just as economic systems or static inventories of natural resources, but also as *environmental systems* that are part of regional and global networks trading goods, information, resources and pollution. At the conceptual level, translating the economic vocabulary of global cities, the spatial division of labour, regional restructuring and technoburbs/edge cities into environmental language would be a worthy start; at the same time, of course, the vocabulary of biodiversity, landscape linkages and carrying capacity should be translated to be understandable by economic interests.

This bilingual translation should extend to the empirical level. I envision extending the concept of the 'trade balance' to include an 'environmental balance' which covers not just commodities, but also natural resources and pollution. Planners should improve their data collection and integration to support the environmental trade balance. They should apply economic-ecological bilingualism not only to the content of data, but also to the spatial framework of the data, by rethinking the geographic boundaries of planning and analysis. Bioregionalists advocate having the spatial scale for planning reflect the scale of *natural* phenomena (eg the extent of a river basin, vegetation zones or the dispersion range of metropolitan air pollution); economic planners call for a spatial scale to match the *social* phenomena (eg highway networks, municipal boundaries, labour market areas, new industrial districts). The solution is to integrate these two scales and overlay the economic and ecological geographies of planning. The current merging of environmental Raster (grid-based) and infrastructural vector-based data in Geographic Information Systems (GIS) recognizes the need for multiple layers of planning boundaries (Wiggins 1993).

Translation can thus be a powerful planner's skill, and interdisciplinary planning education already provides some multilingualism. Moreover, the idea of sustainability lends itself nicely to the meeting on common ground of competing value systems. Yet translation has its limits. Linguistic differences often represent real, intractable differences in values. An environmental dispute may arise not from a misunderstanding alone; both sides may clearly understand that their vested interests fundamentally clash, no matter how expressed. At this point, translation must give way to other strategies. The difficulties are exacerbated when one party has greater power and so shapes the language of the debate as well as prevailing in its outcome. In short, translation, like conflict negotiation, reveals both the promises and the limitations of communication-based conflict resolution.

Other Procedural Paths

Two other, more traditional approaches deserve mention. One is political pluralism: let the political arena decide conflicts, either directly (eg a referendum on an open space bond act or a California state proposition on nuclear power), or indirectly (eg elections decided on the basis of candidates' environmental records and promised legislation). The key elements here, political debate and ultimately the vote, allow much wider participation in the decision than negotiation does. However, a binary vote cannot as easily handle complex issues, address specific land-use conflicts, or develop subtle, creative solutions. Choosing the general political process as a strategy for deciding conflict also takes the process largely out of the hands of planners.

The other traditional strategy is to develop market mechanisms to link economic and environmental priorities. Prices are made the commonality that bridges the gap between the otherwise non-commensurables of trees and timber, open space and real estate. The market place is chosen as the arena where society balances its competing values. This economistic approach to the environment reduces pollution to what the economist Edwin Mills (1978, p 15) called 'a problem in resource allocation'. This approach can decide conflicts along the economic-environmental axis (the resource conflict), but often neglects equity. However, the market does seem to be dealing better with environmental externalities than it did 10 or 20 years ago. Internalizing externalities, at the least, raises the issues of social justice and equity: eg who will pay for cleaning up abandoned industrial sites or compensate for the loss of fishing revenues due to oil spills. The recent establishment of a pollution credit market in the South Coast Air Quality Management District, for example, is a step in the right direction – despite criticism that the pollution credits were initially given away for free (Robinson 1993).

The role of the planner in all four of these approaches is to arrange the procedures for making decisions, not to set the substance of the actual outcomes. In some cases, the overall structure for decision-making already exists (the market and the political system). In other cases, however, the planner must help shape that structure (a mediation forum; a common language) which, done successfully, gives the process credibility. The actual environmental outcomes nevertheless remain unknowable: you don't know in advance if the environment will actually be improved. For example, environmentalists and developers heralded the Coachella Valley Fringe-Toed Lizard Habitat Conservation Plan as a model process to balance the interests of development and conservation; yet the actual outcome may not adequately protect the endangered lizard (Beatley 1992, pp 15–16). Similarly, although the New Jersey State Development Plan was praised for its innovative cross-acceptance procedure, the plan itself arguably has not altered the state's urban sprawl.

The final issue that arises is whether the planner should play the role of neutral moderator or of advocate representing a single party; this has been a long-standing debate in the field. Each strategy has its virtues.

Substantive Paths to Sustainable Development: Land Use and Design

Planners have substantive knowledge of how cities, economies and ecologies interact, and they should put forth specific, far-sighted designs that promote the sustainable city. The first area is traditional planning tools of land-use design and control. The potential for balance between economic and environmental interests exists in design itself, as in a green-belt community (Elson 1986). Sometimes the land-use solution is simply to divide a contested parcel into two parcels: a developed and a preserved. This solution can take crude forms at times, such as the 'no-net-loss' policy that endorses the dubious practice of creating wetlands. A different example, Howard's turn-of-the-century Garden City (1965), can be seen as a territorially symbolic design for balance between the economy and the environment, although its explicit language was that of town-country balance. It is a design's articulated balance between the built development and the unbuilt wilderness that promises the economic-environmental balance. Designs for clustered developments, higher densities and live-work communities move toward such a balance (Rickaby 1987; Commission of the European Communities 1990; Hudson 1991; Van der Rys and Calthorpe 1991). Some dispute the inherent benefits of the compact city (Breheny 1992). A further complication is that not all economic-environmental conflicts have their roots in spatial or architectural problems. As a result, ostensible solutions may be merely symbols of ecological-economic balance, without actually solving the conflict.

Nevertheless, land-use planning arguably remains the most powerful tool available to planners who should not worry too much if it does not manage all problems. The trick in resolving environmental conflicts through land-use planning is to reconcile the conflicting territorial logics of human and of natural habitats. Standard real estate development reduces open space to fragmented, static, green islands – exactly what the landscape ecologists deplore as unable to preserve biodiversity. Wildlife roam and migrate, and require large expanses of connected landscape (Hudson 1991). So both the ecological and the economic systems require the interconnectivity of a critical mass of land to be sustainable. Although we live in a three-dimensional world, land is a limited resource with essentially two dimensions (always excepting air and burrowing/mining spaces). The requirement of land's spatial interconnectivity is thus hard to achieve for both systems in one region: the continuity of one system invariably fragments continuity of the other.[10] So the guiding challenge for land-use planning is to achieve simultaneously spatial/territorial integrity for both systems. Furthermore, a sustainable development that aspires to social justice must also find ways to avoid the land-use manifestations of uneven development: housing segregation, unequal property-tax funding of public schools, jobs-housing imbalance, the spatial imbalance of economic opportunity, and unequal access to open space and recreation.

Substantive Paths to Sustainable Development: Bioregionalism

A comprehensive vision of sustainable land use is bioregionalism, both in its 1920s articulation by the Regional Planning Association of America (Sussman 1976) and its contemporary variation (Sale 1985; Andrus et al 1990; Campbell 1992). The movement's essential belief is that rescaling communities and the economy according to the ecological boundaries of a physical region will encourage sustainability. The regional scale presumably stimulates greater environmental awareness: it is believed that residents of small-scale, self-sufficient regions will be aware of the causes and effects of their environmental actions, thereby reducing externalities. Regions will live within their means, and bypass the environmental problems caused by international trade and exporting pollution.

The bioregional vision certainly has its shortcomings, including the same fuzzy, utopian thinking found in other writing about sustainable development. Its ecological determinism also puts too much faith in the regional 'spatial fix': no geographic scale can, in itself, eliminate all conflict, for not all conflict is geographic. Finally, the call for regional self-reliance – a common feature of sustainable development concepts (Korten 1991, p 184) – might relegate the regional economy to underdevelopment in an otherwise nationally and internationally interdependent world. Yet it can be effective to visualize sustainable regions within an interdependent world full of trade, migration, information flows and capital flows, and to know the difference between *healthy interdependence* and *parasitic dependence* – that is, a dependence on other regions' resources that is equivalent to depletion. Interdependence does not always imply an imbalance of power, nor does self-sufficiency guarantee equality. Finally, the bioregional perspective can provide a foundation for understanding conflicts among a region's interconnected economic, social and ecological networks.

Other Substantive Paths

One other approach is technological improvement, such as alternative fuels, conservation mechanisms, recycling, alternative materials, and new mass transit design. Stimulated by competition, regulation or government subsidies, such advances reduce the consumption of natural resources per unit of production and thereby promise to ameliorate conflict over their competing uses, creating a win-win solution. However, this method is not guaranteed to serve those purposes, for gains in conservation are often cancelled out by rising demand for the final products. The overall increase in demand for gasoline despite improvements in automobile fuel efficiency is one example of how market forces can undermine technologically achieved environmental improvements. Nor, importantly, do technological improvements guarantee fairer distribution.

The role of the planner in all these substantive strategies (land use, bioregionalism, technological improvement) is to design outcomes, with less emphasis on the means of achieving them. The environmental ramifications of the solutions are known or at least estimated, but the political means to achieve legitimacy are not. There also is a trade-off between comprehensiveness (bioregions) and short-term achievability (individual technological improvements).

Merging the Substantive and Procedural

The individual shortcomings of the approaches described above suggest that combining them can achieve both political and substantive progress in the environmental-economic crisis. The most successful solutions seem to undertake several different resolution strategies at once. For example, negotiation among developers, city planners and land-use preservationists can produce an innovative, clustered design for a housing development, plus a per-unit fee for preserving open space. Substantive vision combined with negotiating skills thus allows planners to create win-win solutions, rather than either negotiating in a zero-sum game or preparing inert, ecotopian plans. This approach is not a distant ideal for planners: they already have, from their education and experience, both this substantive knowledge and this political savvy.

In the end, however, the planner must also deal with conflicts where one or more parties have no interest in resolution. One non-resolution tactic is the NIMBY, Not In My Back Yard response: a crude marriage of local initiative and the age-old externalizing of pollution. This 'take it elsewhere' strategy makes no overall claim to resolve conflict, though it can be a productive form of resistance rather than just irrational parochialism (Lake 1993). Nor does eco-terrorism consider balance. Instead, it replaces the defensive stance of NIMBY with offensive, confrontational, symbolic action. Resolution is also avoided out of cavalier confidence that one's own side can manage the opposition through victory, not compromise ('My side will win, so why compromise?'). Finally, an 'I don't care' stance avoids the conflict altogether. Unfortunately, this ostensible escapism often masks a more pernicious NIMBY or 'my side will win' hostility, just below the surface.

PLANNERS: LEADERS OR FOLLOWERS IN RESOLVING ECONOMIC-ENVIRONMENTAL CONFLICTS?

I turn finally to the question of whether planners are likely to be leaders or followers in resolving economic-environmental conflicts. One would think that it would be natural for planners, being interdisciplinary and familiar with the three goals of balancing social equity, jobs and environmental protection, to take the lead in resolving such conflicts. Of the conflict resolution scenarios mentioned above, those most open to planners' contributions involve the built environment and local resources: land use, soil conservation, design issues, recycling, solid waste, water treatment. Even solutions using the other approaches – environmental economic incentives, political compromise and environmental technology innovations – that are normally undertaken at the state and federal levels could also involve planners if moved to the local or regional level.

But the planners' position at the forefront of change is not assured, especially if the lead is taken up by other professions or at the federal, not the local, level. The lively debate on whether gasoline consumption can best be reduced through higher-density land uses (Newman and Kenworthy 1989) or through energy taxes (Gordon and Richardson 1990) not only reflected an ideological battle over interpreting research results and the merits of planning intervention, but also demonstrated how local planning can be made either central or marginal to resolving environmental-economic conflicts. To hold a central place in the debate about sustainable development, planners must exploit those areas of conflict where they have the greatest leverage and expertise.

Certainly planners already have experience with both the dispute over economic growth versus equity and that over economic growth versus environmental protection. Yet the development conflict is where the real action for planners will be: seeking to resolve both environmental and economic equity issues at once. Here is where the profession can best make its unique contribution. An obvious start would be for community development planners and environmental planners to collaborate more (an alliance that an internal Environmental Protection Agency memo found explosive enough for the agency to consider defusing it) (Higgins 1994). One possible joint task is to expand current public-private partnership efforts to improve environmental health in the inner city. This urban-based effort would help planners bypass the danger of environmental elitism that besets many suburban, white-oriented environmental organizations.

If planners move in this direction, they will join the growing environmental justice movement, which emerged in the early 1980s and combined minority community organizing with environmental concerns (Higgins 1994). The movement tries to reduce environmental hazards that directly affect poor residents who are the least able to fight pollution, be it the direct result of discriminatory siting decisions or the indirect result of housing and employment discrimination. The poor, being the least able to move away, are especially tied to place and therefore to the assistance or neglect of local planners. Understandably, local civil rights leaders have been preoccupied for so long with seeking economic opportunity and social justice that they have paid less attention to inequities in the local environment. The challenge for poor communities is now to expand their work on the property conflict to address the development conflict as well – that is, to challenge the false choice of jobs over the environment. An urban vision of sustainable development, infused with a belief in social and environmental justice, can guide these efforts.

Yet even with the rising acceptance of sustainable development, planners will not always be able, on their own, to represent and balance social, economic and environmental interests simultaneously. The professional allegiances, skills and bureaucracies of the profession are too constraining to allow that. Pretending at all times to be at the centre of the planner's triangle will only make sustainability a hollow term. Instead, the trick will be for individual planners to identify their specific loyalties and roles in these conflicts accurately – that is, to orient themselves in the triangle. Planners will have to decide whether they want to remain outside the conflict and act as mediators or jump into the fray and promote their own visions of ecological-economic development, sustainable or otherwise. Both planning behaviours are needed.

ACKNOWLEDGEMENTS

The author thanks Elizabeth Mueller, Susan Fainstein, Diane Massell, Jonathan Feidman, Karen Lowry, Jessica Sanchez, Harvey Jacobs, Michael Greenberg, Renée Sieber, Robert Higgins, the Project on Regional and Industrial Economics (PRIE) Seminar, and three anonymous reviewers for their comments.

NOTES

1   A curious comparison to this equity-environment-economy triangle is the view of Arne Naess (1993), the radical environmentalist who gave Deep Ecology its name in the 1970s, that the three crucial postwar political movements were the social justice, radical environmental and peace movements, whose goals might overlap but could not be made identical

2   Perhaps one can explain the lack of a universal conflict in the following way: if our ideas of the economy, equity and the environment are socially/culturally constructed, and if cultural society is local as well as global, then our ideas are locally distinct rather than universally uniform

3   For planners, if one is simply 'planning for place', then the dispute about suburban housing versus wetlands does indeed reflect a conflict between an economic and an environmental use of a specific piece of land. But if one sees this conflict in the light of 'planning for people', then the decision lies between differing social groups (eg environmentalists, fishermen, developers) and between their competing attempts to incorporate the piece of land into their system and worldview. (This classic planning distinction between planning for people or for place begs the question: Is there a third option, 'planning for non-people, ie nature'?)

4   Schiller, using Kant's logic, recognized 200 years ago this human habit of positing the future on the past: 'He thus artificially retraces his childhood in his maturity, forms for himself a *state of Nature* in idea, which is not indeed given him by experience but is the necessary result of his rationality, borrows in this ideal state an ultimate aim which he never knew in his actual state of Nature, and a choice of which he was capable, and proceeds now exactly as though he were starting afresh... '

5   Some radical ecologists take this lost world a step further and see it not as a garden, but as wilderness (eg Parton 1993)

6   I use the term diaspora to mean the involuntary dispersal of a people from their native home, driven out by a greater power (Hall 1992). The curious nature of the diaspora implied by the en-

vironmental worldview is that it is ambiguously voluntary: Western positivistic thinking is the villain that we developed, but that eventually enslaved us. Then, too, diasporas invariably combine dislocations across both time and space, but the mythic 'homeland' of this environmental diaspora is only from an historical era, but from no specific place

7   The reverse may also not be automatic. David Johns (1992, p 63), in advocating a broad interspecies equity, reminds us that not all forms of equity go hand-in-hand: 'The nature of the linkages between various forms of domination is certainly not settled, but deep ecology may be distinct in believing that the resolution of equity issues among humans will not automatically result in an end to human destruction of the biosphere. One can envision a society without class distinctions, without patriarchy, and with cultural autonomy, that still attempts to manage the rest of nature in utilitarian fashion with resulting deterioration of the biosphere... But the end of domination in human relations is not enough to protect the larger biotic community. Only behavior shaped by a biocentric view can do that.'

8   The ambiguity of the term sustainable development is therefore not coincidental, given that reasonable people differ on which corner of the triangle is to be 'sustained': a fixed level of natural resources? current environmental quality? current ecosystems? a hypothetical pre-industrial environmental state? the current material standards of living? long-term economic growth? political democracy?

9   These issues of language and translation were raised by Ngũgĩ wa Thiong-o and Stuart Hall in separate distiguished lectures at the Center for the Critical Analysis of Contemporary Cultures, Rutgers University (31 March and 15 April 1993)

10 Conservationists have, in fact, installed underpasses and overpasses so that vulnerable migrating species can get around highways

REFERENCES

Altshuler, Alan 1965 The Goals of Comprehensive Planning. *Journal of the American Institute of Planning* 31,3: 186–94

Andrus, Van, et al (eds) 1990 *Home: A Bioregional Reader.* Philadelphia and Santa Cruz: New Catalyst/ New Society

Barrett, Gary W, and Patrick J Bohlen 1991. Landscape Ecology. In *Landscape Linkages and Biodiversity,* edited by Wendy E Hudson. Washington, DC and Covelo, CA: lsland Press

Beatley, Timothy 1992. Balancing Urban Development and Endangered Species: The Coachella Valley Habitat Conservation Plan. *Environmental Management* 16,1: 7–19

Beatley, Timothy, and David J Brower 1993. Sustainability Comes to Main Street. *Planning* 59,5: 16–19

Beltzer, Dena, and Cynthia Kroll 1986. *New Jobs for the Timber Region: Economic Diversification for Northern California.* Berkeley: Institute of Governmental Studies, University of California

Bingham, Gail 1986. *Resolving Environmental Disputes: A Decade of Experience.* Washington, DC: The Conservation Foundation

Bird, Elizabeth Ann R 1987. The Social Construction of Nature: Theoretical Approaches to the History of Environmental Problems. *Environmental Review* 11,4: 255–64

Bramwell, Anna 1989. *Ecology in the Twentieth Century, A History.* New Haven: Yale University Press

Breheny, M J, (ed) 1992. *Sustainable Development and Urban Form.* London: Pion

Bryant, Bunyan, and Paul Mohai (eds) 1992. *Race and the lncidence of Environmental Hazards.* Boulder, CO: Westview Press

Bullard, Robert D 1990 *Dumping in Dixie: Race, Class, and Environmental Quality.* Boulder, CO: Westview Press

Bullard, Robert D (ed) 1993 *Confronting Environmental Racism: Voices from the Grassroots.* Boston: South End Press

Callenbach, Ernest 1975. *Ecotopia: The Notebooks and Reports of William Weston.* Berkeley, CA: Banyan Tree Books

Campbell, Scott 1992. Integrating Economic and Environmental Planning: The Regional Perspective. Working Paper No 43, Center for Urban Policy Research, Rutgers University

Clawson, Marion 1975 *Forests: For Whom and For What?* Washington, DC: Resources for the Future

Commission of the European Communities. 1990 *Green Paper on the Urban Environment.* Brussels: EEC

Crowfoot, James E, and Julia M Wondolleck. 1990. *Environmental Disputes: Community Involvement in Conflict Resolution.* Washington, DC and Covelo, CA: Island Press

Daly, Herman E 1991 *Steady State Economics,* 2nd edition, with new essays. Washington, DC and Covelo, CA: Island Press

Daly, Herman E, and John B Cobb, Jr 1989. *For the Common Good: Redirecting the Economy toward Community, the Environment, and a Sustainable Future.* Boston: Beacon Press

Davidoff, Paul 1965. Advocacy and Pluralism in Planning. *Journal of the American Institute of Planners* 31,4: 544–55

Duerr, Hans Peter 1985. *Dreamtime: Concerning the Boundary Between Wilderness and Civilization.* Oxford: Basil Blackwell

Elson, Martin J 1986. *Green Belts: Conflict Mediation in the Urban Fringe.* London: Heinemann

Fainstein, Susan S, and Norman I Fainstein. 1971. City Planning and Political Values. *Urban Affairs Quarterly* 6,3: 341–62

Findhorn Community, The 1975. *The Findhorn Garden: Pioneering a New Vision of Man and Nature in Cooperation.* New York: Harper and Row

Foglesong, Richard E 1986. *Planning the Capitalist City.* Princeton: Princeton University Press

Friedmann, John, and Clyde Weaver 1979. *Territory and Function: The Evolution of Regional Planning.* Berkeley and Los Angeles: University of California Press

Goldstein, Eric A, and Mark A Izeman 1990. *The New York Environment Book.* Washington, DC and Covelo, CA: Island Press

Goodland, Robert 1990. Environmental Sustainability in Economic Development – with Emphasis on Amazonia In *Race to Save the Tropics: Ecology and Economics for a Sustainable Future,* edited by Robert Goodland. Washington, DC and Covelo, CA: Island Press

Gordon, Peter, and Harry Richardson 1990. Gasoline Consumption and Cities – A Reply. *Journal of the American Planning Association.* 55,3: 342–5

Hall, Stuart 1992. Cultural Identity and Diaspora. *Framework* 36

Harvey, David 1985. *The Urbanization of Capital.* Baltimore: Johns Hopkins University Press

Higgins, Robert R 1994a. Race and Environmental Equity: An Overview of the Environmental Justice Issue in the Policy Process. *Polity,* forthcoming

Higgins, Robert R 1994b. Race, Pollution, and the Mastery of Nature. *Environmental Ethics,* forthcoming

Hoffman, Lily 1989. *The Politics of Knowledge: Activist Movements in Medicine and Planning.* Albany: SUNY Press

Howard, Ebenezer 1965. *Garden Cities of To-Morrow* (first published in 1898 as *To-Morrow: A Peaceful Path to Real Reform).* Cambridge, MA: MIT Press

Hudson, Wendy E (ed) 1991. *Landscape Linkages and Biodiversity.* Washington, DC and Covelo, CA: Island Press

Jacobs, Harvey 1989. Social Equity in Agricultural Land Protection. *Landscape and Urban Planning* 17,1: 21–33

Johns, David 1992. The Practical Relevance of Deep Ecology. *Wild Earth* 2,2

Korten, David C 1991. Sustainable Development. *World Policy Journal* 9,1:157–90

Krumholz, Norman, et al 1982. A Retrospective View of Equity Planning: Cleveland, 1969–1979, and Comments. *Journal of the American Planning Association* 48,2: 163–83

Kumar, Krishan 1991. *Utopia and Anti-Utopia in Modern Times.* Oxford and Cambridge, MA: Basil Blackwell

Lake, Robert 1993. Rethinking NIMBY. *Journal of the American Planning Association* 59,1: 87–93

Lake, Robert (ed) 1987. *Resolving Locational Conflict.* New Brunswick, NJ: Center for Urban Policy Research

Lee, Robert G, Donald R Field, and William R Burch, Jr (eds) 1990. *Community and Forestry: Continuities in the Sociology of Natural Resources.* Boulder, CO: Westview Press

Lindblom, C E 1959. The Science of Muddling Through. *Public Administration Review* 19 (Spring): 79–88

MacKaye, Benton 1962 (first published in 1928 by Harcourt, Brace and Co) *The New Exploration: A Philosophy of Regional Planning.* Urbana: University of Illinois Press

Marcuse, Peter 1976 Professional Ethics and Beyond: Values in Planning. *Journal of the American Institute of Planning* 42, 3:264–74

McPhee, John 1989. *The Control of Nature.* New York: Farrar, Straus, Giroux

Mills, Edwin S 1978. *The Economics of Environmental Quality.* New York: Norton

Naess, Arne 1993. The Breadth and the Limits of the Deep Ecology Movement. *Wild Earth* 3, 1: 74–5

Newman, Peter W G, and Jeffrey R Kenworthy 1989. Gasoline Consumption and Cities – A Comparison of US Cities with a Global Survey. *Journal of the American Planning Association* 55, 1: 24–37

Paehlke, Robert C 1994. Environmental Values and Public Policy. In *Environmental Policy in the 1990s*, 2nd edition, edited by Norman J Vig and Michael E Kraft. Washington, DC: Congressional Quarterly Press

Parton, Glenn 1993. Why I am a Primitivist. *Wild Earth* 3, 1:12–4

Rees, William 1989. *Planning for Sustainable Development.* Vancouver, BC: UBC Centre for Human Settlements

Reisner, Marc 1987. *Cadillac Desert: The American West and its Disappearing Water.* New York: Penguin Books

Rickaby, P A 1987. Six Settlement Patterns Compared, *Environment and Planning B: Planning and Design* 14: 193–223

Robinson, Kelly 1993. The Regional Economic Impacts of Marketable Permit Programs: The Case of Los Angeles. In *Cost Effective Control of Urban Smog.* Federal Reserve Bank of Chicago (November): 166–88

Ross, Andrew 1994. *The Chicago Gangster Theory of Life: Ecology, Culture, and Society.* London and New York: Verso

Sale, Kirkpatrick 1985. *Dwellers in the Land: The Bioregional Vision.* San Francisco: Sierra Club Books

Schiller, Friedrich 1965. *On the Aesthetic Education of Man* (translate by Reginald Snell). Originally published in 1795 as *Über die Äesthetische Erziehung des Menschen in einer Reihe von Briefen.* New York: Friedrich Unger

Sessions, George 1992. Radical Environmentalism in the 90s. *Wild Earth* 2,3: 64–7

Smith, Neil 1990. *Uneven Development: Nature, Capital and the Production of Space.* Oxford, UK: Blackwell

Soja, Edward 1989. *Postmodern Geographies: The Resurrection of Space in Critical Social Theory.* London and New York: Verso

Susskind, Lawrence, and Jeffrey Cruikshank. 1987. Mediated Negotiation in the Public Sector: The Planner as Mediator. *Journal of Planning Education and Research* 4: 5–15

Sussman, Carl (ed) 1976. *Planning the Fourth Migration: The Neglected Vision of the Regional Planning Association of America.* Cambridge, MA: MIT Press

Tuason, Julie A 1993. Economic/Environmental Conflicts in 19th-Century New York: Central Park, Adirondack State Park, and the Social Construction of Nature. Unpublished manuscript, Dept of Geography, Rutgers University

Turner, Frederick W 1983. *Beyond Geography: The Western Spirit Against the Wilderness.* New Brunswick, NJ: Rutgers University Press

Van der Ryn, Sim, and Peter Calthorpe 1991. *Sustainable Communities: A New Design Synthesis for Cities, Suburbs and Towns.* San Francisco: Sierra Club Books

Wiggins, Lyna 1993. Geographic Information Systems. Lecture at the Center for Urban Policy Research, Rutgers University, 5 April

Wilson, Alexander 1992. *The Culture of Nature: North American Landscape from Disney to the Exxon Valdez.* Cambridge, MA and Oxford, UK: Blackwell

World Bank 1989. *Striking a Balance: The Environmental Challenge of Development.* Washington, DC

World Commission on Environment and Development (The Brundtland Commission) 1987. *Our Common Future.* Oxford: Oxford University Press

Chapter 13

Resources: Resource Conservation and Waste Management

UN Centre for Human Settlements

(Extracted from Chapter 12, 'Environmental Protection and Resource Management' in UNCHS (Habitat), *An Urbanizing World: Global Report on Human Settlements, 1996*, Oxford University Press, Oxford and New York, 1996)

LIMITATIONS TO CURRENT APPROACHES

There is no shortage of innovative examples of buildings or settlements in which the level of resource use and waste generation has been greatly reduced. There are also many examples of companies and city governments that have greatly reduced resource use and wastes. There are the many traditional buildings and settlements that have always used resources efficiently and kept wastes to a minimum. What is less evident is governments prepared to develop national frameworks to promote resource conservation and waste minimization in all sectors and at all levels. This chapter includes many examples of innovations – for instance, the great improvements in energy efficiency in most aspects of housing and housing appliances, the trend towards recognizing waste streams as resource streams, and innovations in urban agriculture and urban forestry that reduce cities' 'ecological footprints'. But these tend to be the exceptions rather than the rule.

There is a growing recognition of the need to make all investment decisions by governments and the private sector respond to environmental issues. This is both in the depletion of the different kinds of environmental assets listed in Box 13.1 and in the environmental hazards that arise within human settlements.[1] Middle- and upper-income households can afford to live in the least polluted areas of the city and to avoid the jobs with the highest levels of environmental risk. The areas in which they live generally enjoy the best provision for basic infrastructure and services, while low-income households often live in the most polluted areas, work in the most dangerous jobs and live in the most dangerous sites – for instance, floodplains, steep slopes or sites contaminated with industrial wastes – with little or no infrastructure and services. There are also examples of lower income groups being more exposed to environmental hazards in the North – for instance, in the systematic siting of the more dangerous waste dumps in or close to low-income areas.[2]

Box 13.1 *Different forms of environmental assets*

Non-renewable assets   **Renewable assets**

Resources   Resources
  Fossil fuels   Soils
  Other minerals   Forests
  Biodiversity   Fresh water
                             Marine resources

Sinks   Sinks
  Non-biodegradable wastes (plastics,   capacity to break down
  persistent chemicals, long-lived nuclear   biodegradable wastes
  wastes, CFCs, many greenhouse gases)

There remain many unresolved questions in improving environmental protection and resource management such as how to value the different kinds of environmental assets widely used in production and consumption[3] and how to ensure that this revaluation contributes to greater inter-generational and intra-generational equity. If one considers the four different kinds of environmental assets listed in Box 13.1, most progress in reducing their depletion has been on two of them. The first is limiting the right of industries to use local sinks for wastes – for instance, disposing of untreated wastes in rivers, lakes or other local water bodies or in high levels of air pollution. Environmental legislation has restricted this right in virtually all countries, although the extent to which the environmental legislation is enforced varies widely and in some countries, there is little enforcement.[4] The second is a less wasteful use of renewable resources; in many countries where fertile soil and fresh water are in short supply, and forests are being rapidly depleted, measures have been taken to protect them or, in the case of fresh water, to promote less wasteful patterns of use. But consumers and businesses in the wealthier nations or cities can 'appropriate' the soils and water resources of distant ecosystems by importing the land- and water-intensive goods from these regions. Thus, the depletion of soil and the over-exploitation of fresh water to meet the demands of city consumers and producers may simply be switched from the city's own region to distant regions. On the third and fourth kinds of environmental assets, the use of non-renewable resources and sinks for non-biodegradable wastes, there has been much less progress. This includes the use of the 'global sink' for greenhouse gases and the direct and indirect economic, social and environmental costs this brings or may bring. The need is to halt or modify investment decisions which imply serious social and environmental costs either in the immediate locality or in distant ecosystems or for future generations. To achieve this implies major changes in ownership rights for land and natural resources.[5] Achieving this is made all the more difficult by incomplete knowledge about the scale and nature of the environmental costs that current production and consumption patterns are passing on to current and future generations.[6]

RESOURCE CONSERVATION AND WASTE MANAGEMENT

The Opportunities for Resource Conservation

There is a great range of opportunities for resource conservation and waste reduction in the wealthier nations of both the North and the South. For many actions taken to improve environmental performance, the economic and environmental benefits greatly outweigh the economic and environmental costs.[7] Capital costs are rapidly repaid by lower running costs – as in lower fuel bills for better insulated buildings or through replacement of inefficient cooling or heating systems – so there is little diminution of economic activity. For others, there are economic and employment costs which will have to be borne in the present or immediate future, but as part of a reduction in the costs passed on to future generations. One example of this is the economic costs of a major programme to cut greenhouse gas emissions – for instance, through some dampening in total economic activity as carbon taxes raise the cost of using motor vehicles, of heating and cooling buildings and of most energy-intensive goods. But on the positive side, not only does this diminish the cost passed on to future generations but in addition, technological innovation can certainly diminish these costs and many new jobs will be created.

One of the main resource issues in the North is the transition to a much less fossil-fuel intensive society. The policies that can promote such a transition are well known and well documented.[8] They include:

- Strong encouragement for improving the energy efficiency of residential, commercial, industrial and public sector buildings, working on the basis of installing new equipment and insulation whose cost will be repaid within a few years (or less) from lower fuel bills. This can achieve very substantial reductions in fuel use with no loss in comfort.
- A range of incentives and the provision of technical advice to industries on how to improve energy efficiency; many industries have multiplied severalfold the energy productivity of their processes in recent decades.[9]
- A rethink of pricing and regulation for road vehicles, of pricing for fossil fuels in general, and of provision for public transport and support for increasing bicycling and walking.

Box 13.2 gives examples of energy savings that are possible in different aspects of buildings and domestic appliances, most of which are already being implemented. There are also many examples of much improved performance in terms of resource use for buildings in general. For instance, in the Netherlands, new homes built in recent years require only a third to a quarter of the energy for heating compared to homes built 20 years ago.[10]

Ensuring the widespread adoption of such energy-saving technologies or techniques implies changes to building norms and codes to encourage conservation and energy-efficient equipment and to public information services to promote this. It also implies the labelling of vehicles and appliances so their energy efficiency (and fuel cost implications) are known to consumers, and the implementation of settlement planning and traffic management techniques that have positive social and environmental impacts. Finally, it includes a reappraisal of the energy-producing sector.

One important concept first developed by some utility companies in the United States is to treat potential savings in fuel or electricity as an alternative energy source.

Box 13.2 *Energy savings in different aspects of buildings and domestic appliances and in their construction*

Walls: Improved insulation can be introduced into the walls of many buildings in Europe and North America, with reductions in fuel demand for heating or cooling by up to 25 per cent.

Windows: New window technology is greatly reducing heat loss both through the glass and as a result of gaps. Between 1984 and 1994, advanced windows with two or three panes of glass have claimed 38 per cent of the residential market in the United States, and this has saved the residents some US$5 billion in energy bills each year.[11]

Roof: Installing or upgrading insulation in the roof of many existing buildings in the North can reduce fuel demand for heating by up to 25 per cent with costs often repaid through lower fuel bills in less than a year.

Space heating and cooling requirements: In addition to improved insulation of walls, windows and the roof noted above, various other measures can reduce space heating and cooling requirements. For instance, light coloured roofing and cladding materials that reflect sunlight can cut peak cooling needs by as much as 40 per cent in hot climates, while planting trees around existing buildings can cut cooling needs by up to 30 per cent.

Lighting: New compact fluorescent lamps that can replace conventional light bulbs require less than a quarter of the electricity of the bulbs they replace, and since their introduction in 1982, they have captured a significant portion of the market in Europe and North America; in Japan, where electricity is particularly expensive, these are now used in 80 per cent of home fixtures.[12]

Appliances: Energy use in domestic fridges has fallen significantly, due mainly to better insulation and more efficient electric motors. Electricity use by fridges in the USA fell by around half between 1972 and 1992, while some 1994 models use 30-50 per cent less than the current average. Further improvements are possible so that overall, refrigerators and home freezers can now consume 80–90 per cent less electricity than conventional models. Major savings in electricity use by televisions, computers and photocopying machines can also be achieved through the use of the most energy-efficient models.[13]

Air-conditioners: The need for air-conditioned buildings in hot climates can be considerably reduced by the measures noted above which reduce heat gain from the sun and also greatly reduce the amount of waste heat produced by lighting and appliances within the building. Air conditioners themselves vary greatly in their efficiency; the most efficient use around a third of the electricity of the least efficient ones.

Space heating: Major advances have been made in the fuel efficiency of space heaters in the last two decades. They are not only highly cost effective for new buildings through the fuel costs they save but in many instances can be used to replace inefficient space heaters in existing buildings.

Building materials: There have been considerable improvements in the energy efficiency in building materials production – for instance, the improved energy efficiency of cement production. Energy inputs into buildings have also been reduced through many innovations in the structural elements of large buildings that reduce the need for energy intensive materials and through measures to recycle building materials.

This has become a common response by electricity companies that are having difficulty meeting peak demand or that are planning to increase capacity. The costs of increasing electricity generation capacity are very high, especially if stringent environmental standards are met. It often proves much cheaper for the company to encourage its main users to invest in insulation and more electricity-efficient equipment than to invest in new generating capacity. Although there are obvious problems in implementing such an approach, especially where a company is privately owned and the conservation option proves less profitable than the option of increasing supply, the advantages to society and to the environment are obvious. For instance, the very rapid expansion in the production and use of refrigerators in China in recent years has also required a large increase in electricity capacity to power them, and the high cost of expanding power supply could have been much moderated, if a more efficient refrigerator design had been chosen.[14] Similarly, the promotion of energy-efficient light bulbs in many cities in the South would often considerably reduce the size of the evening peak demand.[15]

In the last few years, several states in the USA have adopted reforms that allow electricity companies to profit from increasing efficiency; in one instance, that of Pacific Gas and Electric in California, three-quarters of its new energy needs during the 1990s should be met through increased energy efficiency programmes with the rest coming from renewable energy sources.[16]

Managing the Transition to Resource-Efficient Cities

In the North and in the wealthier cities in the South, the potential for employment creation in greatly reducing resource use and wastes and in recycling or reusing the wastes that are generated are very considerable. The main reason is that levels of resource use, waste generation and pollution are so high that there are many possibilities for substituting labour and knowledge for resource use and waste. There is great potential for combining employment generation with the transition to a more resource-efficient, minimum waste production and consumption pattern in:

- improving insulation levels in residential, commercial and industrial buildings and in adopting other innovations which limit electricity or fossil fuel consumption;
- the manufacture, installation and maintenance of machinery and equipment that are more resource efficient and less polluting; and
- the industrial and service enterprises associated with waste minimization, recycling, reuse and resource reclamation.

Extending the life of capital goods to reduce levels of resource use also generally means more employment in maintenance and repair, although for many old capital goods and polluting equipment, the focus should be on replacement (including inefficient, high-pollution level motor vehicles, poorly insulated CFC-coolant fridges, and inefficient space and water heaters and electric lights).

One of the factors constraining action by governments towards resource conservation and waste reduction is the worry about the employment costs. There are employment losses arising from the greater cost of certain goods or services, especially those whose production or use requires major changes to reduce unacceptable levels of resource use or waste generation. But there are many examples of industrial processes where resource use and pollution levels have been cut with no overall increase in costs and, in some cases, with significant cost savings. In addition, even if costs do rise, they only do so to compensate for environmental costs that previously had been ignored.

A shift to patterns of production that are far more resource conserving with wastes also minimized implies shifts in employment, including:

- Declining employment in the manufacture of automobiles and the material inputs into this process with expanding employment in public transport equipment and systems, traffic management, air pollution control equipment for motor vehicles and reclamation and recycling of materials used in road vehicles. A study in Germany suggested that investment in public transport equipment and infrastructure creates more jobs than those lost in car manufacture.[17]
- Declining employment in the coal, oil, natural gas and electricity industries and increasing employment in energy conservation in all sectors and in the manufacture and installation of energy-efficient appliances; also in the means to tap renewable energy sources. It is quite feasible in the North for living standards and the number of households to continue growing but with a steady decline in the level of fossil fuel use.[18] Investments in energy conservation are generally far more labour intensive than investments in increasing the energy supply, especially when comparing the cost of increasing the electricity supply with the cost of reducing demand through conservation or the use of more efficient appliances, so that supplies no longer need to increase.
- Declining employment in mining and primary metals industries and paper and glass industries (and other industries associated with packaging production) and expanding employment in urban management systems that maximize recycling, reuse and reclamation, and promote waste minimization.
- Declining employment in producing and selling the fertilizers and biocides now widely used in industrial agriculture and horticulture but with increased employment in lower input farming, ecologically based farming and land management, and resource efficient, high intensity crop production systems such as those based on hydroponics and permaculture.

In many areas, there are likely to be substantial increases in employment opportunities – for instance, in the water supply and sewage treatment industries as higher standards are met and water conservation programmes implemented, and in the managerial and technical staff within municipalities and companies or corporations whose task is environmental management.

There are also the employment benefits that arise from cost savings in conservation as highlighted by the Rocky Mountain Institute in the United States. For instance, the output from a $7.5 million compact fluorescent lamp factory saves as much electricity as a $1 billion power plant makes, as its products are installed to replace conventional light bulbs. While consuming 140 times less capital, the factory also avoids the power plants' fuel cost and pollution. A $10 million 'superglass' factory making windows that block heat but allow light to pass can produce more comfort than the air conditioners run by $2 billion worth of generating stations. Over 30 years, a single glass factory's output would save $12.25 billion in power investments.[19]

Although overall there are employment benefits in moving towards more ecologically sustainable patterns of production and consumption, the employment losses fall heavily on certain employees and on urban centres or regions that have the traditional logging, 'smokestack' and mining industries. Most of the job losses in these industries in Europe and North America over the last two decades have little to do with environmental regulation and much more to do with the gradual shift in production to cheaper areas or to new technologies that greatly reduce the need for labour. But it is little comfort to the miners and steelworkers and their families when jobs disappear, and there are few prospects for new employment in towns where unemployment rates are often 30 per cent or more, to know that policies promoting resource conservation and waste minimization are creating more employment elsewhere. Thus, one important role for government is addressing the needs of the workforce of the resource and waste intensive industries that lose their employment.

Certain cities in the North have managed the transition from centres of 'smokestack' industries towards the development of alternative economic bases, as industries close down, move elsewhere or reduce their workforce. There are also examples of city or regional governments which have begun such a process – for instance, Hamilton-Wentworth in Canada whose programme is described in an annex to this chapter[20] or Leicester in the UK,[21] or the state of Nord-Rhine-Westphalia in the Emscher region in the Ruhr valley in Germany[22] or certain 'eco-municipalities' in Sweden.[23] Many urban regeneration programmes in Europe have also included ecological goals, from ensuring high levels of energy efficiency and reduced water use in the rebuilt or renovated buildings to the development of new parks or green areas.[24]

There is also an important international dimension to this as resource conservation and waste minimization in the North implies less purchase of goods from the South. For instance, strong support in the North for waste minimization and recycling may substantially reduce demand for paper and pulp from the South, while any general tax applied globally on petroleum fuels would penalize exporters of high-volume, low-value goods, most of whom are also in the South. Measures must be sought to reconcile the 'green trade' aspects of more sustainable patterns of production and consumption with support for more prosperous economies in the poorer southern nations.

For practices such as those noted above that are currently the exceptions to become the norm requires a strong commitment and coherent support for local, city and regional action from national government. Such a commitment is also required to address the needs of the inhabitants of cities with the least comparative advantage in the transition to resource conservation and minimum waste. There are likely to be major long-term advantages for cities and nations which are among the first to promote such moves, as enterprises and municipalities there develop the kinds of products, services and knowledge that will be in high demand worldwide. A high quality living and working environment has also become an increasingly important factor in attracting many kinds of new or expanding enterprises in the North and in some city-regions in the South.

Resource Conservation in the South

In most cities in the South, the potential for new employment in resource conservation (including recycling) is rather less, given that levels of resource use are so much lower and levels of recycling, reclamation and reuse often much higher.[25] Ironically, many cities in the South, where housing and living conditions are very poor, are at the same time models of 'ecological sustainability' in that levels of resource use and waste generation are low and so much waste is reused or recycled.[26] Very low levels of resource and waste generation reflect very inadequate incomes for a high proportion of the population. Very low averages for water use per person are usually the result of half or more of the city's population having no piped water supply to their shelter or plot. Having to fetch and carry water from public standpipes greatly reduces consumption levels, often to below that needed for good health. High levels of reclamation and recycling are the result of tens of thousands of people eking out a precarious living from reclaiming or recycling metals, glass, paper, rags and other items from city wastes – and often with very serious health problems for those so engaged and with the work unpleasant and laborious. For instance, as Christine Furedy points out, '... Asian cities have extensive "waste economies", structured through itinerant waste buyers, waste pickers, small waste shops, second-hand markets, dealers, transporters, and a range of recycling industries.'[27]

Most city authorities in the South seem set on copying Northern models for solid waste collection and management, although usually only providing garbage collection services to the middle- and upper-income areas and the main commercial and industrial areas. This indicates very little commitment to recycling or waste reduction and no consideration for the current or potential role of those who make their living picking saleable items from waste. Indeed, waste pickers may lose their source of income as technical changes in waste collection inhibit informal recovery – for instance, through requiring that all households put out their garbage in plastic bags, making it difficult for pickers to sort through the garbage. The conventional Northern model also collects and compresses all wastes, with waste pickers only able to obtain access to such waste at municipal dumps; waste picking is more profitable and less hazardous if waste pickers can sort through the waste at neighbourhood level 'transfer stations' before wastes become too compressed and mixed-up.[28]

However, over the last ten years, an increasing number of city authorities have moved from what can be characterized as 'waste management' to 'resource recognition' – see Box 13.3. Some city authorities are seeking to introduce social and environmental goals into their solid waste collection and management. In some cities, there is a recognition that the people previously regarded as 'scavengers' and 'pickers' are, in fact, recyclers and reclaimers who can be incorporated into city-wide waste-management schemes in ways which benefit them and the city environment. For instance, in Bogotá, waste pickers have formed co-operatives that have successfully bid for some municipal waste collection contracts.[29] In Cairo, the Environmental Protection Company that developed out of a group of informal garbage collectors (the *zabbaleen*) and local contractors have been awarded the contract for waste collection in several parts of the city and the Cairo Governorate is seeking to extend this company's services to other parts of the city.[30] There may be possibilities for further developing the contribution of waste pickers towards a clean and resource-efficient city while also improving the returns that they receive from this work and addressing the health problems which accompany this work. An increasing number of initiatives, most started by Southern NGOs, are seeking to improve solid waste collection and recycling and improve conditions for low-income groups which make a living as waste pickers.[31] There are obvious linkages to be developed between social goals such as increased employment, better working conditions and higher wages for waste pickers, and environmental goals such as better quality collection services, greater coverage for solid waste collection (especially in the illegal or informal settlements where regular collection services are needed) and improved levels of recycling.

Some caution is needed in setting up recycling schemes, as can be seen by the number of schemes that have failed. There are also conflicts or potential conflicts be-

---

Box 13.3 *Resource recognition, not waste management*

A new philosophy of resource management is beginning to transform solid waste management worldwide, grounded in what can be called 'resource recognition'. Most waste material can be regarded as unused resources, so environmentally sound waste management entails the reduction of waste in production and distribution processes and the enhancement of reuse and recycling. In Northern cities these principles are being translated into practice through government regulation, stakeholder cooperation and citizens' initiatives. In Southern cities, solid waste management is still focused on improving the conventional engineering systems (essentially, the collection, transport and disposal of solid wastes). Established environmental movements are not yet much interested in this subject, while city cleansing departments tend to look to higher technology and privatization for solutions to the environmental problems of uncollected and unsafely dumped wastes.

However, there are many small scale non-conventional approaches to solid waste management in cities of the South which not only change the conventional collect-transport-dispose organization of waste services but also have *some general social and ecological goals* linking 'resource recognition' to social betterment and attitudinal change at the local level. These include: assisting poor people whose livelihoods depend on wastes to do safer, more acceptable work; promoting the separation of wastes to facilitate more thorough or more efficient recycling (including decentralized compost-making); developing community/private sector/municipal partnerships; furthering environmental education; and pragmatic accommodation of informal activities in waste recovery and recycling.

Source: Furedy, Christine, 'Garbage: exploring non-conventional options in Asian Cities', *Environment and Urbanization*, Vol 4, No 2, October 1992, pp 42–61

---

tween different goals. For instance, promoting the separation by each household of recyclables and organic wastes from the rest of their wastes ensures much higher levels of recycling, and safer working conditions for those who collect the recyclables, compared to waste picking. It probably means an overall increase in employment. But it also reduces the returns for waste pickers, or may even remove their livelihood as most material with any value is removed from the garbage before they can pick through it. The crews of conventional garbage trucks may oppose a separate collection of recyclables from households since they also make money separating out the more valuable recyclables or items that can be resold as they collect garbage. Some schemes to promote household separation have sought to employ former waste pickers in household collection of recyclable materials,[32] whilst others have concentrated on making the tasks of waste pickers at city dumps less hazardous.[33]

Perhaps the most important way to promote the successful integration of social and environmental goals into conventional solid waste collection and management is the careful evaluation of initiatives to date and a greater sharing of experiences.[34] The experiences documented to date suggest that all new initiatives should be based on a detailed city-specific understanding of how wastes are currently generated and managed in each city, formally and informally from household level through to city level. They must recognize that there are often a great range of actors involved in some form of waste separation and reuse or recycling including:

- Households themselves who often keep separate some recyclables for direct sale.
- Waste pickers who may 'pick' from household garbage cans or garbage on the street or at transfer stations or at the city dump.
- The staff of garbage collection trucks who look for the more valuable recyclable materials or items that can be resold as they collect garbage.
- Waste buyers who range in the scale of their operation from itinerant buyers who go from house to house or from business to business to small waste-purchasing shops or enterprises, to larger buying operations, to factories or businesses who use the waste.
- Those involved in collecting, repairing and selling goods or items working in second-hand markets.

New initiatives need to be assessed in terms of how far they help poorer groups meet their needs and earn sufficient income and how far they reduce exploitation and discrimination against waste pickers and other people making a living from wastes, as well as how much they increase the efficient use of wastes as resources.[35] The ideal would be for no one to need to make a living picking recyclable or reusable waste from a city dump, both because this is a dangerous and unpleasant job and because separation of recyclables at source is a far more efficient way to reduce overall resource use.

Minimizing Wastes[36]

While the initial interest in waste management centred on better ways to collect and dispose of it, there has also been a growing interest in what is termed 'waste minimization'. This seeks to reduce wastes at all points from the extraction of raw materials, their use in production, in packaging and distribution and in use and disposal. As a review of business perspectives on the environment and development prepared for the Earth Summit noted:

> Under the pressure of tightening regulations, increasingly 'green' consumer expectations and new management attitudes towards extended corporate responsibility, companies are recognizing that environmental management now requires the minimization of risks and impacts throughout a product's life cycle, from 'cradle to grave'. This is in turn leading to the industrial ideal of an economic system based on 'reconsumption' – that is the ability to use and reuse goods in whole or in part over several generations.[37]

Waste minimization can bring many advantages. For instance, there are many examples of industries that reduced costs or increased profits at the same time as reducing solid and liquid wastes.[38] One of the best known examples is that of the 3M Company in the US whose 'Pollution Prevention Pays' programme has been applied to more than 3,000 projects and which has brought major reductions in air pollution, waste water and solid wastes, with the company managing to save $537 million.[39] New plant designs often allow process chemicals that were formerly dumped as wastes to be recovered and used again. In other instances, what was originally a production-waste from one factory has become a feedstock for another industry – for example, the organic residues from many industries serve as feedstock for the manufacture of animal feed, packaging material, chemicals and pharmaceuticals, fertilizers, fuel, food and construction materials.[40]

For a municipality, encouraging waste minimization among households and commercial enterprises can considerably reduce the costs of collecting and disposing of solid wastes. Such encouragement could include providing recycling credits which the local authority pays to a household or business for paper, glass, metal or other materials they separate and make available for collection or lower charges for households or enterprises who generate very little waste for collection. This can be paid for through the amount the authority saves from not having to collect and/or dispose of the waste and through the revenue from selling the materials for recycling. But national governments are often reluctant to encourage waste minimization by, for instance, taxing packaging, as they fear that the increased taxation will dampen economic activity, even though this also means a cleaner environment and less pressure on the authorities responsible for solid waste collection and management.

Various governments have taken measures to encourage waste minimization within industries. One is the use of 'take-back' agreements through which industry has to take back the waste that it generates. Take back initiatives have also been developed in voluntary agreements between governments and industry, or between companies themselves, as in the example in Box 13.4. Charging companies the full cost of waste disposal, including paying for the short- and long-term environmental costs, can also promote waste minimization. As the review of business perspectives noted above stresses, one powerful stimulus to waste minimization and to recycling process chemicals within OECD countries is the growing cost of waste disposal; waste processing can cost companies an average of $380 a ton rising to $3,000–10,000 per ton for toxic and hazardous wastes.

Box 13.4 *An example of waste minimization*

The Upper Canada Brewing Company in Toronto has managed to reduce the amount of waste it generates by 99 per cent, resulting in savings of over US$200,000 a year from fees associated with landfill and collection costs. Initiatives to reduce wastes were primarily targeted at the company's suppliers through requests to eliminate excess packaging. For suppliers that were uncooperative, the company sent back excess packaging at the suppliers' expense. The company also arranged for supplies to be shipped using packing material consisting of compostable materials such as popcorn or newspaper. Recycling initiatives focused on fine paper, beverage containers, newsprint, corrugated cardboard, plastics and organic materials. Spent grains generated from the brewing process were used as feed grain. The costs of starting up this initiative was around $15,000.

Source: McRae, L S '3 RS regulations in Ontario; compliance and cost savings', proceedings of R'95 International Congress, Geneva, 1995

Box 13.5 *Hamilton-Wentworth's plan for sustainable development*

Hamilton-Wentworth is a regional municipality in Canada, located in the centre of Canada's manufacturing heartland. Covering an area of 1,140 square kilometres, it has around 452,000 inhabitants. Since 1989, it has been developing its own sustainable development plan with strong social, economic and ecological objectives. These include helping to reorient its economic base away from steel production towards knowledge based industries and enterprises involved in environmental improvement while also protecting its natural resource base, limiting urban expansion, reducing resource use and greatly improving the quality of the environment.

During the 1950s and 1960s, Hamilton-Wentworth's prosperity depended heavily on the steel mills located there and it was the key steel-maker for Toronto, Canada's largest metropolitan centre, 60km away. Since then, especially during the 1980s, a new economic base became increasingly necessary with the decline in steel production and with technological changes in steel mills which greatly reduced the number of jobs. Some local industries also closed or moved away after the 1990 Canada–US Free Trade Agreement. There was the legacy of a large steel town with a heavily polluted bay and contaminated land around the steel mills. In recent years, there has been a major clean-up with salmon and trout returning to the Hamilton harbour which had become almost devoid of fish. The soil around the harbour was also decontaminated and air pollution considerably reduced. The environmental clean-up also helped develop local enterprises based on waste management or environmental improvement.

In 1989, the regional government's management team found that they lacked a framework with which to evaluate proposals put forward for budget approval. They requested the formation of a Task Force on Sustainable Development which was set up in 1990 to explore the concept of sustainable development and its application to Hamilton-Wentworth. Over a three-year period, this Task Force sought the opinion of a wide range of local citizens and specialists through town hall meetings, focus group discussions, community fora and specialized working teams. They produced a report entitled Vision 2020 – a Sustainable Region with two additional reports, the first on directions needed to achieve this, the second on strategies and actions. These covered topics such as air and water quality, the protection of natural areas, waste reduction, energy consumption, transport, land-use planning, agriculture and other economic activities and personal health. They also identified the decisions and actions which the regional government and other levels of government, community groups, business and individual citizens need to make to achieve sustainable development goals. The Task Force's outreach programme also increased people's awareness and knowledge about sustainable development. These documents helped the regional government develop a draft plan Towards a Sustainable Region which is currently being discussed and amended, before implementation begins.

One notable aspect of the draft Plan (and the Task Force documents) is the integration of resource conservation, land-use planning, transport and energy conservation. For instance, energy conservation will be promoted through promoting a compact urban form. The Plan seeks to accommodate 96 per cent of future growth up to the year 2020 within existing urban areas, with the promotion of compact mixed land-use in the regional centre and municipal centres and along corridors. As the draft plan states, mixed forms of development within an urban area are preferable to widespread low-density residential development and scattered rural development because:

Box 13.5 *Continued*

- 'growth can be accommodated by building on vacant or redeveloped land, without taking up agricultural lands or natural areas;
- higher density development can reduce per capita servicing costs and makes more efficient use of existing services;
- efficient and affordable public transit systems can be established;
- effective community design can ensure people are close to recreation, natural areas, shopping and their workplace; and a compact community makes walking and bicycling viable options for movement.' (page C-13).

The Plan has a strong commitment to protecting good quality farmland from urban encroachment, and also of ensuring that farmers can obtain an adequate livelihood and do so, through sustainable farming practices. For instance, it supports the establishment of value added or food-processing facilities on or close to farms and encourages local authorities to support farmer markets.

The linkages between land use, transport, energy and resource conservation are also explicit in the draft Plan's subsection on transport which states that 'because there is a direct link between land-use planning (densities, mix and proximity of uses) and transportation, emphasis will be placed on accessibility and reducing reliance on the automobile by promoting alternative modes of transportation, such as public transit, walking and cycling to all urbanized areas of the Region.' (page C-28). A regional bicycle commuting network plan has been developed to guide improved provision of bicycle lanes and other facilities to support increased bicycle use.

Energy conservation is also encouraged through incorporating energy conservation practices in the design, construction and operation of the regional government's capital works and equipment (and requests that other local government also do so). Public and private agencies, industrial and commercial operations and individuals are also encouraged to take part in energy conservation programmes and the regional authorities aim to promote innovations in housing design to encourage the construction of energy-efficient housing and the utilization of solar energy for space heating, where feasible.

Many other initiatives are also planned to continue improving air and water quality. Vision 2020 outlined a plan to develop a system of interconnected protected natural areas threading through both rural and urban areas in the region, including natural core areas such as wetlands, forests and other ecologically significant habitats used by local wildlife which will be linked by stream corridors, farm hedgerows and newly created linear links with vegetative buffers. These will allow wildlife to move from one geographic area to another and also link natural areas to municipal parks, rights-of-way, bike paths and hiking trails, making open space and natural areas more easily accessible to a higher proportion of the population. Vision 2020 also emphasizes that a new ethic must be adopted on waste reduction, minimizing consumption and substantially reducing the amount of waste.

Apart from the guidance set by Vision 2020 for the different government sectoral plans and reviews, there is also a Staff Working Group on Sustainable Development which is mandated by the regional government to help integrate the principles of sustainable development into the capital budget and departmental work programmes. There is also a programme to involve the population in evaluating what has been achieved and helping set priorities.

Box 13.5 *Continued*

Sources: Wilkins, Charles, 'Steeltown charts a new course', *Canadian Geographic*, Vol 113, No 4, July/August 1993, pp 42–55; Regional Municipality of Hamilton-Wentworth, *Implementing Vision 2020; Directions for Creating a Sustainable Region*, The Regional Chairman's Taskforce on Sustainable Development, 1993; and Regional Municipality of Hamilton-Wentworth, *Towards a Sustainable Region: Hamilton-Wentworth Region, Official Plan (Draft)*, September 1993, Regional Planning and Development Department, September, Hamilton-Wentworth, 1993; Staff Working Group on Sustainable Development, *Hamilton-Wentworth's Sustainable Community Decision-Making Guide*, Regional Municipality of Hamilton-Wentworth, August 1993

NOTES AND REFERENCES

1 Chapter 4 of the volume from which this text is drawn described the direct health costs that environmental hazards impose on the population and how such costs are most evident in cities in the South where the level of environmental risk experienced by citizens is strongly associated with their income

2 Bullard, Robert D, 'Anatomy of environmental racism', in Richard Hofrichter (ed), *Toxic Struggles: The Theory and Practice of Environmental Justice*, New Society Publishers, Philadelphia, 1992, pp 25–35.

3 Serageldin, Ismail, 'Making development sustainable', *Finance and Development*, Vol 30, No 4, December 1993, pp 6–10; Winpenny, J T, *Values for the Environment: A Guide to Economic Appraisal*, HMSO, London, 1991

4 Hardoy, Jorge E, Diana Mitlin and David Satterthwaite, *Environmental Problems in Third World Cities*, Earthscan Publications, London, 1992

5 von Amsberg, Joachim, *Project Evaluation and the Depletion of Natural Capital: an Application of the Sustainability Principle*, Environment Working Paper No 56, Environment Department, World Bank, Washington DC, 1993

6 Serageldin 1993, op cit

7 Lovins, Amory B and L Hunter Lovins, 'Least-cost climatic stabilization', *Annual Review of Energy and Environment*, Vol 16, 1991, pp 433–531.

8 See, for instance, Lovins and Lovins 1991, op cit

9 Schmidheiny, Stephan, with the Business Council for Sustainable Development, *Changing Course: A Global Business Perspective on Development and the Environment*, The MIT Press, Cambridge, 1992

10 'Living under a grass roof', *Environmental News from the Netherlands*, No 4, Ministry of Housing, Spatial Planning and the Environment, The Hague, 1994, pp 5–6.

11 Roodman, David Malin and Nicholas Lenssen,'Our buildings, ourselves', *World Watch*, December 1994, pp 21–29

12 Roodman and Lenssen 1994, op cit

13 Fickett, Arnold P, Clark W Gellings and Amory B Lovins, 'Efficient use of electricity', *Scientific American*, September 1990, pp 65–74.

14 Lovins, Amory B, 'Energy, people and industrialization', paper presented at the Hoover Institution conference on 'Human Demography and Natural Resources', Stanford University, 1–3 February, 1989

15 Lovins 1989, op cit

16 Webb, Jeremy, 'Rebel with a cause; a profile of Amory Lovins', *New Scientist*, Vol 145, No 1964, 1995, pp 32–35

17 Hesse and Lucas, *Die Beschaftigungspolitische Bedeutung der Verkehrswirtschaft in Nordrhein-Westfalen*, Institut fur Okologische Wirtschaftsforschung, Wuppertal, 1990 quoted in Wikima Consulting, *The Employment Implications of Environmental Action*, Report prepared for the Commission of the European Communities, Directorate-General on Employment, Industrial Relations and Social Affairs, London, 1993

18 Several studies in the late 1970s and early 1980s demonstrated this – for instance, see Leach, Gerald et al, *A Low Energy Strategy for the United Kingdom*, London, Science Reviews Ltd, 1979 for details of how increasing prosperity need not imply increased fossil fuel use in the UK

19 Lovins and Lovins 1991, op cit

20 See Box 13.5

21 Environ, *Environmental Achievements in Leicester – Britain's First Environment City*, Leicester, September 1993

22 European Union Expert group on the Urban Environment, *European Sustainable Cities*, first report, October 1994, XI/822/94-EN

23 Mansson, Tommy, 'The new urban dream', *Down to Earth*, 31 May 1993, pp 26–31

24 European Union Expert group on the Urban Environment 1994, op cit

25 This and the following paragraphs on solid waste management draw heavily on the work of Dr Christine Furedy from York University, Toronto, Canada

26 Hardoy, Jorge E, Diana Mitlin and David Satterthwaite, 'The future city', in Johan Holmberg (ed), *Policies for a Small Planet*, Earthscan Publications, London, 1992, pp 124–156

27 Furedy, Christine, 'Garbage: exploring non-conventional options in Asian cities', *Environment and Urbanization*, Vol 4, No 2, October 1992, pp 42–61

28 Furedy, Christine, 'Socio-environmental initiatives in solid waste management in Southern cities: developing international comparisons', paper presented at a workshop on 'Linkages in Urban Solid Waste Management', Karnataka State Council for Science and Technology, University of Amsterdam and Bangalore Mahanagara Palike, Bangalore, 18–20 April 1994

29 Pacheco, Margarita, 'Recycling in Bogotá; developing a culture for urban sustainability', *Environment and Urbanization*, Vol 4, No 2, October 1992, pp 74–79

30 UNCHS (Habitat), *Sustainable Human Settlements Development: Implementing Agenda 21*, paper prepared for the Commission on Sustainable Development, United Nations Centre for Human Settlements (Habitat), Nairobi, 1994

31 Furedy, Christine, 'Social aspects of solid waste recovery in Asian cities', *Environmental Sanitation Reviews*, No 30, December, ENSIC, Asian Institute of Technology, Bangkok, 1990, pp 2–52. Also Furedy 1992, op cit, Huysman, Marijk, 'Waste picking as a survival strategy for women in Indian cities', *Environment and Urbanization*, Vol 6, No 2, October 1994, pp 155–174

32 See, for instance, the experience of the 'garbage recycling project' in Metro Manila described in Furedy 1992 (op cit) and Furedy 1994 (op cit) and that of Waste Wise and Civic Exnora in India (Furedy 1992, op cit)

33 See, for instance, the GTZ funded project in Kathmandu described in Furedy 1992, op cit

34 Furedy 1994, op cit

35 Furedy 1990, op cit

36 This draws on a background paper by Graham Alabaster on *Waste Minimization Strategies for Developing Countries*, UNCHS, Nairobi, 1995

37 Schmidheiny, Stephan, with the Business Council for Sustainable Development, *Changing Course: a Global Business Perspective on Development and the Environment*, The MIT Press, Cambridge, 1992, pp 98–99

38 Schmidheiny 1992, op cit

39 Schmidheiny 1992, op cit

40 Vimal, O P, 'Recycling of organic residues – status and trends in India', *Industry and Environment*, UNEP Europe, Paris, April–June 1982, pp 7–10

Further Reading

Health

For a general discussion of the multiple links between the environment and health with special sections on urban areas and industry, see *Our Planet, Our Health*, Report of the WHO Commission on Health and Environment, World Health Organization (WHO), 1992. Available from WHO Publications, WHO, 1211 Geneva 27, Switzerland

See also: 'Health and sustainability in the urban environment', Trevor Hancock, *Environmental Impact Assessment Review*, Vol 16, Nos 4-6, July–November 1996, pp 259–277

Our Cities, Our Future: Policies and Action Plans for Health and Sustainable Development, Charles Price and Agis Tsouros (eds), WHO, 1996. Published by WHO Healthy Cities Project Office, Scherfigsveg 8, DK-2100 Copenhagen, Denmark

Two issues of *Environment and Urbanization* have concentrated on urban health. The first was Vol 5, No 2 (October 1993) on *Health and Wellbeing in Cities*; the second was Vol 11, No 1 (April 1999) on *Healthy Cities, Neighbourhoods and Homes* and included a description of the Healthy Cities movement (with summaries of healthy city projects in Egypt, Brazil and India), case studies of León (Nicaragua) and Chittagong and Cox's Bazar (Bangladesh), and various papers considering different aspects of 'healthy cities' including provision for water and sanitation and the control of malaria. These are available from *Environment and Urbanization*, IIED, 3 Endsleigh Street, London WC1H ODD, UK, e-mail humans@iied.org

Transport

Newman, Peter and Jeffrey R Kenworthy, *Sustainability and Cities: Overcoming Automobile Dependence* Island Press, Washington DC, 1999

Zegras, Christopher, 'Urban transportation', Chapter 3 in *World Resources 1996–97; The Urban Environment*, Oxford University Press, Oxford and New York, 1996, pp 81–102

Banister, D, 'Energy use, transport and settlement patterns', in M J Breheny (ed), *Sustainable Development* and Urban Form, European Research in Regional Science 2, Pion, London, 1992, pp 160–181

Patel, Sheela and Kalpana Sharma, 'One David and three Goliaths: avoiding anti-poor solutions to Mumbai's transport problems', *Environment and Urbanization*, Vol 10, No 2, 1998, pp 149–159

See also Elsom, Derek, *Smog Alert: Managing Urban Air Quality*, Earthscan, London, 1996

Urban Agriculture

There is a very good global overview of this subject – *Urban Agriculture: Food, Jobs and Sustainable Cities*, Jac Smit, Annu Ratta and Joe Nasr, 1996. Publication series for Habitat II, Vol One, UNDP, New York. Available from United Nations Publications through their distributors within each country or region, or from UN Publications, 2 UN Plaza DC-2-853, New York, NY 10017, USA

See also the following two volumes:

Cities Feeding People: an Examination of Urban Agriticulture in East Africa, Axumite G Egziabher, Diana Lee-Smith, Daniel G Maxwell, Pyar Ali Memon, Luc J A Mougeot and Camillus J Sawio, IDRC, 1994

Further Reading

For Hunger-proof Cities: Sustainable Urban Food Systems edited by Mustafa Koc, Rod MacRae, Luc J A Mougeot, and Jennifer Welsh, IDRC 1999

Both volumes are published by and available from International Development Research Centre, PO Box 8500, Ottawa, ON, Canada K1G 3H9

For a case study which combines an interest in urban agriculture with ecological change, see Losada, H, H Martínez, J Vieyra, R Pealing, R Zavala and J Cortés, 'Urban agriculture in the metropolitan zone of Mexico City: changes over time in urban, suburban and periurban areas', *Environment and Urbanization*, Vol 10, No 2, 1998, pp 37–54

For a paper considering the health implications of urban agriculture, see Birley, M H and K Lock, 'Health and peri-urban natural resource production', *Environment and Urbanization*, Vol 10, No 1, 1998, pp 89–106

Building and Designing with Nature

Greening Cities: Building Just and Sustainable Communities by Joan Roelofs, from which the chapter by Joan Roelofs reprinted earlier in this section is drawn, covers many other aspects of building and designing with nature. The book is published by the Bootstrap Press, New York, 1996. For orders in Europe, available from Jon Carpenter Publishing, the Spendlove Centre, Charlbury, Oxfordshire OX7 3PQ, UK

Regenerative Design for Sustainable Development, John Tillman Lyle, John Wiley & Sons, New York and Chichester, 1994

Urban Form and Planning

Sustainable Cities, Graham Haughton and Colin Hunter, Regional Policy and Development Series 7, Jessica Kingsley Publishers, London, 1994

Most of the detailed discussions of urban form and planning have been within the context of Europe, and this is reflected in most of the publications listed below

Blowers, Andrew (ed), *Planning for a Sustainable Environment:* A Report by the Town and Country Planning Association, Earthscan, London, 1993, especially Breheny, Michael and Ralph Rookwood, 'Planning the sustainable city region' pp 150–189

Sustainable Development and Urban Form, M J Breheny (ed), European Research in Regional Science 2, Pion, London, 1992

Rydin, Yvonne, *Urban and Environmental Planning in the UK*, Macmillan Press, London, 1998

Owens, Susan, 'Lands, limits and sustainability', *Transactions of the Institute of British Geographers*, Vol 19, No 4

European Sustainable Cities Part 1, Expert Group on the Urban Environment, European Commission, X1/95/502-en, Brussels, October 1994

Many of the works recommended under the Further Reading of the next section are also relevant for planning

Resource Conservation and Waste Management

Factor Four: Doubling Wealth, Halving Resource Use, Ernst Von Weizsäcker, Amory B Lovins and L Hunter Lovins, Earthscan, London, 1997. Available from bookstores or direct from Earthscan, 120 Pentonville Road, London N1 9JN, UK e-mail:earthinfo@earthscan.co.uk, price £15.99 plus postage

Reviving the City; Towards Sustainable Urban Development, Tim Elkin, Duncan McLaren and Mayer Hillman, Friends of the Earth, London, 1991.

Part IV
Seeking Action
at City Level

Chapter 14

Agenda 21: A Form of Joint Environmental Management in Manizales, Colombia

Luz Stella Velásquez

(Reprinted from *Environment and Urbanization*, Vol 10, No 2, October 1998, pp 9–36)

Summary: This paper describes the development of Bioplan-Manizales, a local environmental action plan (LEAP) for the city of Manizales and the different groups that contributed to its development; also, how this plan became integrated into the municipal development plan and the municipal budget. The measures taken to monitor and evaluate the social, economic and environmental effects of the environmental policy are also described and these include a series of urban environmental observatories. The paper also describes the broader national and international context for the innovations in Manizales, including the political, legislative and fiscal changes in Colombia that have encouraged local authorities to develop local environmental agendas. Manizales' own historical development is described, including the environmental changes that this development brought and the environmental problems that it precipitated.

INTRODUCTION

Colombia, a tropical country rich in ecological and cultural diversity and facing multiple political and social conflicts, today faces the challenge of strengthening local environmental management in 1,134 municipalities, home to some 38 million people. In Colombia, following the UN Earth Summit in Rio in 1992, all the legal instruments needed to facilitate broad community participation in environmental decisions have been put in place. But the capacity for popular management that environmental decisions require has yet to be achieved. Responsibility for the environmental management of regions, municipalities and cities cannot rest solely with the state. In Manizales, a plan for local environmental action (Bioplan), an interesting scheme of joint environmental management, is developing, linked to the principles of Agenda 21. A continuing commitment by local government and the state university to environmental research and to the sustainable development of the municipality and the region has succeeded in consolidating a programme of continuous environmental action which is addressing the social, economic and environmental problems of this geographically complex area.

As a result of continuous leadership by the universities and the NGOs, and the ownership and commitment of the communities, the environmental policy is underpinned by a continuous investigation into the area's environmental problems and potential and broad popular participation. The public sector, the private sector and the communities have all come together in this constantly growing participative process. As a result, Bioplan's various programmes and projects are being implemented and Manizales has succeeded in improving the quality of life of its residents and in increasing the capacity for environmental management of the poorest communities.

THE DEVELOPMENT OF THE CITY AND THE SHAPING OF ITS ENVIRONMENT

The municipality of Manizales lies in the tropical zone, to the west of the Andes, Colombia's central mountain range. Its physical geography, soil characteristics, rainfall and water resources are determined by the influence of the Cumanday massif. Among the active volcanoes of this massif, at a height of 5400 metres above sea level, is the snow-capped volcano of the Ruiz, whose eruption (and resulting thawing of snow) in 1985 led to avalanches of stones and mud which destroyed the town of Armero and other small riverside communities where over 35,000 people lived. In Manizales and the surrounding area, this event generated a 'culture of disaster prevention' which is now an integral part of the research and environmental planning programmes of the region.

By virtue of Manizales' geographical location, with marked variations in altitude, the territory of the municipality is characterized by great climatic and ecological diversity:

- moist tropical forest at 880 metres above sea level, with an average temperature of 30°C, occupying 19 per cent of the municipality's territory;
- very moist forest in the foothills at 1500 metres above sea level, with an average temperature of 23°C, occupying 62 per cent of the municipality's territory;
- very moist forest in the mountains at 2100 metres above sea level, with an average temperature of 18°C, occupying 12 per cent of the municipality's territory; and
- very moist forest in the mountains at 3800 metres above sea level, with an average temperature of 4°C, occupying 6 per cent of the municipality's territory.

At present, rural areas account for 397.1 square kilometres of the municipality's territory; in 1997, they had a population of 57,057 inhabitants concentrated in seven administrative entities known as *corregimientos*. The urban area covers 42.9 square kilometres, with a population in 1997 of 358,194 inhabitants concentrated in 11 administrative entities called *comunas*. The urban area of Manizales lies in the very moist forest of the mountains and its topography of steep slopes, its high rainfall (2200 mm per annum) and its 78 per cent humidity restrict urban expansion on to the hillsides. It could be said that Manizales has already surpassed the natural limits to its expansion and must seek alternative ways of managing growth – for instance, through increasing density in selected areas and through reusing existing buildings and lots. For this reason, proposals to define and allocate land use will be developed, linked to the restrictions of the hillsides.

According to data in the municipal environmental profile, the environmental problems of Manizales can be summarized as follows:

- inappropriate transformations in its ecosystems, including felling of trees to make way for permanent and temporary crops, the impact of agricultural expansion on the buffer zone of the snow-capped volcano of Ruiz and the transformation of green protection zones by urban expansion;
- pollution of rivers and water catchment areas by industrial, agricultural, mining and domestic pollutants; and
- high seismic and geological risks as a result of the steep slopes and high levels of soil humidity.

Impacts within the urban area arise from:

- a transport and road infrastructure system inappropriate to the city's topography;
- dwellings located in high-risk areas due to the increase in urban poverty;
- industrial contamination of the city's rivers;
- degradation of the landscape, including a loss of urban and architectural heritage;
- shortage of green spaces and public recreation areas; and
- problems arising from a lack of education and training in participative environmental management.

Manizales' environmental potential lies in the biodiversity of its ecosystem, the variety of climates within the municipality's territory, the quality and quantity of water in its catchment areas, the hydroelectric and geothermal potential of its water resources, the agricultural quality of its soil and in the scenic quality of the landscape. Also central to its potential are the credibility of its institutions (including local government), the efficient size of the city's urban area, the many community environmental action groups, and the NGOs and universities.

Manizales municipality has always had a moderate rate of population growth; in 1997, it was 2.1 per cent lower than the national average. Of the economically active population of 137,000, 28 per cent work in commerce, 17 per cent in industry, 11 per cent in education, 12 per cent in agriculture and 9 per cent in construction, while a variety of service-sector occupations account for the remaining 23 per cent. At present, due to the 'coffee crisis', local investment has fallen and the current unemployment rate of 12.4 per cent is four points above the national average. This is just one of the challenges that Manizales has faced in the course of its history and, in considering its settlement process, one must bear in mind two factors, popularly known as 'the culture of coffee' and 'the culture of prevention'.

The striking geographical location of Manizales' urban area amidst steep slopes is the result of the historical dynamic of settlement of a country which, as a result of the Spanish conquest in the 16th century, lost almost all of its indigenous population with only a few small local settlements in inaccessible mountain areas remaining. Manizales remained unchanged until the end of the 19th century when, as a result of the poverty prevailing in the state of Antioquia in the west of the country, a small group of inhabitants migrated in search of gold for use by craftsmen. They settled in a large part of the territory which today makes up the municipalities of Salamina, Neira and Manizales. This internal migration gave rise to what is known in Colombia as the 'Antioquian settlement' which forms part of the identity of the local and regional culture. The new inhabitants transformed the ecosystem of the Andean cloud forests, constructing small settlements which served as temporary dwelling places, while dedicating themselves to mining and growing food crops.

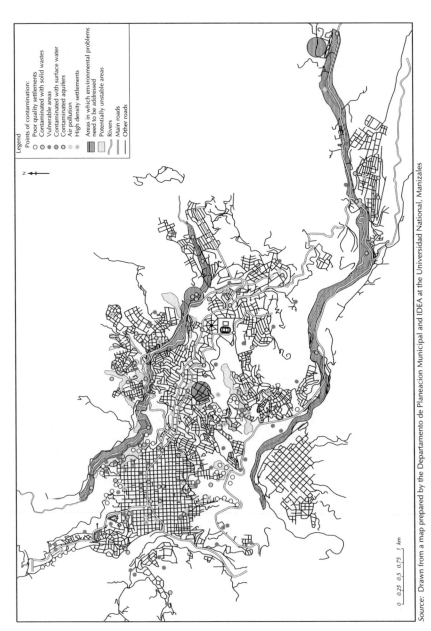

Legend

Points of contamination:
○ Poor quality settlements
● Contaminated with solid wastes
● Vulnerable areas
● Contaminated with surface water
● Contaminated aquifers
● Air pollution
● High density settlements

Areas in which environmental problems need to be addressed

Potentially unstable areas

Rivers

Main roads

Other roads

0 0.25 0.5 0.75 1 km

Source: Drawn from a map prepared by the Departamento de Planeacion Municipal and IDEA at the Universidad National, Manizales

Figure 14.1 *The city of Manizales, highlighting the location of some of the most serious environmental problems*

These settlements were strategically sited in the highest parts of the mountain range so as to dominate the territory visually and allow the defence of the mining activities. This explains how, later, towns became consolidated around roads that were relatively inaccessible, in areas with such steep slopes.

However, it was the cultivation of coffee at the beginning of the 20th century that transformed the region socially, economically and environmentally. The optimal ecological conditions for coffee-growing provided by the moist forests of the mountains, together with the internationalization of the coffee trade, generated significant economic surpluses. The area allocated to cultivating coffee grew steadily and it now accounts for 72 per cent of the municipality's total agricultural production. The temporary settlements remained and make up what today are known as the 'coffee axis' where a network of medium-sized towns and rural and urban communities are home to a population of 2.3 million inhabitants in what is considered one of the regions with the highest quality of life in Colombia. The 'reurbanization' of the municipality of Manizales, where countryside and city merge without any well-defined territorial boundaries, also derives from the coffee economy and the construction of a road network and of services for the transport and commercialization of the coffee bean. Research on aspects of the economic and environmental history of the settling of Manizales has been important for the environmental planning of its territory. This history can be summarized into the following periods.

The Coffee Boom; the New City Following the Fires

As a result of coffee exports and its commercialization in international markets, between 1920 and 1930 Manizales was Colombia's main supply centre for merchandise coming from Europe and the United States. It became the country's second most economically and politically important city. In 1927 and 1928, two conflagrations destroyed almost the entire city, leaving only a few buildings standing on the periphery of the city centre. The prosperity of the majority of the population enabled work to go ahead on reconstruction. However, the new city changed from being a mountain city of the Antioquian settlement to being one whose architecture, parks and urban structures were designed by firms from Paris or London who had won international competitions. The construction of the new projects required substantial modification of the topography and the tropical Andean forest trees were replaced by species brought from Europe, while the bamboo framework used in traditional building was replaced by cement and steel which had to be imported from Europe. Subsequently, using technology imported from Europe, a system of transport to and from Manizales using aerial cables for carrying cargo and passengers for up to 80 kilometres facilitated communication with the Magdalena river, from where coffee was sent to the embarkation port of Barranquilla on the Atlantic coast. During this period, Manizales succeeded in overcoming the physical isolation resulting from its mountainous topography and rebuilding a new city following the fires.

The Coffee Crisis and the Celebration of the Centenary

Towards the end of 1930, coffee prices fell on the international market and the former production boom declined. Communications within Colombia had been expanded and modernized, and Manizales was no longer the point of confluence of roads linking what became Colombia's three largest cities – Cali, Bogotá and Medellín. Manizales was now a terminal city on the crest of the mountain range and on the margin of the principal road and rail links. None the less, it retained its political importance and, for this reason, on the occasion of the 1950 centenary of its foundation, the government provided significant funding for the construction of new infrastructure in the city. It also decided to establish two universities of national rank in Manizales and the city began to distinguish itself in the educational and cultural fields. From that moment on, the universities played an important role in the development of the region, including participation in its planning. Today, the city's eight universities have approximately 20,000 students and, together with the municipality, are managing the consolidation of Manizales as a university city.

The Second Coffee Boom and its Environmental Impact

In 1975, coffee prices went up on the international market, generating significant economic surpluses for the city and the region which lasted for five years. Coffee's high profitability led to increased cultivation of a new variety (Caturro coffee) which needs more sun for increased production. This led to serious damage to the moist mountain forest ecosystem as a result of deforestation of large areas of secondary woodland which had provided shade for the existing variety (arabica coffee). Thus began a rapid exhaustion of the soils and a decline in the productive diversity associated with other food crops and fruit trees. In addition, large areas of woodland with great biodiversity were lost. The increase in coffee production also raised the demand for water for growing and washing the beans to the point where demand exceeded possible supply from the region's catchment areas. For this reason, in 1979, the national coffee growers' federation began a programme of rural environmental education, environmental action, reforestation and research on clean, appropriate technologies for coffee production which would minimize the impact on the ecosystem and take account of integrated resource management. This programme had a positive outcome for the region and the country, and achieved its objectives.

However, the boom also had negative environmental effects on Manizales' urban area due to the rise in investment in construction. At the time, Miami, not London, was more influential, along with a drive to 'modernize the city'. This led to the destruction of much of the urban and architectural heritage which had been completed for the centenary in 1950. The city began to transform its roads, which had to fit into the steep slopes, and construct high-speed avenues and increase the density of the central areas. The architecture also became more homogeneous. In this period of what was called 'urban renovation', the expansion of the urban area coincided with the gradual deterioration of the natural and constructed landscape. In many cases, this surpassed the capacity of the surrounding environment and overstepped natural limits during 'adaptation' of the hillsides for the large-scale erection of housing and urban structures. The technological and architectural solutions used within town planning were not the most appropriate ones, and the quality of the landscape and of Manizales' public and historic places suffered.

Manizales' history is full of events that illustrate the topographical conditions adverse to the city's urban construction: the construction of building lots by 'terracing'; the diversion of river courses; and deforestation for the construction of buildings and roads. When, in 1979, a major earthquake destroyed a large proportion of the 'modern structures' and the new 'infrastructure works', intensive work was begun to investigate the links between seismic and geological risks and construction characteristics. At the time, the municipality developed a new building code which related the appropriateness of the terrain to the possibilities of earthquake-resistant constructions, and a project on seismic micro-zoning was initiated to generate knowledge of the carrying-capacity of the city's different areas.

The Eruption of the Ruiz Volcano: Environmental Crisis and Economic Recovery

In November 1985, the volcano Arenas del Nevado del Ruiz erupted. One of the social consequences of this was that part of Manizales' population moved to other cities because of the risk of a fresh eruption affecting Manizales and the surrounding region. Meanwhile, all new investment in the city came to a halt. This had drastic repercussions on the local economy and the national government declared an economic emergency in Manizales and the region affected by the eruption. The economic emergency decrees sought to stimulate investment by allowing the tax-free import of machinery and products associated with industrial production and by supporting employment generation. During the three years for which these provisions were valid, a total of 76 national and international businesses were set up in Manizales' industrial zone, of which 42 remain active. Although this was important for restarting Manizales' economy, it also brought negative environmental impacts in the form of increased environmental pollution in the Chinchiná river and the Manizales stream. In addition, the increased demand for water outstripped the installed capacity of the industrial zone's aqueduct. At present, work is being done under a business co-operation agreement, together with the National Industrialists' Association and the environmental authorities, to reduce the environmental impact by improving the technology.

The Present Coffee Crisis and Regional Integration for Sustainable Development

From 1994 to the present, Manizales and its surrounding region have been undergoing one of the greatest coffee crises. The international pricing agreement between producer and consumer countries was ended and the way opened for the free market. A consequence of this has been a fall in coffee prices because of excess supply at the international level. The economic impact both on the region and on the country is significant. The signs of poverty in the cities and countryside of the 'coffee axis' are obvious. In Manizales, because of its dependence on coffee-growing, the result has been a major fall in people's quality of life. Much of the city's commerce is linked to investments which were made possible by the profits and surpluses arising from the commercialization and sale of coffee. The proportion of Manizales' population that is below the poverty line has risen from 18 per cent in 1994 to 27 per cent in 1998. Since this phenomenon affects not only Manizales but the whole region, it is interesting to note that those in power have joined together to implement a regional agenda of sustainable development. Today, programmes and projects aiming at economic recovery, the construction of macro-projects of regional urban infrastructure, and the environmental recovery and territorial definition of the Cumanday massif bioregion are being supported at international level.

Municipal Environmental Autonomy and Environmental Territorial Conflicts

Municipal autonomy has been important for Manizales and the outcome of the process of decentralization which has been taking place in Colombia since the mid-1980s has been very positive in making possible the integration of municipalities in decisions on economic and political issues and on regional and metropolitan action. But this autonomy has been less positive for the environment and, today, there are frequent conflicts between neighbouring municipalities, departments and regions throughout the national territory on issues of environmental administration. In Colombia, environmental regions do not coincide with politico-administrative regions. This is why it is so difficult for the environmental authorities to work within the territory's politico-administrative jurisdiction. Decentralization and local autonomy for environmental management give rise to problems because of the existence of economic and political interests at odds with the principles of environmental planning. In addition, environmental management has barely started to consolidate processes of community participation and environmental education. The municipalities are still not ready to administer their environmental territory sustainably.

In 1997, conflicts along these lines between Manizales and Villamaría, its neighbouring municipality, became sharper as a result of the application of measures to restrict land use with respect to shared areas and resources, both natural and urban. However, through the implementation of Villamaría's local environmental action plan (LEAP), linked to the goals of the Local Agenda 21 and developed by the urban environmental study groups of both municipalities, the National University of Colombia's Institute of Environmental Studies (IDEA) and the Ministry of the Environment, co-operation around joint environmental actions to manage water, tourism, transport and recreation was achieved. Similarly, projects were formed for municipal environmental integration and the establishment of an intermunicipal environmental committee to work towards solving 'environmental conflicts'.

ENVIRONMENTAL POLICY IN COLOMBIA AND IN MANIZALES

Environmental policy in Colombia has important antecedents with regard to popular participation and interinstitutional commitment to environmental management. The National Institute for Natural Resources (INDERENA) was founded in 1974 and initiated a diagnosis of the country's environmental situation which alerted the national government to problems which continue to receive priority on its environmental policy agenda. The regions' and municipalities' responsibility with respect to these problems was assessed and the Green Municipalities of Colombia programme was established to address them. This was an important milestone and support was given to the green councils, and broad popular participation in environmental management was generated. Subsequently, with the commitment to seek a sustainable form of national development, the development of environmental policy has been closely linked to the 1991 constitution and the 1992 UN Earth Summit whose outputs included support for Local Agenda 21. Below is a summary of some of the key components of Colombia's environmental management.

The Environmental Profile of Colombia (1990)

Colombia's environmental profile described the country's environmental situation and problems, including those arising from unequal socio-economic development, the use of inappropriate technologies, the growing urbanization resulting from unemployment and violence in the countryside, natural processes that were transforming ecosystems, such as earthquakes, volcanic eruptions and floods, and atmospheric changes. The profile also pointed to the difficulties for environmental management arising from a centralized administration in a country with such a complex and varied geography and with such a high percentage of autonomous municipalities and urban centres. For this reason, it put forward proposals of an institutional nature for participative environmental management and for consolidating a national system of environmental management. It also provided the basis for producing regional environmental profiles and urban environmental profiles.

The New Political Constitution of Colombia (1991)

The new constitution established the ecological function of property and indicated the environmental rights and duties falling to the state and to its citizens. It also decreed that the formulation of environmental policies was part of the national development plan and that sustainable development was a political goal for the country.

Creation of the Ministry of the Environment (1993)

In accordance with the constitutional mandate and following Colombia's participation in the UN Earth Summit in 1992, the conditions were in place for drawing up Law 99 of 1993 (the environmental law) and the Ministry of the Environment and the National Environmental System (SINA) were created. Thus, principles were established for an environmental policy with the institutional, technical and financial legislative bases to support local, regional and national environmental management.

The Urban Environmental Profile of Colombia and the Manizales Case Study (1993)

Colombia's environmental profile recommended the production of urban environmental profiles, emphasizing that 75 per cent of all Colombians live in urban areas and that the main environmental problems are concentrated there, due to pollution, lack of basic services and inadequate housing (in turn linked to unemployment and poverty). In Manizales, with national and local support and with the participation of universities, local government and the environmental authority, a municipal environmental profile was produced which served as a pilot research project for other cities in the country and as a basis for environmental planning for the municipality of Manizales and its region.

Bogotá's Local Environmental Agendas (1993)

The Institute of Environmental Studies (IDEA) and the Administrative Department of the Environment developed environmental agendas for Bogotá directly related to the Local Agenda 21. This was the first experience of its kind in the country and succeeded in consolidating a management process for environmental problems and possible solutions in Bogotá's various areas. These agendas have become an important instrument of local planning. They have also served as a methodological basis for developing environmental agendas in the rest of the country, including Manizales.

The Environmental Policy of the National Development Plan (1994–1998) – the 'Social Leap'

The environmental policy of the National Development Plan (1994–1998), entitled the 'Social Leap' (*Salto social*), engendered the organization of the National Environmental System (SINA) and set it in motion. It also ensured the inclusion of the environment as a factor of development in the policies and programmes to be promoted by the state. Priorities were defined for a national environmental agenda to halt the accelerated environmental decline and the loss of the country's natural resources. The agenda's priority themes included:

- reducing the rates of extraction of natural resources;
- implementing mechanisms to reduce the environmental impact of industry;
- improving the quality of life in cities and towns;
- reducing poverty in urban and rural areas;
- preventing disasters caused by the inappropriate management of natural resources;
- reducing wasteful consumption patterns;
- increasing research on renewable natural resources;
- implementing environmental information and monitoring systems; and
- training public officials to improve environmental administration.

Colombia's Urban Environmental Policy (1995–1996)

The Colombian government's commitment to improving urban environmental quality finds clear expression in the environmental policy principles of the national development plan: better cities and towns. These principles provided a basis on which the Ministry of the Environment and IDEA could design the urban environmental policy which is being driven by the SINA in the country's 1134 municipalities. Local Agenda 21 and its methodological and practical applications to the Manizales Bioplan and to the environmental agendas of Bogotá were very important in defining the policy's participatory character and in prioritizing action. The priorities of urban environmental policy were centred on:

- the promotion of urban environmental research;
- better management of energy consumption in the cities;
- an increase in public and a reduction in private transport;
- waste recycling and improved environmental sanitation;
- industrial production with minimal environmental impact and wastes;
- functional and self-managed growth of the cities with improvements in the quality of the surroundings in marginal communities, the regeneration of city centres and urban public spaces, and increased provision for recreation in urban areas; and
- popular environmental education for participation and support for the implementation in all of Colombia's cities and towns of the local environmental action plans linked to Local Agenda 21.

The Local Environmental Action Plans (LEAPs) – Local Agenda 21 (1997–1998)

Colombia's urban environmental policy proposed developing local environmental action plans (LEAPs) as the main means of implementing Local Agenda 21. It is hoped that all of Colombia's municipalities will implement the plans, with the aid of a methodological guide to be supplied by SINA. The guide will be developed by the Ministry of the Environment and IDEA, after evaluating Manizales' Bioplan and Bogotá's environmental agendas and constructing four pilot plans in different areas of the country:

- Villamaría (within the coffee zone and with its urban area contiguous to Manizales);
- Buenaventura (a port city on the Pacific Ocean);
- Yumbo (a major industrial conurbation that is within the Cali metropolitan area); and
- Yopal (a petroleum-producing area).

These towns, each with different environmental problems, are considered a priority for the development of LEAPs. These pilot projects have already had multiplier effects. For instance, the government of the department of Caldas (of which Manizales is the capital) has committed itself to providing financial and technical support to the implementation of LEAPs in the 24 municipalities under its jurisdiction. The most important aspects of this process have been the active participation of citizens and NGOs in the phases of socialization and of commitment to the programmes, and the co-ordinated financial support for its implementation from the various governmental and environmental authorities.

AGENDA 21 IN MANIZALES: JOINT ENVIRONMENTAL MANAGEMENT

The consolidation of environmental management in Manizales is just as recent as in the rest of Colombia. Its development has been closely linked to national and international environmental policy. In 1992, as a result of the political decisions emerging from the UN Earth Summit, the National University persuaded the municipal government to take up the theme of the environment and integrate it as policy in the municipal development plan. It took concrete form in 1993 in the first municipal environmental agenda. This first, rather general, agenda was gradually integrated into local management. From this moment, inter-institutional actions were being consolidated among the universities, local government, the regional environmental authority, NGOs and residents' associations in order to develop programmes and projects on environmental education and the recovery of marginal areas.

Today, this shared commitment to the sustainable development of Manizales is receiving recognition at national level. Similarly, the positive results coming from programmes and projects to resolve the concrete environmental problems of the poorest communities make these a model for environmental management throughout the country. This joint action between the municipality and the university has gradually strengthened the link between research and management. A detailed knowledge of Manizales' social, economic and environmental reality was essential to the formulation of the LEAPs linked to Agenda 21.

To better understand how environmental planning developed in Manizales, the next section has a summary of the last three periods of government and includes an assessment of the most important factors for developing a form of environmental management that meets the priorities of municipal development.

1990–1992: Social Welfare and Disaster Prevention as the Environmental Priorities

Although projects were being developed in Manizales for the recovery and improvement of the environment, the hillsides posed serious problems of degradation and a high risk of landslides. In these areas, the building of illegal settlements by invaders had increased and the number of families belonging to the marginal sectors had risen considerably. A total of 4239 dwellings, housing 7 per cent of the urban population, were located in substandard areas as a result of critical overcrowding and a lack of urban infrastructure. The problems had become even more severe due to the rising population in risk areas and the increased need for civil works to protect the slopes. For this reason, the central goal of the municipality's environmental planning during this period was to improve the welfare and safety of the poorest population whose dwellings were located on hillside areas with a high risk of landslides.

Work was done on disaster prevention and disaster readiness, drawing on studies on the municipality's physical vulnerability. From this moment on, environmental management emphasized the development of integrated programmes and projects on habitat. The first environmental agenda was formulated with the aim of improving dwellings and providing security to the inhabitants while also considering the physical risks of the terrain. These projects were implemented in association with the local university. During this period, 2320 dwelling units were built for people from among the lowest income groups. At the completion of the government programme, the number of dwellings located in high-risk zones had been reduced by 63 per cent and a total of 360 hectares had been reforested as protected green areas.

There were some problems in defining the boundaries of these 'protected green areas' and in determining the use of the soil – they were subsequently converted into eco-parks for environmental education and research. Eco-parks combine provision for recreation, environmental education and conservation while also keeping buildings off sites that are prone to landslides or hazards – see Box 14.1. During this period, 168 hectares of protected green areas were incorporated into the municipality, corresponding to 9 per cent of its total area. In addition, the municipality established a new city boundary which incorporated environmental conservation as an alternative means of disaster prevention and provided tax incentives for the owners of these areas. For the owners of dwellings in high-risk areas, there were land-exchange schemes so that they could resettle on safer sites, with the high-risk areas recovered for use as forest. Also during this period, the Office for Preventing and Dealing with Disasters was created within the municipality and corresponding policy was formulated integrating the themes of the city's physical vulnerability and its physical suitability for urban expansion.

Box 14.1 *The eco-parks*

The eco-parks are protected green areas located within the municipality's urban area. Most are owned by the municipality or have been acquired through donations from individuals. Only buildings for recreation and education and the infrastructure required for its ecological conservation are allowed in the eco-parks. The eco-parks set natural limits on the expansion of the built-up areas and prevent construction on areas at high risk from landslides.

The environmental education programme developed in the eco-parks is managed by different institutions, including non-government organizations and the National University. For example, in eco-park Alcazares Arenillo, the university is developing environmental educational programmes. The Recycler's Association manages this eco-park through an annual contract with the municipality.

Some examples of the different eco-parks:

- Eco-park Alcazares Arenillo (78 hectares) has a focus on conserving biodiversity. It is used for scientific research linked to environmental education.
- Eco-park Montele-Yarumales (36 hectares) is an ecological reservation for scientific and technological investigation and citizen environmental education.
- Eco-park Sancancio is a symbolic hill with the city. The park also includes an archaeological site of regional importance.
- Eco-park Rioblanco is a strategic ecosystem providing water to the municipality.
- Eco-park Bosque Popular (53 hectares) is the most important place for popular recreation and sport.

During this period, the municipality invested 17 per cent of its budget in the environment and disaster-prevention area. The National University supplied 83 per cent of the budget for the joint extension programme and the regional corporation invested 23 per cent of its budget in infrastructure works to reduce the risk of landslides on the hillsides. The municipality also received significant national contributions towards the implementation of its plan for preventing and dealing with disasters. The affected communities were linked to this mix of technical and financial support and the first local disaster-prevention committees were set up.

1993–1995: Priority – Economic Growth without Environmental Deterioration; public-private Environmental Co-operation

The years 1993–1995 were a significant period in Manizales' economic growth, as reflected in the municipality's fiscal performance and the growth of its revenues in real terms. Current revenues increased by some 64 per cent by the end of 1995, with capital investment up by 139 per cent and municipal incomes up by 56 per cent. At the end of the period, public finances were in surplus. For 1995, investment accounted for 59.9 per cent of the municipal budget, while municipal spending on administration fell to 23.5 per cent of the budget.

The process of administrative and fiscal decentralization within Colombia obliged the municipalities to transform public enterprises into mixed ownership entities which took over the administration of parks and green areas (Regreening Manizales), the management of the water supply (Waters of Manizales – Pure Water), the management of solid wastes (Green City) and the sanitation services (Sanitation Enterprise of Manizales). It is important to emphasize the efficiency of these businesses and the importance of the public-private associations as well as the participation of community associations as members of the enterprises.

This was an important period in the consolidation of environmental management in Manizales because of the municipality's support for the university's initiative to develop the urban environmental profile of Manizales as a pilot case in Colombia. The profile provided the technical basis for management and it proved possible to assemble an inter-institutional work team to carry out the research. Programmes and projects of importance to community environmental education were formulated and the first community environmental committees were set up. The first community environmental agenda was developed and environmental priorities for Manizales were established.

The first phase of the large-scale transport plan was developed and got underway. This included the renovation of roads, the installation of traffic lights and the development of connections between the city's main road corridors. There was also a programme of environmental education for drivers and pedestrians which sought to discourage the use of private transport. The use of private vehicles had grown considerably due to low prices and incentives for the free import of vehicles resulting from the opening up of the country's markets. Other transport alternatives were sought and the first aerial cable project for public transport was developed. With the new scope for municipal autonomy, the local government approved a tax surcharge on petrol with the proceeds going to the large-scale transport project.

For the first time, Manizales had a budget explicitly allocated to environmental policy into which a large part of the municipality's financial surplus was invested. The budget equalled 21 per cent of the total municipal investment budget, of which 15 per cent went to environmental education programmes, community training and tax incentives for those protecting areas of ecological importance to the city, while the remaining 6 per cent was used to purchase land for use in environmental protection and conservation. However, unusually heavy rain resulted in landslides in areas which had not been considered high-risk areas. Two hundred and twenty-six families lost their houses and lives were lost. As a result, the municipality had to spend much of the budget it had set aside for environmental policy on dealing with this emergency, on constructing new infrastructure works and on preparing land on which the displaced population was to be resettled.

1996–1998: Community Environmental Training and International Management of the Bioplan

During this period, significant advances were made in developing participative methodologies for strengthening local entities' and communities' capacity to manage environmental issues and disaster prevention. The Municipal Training Institute (ICAM) and the Secretariat of Community Development developed programmes and supported the community environmental committees in the implementation of projects. The municipality also contracted several community associations to manage and administer two eco-parks, two community plant nurseries and 15 neighbourhood parks. Community participation was established in three mixed economy enterprises (with public and private members), running rubbish dumps, the recycling plant and the centre for supplies. The integration of policies for economic growth, social welfare and environmental improvement, and the design of a system to monitor and evaluate sustainable development in Manizales were significant contributions of this period. The first stage of this system will be implemented in 1998 and it will put into operation the urban environmental observatories for the 11 *comunas* and seven *corregimientos* of the municipality's urban and rural area.

Manizales' participation in the UN Habitat II Conference in 1996 with the Bio-Manizales project as an example of successful practice was important because its environmental policy became known nationally and internationally. This led to co-operative actions to support sustainable development in Manizales. Following Habitat II, the municipal administration and IDEA signed six co-operation agreements with Latin American and European cities on technical exchanges and support for urban environmental management, community environmental education, environmental sanitation and environmental monitoring. These agreements have strengthened co-operation between cities and have had a definitive role in providing continuity to the LEAP:Bioplan.

During this period, municipal investment in environmental work continued to grow with the municipality allocating 23 per cent of its investment budget to environmental policy and disaster prevention. Furthermore, international support made possible investments equivalent to 4 per cent of the municipal environmental budget. The local universities contributed technical and infrastructure resources equivalent to 60 per cent of the budget allocated to activities in support of the community, and international and national support enabled the NGOs to establish projects equivalent to 6.3 per cent of the municipal environmental budget. The municipality and IDEA received technical and financial support from the United Nations Environment Programme, the Organization of American States, the Inter-American Development Bank, the UN Economic Council for Latin America and the Italian, Spanish and Brazilian governments.

During this period, the municipal environmental budget was increased through a 1.2 per cent extra charge on urban and rural properties, representing an environmental surcharge. Colombian national law requires municipal governments to invest this tax in addressing the main local environmental problems. In Manizales, this tax expanded the municipality's financial capacity to implement the Bioplan's programmes and projects. The extra funds went towards the construction of infrastructure to protect the hillsides, towards reforestation programmes, the purchase and preparation of geologically high-risk land for conversion into eco-parks, and the programme for popular environmental education and the creation of the university of the environment.

Luz Stella Velásquez

THE LOCAL ENVIRONMENTAL ACTION PLAN FOR MANIZALES

The Bioplan

From 1994 onwards, the municipal development plan has had the sustainable development of the municipality and the region as its fundamental aim. For this reason, the Bio-Manizales project was approved as its environmental policy goal in the medium and long term in order to:

- stimulate knowledge of the local and regional ecosystem;
- conserve the municipality's natural and cultural resources;
- increase energy efficiency in the running of the city;
- improve urban living conditions for the whole population with attention to environmental sanitation, integrated waste management and recycling, and improved security for citizens in public spaces;
- the application of appropriate technologies in industrial production;
- efficient supply of public services and transport; and
- environmental education for popular participation.

In addition, the projects and infrastructure works that were needed to environmentally reclaim, revitalize and reconstruct the municipality were designed: eco-parks, water parks, biocycles, urban lifts, urban outlook points, urban washing parks, biomarkets, community plant nurseries, green corridors, bio-communities, the university of the environment and biotourist routes. A plan has also been drawn up to develop the historic cable-car system that functioned in Manizales until 1958. The plan is for a network of cable-car lines using small wagons each seating up to 20 persons. The central station of this system would be situated close to the viaduct of the Autonomous University with four routes covering the most important urban and intermunicipal flows: Manizales-Villamaria, Centre-North, Centre-South and North-West. These different projects were presented by the municipality to the industrial and construction guilds as a way of revitalizing the municipality and the region's economy.

However, in 1996, when the development plan was carried out and no modifications were made in the commitment to implementing the municipal environmental policy, with Bio-Manizales once again remaining a long-term goal, there were swift reactions from the universities, residents' associations, ecological groups and environmental NGOs. The environmental sector's representative to the territorial planning council publicly called a citizens' forum which, after several days of discussion with the municipal council, was able to formalize an agreement for the implementation of the LEAP:Bioplan 1997–2000. Thus, the political commitment to improving the environmental quality of the municipality of Manizales passed from the realm of theory to that of action and the investment budget for environmental policy was increased to carry out the programmes and projects.

For this reason, it is very important that the LEAP be converted into the principal driving force of the environmental policy linked to Agenda 21. Problems that require priority need to be selected; there is also the need to encourage the institutions and communities to support the development and implementation of the Bioplan. Following an extensive process of meetings and co-ordination led by the Institute of Environmental Education and the territorial planning council, the following were defined as LEAP programmes: biotourism, biotransport, popular environmental education, integrated waste management and the action plan of Olivares Bio-*comuna*.[1]

Community Environmental Action Plans

As part of the Bioplan, plans were designed for the 11 *comunas* into which Manizales is divided. These plans have already been implemented and evaluated. Most show shortcomings in terms of commitment to participation on the part of institutions and residents so that, in future, the communities need to prepare better for the coordination and decision-making phases. Some environmental conflicts also arose which usually revolved around problems of land use, individual economic interests or political group interests. Recently, this has posed difficulties for project implementation and has limited the participation of many community leaders.

EVALUATION AND MONITORING OF THE ENVIRONMENTAL POLICY

The Need for Monitoring and Evaluation

An effective local environmental action plan in Manizales needs careful and detailed monitoring of conditions and trends. It is also important to monitor programme and project progress and the extent of citizen involvement in all aspects of the plan. The monitoring must also allow a constant evaluation of progress and of difficulties in the application of the policies, investments, programmes and projects in accordance with the plan's declared objectives of social equity, economic efficiency, effective research and protection or restoration of the environment. But it must also produce indicators that are useful for, and easily understood by, the population.

The Environmental Quality Traffic Lights

As will be described in more detail later in this section, a great range of data are collected on social conditions, the economy and the environment, and these form the basis for monitoring conditions and trends. Most are available for each of the territorial units for the city (the 11 *comunas*) and for the wider municipality (*corregimientos*) at least annually. Many are available each month or every three months. Based on this data, ten composite indicators have been developed reflecting overall environmental quality – see Table 14.1. For each of these, scores have been derived which fall into one of three categories:

- red which indicates problems;
- yellow which gives a warning of possible problems;
- green which indicates good quality.

As Table 14.1 shows, this allows a visual representation of where environmental problems are concentrated in terms of sector and in terms of area within the city.

Table 14.1 The Environmental Traffic Lights; how each comuna scored for composite indicator of environmental quality

COMPOSITE INDICATORS	The different comunas into which Manizales is divided										
	1	2	3	4	5	6	7	8	9	10	11
Social well-being (including indicators of health, education, social security and income)	G	R	Y	Y	R	Y	Y	G	Y	Y	Y
Quality and accessibility of public services (based on provision for piped water, sanitation, electricity, gas, public telephones)	G	Y	G	G	Y	G	G	G	G	Y	G
Housing quality (based on quality of construction, density and provision of community services)	G	R	Y	G	Y	Y	Y	G	Y	Y	Y
Healthy environment (based on air and water quality and extent of noise and pollution)	G	Y	G	G	Y	Y	Y	G	G	Y	G
Possibility of enjoying public space (based on, among other things, access to parks and ecological reserves)	G	R	R	Y	R	Y	G	G	Y	Y	Y
Aesthetic and symbolic value of landscape (related to richness and variety of natural and built environment)	G	R	Y	Y	Y	Y	Y	Y	Y	Y	Y
Physical security of the area (based on level of risk from earthquakes, eruptions, landslides and floods)	Y	R	Y	Y	R	Y	Y	Y	Y	Y	Y
Citizen security (based on frequency of assaults, murders, traffic accidents, vandalism of public space)	Y	R	Y	Y	Y	Y	Y	Y	Y	Y	Y
Quality and efficiency of transport	G	Y	Y	Y	Y	Y	Y	Y	Y	Y	Y
Citizen participation in environmental issues (related to extent of participation in different projects and programmes)	R	G	Y	G	G	Y	G	G	Y	Y	R
SUMMARY	Y	R	Y	Y	Y	Y	Y	Y	Y	Y	Y
SCORE	4912	2900	4241	5035	4095	4781	4834	5433	4348	4177	4290

R: red which indicates problems; Y: yellow which gives a warning of possible problems; G: green which indicates good quality

Table 14.1 shows the scores for the 11 *comunas* into which the urban area of Manizales is divided.

Since the completion of the Manizales municipal environmental profile in 1994, environmental quality traffic lights scoring has been applied as a manually operated monitoring system. Its methodological advantages have proved themselves over the course of four years as it has proved possible to monitor the ten environmental quality indicators listed in Table 14.1.

Many communities have helped to gather the data needed for this monitoring with help from the university. The simple methodology has also allowed communities to apply and interpret the system directly and to use the system to help define their community environmental agendas.

However, at present, there are still difficulties in covering the whole territory and in processing, verifying and analysing the data. Systematization of the results is very slow and the information is not distributed regularly to the institutions and communities. Problems have also arisen in relation to the municipal office which collates, centralizes and distributes the information, as well as the commitment of the institutions supporting the process due to the magnitude of the human resources required during the evaluation of the results. As a result, IDEA and the Autonomous University of Manizales, using the environmental quality traffic lights methodology, technical advances in information technology and georeferenced information, with technical support from the United Nations' ECLA and financial assistance from the Italian government, designed a system of urban environmental observatories for Manizales. The first stage of this will be implemented in 1998 with technical and financial support from Colombia's Ministry of the Environment.

The Urban Environmental Observatories

It is important to describe some of the main features of this system of observatories because it brings together much of the technical, economic and managerial effort which has succeeded in making popular participation in sustainable development a priority in Manizales today.

The urban observatories are the physical locations where the community has access to environmental information. They are also the places where the programmes of environmental education for the implementation of the LEAP-Bioplan unfold and where the community is encouraged to improve the environmental quality indicators. For this reason, their operational budget includes the resources necessary to develop activities which complement the planning process.

Figure 14.1 illustrates the role of the urban environmental observatories as intermediaries and information sources, linking the community and the municipal administration. They serve both as key points for collecting data and for analysing and disseminating it.

It is around the action plan of these sites that the joint work for carrying out the programmes and projects are to be formulated and promoted. The observatories need not be separate from existing community meeting places. In each community, existing facilities were evaluated and the most suitable site was chosen, thus reducing running costs.

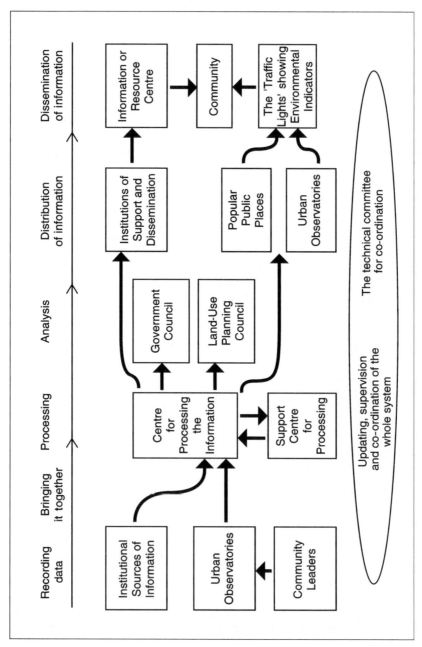

Figure 14.2 *The system in Manizales to monitor, follow up and manage the implementation of the development plan*

The Operation of the System

To help run the system, agreements were reached and an accord signed between the municipality, IDEA and the Ministry of the Environment. The system is part of the Bank for Programmes and Projects with Municipal Investment (BPIM) which will be responsible for supervising LEAP investments. At the BPIM, the technical and financial viability of the Bioplan's projects will be evaluated. These projects should be able to solve environmental problems and also draw on local resources in order to reduce costs and implementation time. The municipal budget provides 80 per cent of the financing and they can receive co-financing from regional or national governmental bodies.

Technical Training of the Communities

In each *comuna*, people were called together to facilitate broad participation by the various working groups, co-operative residents' associations and community leaders. This led to the selection of individuals to receive technical training, leading in turn to subsequent selection of the operators and co-ordinators of the observatories.

The Indicators for Monitoring the Environmental Action Plan – Bioplan

Following a careful bibliographic review of recent experiences with environmental management indicators, the components, factors, variables and indicators of the environmental quality traffic lights system were agreed, taking into account which were feasible in the municipality of Manizales. Thus, the most relevant and feasible indicators for implementing the system of environmental observatories took shape. A relatively simple way of classifying the factors into groups and, in turn, the groups into variables and subvariables was chosen because of the desire for the procedure to be comprehensible to all, not only to experts. For Manizales, the system is made up of three components: the social component, the economic component and the environmental component. These are summarized briefly below, with Tables 14.2 and 14.3 giving more details of the indicators used for monitoring social and environmental conditions and trends.

The Social Component

- *Welfare:* This concentrates on measuring the population's quality of life so it is a decisive factor for interpreting municipal environmental quality. As shown in Table 14.2, a variety of indicators are available for the quality and coverage of education, health, social security, citizen security and recreation and culture.
- *Equity:* This is intimately linked to the urban quality offered by the municipality to the lowest-income population. Within each *comuna*, and for the whole municipality, the quality of housing is monitored, including the proportion of households with basic services, as is the proportion of the population that is below the poverty line or which has unsatisfied basic needs.

Luz Stella Velásquez

Table 14.2 *Examples of the indicators used in monitoring social conditions in Manizales*

WELFARE

Sector	Indicators	Area for which available	Frequency
Education	Percentage of population who are literate	*Comuna* and	Annual
	Staff to student ratio	municipality	Annual
	Percentage of school age children not at school for: preschool; primary school; and secondary school	*Comuna* and municipality	Annual
	Percentage of students not attending: preschool; primary school; and secondary school	*Comuna* and municipality	Annual
Health	Morbidity	Municipality	Monthly
	General mortality rate		Monthly
	Maternal mortality rate		Annual
	Perinatal mortality rate		Annual
	Infant mortality rate		Annual
	Life expectancy at birth	Municipality	Annual
Social security	Proportion of population covered by social and family security	*Comuna* and municipality	Annual
	Number of persons by subsidized health care services		
Citizen security	Number of murders per month	*Comuna* and	Quarterly
	Number of traffic accidents relative to number of automobiles	municipality	
	Number of traffic accidents per month		
	Number of assaults and homicides in public space per 10,000 persons		
	Number of murders per month		
Recreation and culture	Percentage green area	*Comuna* and	Six-monthly
	Number of inhabitants in relation to the number of cultural buildings	municipality	

NB This list is to illustrate some of the social indicators collected or calculated; it is not a complete list and does not include the many economic indicators also collected.

EQUITY

Sector	Indicator	Area for which available	Frequency
Housing	Percentage of housing: that is overcrowded with good quality construction with piped water, sewers, gas, electricity in areas served with public telephones	*Comuna* and municipality	Every three years
Income	Dependency ratio	For low-income *comuna*	Six-monthly

314

Table 14.2 *Continued*

Urban poverty	Level of SISBEN (municipal indicators of poverty)	*Municipality* and for poorer *comuna*	*Annual*
	Proportion of population with unsatisfied basic needs		
	Proportion of population below poverty line		
	Proportion of population in each socio-economic stratum		
	Income per nuclear family for the vulnerable population		
	Social composition; diversity of social strata		

ORGANIZATION FOR CITIZEN PARTICIPATION

Sector	Indicator	Area for which available	Frequency
Participation in politics	In relation to the population of voting age: number of active political groups number of people who vote	*Comuna* and municipality	Whenever elections take place
Community participation	Number of active community representatives Number of community organizations Number of projects presented by the community to the BPIM Number of projects executed by the community	*Comuna* and municipality	Annual Annual Annual Annual
Governmental	Number of public projects Percentage of municipal budget for interinstitutional co-operation Number of international agreements	Municipality	Annual Annual Annual
NGOs	Percentage of municipal budget going to projects executed by NGOs	Municipality	Annual
Private sector	Percentage of municipal budget for projects and programmes executed by the private sector	Municipality	Annual

- *Organization for citizen participation:* Improving the population's quality of life depends, to a considerable degree, on this factor. It is necessary to evaluate the degree of genuine popular participation in management processes and the options for such participation offered by the municipality. As shown in Table 14.2, a variety of indicators are used to monitor the level of participation in politics, community action and public programmes, and the extent of NGO and private sector involvement.
- *Investment:* Here, the interest lies in evaluating and measuring the implementation of programmes and projects in the municipality which improve the population's quality of life. Among the variables to be taken into account are investment in infrastructure for community services, investment in education for participation, and investment in improving dwellings and their surroundings.

The Economic Component

- *Efficiency:* Various indicators are used to measure and monitor the proportion of regional and national production that the municipality contributes; the main sources of funds for the municipality including local, national and international sources; the management of the debt; and administrative efficiency.
- *Production:* Various indicators are used to monitor the scale and nature of economic activity and of the labour force within the municipality.
- *Investment:* Here, the main interests are in monitoring the number of projects started and completed by BPIM; the efficiency of tax collection; the proportion of the municipal budget destined for technical assistance to the productive sector; and the level of investment within the municipality.

The Environmental Component

- *Natural resources:* As Table 14.3 shows, a variety of indicators are available to monitor the quality and use of water, soil and air.
- *Physical security of the surroundings:* Including the levels of risk arising from floods, landslides, avalanches, forest fires, and geological and seismic risks.
- *Energy efficiency:* Here, the interest lies in monitoring the proportion of industries using clean production methods and alternative energies; the extent of recycling; the efficiency with which energy is being used; and the performance of the transport sector.
- *Cleaning up:* Here, the interest lies in monitoring the extent of particular environmental hazards such as the percentage of the population affected by water related diseases or by respiratory diseases (see Table 14.3 for more details).
- *Investment:* This includes investment in environmental education and investment in infrastructure (see Table 14.3).

Table 14.3 *Examples of the indicators used in monitoring environmental conditions in Manizales*

NATURAL RESOURCES

Sector	Indicators	Area for which available	Frequency
Air, water, soil, flora and fauna	Volume of water extracted by sector	Municipality and the wider region; some data also available at the level of the *comuna*	Monthly
	Water quality		Monthly
	Proportion of total potential of the river basin/ catchment area used		Annual
			Quarterly
	Proportion of area deforested		
	Proportion of protected watershed areas reforested		Quarterly
	Proportion of land covered with primary and secondary forest		
	Relative importance of vehicles, commerce and industry in air pollution		

Table 14.3 *Continued*

	Percentage of land area:
	    subject to erosion
	    with potential for agriculture
	    unstable geologically
	    protected from development
			Annual

Physical
security
	Number of registered events in attending to
	and preventing disasters (broken down by
	income group)
	Proportion of housing:
	    with earthquake resistant construction
	    in zones of high risk
	Proportion of municipal budget allocated to
	research on disaster prevention
	Proportion of municipal budget going to
	improvement of degraded areas
		Municipality
		and
		comuna
			Annual

ENERGY EFFICIENCY

Sector	Indicators	Area for which available	Frequency
Clean production	Percentage of industries using clean technologies Percentage of industries using alternative energy	Municipality	Annual Annual
Efficient production	Percentage of plant wastes recycled Percentage of industries internalizing their environmental costs	Municipality	Monthly Annual
Energy consumption	Total energy consumption by sector Total energy consumption relative to municipal GDP	Region and municipality	Monthly
Urban system	Number of industries who are re-using or recycling	Municipality	Annual
Transport	Average velocity of road traffic Number of vehicles relative to road length State and type of road paving Percentage of vehicles that are for public transport Number of passenger-km travelled per km of road Indices of accidents	Municipality and some *comunas*	Monthly Annual Six-monthly Annual Annual Monthly

CLEANING UP

Sector	Indicators	Area for which available	Frequency
Particular impacts	Percentage of population affected by water- related disease (by social group) Percentage of households without treated water Proportion of water bodies contaminated	Municipality	Monthly Annual Monthly

Table 14.3 *Continued*

	Percentage of population suffering respiratory diseases		Annual
	Concentration of different polluting gases at certain critical points		Annual
	Noise levels		Annual
	Population relocated from areas of high risk		Annual

INVESTMENT

Sector	Indicators	Area for which available	Frequency
Infrastructure	Percentage of municipal budget for infrastructure investment	Municipality	Annual
	Percentage of investment for managing and treating water		Annual
	Percentage of investment on research on biodiversity		Annual
	Percentage of public and private investment in control of contamination		Annual
	Municipal budget for funds for local emergencies		Annual
	Scale of construction of basic infrastructure		Annual
Environmental education	Number of programmes for environmental education within higher education	Municipality	Annual

Developing the System's Computerized Logical Support (software)

This involves writing computer programmes to support the processes of recording and processing the data and of distributing the information produced by the system. It includes tests of the software's reliability and consistency, and the production of complete documentation (user's manual, administrator's manual, and maintenance and updating manual).

Data-processing

This includes all the activities of grouping, arranging and performing calculations on the data in order to obtain all the indicators showing the state of the environment in the municipality and in particular the impact of the actions considered in the LEAP. These indicators are produced in detailed form for each *comuna* as well as for each evaluation factor aggregated at the level of the whole municipality. As a result of this process, it is possible to make changes in the indicators. Similarly, a relationship is to be established of projects and investments associated with improvements in each indicator, comparing the positive or negative variations achieved by the investment.

Continuous Assessment

All the indicators determining environmental quality and the achievements of the LEAP are to be assessed by the technical committee, the council of municipal government and the territorial planning council. Once values for the indicators have been obtained for a set period, they need to be analysed by the municipal government with the aim of evaluating the advances achieved and seeking explanations for the setbacks. This should allow corresponding decisions to be taken to promote the desired goals. In order for the mayor and his group of immediate collaborators to make a complete analysis of the results, they need to have available all the indicators calculated and to have at their disposal their variation over time; also, the indicators applicable to the *comunas* or the territorial unit, as a point of reference. The system will supply this information, with the values corresponding to investments in the BPIM's projects and programmes.

Socialization and Dissemination of the Information to the Residents

To achieve effective dissemination of environmental information, the mass media (press, radio and television) will be used, supported by the production and distribution of printed leaflets and direct interaction with the community through activities co-ordinated by the secretariat of community development and the university. An intense campaign of information dissemination regarding the system is to be carried out, telling people about the system's goals, its manner of operation, the function of the urban observatories and, above all, about the role which the community is to play in the system's operative structure. The most suitable locations for the dissemination of information about the system's results are, in the first instance, the urban environmental observatories which will assume responsibility for the continuous promotion of training and actions to address social, economic and environmental problems in the communities corresponding to their respective areas of influence. Other information dissemination sites are busy public places, such as the airport, the transport terminal, Bolivar Square and the commercial centres, among others, where it would be appropriate to have effective means of communicating the state of the indicators – for example, with an electronic panel displaying the environmental quality traffic lights.

The Environmental Bulletin

To help disseminate the results in the urban observatories and public places, it would be useful to produce periodically a bulletin containing the most important indicators, together with explanatory notes and commentaries in order to motivate action. The bulletins should be oriented towards producing greater popular awareness of the need to improve certain aspects of the city and the importance for this of popular participation. It would also be useful to employ the mass media such as radio, the press and television to disseminate results and to educate citizens to interpret these and to assume responsibility vis-à-vis the variations.

The establishment of the system of environmental observatories for monitoring and evaluating the LEAP-Bioplan aims to facilitate decision-making and provide a continuous evaluation of the indicators making up social, economic and environmental components. For the construction and activation of the system, various technological alternatives were considered and their respective set-up and running costs compared. As a result of analysing and comparing them, it was possible to select the one offering the greatest possibility for the integration of interinstitutional management and for socialization among the population.

NOTES AND REFERENCES

1   The October 1999 issue of *Environment and Urbanization* will form the second volume on 'Sustainable Cities Revisited' and will include a second paper by Luz Stella Velásquez on the development of a local environmental action plan (LEAP) in Olivares, one of the 11 *comunas* into which the urban area of Manizales is divided. Olivares is one of the poorest and most environmentally deteriorated areas of the city and the plan developed there serves as a model for encouraging similar local action plans with strong commitments to participation and to combining social, economic and environmental goals

Chapter 15

Let's Build Cities for Life – the National Campaign of Local Agenda 21s in Peru

Liliana Miranda and Michaela Hordijk

(Reprinted from *Environment and Urbanization,* Vol 10, No 2, October 1998, pp 69–102)

Summary: In March 1996, representatives from several Peruvian cities, grass-roots organizations and NGOs, together with scientists and staff from universities and local government authorities, decided to establish a national forum to promote the development and implementation of Agenda 21 in cities in Peru. This came to be called the 'Cities for Life' Forum which today brings together representatives from 41 institutions in 18 cities. This paper describes the origin and early development of the Forum, and its vision, strategies and work to date. It seeks to show how this Forum developed beyond what was initially a conventional project which depended upon technical assistance and the initiatives of a local NGO into a network of many different actors from many urban centres in Peru who together form an autonomous and independent entity. The Forum has encouraged and supported its members in developing and implementing local environmental action plans and in learning from each other's experiences. The paper also outlines the main environmental problems in Peru's urban areas and the unsupportive national framework within which urban authorities and other urban actors strive to address environmental problems.

INTRODUCTION

This paper aims to share with the reader the spirit of the Cities for Life Forum. We believe that our experience is valuable for two reasons. First, because of the capacity developed by the different local actors (both individuals and institutions) since 1994 whose work has ensured changes and improvements in our cities, and second, because it shows how we learn from our own experience and construct theories, concepts, methodologies and instruments that are suited to our problems and thus to concrete possibilities for action.

We want Cities for Life to be for Peruvians, rooted in the knowledge and culture of Peruvians. This paper is an affirmation of Peruvian knowledge, of learning from experience and of the capacity, both individual and institutional, of our communities, technicians, authorities, business people and institutions. Box 15.1 outlines the shared vision of the Forum, a vision which is the result of joint efforts by all the Forum members. In fact, most of the contents of this paper – the working methodology developed, the mission, the strategy and objectives, and the activities described – are the result of joint action and reflection by Forum members, although the opinions expressed are those of the authors.

Box 15.1 *Our vision*

We want 'cities for life' that are an expression of sustainable development, which offer their inhabitants an adequate quality of life and equitable opportunities for healthy, safe and productive lives that are rooted in solidarity. Such 'cities for life' should also be in harmony with nature and the rural surrounds, cultural traditions and spiritual values, and adapted to the diversity of our country.

We want 'cities for life' whose inhabitants identify themselves with their city's development, who are proud of their culture and the natural beauty of the place where they live, who work collaboratively, are competitive but also practise solidarity.

We are convinced that it is a mistake to develop a single proposal for national development without taking into consideration local characteristics, resources, capacities or political will. To be viable and implementable, national development has to be linked to local development. The experience and, especially, the reality of Peru today are in need of a policy of this kind.

The strategic problem of our cities is one of management. Effective management requires both individual and institutional actors capable of leading and sustaining it. It requires the bringing together and harmonization of different sectoral actions and institutions. It has to be built on the lessons of experience that help give us practical models and replicable operations. The proposals and recommendations within international agreements, such as Agenda 21 coming out of the UN Earth Summit in Rio de Janeiro in 1992 and the Habitat Agenda coming out of the UN City Summit in Istanbul in 1996, can be valuable instruments if we know how to adapt them to our national and local realities and contexts. Local Agenda 21s are valid where they have been interpreted as concrete and operative action plans, formulated with leaders who practise *concertación*,[1] who realize concrete actions which address the problems of the poorest and contribute to local urban sustainable development in Peru.

Thus, environmental management within Peruvian cities must look at the short and long term to be effective and must overcome the electoral instability of the authorities in order to construct a shared vision of the future that incorporates an environmental focus in all its actions. It must develop concerted processes which are truly democratic, decentralized and participatory. These processes must institutionalize an integrated system of local environmental management which organizes the course of action and promotes the mobilization of local resources that can ensure a continuous process of urban investment, as an essential component of the Local Agenda 21.

The Cities for Life Forum is without precedent in Peru. It consists of 41 institutions (municipalities, NGOs, grass-roots organizations, universities) from 18 different

Peruvian cities – see Box 15.2. It constitutes an institutional framework for supporting the development of management capacities. It is also a concrete example of bringing different actors to work together in capacity-building and the formation of leaders committed to achieving cities for life.

Box 15.2 *Members of the Cities for Life Forum*

Municipalities: Banda del Shilcayo, Cajamarca, Cayma-Arequipa, Cerro de Pasco, Chancay, Huancayo, Ilo, La Oroya-Yauli, Nuevo Chimbote, Moquegua-Mariscal-Nieto, Paita, Paracas, Piura, San Marcos-Cajamarca, Tarapoto and Trujillo (all of which are secondary cities), plus the Municipality of Metropolitan Lima.

Civil Society: ADECOMAPS (Asociación para el Desarrollo y Conservación del Medio Ambiente de la Provincia del Santa), Bartolome de las Casas (Centro de Estudios Regionales Andinos), Calandria (Asocación de Comunicadores Sociales), CENCA (Instituto de Desarrollo Urbano), CIDAP (Centro de Investigación, Documentación y Asesoría Poblacional), DESCO (Centro de Estudios y Promoción del Desarrollo), Ecociudad, Comunidad Urbana Autogestionaria de Huaycán, Cooperaccion (Accion Solidaria para el Desarrollo), IDEAS (Centro de Investigación, Documentación, Educación, Asesoría y Servicios), INDES (Instituto Nor Peruano de Desarrollo Económico Social), IRESIMA (Instituto Regional Salud Integral y Medio Ambiente), IPES (Instituto de Promoción de la Economia Social), IPEMIN (Instituto de Pesca y Mineria), FOVIDA (Fomento de la Vida), Fundación Maria Elena Moyano, LABOR/Ilo (Asociación para el Desarrollo), LABOR/Pasco (Asociación para el Desarrollo), NATURA (Instituto Ecológico) and OACA (Oficina de Asesoria y Consultoria Ambiental).

Universities: UNI (Universidad Nacional de Ingenería)/Masters School for Architecture, Urbanism and the Arts (FAUA) in Lima; UNSA (Universidad Nacional de San Agustín)/Postgraduate programme of Architecture and Urbanism (FAU) in Arequipa; and UPAO (Universidad Privada Antenor Orrego)/Faculty of Architecture and Urbanism (FAU) in Trujillo.

Thus, this paper seeks to share the lessons we have drawn from experience, from the practice of negotiation, from the wide-ranging exchange of information, from the self-development of empowerment and from our permanent efforts and capacity for dissemination.

THE URBAN ENVIRONMENTAL REALITY OF PERU

Throughout Peru's long colonial and republican history, the state and civil society placed very little importance on environmental issues. The Inca and pre-Inca knowledge of sustainable management of the land and its harmonious relation with nature have been forgotten or undervalued for hundreds of years. This absence of political will within government to address environmental problems remains one of the most serious problems and also one that is difficult to turn around.

Figure 15.1 *Cities in Peru where there are members of the Forum*

One example of this lack of political will can be seen in a meeting in Arequipa in 1996 which brought together top and medium-level business people from all over Peru. President Alberto Fujimori told the press that the main national priority was economic development and pacification, expressly relegating environmental concerns to a secondary concern. A reinsertion of the Peruvian economy within the world economy, financial stability, growth in Peru's gross domestic product, fiscal austerity, more foreign investment and poverty reduction were the priorities of national policy.[2] The president's absence from both the first and the second Eco-dialogue, in 1996 and 1997, organized by the National Environmental Council[3] in Ica is another example of the national government's lack of interest in environmental issues.

One strength of our country is that it is characterized by a strong culture of solidarity, mutual aid and people's capacity to work together, particularly at a local level. In part, this comes from the Andean tradition. Fortunately, these values are now also part of the life of the population, especially the urban population. It can be identified in the illegal or informal settlements in urban areas, where the population must work together in order to improve their living conditions, and amongst poor municipalities which depend on such a strategy to achieve results.

Peru experienced one of the most interesting decentralizing initiatives in the 1980s. In that decade, power, responsibilities and financial resources were transferred to the municipalities (see Box 15.3). It was the decade in which a new municipal law, *la ley organica de municipalidades*, was adopted and, for the first time, municipal responsibilities, functions and powers were laid down in a coherent framework. This included responsibilities and functions relating to environmental issues such as water and sanitation, garbage collection and the management of public space. Unfortunately, the responsibilities and functions of other authorities were not equally curtailed, so the legal framework gives rise to many conflicts over who is responsible for different tasks. But a local government that knows how to work within this law can still operate with a lot of autonomy.

In spite of the leadership of President Alberto Fujimori from 1990, during which an accelerated process of 'recentralization' was introduced, municipal autonomy persists especially outside the national capital, Lima. This allows mayors with the capacity to develop and implement proposals to lead in the promotion of local sustainable development.

Box 15.3 *The decentralization of responsibilities to the municipal level*

In the *Ley organico de municipalidades* the following issues were delegated to the competence of the municipal authorities:

- planning of roads, urban transport and traffic management (including, for instance, organizing and maintaining traffic lights);
- planning of basic social services (health and education) for kindergartens and primary schools; campaigns for literacy; and primary health-care centres;
- planning and remodelling the squatter settlements, providing technical support in the process of legalization of the squatter settlements;
- expropriation of private land that had been invaded;
- giving out land titles;
- licensing of buildings and of commercial activities;
- control of markets and street vendors;
- protecting and promoting parks, squares and monuments and, more broadly, protecting cultural heritage;
- promoting cultural activities and sport and recreation.

Liliana Miranda and Michaela Hordijk

ENVIRONMENTAL PROBLEMS IN PERUVIAN CITIES

Peru is a predominantly urban country. Close to three-quarters of its population already live in urban areas and projections suggest that nine out of ten Peruvians will soon live in urban areas.[4] Most of our population is poor. Four million families live in poverty and, of these, 2.5 million live in 'extreme poverty', mostly in urban areas.[5] Urban authorities can be said to suffer from institutional poverty; the 2000 local governments in Peru receive only 4 per cent of the national budget from central government.[6] The vast majority of the state's resources are earmarked for repayments of the national debt or for military expenses. If social investment has increased in recent years, it continues to be far below what is needed, and virtually all of it is managed by the Ministry of the Presidency.

Figures from the 1993 census show that, at the time, 67.7 per cent of the population was concentrated in 462 urban centres. The high level of government centralization in Peru is reflected in the fact that the national capital, Lima, with 6.7 million inhabitants in 1993 accommodated 43.8 per cent of the urban population. This was also one-third of the total population. The data also show that eight further cities had populations of between 250,000 and 1 million (representing 20.2 per cent of the urban population) and 21 cities between 50,000 and 250,000 inhabitants (representing 14.4 per cent of the urban population). Thus, 34.6 per cent of the urban population of the country is found in the 29 largest cities after Lima, which, together, still have a smaller combined population than Lima. Centralism continues to be one of the main structural problems that inhibits development possibilities for all localities.

The vast majority of the 29 cities suffer from severe deficiencies in their basic infrastructure – for instance, in the provision of safe and sufficient piped water supplies, and of sanitation and drainage. In many, industrial and mining activities generate dangerous levels of air pollution while their wastes cause serious land and water pollution, endangering human life and damaging ecosystems. For instance, the entire population of Cerro de Pasco show signs of lead residues in their lungs due to the activity of a mining company owned by the Peruvian government. In Ilo, the second highest cause of death is lung cancer and this is linked to the high levels of pollution coming from the copper refinery of the Southern Copper Corporation of Peru. In Chimbote, average life expectancy is ten years lower than the national average and premature death among the population is linked to high levels of pollution caused by the steel plant owned by the government, and to the operations of canneries and fishmeal producers. All of these cities are members of the Forum.

In its National Agenda on Environmental Action, the National Environmental Council (CONAM) has stated that poverty is the principal environmental problem in Peru. This can be understood in two ways. First, poverty and environmental risks go together in most cities. The poor are more exposed to the most common urban environmental problems such as the diseases linked to the inadequate provision of urban services, air and noise pollution, contaminated food and a lack of access to natural resources and green areas. They are generally more vulnerable to disasters as they have no alternative but to live on land sites that are more at risk from floods, landslides or other hazards. They also suffer directly from the absence of appropriate urban planning and management systems. This has obvious impacts on their quality of life since it affects their health and reduces their productivity and their economic capacity. It also brings a serious deterioration in the historical and natural heritage of neighbourhoods and cities.

Secondly, poverty, more than any other factor, inhibits the possibility of improving environmental conditions. To confront both problems requires integrated, long-term strategies, but these problems should be recognized as the symptoms of certain underlying structural causes:

- The inability of technicians and authorities, as much at local as at national level, to recognize and manage imbalances generated by the concentration of population in the cities.
- Insufficient supply of housing and urban services, especially in relation to the rapid population growth.
- A short-term view by national government, local authorities and the population which may resolve some current problems, but without taking the action that would prevent or greatly reduce problems in the future.
- Allowing the cities to concentrate industrial, mining and other economic activities which can maximize profits without taking action to control the high environmental costs they generate for the population or ensuring the long-term sustainability of their activities or their use of natural resources.
- Urban land markets which remain speculative and exclusionary.
- The double tendency of spatial concentration and specialization of land use which leads to 'over-exploitation' of certain areas in cities. This causes high pollution levels and social problems in particular districts. Enterprises are concentrating because of economies of scale, within cities whose authorities fail to control pollution.
- The weakness of local institutions, both governmental and within civil society. This is particularly the case for local government which lacks not only resources but also the capacity to make good use of the resources that do exist. One factor in this is the lack of specialized professionals trained in environmental management.
- The lack of political will to face environmental problems, whether due to ignorance of the subject or to vested interests.

TRENDS

Unless action is taken, urban environmental deterioration is set to rise since projections suggest that, by the year 2010, Peru will have 30 million people living in 21 cities of more than 100,000 inhabitants.[7] The low coverage and poor quality of the principal urban services (water, sanitation, collection and disposal of garbage, provision and maintenance of green areas and other public spaces) will continue and industrial pollution will rise until immediate corrective action is taken.[8]

For the country as a whole, environmental deterioration has become a permanent feature. For instance, large areas of irrigated land are no longer productive and soil erosion affects large areas; 60 per cent of coastal lands are suffering from accelerated erosion, while 42 per cent of the Amazon territories are suffering from light to serious erosion. Some 5 million hectares of forest have been destroyed in recent years and current estimates suggest that a further 380,000 hectares are being lost each year, which is equivalent to an area the size of a football field, each minute.[9]

Peru's economy and society depend on its ecology, especially on a diversified agriculture, hydroelectricity, mines and tourism, and with the latter dependent on Peru's rich ecological and cultural heritage remaining intact. This rich ecological heritage can be seen in the fact that Peru is considered one of the seven countries exhibiting 'mega-biodiversity' due to the exceptional range of local ecosystems.[10]

THE INSTITUTIONAL NATIONAL FRAMEWORK

Negotiation as an Option

Peru has a legislative framework for environmental protection and management that is contradictory and inconsistent. CONAM, the highest environmental authority in the country, states that there are over 7,000 environmental norms that have been approved since 1904 that remain in force.[11] Many either contradict or replicate each other. This contributes to a spread of responsibility (and lack of co-ordination), institutional weakness, centralization and sectoral approaches when intersectoral approaches are needed. To this are added a lack of capacity for co-ordination, integration and supervision, as well as a lack of effective mechanisms for citizen participation.

Positive changes are hoped for since, recently, Congress announced the revoking of thousands of these laws to reorder the legislative framework. Meanwhile, CONAM is completing a study for the establishment of the National Environment System. This includes a recognition of the need to establish intersectoral processes which help develop both market and political capacities, and instruments that are participatory and transparent.

The different bodies within central government and its decentralized agencies have the most important role in the development of policy and environmental management under the co-ordination of CONAM (which was created in 1994). However, to date, the process of untangling and reforming the legislative base has hardly begun.

Thus, as with many other issues, environmental issues are neither integrated nor co-ordinated within the government bodies. *Concertatión* on environmental issues is even further away. The spread of authority and of responsibility for environmental management between a series of public bodies has brought many problems of lack of co-ordination and communication. It has also contributed to a large number of judicial conflicts which the contradictory laws helped cause.

The National Environmental Code, approved by law in 1994, entrusted CONAM with the mission to '...promote sustainable development which brings a balance between socio-economic development, use of natural resources and the preservation of the environment'.[12] The Director and Executive Secretary were installed in 1995 and report to the President of the Council of Ministers. This agency's responsibilities are cross-sectoral, however; the results of its work will not be seen for some years to come.

CONAM is also meant to co-ordinate the policies of all the other institutions with some responsibility for urban environmental issues – for instance, each Ministry has an environmental office, all of which are meant to co-ordinate their policies through CONAM. Table 15.1 outlines the many different institutions with responsibilities in this area.[13]

In addition, there is a series of local organizations working on urban environmental issues, generally set up by municipal authorities. The municipalities have developed the functions and responsibilities of environmental management using the Law of Municipalities, within which these responsibilities fall principally upon

Table 15.1 *The key executive and legislative institutions for urban management in Peru*

PERU	Policies and actors for the provision of urban environmental management and basic services	Institutions for planning and implementation of environmental management and pollution control	Institutions for planning and implementation of basic infrastructure (water, sewage, solid waste)
National	1993 Constitution International agreements and laws Law No. 2641 (CONAM) Code of the environment and natural resources Ministerial rules and regulations	Parliamentary Commission of Natural Resources and the Environment National Environment Commission Ministry of Health Ministry of the Presidency Ministry of Energy and Mining Ministry of Housing, Transport and Communication Ministry of Agriculture Ministry of Women Ministry of Fisheries National Oceanographic Institute Ministry of Industry, Tourism and Integration Ministry of Defence National Office of Meteorology and Rivers (SENHAMI) National Institute of Civil Defence and Disaster Preparedness (INDECI)	General Directorate of Health and the Environment (DIGESA) National Institute of Protection of the Environment and Health (INAPMAS) National Institute of Development (INADE) National Housing Fund (FONAVI) National Company of Building and Construction (ENACE) National Foundation for Social Development and Welfare National Programme (PRONAMACHS)
Regional	Law of regionalization Law of decentralization	Regional governments	Secretariats of Natural and Environmental Resources
Local	Municipal laws	Local governments consisting of 189 provincial municipalities and 1973 district municipalities	Water companies Grass-roots organizations Non-governmental organizations Private business and municipal services Municipal basic services areas

local governments. Despite the limitations and confusions within the law, these have permitted or facilitated some processes or actions for environmental protection and conservation. One example can be found in San Marcos-Cajamarca – see Box 15.4.

Box 15.4 *Inter-institutional consultation in San Marcos*

San Marcos-Cajamarca, in the northern Andes of Peru, was one of the regions hardest hit by the cholera epidemic in 1993. The provincial government and seven district munici-palities and public and private organizations joined forces in an effort to improve sanitary infrastructure. Without relying on predetermined, formally approved plans or budgets, they established an agreement and a co-ordinated action plan and investment programme. The results of this approach – bringing together funds and co-ordinating investments and interventions – was so successful that they continued working together when the cholera epidemic was over. Their joint investments in sanitation and awareness-raising developed into a wider programme which included land management and waste disposal. This pro-cess of negotiation and joint action through the body they formed – CINDESAM (the Inter-institutional Consultation and Urban Environmental Management in San Marcos) – is not formalized by any specific norm or rule but is perfectly legal in the sense that the existing legislation does not prohibit such an approach. Today, it is the most influential institutional space in the province. In a country as highly politicized as Peru, it is quite an achievement that mayors from different political parties, departments of national govern-ment, local NGOs and international donors manage to work together. One of the key lessons, according to the mayor of San Marcos, is that they only work together on issues they can agree upon. In other words, all those issues where conflicting opinions or inter-ests exist are accepted but these conflicts are not allowed to inhibit joint action where agreements can be reached.

San Marcos-CINDESAM serves as an example of the effective use of the (legal) au-tonomy of local municipalities and other actors, that also builds on the potential of the population and other actors.

Thus, a contradictory national framework and the absence of political will within central government to address environmental problems do not stop local govern-ments, institutions and populations coming to agreements and forming successful environmental action plans in their cities. The most important factors in develop-ing such action plans are the perseverance and capacity of local institutions, lead-ers, community representatives, professionals and local authorities to negotiate agree-ments. No central or regional government and no company has had the capacity to contradict or ignore actions which develop from negotiations of this kind, at least in the long term.

This level of agreement is generally achieved when the population understands the environmental problems, is aware of the risks from high pollution levels and sees the consequences of the problems within their families; also, when they see that they can take action, and work with local government and make use of local resources. Local leaders emerge and develop their leadership qualities as the seri-ous health impacts of pollution become evident over a number of years. They be-come a powerful instrument for change and for the promotion of local sustainable development.

Thus, despite the many problems and the contradictory and unsupportive legislative base, opportunities and strengths also exist. Cities are not only centres of pollution but also sources of local economic development and innovation.

HOW THE CITIES FOR LIFE FORUM DEVELOPED

The process by which the Cities for Life Forum was constituted and consolidated was never a theoretical exercise. The principal strategy was, and remains, to develop the capacities of leaders, citizens, authorities and institutions, supporting those who are already active in resolving problems in their own cities.

This began as a traditional project. During preparations for Habitat II (the second UN Conference on Human Settlements in Istanbul in 1996), the Dutch government decided to fund an international exchange project. Its objective was to compare and analyse best practices in urban environmental management in three countries – namely, India, Peru and Bolivia – and to disseminate the findings. The project was co-ordinated by the Institute for Housing and Urban Development Studies (IHS) in Rotterdam. In Peru, the work was co-ordinated by the Institute for Local Development (IPADEL), a Peruvian NGO specializing in local government development, whose function was to supervize the research projects, make an analysis of best practices and organize meetings and seminars relevant to the project. IHS provided some technical assistance.

From the outset, the project in Peru took on its own dynamic. The co-ordinating team, in consultation with IHS, decided to develop its own strategy which included obtaining more information and involving more people and institutions than had originally been envisaged. What was initially conceived as a project for designing training strategies for capacity-building was transformed into an exercise in the development of capacities where we Peruvians learnt from ourselves.

The project began with a seminar bringing together a large number of people and institutions who worked together to develop terms of reference for the national competition 'Best Practices in Urban Environmental Management'. Here, the process of learning began to take shape as, at the time, urban environmental management was a new topic in Peru. Although many Peruvian institutions already had significant experience in environment-related issues, they did not consider that they were working in urban environmental management. The project's co-ordinating team had to make several field trips to 'awaken' the capacities of people working on this theme and to develop a basic inventory of available experts and experience. In effect, this first seminar brought together people and institutions who were working in urban environmental management, even if many of them did not realize they were doing so. It was also the first attempt at a collaborative effort to incorporate local agenda 21s into existing initiatives in Peru, although many of the participants were not familiar with the concept of local agenda 21s.

From the outset, urban planning was linked with environmental planning. This produced much discussion and gave rise to certain conceptual and practical disagreements. At the root of these disagreements were conflicts of interest. The conventional urban planners and members of the 'old guard' institutions usually have common links. Today, their work is threatened by constant budget cuts and they feel threatened by the appearance of various environmental institutions who work with the interests and demands of foreign donors who, in turn, are becoming increasingly sensitive to environmental issues. The seminar provided the opportunity for these different groups to convince us that if efforts were united, we could all benefit. But it also made clear that united efforts required substantial efforts at negotiation.

It was from this first seminar that an informal network began. The seminar also produced the terms of reference for the first competition for Best Practice in Urban Environmental Management. An independent jury selected the five best practices which became eligible for a prize that funded a scientific analysis of their experiences. This research should identify the key factors underpinning the best practices and indicate the conditions necessary for supporting comparable practices in other locations.

From the five 'best practice' cases selected, three were innovative practices in integrated environmental management:

- The protection of the Pantanos de Villa, which was one of the last green areas in Lima after decades of rapid urban expansion. This was implemented by different government and non-government actors who worked together to protect the marshland, each having their responsibilities. Within a few years, Pantanos de Villa had been converted into an attractive park with visitors, provision for exhibitions and resources for scientific and other work.
- Environmental management in the city of Ilo in southern Peru, which owed much to the efforts of the charismatic leaders of the local governments, NGOs, community-based organizations, public utilities and, to some extent, the private sector were brought together around 'a positive vision of the future of Ilo'. This participatory development of a 'shared vision of the future' was implemented through an incremental approach, starting with small-scale pilot projects that proved the viability of the approach.[14]
- Inter-institutional co-ordination and environmental improvement in San Marcos-Cajamarca in response to the cholera epidemic. Here, a team led by the provincial government was formed to ensure co-ordinated action. This began with just a few actors working in water supply and hygiene but developed into an organization which brings together the governments of the province and six districts, national government entities, local NGOs, multilateral donors and some grass-roots organizations. It works in many different areas, including research (for more details, see Box 15.3).

The other two 'best practices' selected by the jury were more sectoral:

- Micro-enterprises for the collection of solid waste in Lima. A local NGO helped the inhabitants in low-income neighbourhoods of Lima to establish micro-enterprises to collect solid wastes, clean streets and maintain green areas. The study judged the specific conditions of waste collection, which used a low-cost technology, to be viable as an alternative to conventional waste-management practices. Over 100 small-scale enterprises were set up, most of them with around eight members, the vast majority of whom were women. Not all of the micro-enterprises survived. The case study also identified which institutional framework offered favourable conditions for the micro-enterprises.
- Rotating credit funds for sanitation and water. A local NGO provided training and credit for the construction of water tanks and latrines in poor districts in southern Lima. The people organized themselves and sought help to implement their projects. A micro-business was formed to take care of the construction of

the tanks and latrines. Over 12,000 people were trained in water management and hygiene and 1187 families received credits for sanitary infrastructure. The study included a careful analysis of the increase in the costs of managing such rotating funds.[15]

Each of these best practices was analysed by its own main actors. This meant that careful monitoring of the analysis was required to avoid focusing on only one point of view. Instead of turning this process into something scientific and academic, we had the option of creating a public event, open to all interested people, seeking in this way a greater political impact. A support group was formed with representatives from three Peruvian NGOs – namely, DESCO, IDEAS and AyD – to carefully monitor the studies of these best practices and also to help in areas such as meetings with interested parties and specialized seminars on the different topics for study. An important part of this monitoring process, which contributed significantly to the project, was the fact that in nearly all of these meetings or seminars, discussions on the specific experience were combined with discussions on urban environmental management – and this helped to develop a policy and a strategy which gave coherence to the whole project.

Among the questions that constantly recurred were:

- What can we learn from our own Peruvian experiences; the best, the good and the bad practices?
- In what way can what has been learnt be fruitful in other cities of Peru? Can best practices be replicated?

Initially, the meetings were attended almost exclusively by specialists, technicians and promoters of this work. But gradually, increasing numbers of central and local government representatives attended, widening the spectrum of actors. This growing interest is seen particularly in those cities where a serious environmental problem exists. It was encouraged by the growing volume of data on the urban environmental reality which the project helped to develop. For example, the mayor of La Oroya, a city in the Andes with serious environmental problems caused by the mining industry, participated in the first seminars and paid his own fare to attend them. This was also the case for the mayor of Cerro de Pasco and his team, who live in the highest mining town in the world where there are very severe environmental problems. The same holds for the district government, an NGO in Chimbote and many others.

One of the project's main strategies was to have as many meetings outside the capital as the funds available permitted. This would assure a decentralized process and a growing presence within the project of provincial institutions and people whose experiences must be included in the project's database.

This entire process of raising awareness, motivating action and disseminating findings was the main input to the first major Cities for Life Forum which took place in Lima in March 1996. Here, the results of the work to date were presented to the many institutions and people interested in the subject. We thought that, at most, 60 people would attend, but in the end, 170 participants came. This included several mayors, councillors and staff from local authorities who paid their own expenses. Once again, we learnt of the participants' enormous need for information. What stands out most is that this need almost spontaneously produced an interest in forming a permanent network of exchange, a place where we could learn from our own experience. There was an understanding that the most important kind of knowledge was not disseminated by co-ordinators of the Forum nor by foreign experts but by those people who had built their own experiences here in the cities.

In the first session of the Cities for Life Forum, we worked on action plans for six different cities. Working in groups, these action plans were put together by the inhabitants of these cities, including their representatives, with support from a guide who analysed the best practices and other interesting experiences. This participatory methodology was very different from what traditionally happens, whereby an expert leads or, in the worst cases, creates, a plan of action. Here, the participants themselves developed their plans. It was most gratifying to see the ex-mayor of Ilo helping his Cerro de Pasco counterpart in the development of an environmental action plan. As participants expressed their need to continue with this exchange of experience, we decided to create the Cities for Life Forum. Box 15.5 summarizes the concrete results obtained through this process.

Box 15.5 *Key events before and during the Cities for Life Forum*

- The national competition for the selection and investigation of five best practices.
- Two expert seminars (November 1994, May 1996) and four Round Tables (during 1997) to develop documents to synthesize the urban environmental situation and the capacity-building strategy proposal.
- The national competition to select two innovative proposals for the best cities.
- A database on best practices (29), institutions (163), documents and experts (273, of whom 35 per cent are women).
- The Bi-national Forum in which the Capacities Development Action Plan for Cities for Life was formulated, as much in the national context (for Peru and Bolivia) as for cities (March 1996).
- The international seminar in Rotterdam for exchange and analysis of the results of similar projects in India, Senegal and Holland as well as in Peru and Bolivia.
- The publication of the book *Cities for Life* edited by Liliana Miranda and presented in Istanbul at the Habitat II conference.
- Establishment of the Cities for Life Forum in the first two assemblies (August 1996 and October 1996) and its public presentation at the fifth Round Table, 'Negotiating the Action Plan for Cities for Life' (November 1997).
- Seminar Trujillo-Cajamarca-San Marcos (February 1997).
- First course for environmental promoters for cities (May 1997).
- Community preparation and response; disaster prevention preparation for El Niño (January 1998).

NATIONAL CITIES FOR LIFE FORUM

The principal institutional result of this process was the constitution of the Cities for Life Forum. With this effort, one can channel the investment and capacities of local authorities, institutions and experts, NGOs, grass-roots organizations, public functionaries, members of the press, university members and the citizens themselves towards addressing the critical environmental problems in cities. As members of the Forum noted, the most significant achievement is '...to have involved different actors into a network whose perspective is to contribute to environmental management in Peru, incorporating NGOs, municipalities, universities and grassroots organizations – in itself an example of inter-institutional negotiation at a national level, creating awareness and authority in the theme of environmental management'.[16]

The Cities for Life Forum agreed to establish a small management team to lead and organize the fulfilment of its main activities. The team consists of a co-ordinator, a principal assessor and a technical co-ordinator, supported by a representative from the Institute for Housing and Urban Development Studies (IHS).

The composition of the Forum reflects the Forum's recognition that effective urban environmental management requires the leadership of local government, but a leadership committed to *concertación* and that invites civil society to combine efforts. Initiatives from civil society cannot substitute for the action of (local) government, and the state's agreement and support is needed. Thus, the Forum brings together local municipalities – represented by their mayors – NGOs, grass-roots organizations, university teachers, experts and academics, integrated within a spirit of common goals since experience shows that sectoral or isolated actions do not lead to sustainable changes. However, we do recognize the capacity of leadership, of mobilization and of pressure from civil society (whether it be NGOs, popular organizations or public opinion in general), especially in those cases where the governmental role is at present indifferent, contrary or even antagonistic to urban environmental management.

The Forum's main task is to disseminate and support the application of lessons learnt from the best practices analysed in the preparatory phase. During the process, some key factors were identified. Environmental management initiatives tend to be more satisfactory when the following conditions co-exist:

- clear evidence of environmental problems;
- awareness-raising and popular motivation;
- favourable environmental policies from local governments;
- availability of some local resources;
- continuity of local leadership;
- interventions which come as a result of a consultative process.

The research findings highlighted the most important factors for success: continuity of leadership; a process of *concertación* among the actors; and a participatory process by which all actors work together to develop a shared vision of the future. Such a vision refers to the development of a long-term vision for the community, region or city in question. Within this process, efforts are made to recognize conflicts of interest and to seek consensus about the common objectives which can unite us.

The lesson learnt on the importance of developing a shared 'vision of a common future' is valid also for the Forum itself. This can be seen in the substantial amount of time invested in collective exercises by all members of the Forum in developing a shared vision.

Thus, the Cities for Life Forum promotes democratic practices by citizens to unite local efforts and resources. In doing so, it outlines a new logic for urban development from the environmental perspective. This new logic must overcome the traditional focus which sees 'environment' only in terms of environmental health, involving urban services such as piped water, sanitation, garbage collection and road-cleaning. To overcome this, the Forum promotes inter-institutional, multidisciplinary and inter-sectoral consultation between public and private actors, between municipalities and between different levels of government (national, regional and local).

The Forum's strategic plan and framework were developed in two successive general assemblies and during the Fifth Round Table, 'Negotiating the Cities for Life Action Plan', in November 1996. These documents are the result of a constant effort to 'peruvianize' the principles, objectives, priorities, discourse and international agreements which have been noted in the Habitat Agenda and in Agenda 21. They are also based as much on lessons from experiences in Peru that have yielded successful results as on negotiation, permanent consultation and the real capacities of the different local actors in Peru. As a result of these meetings, we, the Forum members, defined our vision, our mission and our main proposals – see Box 15.6.

Box 15.6 *The Cities for Life Forum mission and objectives*

Our mission:

- To strengthen the institutionalization of the process of organizing cities within the framework and goals of sustainable development.
- To reinforce the role of local governments and of concerted leadership.
- To promote participation.
- To incorporate appropriate technologies.
- To promote exchange and sustain networks for pressure and information.
- To formulate instruments for the prevention and control of environmental problems.
- To foster and develop investment and processes of urban environmental management.

Objectives:

The strategic objective of the Forum's action plan for 1997–2000 is to foster the realization of concrete actions between the different actors that resolve a critical urban environmental problem.

Three major lines of action have been formulated:

- to generate, develop and strengthen institutional capacity;
- to foster concerted leadership and a culture of prevention for environmental problems;
- to promote and strengthen participatory processes, education and capacity-building.

Within these lines of action, four themes are defined:

- Local Agenda 21;
- disaster prevention and risk management;
- mining cities;
- coastal fishing cities.[17]

This way of working might be considered an inefficient way of investing our time, but it is justified by the results that have been achieved. A collective leadership has been achieved, in itself the fruit of consensus. Constant consultation between all members means that all feel part of the Forum and consider themselves co-owners of what the Forum produces: they are the Forum. They are aware of their contribution, are aware of the fact that their information is valuable for others and they know that sharing this information enables them to obtain more.

As must now be evident, the Forum seeks to strengthen existing activities in each city before developing new activities. The introduction of Agenda 21, and within this of Local Agenda 21, gives them a new perspective on the progress of their work. The concept of Local Agenda 21 is relatively new, coming out of the UN Earth Summit in 1992. But it is a powerful instrument, both in political and technical terms, which brings coherence to many scattered interventions. None of the practices analysed in the investigation phase took into account local agenda 21s. But the three integrated environmental management experiences showed many Agenda 21 characteristics.

The current mayor of Ilo, who was working on the environmental management plan before the Rio Summit, explained in the Forum's seminar: 'After the fall of the Berlin Wall, I lost confidence in ideologies and concepts. In effect, the ground fell from underneath me. Now, within the Agenda 21 scheme, I can once again find useful guidelines for the development of my city. Amongst those people who are working in these issues, I can find again a strong agreement with ideals which make me think with gratitude of my political past as a man of the left. However, now is the time to establish for ourselves more viable and concrete goals.' The mayor of La Oroya responded: 'You are indeed correct, my friend. But there are also some differences. Remember how many times we went to the wives of the presidents to push for decentralization, to have the power to make local decisions and we always blamed others for our slow progress. Agenda 21 clearly indicates to us that we, as local government, can help ourselves. This is our responsibility, which we must take, without wishing that others do it for us.' The Forum unites people who have long worked in isolation. To meet others working in the same spirit strengthens their commitment and their leadership in their own locality.

ENSURING SUPPORT FOR THE ACTIONS OF ALL OUR MEMBERS

The need to support and strengthen existing activities requires the Forum to organize as many events as possible outside Lima. The presence of the Forum in its members' cities requires a mobilization of local expectations. This can be illustrated by the third 'Expert Seminar' which is the story of the participants' attempts to visit three Forum cities in three days in February 1997.

It is quite a challenge to visit three cities in three days and combine a full work programme with visiting interesting experiences in participating cities. Although all Forum members had to find the funds to come to Lima, this did not prevent them. The 64 participants, including national government officials, mayors and council members, first embarked on buses to look around Trujillo. As always, the programme was organized by the receiving city. The University had organized two guides but, within ten minutes, the mayor of Trujillo had taken the microphone and started telling the participants his story of the city, both the successes and the failures. We visited both the recovered beach areas, a new irrigation/forestation project and the settlements under serious threat of disaster. At the municipality offices, we were given an official presentation, with all the local press present, of the environmental management plan of Trujillo.

After dinner, we travelled overnight to Cajamarca where there were presentations on how to develop a Local Agenda 21 and on the current legal framework and proposals for change. Here, the network approach seems to be successful. The presentations were all given by Forum members and that for the Local Agenda 21 drew heavily on what had been learnt from the best practices analysed. The introduction of the legal framework was a joint effort by various lawyers in the Forum. The issue was immediately taken up by some of the mayors present and a separate working group formed to develop the proposal into something that could be presented at the Fifth Congress of the AMPE (bringing together 500 Peruvian mayors) later that week.[18] Other working groups were formed to cover different areas of the draft manual for developing a Local Agenda 21 and a fifth working group worked on finalizing the Forum's plan of action.

After a few hours of tough discussions, there was an abortive attempt to visit some of the experiences in Cajamarca but, in a later presentation, the participants got a clearer idea of what is actually going on in the city, which won the first prize in the national 'Best Practices' contest.

In the third city, San Marcos (whose programme is outlined in Box 15.4), the participants were met by seven new mayors: the provincial mayor and six of his seven district mayors. Although political colours differ, planning is a joint effort leading to a coherent policy. One of the secrets of San Marcos' success is that the committee decides to work only on those issues they agree upon. They never wait for a final consensus on all problems to be solved but focus on concrete actions that all want to support.

The working groups met again and the action plan, the manual and the legal proposal were edited. In a final official meeting at the municipality offices, we were all named 'honoured visitors of San Marcos' and received a certificate and an official municipal resolution of our presence.

Visiting member cities with the whole Forum has several objectives. It strengthens the network, especially the important personal relations between those who are experienced and those who are still at the beginning of a process. It enables Forum members to know every locality that plays a role in the training materials. But it also strengthens the group taking the lead in urban environmental management in the city. Wherever we go there are official events, press and cameras. Our presence gives recognition to the work done locally, helping to bring it to the forefront of city activity, and supports the pioneers in their difficult work.

The seminar ended in a glorious party and the following day, the conclusions regarding the proposal to improve the legal framework were disseminated at the 500 mayor AMPE Congress. The president of the AMPE – the mayor of Cajamarca and a Forum member – ensured the presentation of the proposal in one of the plenary sessions of the Congress. Many elements are included in the Congress' official conclusions and recommendations. A few days later the text was published in one of the most important national newspapers.

The Forum has put forward many initiatives to stimulate the development of local agenda 21s. The basic strategy of the action plan is to establish a system of annual prizes for a 'City for Life', to tackle one critical aspect of its Local Agenda 21 or sustainable local development action plan. Round Table participants called this action plan the principal instrument for achieving Cities for Life in Peru. But the Forum members also pointed to the urgent need to develop the management capac-

---

Box 15.7 *The strategy of the City for Life Forum*

- To systematize the lessons learnt, both of good and bad practices in Peruvian urban environmental management, and follow the developments through time.
- Best and good practices, contributions to events and scholarships for courses are selected in a contest with independent juries.
- Each locality requires its own approach but common features of the best practices serve as guidelines, without claiming to represent blueprints, to promote Cities for Life.
- Permanent and open *concertación* with all members.
- A constant update on 'the state of the art' and of the areas of conflict in the field of Peruvian urban environmental management.
- Developing strategies for incremental improvement, starting with small-scale commitments and investments to stimulate larger investments and actions.
- An open and democratic call for participation, information exchange and dissemination, aiming at the participation of the most interested and most committed actors. This includes constantly calling upon those local government and national government representatives who have been supportive during the establishment of the Forum.
- Offering a constant forum for discussion of proposals, policies and investments.

---

ity to be able to use this action plan in each locality, thus encouraging a larger number of cities to use this instrument, with or without the incentive of a prize (although with the incentive of recognition and accompaniment throughout the process). Thus, the Forum's action plan contains three major kinds of activity for which funds are currently being sought:

- annual city prize for a convincing proposal for a Local Agenda 21;
- decentralized training and capacity-building for different actors;
- consultation on and proposals for the establishment of environmental norms, standards and regulations.

The action plan as a whole is not yet funded. The work is mainly supported by voluntary work and has limited financial support from member institutions. With limited staff capacity and much goodwill, and a lot of (mostly voluntary) work by the Forum members, technical assistance has been provided to several member municipalities. Owing to a diversification of the funding sources, several municipalities have been supported in the development of their environmental development plan.[19]

The objective of decentralized training has been taken up by the Education Programme in Urban Management for Peru (PEGUP) which began in March 1998 and which will run for four years. The Forum launched this with its principal alliance, the Institute for Housing and Urban Development Studies (IHS). PEGUP concentrates training and capacity-building activities along two lines of action:

- An academic line, by creating three Masters Courses in Urban Environmental Management in the three member universities of the Forum (UNSA in Arequipa, UPAO in Trujillo and UNI in Lima); and training of trainers.
- An extra-academic line which will be developed in *concertación* with the newly constituted regional nucleus of the Forum, consisting of high level seminars,

national fora, development of training materials for long-distance learning, radio programmes, Internet pages and courses for community leaders. Several member municipalities and NGOs have already expressed the intention of sending staff to be trained and even two mayors are considering applying.

To enable the implementation of PEGUP, the Forum recently changed its organizational structure. The secretary of PEGUP was installed in the Forum's offices and three decentralized management nuclei of the Forum were formed in addition to the national nucleus: one each in the South, the North, and the Central and Amazonian regions. The decentralized management nuclei are led by the most active and enthusiastic members of the Forum in the process prior to PEGUP.

The decentralized training started on a small scale with a course for environmental promoters held at the university of Arequipa in which the concept of the manual, as discussed during the seminar in Cajamarca, was a major training tool.[20]

TRAINING ENVIRONMENTAL PROMOTERS

In April 1997, a national competition was convened with 25 grants available to help fund representatives from nine different cities to participate in a course for environmental promoters for cities. To obtain one of the grants, the applicants had to form a team in their city with at least one representative each from local government, NGOs and community organizations. Each team prepared a preliminary environmental profile. The grants were awarded according to the following criteria:

- availability and use of urban environmental information and indicators collected by the team;
- combined presentation of candidates for each city or locality;
- experience, management and commitment to the theme within their city;
- whether they are members of the Forum and whether they have participated in other Forum events;
- whether there exists any Local Agenda 21 process initiated in their city of which they are already a part.

The winning teams received three grants, encouraging them to send four or five members of their city on the course. By using the grants as seed money, 12 city teams were formed to take part in the course.

The course took place over ten days in May 1997 in Arequipa and Ilo, in association with various local, national and international institutions.[21] As usual, participation was much higher than had been anticipated; instead of 30 participants, 62 came from 18 secondary and intermediate cities of Peru, including five mayors. Most course participants paid their own fares and accommodation costs; the only subsidy they received was to cover the registration fee.

The course's main objectives were to promote the formation of Local Agenda 21 committees in the cities and to train the participants to take the lead in the process of formulating these local agenda 21s. The course combined theory and practice and was based around four themes:

- *Conceptual theory:* developing the concepts of sustainable development, urban management and environmental management of cities.

- *Experiences:* presenting different Peruvian and international experiences in environmental management for cities such as Tilburg, Holland (with the collaboration of the Association of Municipalities of Holland, VNG), San Marcos, Cajamarca and Ilo, and a visit to Arequipa including a Round Table discussion.
- *Instruments:* in which concepts and methodology are developed for:
  - participatory discussion in Local Agenda 21s;
  - environmental profiles of cities;
  - the promotion plan for Local Agenda 21s;
  - the national legislative institutional framework;
  - evaluating environmental risks (Ecorisk Project).

- *Practice:* with the constitution of 12 working groups, each including three or four representatives from the same city and, in some cases, from some cities whose participants had arrived individually, 12 environmental profiles were drawn up of the following cities: Cerro de Pasco, Ilo, Piura, Trujillo, Tarapoto, Chimbote, Villa El Salvador (within Lima), Arequipa, San Marcos, Tiripata, Sullana and Paita. In addition, 13 Local Agenda 21 promotion plans were developed including a Local Agenda 21 National Campaign group with members from AMPE, CONAM and the Vice-Ministry of Housing and Construction, strategic allies of the Forum.

In addition, a Manifesto of Arequipa was created, in which citizens, authorities, institutions and businesses were called together to participate actively in collaborative processes to create their local agenda 21s.

SUCCESSES

Three factors turned out to be key, both in the best practices analysed and in the subsequent process of the Forum's constitution and consolidation:

- favourable political will from governors;
- large-scale, organized and permanent participation from the population and its institutions; and
- a growing knowledge, awareness and information about the urban environment.

Until the end of 1994, international agencies working in Peru did not pay much attention to the urban environment; indeed, there were no formal agendas for its protection. The process described above and the activities of the Forum have been particularly valuable in bridging this gap now that the agreements from the UN Habitat II Conference (especially the Habitat Agenda) have highlighted the importance of urban issues. From these lessons, better and probably different experiences from those in the past are now being promoted.

With the building of a strong network, where members share experiences, information is open and available to all. This strengthens innovative practice through recognition being accorded to those who were responsible for the innovations, and helps to reduce isolation. Today, of the 18 municipalities which are members of the Forum, 12 are working on their environmental profiles and implementing local agenda 21s in their cities. Most do so without needing outside help and this strong network, the Forum, is a network of learning. As Forum members often stress, each has been able to draw on each other's real experiences, especially in developing collaborative planning. This has helped them to learn how to implement urban management action without committing unnecessary errors. The Forum also provides an important professional back-up for local initiatives, since it offers not only consultancy but also a presence, whenever possible, at important events.

Several other institutions are starting similar initiatives; some have become members of the Forum, including the NGOs OACA, Calandria and Co-operacción. More municipalities have joined, including those of Huancayo, Tarapoto, Qoishco and La Banda de Shilcayo (four Peruvian cities with serious environmental problems) who were integrated into the Forum at the Third Assembly, in October 1997. The Forum has helped to introduce, promote and strengthen the environmental focus in the promotion of urban development within the principal Peruvian cities and also at a national level. As the consulted Forum members point out, '...we have managed to put into practice and into the agendas of Peruvian development institutions a new development paradigm: collaborative and participatory urban environmental management'. Now, local and regional development plans need to consider the environmental dimension to become complete; in addition, local management processes need to be supported by the participation of the actors themselves, whether at the planning stage or in management itself.

The Forum has been set up in its own institutional space, recognized, respected, consulted and accepted by most of the main actors in sustainable urban development (central government, municipalities, NGOs, universities, professional colleges and, to some extent, community leaders). However, we are conscious that there is still work to be done with business and with continuing to strengthen work with grass-roots community organizations.

The capacities of key local actors have been developed, with more professionals and local promoters available to support the process. So, too, has provision for the exchange of experiences among fellow Peruvians and also internationally with Bolivia and with other countries. Forum members can also draw on each other's knowledge and experience which, in turn, strengthens their capacity for negotiation and leadership.

The Forum has also allowed a more systematic understanding of best Peruvian practices. The recognition of 'best practice' has strengthened the work in the cities who were judged to have achieved it and has allowed a permanent exchange of things learnt, including both positive and negative factors. This encourages and helps in the development of proposals, methodologies and instruments for democratic negotiation and participation in the environmental management of the city. This is recognized by Forum members, who stress that '...the most important provision of the Forum is that it provides us with simple but effective management tools. The training offered is based on existing practices in the institutions. In the same fashion, it has incorporated the theme of strategic planning, specifically in urban environmental management'. In short, Forum members understand the value of developing a specific methodology for the process of planning, specifically in the environmental field.

Another important change to which the Forum has contributed is to ensure that cities' environmental problems are considered and better understood within the traditional environmental networks, and also by key institutions within national and local government, including the municipality of Metropolitan Lima (whose present Director of the Institute of the Environment, the architect Arnold Millet, won the competition with the Pantanos de Villa experience), CONAM itself and a number of municipalities. This has helped to ensure that the understanding of environmental problems in Peru has moved beyond an exclusively 'green' focus. Industrial and urban pollution is a subject which NGOs, professionals and central and local governments are starting to discuss and act upon.[22] As the consulted members of the Forum say, '…the construction of visions of sustainable cities, that the City for Life is the goal to which we all aspire, and one that can be realized, that a balance between the environment and development is needed, and that a city that will be inherited by our children must be cared for, today more than ever – all these make up the vision that gives the Forum its power of leadership and of bringing people together'.

PROBLEMS ENCOUNTERED

Unfavourable Political Will

As noted earlier, one of the main problems encountered is the absence of political will at national level. The Forum lost a lot of time and opportunity in its attempts to interest and involve many central and regional government bodies. One example of the lack of interest by national government was when the Vice-Minister of Housing and Construction, in spite of being president of the official Habitat II Commission, was relieved of his responsibilities by orders from above. He was removed from the official delegation in Istanbul and replaced by the manager of the Banco de Materiales, thus disassociating the activities of the unofficial Peruvian delegation from those of the official one.

There is a comparable lack of political will in some cities. For instance, in Chimbote, the mayor has made no commitment to environmental action, despite the existence within his city of a strong and legitimate space for negotiation, incorporating 41 organizations from civil society, district municipalities and regional government. This body, the Association for the Development and Conservation of the Environment in the Province of Santa (ADECOMAPS), is fighting to save El Ferrol Bay which is seriously damaged by pollution from fishing and fishmeal production activities.

Urban vs Environmental Focus

Many disagreements emerge in the numerous discussions between professionals working on urban issues and those working on environmental issues. Some of those who have long experience in working on urban issues can provide much needed advice and technical knowledge to the Forum. But when these people do not find themselves in positions of leadership due both to the relative 'newness' of the subject and to their lack of experience in terms of urban environmental issues, conflict often develops.

On the other hand, the 'pure environmentalists' see themselves as those who really know the subject. They generally insist on working on the subject exclusively from a high scientific level which excludes the non-scientific majority of Forum members from the discussions. This process of exclusion can repeat itself in the work in the cities.

Addressing these problems requires careful management by the Forum staff. It also means accepting that, sometimes, the process may be slower in order to avoid and/or resolve the tensions generated.

Liliana Miranda and Michaela Hordijk

The Environment as a New Subject

Another difficulty we face is the fact that the theme of environment in the management of cities is a relatively new one. There is very little information available on
environmental conditions in cities. Nineteen ninety-four was the first time that surveys were used to identify experiences in urban environmental management and the
very limited response from institutions was because most of those consulted did not
consider their activities to be 'environmental'. So, in spite of the fact that they were
working in water supply, garbage and even forestation, they did not regard these
activities as 'environmental' but as 'urban promotion' or 'urban sanitation'. Only
after we interviewed them or visited the organization (93 institutions were visited
during the first mission of the IHS) did they recognize that much of their work was
'environmental'. In subsequent years, this problem invariably repeated itself with
a large number of organizations contacted for the first time.

Competition as a Uniting or Dividing Factor?

Asking cities to take part in competitions can present problems. For instance, how
can one ensure a 'level playing field' for all if, in reality, we know that neither cities
nor the actors within them have the same level of knowledge and resources? Holding competitions risks rewarding the stronger and better endowed cities over those
that may have the greatest need. The better placed institutions and municipalities,
with better prospects of financing and with a higher capacity, are better placed to
win prizes. We have sought to help the weaker institutions and municipalities with
information packs and the Local Agenda 21 manual, although we have not found a
way of giving opportunities to those actors who cannot count on so much capacity.

The question remains – up to what point is the Forum's life and range of activities directly related to the spirit of competition for prizes or for public recognition?
This question was raised by one of the AMPE assessors. The strength of the strategy can also be a source of weakness for institutionalizing the Forum. What will
happen when the Forum cannot count on funds for prizes?

Low Levels of Response, Outside of Meetings

Another of the problems identified is the difficulty in getting high levels of participation outside the meetings. For example, the response rate to surveys sent out by
post or e-mail is only about 50 per cent or less. Similarly, the response rate for comments on proposals for legislative changes not discussed in Forum events is very
limited. High levels of participation and activity are only achieved at events where
Forum members meet and work together to produce proposals and agreements but,
even so, a group of Forum members has yet to take up a common proposal for Cities for Life. There is also the problem that some members do not work with each
other outside of Forum events, even when they live in the same city (as in Trujillo
and Arequipa). Forum members recognize that this is a serious management problem; they also recognize that information flows are slow from both sides. There is
still no constant flow of communication allowing rapid exchange of information.

Some members maintain that this is because most decisions are being taken in Lima, which exacerbates the lack of communication. They suggest that the Forum should send, on a monthly basis, bibliographic material, opportunities for empowerment and accounts of experiences in urban environmental management.

Being a member of the Forum does not in itself guarantee a change in attitude in urban environmental management and in *concertación*. The Forum can count on members with a great capacity for collaboration but other organizations exist whose representatives do not necessarily practise collaborative strategies and who have been absent from recent events.

Limited Participation of Community Leaders and Business People

The Forum has had difficulty encouraging the involvement of community leaders and business people, with some meetings lacking a community leader presence. The academic level of the environmental promoters course also appeared to be a problem since the five community leaders who took part had difficulty in understanding some of the content.

There is also the continuing, almost complete absence of the business sector in spite of attempts to address this. (A representative from the Peruvian Chamber of Constructors was invited to the Round Table. The representative made no mention of the environment but instead expounded exclusively on proposals for the financing of housing.) However, an analysis of experience has shown that the business sector (both medium and large organizations) does not play a role in managing the urbanization process. Rather, it is a source of permanent conflict due to its unchanging attitude towards transferring its environmental responsibilities to city councils.

At present, the relationship between the Forum and the business community is one of conflict and mistrust. Examples of this include the invention of all kinds of excuses to unsettle and denigrate the Forum's work – for instance, an editorial in *El Comercio*, on the same day as the closing of the Fourth Round Table, stated that '...we must beware of the environmentalists since they are like watermelons – green on the outside, red on the inside'. Although we have not developed a special strategy to relate to the business community, it is something that must be tried, although there are few successful experiences of collaborative relationships with the private sector from which to draw in developing our strategy.

Financial Instability

The inter-institutional relations of the Forum are not formal. This is a problem in terms of setting specific quotas for each member, signing financial contracts and instituting agreements made in the assemblies. This keeps the network weak and its future uncertain. However, it does also ensure considerable flexibility in its operations.

But there is the problem of funding and the uncertainty of when funds that the Forum needs to continue its work will arrive. Problems include changes in the executive structure of the Dutch Embassy, a lack of clarity from staff at the Peru–Canada Contravalor Fund and the silence and slowness in the confirmation of funding from United Nations agencies. This contributes towards an unstable income for the management team and the weakness of the Forum's internal organization team. This greatly limits the capacity of Forum staff to ensure that each city member receives the co-ordination and support they need. This has been partly resolved by the substantive support given by the PEGUP to the national management nucleus by installing its executive secretariat in the offices of the Forum. But problems remain for the decentralized nuclei as they have difficulties paying their telephone bills (a heavy burden) and have other logistical problems on which the professionals have to spend some time.

Problems also relate to the fact that international agencies traditionally gave priority to rural issues even in a country such as Peru where most of the population lives in urban areas. This is often founded on inaccurate assumptions about the countryside being systematically 'exploited' by the city – assumptions that are no longer valid in Peru. But as more international agencies begin to work on urban issues, they usually begin by supporting action at the neighbourhood level, avoiding the local or city level and leaving aside experiences such as those of the Forum which seek to promote change on a larger scale and to exchange experiences at city level throughout the country. This tendency to support only neighbourhood level action also helps explain why we cannot find many examples of NGOs working at city level in urban environmental management. Since government authorities have also not prioritized environmental issues, the Forum finds few successful experiences from which it can learn.

LESSONS

We present below what we consider to have been the main lessons learnt from our work within the Forum:

- The exchange of experiences between cities and projects must be of similar practices which have some relevance to those who visit or get to know of them. Documenting experiences must include the 'bad' as well as the 'good' points. Ensuring such honesty and generosity requires trust and tolerance from those who present the experiences as well as from those who receive the information.
- Urban environmental management requires an integrated vision of the city and its surrounds. Much of the urban work of the 1980s, oriented more towards the sociological viewpoint and towards social science professionals (eg studies in urban social movements), concentrated work in urban promotion only in the poorest part of the city. By doing so, it obscured the need to manage the city as one entity, of managing the whole in a more complete and effective way. Environmental management of the city requires a holistic vision which does not exclude its agricultural or rural surrounds and which involves rich and poor zones. It needs to avoid competing conceptual foci (urban versus sustainable urban; Habitat II versus Agenda 21), but instead to construct new foci from existing facts and from our reality.
- The establishment of a strong tapestry of relationships between Forum members (representative institutions and people) and institutions that are supportive has been fostered by the relative 'newness' of the subject. It has been rooted in the transparent management of information, in teaching *concertación* by practising it, in working with the people who want to work and in developing activities only where agreements have been reached (leaving to one side those on which agreement cannot be reached). We must recall that these types of problems have

not been attended to for a long time. Also, that these strong institutional and personal relations are strengthening and expanding in each new Forum event.

- The decentralization of Forum activities is a key factor in its strength and its continuity. The fact that the Forum is not giving priority to Lima (neither in the conformation of its members nor in the development of its main activities) has contributed to the strengthening of the capacities of those who really need it most. Even today, for too many people, Lima is seen as the 'model'. Several Forum members have expressed their satisfaction at seeing that Lima's problems and strategies do not deserve to be replicated and that in their proposals they cannot continue to assume that policies and practices in Lima have to be copied. The Forum has helped to demonstrate that Lima is not the ideal; indeed, it is not even better than any other city. This has been greatly appreciated by representatives from other provinces or cities whose achievements had previously gone unrecognized or ignored and has been a motivating factor in their involvement. This has turned into a powerful instrument for strengthening collective capacities and self-esteem. It also gets results. As one of the provincial participants on the environmental promoters course noted: 'We have greater confidence in what we are doing... now they are not the same professionals as before.'

This manifested itself when AMPE requested participation in a series of strategic planning workshops run by the Associations of Regional Municipalities (AMRES) by Forum members who had attended the Local Agenda 21 conference. The first reaction, before the designation of provincial staff to attend the conference, was one of envy on the part of the AMPE and AMRES staff. After one presentation (by the ADECOMAPS president about their work in Chimbote), the national co-ordinating body received a special call of thanks and congratulations from the AMPE organizers who recognized that the local professionals were the people most adept at carrying out these presentations.

> Contact key actors and key people from key cities and bring them together in an environment suitable for developing Peruvian solutions for Peruvian problems. The key actors are those who suffer from or cause urban environmental problems, or those who lead the process to resolve or cause the problems. And the key cities are those with clear and evident environmental problems, with conscious and motivated populations who will use local resources to resolve them.[23]

- Do not work with set plans. Each city has its own characteristics and capacities. Solutions must be developed with a foundation in local initiatives and capacities that can be strengthened.
- The influence of the personalities of institutions' representatives can be very significant and often ignored. Individual capacity to lead a process sometimes contributes to and sometimes detracts from the process. A democratic attitude, open in its decision-making, stimulates negotiation and gives credit to the individual role of each actor. This stimulates participation in and the development of new initiatives.
- The entire process depends on how much information is shared. The more information there is available to all, the higher the level of participation. Sharing as much information as possible is encouraged by receiving information. On the other hand, encouraging cities to share information amongst themselves fosters a healthy spirit of competition since each wishes to convert itself into an example for the rest of Cities for Life.

- Finally, as noted earlier, the understanding of environmental problems in Peru has moved beyond an exclusively 'green' focus. Industrial and urban pollution is a subject which NGOs, professionals and central and local governments are starting to discuss and act upon.

MEASURING THE FORUM'S ACHIEVEMENTS

The Forum's most important achievement is that the subject of urban environmental management is now better known, both by municipalities and NGOs, notwithstanding the fact that there was already a strong trend towards working on environmental issues. It is impossible to identify the precise influence of the Forum's many activities on what is planned and done in member cities; the real advances are due to local efforts. Yet it is clear that the Forum provides an important role of promotion, support and awareness-raising. Here are a few examples.

- As described earlier, in the city of Chimbote/Nuevo Chimbote and its province, Santa, has been the formation of ADECOMAPS. This organization has 41 different public and private institutions which together make up a Local Agenda 21 committee. They are designing their first project, cleaning up highly polluted beaches and addressing the rapid growth of shanty towns. The beach project can now count on funding from CONAM. All this work is being developed and co-ordinated with the co-operation of the Forum.
- Arequipa had an environmental committee, formed independently a few years ago. At the course in Arequipa/Ilo, organized by the Forum, many members of that committee met up once again. This had not been planned but was motivated by the course and encouraged by the course co-ordinators. They developed an environmental profile and an action plan. After the course, the committee continued its work and the University of Arequipa set up a postgraduate course within the Centre for Urban Environmental Studies. The course co-ordinator in Arequipa won a public prize for her efforts to improve environmental conditions in Arequipa.
- The Cerro de Pasco working group continued with what they had planned on the course they had attended in Arequipa. Three months later, the Forum's co-ordinating team was invited (with their costs paid by the municipality) to attend the first 'Environmental Action Plan Creation' workshop, in which working groups were set up, combining the methodology of the manual with the aims of the provincial development plan team. A course in October 1997 followed, again funded by the municipality.
- The 'Water for Villa El Salvador' committee, formed during the Bi-national Forum, works independently, building and improving water management for Villa El Salvador. They keep us informed about the progress achieved.
- The Executive Environmental Council in the city of Tarapoto (CEPMA) developed their environmental management plan with help from the Forum.[24]

However, it is not easy to show that the relationships of confidence and the legitimacy that the Forum has fostered through its platform for proposals, visions and ideas really can contribute to improving the management capacities of actors striving for Cities for Life in Peru.

FACTORS THAT CAN BE REPLICATED IN OTHER COUNTRIES

A high proportion of urban environmental problems are basically the negative re-sults of certain practices by city businesses, institutions and residents. The points below seek to draw on our experience to suggest key factors that can be replicated.

- Building cities in which sustainable development goals are met must be based on management systems which create a higher awareness of and give greater priority to urban environmental problems caused by different social actors – which, in turn, mobilizes their active involvement and participation at grass-roots level in a new local institutional setting which integrates and does not exclude.
- An integrated system of collaborative local environmental management needs to be established in all cities. Clear leadership is a key part of this. Processes need to be established into which are built consent or modest collective agree-ments about critical or prioritized problems but without losing sight of future necessities. This must be done while promoting democratic citizen practices which allow efforts and resources at local, institutional and business levels to be united, outlining a new logic in urban development from the environmental viewpoint: sustainable urban development.
- Develop consultative leadership capable of influencing a positive vision of the future for its cities.
- Develop skills, values and mental models open to innovation and creativity which facilitate co-ordination, mutual assistance, solidarity and equal competition; in summary, collaboration in practice.
- Promote the integrated management of initiatives, especially in those NGOs which are still working in specific experiences. In doing so, aid agencies have to be encouraged to prioritize these types of integrated activities, avoiding the com-mon practice of supporting isolated initiatives with short-term results.
- Develop technical and legislative capacities and the capacity to prepare policies that propose alternative norms which give priority to urban environmental poli-cies (local agenda 21s). These must be rooted in the process through which pub-lic and municipal budgets are formulated and be linked to redistributive tax policies, standards and indicators of urban environmental quality, and meth-ods of environmental conflict negotiation such as urban environmental fora.
- Strengthen local and national networks, empowering them in their linkages and interaction with different urban actors and prioritizing their interrelationship with local government.
- Share and disseminate lessons of successful experiences. This should include developing manuals to encourage replication. It should also include exchange programmes and internships.
- Maintain a register of organizations, experts and experiences which will contrib-ute to sustainable development of cities at local and national level. This allows the publication of directories which indicate who is doing what in urban envi-ronmental issues (and which are available to the public via the Internet, news-papers, etc) and which include details of staff and contact addresses.

If we consider our experience, we should also take into account the opinions of some members which suggest that the actions of any national Forum should be even more decentralized, in such a way that grass-roots leaders are those who benefit most directly from its activities. A more direct presence by Forum members is needed at local and/or regional events, particularly from specialists in specific subjects. Thematic groups could be formed within each region. There is also the suggestion that the Forum develop a new means of dissemination such as a bulletin or magazine, where its ideas, experiences and accounts of its activities can be published.

Each day, there is a greater awareness of the importance of the formal education system in the preparation of the environmental city. In the light of this, some Forum members suggest that the Forum should develop a strategy to incorporate the role of schools in urban environmental management.

NOTES AND REFERENCES

1   The concept of *concertación* is difficult to translate. It goes beyond consultation and brings the different stakeholders around the table so that solutions can be negotiated and responsibilities assigned. This includes conflicting interests, where these exist

2   Documents from Prom-Peru (1997), *Perú, País en Marcha* (Peru, Country on the Move), Lima

3   CONAM: Concejo Nacional del Ambiente (National Environmental Council)

4   Instituto Nacional de Estadisticas y Informaciones (INEI) *Proyecciones as año 2010*, Lima

5   Censo Nacional de Población y Vivienda (1993), INEI, Lima

6   According to the IIEP (1996), other funds transferred for specific uses (eg 'Glass of Milk') have been raised to 8 per cent

7   Instituto Nacional de Estadisticas y Informaciones (INEI) op cit

8   Dr Mariano Castro, CONAM, in a presentation at the first course for environmental promoters for cities, Arequipa, May 1997

9   Ibid

10 The other countries are Colombia, Mexico, Brazil, Madagascar, Australia and the Congo (formerly Zaire)

11. Dr Mariano Castro op cit

12 CONAM, *Política Ambiental Peruana* (Peruvian Environmental Policy), Lima

13 Irigoyen, M (1996), 'Concertación interinstitucional y mejoramiento ambiental en San Marcos-Cajamarca' in *Ciudades para la Vida, experiencias exitosas y propuestas para la Acción*, Lima

14 For more information, see Balvín Díaz, Doris, José, Luis López, Follegatti and Michaela Hordijk (1996), 'Innovative urban environmental management in Ilo, Peru' in *Environment and Urbanization* Vol 8, No 1

15 The studies and several other articles are published in Spanish by the Urban Management Programme's Office for Latin America and the Caribbean in Quito (1996), *Ciudades para la Vida, experiencias exitosas y propuestas para la acción, Serie Gestión Urbana*, No 6, Lima, available from Ecociudad. English versions published as working papers are available from IHS (Rotterdam)

16 A member of the Forum in response to a questionnaire on the Forum's successes and failures

17 Based on the Action Plan 1997–2000 and the minutes of the general assemblies

18 The AMPE is the Associación de Municipalidades Peruanos (the Association of Peruvian Municipalities) which brings together all Peruvian district and provincial municipalities. AMPE organizes national congresses to define and defend the municipal interests and functions with an executive council and representatives from the ten regions of Peru. Elections for the new council and the regional representatives will be held in February 1999 after local elections in October 1998. The Forum has a covenant with the AMPE

19 These environmental development plans are very similar to Local Agenda 21. Each municipality chooses the name for the plan they develop

20 Drafts of 'The Cities for Life Manual on Developing a Local Agenda 21' were prepared by the former mayor of Ilo, Dr Julio Díaz Palacios, one of the driving forces behind the Forum, drawing both on international documents and on all lessons learnt from the Peruvian best practices. The drafts were discussed in many Forum meetings. The document is currently being revised and publication is planned for 1999

21 San Agustín University, Arequipa (UNSA) and the National University of Engineering (UNI), both members of the Forum, and the Institute for Housing and Urban Development Studies (IHS) of Holland

22 See, for instance, a series of events organized by AMPE, '*La Ciudad y sus Valles*' (The City and its Valleys), OACA '*Ciudades Sostenibles*' (Sustainable Cities) and the Comisión Habitat '*La Ciudad Sostenible, perspectivas futuras*' (Sustainable Cities, Perspectives for the Future) between July and October 1997 in Lima; these show the interest of institutions in investigating these themes more deeply

23 Presentation at the Australian conference 'Pathways to Sustainability', Liliana Miranda and Michaela Hordijk, May 1997

24 This technical assistance has been made possible thanks to a direct contract with the Programme for Development of Local Government, financed by US-AID and executed by the Postgraduate School for Business Administration (ESAN)

Chapter 16

Developing Indicators of Sustainable Community: Lessons from Sustainable Seattle

Alan AtKisson

(Reprinted from *Environmental Impact Assessment Review* Vol 16, 1996, pp 337–350.)

'What legacy are we leaving to future generations?' That was the question that drew 70 Seattle citizens to a one-day forum in November 1990, sponsored by several local organizations and a Washington, DC-based coalition of businesses and environmental groups. The 'Sustainable Seattle Forum' discussed the range of environmental, social and economic problems affecting the city's long-term well-being; struggled with definitions of sustainability; and wondered how a city's progress toward that goal might be measured.

The group reached no conclusions at that initial meeting, but it did give birth to a continuing civic effort called Sustainable Seattle, which identified itself as a 'Volunteer Network and Civic Forum'. As its first task, the group decided to define, research and publish a set of 'Indicators of Sustainability', as a way of introducing the concept and establishing a foundation for future activism and policy work.

Five years later, Sustainable Seattle finally accomplished that goal. What were the key steps in the process? Why did the work take so long to complete? What achievements and obstacles did the group experience along the way? What do the Indicators themselves say, and what do they suggest about the challenge of promoting change in the direction of sustainability? This paper tells the 'story so far' of the Sustainable Seattle project, presenting it as a case study so that others can learn from the successes, avoid some of the pitfalls, and share in the remarkable sense of motivation and commitment displayed by its volunteers.

The story is presented in chronology format since each phase of the project corresponds to specific issues in indicator selection and development. Key lessons are highlighted throughout and summarized in the conclusion.

1991: DEVELOPING MULTI-SECTORAL RELATIONSHIPS AND DEFINING THE TASK

When Sustainable Seattle participants first began meeting in the early spring of 1991, 'sustainability' was a new concept to most people in public life. For many nations, the Brundtland Commission report, *Our Common Future*, and its classic definition of sustainable development ('meet[ing] the needs of the present without compromising the ability of future generations to meet their own needs') became a call to action.[1] But the US government had expressed little interest in the concept, leaving most members of the public uninformed. For most people in attendance, the initial meetings of Sustainable Seattle were a first introduction to the challenging idea of integrating environmental, social and economic goals over the long term.

Early participants came from many different sectors of Seattle society: big business, small business, labour, city and county government, environmental groups, the religious community, educators, social justice activists and civic clubs were all represented. Issues of trust were paramount and relationship-building was a high priority. Six months were spent on ratifying the effort's name, developing a tentative organizational structure and creating a definition of sustainability by consensus process: 'long-term cultural, economic, and environmental health and vitality'. To underscore the delicacy of this process, note that the three key elements of that definition – 'cultural, economic, and environmental' – are listed in alphabetical order. This assured participants that the effort would not have too much of a 'slant' in any one of those directions.

Initial discussions touched on key issues facing the community, ranging from increasing child poverty to rapid development, and from regulatory pressures on small businesses to the potential impact of global warming on local climatic conditions, and sought to find relationships between them. Given the breadth of the group's concerns and its diverse constituencies, finding common ground for a joint initiative posed a significant challenge.

Focusing on the practical question of how to *measure* sustainability, in all its facets, emerged as the best way to explore the issues in more depth and to develop a sense of common understanding. Sustainable Seattle, while also hosting speakers and round-table discussions and giving birth to a newsletter, created an all-volunteer 'Task Team' of diverse professionals whose charge was to design a system of sustainability indicators and to draft a proposed list of items to be measured. Although the initial meetings of Sustainable Seattle were hosted by the City in its office buildings, the indicators project was kept non-governmental and all-volunteer for two reasons: (1) local government officials were not yet sufficiently interested in sustainability or in benchmarking progress toward it, and (2) a volunteer citizens' effort was believed to have greater potential for long-term impact than a government-led project. Volunteers could take risks and try experimental approaches that government would be less likely to attempt. Since they would be less affected by shifts in the political wind, citizen volunteers would be better able to focus on tough issues and long-term trends.

Starting from the existing literature (including the pioneering work of Hazel Henderson, the Oregon Benchmarks programme and the Jacksonville 'Quality Indicators for Progress'), the Seattle group defined three types of indicators. A limited number of 'Key Indicators' would be considered the basic measures of sustainability, but they would be supported by (or even aggregated from) a larger number of 'Secondary Indicators'. To allow for creativity and to attract the media, the group also proposed the development of 'Provocative Indicators', measures that might have little scientific interest but that would reflect sustainability trends in humorous or surprising ways (eg the number of paper cups consumed by Seattle's famously addicted coffee drinkers).

The Task Team concentrated primarily on the development of Key Indicators and this task proved sufficiently large. Team members (including professional economists, scientists, environmentalists, social workers and government planners) pooled their knowledge and debated different measurement strategies, criteria and lists of indicators. By the beginning of 1992, they had produced the fourth iteration of a proposed list, which they finally presented to the leadership for review.

1992: CONVENING A COMMUNITY PANEL TO REVIEW AND LEGITIMATE INDICATOR SELECTION

When presented with the Task Team's work, the newly formed Trustees of Sustainable Seattle, drawn from the initial group of volunteers and civic representatives, decided that some form of community involvement was needed to give the project additional legitimacy and to enhance the quality of the indicators themselves. This idea grew into the formation of the Sustainable Seattle Civic Panel, an invitational process designed to bring a wide spectrum of community leaders and active citizens into an intensive dialogue on the meaning of sustainability and the best ways to measure it.

Sustainable Seattle sent invitations to 300 people in positions of responsibility, in government, business and a wide variety of civic organizations. It asked for a commitment of six months, including four plenary workshops and significant outside committee and review work. Given the busy schedules of the invitees, organizers expected perhaps 50 of them to accept the invitation. They were astonished to receive over 200 initial acceptances. Ultimately, 150 people participated in the process, with over 100 present at each of the four plenary meetings. Organizers interpreted this 'indicator' as a signal that many in the community were concerned about the future and interested in the more systemic perspective that sustainability provides.

Civic Panel members were first sent a packet that included some introductory materials on sustainability, a reading list and the 'Draft Indicators Version 4', the Task Team's list of 29 proposed items to measure. After an initial orientation and visioning session, panelists spent the summer reviewing the document and filling in a six-page feedback form. Again, participation exceeded expectations, with some panelists adding pages of typewritten notes about the draft. Task Team members synthesized all this feedback into 'Draft Indicators Version 5'.

In the Fall of 1992, Civic Panel members met in three plenary sessions and numerous subcommittees, dividing up into ten topic areas: resource consumption, education, economy, transportation, natural environment, health, social environment, culture and recreation, population, and community participation. With Version 5 as their starting point, they worked in structured, facilitated sessions using a consensus process. They hotly debated the criteria for sustainability in each topic and which indicators would provide the most crucial information about the basic systems on which a community's health depends. Their goal was to recommend indicators that met four overall criteria, set by the organizers. The selected indicators had to be:

- reflective of trends that were fundamental to long-term cultural, economic and environmental health;
- statistically measurable, with data preferably available for one or two decades;
- attractive to the local media; and
- comprehensible to the average person.

While these criteria guided indicator selection, they sometimes proved impossible to meet. Compromises were struck to achieve consensus. Some indicators that were

354

technically unfeasible, too complicated for the average person or unlikely to attract media attention were retained for the purposes of group politics. Others that were likely to lack historical data were deemed important to start measuring now. Some groups (such as those working on education and social welfare) met their assigned goal of recommending no more than five indicators for final acceptance; but others (such as the economics and natural resources groups) could only reach consensus by agreeing to an expanded list.

In addition, debates were engaged on a host of questions that affected indicator selection. These questions can be summarized as follows:

- *Local vs Global.* One key question that emerged was the tension between local and global issues. Clearly, Seattle's well-being is intimately tied to the world at large. Its economy is dependent on international trade and its environmental well-being is impacted by conditions far away from its borders. Should some of Seattle's indicators be, in fact, global measures, or specifically linked to global trends? After much discussion, this was deemed impractical from a research perspective and potentially confusing to a local education campaign aimed at changing local behaviour. The decision was made to stay locally focused, and indeed to find some indicators that measured progress toward (or away from) greater local self-reliance, particularly in the area of resource use.
- *Inputs vs Outputs.* In systems terms, indicators can measure input variables (such as the amount of money budgeted for some programme) or outputs (such as the measurable results of that programme's implementation). Panelists decided early on to focus on outputs.
- *Problems vs Solutions.* Should indicators highlight negative trends or concentrate on the positive? Most panelists seemed to believe that an optimistic, solutions-oriented approach would attract more attention, and efforts were made to identify measures of progress toward desired outcomes. It was impossible, however, to find such measures in most cases, leading to a mixed approach. For example, the problem of toxic releases (as measured by the EPA's Toxic Release Inventory) was paired with the (mostly unrelated) solution of increases in recycled paper use to provide an indicator of trends in sustainable management of resources.

In the end, the Civic Panel recommended a total of 99 indicators. This list – Version 7 – was first presented at the final meeting (in November 1992) in the form of a 'dramatic reading', with relevant poems and stories punctuating the reading of the indicators themselves. Then panelists used a simple voting scheme to register which indicators they thought most likely to capture the public's imagination; 'Wild Salmon' was by far the most popular vote-getter. Finally, the panelists brainstormed applications for the indicators, and ways to publicize them in the media.

Since nearly everyone agreed that 99 indicators was too large a set for the public to digest, the Civic Panel agreed to let a technical review group winnow the list down to a manageable number. This group, formed of members from the original Indicators Task Team and several Civic Panelists, met several times over the winter of 1992–93, eliminating those indicators that were unmeasurable or difficult for the layperson to understand, and paying attention to the preference voting results from the final Civic Panel meeting. They did their best to interpret the intentions of the Panel while developing a technically sound array of measurables. The result was a final list of 40 indicators – see Table 16.1.

Table 16.1 *A Summary of the Sustainable Seattle Indicators of Sustainable Community, 1995*

Key: For each indicator, the leading arrow or dash connotes the sustainability trend evaluation: '<–' means moving away from sustainability; '–' means unchanged or no discernible trend, and '–>' means moving towards sustainability. The description in parentheses summarizes the data interpretation.

ENVIRONMENT

<– Wild salmon returning to spawn in King County streams (an indicator of water quality, overall environmental health and biodiversity; declining sharply)
<– Wetlands health (as measured by water quality, water level fluctuation and amphibian health; all declining)
<– Biodiversity (as measured by amphibian and plant diversity in King County wetlands; declining)
<– Soil erosion (as measured by turbidity levels in King County waterways; increasing)
– Percentage of Seattle streets meeting 'pedestrian-friendly' criteria (an indicator of urban environmental quality; insufficient data to determine trend)
– Impervious surface area in the City of Seattle (linked to surface water run-off and water quality problems; insufficient data to determine trend)
–> Air quality (as measured by EPA Pollutant Standards Index; improving since 1980)
– Open space (surveys of the amount accessible compared to city planning goals; current levels are below desired levels and there is insufficient data to determine a trend)

POPULATION AND RESOURCES

–> Population growth rate (declining from current level of 0.8 per cent)
<– Residential water consumption (per capita is declining, total is still increasing)
–> Solid waste generated and recycled (per capita generation is still increasing, but per capita recycling is increasing at a faster rate)
–> Pollution prevention and renewable resource use (toxic release as measured by EPA Toxic Release Inventory is declining; use of recycled paper products is increasing)
<– Farm acreage in King County (decreasing)
– Vehicle miles travelled and fuel consumption (levelling off after 20 years of steady increase)
<– Renewable and non-renewable energy use (a measure of long-term energy sustainability; dependence on non-renewables increasing)

ECONOMY

–> Percentage of jobs concentrated in top ten employers (a negative indicator of economic diversity and resilience; decreasing)

Table 16.1 *Continued*

- Real unemployment (currently declining, following traditional business cycles, but jobs are inequitably distributed)
<- Distribution of personal income (an indicator of economic equity; the gap between the wealthy and poor is widening and the middle class is losing ground)
<- Health-care expenditures (selected because of its perceived urgency and potential impact on economic viability; rapidly increasing)
- Hours of work at the average King County wage required to meet basic living needs (a measure of purchasing power; unchanged since 1982)
<- Housing affordability (improving for home-buyers, declining for low-income renters)
<- Children living in poverty (a negative indicator of social health and intergenerational equity; increasing)
<- Emergency room use for non-emergency purposes (a negative indicator of health-care accessibility; increasing)
- Community capital (resources available for local economic development, as measured by deposits in local banks; declining)

YOUTH AND EDUCATION

- Adult literacy (an indicator of social intellectual capacity; insufficient historical data to determine a trend)
- High-school graduation (a basic measure of educational success; insufficient data to determine long-term trends)
- Ethnic diversity of teachers (a measure of equity; currently equivalent to diversity of adult population, but not that of students and insufficient data to determine trend)
- Arts instruction (a measure of educational investment in creative thinking; no data available)
- Volunteer involvement in schools (a measure of community investment in the well-being of next generation; insufficient data to determine trend)
<- Juvenile crime (a negative indicator of current and future public safety; increasing)
-?- Youth involved in community service (a positive indicator of current and future good citizenship; no data available)

HEALTH AND COMMUNITY

- Equity in justice (a basic equity indicator, as measured by differences in judicial handling among juveniles of differing ethnicities; insufficient data to determine a trend, but sharp inequities exist)
- Low birth-weight infants (a negative leading indicator of future social problems; finally stabilizing after years of increases, especially among disadvantaged groups)
<- Asthma hospitalization rate for children (an indicator linked to poverty and local environmental quality; rapidly increasing)

Table 16.1 *Continued*

-> Voter participation in off-year primary elections (an indicator of committed citizenship; currently increasing after years of decline)
-> Library and community centre usage (a positive indicator of healthy community development; increasing)
- Public participation in the arts (a measure of cultural vitality; levels are high, but insufficient data to determine a trend)
- Gardening activity (a measure of connection between people and environment; levels are high, but insufficient historical data to determine a trend)
- Neighbourliness (a measure of community vitality and resilience, as measured by surveys of reported interactions with neighbours; levels are high, but insufficient historical data to determine a trend)
-> Perceived quality of life (a measure of personal happiness, as measured by surveys of people's individual sense of well-being; levels are high and respondents expect them to remain high or even improve)

Source: 'Indicators of Sustainable Community 1995', Sustainable Seattle, 1995. Complete report is available for $15 from Sustainable Seattle, e-mail sustsea@halcyon.com

1993: RESEARCH AND PRELIMINARY PUBLICATION

Once the indicators were defined, Task Team members immediately began to research them. The intent was to establish long-term trends, with data reaching back 10 or 20 years wherever available. For indicators that had never before been measured, Sustainable Seattle would be creating a baseline for the future. It quickly became apparent that data availability was often quite limited, so an initial subset of 20 indicators was selected for initial publication, based on the likelihood that reliable data could be found. Even these proved very challenging to research: Sustainable Seattle volunteers pored over piles of public documents and databases, and called dozens of agency officials in local, state and national government, looking for the best available numbers.

Data availability (or lack thereof) forced more changes in the indicator list itself. Every change had to be weighed against the original intentions of the Civic Panel, who sometimes had identified a social, economic or environmental issue they wanted measured, but not the technical definition of the indicator. 'Homelessness', for example, was changed through the research process into 'Housing Affordability', which experts all said was a more reliable source of data as well as a better indicator of the conditions that breed homelessness. 'Wild Salmon' was narrowed down to the salmon runs in two specific streams, reflective of the Puget Sound system as a whole. Similar technical adjustments were made to virtually every indicator, but the wishes of the Civic Panel remained the guiding beacon for each of those decisions.

Some indicators had to be dropped for lack of data, but others were considered too important to drop, even when research could turn up no reliable information. For example, there was virtually no tracking of the number of youth involved in community service or the hours spent on arts instruction in the schools, but these indicators were retained because the Civic Panel considered them essential to the health of the next generation. Sustainable Seattle members believed that by reporting on these indicators and noting that no data existed, public or private agencies would be spurred to begin tracking the information.

Key reporting questions were also settled during this period, such as whether to aggregate the indicators together into a single number or 'Sustainability Index'. The group's answer was no, because it would hide the systemic complexity the project was trying to emphasize and because assigning the indicators relative weights would be difficult at best. Another key question was whether to set benchmarks or 'sustainability levels' against which to evaluate the indicators. Again, the answer was no because these levels were often impossible to determine. For example, how could one calculate a 'sustainable' level of child poverty or fossil fuel use? The question of setting targets and benchmarks was therefore tabled for future consideration.

Instead, it was finally agreed that the *direction* of sustainability would be determined for each indicator and the trend evaluated in terms of that direction. For instance, declining salmon runs, rising child poverty and widening gaps in the distribution of income would all be considered trends *away* from sustainability (and alarming ones at that) because they threatened the long-term health of the community. Improvements in air quality, reductions in per capita water use and increasing diversity of the employment base would all be considered trends *toward* sustainability. A main goal of the Indicators report was to present these overall trends in a way that quickly communicated the state of the city and its direction of change, while not hiding the complexity of the systems on which its health depended. Organizers used the image of an instrument panel, where the general state was discernible at a glance, but where detailed evaluations were still available for those who wanted them.

Perhaps the most difficult indicator to evaluate was population growth. There was no consensus in the group, with its diversity of representation, on whether population growth was inherently unsustainable. Those from the business community felt that some growth was healthy and necessary and were unmoved by arguments about carrying capacity. Those from environmental groups felt any growth was simply a further tax on already damaged ecosystems. Some thought population should be in a category all its own, as a kind of 'meta-indicator' against which all the others would be referenced. Finally, a compromise was struck: everyone could agree that growth rates were too high to permit effective planning on the part of local authorities, causing too much stress to human and natural systems alike. Hence, the rate of population growth up to 1993 was deemed unsustainable.

Organizers had hoped that the Indicators would quickly be accepted as an important resource for policy-makers and citizens, because they would illuminate key long-term trends, the connections between the trends, and the priorities for action. But when the research was completed and the 'Indicators of Sustainable Community 1993' finally published,[2] their initial reception was mixed. Local newspapers did not cover it. Talk radio, however, covered it extensively, inviting Sustainable Seattle organizers to their studios for call-in shows. Some local government officials promoted it as a quasi-official addition to the City's comprehensive planning process then under way (even naming the City's official Comprehensive Plan, 'Toward a Sustainable Seattle'); but others in government paid little attention. The Indicators became quite well known in planning circles, but most citizens – to whom the report was primarily addressed – never heard of it. Ironically, the group's work became much more well known outside Seattle than at home.

1994: INTERNATIONAL DISSEMINATION
AND FURTHER RESEARCH

Sustainable Seattle organizers spent much of 1994 promoting and distributing the indicators not just around Seattle, but around the world. Quite unexpectedly, the indicators became seen as a model effort, and cities and civic groups from Europe to Taiwan expressed interest in adapting them. The 1993 report was presented to the US President's Council on Sustainable Development, the Global Forum in Manchester, UK (a follow-up to the Earth Summit), the European Commission, international forums from Hungary to Argentina, and in many American cities. The group distributed 2500 copies of the report to colleges, government agencies, companies and individuals all over the world.

One reason for the report's success was its focus on *linkages*, the connections between various indicators and the systems they measure. Many people cited its example of the link between wild salmon and child poverty: poor children are more likely to enter lives of crime, creating unsafe streets, causing people to drive more often rather than walking or biking (or move to the suburbs), leading to increased non-point source pollution in local streams, killing salmon. While hardly an exact science, such descriptions of linkages can help citizens, planners and decision-makers to keep the 'big picture' in mind when facing major policy decisions, contributing at least to an intuitive understanding of systems, feedback loops and unintended consequences.

Meanwhile, volunteers were gearing up for researching the remaining 20 indicators, many of which had never been researched before. Sustainable Seattle commissioned a local survey firm to study more subjective trends such as perceived quality of life or the 'neighbourliness' of Seattle-area citizens. It sent college interns into libraries to wade through the literature on biodiversity and food production. Volunteers again pored over the numbers and, again, some indicators selected by the Civic Panel had to be altered for lack of meaningful data (such as the amount of Seattle's food that had actually been grown in Washington State, impossible to determine given the complexity of agricultural trade and transport). Others were added based on their clear affinity with the Civic Panel's intentions (such as childhood asthma, linked to indoor air quality and child poverty).

But progress was much slower than anticipated, for three reasons: first, the second set of 20 indicators was far more difficult to research, raising exceedingly difficult questions about data availability, reliability and interpretation. Second, and more importantly, the group's volunteer-based structure began to show signs of stress. Project leaders were also professionals with increasingly busy schedules and the added difficulty of the indicators' research stretched their capacities to the maximum. Finally, the group felt pressured to meet and exceed the quality standard it had set in its 1993 report, adding another layer of challenge to the task.

1995: PUBLICATION OF COMPLETE REPORT

Several delays ensued, and ultimately the report was published almost a year behind its original schedule. However, the delays may have worked in the group's favour. By the time the 'Indicators of Sustainable Community 1995' were published in November,[3] the extra year had allowed the group to build stronger relationships with city governments and the media. Seattle's Mayor and the President of its City Council both made strongly supportive statements about the project to the press. The result was that the release of the document made front-page news in one daily paper and it received extensive coverage on the front of the local news section in the other.[4] It also received prominent coverage in the major business daily.[5]

Finally, after nearly five years of steady work by legions of volunteers (and in 1995 by two part-time staff), Sustainable Seattle had achieved its goal of bringing a full array of indicators to the attention of the public. It had overcome numerous barriers, including the need to (1) build trust among diverse participants, (2) establish credibility and legitimacy in the eyes of decision-makers and the media, (3) mobilize and retain highly skilled volunteers, (4) include the creative participation of hundreds of citizens, and (5) meet the technical challenge of finding and presenting data for 40 long-term trends. But since its inception, production of the Indicators report – now projected to be updated every two to three years – was only step one in a long-term strategy for creating a more sustainable city. The real work of the group had just begun.

THE PROCESS: SUMMARY OF LESSONS LEARNED

Maintaining a volunteer effort of this magnitude and complexity is no small task and there were several factors that contributed to the group's ultimate success:

- *An administrative base.* While the indicators' effort was nearly all-volunteer, Sustainable Seattle was fortunate in having several businesses, organizations and institutions who provided it with in-kind support from the outset. Chief among these was Metrocenter YMCA, a community service branch of downtown YMCA, which provided it with office and meeting space (and where staff are now employed). Several local consulting firms, foundations, non-profits and government agencies also contributed significantly.
- *Good timing.* The first Civic Panel meeting in 1992 coincided almost exactly with the convening of the Earth Summit in Rio de Janeiro, and Sustainable Seattle timed its activities to catch the new wave of media attention and public interest in sustainable development. Also, the parallel development of the City's Comprehensive Plan facilitated relationship-building with City officials, who saw value in supporting this non-governmental effort because it had complementary goals.
- *Skilled facilitation.* Several of the key organizers were professional facilitators with years of experience in collaborative process design and sustainability-related issues. Their long-term commitment to the project provided leadership continuity and helped to create an inclusive, participatory organizational culture, while ensuring that meetings were well organized and productive.

Still, there were many obstacles that, in retrospect, might have been more skilfully negotiated. The group's all-volunteer status, while adding grass-roots legitimacy, slowed the work considerably. The prospect of citizen volunteers taking on something so technical was difficult for many local academics, journalists and professionals to accept (unless they were also involved as volunteers). The focus on the long-term, comprehensive 'big picture' of sustainability initially alienated groups focused on single issues like water quality or small business development. But these obstacles have largely been overcome, as evidenced by the report's completion and its growing acceptance within the community.

In addition to the specific points described in this article, several general conclusions can be drawn from the Sustainable Seattle process and from the experience of indicators' projects in general:

- Indicators can provide a sense of common ground on which to build community relationships, consensus and understanding about sustainability.
- Special care must be given to balancing environmental, economic and social
  interests in the development of community sustainability indicators.
- Selection of indicators must balance the requirements of technical sophistication against the capacity of the public to understand and respond to the information.
- While data availability will necessarily affect indicator selection and development,
  it should not be the deciding factor. Lack of data availabilty on a key sustainability
  issue is itself an indicator that the issue is receiving insufficient attention.
- Key indicators of sustainability may not always have immediate and clear links
  to current policy issues. Such issues should influence selection, but again, they
  should not be the deciding factor when long-term sustainability is the focus.
- Getting media attention to sustainability indicators is a challenge requiring
  dogged persistence. Reporters and editorial boards must be educated about
  the value of the approach and persuaded to give complicated long-term trends
  the attention they deserve. Highlighting urgent negative trends together with encouraging success stories is often the most effective formula.

THE NEXT CHALLENGE: ACTION FOR SUSTAINABILITY

The Sustainable Seattle Indicators paint a vivid picture of a city where quality of life
is celebrated and most people feel good about their individual prospects, but where
many of the things that comprise *sustainability* are on the wane. Of the 40 trends
surveyed, ranging from air quality and biodiversity to energy use and public participation in the arts, only 8 are moving the city in the direction of long-term health.
Fourteen are carrying the city in the wrong direction, often at an alarming pace. The
remaining 18 indicators are either unchanged or do not yet have enough data to
show a discernible trend, but half of these are currently at levels the group considers to be untenable in the long run (see Table 16.1).

The good news is encouraging: Air quality by some measurements has steadily
improved, thanks to effective regulation. The economy is reasonably healthy in conventional terms. People generally enjoy their lives here on the shores of Puget Sound
and they are showing an increased sense of stewardship in their rising recycling
rates, their decreased toxic emissions, their growing use of recycled paper and their
shrinking per capita consumption of water (though overall water use is still increasing because of population growth).

But wild salmon are rapidly disappearing, as are wetlands, farmlands and
biodiversity. Reliance on fossil fuels – an unsustainable energy source that adds
to global warming – is going up, not down. More children are being born into poverty. And a very basic measure of educational success, high school graduation, is
not even being effectively measured by local school administrators. Today's citizens
may be enjoying 'the good life', but if current trends continue, their children will
inherit a seriously degraded environment, a more fragile economy and a severely
stressed social system.

Can a report like this make a difference? Only time will tell. But the fact that it is a *citizens'* report, rather than a government one, improves the odds. For all the delays and difficulties posed by tackling this sophisticated project using volunteers and participatory processes (rather than a small team of paid government professionals), the long-term results may be well worth it. The Sustainable Seattle Indicators represent the work of hundreds of people who now have an intimate knowledge of sustainability. They are spreading that knowledge into their homes, schools and workplaces. Their five years of work represents a remarkable investment in the community's future. Many are now shifting their efforts into new projects designed to move the indicators in the right direction. By their actions, these volunteers have demonstrated that they will not wait for government to respond; instead, they will hold government, citizens and themselves accountable for ensuring the city's long-term health.

In short, the volunteers of Sustainable Seattle will make sure that the indicators do not remain an abstract exercise or a report on a shelf. They will ensure that the indicators are seen as a call to action, a continuing inspiration for citizenship today and an abiding legacy for future generations.

NOTES AND REFERENCES

1   World Commission on Environment and Development, *Our Common Future*, Oxford University Press, 1987, p 1
2   Sustainable Seattle, *Indicators of Sustainable Community 1993* (out of print)
3   Sustainable Seattle, *Indicators of Sustainable Community 1995*, Metrocenter YMCA, 1995
4   Bill Dietrich, 'Robust? Going Bust? Taking city's pulse,' *Seattle Times* 15 November 1995, p A1; and Scott Maier, 'Seattle's long-term health is on the wane, survey shows,' *Seattle Post-Intelligencer*, 16 November 1995, p B1
5   Gagandeep Saini, 'Can this way of life be sustained?', *Daily Journal of Commerce*, 16 November 1995, p 1

Chapter 17

Indicators and Information Systems
for Sustainable Development

Donella Meadows

INTRODUCTION

This text is drawn from Chapters 6 and 7 of *Indicators and Information Systems for Sustainable Development* by Donella Meadows, published by the Sustainability Institute, Hartland (USA) in 1998.* This report grew out of a five-day workshop on sustainable development indicators attended by a small subset of the 200 members of the Balaton Group (an international network of scholars and activists who work on sustainable development in their own countries and regions).

The discussions that go before and after these two chapters will also be of interest to any person or group involved in developing indicators for sustainable development for cities. Chapter 1 discusses what indicators are and from what they arise – the desire to measure what we care about – and stresses their importance (not least because they sit at the centre of the decision-making process). It also points to how dangerous they can be if they are poorly chosen, as they can give a false or incomplete picture. Chapter 2 describes how indicators are always only partial reflections of reality (the map is not the territory it seeks to represent) and are generally based on uncertain and imperfect models. Chapter 3 discusses why we need indicators of sustainable development, with Chapter 4 discussing the difficulties in coming up with appropriate indicators. It also discusses why we need a coherent information system from which indicators can be derived. Chapter 5 discusses the key characteristics of such an information system and how its organization must meet the needs both for detail and specificity at local level and for more aggregation for higher levels. It explains why the process of developing indicators is as important as the indicators selected and how this process must involve both specialists and non-specialists. This chapter also describes how indicators must help identify critical linkages, dynamic tendencies and leverage points of action. It stresses the need to distinguish between stocks and flows. Stocks are indicators of the state of the system (the amount of trees, the quantity of water in the aquifer...). They are generally

---

* The full report is available from The Sustainability Institute, PO Box 174, Hartland Four Corners, VT 05049, USA, price US$10; orders from outside the US should add $5 for postage and packing. Payment through dollar cheques drawn on US bank accounts or international money orders.

the most countable elements of systems and so make obvious indicators, while the size and lifetime of stocks give useful indicators of response rates. Flows are inputs or outputs (measured per unit time) that increase or decrease stocks – for instance, the harvest and growth of trees or the build-up of greenhouse gases. Chapters 6 and 7, which are reproduced below, suggest a framework for sustainable development indicators and give some sample indicators. The report ends with a short Chapter 8, discussing the importance of getting indicators actually measured, reported and used. It stresses the need to get some preliminary indicators into use, even if our knowledge is imperfect, but within a commitment to search for better indicators and to monitor, test, evaluate and improve those that are used.

A SUGGESTED FRAMEWORK FOR SUSTAINABLE DEVELOPMENT INDICATORS

> That which is good and helpful ought to be growing and that which is bad and hindering ought to be diminishing... We therefore need, above all else ... concepts that enable us to choose the right direction of our movement and not merely to measure its speed.
>
> *E F Schumacher*

The Hierarchy from Ultimate Means to Ultimate Ends

The 'Daly Triangle', which relates natural wealth to ultimate human purpose through technology, economy, politics and ethics, provides a simple integrating framework (see Figure 17.1).

So what information needs to be displayed on the cockpit, to allow society to steer successfully toward sustainable development? What organizing framework makes intuitive sense, captures the relative importance of various indicators and illustrates their relationship to one another? What could deliver at a glance the essence of the present situation and its rate and direction of change, and the policy levers that might alter the rate and direction of change?

Several tentative frameworks have been suggested and discussed, among them the 'pressure-state-impact-response' model used to organize the first indicator efforts of the UN Commission on Sustainable Development and other international bodies,[1] the 'ecological footprint',[2] the 'four capitals' (economic, natural, human and social capital) arising from the World Bank,[3] and the idea of 'genuine savings'.[4] The Balaton Group workshop found these forerunners useful; each seemed to capture an important piece of the puzzle, but not the whole puzzle. We struggled to bring them together, to distil the message that each seemed to carry, and to find a more whole-system context within which to place them. We looked for a framework that would make sense on its own terms and that would lend itself both to a comprehensive underlying information system and to underlying dynamic models. We wanted a 'database organizer' that could be comprehended at all levels, in which one would not be likely to lose one's way, in which one would never lose sight of what is most important for sustainable development.

I believe we found it, but before I describe it, I must state that several of my Balaton colleagues have reservations about this scheme, more on the symbolic and philosophical levels than on the level of logical concepts. No scheme we came up

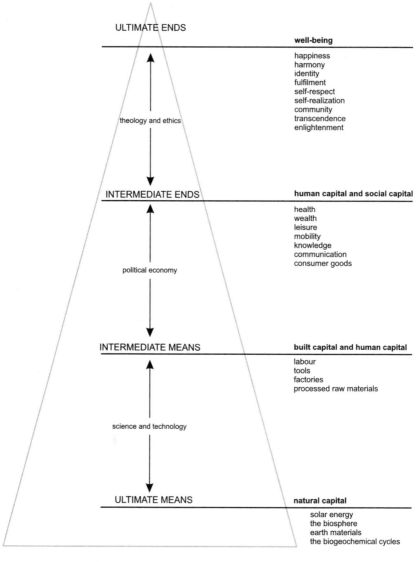

Figure 17.1 *The relationship between the human economy and the earth*

with was embraced by all without reservation. Our discussions of our doubts about each scheme were revealing, showing the power of symbols and the different interpretations different cultures can bring to the same symbol. I see no way around that difficulty, except to choose a framework that seems to capture the central logic one is trying to communicate, and then, through use and example, to imbue that framework with the intended meaning. That is how every large-scale indicator, from the GDP to the Dow-Jones Index, has evolved.

The framework I suggest is based on a diagram Herman Daly drew more than 20 years ago.[5] It pictures the relationship between the human economy and the earth in a way that is, to me, logical, systematic and clarifying. Daly originally drew it as a triangle or pyramid, and for historical purposes I will use that symbolism, though the shape is not necessary to the logic.[6] Daly himself abandoned it in later texts and simply drew a vertical line. The important idea is to situate the human economy within a hierarchy, resting on a foundation of natural resources and reaching to the height of ultimate purpose.

At the base of the triangle, supporting everything, are what Daly calls the *ultimate means* out of which all life and all economic transactions are built and sustained. This is *natural capital*, the matter of the planet, the sun's energy, the biogeochemical cycles, the ecosystems and the genetic information they bear, and the human being as an organism. These ultimate means are not created by us; they are the heritage we were born into and out of them we fashion everything we have or know. They are studied by the sciences and converted through technology to intermediate means.

The *intermediate means* are tools, machines, factories, skilled labour, processed material and energy – *built capital* and *human capital* and raw material. These intermediate means define the productive capacity of the economy. Economists call them inputs to the economy (systematically ignoring nature's unpriced inputs from the level below). Intermediate means are necessary but not sufficient to accomplish all higher purposes. Managing, valuing, distributing, maintaining and using these intermediate means is the concern of economics and politics, or the political economy.

The *intermediate ends* are the goals that governments promise and economies are expected to deliver – consumer goods, health, wealth, knowledge, leisure, communication, transportation – what economists call output. They are what everyone wants, but they by no means guarantee satisfaction, as is revealed by societies where intermediate ends are abundant but people still feel their lives are empty. That is because intermediate ends are not ends in themselves, but instruments to achieve something yet higher. The conversion of intermediate ends to ultimate ends depends on an effective ethic or religion or philosophy that can answer the question: what are health, wealth and education for?

At the top of the triangle is the ultimate end, desired for itself, not the means to the achievement of any other end. The definition or measurement of the ultimate end is fraught with difficulties, especially for people of Western cultures. Daly was vague about it: 'Our perception of the ultimate is always cloudy, but necessary none the less, for without a perception of the ultimate it would be impossible to order intermediate ends and to speak of priorities.'[7] He called the ultimate end the 'summum bonum', and insists, from his own monotheistic point of view, that it is singular, not plural.

I have added to the diagram some other words that people use to define the ultimate end of human economic activity and human life – happiness, harmony, fulfilment, self-respect, self-realization, community, identity, transcendence, enlightenment. The impossibility of defining these words, or agreeing on ultimate end or ends, demonstrates that we are discussing *quality*, not quantity, something immaterial, not material, though it requires the whole material triangle underneath to support it.

Now for the reservations. Several members of the Balaton Group have problems, not with the basic idea behind this triangle, but with its symbolism. It is too hierarchical and 'Western minded' for some; too anthropocentric for others; or too static; or there's too much vagueness about the top of the triangle, where objective physical stuff somehow gets transformed into subjective human satisfaction or arguable spirituality.

We all like the idea of the economy being borne up by and drawing from nature and the idea of the economy serving higher goals and not being an end in itself. We regard those two ideas as essential to the understanding of sustainable development. We tried redrawing the Daly diagram, turning it into concentric circles of 'nested dependencies', into a flower (see the title page of this report), even into a Möbius strip. We made it into a compass (a likely indicator to find on a cockpit instrument panel), with N=Nature, E=Economy, S=Society and W=Human Welfare. We got into snarls with the compass symbol too; some people interpreted it as saying that N is the best direction to go, or that if you go E, you can't simultaneously go W, etc, etc, etc. The compass, while preserving most of the content of the Daly triangle (except the ultimate end, which some people are glad to get out of the picture), loses the sequential, dependent relationships among the various levels.

The whole discussion, which became very emotional, taught us a lot about the humourlessness with which human beings take their symbols – a vital lesson for the design of indicators!

I don't insist on the triangle, though out of deference to Daly's original vision, I use it here. I certainly don't intend to convey by it the idea that the only purpose of nature is to fulfil human ends, an interpretation to which most Balaton members strongly object. (Rather, I see the triangle as saying there's no way human ends can be realized without healthy, functioning natural and economic and social systems. Others see no problem, because they assume that high human purposes must naturally include valuing nature in its own right, independent of its ability to supply human ends.) The logical relationship among the levels of the hierarchy is what's important to me, along with the challenge of orienting indicators towards the two things that ultimately count for me – the health of nature and real human well-being. I find the Daly pyramid the most intuitive of the many frameworks I have seen for organizing indicators, one that organizes the links among many aspects of sustainable development, and one which, as I will demonstrate here, lends itself naturally to dynamic modelling, pressure-state-response schemes, ecological footprints and various kinds of capital.

Sustainable development is a call to expand the economic calculus to include the top (development) and the bottom (sustainability) of the triangle. Industrial society has thousands of indicators from the middle of the pyramid, but few from the bottom and almost none from the top. That is probably why 'sustainable development' has become a global rallying cry. Obviously, the purpose of life is more than economic, and life is supported by more than that to which we can assign an economic price. Sustainable development asks us to pay attention to the bottom and the top of the pyramid, the health of nature and the well-being of people, one measured in physical terms, one measured in subjective terms; one the domain of science, the other the domain of philosophy and psychology. Seemingly incommensurable, essentially undefinable, sometimes apparently at odds with each other, the two concepts of sustainability and development clearly derive from the top and bottom of the pyramid and are linked through the intermediate steps.

Indicators can be derived from each level of the triangle separately (as I will illustrate), but the most important indicators will reflect the connections between one level and another.

The three most basic aggregate measures of sustainable development are the sufficiency with which ultimate ends are realized for all people, the efficiency with which ultimate means are translated into ultimate ends, and the sustainability of use of ultimate means. It is conceivable that health, education, happiness and harmony could increase, even if the mobilization of energy, materials, capital and labour decreased. That would obviously be a step in the direction of sustainable development. *In fact, it would be a primary goal of a sustainable society to produce the greatest possible ends with the least possible means.*

Sustainable development indicators could rise if, say, total electricity use goes down through more efficient technology that provides light or turns motors with less current. The indicators could rise if more comfortable and convenient mobility were provided with fewer cars (or, if unnecessary mobility were eliminated, by better spatial planning). They could rise if people learned to satisfy their non-material needs (such as self-esteem) through non-material means, instead of through heavily marketed material substitutes (such as clothes or cars).

To provide more ends with fewer means, the entire triangle, from technology through philosophy, must be balanced and integrated. If there is wisdom about ultimate ends but no technology for tapping ultimate means, the wisdom will rest on a foundation of physical scarcity. If there is technical proficiency supplying an abundance of intermediate means, but unjust politics and distorted economics, there will be plentiful capital, labour and energy, but poorly distributed health, education and wealth. Powerful technologies and an efficient, equitable economy may make a society rich in intermediate ends, but if that society is spiritually barren, its abundance will not bring fulfilment. If technologies are destructive of the ultimate means, the entire structure will crumble at its foundation, regardless of the excellence of its upper levels.

Integration of the triangle from bottom to top requires good science and just and efficient political and economic systems, and a culture that illuminates the higher purposes of life. The focus of such a society would be wholeness, not maximizing one part of the system at the expense of other parts. The goal of perpetual economic growth would be seen as nonsensical, partly because the finite material base cannot sustain it, partly because human fulfilment does not demand it. The focus would be on quality, not quantity, and yet quantity sufficient for the physical needs of all would not be lacking.

Therefore, the most basic indicators of sustainable development would be the sufficiency, efficiency, and sustainability of the entire triangle, determined by some kind of aggregate measures of:

- real human welfare;
- environmental integrity; and
- the ratio between the two, which is a measure of the efficiency with which environmental resources are translated into human welfare.

It's easy enough to say 'some kind of aggregate measures of human welfare and environmental integrity', but not at all easy to produce these measures. The rest of this document is an attempt to begin to think through how to do it. I invite others to join in the thinking.

In order to develop these aggregate indicators, we need an information system for each step in the triangle. Those information systems depend upon the notion of several kinds of capital. Extending the definition of capital to natural, human and social capital could provide an easily understood base for calculating and integrating the Daly triangle.

To a bank or a university or a business or an endowed charitable foundation, 'development' means increasing your stock of wealth and 'sustainability' means living on the income from that wealth, not eating into principle. No accountant would credit as 'income' a temporary burst of money that comes from the drawing down of capital faster than it is replenished.

That idea extends easily to 'natural capital'. We should draw water from the out-flow of a lake, not drain down the lake; catch fish at the rate at which they regenerate, not consume the breeding population; harvest forests no faster than they can grow back; farm so the soil doesn't erode.

Herman Daly captured the concept of natural capital in the three basic 'Daly Rules' for sustainability:[8]

- Renewable resources (fish, forests, soils, ground waters) must be used no faster than the rate at which they regenerate;
- Non-renewable resources (mineral ores, fossil fuels, fossil ground waters) must be used no faster than renewable substitutes for them can be put into place;
- Pollution and wastes must be emitted no faster than natural systems can absorb them, recycle them, or render them harmless.

These three rules suggest sustainability indicators for each resource that flows through the human economy. More on that in the next section.

The World Bank is now trying not only to establish natural capital accounts, but also to extend the concept to human and social capital.[9] Surely there is a stock or endowment of health, skills and knowledge that can be invested in, enhanced, and used to produce a steady stream of productivity, or that can be overused, eroded, allowed to depreciate. Surely there must be social capital in the form of functioning civic organizations, cultures of personal and community responsibility, efficient markets and governments, tolerance and public trust.

The Balaton working group agreed unanimously that the idea of capital – all forms of capital – is central to information systems for sustainable development. Combined with the Daly triangle, various capital structures can capture development and sustainability and their relation to each other. They allow the stock-flow analysis that can make indicators dynamic. And they begin to suggest a conceptual framework to keep track of the linkages among many forms of capital and to derive indicators that could help people and nations build up the several kinds of wealth that are necessary for a people-enriching, nature-preserving system.

NATURAL CAPITAL (ULTIMATE MEANS)

It would be a real achievement if ... capital assets, natural assets, and environmental assets were equally 'real' and subject to the same scale of values, indeed the same bookkeeping conventions. Deeper ways of thinking might be affected. *Robert Solow*

Natural capital consists of the stocks and flows in nature from which the human economy takes its materials and energy (sources) and to which we throw those materials and energy when we are done with them (sinks). The materials and energy used in the human economy do not appear from nowhere. Nor, when we are done with them, do they disappear. They are taken from and return to the Earth's biogeochemical systems (see Figure 17.2).

To borrow some useful but unbeautiful terms from engineering, we can call the flows of material and energy from nature into the economy inputs, the flows of wastes back to nature outputs, and the combined flows throughputs. Then the capital/income idea can be stated clearly. Throughput is the income derived from a natural capital stock. A throughput stream of lumber and paper and wood fuel comes from the natural capital of a forest. Ground water is pumped up from the natural capital

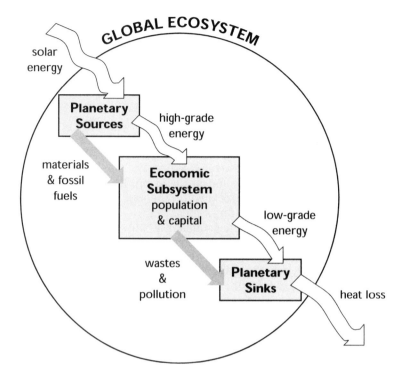

Figure 17.2 *Flows of materials and energy through the global ecosystem*

in the aquifer. A stream of food can be obtained from the natural capital of the nutrients in the soil. On the sink side, an output flow of sewage can be released to the natural capital of organisms that break the sewage back down to nutrients. The carbon dioxide from burning fossil fuels can be removed from the atmosphere by the natural capital of green plants photosynthesizing.

Notice that forests are source capital for the input of wood products and sink capital for the output of carbon dioxide. Many forms of natural capital play both source and sink roles. Aquifers provide drinking water but also may be sinks for leached pesticides or leaked petroleum. Soil provides nutrients for growing crops and receives deposits of heavy metals from the atmosphere. The connections among the elements of natural capital – the oneness of the global system – is a major cause of sustainability problems and a major reason why indicators (and formal models of our complex natural support systems) are so badly needed.

The human economy uses many kinds of throughput streams, each associated with natural capital on both the source and sink end of the flow. Think of the throughput flows summoned continuously and in great volume by any city or nation. Water and many kinds of food. Oil, coal, natural gas and other fuels. Construction lumber, plywood, cardboard, paper. Steel, copper, aluminum, and a host of other metals. Rubber, plastics, glass, cement. Tens of thousands of kinds of chemicals.[10]

All these substances flow in from nature and flow out after use, usually in haphazard mixes, into air, water, soils. To keep track of these many throughput flows is a large but not impossible task, no worse in principle than keeping track of the money flows through all industrial sectors that make up the GDP. Input-output tables are easily adapted to the task. Material and energy-flow tables, combined with money-flow tables, should and could be an essential part of national accounting.[11]

Material and energy flows through the economy are at least theoretically measurable, even though they are not yet always measured. It is more difficult to keep track of the natural capital stocks that are the sources and sinks of the flows – difficult because for some we haven't done it before, for others the people who do the measuring (foresters, soil scientists, atmospheric chemists) are not in regular contact with national accountants, and for some (ocean fish, soil bacteria, oil under the ground) accurate measurement is very difficult to do.

Nevertheless, we could compile and organize many kinds of natural capital measures and relate them to their associated throughput flows. That would form the basis for a natural capital accounting system.

Natural capital is being used unsustainably if sources are declining or sinks are increasing. The indicators of the sustainability of use of most forms of natural capital are obvious; they are the directions and rates of change of sources and sinks. As previously discussed, they could be expressed dynamically as the ratio between use rate and restoration rate (with 1.0 standing for sustainability) or as the amount of time until the resource can no longer be a source or sink.

If a forest is cut faster than it grows, the throughput stream of products from the forest will not be sustained. Natural capital is being spent, reducing future productivity. Whatever the indicator, the value of the excess harvest should be counted not as income but as depletion of capital.[12]

If ground water is pumped down to irrigate farmland and there is no investment in an alternative water source to keep that land in production after the ground water is gone, that is drawdown of capital.

On the sink side, if an output stream builds up wastes that are not recycled or rendered harmless, then that practice cannot be sustained without serious repercussions somewhere. An indicator can signal how far above a sustainable absorption rate the output is, or how long it will be until an unacceptable level of waste accumulates. The value of the throughput stream creating the waste ought to be discounted either by the eventual cost of dealing with the pollution or by the actual damage that pollution is causing to built capital, human capital (such as health), or some other form of natural capital.

Indicators can signal unsustainability long before a resource 'runs out' or a sink overflows, even if natural capital cannot be measured directly. It's hard to measure ocean fish populations, for example, but a leading indicator of their decline is decreasing catch per fishing effort (per boat, per hour of trawling, per dollar of operating or investment cost, per gallon of fuel burned). We do not know the exact size of undiscovered petroleum reserves, but a drop in yield per discovery effort is a leading indicator of a depleting resource.

'Daly rule' indicators such as these are simple, leading sustainability measures easily understood and readily measured for many throughput streams. They should be implemented wherever possible. However, it is important to note that the 'Daly rules' are static, and they are stated with regard to quantitative flows of separate throughput streams. They may not capture either qualitative degradation nor interactions between one form of natural capital and another, nor do they necessarily reveal the seriousness of unsustainability through 'time to exhaustion' or 'time to unacceptable threshold'. Indicators that reveal these important factors will require integrated dynamic models.

Indicators should highlight limiting natural capital stocks. If nitrogen is lacking in the soil, it doesn't help that there is plenty of phosphate. If chromium is lacking to make stainless steel, it doesn't matter that there's an excess of iron. If the output from burning coal stresses an atmospheric sink, it is of little comfort to know that on the source side coal is abundant. Like all complex systems, the physical economy depends not on its most abundant throughputs, but on its most limiting. The limits can come from either the source or the sink side of the flow.

Ideally a complete information system would keep track of all forms of natural capital and their throughputs, but cockpit indicators would emphasize the most limiting factors. (Like lights on an instrument panel, you only need to pay attention to the ones blinking red.) The warning lights must blink far enough in advance to allow preventive action and must illustrate interconnections, so the preventive action will not simply throw the load on to another natural capital stock, which would then become limiting. Again, this is a research agenda and a task for dynamic modelling.

Natural capital should be monitored at whatever geographic level makes sense. The stock of nutrients in soil is measured most meaningfully at the field or farm level. It can be aggregated to the national level as the percentage of agricultural land that is losing nutrients faster than they are replaced.

The stock of greenhouse gases in the atmosphere makes sense only at the global level. At the national level one can keep track of the national contribution to the global imbalance in that stock.

The appropriate geographic level for measurement is obvious for most resources. More tricky is the question of imported resources. It should be a concern at the national level to know the sustainability of whatever natural capital outside the country supplies a critical stream of resources to the country. This could be done by calculating a national ecological footprint.

The ecological footprint, invented by William Rees of the University of British Columbia, measures a person's, city's, industry's or nation's environmental impact by the amount of land (anywhere on earth) that entity requires for its maintenance.[13] For example, Rees calculates that the city of Vancouver, through its food, water, energy and waste-disposal demands, actually occupies an area of land (an ecological footprint) fourteen times the area of the city.

The use of land as a numeraire, rather than money or energy, makes the footprint easy to understand and also permits provocative calculations. For example, Rees calculates that if all people on earth had the same footprint as the average American (5 hectares), we would need three Earths to supply everyone! He calculates a 'fair earthshare' (total productive land area divided by world population) of 1.5 hectares, a number that goes down as the population grows. He points out that the average footprint of a citizen of India is just 0.5 hectares, but because there are 910 million Indians, the total footprint of India is 35 per cent greater than the actual area of India.

The ecological footprint captures many useful ideas within one number, and it has a strong intuitive and metaphorical appeal. It is an excellent summary indicator of sustainable development, with the following caveats. There needs to be a considered scientific review to codify its calculation. (Rees' method is rough and ready, fairly easy to implement, but oversimplified.) As Rees himself points out, it should have a marine resources equivalent. And it needs to be made dynamic, so it reflects not only present footprints, but implications for future ones.

We need to allow estimates in our indicators for life support systems that we do not yet understand. Most of us didn't understand the life-sheltering function of the stratospheric ozone layer until scientists noticed that that layer was eroding. Whole communities of poorly understood soil microbes serve as fertilizer-generating factories in healthy organic soils.

The unpriced value of nature's direct services to the human economy (through pollination, flood control, drought protection, pest control, waste recycling, species protection, nutrient regeneration, soil formation and a dozen other critical functions) has been conservatively estimated at $33 trillion per year (as compared with the economic system's output of $18 trillion per year).[14]

We only dimly understand the intricately woven web of geophysical processes and life forms that make up Planet Earth and support our endeavours. Therefore we should create at least one indicator to measure the amount of nature we have left untouched, an 'insurance factor' for the knowledge we don't yet have about the forms of natural capital we don't know enough to value.

BUILT CAPITAL (INTERMEDIATE MEANS)

Built capital is human-built, long-lasting physical capacity – factories, tools, machines – that produces economic output. We have come to think of money capital as interest-bearing – able to produce a steady stream of income without itself being depleted – because there is a form of real capital that can behave that way. It is 'built capital' – the human-made tools, machines, factories, smelters, electric generators, pumps, trucks that create output without themselves being consumed (or at least that create output while themselves depreciating only slowly).

Built capital is the physical stock of productive capacity of an economy. It is steel mills, cement plants, car factories, construction equipment, lathes, tractors, buildings, oil wells, chainsaws, power plants, the most solid measures of economic development. Built capital is increased by investment (usually after a construction delay). It is decreased by depreciation or obsolescence (which can be postponed by maintenance and retrofitting).

Built capital usually lasts for decades, providing both stability and inflexibility to the economy. Built capital has an age structure just as population does. New steel mills age into old steel mills that may be technically obsolete long before they actually wear out.

One simple development indicator is built capital per person. An efficiency indicator would measure the amount of built capital (and throughput) necessary to meet final demand for intermediate ends – the lower the number, the more efficient the capital. Capital lifetime is another good indicator – the longer the lifetime, the more value over time each piece of capital supplies (assuming no technical obsolescence).

The nature and amount of built capital determines the standing demand for human capital (labour and skills) and for throughput from natural capital (materials and energy). That fraction of built capital that produces more built capital (investment) determines the rate of economic growth.

Built capital sits on the second level of the Daly pyramid; it is intermediate means. It is a key element in integrating the pyramid because a piece of built capital

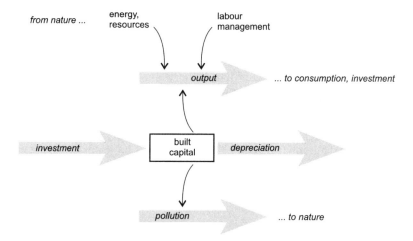

Figure 17.3 *From nature to consumption, investment ... to nature*

– a furnace, say, or a paper mill, or an irrigation system – requires a specific stream of throughput from natural capital (materials, energy, water) in order to function. It releases a specific stream of waste and pollution. It requires particular types of labour and management (human capital). As long as it is running to capacity, it produces a known stream of output, which is either consumption (on the next level of the Daly pyramid, intermediate ends) or investment (some other form of capital).

Built capital is usually measured in money terms – the accumulated amount invested in it, or the amount it would take to replace it at current prices. There are problems with this way of measuring, primarily because money is an insufficient proxy for something that is actually concrete, that comes in many different forms and capacities, that does not inflate but does wear out physically, that does not physically change even if prices change. For the moment we probably must construct indicators of built capital in money terms, but in a more elaborate information system for sustainable development, we may want to specify them in terms of output capacity (megawatts, tons of steel per year, cars per year) and input requirements (fuel, labour, material per year).

Sustainability on the level of built capital means investing at least as fast as capital depreciates. Across levels it means keeping the throughput needs of built capital appropriate to the sustainable yields and absorptive capacities of natural capital and keeping labour and management needs appropriate to the sustainable use of human capital.

To sustain built capital, investment must replace depreciation (in actual productive capacity, not in money terms). Capital grows if investment is faster than depreciation. The self-generating growth of built capital (it takes capital to produce more capital; the more capital you have, the more new capital you can build) is one of the sensitive positive feedback loops that provides a central indicator of both sustainability and development.

Development indicator: real investment (measured in concrete productive capacity) divided by real depreciation (measured in physical terms). If greater than 1, productive capacity is growing. If equal to 1, productive capacity is just being maintained. If less than 1, the built capital stock of the economy is not being sustained.

Note: such an indicator is common in money terms, but doing it in physical terms would reveal new information – for example, it would signal the erosion of capital through deferred maintenance much faster than money accounts can do.

Sustainability indicator: throughput need of built capital divided by sustainable yield from natural capital. If greater than 1, the economy has built itself beyond the capacity of the resource base to supply it.

Sustainability and development indicator: labour and management need of built capital divided by labour and management capacities of human capital (which will be discussed in the next section). Greater than 1 indicates insufficient human capacity to run and maintain the capital plant. Less than 1 indicates human resources going unused. (An information system that tracks built capital could also track jobs and employment relatively easily.)

There are many categories of built capital. A useful indicator would reflect the proper balance among categories to permit the most productive use of all forms of capital. Built capital accounts could be kept for every industrial sector, every city, every company. In some countries, they are already measured on all those levels, because on each level there are decision-makers who need to monitor capital accounts. (The job is not only similar to keeping accounts for GDP, or national input-output tables, it naturally complements those accounts.)

For indicators of sustainable development at the national level, a few categories of built capital can be aggregated according to their large-scale system function:

- *Industrial capital* is capital that can build more capital – the steel mills that make steel for more steel mills, the machine tools that make machine tools. This is the fraction of built capital that provides real physical investment, the engine of economic growth.
- *Household capital* consists of homes, cars, refrigerators, home computers, durable goods owned by families. It is a supporter or enhancer of human capital and a better measure of material well-being than income.
- *Service capital* is hospitals, schools, government buildings, banks – capital that provides services, some of which enhance the functioning of other kinds of capital, some of which enhance human and social capital.
- *Consumer goods capital* produces non-durable consumer products (food, paper, clothing), another measure of material well-being.
- *Public infrastructure* is roads, bridges, ports, water lines and other public investments that serve the whole economy.
- *Resource-obtaining capital* consists of mines, oil wells and other built equipment that extracts throughput from natural capital.
- *Pollution-abating capital,* such as sewage treatment plants, trash incinerators or stack scrubbers, ameliorate damage when throughput is released back to nature.
- *Military capital* maintains the security of natural capital, economy and society.

The last three types of capital are not directly productive; they are costs of supplying or keeping safe other kinds of capital. An efficient society will be structured to need as little of them as possible. So a useful indicator would be the ratio of the last three protective kinds of capital to the first five productive kinds of capital. (But if, for example, necessary pollution-abating capital is not built, some other form of capital, probably natural or human capital, will be degraded. A proper capital accounting system should assess those costs.)

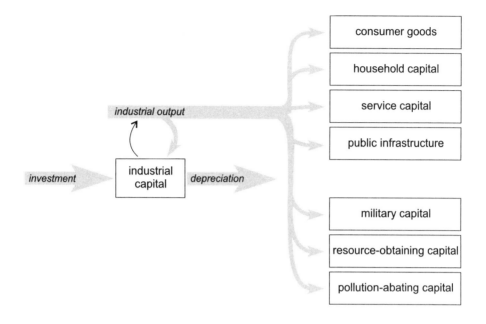

Figure 17.4 *Built capital*

For some kinds of capital, national accounts would need to distinguish that which is used for 1) domestic production, 2) export production, and 3) import production ('virtual capital' in other countries). The first two of these generate in-country jobs, pressure on natural capital and pollution. The first and third generate in-country consumption.

Another important indicator would be the balance among various kinds of capital. There are countries, for example, with roads so bad that vehicles get shaken apart by potholes. This is unnecessary depreciation of household capital because of an underinvestment in public infrastructure capital. In other countries, underinvestment in energy production (resource-obtaining capital) occasionally shuts down industrial or household capital. There are places where insufficient service capital hampers the functioning of all other forms of capital because of an unskilled or unhealthy labour force.

Therefore, an indicator should measure the balance among the kinds of capital (what fraction of total capital is represented by each), to reflect the extent to which they enhance rather than undermine each other's productivity. Ideally, lights should start to blink on the social instrument panel when over- or underinvestment in one kind of capital degrades the effectiveness of another kind of capital. (It is widely believed that the free market automatically takes care of such capital imbalances, but the widespread existence of capital imbalances illustrates that delays and imperfections keep the actual market a long way from fulfilling theoretical expectations.)

HUMAN CAPITAL (INTERMEDIATE MEANS/ENDS)

> Development does not start with goods; it starts with people and their education, organisation, and discipline. Without these three, all resources remain latent, untapped, potential... We have had plenty of opportunity to observe the primacy of the[se] invisible factors after the war. Every country, no matter how devastated, which had a high level of education, organization, and discipline, produced an 'economic miracle.' *E F Schumacher*[15]

Human and social capital are difficult to define; indeed, it is a significant question whether 'capital' is the right conceptual framework for them. Neither human nor social capital can be adequately denominated in terms of materials, energy or money. Furthermore, drawing a line between the 'human' and the 'social' is dependent on worldview. What is seen in some cultures as human capital (because it is carried within the minds and bodies of individuals) is seen by others as social capital, because the individual is only given identity and purpose by the group.

However, given those caveats, it is possible and useful to talk about and create indicators for human and social capital, both of which can accumulate over time, can be invested in, can depreciate and must be essential factors in sustainable development.

The base of human capital is the population, including its age and gender structure. Demographic models, derived from fairly accurate censuses in most countries, are already available. Populations are countable stocks, increased by births and in-migrations, decreased by deaths and out-migrations. Each person in the population carries with him or her a set of attributes, the most obvious of which – age and sex – are already reported in the census.

Because of the long lifetimes of most people, populations change only slowly, with great momentum. Much about their future is predictable from their age structures – this year's 5-year-olds will be (minus migration and mortality) the 20-year-olds of 15 years from now and the 65-year-olds of 60 years from now. Demographic modelling can spin out the future implications of today's population events.

Modelling can also calculate the future consequences of a crucial exponential growth indicator: net population growth rate.[16]

Along with numbers, ages and genders, human capital can be measured by attributes such as health and education. Demographic databases can also include information about attributes imbued within the minds and bodies of people – most obviously their levels of education and health. Investment (especially in service and human capital) can build up those attributes. Neglect can allow them to depreciate. Investment in human capital can also be seen as a positive feedback loop – the more education in a population, the more educated parents and teachers build that education level still further.

I will define attributes that inhere not to individuals but to groups as social capital and discuss them in a moment.

Human capital is in one sense an intermediate means, in another sense an intermediate end. Seen as a labour force, human capital is an intermediate means, a factor of production, which interacts with built capital and throughput from natural capital to produce economic output. As the health and education of a population increase, other forms of capital can be more productive. Human capital, if we had a way of accounting for it in money terms, might prove to be at various stages of development the most lucrative possible investment on pure grounds of economic return. (That becomes again a matter of balancing the various types of capital so they do not hold each other back.)

Human capital is also, however, an intermediate end. Education and health (and other individual attributes) have purposes beyond making a person more productive in the economy. They also serve the top of the triangle – the ability to lead a joyful, fulfilling life. If we could measure the degree to which human capital serves ultimate goals, investment in it might look like an even better deal. Relative to built capital, human capital probably delivers more well-being from less money, less built capital, and less material and energy throughput than any other investment (with the possible exception of social capital).

Population with its attributes, like built capital, is an indicator of the necessary throughputs and potential outputs of a society. Human capital relates to the top of the triangle through well-being. It relates to the bottom of the triangle through the flows of material and energy necessary to maintain a person. It relates to the middle of the triangle through the flows of economic output that a person (with the aid of built capital) is capable of producing and consuming.

Thus, human capital, like built capital, can be seen as a standing demand for material and energy throughput. Different people with different attributes and in different cultures require very different throughputs. (They have very different Ecological Footprints.) They are capable of producing very different outputs. (They have different labour productivities.)

In order to avoid double counting, we need to distinguish the throughput needs and output potential attributable to human capital and to built capital. Economists have been trying to untangle this knot for years. It might be clearer not to try to

Table 17.1 *Women's and men's use of time in India (per cent of total hours)*

	Forest tribe	Hill tribe	Landless rural	Landed rural	Urban 'slum'	Middle class
Women						
Sleep	40	33	34	50	34	39
Survival	12	27	17	13	17	11
Reproductive work	12	17	13	8	14	10
Wage work	13	10	26	–	19	17
Learning	2	3	2	8	4	7
Recreation	17	5	5	8	8	11
Religion	4	4	3	13	4	5
Men						
Sleep	43	49	47	48	47	48
Survival	9	6	6	2	3	2
Reproductive work	6	2	2	1	2	1
Wage work	19	22	30	26	28	26
Learning	5	4	3	6	6	8
Recreation	15	14	10	13	11	13
Religion	4	4	2	4	4	3
Life expectancy (years)	45	60	60	60	60	75

Source: Aromar Revi, TARU, New Delhi, personal communication

make a clean separation of what is actually a systematic partnership. Throughputs and outputs might best be specified for the human-and-built-capital system as a whole.

The universal resource available to all human beings, and the currency of most value to them, is time. Time accounting may be key to human capital accounting. In Table 17.1 is an example from India of the kinds of information revealed by data systems built upon time. Notice the strong differences between women and men, and between landless and landed women.

We each have an equal endowment of 24 hours a day. Much of real economics has to do with commandeering the time endowments of some people to serve other people's intermediate or ultimate ends. We had the feeling in the workshop that time budgets could be even more revealing than money budgets, especially as we begin to relate to the top of the triangle. We're not sure yet how to integrate them, but clearly another attribute that could be correlated with each person in a human capital stock would be the allocation of that person's time.

Human time can be sorted into many possible categories, such as:

- *Survival tasks:* eating, sleeping, preparing food, gathering fuel, etc.
- *Learning:* acquiring the skills necessary to survive and to exchange in the time economy.
- *Wage work:* time exchanged in the market for compensation.
- *Child rearing:* time invested in the next generation of human capital.
- *Leisure:* time spent on psychological maintenance, spiritual development, building and maintaining relationships, entertainment, sports, etc. Viewed in some cultures as time of little value; viewed in others as time invested in health, productivity and realization of the top of the triangle.
- *Community time:* time devoted to the needs of others, to community functions, volunteer groups, neighbourhood duties, discussion and co-ordination of work in groups.

A key indicator is how much healthy time is available to people (subtracting time spent sick, immobile or aged to the point of feebleness).[17] A second would be how that healthy time is distributed among different genders, ages and social classes or income groups. Time spent on survival tasks, indexed for equity, is essentially a proxy for depreciation rates of human capital.

A set of indicators based on 'time' could be a fruitful topic for research, for indicators of sustainable use of human capital and indicators of sustainable development. Some of us think the prime characteristic of a sustainable society would be that life would slo-o-o-w down so there would not be a perpetual sense of scarcity about time. But we didn't have time in our hectic five-day workshop to develop this idea!

SOCIAL CAPITAL (INTERMEDIATE ENDS)

Equally important is the social side, and here we mean equity, social mobility, social cohesion, participation, empowerment, cultural identity, and institutional development... It is, to my mind, an essential part of the definition of sustainability, because, let me remind you, the neglect of that side leads to institutions that are incapable of responding to the needs of society. We see the consequences of that in tragedies from Somalia to Rwanda and from Liberia to Bosnia. *Ismail Serageldin*

Social capital is a stock of attributes (knowledge, trust, efficiency, honesty) that inheres not to a single individual, but to the human collectivity. When you start thinking about social capital, you begin seeing it around you. Knowledge is clearly an accumulated stock which grows through inflows of research, experiment, new understanding and is drained by outflows of forgetting. Parliamentary rules and other social behaviours that allow large groups to have fair and purposeful discussions are learned painstakingly over time and must be maintained against depreciation. The ability of a household to clean itself, of a community to police itself, of businesses to make and enforce contracts, of citizens to propose, debate, pass and obey laws – all these could be considered social capital. They can be invested in. They depreciate. They don't change quickly. They bear the history of all past investments and depreciations.

We could think of public trust as a stock of capital, decreased by telling lies and increased by telling the truth. (Perhaps each lie or truth should be weighed by the number of people who hear it. That way each of us every day builds or depreciates the public trust, but public figures who speak to millions can build or erode the public trust far more quickly than can ordinary citizens.)

Tolerance of ethnic, religious or other diversity might be a social capital stock, built up by actions and words that demonstrate good will, torn down by actions and words that express hatred.

- Efficient, well-regulated markets.
- Technology and the ability to evolve new technology.
- Orderliness, reliability, creativity, culture.
- The ability to treasure what is valuable in the old and to seize what is useful in the new.
- Museums, folksongs, jokes, city parks, sports teams, scouts.

All these things must have something to do with social capital. Adaptability, resilience, the capacity to learn and reorganize, repair damage or change direction, maintain a steady course, muster resources for major efforts – all of these are dependent on having an adequate 'stock' of social 'capital'.

Indicator selection for social capital is difficult indeed. Suggested social capital indicators often measure depletion or malfunction – crime, for example. Crime is surely an indicator of decline in social capital, driven by inadequate investment in other kinds of capital.

Social capital is terrifically varied, incredibly hard to measure, but most of us not only acknowledge its existence but can sense its presence or absence. 'You can feel it when you walk down the street,' one member of our workshop said. It is based in the integrity and efficiency of institutions, information systems and human relationships.

Just as time is a key currency for human capital, information may be a key currency for social capital. Social capital is generally understood in terms of 'cohesion', but its primary component is information. More accurately, social capital is embodied in dense, meaningful and truthful information flows.

Indicators of social capital would be especially useful if they could discriminate not only quantity of information (which can be measured by stocks and flows of megabytes), but quality of information – the difference between data, information, knowledge and wisdom. Data are bits of information which can rapidly become distracting, overwhelming, stupefying or a management nuisance (as is currently the case with most of the Worldwide Web). Information is data sorted and selected to 'make a difference' to some system or some decision. Knowledge is understanding of the way information streams are organized and accessed. Wisdom is the capacity to utilize knowledge in decision-making, to integrate knowledge and information with new experience, to see the system whole, to grasp the necessity and yet the uncertainty of models, to move between and within levels in a model, to be able to distinguish between the system itself and models of the system, and to make adjustments to models as necessary.

Trust, relational capacity and the efficacy of a society's institutions all depend on the quality of information flows within a society. It is a central tenet of systems theory that a system cannot be managed without adequate flows of information.

Another possible measure of social capital would be density or frequency or intensity of human relationships. How often do you see your relatives and for what length of time? Does that measure the stability, resilience, functionality of your family? How many neighbours do you know by name, talk to often, understand something about their lives? Does that give an idea of the social integrity of your neighbourhood? Do you have a face-to-face human relationship with your employer or employees? With the makers and suppliers of the things you buy? With the people who teach your children, who heal your body, to whom you grant the power of governance? Is social capital enhanced or decreased as institutions become bigger and more powerful but human relationships become more distant and abstract?

Decentralized, relatively immobile societies such as traditional villages have a high density and frequency of face-to-face interactions, which builds up a palpable, functional social capital. A society based on long-term personal relationships needs few, if any, contracts, papers, lawyers, rules, courts, judges. It's probably the absence of such relationship-based interactions in our lives that makes us romanticize such a decentralized system – and it does have real advantages.

On the other hand, a decentralized society can suffer from insularity, inbreeding, narrowness of ideas and viewpoints, suspiciousness of innovation, suppression of deviance. Perhaps a 'cosmopolitan-ness' index could counterbalance the human relationship index, to measure the breadth of a society's information contacts and idea-base.

Then comes the question, is it possible to devise a society that could score high on both indices?

The 'forbidden numeraire', whose stocks, flows and distribution could lend itself to indicators, is power. I have no idea how to measure power. I don't think many of us do. I suspect that is not so much because it is unmeasurable as because it is not politically acceptable to raise the topic (especially among those who have accumulated large quantities of power). All the more reason to try to measure it. Clearly, power has to do with the ability to force people to do things they would not independently choose to do. (It may be inversely related to freedom, creativity, social resilience and evolutionary potential.)

Here are some ideas for measures of power:

- number and strength of weapons and distribution among the population;
- ratio of number of employers to number of employees;
- income distribution, particularly the ratio of extremely rich to extremely poor;
- concentration of ownership of the media (public and private);
- political prisoners as per cent of the population;
- per cent of GDP earned by the 10 or 50 largest corporations.

Social capital can be a high-leverage transformative factor in the process of channelling ultimate means into ultimate ends.

> If the world's population had the productivity of the Swiss, the consumption habits of the Chinese, the egalitarian instincts of the Swedes, and the social discipline of the Japanese, then the planet could support many times its current population without privation for anyone. On the other hand, if the world's population had the productivity of Chad, the consumption habits of the United States, the inegalitarian instincts of India, and the social discipline of Argentina, then the planet could not support anywhere near its current numbers. *Lester Thurow*[18]

If a society has a low crime rate, a history of common endeavour, and habits of timeliness and cleanliness, then it probably can organize a pleasant, efficient, mass-transportation system that gives its citizens high mobility with minimal cost in household capital (cars) and natural capital (steel, glass, rubber, fossil fuels, concrete, air pollution). High mobility can be obtained at low cost because of the high level of social capital.

If a culture allows men to feel manly without having to be surrounded by tons of polished steel propelled at high speeds, that culture could allow the realization of an important ultimate end with great savings of all kinds of ultimate and intermediate means.

It is well established for most of the industrialized nations that efficiency in the design of built capital can produce the same amounts of economic output with half as much, or even one-tenth as much, energy.[19] It could be true that efficiency in the design of social capital could produce equivalent well-being with one-hundredth or one-thousandth as much energy, materials and built capital. This possibility gives hope that truly sustainable means of meeting the highest and most important ends could be attained for all people on Earth. Somewhere within the concept of social capital, combined with clever technical design of built capital and loving development of human capital, is the capacity to meet material needs materially and non-material needs non-materially with great efficiency in the use of ultimate means.

Rough indicators of social capital are better than nothing. It is tempting to refuse to deal with anything so messy (and politically touchy) as social capital. It's all too easy for experts in science or economics who like to deal in clean concepts and precise numbers, to shift the topic quickly to prices or kilojoules or numbers of species.

While we didn't make enormous headway on social capital in our own workshop, we recommend that this topic become a major area of discussion, involving many kinds of people.

We believe it is possible and vitally important to find ways to measure social capital, even if those ways are subjective (remember, all indicators are subjective). It is important partly because social capital can be such a powerful mediator in the translation of ultimate means to ultimate ends, and partly because without any measure of social capital, many purported 'development' plans may eat into this kind of capital without counting the cost. (Dams that flood out long-standing communities, employment patterns that break up families, mass-information systems that swamp local cultures.)

Participatory indicator selection processes can be especially creative in coming up with indicators of social capital. Even if they can only produce agreement about the general direction of change (pedestrian streets in cities increase social capital, freeways decrease it; many small, local-based retail stores increase social capital, one or two large 'chain' distributors decrease it), the exercise is worth doing.

Box 17.1 *Examples of social capital indicators from community indicator projects*

Sustainable Seattle's participants were determined to measure 'neighbourliness' some-how. They invented a telephone survey to ask: How do you define 'neighbour?' How many neighbours would you say you have? How many of them do you know by name? What kinds of interactions do you have with them? The answers revealed strong differences by neighbourhood and by income class, and suggested that the city was not actually very neighbourly.[20]

Among draft indicators in the 'social' dimension for the US Interagency Working Group on Sustainable Development Indicators are:[21]

- per cent of children living in one-parent families;
- per cent contributing time or money to charities;
- crime rate;
- participation in the arts and recreation;
- number in census tracts with over 40 per cent poverty.

The World Bank provides a long list of possible indicators of social capital, among them:[22]

- index of democracy;
- index of corruption;
- independence of court system;
- contract enforceability;
- strikes, riots, protests;
- prisoners per 100,000 people;
- extent of trust in government, trade unions;
- small credit availability;
- index of political and/or economic discrimination;
- index of civil liberties;
- voter turnout.

Social capital is, essentially, a 'shared wisdom index'. Defining it requires a significant amount of wisdom!

WELL-BEING (ULTIMATE END)

It [the GNP] does not include the beauty of our poetry or the strength of our marriages, the intelligence of our public debate or the integrity of our public officials. It allows neither for the justice in our courts, nor the justness in our dealings with one another. The Gross National Product measures neither our wit nor our courage, neither our wisdom nor our learning, neither our compassion nor our devotion to country. It measures everything, in short, except that which makes life worthwhile. *Robert Kennedy*

If social capital was hard, how are we ever going to define ultimate human fulfil-ment? Not by going around doing shallow polls that ask, simply, 'Are you happy?' (Think what answers might come forth if we asked, 'Does your life allow you to contribute all you have to give to society? If you had complete control of your own time, would you spend it the way you do now? Do you see a purpose to your life and are you able to achieve that purpose? Are you lonely? Are you loved? Is there beauty in your life? Joy? Transcendence? If you knew you would die tomorrow, would you be satisfied?'.)

The question of ultimate ends, happiness, well-being has been a topic of discussion for thousands of years. That discussion has not produced nothing. Through many different cultures and historical periods it has produced some strikingly constant insights, one of which is that 'man does not live by bread alone'. Well-being requires a basic amount of material throughput to sustain life, but after that point, more wealth is only loosely associated, if at all, with more happiness.

So how to measure the most qualitative, personal, culture-bound, subjective and important part of the pyramid? We're not sure. We suspect that it should be a participatory, not an expert-dominated activity. We do know that, however uncomfortable or difficult the topic, discussing the top of the pyramid is the most important task on the road to sustainable development.

The most important indicator, without which the others make no sense, is an indicator of ultimate ends. If we can't define what our ultimate ends are, how can we know whether we are approaching them, or with what efficiency, or even whether we're going the right direction? The qualitativeness, subjectiveness, elusiveness and culture-specificity of the ultimate ends does not for a moment diminish their importance. If the system orients itself around indicators that do not reflect real well-being, then it will produce whatever those indicators do measure (money flow, size of the economy, personal material possessions) rather than real well-being.

We need to press courageously to discuss well-being and define indicators that reflect it, even if we suspect that this process will shake up our worldviews and challenge our power structures and our lives. If those power structures and lives are in fact creating well-being, then they won't be challenged. If they are not, then they should be shaken.

Indicators of ultimate ends may not be numerical or precise, but they are findable and usable. The literature on human happiness/fulfilment/purpose/satisfaction/quality of life is far too extensive to review in this short paper. I will quote here only one scheme by which indicators could be derived, more to illustrate that such schemes are possible than to defend this particular one as best – though I personally find it thought-provoking and as good a basis for building 'quality of life' indicators as any other I know.

Manfred Max-Neef, after many cross-cultural studies, has come up with a list of nine universal 'basic human needs'.[23] Only the first of them – subsistence – is clearly material. The others may have material underpinnings, but they are essentially qualitative:

- subsistence;
- protection (security);
- affection;
- understanding;
- participation;
- idleness (leisure, rest);
- creation;
- identity;
- freedom.

Max-Neef insists that these needs are not hierarchical or substitutable. All are necessary; none is more important than the others. One can't compensate for a deficiency in one by an excess in another – for lack of affection, say, by an increase in protection, or for a loss of freedom by an improvement in material subsistence.

Cultures differ, says Max-Neef, not in these needs, which are essentially human, but in their satisfiers, their specific ways of satisfying the needs. Participation may be realized in some societies by democratic voting, in others by long discussion, in others by a formal process of consensus. Identity could be established by particular kinds of decoration or clothes, by possessions such as cars or houses, by celebrity in the mass media, by local nicknames or affectionate jokes or a small community knowing and respecting one's unique set of strengths and weaknesses. Some satisfiers can meet multiple needs. (Max-Neef cites breast-feeding which serves subsistence and affection, or barefoot-doctor programmes which serve subsistence, participation, understanding and identity.) Some pseudo-satisfiers can appear to meet needs but actually fail to meet them or even undermine them. (Expensive brand-name sneakers may purport to establish identity or freedom, but actually make their wearers look alike and manipulate them for the benefit of corporations that make and market the sneakers.)

Satisfiers are the equivalent of intermediate ends on the Daly triangle. The list of basic needs might be a fruitful beginning for indicators of ultimate ends. (I could think of others I might add, such as beauty and transcendence/enlightenment/grace.)

If we search sincerely and if we are open to answers that may not look like scientific formulae, I believe that ultimate ends can be defined, at least qualitatively, and that the definitions are not so different from one human soul to another. We may disagree hotly about our models of what means can lead to the ends, but when it comes to the ends themselves, the essential human values, we are, quite simply, all human.

Even if we agree on no more than this – that the dominant cultures are mobilizing enormous flows of resources, spewing out unsupportable quantities of wastes, building huge capital structures and not clearly achieving happiness – then there is already a strong reason to stop using indicators that count a larger physical economy as 'good' and to search for indicators of more importance.

INTEGRATION (TRANSLATING ULTIMATE MEANS INTO ULTIMATE ENDS)

We will know we're really talking about sustainable development when the conversation shifts from efficiency to sufficiency. Efficiency is quantifiable and satisfies the Cartesian mind. Sufficiency will drive the Cartesian mind crazy. *Wes Jackson*

The central indicators of sustainable development will integrate the whole Daly triangle – see Figure 17.5.

Suppose that we could, by whatever means you can imagine, assess the well-being of a given society. And suppose we could measure the throughput from nature that is being used to achieve that well-being. Then we would be able to come close to the three indicators that answer the central questions of sustainable development.

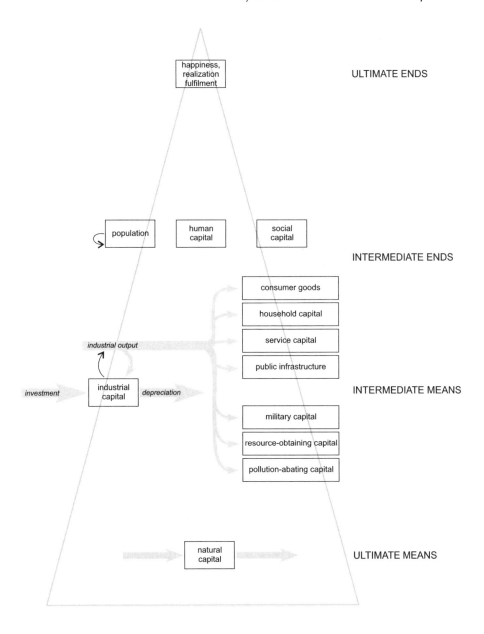

Figure 17.5 *From ultimate means to ultimate ends*

- Are people well-off, satisfied, happy? (Sufficiency and equity – top of the triangle.)
- Is the most possible well-being achieved with the least possible throughput of material and energy? (Efficiency of the translation mechanisms from the bottom to the top of the triangle.)

- Are the natural systems that support the material and energy throughput healthy, resilient and full of evolutionary potential? (Sustainability, bottom of the triangle.)

The information system from which these central indicators can be derived will measure capital stocks at every level and the flows that increase, decrease and connect those stocks. An integrated account of the interlinked stocks and flows at all levels of the pyramid, quantified where possible, estimated otherwise, could provide the information base from which sustainable development indicators are derived. (Just as underlying accounts of interlinked money flows provide the base from which the GDP is derived.)

These stocks and flows should be measured in whatever units make sense; units that will be quite different at different levels of the system. There is a tendency in economics, which measures almost everything with the numeraire of money, to assume that because money is interchangeable, then all forms of capital are inter-substitutable. If there is not enough labour, substitute built capital. If there are not enough resources, compensate with more resource-obtaining capital.

To some extent intersubstitutability is possible, and within that possibility arise all the marginal cost and benefit questions that are interesting to economists. But, as Herman Daly points out, it just doesn't work to substitute fishing boats for fish or sawmills for trees. The absence of trees renders sawmills valueless, as the absence of fish does for fishing boats. Larger pumps can counter a falling groundwater table for a while, but this substitution is not sustainable. Built capital and natural capital are more complementary than substitutable. The same could be said for human and social capital and built capital.

The assumption of total substitutability of any form of capital for any other is just as simple-minded as is the assumption of no substitutability. Therefore indicators should be sought that capture, up and down the pyramid, the extent to which the various forms of capital complement and enhance or undermine and undercut each other.

There are systematic schemes for assessing the total viability of a system. These schemes can serve as checklists for sustainable development indicators. One of these schemes is Hartmut Bossel's set of orientors, which measure the ability of any system to meet environmental challenges by appropriate system responses.[24] There are seven Bossel orientors which can be measured for systems at any level, from a single organism to a whole society. They are:

- existence (the ability to sustain physical needs);
- psychological needs (the ability to generate internal well-being, satisfaction, happiness – applicable to human systems only);
- effectiveness (the ability to take actions that produce desired effects);
- freedom of action;
- security;
- adaptability;
- co-existence (the ability to live in harmony; not to create costs from incompatibility with others or with the environment).

Although Bossel derived these orientors from systems theory rather than from social science, they bear a resemblance to Max-Neef's list of basic needs. Like Max-Neef, Bossel emphasizes that these orientors are complementary, not substitutable. Each of the orientors has to be satisfied to a certain degree if the system (or person or society) is to be functional. A viable system requires balanced attention to all needs. Where one attempts to compensate a needs deficit by excess satisfaction of another need, pathological behaviour results.

I find the Bossel scheme a useful checklist to see that a proposed set of indicators is comprehensive. It suggests to me areas I might not have thought about, parts of the system that must be monitored, to be sure that the entire system can achieve sustainable development.

Other more informal kinds of 'integrative checks' emerged from our workshop conversations. We invented the 'Nazi test' – if we applied any suggested set of indicators to Nazi Germany, would it have revealed the obvious problems of that society? Or the 'Maya test' – if we could have measured these indicators for the Maya empire, would they have revealed its incipient collapse? In time to prevent that collapse?

SAMPLE INDICATORS

> While you and I have lips and voices which
> are for kissing and to sing with
> who cares if some one-eyed son of a bitch
> invents an instrument to measure Spring with? *E E Cummings*

The proof of any indicator scheme is in the indicators it produces and the societal behaviour those indicators help to inform. The scheme suggested in this report calls not only for indicators, but for an underlying information system and set of dynamic models, none of which currently exist (though there are plenty of prototypes).

Where to start? What indicators to start with? There is no 'best' answer to that question. I have given many sample indicators throughout this report, hoping to stimulate creative thinking and even outrageousness on the part of many people, in order to shake loose old thinking, welcome new worldviews, and begin to suggest indicators that can actually move us toward sustainable development. I'll give some more examples here.

The Balaton Group workshop participants came up with this list in Box 17.2. A thoughtful list of 41 indicators developed for the United States is included in Box 17.3, all of which are available with significant time series.[25] Notice that many are grounded in critical capital stocks and in leading-indicator rates of flow.

If I played the 'ten indicators or you'll be shot at dawn' game with myself, I'd come up with a list like the following (assuming that I am working on national-level indicators). I am aware that many items on this list are hard to define and measure. I'd use any quick and dirty surrogate measure I could find to start with and then work to make them better. I assume that these would be aggregate indicators, with a 'click' revealing the disaggregated source data.

- Ecological footprint and rate of change (ultimate means).
- Aggregate measures of natural, built, human and social capitals and rates of change (ultimate and intermediate means, intermediate ends).
- Real well-being – measured by survey data if necessary – and rate of change (ultimate ends).

Box 17.2 *Sample indicators*

For natural capital:

- Renewable resources used/total natural resources used.
- Time to oil or gas depletion/lead time for renewable substitute.
- Agricultural land loss (to urbanization, desertification, erosion)/total arable land.
- Loss of primary forests/total primary forests remaining.
- Unit of effort (money, labour, investment, time) necessary to add a unit to identified reserves of non-renewables.
- Fish caught per unit of fishing effort.
- Soil organic matter content (time trend).
- Output to sink/capacity of sink to absorb or assimilate (especially for CO_2).
- CO_2 emission per capita, relative to 'fair earthshare'.
- Quality of river water entering country or city/quality leaving country or city.
- Number of synthetic chemicals in use.
- Area used for organic agriculture/area used for chemical intensive agriculture.

For built capital:

- Average productive lifetime of capital.
- Maintenance inputs to capital stock/productive output of capital stock.
- Capital stock/end use output.
- Resource (material and energy) throughput/end use output.
- Ratios (balance) between various forms of built capital.

For human and social capital:

- Infant and child mortality rate.
- Total fertility rate (births per woman over that woman's expected lifetime).
- Education level of the bottom 10 per cent of 20-year-olds.
- Education and skills attributes of population matched with education and skills requirements of built capital.
- Average layers of management between employees and owners.
- Income of the top 10 per cent/income of the bottom 10 per cent.
- Per cent of government office-holders' total income coming from bribes, pay-offs and private campaign contributions.
- Per cent of time necessary to secure survival needs.
- Per cent of time contributed to civic, religious and other non-profit causes.
- Juvenile crime rate.

For ultimate ends:

- Population of the local 'totem' species (salmon in Seattle, eagles in Maine, seals in the Netherlands).
- Proportion of leisure time per person (and equity of its distribution).
- Human openness in the streets and squares.
- Number and size of places of rest and beauty (eg forests, parks, temples).
- Flexibility in choosing transport mode and housing.
- Per cent of people who say they have 'enough'.

Box 17.3 *Sample indicators for the USA*

Economic:

- Capital assets.
- Labour productivity.
- Federal debt to GDP ratio.
- Investment as a per cent of GDP.
- Energy consumption per capita and per $ of GDP.
- Materials consumption per capita and per $ of GDP.
- Inflation.
- Investment in R&D as a per cent of GDP.
- GDP per capita.
- Income distribution.
- Consumption expenditures per capita.
- Unemployment.
- Percentage of households in problem housing.

Environmental:

- Surface water quality.
- Acres of major terrestrial eco-systems intact.
- Contaminants in biota.
- Accumulated quantity of spent nuclear fuel.
- Status of stratospheric ozone.
- Greenhouse gas emissions.
- Ratio of renewable water supply to withdrawals.
- Fisheries utilization (per cent overfished).
- Invasive exotic species.
- Conversion of cropland to other uses.
- Soil erosion rates.
- Timber growth/removal.
- Identification and management of toxic waste sites.
- Outdoor recreational activities.
- Extreme weather events.

Social:

- Population.
- Children living in families with only one parent.
- Teacher training level.
- Contributions of time and money to charity.
- Births to single mothers.
- School enrolment by level.
- Participation in arts and recreation.
- People in census tracts with 40 per cent or more poverty.
- Crime rate.
- Life expectancy.
- Educational achievement rates.
- Homeownership rate.

- Physical throughput/well-being (throughput efficiency from ultimate means to ultimate ends).
- Four kinds of capital/well-being (intermediate means and ends to ultimate ends).
- Built capital balances (intermediate means).
- Most limiting sources and sinks and rates of change (ultimate means).
- Most critical respite/response areas (throughout the triangle).
- Untouched natural areas and rates of change (ultimate means).
- Something wacky and human – smiles on faces on the street, hugs per day, clowns per capita (ultimate ends).

I present all these lists not as final, considered opinions, but as challenges. What would you choose?

NOTES AND REFERENCES

1   See, for example, 'Work Programme on Indicators of Sustainable Development of the Commission on Sustainable Development,' United Nations Department for Policy Coordination and Sustainable Development, February 1996, and 'OECD Core Set of Indicators for Environmental Performance Review,' OECD Environment Directorate, October 1993

2   Mathis Wackernagel and William Rees, *Our Ecological Footprint – Reducing Human Impact on the Earth*, New Society Publishers, 1995

3   I Serageldin, *Sustainability and the Wealth of Nations: First Steps in an Ongoing Journey*, World Bank Discussion Draft, Second Edition, March 3, 1996

4   World Bank, Monitoring Environmental Progress: A Report on Work in Progress, ESD Series, 1995

5   H E Daly, *Toward a Steady-State Economy*, San Francisco: W H Freeman & Company, 1973, p 8

6   This issue is discussed in more detail on p 42 of the original report

7   Daly 1973, op cit pp 7–8

8   Herman Daly, 'Toward Some Operational Principles of Sustainable Development', *Ecological Economics* 2 (1990): 1–6

9   Serageldin, op cit

10 For illustrative throughput numbers for the city of London, see H Girardet's paper in Chapter 19 of this Reader; also his book *The Gaia Atlas of Cities: New Directions for Sustainable Urban Living*. New York: Doubleday, June 1993; for Hongkong, see S Boyden, *An Integrative Ecological Approach to the Study of Human Settlements*. Paris: Unesco, International Co-ordinating Council of the Programme on Man and the Biosphere, 1979

11 For a pioneering example, see A Adriaanse et al, *Resource Flows: The Material Basis of Industrial Economies*. Washington DC: World Resources Institute, 1997

12 See R Repetto et al, *The Forest for the Trees? (Government Policies and the Misuse of Forest Resources); Wasting Assets (National Resources in the National Income Accounts); and Accounts Overdue (Natural Resource Depreciation in Cost Rica)*. Washington, DC: World Resources Institute, 1988–1991.

13 Wackernagel and Rees, op cit

14 R Costanza, R d'Arge, R de Groot, 'The Value of the World's Ecosystem Services and Natural Capital,' *Nature* 387 (15 May 1997): 253–60; G Daily (ed), *Nature's Services: Societal Dependence on Natural Ecosystems*, Washington, DC: Island Press, 1997

15 E F Schumacher, *Small is Beautiful*. New York: Harper & Row, 1973

16 Earlier chapters in the original report have more discussion of positive feedback loops

17 C J L Murray, 'Quantifying the Burden of Disease: The Technical Basis for DALYs', *Bulletin of the World Health Organization* 72, No 3 (1994): 429–445.

18 Technology Review, August/September 1986

19 See E von Weiszacker, A Lovins, and H Lovins, *Factor Four: Doubling Wealth – Halving Resource Use*, London, Earthscan, 1997

20 *Sustainable Seattle, Indicators of Sustainable Community 1995*, available from Sustainable Seattle, 909 Fourth Avenue, Seattle, WA 98104 USA. See also the paper by Alan AtKisson in Chapter 16 of this Reader

21 U.S. Interagency Working Group on Sustainable Development Indicators, *Sustainable Development in the United States*, Interim Report, draft, April 1998

22 The World Bank, *Expanding the Measure of Wealth: Indicators of Environmentally Sustainable Development*, 1997

23 M A Max-Neef, *Human Scale Development*, New York: Apex Press, 1991

24 H Bossel, *Concepts and Tools of Computer-Assisted Policy Analysis*, Basel: Birkhaeuser, 1977

25 U.S. Interagency Working Group on Sustainable Development Indicators, op cit

Chapter 18

Is There Method in our Measurement? The Use of Indicators in Local Sustainable Development Planning

Jeb Brugmann

(Reprinted from *Local Environment* Vol 20, No 1, February 1997, pp 59–72.)

Summary: 'Sustainability indicators' are being used in local communities to serve multiple and sometimes vague or contradictory objectives. This can add to confusion about sustainable development among the public and policy-makers. The case of Seattle, USA, is used to illustrate how a set of well-developed indicators can fail to meet their objectives if they are unrelated to a methodical planning process. The cases of the State of Oregon, USA, and Santa Monica, USA, are then presented to demonstrate how indicators can be used effectively in sustainable development planning to measure performance and to promote positive change. The author concludes that, at the local level, indicators are ideally suited for performance measurement. Indicators are a suboptimal tool for technical assessment and even public education. Applications of indicators for these two purposes can compromise the performance measurement function.

INTRODUCTORY MUSINGS

The Context

No sooner was the concept of sustainable development legitimized by the 1992 UN Earth Summit than numerous central governments sought to blend the concept into a less rigorous ideology of economic growth.[1] United Nations support for sustainable development became a central focus of debate at the 1996 UN Habitat II Conference, where member states modified most references to sustainable development in the Conference's 'Habitat Agenda' by appending to it the phrase 'and sustained economic growth'. Such a well-orchestrated consensus in the fractious and ethereal world of UN inferences reflects the advent of a fuzzy, popular notion about 'sustainability' – a notion with growing resonance among populations experiencing less economic opportunity and security – which could be stated as follows:

> Economic (ie capitalist) development can be sustained if we pay more attention to environmental and social concerns. These concerns are best addressed by opening markets to

accelerate the transnational transfer of information, technology and private capital and by replacing government regulation with voluntary partnerships. In particular, partnerships based on mutual self-interest should ensure that growth can be sustained – at least for as long as we presently are willing to concern ourselves.

Glaring global trends in poverty, health, natural resources, pollution and population stand in counterpoint to such revisionism and demonstrate the unsustainable nature of current forms of economic development in our countries and towns. In the light of these trends, the Habitat II debates over sustainable development appear for what they are – as efforts to buy time and resist necessary change. The trends illustrate that meaningful use of the concept of sustainability and the related application of sustainable development planning implies dramatic and immediate reform of economic processes and the public institutions that regulate them, ranging from global trade regimes to resource management procedures to household consumption patterns.

At the local level, a growing group of local government officials and volunteer leaders have been making a first, earnest attempt at applying the sustainable development concept. In the first instance, these planning efforts generate much public enthusiasm and support. Later, when governments, corporations and households are confronted with implementing the resulting action plans, the credibility or necessity of development reforms often are called into question. In the face of organized critics of reform, continued sustainable development planning depends upon the articulation of a consistent method and the indication of concrete positive results.

I believe that a methodology is arising from the past eight years of local experimentation with sustainable development planning. However, in one aspect of such planning – the use of 'sustainability indicators' – we have failed to be both methodical and articulate. The resulting lack of ability to demonstrate the positive impacts of new policies and practices can be used to create public confusion or to weaken public acceptance of the sustainable development agenda.

What are We Measuring?

Evaluating the objective ability of a community to sustain itself (and thereby the planet's ecosystem, the global economy, etc) and its quality of life (within the context of shifting local perceptions of 'quality') requires levels of scientific sophistication and local values clarification that are rarely available to a local community. This is a worthy effort upon which great progress might be made in one city with tens of millions of dollars.

Informing local residents and institutions about our imperfect understanding of this desirable but complex state called 'sustainability' and finding out what they most want to sustain is an equally noble yet essentially different task.

Making sure that the efforts and investments of local residents and local institutions are having their intended effects and are achieving agreed targets is yet another important task which is fundamental for any movement of a complex social system, eg a 'community', from point A to point B.

'Sustainable development' at the local level requires these three activities, and more. These activities can be undertaken in an integrated way. But the rigours of methodology require that we view them as distinct tasks. Indicators are one tool that can be applied in achieving each task but, methodologically speaking, we need to keep clear that, in each instance, indicators are being used for different functions. Each function places quite distinct requirements on the methods and standards of their development and use. The following three brief cases illustrate this point and begin to demonstrate how, at the local level, indicators are most optimally used for performance measurement purposes, and provide only a faint portrait of the complex sustainability challenges facing a late 20th-century city.

A TALE OF THREE CITIES

Three cases have been selected on the basis of (a) their comparability and (b) their ability to highlight the different applications of indicators in local sustainable development planning (Zachary 1995; ICLEI 1996). The projects – in Seattle, Washington; the State of Oregon; and the City of Santa Monica, California – have all taken place during the same general period of time in a single region of the United States where there is considerable communication and cultural, institutional and legal homogeneity. The three cases differ with regards to the primary actor in each indicator project, but these differences only highlight the methodological questions we seek to explore through their comparison.

Seattle, Washington, USA: 'Sustainable Seattle' Revisited

The case of the 'Sustainable Seattle' Project, a voluntary sector indicators project, hardly requires description. The Project has been heralded throughout North America and Europe and has been used frequently as a 'best practice' model in the United Kingdom. We can continue to learn from this interesting experiment by factoring Seattle's more recent developments.

Established in 1990, the four primary objectives of the Sustainable Seattle Project were (1) to establish 'bell-wether tests of sustainability', (2) to catalyse the public 'to reconsider our priorities, (3) to explore the linkages and causal connections between these trends and (4) to change our personal and collective behaviour in ways that will steer our community on a more sustainable course [author's numbers]' (Atkisson et al 1995). Five years later, how successful has the project been in meeting its objectives?

Problems of scientific method cloud any assessment of the project's success with objective one, eg the effectiveness of the indicators in testing the city's 'sustainability'. To the project's credit, a number of the selected indicators are defined and measured with a high degree of technical sophistication. Nevertheless, the inherent simplicity of the limited set of measures makes it difficult to say whether the indicators will ever provide a complete enough snapshot of reality to rigorously evaluate the sustainability of the project's desirable 'Seattle'.

The project's status report also reveals – although judgement may be premature – that, it would be difficult to claim success with the project's fourth objective, ie to use the indicators to change collective behaviour. Since 1993, 14 indicators showed a declining 'sustainability trend'. Eighteen indicators had no discernible trend or remained unchanged. Only 8 indicators showed an improving trend. In particular, 11 indicators on the environment and resource management declined while only 3 in these areas improved. The environmental indicator that improved is air quality, a condition that is strongly regulated by both national and state legislation and has been improving since 1980 – long before the indicators project. In the resource management area, positive trends since the 1970s have continued, largely due to existing public-sector measures.

What we can say is that, by all accounts, the project implemented its activities in a creative way, establishing a credible local stakeholder organization to raise awareness and establish the 'sustainability' agenda in the city. Based on the project's own reports and on recent discussions with local participants and municipal officials,[2] it is fair to say that the project has made and continues to make a recognizable impact in the community in objectives two and three – that is, to engender debate about priorities and the connections between local trends. However, the very method that the project has been using to succeed in these two areas consigns it to continued uncertain achievements with objectives one (ie measurement of sustainability) and four (ie behaviour change).

Participation versus measurement of 'sustainability'. The Sustainable Seattle approach suffers from a common notion that the measurement of 'sustainability' can be achieved through a public participation process. A recent article by Professor Virginia W Maclaren in the *American Planning Association Journal*[3] inadvertently highlights the tension in this notion.

Maclaren's aim is to combine the experiences of projects like Sustainable Seattle with current environmental and social reporting theory to establish a general framework for 'urban sustainability reporting'. To begin, Maclaren correctly catalogues the variety and technical complexity of indicators that would need to be employed 'to characterize the different dimensions or aspects of a situation', because 'indicators are simplifications of complex phenomena' (Maclaren 1996, p 186). She convincingly describes how a local effort to characterize sustainability might require:

- *integrating indicators or indexes,* to portray linkages between economic, social and environmental phenomena;
- *trend indicators,* linked to targets and thresholds;
- *predictive indicators,* relying upon mathematical forecasting models or, alternatively, *conditional indicators* using 'if/then' scenarios to estimate future conditions;
- *distributional indicators,* measuring intergenerational equity and specifying local, upstream and downstream effects through the use of highly disaggregated data;
- and, depending upon the framework applied, *condition-stress-response indicators* that provide simple causal models for local conditions.

Each of these different types of indicators, Maclaren shows, would be useful in evaluating different aspects of sustainability in a community. At the same time, each has its own methodological complexities, data requirements and application standards.

Having highlighted, perhaps unintentionally, the complexity of using indicators as a tool for evaluating the objective condition of sustainability, Maclaren then points out that sustainability indicators, in particular, need to be developed with input from a broad range of stakeholders 'since sustainability is such a value-laden and context sensitive concept' (Maclaren 1996, p 188). The tension between scientific rigour and public values and perceptions is never addressed, but it is exactly this tension – which arises, in fact, from the ambiguity of the sustainability concept itself – that compromised the achievement of Sustainable Seattle's first objective.

If Seattle's sustainability is, in fact, a complex, ecologically determined condition, then the ability of Sustainable Seattle's dedicated generalists (ie stakeholders) to define and apply indicators to evaluate this condition accurately would appear problematic. In fact, the evaluation of the condition of sustainability would require quite advanced scientific scrutiny and use of the simple tool of indicators itself would seem questionable. If, on the other hand, Seattle's sustainability is primarily a social construct, then Maclaren's catalogue of diverse indicators is not necessary. Emphasis, then, must be given to the social process of clarifying and resolving conflicting values and establishing a social consensus – a process that the self-selected stakeholders in the Sustainable Seattle project were also unable to perform with rigour.

In the end, it appears that Sustainable Seattle's method of deriving sustainability indicators was little related to a clear understanding of what sustainability means. The indicators fail as 'bell-wether tests of sustainability' because the condition that they are intended to measure remains undefined. Instead, Sustainable Seattle is actually more dedicated to its third objective – that is, 'understanding ... all [sic] the connections between various elements of a healthy society, and thinking in longer time spans than we may be accustomed to' (Atkisson et al 1995, p i). Sustainable Seattle was primarily a public education and advocacy exercise, and a valuable one at that. The Sustainable Seattle Project chose simplicity and participation over complexity and depth of understanding. The project's indicators are highlighting key local values and amenities more than tracking the complex course of its city into the future.

The complexity of the reporting system presented by Maclaren would be likely to undermine the educational objectives which are pre-eminent in a Seattle-styled indicators project. In the end – and this is a point that Maclaren's framework seems to avoid in the current fascination with indicators as an all-purpose tool – the city's actual sustainability trends might be more effectively evaluated by the more technical and comprehensive assessment that can be achieved through, say, a modified State of the Environment Reporting procedure. Related to such a procedure, certain core indicators could be defined by stakeholders in order to inform the public about trends in key community values. But final determinations about the sustainability of different conditions would be handled through a more extensive and technically informed assessment effort.

The uncertain relationship between information and behaviour change. The other challenge facing an indicator project on the model of Sustainable Seattle, or any 'sustainability' reporting process, is the complex relationship between information, discussion and data on the one hand, and behaviour change, investment and policy on the other. In an open society, the well-organized clarification of public values, as embodied in key indicators, can draw political attention to new priorities. Reports from the City of Seattle Office of Management and Planning verify that Sustainable Seattle, by raising public awareness, increased the inevitability that the City would address sustainability issues in its strategic planning activities.[4] But Sustainable Seattle itself, organized as it was without connection to major institution generally, and the City's strategic and statutory planning processes specifically, neither provided a blueprint nor stimulated commitments, nor even a consensus, for action. Its impact in driving change in local conditions was therefore, at best, catalytic.

Reflecting this gap in the Sustainable Seattle approach, the City of Seattle established a quite separate citywide task force in 1995 to develop a municipal strategic plan which is linked to the statutory 'Comprehensive Plan' required of all municipalities by the State of Washington. This task force identified its own long-term goals for Seattle. The senior management and leadership of the municipality used this opportunity to link the statutory plan to a new performance management system for municipal operations and services. For this purpose, a completely new set of performance indicators was established. These indicators were derived from the nearly 500 goals and policies set forth in the Comprehensive Plan. An initial set of 100 indicators was prepared by city staff. One indicator was assigned to each goal or policy in the Comprehensive Plan. Following this exercise, a shorter list of 28 indicators was established to highlight the 'most critical' elements of the plan. The key criteria used in selecting these core indicators were:

- a direct and understandable relationship to one or more of the plan's goals or policies, or to its vision;
- the availability of reliable, regular information to cost-effectively track the indicator;
- 'The total list of selected indicators describes progress towards the core values that underlie the Plan.' (City of Seattle 1996)

While Sustainable Seattle set the stage for sustainability issues to be integrated into the Comprehensive Plan – and although there are thematic overlaps between the Sustainable Seattle indicators and the city's indicators – the municipality's indicators are not only different but, more importantly, are embedded in development policies that the municipality has a political and legal obligation to implement. The City's performance indicators are, therefore, more likely than Sustainable Seattle's to guide

Table 18.1 *Sustainability indicators for Seattle – a comparison of selected indicators*

Sustainable Seattle Project	City of Seattle	A	B	C
Puget sound air quality Control agency index	Puget sound air quality Control agency index	x	–	–
Total water consumption	Per capita water consumption	–	x	–
Villages meeting open space requirements in comprehensive plan	Acres of open space	–	x	–
Volunteering in schools; youth community service	Survey of volunteering in community activities	–	x	–
Survey of average residents' perception of no of 'neighbours'	Survey of perception on neighbourhood safety	–	x	–
Real unemployment	Ratio of jobs to households	–	x	–
Juvenile crime	Number of violent and property crimes	x	–	
Per capita waste generation and recycling rate	Rate of recycling	x	x	–
Medium household income by $10,000 ranges	Medium household income (quartiles)	x	x	–
Plant and amphibian biodiversity vs remaining natural habitat	Tree coverage	–	–	x
Equity in justice	Population distribution by race	–	–	x

Note: A = consistent
        B = conflicting measurements of similar conditions
        C = conflicting or alternative definitions of sustainability

change in policy, public investment and, therefore, 'collective behaviour'. Table 18.1 presents a comparison between the indicators used by the City and Sustainable Seattle.

Recent developments in Seattle highlight the fundamental importance of taking a methodical approach to indicators development and application at the community level. The first step in being methodical is to identify and focus on the primary objective of the indicators. Other tools can then be considered to achieve any secondary objectives.

Sustainable Seattle tried to use one set of simple indicators to serve a number of complicated objectives simultaneously, setting itself up for failures and adding to confusion in Seattle about the use of indicators. Where Sustainable Seattle failed, such as in the area of performance measurement, the City established a second set of indicators to link sustainability reporting to key municipal planning and policy processes. As a result, Seattle's neighbourhoods and residents are confronted with two sets of competing 'core' indicators whose functions are overlapping and ill-defined.

In cities where the municipality and other major institutions are prepared to change development practices and trends, stakeholders would ideally focus on preparing the goals and targets of a strategic plan that has legal standing with these institutions. Indicators would then be developed after these goals and targets are established in order to serve as performance measures in a reporting, ie accountability, system. Of course, and as the following cases will illustrate, such an approach implies a quite different and more limited function for the indicators: they are employed less as a tool to 'measure sustainability' – which in the face of effecting real change takes on a more academic or pedagogical appeal – than as a tool to maintain accountability to locally and popularly mandated change.

The State of Oregon, USA: a Participatory Performance Measurement Model

In 1988, the Governor of Oregon, USA (estimated population 3 million) initiated a strategic planning process focused on maintaining the quality of life and economic competitiveness of the state. The state's effort was influenced from the outset by the emergent North American interest in public-sector performance measurement (Oregon Economic Development Department 1989).

In 1989, the State Legislature created an independent state planning and oversight agency, called the Oregon Progress Board, to facilitate stakeholder input into strategic planning and to oversee the implementation of the 20-year plan. In order to evaluate progress, in 1990 the multi-stakeholder Progress Board established citizen steering committees involving more than 200 organizations and individuals in the preparation of 160 benchmarks tied to the strategic plan. These benchmarks, each with a common baseline year (1990) and desired targets for 1995, 2000 and 2010, were adopted as policy by the State Legislature in 1991. Following adoption, the Progress Board has continued to oversee the application of the benchmarks by all state agencies, the periodic public review of the benchmarks, and the ongoing development of a performance accountability system in the state. As a result of such review and application, the benchmarks have been continuously refined and expanded. Today, the state uses a total of 269 benchmarks (Oregon Progress Board 1990, 1996).

As performance measurement procedures became the *modus operandi* in all Oregon state agencies and departments, a further law was passed in 1993 directing all state and state-supported agencies to use the benchmarks in performance measurement, planning and budgeting decisions. In addition, 14 local Progress Boards, in partnership with municipalities such as Portland, the state's largest city, have been established voluntarily and employ the Oregon Benchmarks to measure local performance as part of the growing statewide system. The Oregon Progress Board, meanwhile, has established a number of programmes to successfully encourage the state's 13 key industries, its 12 economic regions, non-profit organizations, citizen groups, charities and one major foundation to tie their efforts to the benchmarks. A report card, *Oregon Benchmarks,* is published every two years to track performance relative to targets (Oregon Progress Board 1994).

In contrast with the Sustainable Seattle approach, this neighbouring initiative appears to be successfully aligning the entire budgeting and policy-making process of the state and a growing number of major institutions to a common set of development objectives and targets. When a benchmark on child immunization demonstrated poor performance, the state mobilized and increased immunizations by 25 per cent in two years. The state's system of County Commissions on Children and Families are legally required to use the benchmark on teen pregnancy in their planning and performance evaluation. A 'Key Industries Program' was established to improve benchmark performance in the area of economic diversification. The state's recent welfare (public assistance) programme reform efforts have been linked to the employment and poverty benchmarks. Indeed, the entire benchmarks effort is oriented towards performance. The Progress Board is currently undertaking a statewide consultation to upgrade the benchmarks system. Part of this effort includes a research partnership with the state's two major universities to determine why performance is lagging on selected key benchmarks (Hatry and Kirlin 1994).[5]

Therefore, in comparison with the Sustainable Seattle Project, the Oregon Benchmarks were clearly identified as a performance measurement tool in a multistakeholder strategic planning process. As such, they were legitimized by diverse sectors and linked to the budgeting, policy development and programme planning activities of both state agencies and other public and private institutions. This has resulted in discernible impacts as well as survivability – not yet assured in Seattle – since the Oregon project is tied to an independent state agency, the Oregon Progress Board, with a policy and budgetary mandate to ensure that the benchmarks are being employed by Oregon institutions. While it may be unfair to compare Seattle's community-based and municipal projects with this state government initiative, the comparison illustrates how much more extensively and effectively indicators can be put to use when linked from the outset to a multistakeholder strategic planning initiative. The continued debate that may ensue in Seattle over the 'right' indicators may instigate public awareness; meanwhile, in Oregon a large number of diverse sectors and institutions are comfortable to apply a common set of state-wide indicators to guide their actions and investments.

The City of Santa Monica, California, USA: Indicators as a Management Tool

The Oregon Benchmarks system, it could be argued, is too ambitious for many local governments, which may have neither the resources nor the sustained political or public commitment to strategic planning. The more recent case of Santa Monica's Sustainable City Program is presented, therefore, to illustrate how indicators can be effectively used as a management tool in achieving long-term targets at the departmental level.

Started in 1992, the Santa Monica Sustainable City Program is an initiative of the municipality's Environmental Programs Division to establish a focused, results-oriented strategy to achieve measurable improvement in environmental and social conditions under the city's control. While embedded in the sustainable development notions of the Brundtland Commission and the 1992 Earth Summit, the programme 'set as its most important priority the creation of a decision-making framework for the city that provides criteria for evaluating long-term as opposed to short-term impacts of decisions'. As such, the programme does not attempt to define or achieve some specific state of 'sustainability'. Indeed, avoiding the hyperbole typical of such initiatives, the programme recognizes that 'it is no more than a good starting point for the tremendous amount of work which needs to be done to ... achieve the vision of sustainability' (City of Santa Monica 1994a). Its primary goal is to *get started* by directing municipal policies, budgets and activities according to development priorities identified by local stakeholders.

To begin this process, the city established a multistakeholder Task Force on the Environment to work with the Environmental Program Division to develop the programme. The Task Force undertook a survey of prominent community members in order to identify priority sustainability issues. The respondents and additional representatives of neighbourhood organizations then were invited to a public meeting to review the results of the survey. At this meeting, the Task Force, with support from the Division, also presented a preliminary draft of the proposed programme, which was openly discussed. The programme was revised on the basis of this discussion. A larger public working conference then was held for final review of the programme. The final draft programme for submission to the City Council was prepared on the basis of discussions at this conference and approved in September, 1994.[6]

The key elements of the resulting programme are eight guiding principles for city decision-making, specific performance goals for each of four policy areas (resource conservation, community and economic development, transportation, and pollution prevention and public health protection), and specific, quantifiable targets to achieve these goals. A common base year of 1990 and target year of 2000 was established for each target (City of Santa Monica 1994b).

Indicators were then established by city staff and Task Force members to evaluate performance in achieving the programme targets. Since the indicators are primarily intended for performance evaluation as opposed to public education, priority was given to the ability of the Division to measure the indicators and to influence their values through municipal programmes.[7] In fact, as evident in Table 18.2, a number of the indicators are defined by the targets themselves.

The result is a quite simple, yet managerially sophisticated system to hold the Division, specifically, and the city, broadly, accountable to the goals and targets accepted in the public consultation process. The Division now prepares its annual work programme and budgets based on these targets. At the same time, the Division is supporting other municipal departments to co-ordinate their programmes with the Sustainable City Program goals and targets. For instance, the Division and the Task Force are currently working with relevant city departments on sustainability criteria

Table 18.2 *The Santa Monica Sustainable City Program: selected goals, targets and indicators*

Policy area	Resource conservation

Goals:
• Promote the use of conservation technologies and practices and reduce the use of non-renewable resources.
• Develop local, non-polluting, renewable energy, water and material resources, and expand recycling technology in these areas.

Targets:
• Reduce energy usage by 16%.
• Reduce potable water usage by 20%.
• Reduce solid waste volumes by at least 50%.
• Achieve a 50% average post-consumer recycled and/or tree-free content in all city paper purchases.
• Convert 75% of the city vehicle fleet to reduced-emission fuels.
• Reduce waste-water flows by 15%.
• Increase total number of trees on public property by 350.

Indicators	1990 (Actual)	1993 (Actual)	2000 (Target)
Energy usage (non-mobile sources)	4.0 million btu/year	4.0 million btu/year	3.36 million btu/year
Water usage	14.3 million gallons/year	12.0 million gallons/year	11.4 million gallons/year
Post-consumer recycled tree-free paper purchases	Unknown	Unknown	50%
Waste-water flows	10.4 million gallons/day	8.5 million gallons/day	8.8 million gallons/day
City fleet vehicles using reduced-emission fuels	Unknown	10%	75%
Trees in public spaces	28,000 trees	28,000 trees	28,350 trees

Policy area	Community and economic development

Goals:
• Encourage the development of compact, mixed-use, pedestrian-oriented projects.

Table 18.2 *Continued*

- Promote the growth of local businesses that provide employment opportunities to Santa Monica residents.
- Facilitate education programmes that enrich the lives of all members of the community.

Targets:
- Provide 750 additional affordable housing units.
- Create three new community gardens.
- Establish partnership with local schools to create and complement a Sustainable Schools Programme.
- Increase total public open space area by 15 acres.

Indicators	1990 (Actual)	1993 (Actual)	2000 (Target)
Deed-restricted affordable housing units	1172 units	1313 units	1922 units
Community gardens	2 gardens	2 gardens	5 gardens
Creation of a Sustainable Schools Program	N/A	N/A	Implemented
Public open space	164 acres	164.8 acres	180 acres

Source: City of Santa Monica, Environmental Programs Division, PO Box 2200, 200 Santa Monica Pier, Santa Monica, CA 90401-2200, USA

for the city's development review process, procurement system and service contracting procedures.

The Santa Monica case could be viewed as a scaled-down, localized version of the Oregon Benchmarks process. However, it differs in that it was initiated by a specific municipal department to focus its own activities. This has created a clearer linkage of accountability between the indicators and the Division than in the case in Oregon, where hundreds of benchmarks were first created and state agencies were then required to find a way to put them to good use.

The Santa Monica case contrasts significantly with Sustainable Seattle. While Santa Monica's indicators now can be used for the same public education purposes as the Sustainable Seattle indicators, their primary purpose is to guide municipal activities and to provide all stakeholders with a tool to hold the municipality accountable to its own goals and targets. This is a purpose that the Sustainable Seattle indicators are poorly situated to achieve. Likewise, without clear targets, the City of Seattle's indicators will be less useful in generating specific responses from the City Council and municipal departments if indicators demonstrate poor performance or progress.

OPTIMIZING POSITIVE CHANGE

These cases highlight four considerations to be factored when determining the optimal use of indicators in local sustainable development planning.

First, local communities are all in different stages of preparedness to adopt and face the sustainable development challenge. Some genuinely may not be ready for planning and/or action but must first dedicate resources to education and the building of public support. In this case, the use of indicators as a public education tool needs to be carefully considered with reference to potential future interest in using indicators for other purposes.

Second, since meaningful use of the sustainable development concept implies, sooner rather than later, dramatic and immediate change in local trends, action is the optimal and ultimate response to the challenge. Applications of indicators to support focused action should be given priority consideration.

Third, indicators are a tool that can be used for diverse purposes – to educate residents, to assess existing conditions, to guide planning decisions, or to focus and evaluate actions. However, each use implies different methods of development and standards of use, and it cannot be assumed that the indicators used for one purpose can be effectively applied for another purpose.

Fourth, there are a variety of tools available for sustainable development planning and it is advisable that, factoring local circumstances, each tool is used to serve its optimal purpose. Therefore, while indicators can be an effective educational tool, we know that there are a plethora of tested educational tools and approaches, some of which may be equally or more effective in a particular local setting. Similarly, as planners we know that a variety of tools or methods are available for technical assessments, tools that are both more sophisticated and more tested than indicators for this purpose. Indicators stand out as a basic and effective tool for performance evaluation. In sustainable development planning indicators have a unique place as a tool to measure performance in implementing each goal or policy of an action plan.

From the standpoint of planning, the use of indicators as a performance measurement tool is also more simple, more justifiable and more precise.

- It is more simple because a performance indicator is methodologically more straightforward than the pantheon of other kinds of indicators. Often, as in the case of Santa Monica, the performance target itself defines the indicator.
- It is more justifiable because the performance indicator is only defined after the extensive process of identifying priorities, assessing conditions, establishing goals, agreeing to programme objectives and negotiating targets is completed. Conversely, the establishment of indicators as an early step in a planning exercise can impose an **a priori** set of values upon a planning process whose realistic findings and outcomes are not yet determined.
- It is more precise because the indicator is being used to measure a very specific condition or activity; the scientific and epistemological issues of whether and how one defines and measures a broad condition such as 'sustainability' are eliminated. However, where public debate has generated agreement about the core elements of 'sustainability' that a community would like to uphold, it can be desirable to establish 'core value' indicators – related to and consistent with the specific performance indicators – for public reporting and educational purposes.

The above-presented cases, and others that can be cited, lend support to these positions. The most results-oriented indicators projects are those that use indicators to hold institutions accountable to their plans and to evaluate whether actions are having the desired effects. The celebrated case of Sustainable Seattle demonstrates that indicators can serve as an effective community education tool, but also shows that education alone does not guarantee change. Change, in the cases of Seattle and Oregon and Santa Monica, is resulting from performance-driven leadership in key institutions, for which purpose all three governments considered indicators as an important management tool.

In conclusion, I believe that we optimally want our indicators to indicate the results of action. This encourages not only accountability, but a sense of local agency. Only with rigorous accountability and focused agency can we assure that the sustainability concept is employed for long-term action and not, as we risk, for action ... but in the long-term.

ACKNOWLEDGEMENTS

I would like to thank Reena Lazar for her research assistance. Thanks also to my UK colleagues, including Roger Levitt and Derek Taylor, whose demands for more rigour forced the writing of this article.

NOTES

1 The effort to scuttle the UN's endorsement of sustainable development was ironically led by a number of developing countries in the G77 group, typically those with highly industrialized economies. The arguments of these countries have evolved since the preparatory debates for the Rio Summit. In the Rio process, sustainable development was challenged as a hypocritical imposition of development controls – or even as a violation of national sovereignty – by rich countries unwilling to reduce their own unsustainable levels of consumption. Rather than argue against sustainable development in the Habitat II process, many of the same countries proposed instead to replace all references to sustainable development with 'sustained economic growth'. Economic growth, they argued, would generate the wealth needed to address the social and environmental problems created by rapid capitalistic development. (Similar arguments have been used in rich countries by coalitions of business, labour and conservative political parties to attack environmental programmes and regulations.)

   The doubts expressed by NGOs about the lack of distribution of the new wealth in many of these growing economies – and related poverty and pollution problems – were ignored. Rich countries could hardly argue against the 'sustained economic growth' proposal. The result was repeated use of these contrasting concepts in tandem throughout the *Habitat Agenda*, further muddling international commitment to and clarity about sustainable development

2 Conversations with Tom Hauger and Bonnie Snedeker, City of Seattle, Office of Management and Planning, July 1996
3 Maclaren, W (1996) Urban sustainability reporting. *Journal of the American Planning Association* 62(2)
4 Conversations with Tom Hauger and Bonnie Snedeker, City of Seattle, Office of Management and Planning, July 1996
5 Interview with Jeff Tryens, Executive Director, Oregon Progress Board, August 1996
6 Interview with Dean Kubani. Santa Monica Environmental Programs Division, August 1996
7 Ibid

REFERENCES

AtKisson, A et al (1995) *Sustainable Seattle: indicators of sustainable community, 1995* (Seattle, Sustainable Seattle)

City of Santa Monica (1994a) *Recommendation to Approve the Santa Monica Sustainable City Program* proposal to the City Council, 20 September (Santa Monica, City of Santa Monica)

City of Santa Monica (1994b) *Santa Monica Sustainable City Program* adopted 20 September (Santa Monica, City of Santa Monica)

City of Seattle, Office of Management and Planning (1996) *City of Seattle Comprehensive Plan Monitoring Report – biennial update on Seattle's comprehensive plan (Draft)* (Seattle, City of Seattle)

Hatry, H P and Kirlin, J (1994) *An Assessment of the Oregon Benchmarks: a report to the Oregon Progress Board* (Eugene, University of Oregon)

ICLEI (1996) *The Local Agenda 21 Planning Guide* (Toronto, ICLEI/IRDC/UNEP)

Maclaren, V W (1996) Urban sustainability reporting, *Journal of the American Planning Association*, 62(2)

Oregon Economic Development Department (1989) *Oregon Shines: an economic strategy for the Pacific century – summary* (Salem, Oregon Economic Development Department)

Oregon Progress Board (1990) *Oregon Benchmarks: setting measurable standards for progress – public review draft* (Salem, Oregon Progress Board)

Oregon Progress Board (1994) *Oregon Benchmarks: standards for measuring statewide progress and institutional performance – report to the 1995 legislature* (Salem, Oregon Progress Board)

Oregon Progress Board (1996) *Governing for Results: using benchmarks to define and measure progress toward strategic priorities* (Salem, Oregon Progress Board)

Zachary, J (1995) *Sustainable Community Indicators: guideposts for local planning* (Santa Barbara, CA, Community Environmental Council)

Further Reading

Case Studies of Cities

On Ilo in Peru: Diaz, Doris Balvin, José Luis Lopez Follegatti and Micky Hordijk, 'Innovative urban environmental management in Ilo, Peru', *Environment and Urbanization*, Vol 8, No 1, April 1996, pp 21–34.

On Chimbote in Peru: Foronda F, Maria Elena, 'Chimbote's Local Agenda 21: initiatives to support its development and implementation', *Environment and Urbanization*, Vol 10, No 2, October 1998, pp 129–147

The October 1999 issue of *Environment and Urbanization* is on 'Sustainable Cities Revisited II' and includes Roberts, Ian, 'The strengths and limitations of partnerships in implementing Local Agenda 21s: the experience of Leicester' and Menegat, Rualdo, 'Environmental management in Porto Alegre'

New case studies of Local Agenda 21s in Durban (South Africa), Surabaya (Indonesia), Jinja (Uganda) and Rufisque (Senegal) will be available towards the end of 1999 or early in 2000; for details, write to the Human Settlements Programme, IIED, 3 Endsleigh Street, London WC1H ODD, UK, e-mail humans@iied.org

Reviews of City Action Plans Within Countries

From the Earth Summit to Local Agenda 21: Working Towards Sustainable Development, Lafferty, William M and Katarina Eckerberg (eds), Earthscan, London, 1998, has separate chapters on progress for local agenda 21s in Finland, Sweden, Norway, Germany, Austria, the Netherlands, the United Kingdom and Ireland, and an introductory and a conclusions chapter which compare and contrast national experiences and suggest factors which help in the implementation of local agenda 21s

For those who read Spanish, *Ciudades para la vida: experiencias exitosas y propuestas para la acción* (Cities for Living: Innovative Experiences and Proposals for Action), Liliana Miranda Sara (ed), 1996, is recommended. Published by IPADEL-IHS-PROA-PGU and Naciones Unidas, Lima, and available from Ecociudad, Vargas Machuca 408, San Antonio, Miraflores, Lima, Peru, e-mail: foro@civdad.org.pe

Participation/Empowerment

For a broad overview of this (covering rural and urban areas) see *Whose Common Future: Reclaiming the Commons*, The Ecologist, Earthscan, 1992. This book is about how people and their community organizations must be permitted to reclaim the right to use, maintain and control local resources as a precondition for a sustainable future

In regard to participation and empowerment in urban areas, see: Douglass, Mike and Malia Zoghlin, 'Sustaining cities at the grassroots: livelihood, environment and social networks in Suan Phlu, Bangkok', *Third World Planning Review*, Vol 16, No 2, 1994, pp 171–200.

Douglass, Mike, 'The political economy of urban poverty and environmental management in Asia: access, empowerment and community-based alternatives', *Environment and Urbanization*, Vol 4, No 2, October 1992

See also *Human Settlements and Planning for Ecological Sustainability: The Case of Mexico City*, Keith Pezzoli, MIT Press, Boston and London, 1998

For case studies of participatory tools and methods in urban areas see *RRA Notes 21: Special Issue on Participatory Tools and Methods in Urban Areas*, Diana Mitlin and John Thomson (eds), IIED, 1994. Most issues of the journal *Environment and Urbanization* published since 1995 have one or more further case studies or discussions of participatory tools and methods

The October 1999 issue of *Environment and Urbanization* includes two case studies of community-level local agenda 21s: Hordijk, Michaela, 'A dream of green and water: Community-based formulation of a Local Agenda 21 in peri-urban Lima, Peru' and Velásquez, Luz Stella, case study of Olivares (Manizales)

See also *The Struggle for Nairobi*, Terry Hirst, assisted by Davinder Lamba, 1994, Mazingira Institute, Nairobi. This is a large format 'documentary comic book' which has considerable detail and analysis in regard to the history of Nairobi and its environmental problems. Available from Mazingira Institute, PO Box 14550, Nairobi, Kenya

Addressing the Needs of Children in Urban Areas

A recently published book reviews how those responsible for urban planning and management can address the environmental needs of children: *Cities for Children: Children's Rights, Poverty and the Urban Management*, Sheridan Bartlett and others, Earthscan, London, 1999

Tools and Methods

Graham Haughton's paper 'Key policy domains for improving the urban environment' (*Environment and Urbanization*, Vol 11, No 2, October 1999) includes discussions of tools and methods for land-use planning, transport planning and solid waste management, and the use of the various tools for environmental assessment (environmental impact assessment, capacity studies, environmental audits, state of the environment reports...)

See also 'Sustainability and methodologies of environmental assessment for cities', Ernie Jowsey and Jonathan Kellett in Cedric Pugh (ed), *Sustainability, the Environment and Urbanization*, Earthscan Publications, London, 1996

Planning (and Indicators)

The paper by Jeb Brugmann reproduced in this Reader generated an interesting response and then 'response to the response' from the original author. See Pinfield, Graham, 'The use of indicators in local sustainable development planning: a response to Jeb Brugmann', *Local Environment*, Vol 2, No 2, 1997, pp 185–187 and Brugmann, Jeb, 'Sustainability indicators revisited: getting from political objectives to performance outcomes – a response to Graham Pinfield', *Local Environment*, Vol 2, No 3, 1997, pages 299-302

A special issue of *Environmental Impact Assessment Review* published in 1996 was on the theme of urban sustainability – see Vol 16, Nos 4–6, July–November 1996. This included the paper on Seattle by Alan AtKisson reproduced earlier and also Brugmann, Jeb, 'Planning for sustainability at the local government level', pp 363–379; and Mehta, Pratibha, 'Local agenda 21: practical experiences and emerging issues from the South', pp 309–320.

As noted in 'Further Reading' for Part II, The International Council for Local Environmental Initiatives (ICLEI) has many general publications of relevance to sustainable development and cities, as well as many case studies of innovative local government action and guides to local government action. See ICLEI's web page http://www.iclei.org or write to ICLEI at City Hall, East Tower, 8th Floor, Toronto, Ontario M5H 2N2, Canada

Assessing, Measuring and Monitoring Progress

Indicators and Information Systems for Sustainable Development by Donella Meadows, A Report to the Balaton Group, Sustainability Institute, Hartland, 1998. This is the full Report from which the extract by Donella Meadows published in this section is drawn. Available from the Sustainability Institute, PO Box 174, Hartland Four Corners, VT 05049, USA, price US$10; for orders from outside USA, add $5 for postage and packing

See also 'Measuring urban sustainability', Marina Alberti, *Environmental Impact Assessment Review*, Vol 16, Nos 4–6, July–November 1996, pp 381–424

Part V
Sustainable Development for Cities within a Regional, National and Global Context

Chapter 19

Sustainable Cities: A Contradiction in Terms?

Herbert Girardet

(Reprinted with permission from Edesio Fernandes (editor), *Environmental Strategies for Sustainable Development in Urban Areas: Lessons from Africa and Latin America*, Ashgate, Aldershot, pp 193–209.)

THE URBAN AGE

City growth is changing the condition of humanity and the face of the earth. In one century, global urban populations will have expanded from 15 to nearly 50 per cent and this figure will increase further in the coming decades. By 2000, half of humanity will live and work in cities, while the other half will depend increasingly on cities and towns for their economic survival. In the UK, a pioneer of large-scale urban development, over 80 per cent of people live in urban centres.

The size of modern cities, too, in terms of numbers as well as physical scale, is unprecedented: in *1800* there was only one city with a million people – London. At that time the largest 100 cities in the world had 20 million inhabitants, with each city usually extending to just a few thousand hectares. In *1990* the world's 100 largest cities accommodated 540 million people and 220 million people lived in the 20 largest cities, mega-cities of over 10 million people, some extending to hundreds of thousands of hectares. In addition, there were 35 cities of over 5 million and hundreds of over one million people.[1]

In the 19th and early 20th centuries, urban growth was occurring mainly in the North as a result of the spread of industrialization and the associated rapid increase in the use of fossil fuels. Today, the world's largest and fastest growing cities are emerging in the South because of unprecedented urban-industrial development and frequently as a consequence of rural decline.

We are used to thinking about cities as places where great wealth is generated and also where *social* disparities and tensions have to be addressed. The urban social agenda is certainly a critical one and much effort has gone into addressing these problems. Cities as *cultural* centres have also received much attention, with ancient cities the world over enjoying an unprecedented tourist boom, and great urban centres such as London, New York or Paris accepted as the epitome of cultural development. However, an issue which has received much less attention is the huge *resource use* of modern cities and the implications of that for both local and global environments.

Worldwide, urban growth is closely associated with increased resource consumption. This tends to increase human living standards in monetary terms which can be witnessed today in countries in the South where urban people, typically, have much higher levels of consumption than rural dwellers, with massively increased throughput of fossil fuels, metals, timber, meat and manufactured products. Increased resource throughput in urban centres often coincides with poor management of wastes, causing threats to the health of city people as they are exposed to high concentrations of disease vectors. Many Third World cities don't have the infrastructures to cope with the appropriate handling of wastes. Diseases such as cholera, typhoid and TB, well known in London 150 years ago, are occurring in many Third World cities, with epidemics threatening particularly the poorest districts.

In global environmental terms, too, increased resource use is becoming a pertinent issue. Asia is currently undergoing the most astonishing urban-industrial development. China alone, with 10 per cent economic growth per year, is planning to double the number of its cities, from just over 600 to over 1200 by 2010. Some 300 million people are expected to be moving to cities, converting from peasant farming and craft-based living to urban-industrial lifestyles. The increased purchasing power is already leading to increased demand for consumer goods and a more meat-based diet, with massive implications for the future environmental impact of the world's most populous country.[2]

CITIES AS SUPERORGANISMS

Urban systems with millions of inhabitants are unique to the current age and they are the most complex products of collective human creativity. They are both *organisms* and *mechanisms* in that they utilize biological re-production as well as mechanical production processes.

Large cities are evolving to have characteristics all of their own, with 'the fine specialisation and extraordinary diversity of skills'.[3] Firms will tend to congregate where there is a large market, but the market is large precisely where firms' production is concentrated. The vast array of productive enterprise, capital and labour markets, service industries and artistic endeavour could be described as a symbiotic cultural system. However, unlike natural systems they are highly dependent on external supplies: for their sustenance large modern cities have become dependent on global transport and communication systems. This is not *civilization* in the old-fashioned sense, but *mobilization*, dependent on long-distance transport routes.

Demand for energy defines modern cities more than any other single factor. Most rail, road and aeroplane traffic occurs between cities. All their internal activities – local transport, electricity supply, home living, services provision and manufacturing – depend on the routine use of fossil fuels. As far as I am aware, no city of more than one million people has ever managed without fossil fuels, with the possible exception of medieval Tokyo (Edo) and ancient Rome, both of which made extensive use of sea transport. Without their routine use, the growth of mega-cities of ten million people and more would not have occurred. But there is a price to pay. Waste gases, such as nitrogen dioxide and sulphur dioxide, discharged by chimneys and exhaust pipes, affect the health of city people themselves and, beyond urban boundaries, forests and farmland downwind. A large proportion of the increase of carbon dioxide in the atmosphere is attributable to combustion in the world's cities.

Concern about climate change, resulting mainly from fossil-fuel burning, is now shared by virtually all the world's climatologists.

Concentration of intense economic processes and high levels of consumption in cities both increase their resource demands. Apart from a monopoly on fossil fuels and metals, humanity now uses nearly *half* the world's total photosynthetic capacity as well. Cities are the home of the 'amplified man', an unprecedented amalgam of biology and technology, transcending his biological ancestors. Beyond their limits, cities profoundly affect traditional rural economies and their cultural adaptation to biological diversity. As better roads are built and access to urban products is assured, rural people increasingly abandon their own indigenous cultures which are often defined by sustainable adaptation to their local environment. They tend to acquire urban standards of living and the mind set to go with these.

Urban agglomerations are becoming the dominant feature of the human presence on earth, with supplies brought in from an increasingly global hinterland. All in all, urbanization has profoundly changed humanity's relationship to its host planet, with unprecedented impacts on forests, farmland and aquatic ecosystems. The human species is changing the very way in which the 'the web of life'[4] on earth itself functions, from a *geographically distributed* interaction of a myriad of species, into a *punctuated system* dominated by the resource use patterns of just the one species: cities take up only 2 per cent of the world's land surface, yet they use over 75 per cent of the world's resources.

With Asia, Latin America and parts of Africa now joining Europe, North America and Australia in the urban experiment, it is crucial to assess whether large-scale urbanization and sustainable development can be reconciled. Whilst urbanization is turning the living earth from a self-regulating interactive system into one dominated by humanity, we have yet to learn the skill of creating a new, sustainable equilibrium.

LONDON'S FOOTPRINT

A few years ago I produced a TV documentary on deforestation in the Amazon basin and the resulting loss of biodiversity. Filming at the port of Belem I saw a huge stack of mahogany timber with 'London' stamped on it being loaded into a freighter. I started to take an interest in the connection between urban consumption patterns and human impact on the biosphere. It occurred to me that logging of virgin forests or their conversion into cattle ranches and into fields of soya beans for cattle fodder (in Brazil's Mato Grosso region) or of manioc for pig feed (in the former rainforest regions of Thailand), was perhaps not the most rational way of assuring resource supply to urban 'agglomeration economies'.[5]

Recently, the Canadian economist William Rees[6] started a debate about the *ecological footprint* of cities, which he defines as the land required to supply them with food and timber products and to absorb their CO_2 output via areas of growing vegetation. I have examined the footprint of London which also happens to be the city that started it all: the 'mother of mega-cities'. Today, London's total footprint, following Rees' definition, extends to around 125 times its surface area of 159,000 hectares, or nearly 20 million hectares. With 12 per cent of Britain's population, London requires the equivalent of Britain's entire productive land.[7] In reality, this land, of course, stretches to far-flung places such as the wheat prairies of Kansas, the tea gardens of Assam, the forests of Scandinavia and Amazonia, and the copper mines of Zambia.

Herbert Girardet

Box 19.1 *London's ecological footprint*

This assessment of London's ecological footprint is based on the work of William Rees and Mathis Wackernagel. They have independently estimated the average footprint of Europeans as around 3 hectares, contrasting with 4-5 hectares for North Americans.

London: 7,000,000 people
Surface area: 158,000 hectares
Area required for food production: 1.2 hectares per person: 8,400,000 hectares
Forest area required by London for wood products: 768,000 hectares
Land area that would be required for carbon sequestration: 1.5 hectares per person; total: 10,500,000 hectares
Total London footprint: 19,700,000 hectares = 125 times London's surface area
Average ecological footprint of Londoners: 2.8 hectares
Britain's productive land: 21,000,000 hectares
Britain's surface area: 24,400,000 hectares

But large modern cities are not just defined by their resource use. They are also centres for financial services. When discussing urban sustainability we have to try to assess the financial impact of cities on the rest of the world.

A friend of mine recently told me about a startling experience: 'A couple of years ago I attended a meeting typical of those which take place every day in the City of London. A group of Indonesian businessmen organized a lunch to raise £300 million to finance the clearing of a rainforest and the construction of a pulp paper plant. What struck me was how financial rationalism often overcomes common sense; that profit itself is a good thing whatever the activity, whenever the occasion. What happened to the Indonesian rainforest was dependent upon financial decisions made over lunch that day. The financial benefits would come to institutions in London, Paris or New York. Very little, if any, of the financial benefits would go to the local people. Therefore, when thinking about the environmental impact of London, we have to think about the decisions of fund managers which impact on the other side of the world. In essence, the rainforest may be geographically located in the Far East, but financially it might as well be located in London's Square Mile.[8]

A crucial question for a world city such as London is how it can reconcile its special status as a global trading centre with the new requirement for sustainable development. London's own development was closely associated with gaining access to the world's resources. How can this be reconciled with creating a sustainable relationship with the global environment and also with the aspirations of people at the local level?

London was a pioneer in large-scale urban development. Today, London's businesses, its few remaining manufacturing companies, as well as its trading corporations and its financial institutions, certainly have the desire to *continue*. They wish to be sustainable in their own right. The question now is how the momentum for sustainable development can encompass the aspirations of business, assuring that people can lead lives of continuity and certainty, whilst together achieving compatibility of the urban metabolism with the living systems of the biosphere.

THE METABOLISM OF CITIES

Like other organisms, cities have a definable metabolism. The *metabolism* of most 'modern' cities is essentially linear, with resources flowing through the urban system without much concern about their origin and about the destination of wastes; inputs and outputs are considered as largely unrelated. Raw materials are extracted, combined and processed into consumer goods that end up as rubbish which can't be beneficially reabsorbed into living nature. Fossil fuels are extracted from rock strata, refined and burned; their fumes are discharged into the atmosphere.

In distant forests, trees are felled for their timber or pulp, but all too often forests are not replenished. Similar processes apply to food: nutrients that are taken from the land as food is harvested and not returned. Urban sewage systems usually have the function of collecting human wastes and separating them from people. Sewage is discharged into rivers and coastal waters downstream from population centres and is usually not returned to farmland. Today, coastal waters are enriched both with human sewage and toxic effluents, as well as the run-off of mineral fertilizer applied to farmland feeding cities. This open loop is not sustainable.

The linear metabolic system of most cities is profoundly different from nature's circular metabolism where every output by an organism is also an input which renews and sustains the whole living environment. Planners designing urban systems should start by studying the ecology of natural systems. On a predominantly urban planet, cities will need to adopt circular metabolic systems to assure the long-term

---

Box 19.2 *The metabolism of Greater London*

These figures will eventually allow a comparison of London's metabolism with that of other cities. However, so far up-to-date figures for other cities are not available.

INPUTS	Tonnes per year
Total tonnes of fuel, oil equivalent	20,000,000
Oxygen	40,000,000
Water	1,002,000,000
Food	2,400,000
Timber	1,200,000
Paper	2,200,000
Plastics	2,100,000
Glass	360,000
Cement	1,940,000
Bricks, blocks, sand and tarmac	6,000,000
Metals (total)	1,200,000
WASTES	
CO_2	60,000,000
SO_2	400,000
NO_x	280,000
Wet, digested sewage sludge	7,500,000
Industrial and demolition wastes	11,400,000
Household, civic and commercial wastes	3,900,000

---

viability of the rural environments on which they depend. Outputs will also need to be inputs into the production system, with routine recycling of paper, metals, plastic and glass, and the conversion of organic materials into compost, returning plant nutrients to keep farmland productive.

The *local* effects of urban use of resources of cities also needs to be better understood. Cities accumulate large amounts of materials within them. Vienna, with 1.6 million inhabitants, every day increases its actual weight by some 25,000 tonnes.[9] Much of this is relatively inert materials, such as concrete and tarmac. Other materials, such as heavy metals, have discernible environmental effects: they gradually leach from the roofs of buildings and from water pipes into the local environment. Nitrates, phosphates or chlorinated hydrocarbons accumulate in the urban environment and build up in watercourses and soils, with as yet uncertain consequences for future inhabitants.

The critical question today, as humanity moves to full urbanization, is whether living standards in our cities can be maintained whilst curbing their local and global environmental impacts. To answer this question, it helps to draw up balance-sheets comparing urban resource flows. It is becoming apparent that similar-sized cities supply their needs with a greatly varying throughput of resources. Most large cities have been studied in considerable detail and in many cases it won't be very difficult to compare their use of resources. The critical point is that cities and their people could massively reduce their throughput of resources, maintaining a good standard of living whilst creating much needed local jobs in the process.

ARE SOLUTIONS POSSIBLE?

It seems unlikely that the planet can accommodate an urbanized humanity which routinely draws its resources from a distant hinterland. Can cities therefore transform themselves into sustainable, self-regulating systems – not only in their internal functioning, but also in their relationships with the outside world?

An answer to this questions may be critical to the future well-being of the biosphere, as well as of humanity. Maintaining stable linkages with the world around them is a completely new task for city politicians, administrators, business people and people at large. Yet there is little doubt that the world's major environmental problems will only be solved through new ways of conceptualizing and running our cities, and the way we lead our urban lives.

Today we have the historic opportunity to implement technical and organizational measures for sustainable urban development, arising from agreements signed by the international community at UN conferences in the 1990s. Agenda 21 and its prescriptions for solving global environmental problems at the local level are well known. Building on Agenda 21, the Habitat Agenda, signed by 180 nations at the recent Habitat II conference in Istanbul, will also strongly influence the way we run cities. It states: 'Human settlements shall be planned, developed and improved in a manner that takes full account of sustainable development principles and all their components, as set out in Agenda 21 ... We need to respect the carrying capacity of ecosystems and preservation of opportunities for future generations. Production, consumption and transport should be managed in ways that protect and conserve the stock of resources while drawing upon them. Science and technology have a crucial role in shaping sustainable human settlements and sustaining the ecosystems they depend upon.'[10]

What, then, is a sustainable city? Here is a provisional definition: A 'sustainable city' is a city that works so that all its citizens are able to meet their own needs without endangering the well-being of the natural world or the living conditions of other people, now or in the future. This definition concentrates the mind on fundamentals. In the first instance the emphasis is on people and their needs for long-term survival. Human needs include good quality air and water, healthy food and good housing; they also encompass quality education, a vibrant culture, good health care, satisfying employment or occupation, and the sharing of wealth; as well as factors such as safety in public places, supportive relationships, equal opportunities and freedom of expression; and meeting the special needs of the young, the old or the disabled. In a sustainable city, we have to ask: are all its citizens able to meet these needs?

CONDITIONS FOR SUSTAINABLE DEVELOPMENT

Given that the physiology of modern cities is currently characterized by their routine use of fossil fuels to power production, commerce, transport, water supplies as well as domestic comfort, a major issue for urban sustainability is whether *renewable* energy technologies may be able reduce this dependence.

London, for instance, with 7 million people, uses 20 million tonnes of oil equivalent per year, or two supertankers a week, and discharges some 60 million tonnes of carbon dioxide. Its per capita energy consumption is amongst the highest in Europe, yet the know-how exists to bring down these figure by between 30 and 50 per cent without affecting living standards, whilst creating tens of thousands of jobs in the coming decades.[11]

To make them more sustainable, cities today require a whole range of new resource-efficient technologies, such as combined heat-and-power systems, heat pumps, fuel cells and photovoltaic modules. In the near future enormous reductions in fossil-fuel use can be achieved by the use of photovoltaics. According to calculations by BP, London could supply most of its current summer electricity consumption from photovoltaic modules on the roofs and walls of its buildings.[12] This technology is still expensive, but large-scale production will massively reduce unit costs.

Looking back, the physiology of traditional towns and cities was defined by transport and production systems based on muscle power. Dense concentration of people was the norm. Many cities in history adopted symbiotic relationships with their hinterland to ascertain their continuity. This applies to medieval cities with their concentric rings of market gardens, forests, orchards, farm and grazing land. Chinese cities have long practised the return of night soil on to local farmland as a way of assuring sustained yields of foodstuffs.[13] Today, most Chinese cities administer their own, adjacent areas of farmland and, until recently, were largely self-sufficient in food.[14]

A major effect of the routine use of fossil-fuel based technologies was for cities to replace this density with urban sprawl. Motor transport has caused many cities to stop relying on resources from their local regions and to become dependent on an increasingly global hinterland.

However, some modern cities have made circularity and resource efficiency a top priority. Cities right across Europe are installing waste recycling and composting equipment. Austrian, Swiss, Danish and French cities have taken the lead. In German towns and cities, at this point in time, dozens of composting plants are under construction. Throughout the South, too, cities have made it their business to encourage recycling and composting of wastes.[15]

Some writers have argued that cities can actually be beneficial for the global environment, given the reality of a vast human population.[16] They suggest that the very density of human life in cities makes for energy efficiency in home heating as well as in transport. Systems for waste recycling are more easily organized in densely inhabited areas. And urban agriculture, too, if well developed, could make a significant contribution to feeding cities and providing people with livelihoods.

Urban food growing is certainly common in the late 20th century and not just in poorer countries – a book published by UNDP proves the point: 'The 1980 US census found that urban metropolitan areas produced 30% of the dollar value of US agricultural production. By 1990, this figure had increased to 40%. – Singapore is fully self-reliant in meat and produces 25% of its vegetable needs. – Bamako, Mali, is self-sufficient in vegetables and produces half or more of the chickens it consumes. – Dar-es-Salaam, one of the world's fastest growing large cities, now has 67% of families engaged in farming compared with 18% in 1967. – 65% of Moscow families are involved in food production compared with 20% in 1970. There are 80,000 community gardeners on municipal land in Berlin with a waiting list of 16,000.'[17]

POLICIES FOR SUSTAINABILITY

Today, we have a great opportunity to develop a whole new range of environmentally friendly technologies for use in our cities. Efficient energy systems are now available for urban buildings, including combined heat-and-power (CHP) generators, with fuel cells and photovoltaic modules waiting in the wings. New materials and concepts of architectural design allow us to greatly improve the energy performance and to reduce the environmental impact of materials use in buildings. And waste-recycling technologies for small and large, rich and poor cities, can facilitate greater efficiency in the urban use of resources. Transport technologies, too, are due for a major overhaul. Fuel-efficient low-emission vehicles are at a very advanced stage of development. In US cities, rapid urban transit systems are starting to reappear even where people had come to depend almost exclusively on private transport.

With over 80 per cent of the population in the UK living in cities and with cities using most of the world's resources, it is critically important to develop new policies for sustainability – social, economic and environmental. Britain has the historic opportunity of developing practical policies for urban redevelopment, benefiting both people and the environment. This means, above all else, self-financing investment in end use efficiency, reducing resource use whilst simultaneously generating urban jobs and business opportunities.

With Britain signed up to Agenda 21 and the Habitat Agenda, we have the opportunity to refocus investment from resource extraction to resource conservation and recycling, with a great many employment and business opportunities. Whilst a policy based on high resource productivity would reduce employment in mining, much of it abroad, it would enhance job creation in end use efficiency – in the building trade, in environmental technology industries and in the electronics sector – in places where they are most needed: in our cities.

Policies proposed here aim to create synergies between various business sectors: the waste outputs of cities can be a basis for new business ventures. Energy efficiency, so far tackled half-heartedly, should be given top priority. Government can do a great deal to facilitate sustainable urban development, using European and national legislation, planning regulation and budgetary signals to initiate change.

Waste

The recent landfill tax is increasing recycling in the UK, helping to achieve the government target of 25 per cent household-waste recycling by 2000. This taxation should be extended, with the purpose of achieving a recycling rate of at least 50 per cent which is already the norm in other countries. In some British cities, such as Bath and Leicester where recycling has advanced a great deal, the benefits for people and the local environment are already clearly in evidence.

In London, where currently only 7 per cent of household waste is recycled, a new initiative by LPAC and London Pride Partnership is expected to bring recycling up to unprecedented levels: by 2000 every London home will have a recycling box with separate compartments instead of conventional dustbins. Progressively more and more municipal waste will be recycled, establishing new reprocessing industries and creating 1,500 new jobs.[18] This figure will go up further early in the new century. Already, composting organic wastes is advancing well, with 'timber stations' composting shredded branches of pruned trees and leaf litter being established in various locations.

Energy

National planning regulations have already greatly improved energy efficiency of homes, but much more can be done, dramatically improving the energy performance of buildings, creating more local jobs in the process and reducing the environmental impact of energy use. Regulating the energy supply industry to further improve generating efficiency and reduce discharge of waste gases could significantly increase the use of modern, clean Combined Heat and Power (CHP) systems in our cities.

The UK is just seeing the first schemes where greenhouse cultivation is being combined with CHP, utilizing their hot water and waste CO_2 to enhance crop growth for year-round cultivation.[19] Policies encouraging CHP could thus also be used for enhancing urban agriculture, bringing producers closer to their markets instead of flying and trucking in vegetables long distance. Once again, beneficial effects on jobs would result.

Another policy area is photovoltaics. Government policy should vigorously encourage the installation of photovoltaic modules on buildings, enhancing the UK's capacity to produce PV systems and creating much needed local jobs in the process. Experimental buildings such as the photovoltaics centre at Newcastle University, a 60s building recently clad with photovoltaic panels, are very promising.[20] Every city in the UK should have such buildings to test the potential of PV and to develop local know-how.

Sewage

A major urban output is sewage, containing valuable nutrients such as nitrates, potash and phosphates. Returning these to the land is an essential aspect of sustainable development. In Bristol, Wessex Water now dries and granulates all of the city's sewage. The annual sewage output of 600,000 people is turned into 10,000 tonnes of fertilizer granules. Most of it is currently used to regreen the slag heaps around Merthyr Tydfil across the Severn in South Wales. In contrast, Thames Water in London is currently constructing incinerators for burning the sewage sludge produced by 4 million Londoners. This is a decision of historic short-sightedness given that phosphates – only available from North Africa and Russia – are likely to be in short supply within decades. Crops for feeding cities cannot be grown without phosphates.

Cities all over the UK should be encouraged to build sewage recycling works using the latest technologies such as the one utilized by Wessex Water. This will be of critical importance for sustainable urban development and will, once again, create jobs in cities as well as benefiting the environment.

SMART CITIES

Cities are centres of communication and new electronic systems have dramatically enhanced that role. Information technologies have given cities a global reach as never before, and particularly in further extending the financial power of urban institutions. The daily money-go-round from Tokyo to London and on to New York and Los Angeles is the most striking example of this. '... the new economy is organised around global networks of capital, management, and information, whose access to technological know-how is at the roots of productivity and competitiveness'.[21] But will this power ever be exercised with a sense of responsibility appropriate to an *urban age*? If this is the global network society, who controls its ever growing power?

The global economic and environmental reach of cities today needs to be matched with communication systems that monitor new impacts, an early warning system that enables city people to ring alarm bells as soon as new, unacceptable developments occur, whether it is the transfer of toxic waste or the transfer of environmentally undesirable technologies from one city or territory to another.

Much more needs to be done to ensure processes by which cities monitor and ameliorate their impact on the biosphere. I would like to postulate that modern cities could develop cultural feedback systems, responding to the challenge of achieving sustainability by limiting urban resource consumption and waste output through technological and organizational measures.

Today, new communication technologies should also be utilized to improve the functioning of cities in many different ways and communications within them. Urban Intranets, now in place in a growing number of cities, should enhance the communication flow between various sectors of urban society. Electronic sampling of opinions should be used to enhance urban decision-making.

In that context it is of critical importance to recognize the great inherent creativity of city people. In the end, only people can implement measures for sustainable urban development – technical fixes are not enough. But people need a good knowledge base. For this purpose the most important thing is the collection and dissemination of best practices to assure that people in cities worldwide actually know about existing projects. Much better use has to be made of new information technologies. That would be an indication that cities were becoming smart in the best sense of the word.

THE LEGACY OF HABITAT II

The Habitat II Conference in Istanbul made a great deal of the fact that cities, more often than not, are considered places where problems are concentrated, yet in reality, given half a chance, people, wherever they are, seek to improve their situation wherever possible. The Best Practices and Local Leadership programme was one of the flagship initiatives of Habitat II. In the course of two years it collected some 700 examples from around the world under the following categories:

1 Poverty reduction and job creation
2 Access to shelter, land and finance
3 Production/consumption cycles
4 Gender and social diversity
5 Enterprise and economic development
6 Waste recycling and reuse
7 Transport and communication
8 Combating social exclusion
9 Crime prevention and social justice
10 Governance
11 Infrastructure, water and energy supply
12 Innovative use of technology
13 Environmental protection and rehabilitation
14 Policy and planning

This information is now available via e-mail[22] and through direct contacts with urban groups all over the world. Exchange programmes for disseminating this information are now reaching some of the poorest urban communities.

In some cities, too, business is recognizing the need to make urban sustainability a central concern and to support local communities, but much more needs to be done.

According to Wally N'Dow, Director-General of Habitat II, there are five lessons that emerged out of the preparations for the conference:[23]

1 *The power of the good examples.* There are fascinating initiatives throughout the world's cities. Habitat and its partners have helped groups from around the world to prepare reports and to make films about their own activities. It is also undertaking the dissemination of best practices. This process will deepen our understanding of urban challenges and opportunities so that realistic steps can be taken at local, national and international levels to develop new partnerships for solving problems and enriching the life of cities.
2 *Complexity of issues.* The contributions Habitat received also illustrated just how complex modern cities are. In this context, obstacles to successful implementation must be analysed and effective processes for implementing projects identified. In situations of rapid urban growth it is particularly important for the development of urban infrastructure problems to be overcome.
3 *Local level action has large-scale repercussions.* Implementation must be tailored very closely to local situations. We then have to ask: how applicable are best practices outside their own regions? For urban best practice to be transferable from one city to another, implementation must be closely tailored to local situations. It is particularly important to establish under what circumstances and with what types of partners successful projects have materialized.
4 *Exchanges take place between peer groups in different cities.* The sharing of best practice between cities is an essential tool for sustainable urban development. Once outside interest in a project has been established, site visits are of critical importance. By learning from example, local transformation can lead to global change.

5   *Changing the way urban institutions work.* The power of allowing people direct access to best practice examples through a dynamic process of decentralized co-operation has become very apparent. The material collected under the Habitat 'best practice initiative' is a gold-mine for the world's cities and its dissemination will be of paramount importance for all the potential partners concerned.

By the time the next century passes its first quarter, more than a billion and a half people in the world's cities will face life- and health-threatening environments unless we create a revolution in urban problem solving. We need a new approach, a creative and constructive effort that can only come if we forge a global partnership between national governments and local communities, between the public and private sectors.

Whether it is the environment or human rights, population or poverty or the status of women, we must deal with these issues in our cities. That is why they have become a priority challenge for the international community; why it is essential that they are at the centre of a growing global effort to make our cities and all communities productive, safe, healthy, more equitable and sustainable.

To make a success of cities we need to extend popular participation in decision-making to restore confidence in local democracy. Consultation is not enough. To strengthen local democratic processes, methods such as neighbourhood forums, action planning and consensus-building should be widely used because in appropriate circumstances these lead to better decisions and easier implementation. With the help of modern communications technologies, wider citizens' involvement can be incorporated into strategic decision-making.

CULTURAL DEVELOPMENT

With the whole world now copying Western development patterns, we need to formulate new cultural priorities. Cultural development is a critical aspect of sustainable urban development, giving cities the chance to realize their full potential as centres of creativity, education and communication. Cities are nothing if not centres of knowledge, and today this also means knowledge of the world and our impact on it. Reducing urban impacts is as much an issue of education and of information dissemination as of the better uses of technology.

Ultimately, that cannot be done without changing the value systems underpinning our cities. Adopting circular resource flows will help cities reduce their footprint, and thus their impact on the biosphere is a cultural issue. Initiatives to that effect are now in evidence all over the world. In many cities there is growing awareness that the urban super-organism can become a sustainable, self-regulatingsystem through appropriate cultural processes. In the end, it is only a profound change of attitudes, a spiritual and ethical change, that can bring the deeper transformations that can make cities truly sustainable.

We need to revive the vision of the city as a place of culture and creativity, of conviviality and above all else of sedentary living. As I have suggested, currently cities are not centres of *civilization* but *mobilization* of people and goods. A calmer, serener vision of cities is needed to help them fulfil their true potential as places not just of the body but of the spirit. Great cities of the past were above all else places of beauty, with their great public spaces, their magnificent bridges and the rising spires of their religious buildings.

Cities are what their people are. The greatest energy of cities should flow *inwards*, to create masterpieces of human creativity, not *outwards*, to bring in ever more products from ever more distant places. The future of cities crucially depends on the utilization of the rich knowledge of their people, and that includes environmental knowledge. Cities cannot claim to be knowledge-led without activating the know-how to beautify their own internal environment for all to enjoy and to reduce their impact on environments worldwide.

Central and local governments are increasingly aware that efforts to improve the living environment must focus on cities. Eco-friendly urban development could well become the greatest challenge of the 21st century, not only for human self-interest, but also for the sake of a sustainable relationship between cities and the biosphere on which humanity ultimately depends.

Cities for a new millennium will be energy and resource efficient, people friendly and culturally rich, with active democracies assuring the best uses of human energies. In northern mega-cities, such as London and New York, prudent inward investment will contribute significantly to achieving higher levels of employment. In cities in the South, significant investment in infrastructure will make a vast difference to health and living conditions. But none of this will happen unless we create a new balance between the material and the spiritual, and to that effect much good work needs to be done in the years to come.

NOTES AND REFERENCES

1   Extracted from UNCHS (Habitat), *An Urbanizing World: The Global Report on Human Settlements 1996*, Oxford University Press, Oxford and New York, 1996
2   Worldwatch Institute, *State of the World 1997*, Earthscan Publications, London, 1997
3   LSE Greater London Group, *London's Size and Diversity*, January 1996
4   Fritjof Capra, *The Web of Life*, Harper Collins, London, 1996
5   LSE Greater London Group (1996) op cit
6   Mathis Wackernagel and William Rees, *Our Ecological Footprint*, New Society Publishers, Gabriola, 1995
7   Herbert Girardet, *Getting London in Shape for 2000*, London First, 1996
8   Mark Campanale, personal communication
9   Prof Paul Brunner, TU, Vienna, personal communication
10   United Nations, *The Habitat Agenda*, New York, 1996
11   Herbert Girardet (1996) op cit
12   Rod Scott, BP Solar, personal communication
13   F H King, *Farmers of Forty Centuries*, Rodale Press, Emmaus, 1911
14   Victor Sit (ed), *Chinese Cities, the growth of the Metropolis since 1949*, Oxford University Press, 1988
15   *Warmer Bulletin*, Summer 1995
16   Richard Gilbert in Richard Gilbert, Don Stevenson and Herbert Girardet, *Making Cities Work, The Role of Local Authorities in the Urban Environment*, Earthscan, 1996
17   Jac Smit, Annu Ratta and Joe Nasr, *Urban Agriculture: Food, Jobs and Sustainable Cities*, Publication Series for Habitat II, Volume One, UNDP, New York, 1996
18   *Evening Standard*, 30 December 1996
19   *Grower Magazine*, 21 March 1996
20   Prof Robert Hill, Northumbria Solar Project, University of Newcastle, 1996
21   Manuel Castells, *The Network Society*, Blackwells, Oxford, 1996
22   On http://www.bestpractices.org
23   Quoted in Herbert Girardet, *The Gaia Atlas of Cities*, second edition, Gaia Books, London, 1996

Chapter 20

The Rural, Regional and Global Impacts of Cities in Africa, Asia and Latin America

Jorge E Hardoy, Diana Mitlin and David Satterthwaite

(Taken from Chapter 4 of Hardoy, Jorge E, Diana Mitlin and David Satterthwaite, *Environmental Problems in Third World Cities*, Earthscan Publications, London. Originally published in 1992, this version is drawn from a new draft of this chapter prepared for a second expanded and updated edition, due for publication by Earthscan in 2000.)

CITIES' REGIONAL IMPACTS AND RURAL-URBAN INTERACTIONS

Cities transform environments and landscapes not only within the built-up area but also for considerable distances around them. This includes environmental impacts in the region around the city which usually includes large areas defined as (or considered) rural. The inhabitants, environment and natural resource base of this wider region are usually affected by:

- the expansion of the built-up area and the transformations this brings – for instance, as land surfaces are reshaped, valleys and swamps filled, large volumes of clay, sand, gravel and crushed rock extracted and moved, water sources tapped and rivers and streams channelled;[1]
- the demand from city-based enterprises, households and institutions for the products of forests, rangelands, farmlands, watersheds or aquatic ecosystems that are outside its boundaries;
- the solid, liquid and air-borne wastes generated within the city and transferred to the region around it which have environmental impacts, especially on water bodies where liquid wastes are disposed of without treatment and on land sites where solid wastes are dumped without measures to limit their environmental impact.

Cities require a high input of resources – fresh water, fossil fuels, land and all the goods and materials that their populations and enterprises require. The more populous the city and the richer its inhabitants, the greater its demand on resources and, in general, the larger the area from which these are drawn, although at any one time, each particular type of natural resource may have its own particular area of supply.[2]

The more valuable and lighter natural commodities such as fruit and vegetables, wood and metals may be drawn from areas hundreds of kilometres away or imported from other countries. So may cheaper foods and other natural resources, if these are not easily produced locally. But the more bulky, low-value materials will usually come from close-by; as Ian Douglas notes, 'the physical structure of fabric of the city, the buildings, the roads, railways, airports, docks, pipe and conduit systems require large quantities of materials for their construction' and 'the bulk of the structures are derived from locally available clay, sand, gravel and crushed rock'.[3] This can be seen in the brick works, quarries, claypits, sand and gravel pits in and around most cities,[4] all of which have environmental impacts.

Cities are also major centres for resource degradation. Water needed for industrial processes, for supplying residential and commercial buildings, for transporting sewage and for other uses is returned to rivers, lakes or the sea at a far lower quality than that originally supplied. Solid wastes collected from city households and businesses are usually disposed of on land sites in the region around the city while much of the uncollected solid waste generally finds its way into water bodies, adding to the pollution. These can be termed regional impacts. We look first at the environmental impact of cities' physical expansion, then at the demand for resources from the wider region (the 'inputs') and then at the impact of wastes generated by city-based activities (especially waste disposal) on the wider region (the 'outputs').

CITIES' PHYSICAL EXPANSION

In the absence of any effective land use plan or other means to control new developments, cities generally expand haphazardly – defined by where different households, residential areas, enterprises and public sector activities locate, legally and illegally. Uncontrolled physical growth impacts most on what might be termed an immediate hinterland around a city; much of this cannot be described as urban or suburban and yet much of it is no longer rural. If the city has been designated a 'metropolitan centre', much or all of this hinterland may fall within the metropolitan boundaries.

Within this area, agriculture may disappear or decline as land is bought up by people or companies in anticipation of its change from agricultural to urban use and of the often very large increases in land value that this brings, as the city's built-up area and transport system expands. There is usually a lack of effective public control of such changes in land use or on the profits that can be made from them. In many nations, it is also encouraged by a lack of other domestic high-return investment opportunities.

Unplanned and uncontrolled city expansion produces a patchwork of different developments, including businesses and many high-density residential settlements, interspersed with undeveloped land – some of it held for speculative gain. Development occurs through legal and illegal action by various landowners, builders, developers and real-estate firms in an ad hoc way, producing an incoherent urban sprawl. There are usually many legal subdivisions in this hinterland for houses or commercial and industrial buildings which have been approved without reference to any city-wide plan. Many cities have a considerable range of new factories and other businesses developing in surrounding 'rural' areas, although their functioning and markets are intimately tied to the city.[5] In more prosperous cities, many new low-density, high-income residential neighbourhoods may also develop here, along with some commercial developments and leisure facilities for higher income groups – for instance, country clubs and golf courses. In many cities, especially those with high levels of crime and violence, there are residential developments enclosed within walls protected by private security firms – the 'walled cities' or *barrios cerados*. There are usually many unauthorized subdivisions as well and where regulation is lax, these may cater for middle- and upper-income developments, too. There are usually illegal squatter communities, too, who originally located here because the inaccessibility, lack of infrastructure and poor quality of the site gave more chance of not being evicted. In many cities (including Buenos Aires, Delhi, Santiago, Seoul and Manila), this hinterland also contains settlements formed when their inhabitants were dumped there, after being evicted from their homes by 'slum' or squatter clearance.[6] The inhabitants of these settlements may again find themselves under threat of eviction as the physical expansion of the urban area and its road network increases the value of the land on which they live.

There may be no citywide plan and in many larger cities, responsibility for land-use planning and development control is held by a large number of individual municipal or other local authorities with few, if any, mechanisms to ensure some coordination between them. Some local authorities may seek to attract new business by lax environmental controls. One interesting case study of this is in Colombia where the cities of Villamaria and Manizales share an ecosystem and both rely on various natural resources, but the local authorities had very different attitudes to environmental management.[7] Manizales is well known for its environmental management and its innovative Local Agenda 21,[8] but neighbouring Villamaria sought to attract new enterprises by keeping down taxes – for instance, on petrol – and having more lax controls on land development and pollution, although there are now institutional measures in place to ensure better joint management of shared resources.[9]

The uncontrolled and unregulated physical expansion of the built-up area usually has serious social and environmental consequences, including problems of soil erosion and its contribution to silting up drainage channels and the segregation of low-income groups in the worst located and often the most dangerous areas. The haphazard expansion of settlements also means greatly increased costs of providing basic infrastructure as new developments needing connection to existing networks of roads, water mains and sewage and drainage pipes spring up far from existing networks. It is also more expensive to provide public transport and social services. One often sees the paradox of extreme overcrowding, serious housing shortages and acute shortages of infrastructure and services in many particular areas and yet large amounts of land left vacant or only partially developed with all that this implies in terms of increasing the cost of providing infrastructure and services. Illegal or informal settlements will also often grow on land sites subject to flooding or at risk from landslides or other natural hazards, especially where these offer the best located sites on which low-income settlers have the best chance of establishing a home or simply avoiding eviction. But these are also land sites to which it is more difficult and expensive to extend basic infrastructure.

It is not only around the major cities that uncontrolled urban expansion produces these kinds of serious social and ecological impacts, as can be seen in a study of Bamenda in Cameroon with a population estimated at 270,400 in 1993.[10] Settlements have expanded up steep hillslopes of the Bamenda escarpment with no public provisions to ensure the more unstable areas are avoided or to minimize soil erosion when sites were cleared. Flooding has become a particular problem, as land clearance-induced erosion contributes to the silting of stream beds or other drains and more rapid water run-off. The impact of the floods is made more serious by the expansion of settlements over flood plains and the inadequate provision for drainage, along with the expansion of paved or otherwise impervious surfaces. The main reason for the expansion of settlements up these fragile slopes is that land here is very cheap and low income households cannot afford the much more expensive but safer sites. But as Acho-Chi points out in his study of Bamenda, it is also very expensive to extend basic services to those living on the steep slopes so a failure to manage urban expansion brings high social as well as ecological costs.[11]

The loss of agricultural land, forests or other land sites with valuable ecological functions – for instance, wetlands – is another consequence of uncontrolled city growth. Cities often expand over some of their nation's most productive agricultural land since so many cities grew up within highly fertile areas. Most cities in Latin America, Asia and North Africa were important urban centres before the development of motorized transport.[12] At that time, no major city could develop too far from the land which produced its inhabitants' daily food and fuel requirements. In addition, many cities first developed as market centres to serve the prosperous farms and farming households around them. For example, almost all the large cities in the nations around the Pacific were established on lowland delta regions and continue to expand into their nation's most fertile agricultural land.[13]

This loss of agricultural land can usually be avoided or minimized if government guides the physical expansion and ensures that vacant or underutilized land is fully used. In most cities, the problem is not a lack of vacant land but a lack of government action to guide new developments on land other than the best farmland. In Egypt, more than 10 per cent of the nation's most productive farmland has been lost to urban encroachment in the last three decades, much of it through illegal squatting or subdivision, while at the same time prime sites within cities remain undeveloped,[14] although Egypt is unusual in having such a small proportion of its national surface as cultivatable since more than 95 per cent of the country is desert. The urban area of Delhi (including New Delhi) has grown nearly 13-fold since 1900, eating into surrounding agricultural areas and absorbing more than 100 villages. This unplanned and uncontrolled expansion has been accompanied by the expansion of brick-making kilns with fertile topsoil being used to make bricks.[15]

Urban land markets can also disrupt agricultural production and the livelihoods of those who depend on it for areas that stretch far beyond sites developed for urban use. There are also conflicts over land-use priorities between urban-based demands and environmental perspectives; examples include the loss of agricultural lands and of forests, wetlands and other undeveloped sites to industrial estates and residential developments or to golf courses and country clubs. These conflicts generally involve social conflicts, too, as the livelihoods of those who depend on the agricultural lands or forests are threatened by urban-based demands.[16] Box 20.1 describes these conflicts in the highly productive agricultural zone to the south of Manila and how national, local and personal forces ensure that land for residential, industrial or other urban developments are favoured over protection and continued use of highly productive farmland.

Uncontrolled physical expansion also destroys natural landscapes in or close to cities which should be preserved as parks, nature reserves, historic sites or simply areas of open space for recreation and children's play. The need to preserve or develop such areas might seem less urgent than, say, land for housing. But once an area is built up, it is almost impossible (and very expensive) to remedy a lack of open space. In addition, the richer groups suffer much less. Their residential areas

Box 20.1 *The politics of land conversion on the rural-urban interface; the case of Cavite in the Philippines*

In the province of Cavite, just to the south of Manila, agricultural land and the rural livelihoods and staple food this supports are being lost to urban and industrial development. Official figures show that 1840 hectares of agricultural land in Cavite were converted to non-agricultural use between 1988 and 1995, more than half for residential developments with most of the rest for industrial and institutional developments. Most land conversions are on irrigated rice lands. But these figures almost certainly understate the land taken out of agricultural production since they do not include land that is lying idle because the owners have removed the tenant farmers but not yet developed it or land converted without the knowledge of the authorities. The land conversion displaces the farming population; the biggest losers are the landless agricultural labourers since at least the tenant farmers receive disturbance compensation.

In terms of environmental impact, farmers in Cavite complain that irrigation canals have been silted up with eroded material from local building sites. In other cases, water supply is also blocked by household wastes as new residents respond to inadequate garbage collection services by discarding these in nearby canals. Farmers have also complained that crop pests have become an increasing problem with the development of residential areas in the midst of farmland.

Despite an agrarian law which is meant to protect rice and corn lands and support the transfer of land to the tenant farmers who work it, various factors at national, local and personal levels ensure a continued loss of agricultural land:

- Landlords keen to avoid losing their land can circumvent the agrarian reform law by converting it to other crops or to non-agricultural uses. In many cases, tenant farmers have been removed and the land has been left idle because leaving a farmer to cultivate rice would make it difficult to obtain a non-agricultural zoning from the local government. In addition, the longer a tenant is allowed to farm land, the higher the compensation that has to be paid. But if land is left idle, after a few years, the owner can claim the land is 'non-productive' and therefore eligible for conversion.
- The government under President Ramos emphasized industrial development and although this was meant to include agro-industrialization, this came to mean industrial development located in agricultural areas rather than the formation of functional linkages between agriculture and industry.
- The legal setting for land conversion has various measures to protect agricultural land but with few provisions for punishing offenders and with numerous opportunities for evasion. Various laws also undermine the control of land conversion by the Department of Agrarian Reform. In addition, the political climate has been one in which industrial development is aggressively promoted while agricultural land is seen as expendable when it conflicts with other priorities. Those with the means and good connections can circumvent the land conversion regulations relatively easy.
- At local level, many towns have no precisely defined or publicly available zoning maps, so local officials (especially mayors) have great scope for land reclassification. As a result, Cavite's municipal mayors have become the province's leading real-estate agents and brokers.[17] In part, this is because municipal revenues increase with residential and industrial growth, but local politicians generally have a more direct stake in land conversion. Since local councils are also in charge of law

---

Box 20.1 *Continued*

farmland. Provincial governments can also become involved, although technically they have little power to influence land-conversion decisions. However, the governor of Cavite in the early 1990s was reported to have ordered the bulldozing of homes and engineered the destruction of irrigation canals so land was cleared of 'squatters' and tenant farmers and made available for Manila-based or foreign companies for 'development' into industrial estates.[18]

- At the level of personal relations, there is little basis for equality as tenant farmers negotiate with landlords who have high social status, sufficient resources to bribe officials and access to legal counsel. This negotiation also takes place within a cultural context of patron-client ties that preclude farmers from asserting their legal rights.

Land has long been the key source of power and conflict in the Philippines but in the past, the struggle has focused on the control of agricultural land as the basis for wealth, patronage and dominance. Now it is the potential of agricultural land for urban-industrial uses that motivates the will to control it in areas such as Cavite.

Source: Kelly, Philip F, 'The politics of urban-rural relationships: land conversion in the Philippines', *Environment and Urbanization*, Vol 10, No 1, 1998, pp 35–54

---

usually have plenty of open space. Their homes often have gardens. And they can afford to become members of the 'country clubs', sports clubs and golf courses which have become common on the outskirts of many cities and so can enjoy walks, playgrounds and facilities for sport.

INPUTS INTO URBAN AREAS – THE DEMAND FOR RESOURCES

It is difficult to draw up any 'balance-sheet' regarding the environmental (and other) benefits and costs of urban-based demand for rural resources. This chapter concentrates on the environmental costs. But urban-based demand for rural resources is also an important (and often the most important) basis for rural incomes and livelihoods, and the incomes produced by urban demand may form the basis for prosperous, well-managed farms, fisheries and forests. This is a point to which we will return in a later section on rural-urban relations.

The demand for rural resources from city-based enterprises and households may limit their availability for rural households. For instance, in cities where wood and charcoal are still widely used for cooking and heating (mostly by lower income households), city-based demand may pre-empt supplies formerly used by rural inhabitants. Where once poor rural inhabitants gathered wood from what was regarded as common land, now they may be barred from doing so, as the wood is harvested for sale. Common land once used for gathering wild produce and grazing is taken over by monoculture tree plantations where such gathering or grazing is no longer permitted.[19] High demand for fuelwood from cities may be a prime cause of deforestation (and the soil erosion which usually accompanies it), and this may be taking place at considerable distances from the city (see Box 20.2). However, some care is needed in assuming that this will be the case, since studies in various African countries showed little or no evidence of large-scale deforestation associated with urban-based demand for wood and fuelwood.[20]

Box 20.2 *Firewood in the cities*

To meet demand for firewood in Delhi, 12,423 railway wagons of firewood arrived at Tughlakabad railway siding during 1981–82, some 612 tons a day. Most of this wood comes from Madhya Pradesh, nearly 700 kilometres away. The Shahdara railway siding also receives firewood daily from the forests in the Himalayan foothills in Assam and Bihar, although in smaller quantities. In addition, the forested area and trees within Delhi yield thousands of tons annually. Yet Delhi has a relatively low per capita consumption of firewood because of the ready availability of kerosene, coal and liquid petroleum gas (which are much preferred as fuel if they can be afforded). In Bangalore, an estimated 440,000 tonnes of commercial firewood are consumed each year, far more than Delhi, even though Bangalore has around half the population of Delhi. Most of it arrives by road – an average of 114 trucks a day. Most firewood comes from private farms and forests within 150 kilometres of Bangalore, but 15 per cent comes from government forests, 300–700 kilometres away.

Source: CSE, The State of India's Environment 1984–5: The Second Citizens' Report, Centre for Science and Environment, New Delhi, 1986

A study of the long-term impact that Jakarta may have on its wider region provides an example of the complex rural-urban interactions taking place between a city and its surrounding areas and shows how serious the environmental consequences can be.[21] The expansion of the urban area and urban activities pushes farmers from agricultural land; productive agriculture is replaced by urban developments or by commercial ventures for tourism and recreation. Agriculture is pushed on to land less suited to such use in hill and upland areas. Soil erosion there lowers agricultural productivity and causes siltation of water reservoirs, flooding after heavy rains, plus reduced flows in rivers during dry periods. Meanwhile, the government must seek new sources of water to supply Jakarta since overpumping of ground water has already resulted in serious salt-water intrusion into what were previously sweet-water aquifers; the supply of water may need to multiply considerably, especially if rising demand from a growing population and expanding productive base is to be combined with improvements in the supply of piped water to city households. But many of the lowland river and watercourses nearby have high concentrations of organic chemicals and heavy metals from agricultural biocides which are not broken down by natural processes, and this limits their use for human consumption (see Box 20.3 for more details).

Depletion of freshwater resources. Many urban centres face similar difficulties to Jakarta in obtaining sufficient fresh water and this is even the case in cities where half or more of the population are not adequately served with safe, sufficient supplies. Many cities have outgrown the capacity of their locality to provide adequate water supplies or are drawing down groundwater resources much faster than the natural rate of

Box 20.3 *Regional impacts of Jakarta*

The Jakarta metropolis now ranks as the eighth largest urban agglomeration in the world. By 1980, most of the growth in population was taking place on the periphery of the metropolis, with the population in previously low-density areas such as Depok and Cibinong growing at rates of 10 per cent a year. A significant proportion of population growth has occurred through the attraction of migrants from other regions of Java.

The first major planning study to deal solely with the spatial dimension of environmental degradation in the Jakarta metropolitan region in 1983 identified problems such as severe water pollution from both urban and agricultural uses, unnecessary loss and degradation of prime agricultural land through urban expansion, potentially serious erosion problems developing in the uplands, extensive loss of natural habitation and severe threats to the remaining areas of natural forest, coastlands and marine ecosystems. Other studies of environmental conditions in Jakarta have noted the existence of mercury poisoning in Jakarta Bay and the absence of concrete government measures to deal with the mounting levels of toxic wastes. These problems are not simply the result of either a unidirectional spread of urbanization into agricultural lands or the movement of rural households into ecologically critical uplands. Rather they are the outcome of negatively reinforcing impacts of both rapid urbanization and the rapid expansion of rural land use in coastal, upland and forest areas in the region reaching beyond the Jakarta agglomeration and along the Jakarta-Bandung corridor.

As the metropolis has expanded, the negative environmental impacts of one activity have been magnified by those of another. Industrial pollution of water systems has occurred alongside that caused by the excessive use of fertilizers, pesticides and herbicides in agriculture which feed into the same water system. Added to these impacts is a situation in which most of the population continues to depend upon natural river flows for daily water consumption and waste disposal.

In a region such as Jakarta, environmental problems go beyond the categories of simple negative externalities and threaten the very sustainability of development. One example is the extraction of ground water at an accelerating rate by a multiplicity of users. The result has been that sea water has now intruded 15 kilometres inland, creating a zone of salinized ground water reaching to the centre of the city.

The expanding population and economic activities have brought about land use changes within the region. As the zone of urban land expands, agriculture is pushed outward and upward towards less suitable agricultural land in hill and upland areas. In upland areas, soil erosion is a particular concern; besides lowering agricultural productivity, it also has potentially severe downstream impacts such as: the siltation of reservoirs; flooding through loss of upland capacity to retain water after heavy rains; and a reduced flow in other seasons which would exacerbate downstream pollution and create 'desertification-like' conditions of rural land in the region.

There is a major dilemma to be faced by efforts to improve the quality of life in metropolitan core regions in Asia. This centres on the fact that the major parameters which need to be guided are neither contained within Jakarta nor are subject to substantial manipulation by the spatial allocation of infrastructure in the capital city region. Mechanization of agriculture and a decline in public spending on rural construction, which are both working to accelerate rural-metropolitan migration; the fall in the prices of outer-island exports, which has reduced the economic pull to direct migration away from Java; import-substitution and, more recently, export-oriented manufacturing policies which have worked to polarize manufacturing employment within the Jakarta agglomeration,

---

Box 20.3 *Continued*

are the major factors propelling the accelerated growth of the Jakarta metropolitan region.

It is already evident that land-use management within the region must be dramatically improved if the negative impacts of land-use changes and conflicts are to be reduced to allow for an environmentally sustainable development process. At present there are three main obstacles to land-use policy implementation: the failure to effectively co-ordinate the programmes of government bureaux responsible for various aspects of land-use control; the absence of sufficient incentives to guide land-use changes by the private sector away from environmentally sensitive areas; and the absence of a clear political will to implement existing policies and regulations.

Drawn from Douglass, Mike 'The Environmental Sustainability of development: coordination, incentives and political will in land use planning for the Jakarta metropolis',*Third World Planning Review*, Vol 11, No 2, 1989

---

recharge. Many have overused or otherwise mismanaged local sources, so these are no longer available – for instance, for many coastal cities, local aquifers that have been overpumped, resulting in saltwater intrusion. Over-exploitation of underground water often causes serious problems of subsidence for many buildings and sewage and drainage pipes in many cities.[22] Problems of water scarcity are particularly acute in the many urban centres in relatively arid areas that have also grown beyond the point where adequate water supplies can be drawn from local or even regional sources. Many urban centres in Africa's dryland areas face particularly serious problems because of a combination of rapid growth in demand for water and unusually low rainfall in recent years, with the consequent dwindling of local freshwater resources. These and many other cities face problems in financing the expansion of supplies to keep up with demand, as the cheapest and most easily tapped water sources have been tapped or polluted, and drawing on newer sources implies much higher costs per unit volume of water.[23]

In Dakar (Senegal), water supplies have to be drawn from ever more distant sources. This is both because local groundwater supplies are fully used (and polluted) and local aquifers overpumped, resulting in saltwaterintrusion; a substantial proportion of the city's water has to be brought in from the Lac de Guiers, 200 kilometres away (see Box 20.4).[24] Mexico City has to supplement its groundwater supplies by bringing water from ever more distant river systems and pumping this water up several hundred metres to reach the Valley of Mexico where the city is located.[25] The energy needed to pump this water represents a significant part of Mexico City's total energy consumption. Overexploitation of underground water has also made the city sink – in some areas by up to nine metres – with serious subsidence damage for many buildings and sewage and drainage pipes.[26] Despite the very high costs of drawing water from outside the valley and the high costs of managing the huge volume of wastes which then have to be pumped out of the valley, little effort has been made to increase the efficiency of water use and encourage water conservation and where appropriate the reuse of waste water.[27]

Box 20.4 *Meeting Dakar's water needs*

In 1961, on the eve of independence, Dakar was a city of approximately 250,000 people. It occupied a peninsular site, open to cooling winds and scoured by ocean currents. Most of the drinking water was drawn straight from the basalt aquifer on which the city was built. By 1988, the population of Dakar had reached 1.5 million.

As the city expanded it overran and polluted the local groundwater supplies, while overpumping of the aquifer resulted in saltwater intrusion. As the basalt aquifer became inadequate, supplies were drawn from sedimentary aquifers 80 kilometres distant. Later, as these were unable to keep up with demand, water was drawn from sedimentary strata further north. As these too were surpassed, a pumping station was established in the Lac de Guiers, a shallow reservoir created in a fossil river valley, 200 kilometres from Dakar. By 1978 the Lac de Guiers was providing approximately 20 per cent of Dakar's water supply, although this figure varied greatly according to the amount of water in the lake. In the late 1970s plans were made for the doubling and tripling of the capacity of the water pipes from the Lac de Guiers to Dakar. The money was never found to finance these schemes. A much larger plan is now on the drawing board, to bring water from the southern end of the Lac de Guiers by an open canal, known as the Canal de Cayor. There is virtually no recycling of water; it is widely believed that there would be serious cultural objections to such a proposal.

An important effect of the overall lack of water is that the sewage and waste-water canals and drains are inadequately flushed. To reduce the amount of household garbage dumped in the canals, some have been cemented over, hiding a growing problem. Sewage and semi-liquid waste are usually the first to have visible negative impacts on the urban system, resulting in increased coliform counts,[28] beaches closed for swimming and reduced catches from the inshore fishery. In 1986 the Senegalese Department of the Environment put into operation its first (mobile) water quality laboratory. It carried out coliform counts for the beaches around the city and it presented the results in the annual (September) warning regarding storms and dangerous tides, which was published in the national newspaper. The results were appalling; for some samples the coliforms were too numerous to count. In the meantime, the combination of household and industrial wastes has polluted the Baie de Hann so badly that algal growths have killed off the inshore fishery. Few local fishermen have the equipment to fish further from the shore. From simply being a nuisance, environmental decline has now begun to undermine the local economy beginning with fishery and tourism.

Source: White, Rodney R (1992) 'The international transfer of urban technology: does the North have anything to offer for the global environmental crisis?', *Environment and Urbanization*, Vol 4, No 2, pp 109–120.

RURAL-URBAN LINKS

For most urban centres worldwide, an examination of the resource flows into them reveals a scale and complexity of linkages with rural producers and ecosystems within their own region and beyond which implies that 'sustainable urban development' and 'sustainable rural development' cannot be separated.[29] The rural-urban linkages can be positive in both developmental and environmental terms. For instance, demand for rural produce from city-based enterprises and households can support prosperous farms and rural settlements, where environmental capital is not being depleted – for instance, as local producers invest in maintaining the quality of soils and water resources. Few governments in the South appreciate the extent to which productive, intensive agriculture can support development goals in both rural and urban areas.[30] Increasing agricultural production can support rising prosperity for rural populations and rapid urban development within or close to the main farming areas – the two supporting each other.[31] There are also many examples of organic solid and liquid wastes that originate from city-based consumers or industries being returned to soils.

There are generally many 'rural' households for whom urban incomes are important components of total incomes. This often includes large numbers of low-income households who live in rural areas around cities and are considered rural inhabitants but who have one or more member who works in the city or commutes there. There is also growing evidence of the importance for livelihoods and for urban consumers of food production in areas close to the built-up area.[32]

The scale and nature of migration flows to urban centres from the regions around them will be influenced by the extent to which government policies support rural livelihoods and good environmental management there. Ironically, many governments claim to want to slow migration to cities yet they do little to support rural livelihoods, protect agricultural land and prevent resource degradation in the areas around cities, as was evident in the case study of land conversion just outside Manila (Box 20.1) and around Jakarta (Box 20.3). Similarly, as noted earlier, a lack of attention to controlling pollution of local water bodies so often means damage or destruction of productive local fisheries which previously supported many jobs and often provided cheap high-quality protein (see Box 20.4). This is not to say that urban expansion (and the conversion of land) has to be halted; prosperous urban centres need more land and constraining the land available for housing pushes up house prices, which so often means that lower income groups face worse, more overcrowded conditions and/or resort to illegal developments. City-based demand can also stimulate and support a considerable range of new 'rural' enterprises and occupations. For instance, many farmers around Mexico City have benefited from the expanded demand for high-value agricultural produce and from tourist demand.[33] There is also evidence of large and diverse non-agricultural economic activities developing in the regions around prosperous cities, although, as noted earlier, from an environmental perspective, care is needed to ensure that the more environmentally damaging enterprises do not locate there because environmental regulations are less strict or less enforced than within the city. The fact that it is common for a diverse range of residential, commercial and industrial developments to develop in the region around cities means that measures are needed to limit their environmental impacts and to protect rural resources, although attention is needed as to the possible social implications of such measures.[34] There is also a need to guard against the potential for intensive agriculture or livestock production to pollute water sources.

The above examples help to show the difficulty in considering 'urban' and 'rural' problems separately. The impoverishment of rural people in a region and their movement to cities may be considered a rural problem, but it may be largely the result of the commercialization of agricultural land markets and crop production because of city-based demand. Deforestation may be considered a rural problem, but it may be intimately linked to urban-based demand, for instance – for timber, fuelwood or charcoal, or for agricultural products which makes it profitable for those who own or control forests to clear them for agriculture. The soil erosion linked to deforestation may be destroying rural inhabitants' livelihoods, with the result that they migrate to the city. The environmental impacts of large hydroelectric dams (eg the loss of agricultural land and the introduction or exacerbation of waterborne or water-related diseases) are usually considered rural even if most of the electricity will be consumed in urban areas. Other examples include the environmental effects of agricultural or mining operations which produce raw materials for city-based activities or poorly designed and located bridges, highways and roads linking smaller settlements with cities which might contribute to problems of flooding.

CITY OUTPUTS – SOLID, LIQUID AND GASEOUS WASTES

Liquid, gaseous and solid wastes generated by city-based enterprises and consumers often have significant impacts in the region surrounding the city. Each is considered here.

Disposal of Liquid Wastes

The contamination of rivers, lakes, seashores and coastal waters is an example both of the impact of city-generated wastes on the wider region and of government's negligent attitude to protecting open areas. In cities on or close to coasts, untreated sewage and industrial effluents often flow into the sea with little or no provision to pipe them far enough out to sea to protect the beaches and inshore waters. Most coastal cities have serious problems with dirty, contaminated beaches and the water there is a major health risk to bathers. Oil pollution often adds to existing problems of sewage and industrial effluents. Pollution may be so severe that many beaches have to be closed to the public. It is usually the most accessible beaches which suffer most and these are among the most widely used recreational areas by lower income groups. Richer households suffer much less; those with automobiles can reach more distant, less accessible and less polluted beaches.

The possibilities for improvement vary greatly. In many of the largest cities in Europe and North America that are located on rivers or by lakes, great improvements have been achieved in reducing water pollution, mostly through stricter controls on industrial emissions and more sophisticated and comprehensive treatment of sewage and water run-off collected in drains. Rather less success has been achieved in reducing polluting discharges to the sea. In most Third World cities, the problems are not so easily addressed as they have much more serious 'non-point' sources of water pollution than cities in the North because of the lack of sewers and drains in many city districts and peripheral areas and the inadequate services to collect solid wastes. A lack of solid waste collection adds to water pollution problems since many of the uncollected wastes are washed into streams, rivers or lakes, adding to the pollution load.

Liquid wastes from city activities have environmental impacts stretching beyond the immediate hinterland. It is common for fisheries to be damaged or destroyed by liquid effluents from city-based industries with hundreds or even thousands of people losing their livelihoods as a result; among the places where major declines in fish catches have been documented are many rivers, estuaries or coastal waters in India, China and Malaysia, Lake Maryut in Alexandria, the Gulf of Paria between Venezuela and Trinidad, Manila Bay, Rio de Janeiro's Guanabara Bay, the Bay of Dakar and the Indus delta near Karachi.[35] The fish may also be contaminated; in a sample of fish and shellfish caught in Jakarta Bay, Indonesia, 44 per cent exceeded WHO guidelines for lead while 38 per cent exceeded the mercury guidelines and 76 per cent exceeded the cadmium guidelines.[36] Perhaps the best known and most dramatic example of water contamination is that of Minamata in Japan. Although Japan has long been too wealthy to be classified as Third World, the example has relevance because it illustrates the scale of damage that can be done (in this case by a single industry). The industry discharged mercury-contaminated waste water into Minamata Bay and the mercury was biologically concentrated in fish and shellfish which were then consumed by people living around the Bay. As of 1990, 2248 people had been recognized as suffering from Minamata disease and of these 1004 had died.[37] It is likely that far more had their health impaired, but were unable to prove this. The costs of dredging the bay to reclaim mercury and of compensation ran to the equivalent of hundreds of millions of US dollars. This illustrates the enormous cost in human life and health, and in the costs of seeking to compensate for the damage done, if environmental regulations are not enforced.

River pollution from city-based industries and untreated sewage can lead to serious health problems in settlements downstream. Paper and rayon factories in India are notorious water polluters and such pollution causes diseases in villagers who live downstream; it often means declining fish catches and declining water volumes as well.[38] Rivers which are heavily contaminated as they pass through cities may become unusable for agriculture downstream or particular contaminants in the water may damage crops or pose risks to human health. For instance, cadmium and lead concentrations in rivers are particular problems downstream from certain industries and if the water is used for growing crops like rice, those regularly eating that rice can easily exceed the WHO defined acceptable daily intake.[39]

This regional impact of water pollution can even extend to international water bodies. For instance, in the Persian/Arabian Gulf (a small, shallow, salty and almost landlocked sea) rapid urban and industrial growth on its shores is threatening its fragile ecosystem. While the major danger of marine pollution comes from oil, especially from tanker deballasting and tank washing, sewage from the rapidly expanding coastal cities and untreated industrial liquid wastes are also having a considerable impact, as are the concentration of desalination plants along the coast.[40] The Caribbean faces problems because of the high concentration of people living on or near the seashore, the concentration of tourist developments and the lack of effective control over coastal developments and of discharges of municipal, industrial and mining liquid wastes. Large quantities of untreated sewage are discharged directly into bays, estuaries, coastal lagoons and rivers and 'highly toxic effluents from rapidly developing light and heavy industries... also often discharged directly into adjacent bays'.[41] Heavy metals from mining operations, metal smelting or other industrial processes pose serious problems to coastal environments in some areas – for instance, the Coatzacoalcos estuary in the Gulf of Mexico and the bays of Cartagena, Guayanilla, Puerto Moron and Havana.[42] There are also problems with oil pollution from illegal discharges by tankers and other ships, offshore oilrigs and the many oil refineries within the region.[43]

Solid Waste Disposal

It is still common for most of the solid wastes that are collected within urban centres to be dumped on some site outside the city with no preparation of the site to minimize the threat of seepage and leaching contaminating local water resources and with no provision to cover the wastes to reduce the breeding of disease vectors and uncontrolled burning. Dump sites are often ecologically valuable wetlands. The inadequacies in provision for handling hazardous wastes was noted earlier; it is also common for hazardous wastes which require special handling, storage and treatment to ensure safe disposal to be dumped on the same land sites as conventional solid wastes, with few (if any) safeguards to protect those living nearby or nearby water sources from contamination.

Box 20.5 gives an example of some of the impacts of Rio de Janeiro on the wider region, including those arising from inadequate attention to the collection, treatment and safe disposal of solid and liquid wastes.

Box 20.5 *Environmental problems in Rio de Janeiro*

By 1990, Rio de Janeiro's population had grown to 9.6 million in a metropolitan area that covered almost 6500 square kilometres. Developing on a narrow piece of land between the sea and the mountains, the city developed within one of the world's most beautiful natural sites, beside Guanabara Bay; despite its name, there is no Rio or river; the Portuguese navigators who named it had assumed that the entrance of the bay was the mouth of a river. This natural beauty is an important economic asset for residents and for tourists (the city alone has 80 kilometres of recreational beaches that can be enjoyed all year).

The main environmental problems include:

- Water pollution from both point and non-point sources. The main point sources are collected but inadequately treated – domestic sewage and industrial effluent from chemicals, petrochemicals and petroleum refining, iron and steel production and other metal-refining industries. The main non-point sources are uncollected and untreated domestic wastes, agricultural run-off, storm-water run-off and improperly disposed of solid waste. The lack of control over water pollution also means widespread coastal pollution, especially around Guanabara and Sepetiba Bays, largely because of uncontrolled disposal of wastes from commercial and industrial activities.
- The incapacity of the municipal governments to manage the vast quantity of solid and liquid wastes generated within Rio de Janeiro; a considerable proportion of this waste goes uncollected. In 1990, more than a quarter of households did not have a garbage collection service. Most sewage is dumped untreated into rivers, bays and near-shore oceanic waters and ends up in Guanabara and Sepetiba bays; the only exception is sewage collected from approximately two million people in the Ipanema area that is disposed of through an outfall located some 3.5 kilometres offshore.
- The rapid and uncontrolled expansion of urban settlements over land on the city's periphery. Some of this is on unsafe land in areas where local governments lack the capacity to guide the expansion of settlements, protect fragile slopes from settlements and provide basic services and infrastructure. By 1991, close to half of the

---

Box 20.5 *Continued*

population lived in peripheral municipalities, compared to 32 per cent in 1960. In 1990, 16 per cent of Rio's households still lacked piped water and 17 per cent lacked adequate sanitation. The annual expenditure per person on sanitation and health care in some of the poorest municipalities was US$8 or less per person 1988–1991.

• Regionwide deforestation has led to severe erosion and degradation of water sources. The removal of vegetative cover from slopes, combined with the development of low-land areas, has led to very poor natural drainage. Rainwater and earth from eroded soils pour down from the mountains during the summer rains, often causing stream channels to overflow and an inundation of floodplains.

One of the main constraints on effective action is the complex institutional structure, combined with a long-established reluctance of state and federal authorities to fund investments in Rio de Janeiro. Municipal authorities do not have total control over development decisions at local level and most lack the staff and funds to administer urban and environmental planning. Many responsibilities for environmental control have been transferred to them from the state but without the resources to permit them to do so. Responsibilities for land use and zoning regulations rest with local governments, but there are many problems of co-ordination between the different public agencies. Local governments have the authority to regulate commercial and residential use as long as their regulations do not conflict with federal and state laws; zoning at federal government level focuses on the protection of forests and ecological reserves, while at state level it is meant to control the location of polluting firms. But overlapping jurisdictions often discourage co-ordination between different bodies and restrict effective action. To compound the problem, all municipalities other than the central Rio de Janeiro municipality have outdated property and other cadastre information, making it difficult to implement projects and enforce the law.

Source: Kreimer, Alcira, Thereza Lobo, Braz Menezes, Mohan Munasinghe, Ronald Parker and Martha Preece, 'Rio de Janeiro – in search of sustainability' and other papers in Alcira Kreimer, Thereza Lobo, Braz Menezes, Mohan Munasinghe and Ronald Parker (eds), *Towards a Sustainable Urban Environment: The Rio de Janeiro Study,* World Bank Discussion Papers, No 195, World Bank, Washington DC, 1993

Acid Precipitation

Consideration must be given to the impact of air pollutants from city-based activities on the wider region. Sulphur and nitrogen oxides discharged by power stations burning high sulphur coal or oil, and from automobile exhausts can make rain acid, with this acid rain falling to earth a considerable distance from the emission sources. The result can be declining or disappearing fish populations and damage to soils and vegetation. Toxic metals may also be leached from the soil into water used for animal or human consumption or copper, lead, cadmium or copper mobilized by acidic drinking-water supplies from piped water systems. Acid precipitation is causing concern in the areas surrounding many cities in Asia and Latin America.[44] The air

Box 20.6 *The impact of air pollution on agriculture*

Air pollution can cause serious losses to crops and animal husbandry, although the levels of loss under different circumstances are difficult to assess experimentally.

Acid pollution: Sulphur dioxide and the oxides of nitrogen coming from fossil-fuel combustion in cities can be deposited directly from the air on farmers' fields (dry deposition) or from rain, clouds/fog or snow acidified by these chemicals. Both can damage plants at high concentrations (causing acute damage, especially to certain species of plants which are particularly sensitive to exposure), although the concentrations needed to achieve this are rare, except in the immediate vicinity of intense sources of emissions – for instance, metal smelters with no pollution controls and lacking high chimneys. At lower concentrations, both sulphur dioxide and the oxides of nitrogen are associated with reductions in yields and growth for many crops, although there are many other factors which can influence this. For acid rain, experimental reports of foliar injury are for pH values of less than 3.5, a level of acidity which rarely occurs. Soils are also at risk since in many tropical and subtropical countries, the soils are already acidic and unable to buffer any further additions in acidity. Further acidification can bring into solution potentially toxic trace elements – for instance, aluminium in acid soils disrupts the metabolic processes of roots and inhibits their growth.

Ozone: Ozone is produced by complex photochemical reactions involving air pollutants which are common over cities (oxides of nitrogen, carbon monoxide and hydrocarbons) reacting in sunlight. Temperature inversions over cities can keep the reactive chemicals in touch by inhibiting the dispersion of pollutants. Ozone continues to be generated in plumes of contaminated air originating in cities but often at a considerable distance from the source, which can make the concentration of ozone in rural areas downwind of cities higher than in the city itself. Plumes downwind of large North American cities produce ozone concentrations of between 130 and 200 parts per billion, often over distances of 100–300 kilometres;[46] ozone concentrations of only 60–100 ppb are sufficient to cause significant loss of yield in a wide variety of crops. The most direct impact on plants is the reduction in the amount of light caused by the photochemical smog. In many cities, ozone also causes visible leaf damage, while concentrations well below those needed to cause visible injury (and also below that of most air quality standards) are also known to significantly reduce crop growth and yields for a wide range of plants, including oranges, lemons, grapes, wheat and rice.

Fluorides: These are typically emitted as hydrogen fluoride from brick, glass and tile works, steel works, potteries, aluminium smelters, phosphate factories and some other industries. Particular industries can cause acute damage over considerable distances, if no measures are taken to limit emissions. For vegetation far from emission sources, the hazard arises from long-term exposure to very low levels, so trees and perennial plants are more likely to suffer damage than annuals. Fluoride may directly damage fruits or accumulate in forage and so present a particular risk to grazing livestock.

Other air pollutants and their interactions: Soot or dust may affect plant growth by reducing the rate of photosynthesis or damaging the plant. Mixtures of pollutants may produce synergistic or antagonistic effects, or one gas may predispose or desensitize a plant to the effect of another. Gaseous pollutants may also stimulate more serious attacks by pests such as aphids or white fly.

Source: Drawn from Conway, Gordon R and Jules N Pretty, *Unwelcome Harvest*, Earthscan Publications, London 1991

pollutants that cause the most damage to forests, soils and agriculture are sulphur dioxide, oxides of nitrogen and ozone (and other photochemical oxidants) and, in certain instances, fluorides (see Box 20.6).[45]

The most dramatic examples of damage to crops (and other flora) come in the immediate vicinity of industries with very high sulphur dioxide emissions. Metal smelters without pollution controls and tall smokestacks can cause severe damage to vegetation over areas of several hundred square kilometres. The emissions from cities do not produce such high concentrations, although a combination of high emissions and a lack of winds to disperse them can mean evidence of damage to vegetation or falling crop yields. The problem is reported to be particularly acute in south-western China – for instance, around cities which have high levels of sulphur dioxide emissions such as Guiyang and Chongqing.[47]

The relative acidity (or its opposite, the alkalinity) of any substance is measured by its pH and the neutral point is a pH of 7.0. Rain with a pH value below 5.6 is generally considered 'acidic'. In the provinces of Guizhou and Sichuan, some 40,000 square kilometres received rainfall with a pH of less than 4.5.[48] At Guiyang itself, the pH of rainfall was reported to be less than 4 from September to January. Around Chongqing, large areas of (rice) paddy have turned yellow, following rainfall with a pH of 4.5 while in Chongqing itself, vegetation has been damaged by rain with a pH of 4.1.[49] Professor Vaclav Smil in his review of environmental problems in China suggests that such cases are 'most certainly just the proverbial tip of the iceberg' and that regional damage to plants and livestock must also be quite considerable near coal-fired power stations, refineries and chemical works with non- (or only rudimentary) controls.[50] There may be many other city-regions where damage to agriculture is visible, although the fact that this needs a high concentration of emissions combined with particular meteorological conditions will make this unusual.

Emissions of fluorides, particulate matter and chemicals which react in sunlight to produce ozone from urban areas may also damage flora in the surrounding regions. Ozone concentrations may not reach a maximum until the urban plume of pollutants is well away from the city.[51] For fluorides, although the damage to crops, pasture and livestock is well known, there are few reports on this outside the North, except for the serious damage reported to sericulture from fluoride emissions from small rural industries in China.[52]

CITIES' ECOLOGICAL FOOTPRINTS

The extent of the environmental changes caused by any urban centre on its surrounds and the size of the area that has been changed is much influenced by the urban centre's size and wealth (as these are key influences on the scale and nature of resource demands and waste generation), as well as the nature of its production base and of the resource endowments of the region around it. It is also much influenced by the quality of environmental management both within the urban centre and in the region surrounding it.

Two issues inhibit more effective measures to limit cities' ecological impacts. One was highlighted by Mike Douglass in his discussion of Jakarta's environmental impact on its region and by Philip Kelly in discussing competition for land around Manila: the fact that there are so many different influences on land use from local concerns – for instance, the competition between agriculture and urban development for land – to regional and national concerns (the promotion of industrialization) to

international concerns (for Jakarta, the fall in the price of export crops for outer islands, reducing the attraction for migrants of areas outside Jakarta and other areas
in Java). The second is the difficulty in co-ordinating actions in different places by
different agencies and different levels of government because cities' environmental
impacts are so diverse and often happen over such distances (as in the example of
Delhi described in Box 20.2 with much of the firewood coming from a region nearly
700 kilometres away).

Although much of the literature on the generation and transfer of environmental costs from cities concentrates on the region around cities, the demands that the
larger and wealthier cities concentrate for food, fuel and raw materials may be increasingly met by imports from distant ecosystems with much less demand placed
on the region surrounding the city, which makes it easier to maintain high environmental standards in this region and, for instance, to preserve forests and natural
landscapes. In addition, the goods whose fabrication involves high levels of fossil-
fuel consumption, water use and other natural resource use, and dirty industrial
processes (including the generation of hazardous wastes) and hazardous conditions
for the workforce can be imported. The possibilities for enterprises and consumers
to import such goods from a greater distance is much helped by the low price of oil.

Other environmental cost transfers are into the future. For instance, air pollution may be controlled with a major decline in some particular pollutants (as has
been achieved in many of the world's wealthiest cities), but emissions of carbon dioxide (the main greenhouse gas) remain very high and in most cities may continue
to rise – for instance, because of increasing private automobile ownership and use,
and with increased use of air-conditioning where this is powered by electricity from
thermal power stations. This is transferring costs to the future through the human
and ecological costs of atmospheric warming. The generation of hazardous non-biodegradable wastes (including radioactive wastes) or non-biodegradable wastes whose
rising concentrations within the biosphere has worrying ecological implications is
also transferring costs to the future. So, too, are current levels of consumption for
the products of agriculture and forestry where the soils and forests are being destroyed or degraded and biodiversity reduced.

It is difficult to estimate the ecological costs that arise from producing all the
inputs that support city production and consumption – the large and diverse range
of raw materials, intermediate goods and final goods. To do so would require not
only an accurate mapping of the scale and nature of resource inputs but also an
assessment of the ecological impacts of their production. As noted earlier, intensive
rural production for urban markets need not be ecologically damaging, while rural
incomes derived from production for urban markets may be providing the means for
better management of land, forests and watersheds. But the scale of the demand
for resources and of waste generation concentrated in cities has encouraged the
development of new concepts to help map out and to begin to quantify the scale and
nature of these interregional or international transfers.

The development of a method to calculate the 'ecological footprints' of cities (and
of particular households, enterprises and nations) by William Rees[53] is one of these
(see Box 20.7). This makes evident the large land area on whose production the inhabitants and businesses of any city depend for food, other renewable resources
and the absorption of carbon to compensate for the carbon dioxide emitted from fossil-fuel use. Rees calculated that the lower Fraser Valley of British Columbia (Canada)
in which Vancouver is located has an ecological footprint of about 20 times as much
land as it occupies – to produce the food and forestry products its inhabitants and

Box 20.7 *The ecological footprint of cities*

All cities draw on natural resources produced on land outside their built-up areas (eg agricultural crops, wood products, fuel) and the total area of land required to sustain a city (which can be termed its ecological footprint) is typically at least ten times or more greater than that contained within the city boundaries or the associated built-up area. In effect, through trade and natural flows of ecological goods and services, all cities appropriate the carrying-capacity of other areas. All cities draw on the material resources and productivity of a vast and scattered hinterland.

Ecologists define 'carrying-capacity' as the population of a given species that can be supported indefinitely in a given habitat without permanently damaging the ecosystem upon which it is dependent. For human beings, carrying-capacity can be interpreted as the maximum rate of resource consumption and waste discharge that can be sustained indefinitely in a given region without progressively impairing the functional integrity and productivity of relevant ecosystems.

Preliminary data for industrial cities suggest that per capita primary consumption of food, wood products, fuel, waste-processing capacity, etc, co-opts on a continuous basis several hectares of productive ecosystem, the exact amount depending on individual material standards of living. This average per capita index can be used to estimate the land area functionally required to support any given population. The resultant aggregate area can be called the relevant community's total 'ecological footprint' on the Earth.

Regional ecological deficits do not necessarily pose a problem if import-dependent regions are drawing on true ecological surpluses in the exporting regions. A group of trading regions remains within net carrying-capacity as long as total consumption does not exceed aggregate sustainable production. The problem is that prevailing economic logic and trade agreements ignore carrying-capacity and sustainability considerations. In these circumstances, the terms of trade may actually accelerate the depletion of essential natural capital, thereby undermining global carrying-capacity.

Because the products of nature can so readily be imported, the population of any given region can exceed its local carrying-capacity unknowingly and with apparent impunity. In the absence of negative feedback from the land on their economy or lifestyles, there is no direct incentive for such populations to maintain adequate local stocks of productive natural capital. For example, the ability to import food makes people less averse to the risks associated with urban growth spreading over locally limited agricultural land. Even without accelerated capital depletion, trade enables a region's population and material consumption to rise beyond levels to which they might otherwise be restricted by some locally limiting factor. Ironically, then, the free exchange of ecological goods and services without constraints on population or consumption ensures the absorption of global surpluses (the safety net) and encourages all regions to exceed local carrying-capacity. The net effect is increased long-range risk to all.

This situation applies not only to commercial trade but also to the unmonitored flows of goods and services provided by nature. For example, northern urbanites, wherever they are, are now dependent on the carbon sink, global heat transfer and climate stabilization functions of tropical forests. There are many variations on this theme, touching on everything from drift-net fishing to ozone depletion, each involving open access to, or shared dependency on, some form of threatened natural capital.

Source: Rees, William E, 'Ecological footprints and appropriated carrying capacity: what urban economics leaves out', *Environment and Urbanization* Vol 4, No 2, October 1992, pp 121–130

businesses use and to grow vegetation to absorb the carbon dioxide they produce.[54] London's ecological footprint is estimated to be 125 times its actual size, based on similar criteria.[55] However, care is needed in comparing the size of different cities' ecological footprints. One reason is that the size of the footprint as a multiple of the city area will vary considerably, depending on where the city boundary is drawn, and this is the main reason why London's inhabitants appear to have a much larger individual ecological footprint than the inhabitants of the Fraser Valley.[56] A second is differences between cities in the quality and range of statistics from which a city's ecological footprint is calculated.

Wealthy and powerful cities have always had the capacity to draw resources from far beyond their immediate region. For instance, imperial Rome drew timber, grain, ivory, stone and marble from North Africa.[57] But the scale of this capacity to draw on the productivity of distant ecosystems has been greatly increased in the last few decades as incomes have risen and transport costs declined. City-based consumers and industries in the wealthy nations have increasingly appropriated the carrying-capacity of rural regions in other nations. This separates the environmental impact of the demand the city concentrates for natural resources from the city itself, to the point where city inhabitants and businesses have no idea of the environmental impact for which they are responsible. One of the advantages of having the environmental impact in a city's own surrounds is the visible evidence of environmental damage that could spur actions to reduce it.[58]

Certain natural resources are essential to the existence of any city – fresh water, food and fuel supplies. Many of the economic activities on which a city's prosperity depends require regular supplies of renewable resources; without a continuing supply of fresh water, agricultural goods and forest products, many cities would rapidly decline in size and have reduced employment opportunities for their residents. Many other formal and informal economic activities, although not directly linked to resource exploitation, depend on such exploitation to generate the income to support their own activities. In the past, the size and economic base of any city was constrained by the size and quality of the resource endowments of its surrounding region. The cost of transporting food, raw materials and fresh water always limited the extent to which a city could survive by drawing resources from outside its region. The high costs of transporting city-generated wastes away from the surrounding region promoted local solutions, and there was a need to ensure that such wastes did not damage the soils and water on which local agricultural production (and often fishing) depended. If local ecosystems were degraded, the prosperity of the city suffered – or, in extreme cases, its viability as a city was threatened. A city's ecological footprint remained relatively local.

Motorized transport systems introduced the possibility of disassociating the scale of renewable resource use in cities from the productivity of its region. Prosperous cities now draw from the entire planet as their 'ecological hinterland' for food, fossil fuels and raw materials. If many consumers in, say, Singapore or São Paulo (and, of course, European and North American cities) are drawing their fruit, vegetables, cereals, meat, fish and flowers from an enormous variety of countries, how can a link be established between this consumption and its ecological consequences?

As noted earlier, fresh water can also be drawn from distant watersheds and even pumped hundreds of metres up hills, as long as little consideration is given to the high energy costs that this entails (usually coming from thermal power stations that also mean high levels of greenhouse gas emissions). Such technology and its high energy requirements obscure the link between a city's renewable resource use and the impact of this use on the ecosystem where the resource is produced. Prosperous cities can also transport their wastes and dispose of them beyond their own region – in extreme cases, even shipping them abroad. Or they can 'export' their air pollution to surrounding regions through acid precipitation and urban pollution plumes with sufficiently high concentrations of ozone to damage vegetation in large areas downwind of the city. Perhaps only when the cost of oil-based transport comes to reflect its true ecological cost in terms both of a depleting non-renewable resource and its contribution to greenhouse gas emissions will a stronger connection be re-established between resource use within cities and the productive capacity of the regions in which they are located.

The calculation of ecological footprints for cities should not obscure the fact that particular enterprises and richer income groups contribute disproportionately to these footprints. For example, Wackernagel and Rees calculate that the average ecological footprint for the poorest 20 per cent of Canada's population is less than a quarter that of the wealthiest 20 per cent.[59] It is also possible to measure the ecological footprints of particular activities. For instance, Wackernagel and Rees' book on ecological footprints consider the ecological footprint of different kinds of housing, different commuting patterns, road bridges and different goods (including tomato production and newspapers).[60] It is also worth noting that high-income households in rural or suburban areas generally have larger ecological footprints than those with comparable incomes living in cities.[61]

Another concept that helps to reveal the reliance of wealthy cities on non-renewable resources is through calculating the 'material intensity' of the goods consumed in that city (or what is sometimes termed these goods' ecological rucksack). The material intensity of any good can be calculated, relative to the service it provides, as a way of providing a quick and rough estimate of its environmental impact.[62] This calculation can include all the energy and material inputs into any good from the extraction or fabrication of materials used to make it through its use to its final disposal. It can also include consideration of how much service that good provides, including how long it lasts – so, for instance, a fridge or car that lasted 20 years would have less material intensity than one that lasted 10 years. It has been calculated that a home fridge designed to lower its 'material input:intensity of service ratio' could be constructed with available technologies and materials to achieve a resource productivity of roughly six times that of currently available models.[63]

There is also the long-established practice of calculating the energy-intensity of different goods which can also take into account the energy used in their fabrication, transport, preparation for sale, sale, use and disposal. Since in most instances most or all of the energy input comes from fossil fuels, this allows an idea of how the use of this good contributes to the use of fossil fuels and the generation of carbon dioxide (the largest contributor to atmospheric warming), and perhaps also some idea of the air pollution implications of its fabrication, use and disposal.

While concepts such as 'ecological footprints' and 'ecological rucksacks' have helped to make apparent the extent to which modern cities can generate environmental costs far from their boundaries, it is difficult to quantify all such transfers. For instance, the long-term health and ecological consequences of many chemical wastes are unknown, including those arising from the accumulation of certain persistent chemicals. It is also difficult to estimate the scale of the health risks faced by the workers and their families who make the goods which the consumers and enterprises within wealthy cities use. It is also difficult to adjust the calculations for a city's 'ecological footprint' to take account of the goods and services that its enterprises produce for those living outside its boundaries. Measures are needed to reduce the ecological footprint of wealthy and large cities, but this must not detract from cities' key roles within the efficient, prosperous, innovative and flexible economies that all nations want to develop. And as Chapter 3 stressed, prosperous cities with high quality environments can also be highly efficient in their use of resources and generation of wastes.

CITIES AND THE GLOBAL COMMONS

No overview of environmental problems in Third World cities would be complete without some consideration of the impacts of city-based activities on the global commons. These impacts include the depletion of non-renewable resources and emissions of 'greenhouse gases' (which contribute to global warming), and of gases which contribute to the depletion of the stratospheric ozone layer. They also include the environmental degradation to which city-based demand for goods and city-generated wastes contribute beyond the city and its surrounding region. There is also the pressing issue of the possible or probable impacts on Third World cities arising from global climate change. This requires some discussion of the difference between the production and consumption patterns that contribute most to climate change (much of which arises outside of Africa, Asia and Latin America and the Caribbean), and the people most likely to suffer from its direct and indirect effects. In general, low income people and many low-income countries are likely to bear much of costs, despite having contributed least to the problem.

The main contribution of city-based production and consumption to greenhouse gases is carbon dioxide emissions from fossil-fuel combustion by industry, thermal power stations, motor vehicles and domestic and commercial energy uses. City-based activities also contribute to emissions of other greenhouse gases – for instance, of chlorofluorocarbons by certain industries or industrial products, of nitrous oxide by motor vehicle engines and of methane by city-generated solid and liquid wastes. City-based demand for fuelwood, pulp and timber also contributes to deforestation in most countries (although it is not so much the demand but inadequate forest management that is the cause). A considerable proportion of the greenhouse gas emissions arising from rural food production – for instance, methane emissions from livestock and from rice cultivation – can be attributed to city-based consumption of such food.

There are few figures available on the scale of greenhouse gas emissions for individual cities, although those that do exist suggest relatively low levels of per capita emissions for carbon dioxide (the main greenhouse gas) for cities in the South when compared to cities in the North.[64] Figures available for different nations' per capita consumption of non-renewable resources and greenhouse gas emissions show much higher consumption and emission levels in the North when compared to the South.[65] This suggests that cities in the North have in aggregate a much higher draw, per capita, on the global commons both in terms of resource consumption and in terms of using the atmosphere and seas as sinks for wastes. Among other evidence which would support this would be: the much lower levels of fossil-fuel consumption per capita in Third World cities, the small proportion of the world's industrial production located there;[66] the lower number of automobiles per inhabitant;[67] and the lower levels of waste generation per capita.[68]

However, the very large differences between Third World cities in (among other things) their production structure, per capita income (and income distribution) and consumption patterns suggests enormous variations in resource use, waste generation and greenhouse gas emissions. Cities such as São Paulo with its high concentration of industry and of middle- and upper-income groups with high levels of resource use (including fossil fuels) and waste generation will put the average per capita resource use and greenhouse gas emissions for the city far above the average forThird World cities. In terms of greenhouse gas emissions per capita, this may also be true for many centres of heavy industry – for instance, some of China's centres of heavy industry, but here the greenhouse gas emissions derive mostly from the widespread use of coal in industry and for domestic and commercial heating, and not as a result of high-consumption levels. By contrast, most cities and smaller urban centres in low- and middle-income Third World nations are likely to have per capita greenhouse gas emissions far below the average.

The very low incomes on which such a high proportion of the Third World's urban population survive is one key reason for this. From the point of view of sustaining the global commons, the rich nations are fortunate that the urban (and rural) poor make such a minimal call on the world's renewable and non-renewable resources and contribute so little to stratospheric ozone depleting chemicals and to greenhouse gas emissions.[69] In regard to the hundreds of millions of people living in urban areas with inadequate incomes and very poor housing conditions, there is no evidence that they are major contributors to environmental degradation on a global scale, despite the suggestion that poverty is a major source of environmental degradation.[70] Most of the urban poor are exposed to very high levels of environmental risk because of the hazards they face from inadequacies in provision for piped water, sanitation, drainage, paved roads, health care and emergency services (as described earlier), but this is not the same as high contributions to environmental degradation. Here, it is so important to distinguish between environmental hazards and environmental degradation. If we consider environmental degradation in terms of loss of environmental capital, then in none of the categories of environmental capital do the urban poor have a significant role in its depletion at a global scale:

- In regard to non-renewable resource use, most of the houses in which low-income groups live (and often build for themselves) make widespread use of recycled or reclaimed materials and little use of cement and other materials with a high-energy input. Such households have too few capital goods to represent much of a draw on the world's finite reserves of metals and other non-renewable resources. Most low-income groups in urban areas rely on public transport (or they walk or bicycle) which ensures low averages for oil consumption per person.[71] Low-income households on average have low levels of electricity consumption, not only because those who are connected use less but also because a high proportion of households have no electricity supply.
- In regard to the use of renewable resources, low-income urban dwellers generally have much lower levels of consumption for fresh water (although this is more due to inconvenient and/or expensive supplies than need or choice) and occupy much less land per person than middle- and upper-income groups. There are examples of low-income populations contributing to particular environmental problems – for instance, where low-income settlements have developed in watersheds – but this is a problem caused by the failure of urban authorities to ensure they have access to other residential sites.
- In regard to waste generation, low-income groups usually generate much lower levels per person than middle- and upper-income groups, and the urban poor

generally have a very positive role from an ecological perspective as they are the main reclaimers, reusers and recyclers of wastes from industries, workshops and wealthier households. There are examples of small-scale urban enterprises (including illegal or informal enterprises) which can cause serious local environmental problems – for instance, contaminating local water sources – but their contribution to citywide pollution problems relative to other groups is usually very small. In addition, it is difficult to ascribe the pollution caused by small-scale enterprises to the urban poor when many such enterprises are owned by middle- or upper-income groups.

- In regard to greenhouse gas emissions, low-income groups usually generate much lower levels per person than middle- and upper-income groups as their total use of fossil fuels or of goods or services with high fossil-fuel inputs in their fabrication and use is so much lower. The only exception may be for some low-income households in urban areas where there is a need for space heating for parts of the year and a proportion of the urban poor use biomass fuels or coal in inefficient stoves or fires. This may result in these households having above-average per capita contributions to carbon dioxide emissions (and also to urban air pollution), but these are exceptional cases and, in general, the consumption patterns of low-income groups imply much lower greenhouse gas emissions per person than those of middle- and upper-income groups.

There is also the issue discussed under the earlier section on cities' ecological footprints regarding the extent to which the population and enterprises in wealthy cities can ensure high-quality environments in their surrounds by drawing most resources and goods from distant regions. The level of greenhouse gas emissions per person from within wealthy cities will be lowered by enterprises and consumers there using energy-intensive goods that are made elsewhere. Similarly, urban centres with a concentration of factories producing energy-intensive goods or materials will always tend to have above-average levels of greenhouse gas emissions per person. This helps to illustrate the difficulties in seeking an 'accounting system' which penalizes locations with high emissions since it is the people who use the energy-intensive goods or materials, not the places where they are made, that should be penalized.

The institutional means do not exist to discourage the fact that so many of the serious environmental implications of the consumption patterns of wealthy citizens and wealthy cities can be displaced to 'foreign' people and their ecosystems or into the future.[72] The need to address such issues has been highlighted by 'green consumerism' and by companies that recognize the need to improve the social and environmental performance both of their own operations and of their suppliers. But there is little progress on the international agreements that could address such problems. The environmental implications of free trade worldwide will have to be addressed if this is leading to serious and sustained ecological deterioration in many Third World nations (as soils and forests are damaged or destroyed by the pressure to produce the 'cheapest' goods) and, within the world system, to increasing greenhouse gas emissions.

The low average for all urban centres in the Third World in regard to greenhouse gas emissions might suggest little need to act there. But with growing urban populations and a large and increasing share of the world's population located there, the future form and content of urban development, both in its built form and in its spatial organization, has major implications for atmospheric warming worldwide. Many of the more prosperous cities in Asia and Latin America (or the more prosperous suburbs) already have spatial structures which build in a high dependence on private automobile use which also implies high greenhouse gas emissions. Few countries or cities have building codes or effective incentives to encourage buildings which minimize the need for heating or air-conditioning. The extent to which middle- and upper-income groups in Third World cities draw on artificial heating or cooling and depend on private automobiles has large implications for countries' greenhouse gas emissions. In addition, the pressure on the global commons would be enormous, if meeting the needs of low-income groups implied the levels of resource use and waste generation now common among most middle- and upper-income groups.

IMPACTS OF GLOBAL WARMING ON THIRD WORLD CITIES

There is still uncertainty about the possible scale of global warming in the future and its likely direct and indirect effects. But atmospheric concentrations of the most important greenhouse gases – carbon dioxide, halocarbons and methane – are increasing. There is evidence of an increase in the global average temperature over the last 120 years and many of the warmest years on record have been in the last 15 years. Glaciers in virtually all parts of the world are receding. These are consistent with global warming induced by greenhouse gases released by human activities, but there are uncertainties as to the extent to which the increase in global temperature is the result of human activities and the extent (and rate) at which it will continue. For instance, non-human induced factors such as volcanic eruptions are also important. The warming trend might be part of a natural variation that may reverse itself. But if global warming arising from human-induced releases of greenhouse gases does continue, it is likely to bring very serious problems for a large part of the world's settlements.

These problems can arise from:

- the direct effects of changes in temperature and the changes in weather that this brings, including changes in the hydrological cycle (and thus water supplies) and altered frequency and/or intensity of extreme weather events; and
- the indirect effects, as the changes in temperature and weather induce changes in, among other things, sea levels, ecological systems and air pollution levels – with these ecological changes also having serious effects on, for instance, food production. Figure 20.1 illustrates the range of possible health impacts of climate change and also of stratospheric ozone depletion.

In regard to cities, among the most immediate effects of climate change would be:

- higher global mean temperatures;
- sea-level rises;
- changes in weather patterns (including those of rainfall and other forms of precipitation);
- changes in river flow arising from increased temperature (and the melting of snow and ice) and changes in precipitation);
- changes in evaporation rates;
- changes in the structure of ecosystems – for instance, as a result of changes in plant growth rates and favoured species and in insect populations; and

- changes in the frequency and severity of extreme weather conditions – for instance, storms and sea surges).[73]

The scale and nature of the consequences will obviously differ depending on the city location, the characteristics of its site and the particular changes in that region in, for instance, precipitation and humidity. There will also be very large differences in the capacity of city authorities and of city-based households and enterprises to take measures to limit an increase in risk – for instance, by better drainage systems and other measures to protect against flooding – and to ensure rapid and effective responses when flooding or some other disaster occurs.

Sea-level rises will obviously be most disruptive to settlements on coastal and estuarine areas and this is where a considerable proportion of the world's population lives. One estimate suggested that 60 per cent of the world's population live within 60 kilometres of a seacoast.[74] Many of the Third World's most densely populated areas are river deltas and low-lying coastal regions. For instance, in the unprotected river deltas of Bangladesh, Egypt and Vietnam, millions of people live within one metre of high tide in unprotected river deltas.[75] The lower reaches of many major rivers that also have high population concentrations present particular difficulties – for instance, on the Hwang Ho and Yangtze (China).[76] The Maldives, the Marshall coastal areas, archipelagos and island nations in the Pacific and Indian Oceans, and the Caribbean are likely to lose their beaches and much of their arable land.[77] Global warming may also increase the incidence and severity of tropical cyclones and expand the areas at risk from them, bringing particular dangers to such places as the coastal areas of Bangladesh that are already subject to devastating cyclones.[78]

Most of the largest cities in Africa, Asia and Latin America are port cities for historic reasons linked to their colonial past. The high cost of land in the central city and/or around ports has often encouraged major commercial developments on land reclaimed from the sea or the estuary and these will often be particularly vulnerable to sea-level rises. So, too, will the many industries and thermal power stations that are concentrated on coasts because of their need for cooling water or as the sea becomes a convenient dumping ground for their waste.[79] Sea-level rises will also bring rising groundwater levels in coastal areas that will threaten existing sewerage and drainage systems and may undermine buildings. Box 20.8 gives an example of the environmental impacts of sea-level rise on a low-lying coastal city – in this instance, Alexandria in Egypt. It also shows how other human-induced changes such as reducing sediment flow and floodwater flows in the Nile have also helped increase the risk of flooding in the city.[80]

Ports and other settlements on the coast or estuaries are also most at risk from any increase in the severity and frequency of floods and storms induced by global warming, with storm-induced tidal surges often being a particular problem.[82] Coastal cities whose economies benefit from tourism may have considerable difficulties protecting tourist attractions such as beaches and nearby wetlands.[83] There are also the impacts of changes in the availability of freshwater resources – for instance, shortfalls because of reduced precipitation levels and the difficulties in protecting groundwater resources from contamination by sea water. The drinking-water supplies of many coastal cities are already threatened by a landward shift in the interface between salt water and fresh water – for instance, Dhaka[84] and, as already noted, Dakar and Jakarta; sea-level rise would further compound this problem.

There will also be serious impacts for many inland cities. One example is an increased intensity of flooding as a result of the changes predicted in rainfall regimes.

	Mediating process	Health outcomes

Temperature and weather changes ↗ ↘

Direct	
Exposure to thermal extremes →	Altered rates of heat- and cold-related illnesses and death
Altered frequency and/or intensity of other extreme weather events →	Deaths, injuries, psychological disorders; damage to public health infrastructure

Indirect

Disturbances of ecological systems	
Effects on range and activity of vectors and infective parasites →	Changes in geographic ranges and incidence of vector-borne diseases
Altered local ecology of waterborne and food-borne infective agents →	Changed incidence of diarrhoeal and other infectious diseases
Altered food (especially crop) productivity due to changes in climate, weather events, and associated pests and diseases →	Malnutrition and hunger, and consequent impairment of child growth and development
Sea-level rise, with population displacement and damage to infrastructure →	Increased risk of infectious disease, psychological disorders
Levels and biological impacts of air pollution, including pollens and spores →	Asthma and allergic disorders; other acute and chronic respiratory disorders and deaths
Social, economic and demographic dislocations due to effects on economy, infrastructure and resource supply →	Wide range of public health consequences: mental health and nutritional impairment, infectious diseases, civil strife

Stratospheric ozone depletion	→	Skin cancers, cataracts and perhaps immune suppression; indirect impacts via impaired productivity of agricultural and aquatic systems

Source: McMichael, A J, A Haines, R Sloof and S Kovats, *Climate Change and Human Health,* WHO, Geneva, 1996

Figure 20.1 *Possible major types of health impact of climate change and stratospheric ozone depletion*

Box 20.8 *The impact of sea-level rise and other human-induced changes on Alexandria, Egypt*

Alexandria is on the north-east fringe of the Nile delta, on the Mediterranean sea. The Nile delta has a rare set of fossilized sand-dunes along its coastal fringe which provide a stable foundation for the city above the low delta plain. The Old City is as much as 12 metres above sea level and is safe from the direct effects of sea-level rise. However, the port area and newer suburbs which have been built on low land with the aid of flood defences are at risk. The low marshes and lagoons which surround the city could be lost or seriously contaminated with salt water due to sea-level rise. Ultimately, the city could become a peninsula, surrounded by the Mediterranean, only reached by bridges and causeways.

Both subsidence and coastal erosion have been enhanced by development projects, which have also increased the city's vulnerability to climate change. The control of floods on the Nile (the most important being through the Aswan High Dam completed in 1964) have produced major benefits for irrigated farming and tourism but have stopped sediment previously brought down to the coast, which has meant some dramatic erosion around the mouths of the Damietta and Rosetta rivers. Sediment starvation may eventually erode the already fragile beaches protecting Alexandria. The control of floodwaters in the Nile has also reduced the volume of water that recharges the aquifers below the delta. This has led to the increased rates of groundwater withdrawal, which in turn increased subsidence and saltwater intrusion into freshwater aquifers. The net result is deeper extraction and more subsidence.

A sea-level rise of just 10–20 centimetres would accelerate significantly the retreat of the coastline. Rises of 30–50 centimetres would probably require expensive and extensive protection measures to reduce the risk to Alexandria (and also to Port Said). Plans to boost beach tourism would certainly be jeopardized. A relative rise of one metre could submerge lowlands to within 30 kilometres of the coast; engineering solutions could mitigate the flooding problem but the capital costs would be high.

Source: Turner, R K, P M Kelly and R C Kay (1990) *Cities at Risk*, BNA International, London[81]

In Latin America, increased flooding will pose serious threats to thousands of city dwellers in many urban centres that are in the foothills of the Andes, including such major cities as Lima, Santiago, Quito and Bogotá.[85] Increasing rainfall or changes in its distribution over the year may seriously affect many cities built next to rivers – for instance, cities such as Formosa, Clorinda, Resistencia and Goya which lie on reclaimed land beside the middle Paraná and lower Paraguay rivers.[86]

Global warming will also mean increased human exposure to exceptional heat waves. The elderly, the very young and those with incapacitating diseases are most at risk from these.[87] Low-income groups will generally be more vulnerable because their housing is less suited to moderating extreme temperatures and they lack air-conditioning.[88] Those living in cities or those parts of cities which are 'heat islands' where temperatures remain significantly above those of the surrounding regions will also be particularly at risk. High relative humidity will considerably amplify heat stress.[89] One study of China suggested that future warming may affect mortality markedly, especially in mid-latitude cities such as Shanghai. Two categories of potentially stressful air masses were identified in Shanghai – the first characterized by hot clear and dry conditions, the second by humid, maritime tropical conditions. Although these two air masses occur for less than a third of the time during the summer, they account for 94 per cent of the top 50 mortality days in Shanghai. It is projected that these air masses would occur much more frequently with climate change.[90]

Increased temperatures in cities are also likely to aggravate air pollution problems. For instance, increased temperatures can increase the concentrations of ground-level ozone (whose health effects were discussed earlier), as it increases the reaction rates among the pollutants that form ozone.[91]

Warmer average temperatures permit an expansion in the area in which 'tropical diseases' can occur – for instance, global warming is likely to permit an expansion of the area in which mosquito species that are the vectors for malaria, dengue fever and filariasis can survive and breed.[92] The same is true for the aquatic snail that is the vector for schistosomiasis and also for the vectors of leishmaniasis and Japanese encephalitis.[93] Rodent populations are likely to increase and with them increased risk of the many infectious diseases in which rodents are involved.[94] Climate-change induced reductions in water supply or increased floods (which contaminate water supplies) could increase the incidence of waterborne and water-washed diseases. Precise predictions are difficult because climate change will bring changes to so many factors which influence disease-causing agents and vectors, including temperature, humidity, precipitation, flora, fauna, predators and competitors.[95]

The more indirect routes by which global warming affects settlements, such as through disturbances to crop production, will probably have as dramatic an impact on urban areas as the more direct effects. These include:

- the changes in rural production caused by the increasing temperatures and changes in weather patterns and their impacts on ecosystems, which then impact on the livelihoods of those who exploit or rely on natural resources for their livelihoods;
- the changes in resource availabilities for urban enterprises – for instance, from changes in rural production or changes in freshwater availabilities.

There are also the broader ecological changes within which these fall: the physical damage, habitat loss and species depletion currently suffered by marine and terrestrial ecosystems such as pastoral lands, ocean fisheries and wetlands may be exacerbated by climate change.[96]

The additional cost of meeting global food demand has been estimated to be up to 10 per cent of world GDP.[97] Changes in rural production will include disruptions to production destined for cities and to rural incomes spent in cities. Many cities will have increased in-migration of people who have lost their homes and livelihoods as a result of the direct or indirect effects of global warming. The economic base of many villages, towns and cities will be altered by the changes brought to agricultural production and productivity from changes in temperature and precipitation, and this will affect existing patterns of regional, national and continental urban development. In some cities and regions, opportunities will increase and incomes rise while other areas will experience economic decline. Both traditional and modern agricultural practices may be vulnerable to the relatively rapid changes in temperature, rainfall, flooding and storms that global warming can bring. Forests and fisheries may also be subject to rapid change. Reduced rainfall in the Sahel has already considerably increased population growth in urban centres in the region, as pastoralists deprived of their livelihood move there. The problems are likely to be most serious in the countries or areas where the inhabitants are already at the limits of their capacity to cope with climatic events – for instance, populations in low-lying coastal areas and islands, subsistence farmers and populations on semi-arid grasslands.[98]

A considerable range of manufacturing and service industries will also be affected. For example, reductions in the availability of water will jeopardize those industries which use large volumes of water, while changes in agricultural production will affect food-processing industries, and changes in the weather will impact on the tourist industry.

Climate-change induced changes in the frequency and magnitude of precipitation will increase flooding, landslides and mudslips in many places and as such bring increased dangers to many residential sites.[99] Storms and other extreme weather conditions may become more frequent in a number of areas, while sea-level rises will also make the impact of 'normal' extremes such as high tides, storm surges and seismic sea waves (tsunamis) more severe.[100] The impacts of disasters often fall particularly heavily on low-income groups because so many of them can only find land for housing in the areas that are most vulnerable to extreme weather events and because they lack the resources to minimize the risk and the damage, and to help them cope in the event of a disaster.

One other aspect of global warming is difficult to predict – the capacity and readiness of societies to respond to the changes that warming and its associated effects will bring. All societies have evolved a range of measures to reduce risk from natural hazards, including long-established traditions through which house design and settlement layout include measures to limit loss of life and property from earthquakes or storms. There are also those that have passed into law and statute books that can be seen in building and planning codes and in health and safety regulations, and the institutional measures developed to enforce them. Where these are appropriate to that particular society and its resources,[101] and where they are enforced, they reduce risk and ensure that the built environment can cope with high winds, accidental fires or sudden heavy rainstorms. Their effectiveness can be seen in the great reductions achieved in accidental death and injury. For instance, even as late as the last century, it was common for accidental fires to destroy large areas of cities in Europe and North America.

This complex set of institutional measures and the built environment that they have influenced will have to change to reflect new hazards or a much increased scale of existing hazards. There is the vast stock of buildings, roads, public transport systems and basic urban infrastructure that was built without making allowance for the changes that global warming will bring.[102] Modifying or replacing these will be expensive and time-consuming, and particularly difficult in low-income countries with weak and under-resourced city authorities, where there are still large deficits in basic infrastructure that need addressing.

NOTES AND REFERENCES

1   Douglas, Ian, *The Urban Environment*, Edward Arnold, London, 1983; Douglas, Ian, 'Urban Geomorphology' in P G Fookes and P R Vaughan (eds), *A Handbook of Engineering Geomorphology*, Surrey University Press (Blackie & Son) Glasgow, 1986, pp 270–283

Jorge E Hardoy, Diana Mitlin and David Satterthwaite

2   See Chapter 3 of Douglas, Ian, *The Urban Environment*, Edward Arnold, 1983, for more details and also examples of maps showing the locations for sources of food or materials for different cities

3   Douglas 1983 op cit p 26

4   Ibid. One recent study of the environmental impact of a city on its surrounds in terms of its draw on soil for construction, timber, wood fuel and other resources is Acho-Chi, 'Human interference and environmental instability: addressing the environmental consequences of rapid urban growth in Bamenda, Cameroon', *Environment and Urbanization* Vol 10, No 2, 1998, pp 161–174

5   Jones, Gavin W, 'Structural change and prospects for urbanization in Asian countries', Papers of the East-West Population Institute No 88, East-West Center, Honolulu, August 1983; and McGee, T G, 'Urbanization of Kotadesasi – the emergence of new regions of economic interaction in Asia', Working Paper, East-West Center, Honolulu, June 1987

6   Asian Coalition for Housing Rights, 'Evictions in Seoul, South Korea' *Environment and Urbanization* Vol 1, No 1, April 1989, pp 89–94; Makil, Perla Q 'Slums and squatter settlements in the Philippines', Concerned Citizens of the Urban Poor Series No 3, Manila, 1982; Shrivastav, P P, 'City for the citizen of citizen for the city: the search for an appropriate strategy for slums and housing the urban poor in developing countries – the case of Delhi' *Habitat International* Vol 6, No 1/2 1982, pp 197–207; and Hardoy, Jorge E and David Satterthwaite, *Squatter Citizen: Life in the Urban Third World*, Earthscan Publications, London, 1989

7   Vélasquez, Luz Stella and Margarita Pacheco, 'Research-management as an approach to solving environmental conflicts in metropolitan areas: a case study of the Manizales-Villamaría conurbation, Colombia', in Adrian Atkinson, Julio D Dávila, Edésio Fernandes and Michael Mattingly (eds), *The Challenge of Environmental Management in Urban Areas*, Ashgate, Aldershot, 1999

8   This is described in the paper by Luz Estella Vélasquez, in Chapter 15.

9   Velásquez and Pacheco 1999, op cit

10   Acho-Chi 1998, op cit

11   Acho-Chi 1998, op cit

12   Although much of the general literature on urban change in the Third World talks about an urban explosion and a mushrooming of cities, most cities in North Africa, Asia and Latin America have a long history as significant urban centres. There are very few major cities in these regions which do not predate the motor car. See Satterthwaite, David, *The Scale and Nature of Urban Change in the South*, IIED, London, 1996

13   Douglass, Mike 'The future of cities on the Pacific Rim', Discussion Paper No 3, Department of Urban and Regional Planning, University of Hawaii, July 1987

14   Kishk, M A, 'Land degradation in the Nile Valley', Ambio Vol XV, No 4, 1986, pp 226–230

15   Chaturvedi, A 'Bricks versus food: Delhi's dilemma', Earthscan Feature, London, 1983

16   See, for instance, Douglass, Mike, 'The environmental sustainability of development – coordination, incentives and political will in land use planning for the Jakarta metropolis', *Third World Planning Review*, Vol 11, No 2, May 1989, pp 211–238 and Kelly, Philip F, 'The politics of urban-rural relationships: land conversion in the Philippines', *Environment and Urbanization*, Vol 10, No 1, 1998, pp 35–54

17   Sidel, J, *Coercion, Capital and the Post-colonial State: bossim in the postwar Philippines*, unpublished PhD thesis, Cornell University, 1995

18   Ibid

19   Agarwal, Anil and Sunita Narain, 'Towards green villages; a strategy for environmentally sound and participatory rural development in India', pp 53–64 and Lee-Smith, Diana and Catalina Hinchey Trujillo, 'The struggle to legitimize subsistence: Women and sustainable development', pp 77–84 in *Environment and Urbanization* Vol 4, No 1, April 1992

20   Leach, Gerald and Robin Mearns, *Beyond the Woodfuel Crisis – People, Land and Trees in Africa*, Earthscan Publications, London, 1989

21   Douglass 1989, op cit

22   Postel, Sandra *The Last Oasis; Facing Water Scarcity*, Worldwatch Environmental Alert Series, Earthscan Publications, London, 1992

23   Bartone, Carl, Janis Bernstein, Josef Leitmann and Jochen Eigen, *Towards Environmental Strategies for Cities; Policy Considerations for Urban Environmental Management in Developing Countries*, UNDP, UNCHS and World Bank Urban Management Program No 18, World Bank, Washington DC, 1994

24 White, Rodney R, 'The international transfer of urban technology: does the North have anything to offer for the global environmental crisis?' *Environment and Urbanization* Vol 4, No 2, October 1992, pp 109–120

25 Connolly, Priscilla, 'Mexico City: our common future?', *Environment and Urbanization*, Vol 11, No 1, April 1999 describes this and other aspects of Mexico City's environmental problems

26 Damián, Araceli, 'Ciudad de México: servicios urbanos en los noventas' *Vivienda* Vol 3, No 1, January–April 1992, pp 29–40; and Postel 1992, op cit

27 Connolly 1999, op cit

28 A coliform count is a good indicator of water quality since faecal coliform bacteria are found in human and animal wastes. Although coliform bacteria themselves do not cause disease, their presence can indicate the presence of bacteria that cause typhoid, cholera, dysentery and other waterborne bacterial diseases. A faecal coliform bacteria count gives the number of bacterial colonies per 100 ml of water and a sample with less than 100 is considered safe to drink while a sample with less than 200 is considered safe for swimming

29 This section draws on the findings of IIED's research programme on rural-urban interactions, and especially from Tacoli, Cecilia, *Bridging the Divide: Rural-Urban Interactions and Livelihood Strategies*, Gatekeeper Series No 77, IIED Sustainable Agriculture and Rural Livelihoods Programme, London, 1998

30 Tiffen, Mary and Michael Mortimore 'Environment, population growth and productivity in Kenya; a case study of Machakos District', *Development Policy Review*, Vol 10, 1992, pp 359–387; Manzanal, Mabel and Cesar Vapnarsky, 'The Comahue Region, Argentina' in Hardoy, Jorge E and Satterthwaite, David (eds), *Small and Intermediate Urban Centres; Their Role in National and Regional Development in the Third World*, Hodder & Stoughton (UK), 1986 and Westview (USA) 1986

31 See Chapter 9 of Hardoy, Jorge E and David Satterthwaite, *Squatter Citizen: Life in the Urban Third World*, Earthscan Publications, London

32 Stren, Richard E, *The Ruralization of African Cities: Learning to Live with Poverty*, Project Ecoville Working Paper No 34, University of Toronto, June 1986; and Mazingira Institute, *Urban Food and Fuel Study*, Nairobi, Kenya, 1987

33 Losada, H, H, Martínez, J Vieyra, R Pealing, R Zavala and J. Cortés, 'Urban agriculture in the metropolitan zone of Mexico City: changes over time in urban, suburban and periurban areas', *Environment and Urbanization*, Vol 10, No 2, 1998, pp 37–54

34 Large 'green belts' or other means of preventing new urban developments on large areas of land may drive up housing prices by restricting land supplies for housing and encourage more dispersed, automobile-dependent patterns of urban expansion

35 For India, Agarwal, Anil, 'The poverty of nature: environment, development, science and technology', IDRC Report No 12, No 3, Ottawa, Canada, 1983, pp 4–6. For China, Smil, Vaclav, *The Bad Earth: Environmental Degradation in China*, M E Sharpe, New York and Zed Press, London, 1984. For Malaysia, Consumers Association of Penang, *Development and the Environment Crisis – A Malaysian Case, 1982*; and reports in *Environmental News Digest*, 1982. For Alexandria, Hamza, Dr Ahmed, 'An appraisal of environmental consequences of urban development in Alexandria, Egypt', *Environment and Urbanization* Vol 1, No 1, April 1989, pp 22–30. For Gulf of Paria, cover story, *The Siren* No 38, UNEP, Nairobi, October 1988. For Manila Bay, Jimenez, Rosario D and Sister Aida Velasquez, 'Metropolitan Manila: a framework for its sustained development', *Environment and Urbanization*, Vol 1, No 1, April 1989. For Rio de Janeiro, Alcira Kreimer, Thereza Lobo, Braz Menezes, Mohan Munasinghe and Ronald Parker (eds), *Towards a Sustainable Urban Environment: The Rio de Janeiro Study*, World Bank Discussion Papers No 195, World Bank, Washington DC, 1993. For the Bay of Dakar, Kebe, Moctar, 'The West and Central African Action Plan', interview in *The Siren* No 37, July 1988, pp 31–34 and White 1992, op cit. For Indus Delta, Sahil, 'Marine pollution and the Indus Delta' , Vol 1 (house journal of National Institute of Oceanography, Karachi, Pakistan), 1988, pp 57–61; and Beg, M Arshad Ali S Naeem Mahmood, Sitwat Naeem and A H K Yousufzai, 'Land based pollution and the marine environment of the Karachi coast', Pakistan Journal of Science, *Industry and Resources* Vol 27, No 4, August 1984, pp 199–205

36 World Bank, *World Development Report 1992*, Oxford University Press, 1992

37 WHO, *Our Planet, Our Health*, Report of the WHO Commission on Health and Environment, Geneva, 1992

38 Gadgil, Madhav and Ramachandra Guha, 'Interpreting Indian environmentalism', paper presented at the UNRISD Conference on the Social Dimensions of Environment and Sustainable Development, Valletta, Malta, April 1992

39 Conway, Gordon R and Jules N Pretty, *Unwelcome Harvest*, Earthscan Publications, London, 1991

40 There is also the massive oil pollution arising from the Gulf War whose long-term effects are not known. See Hinrichsen, Don, *Coastal Waters of the World: Trends, Threats, and Strategies*, Island Press, Washington DC, 1998

41 Lopez, José Manuel, 'The Caribbean and Gulf of Mexico', *The Siren* No 36, April 1988, pp 30–31

42 Hinrichsen 1998, op cit

43 Hinrichsen 1998, op cit

44 McCormick, John, *Acid Earth: The Politics of Acid Pollution*, Earthscan, London, 1997. See also for China, Smil 1984, op cit. For India, Centre for Science and Environment, *The State of India's Environment – a Citizen's Report*, Delhi, India, 1983

45 This paragraph draws on Conway and Pretty 1991, op cit

46 Krupa, S V and W J Manning 'Atmospheric ozone: formation and effects on vegetation' *Environmental Pollution*, Vol 50, 1988, pp 101–137 quoted in Conway and Pretty 1991

47 Conway and Pretty 1991, op cit

48 Zhao, D and J Xiong, 'Acidification in southwestern China' in H Rohde and R Herrera (eds), *Acidification in Tropical Countries*, SCOPE Report No 36, John Wiley & Sons, Chichester, 1988

49 Conway and Pretty 1991, op cit

50 Smil 1984, op cit

51 Conway and Pretty 1991, op cit

52 Wang, Jia-Xi and Yong-Mei Bian, 'Fluoride effects on the mulberry-silkworm system' *Environmental Pollution* Vol 52, 1985, pp 11–18, quoted in Conway and Pretty 1991, op cit

53 Rees, William E 'Ecological footprints and appropriated carrying capacity: what urban economics leaves out', *Environment and Urbanization*, Vol 4, No 2, October 1992, pp 121–130; Wackernagel, Mathis and William E Rees, *Our Ecological Footprint: Reducing Human Impact on the Earth*, Gabriola (Canada): New Society Publishers, 1995

54 Rees 1992, op cit

55 Jopling, John and Herbert Giradet, *Creating a Sustainable London*, Sustainable London Trust, London, 1996. See Herbert Giradet's paper in Chapter 19 for more details

56 The calculation for London was based on an area of 1,580 square kilometres (virtually all of which is built-up area) with a population of seven million. The calculation for the lower Fraser Valley was for an urban-agricultural region of 4,000 square kilometres with 1.8 million inhabitants

57 Giradet, Herbert, *The Gaia Atlas of Cities*, Gaia Books, London, 1992

58 Rees 1992, op cit

59 Wackernagel and Rees 1995, op cit

60 Ibid

61 Middle- or upper-income city dwellers generally have fewer cars and use them less than those living in suburban or rural areas with the same per capita income. City dwellers also generally have smaller homes and have lower fossil-fuel or electricity consumption for heating or air-conditioning them

62 Schmidt-Bleek, F, 'MIPS revisited', *Fresenius Environmental Bulletin* Acho-Chi 1998, Vol 2, No 8, 1993, pp 407–412

63 Tischner, Ursula and Friedrich Schmidt-Bleek, 'Designing goods with MIPS', *Fresenius Environmental Bulletin*, Vol 2, No 8, 1993, pp 479–484

64 Nishioka, Shuzo, Yuichi Noriguchi and Sombo Yamamura, 'Megalopolis and climate change: the case of Tokyo' in James McCulloch (ed), *Cities and Global Climate Change*, Climate Institute, Washington DC, 1990, pp 108–133

65 WHO 1992, op cit; and Agarwal, Anil and Sunita Narain, *Global Warming in an Unequal World – a Case of Environmental Colonialism*, Centre for Science and Environment, Delhi, 1991

66 The ratio of greenhouse gas emissions to unit value of output may be significantly higher, both because of old, inefficient equipment and, for some nations, a greater reliance on heavy industries within the industrial sector

67 In some of the larger and wealthier Third World cities, the number of automobiles per inhabitant may be comparable to some of the major cities in Europe and North America

68   WHO 1992, op cit
69   Despite the claim by so many international reports that poverty is a major cause of environmental degradation – a claim that was included in the World Commission on Environment and Development's report, *Our Common Future* (Oxford University Press, Oxford and New York, 1987), and then repeated and amplified in many subsequent publications – there is very little evidence that this is actually the case *on a global scale*. The text in this chapter considers this in regard to the contribution of the urban poor to environmental degradation. For a discussion of whether poor rural populations can be implicated, see Satterthwaite, David, 'Cities and sustainable development; what progress since *Our Common* Future' in Softing, Guri Bang, George Benneh, Kjetil Hindar, Larse Walloe and Anders Wijkman, *The Brundtland Commission's Report – 10 years*, Scandinavian University Press, Oslo, 1998
70   World Commission on Environment and Development 1987, op cit
71   A small proportion of the urban centres in the developing world do have high levels of automobiles relative to populations; some have higher ratios of automobiles to population than many cities in the North. But an average figure for per capita fuel consumption taken across all urban centres would produce a much lower figure than that for urban centres in the North
72   This issue is discussed in more detail in Chapters 5 and 6 of this Reader
73   Scott, M J, draft paper on Human settlements – impacts/adaptation, IPCC Working Group II, WMO and UNEP, 1994
74   Scott, Michael J and others, 'Human settlements in a changing climate: impacts and adaptation', Chapter 12 in Robert T Watson, Marufu C Zinwowera and Richard H Moss (eds), *Climate Change 1995; Impacts, Adaptations and Mitigation of Climate Change: Scientific-Technical Analyses*, published for the Intergovernmental Panel on Climate Change by Cambridge University Press, Cambridge, 1996, pp 399–426
75   Scott 1994, op cit
76   Scott 1994, op cit
77   Scott 1994, op cit
78   WHO 1992, op cit
79   Parry, Martin, 'The urban economy', presentation at *Cities and Climate Change*, a conference at the Royal Geographical Society, 31 March 1992
80   Turner, R K, P M Kelly and R C Kay, *Cities at Risk*, BNA International, London, 1990
81   This source drew on: El Raey, M, S Nasr and O Frihy, 'National assessment of the impact of greenhouse induced sea level rises on the northern coastal regions of Egypt' in S P Leatherman (ed), *National Assessments of Sea-level Rise Vulnerability*, Centre for Global Change, University of Maryland, Maryland, 1990; El Sayed, M K, 'Implications of relative sea level rise on Alexandria' in R Frassetto (ed), *Cities on Water: Proceedings of the First International Meeting of Sea level Rise on Cities and Regions*, Venice, December 1989; Meith, N, *High and Dry: Mediterranean Climate in the 21st Century*, United Nations Environment Programme, Athens, 1989; and Sestini, G, L Jeftic and J D Milliman, *Implications of Expected Climatic Changes in the Mediterranean Region: an Overview*, UNEP Regional Seas Reports and Studies No 103, UNEP, Nairobi, 1990
82   Smit, Barrie, 'Planning in a climate of uncertainty' in James McCulloch (ed), *Cities and Global Climate Change*, Climate Institute, Washington DC, 1990, pp 3–19; Turner, Kelly and Kay 1990, op cit
83   Turner, Kelly and Kay 1990, op cit
84   Muhtab, F U *Effect of Climate Change and Sea level Rise on Bangladesh*, Report prepared for the Commonwealth Expert Group on Climate Change and Sea Level Rise, Commonwealth Secretariat, London, 1989, quoted in Turner, Kelly and Kay 1990, op cit
85   di Pace, Maria, Sergio Federovisky, Jorge E Hardoy, Jorge E Morello and Alfredo Stein 'Latin America' Chapter 8 in Richard Stren, Rodney White and Joseph Whitney (eds), *Sustainable Cities: Urbanization and the Environment in International Perspective*, Westie Press, Boulder, 1992, pp 205–227
86   di Pace et al 1992
87   WHO 1992, op cit
88   McMichael, A J, A Haines, R Sloof and S Kovats, *Climate Change and Human Health*, WHO, Geneva, 1996
89   WHO 1992, op cit
90   McMichael and others 1996, op cit

Jorge E Hardoy, Diana Mitlin and David Satterthwaite

91 Gupta, Joyeeta, 'A partnership between countries and cities on the issue of climate change – with special reference to the Netherlands' in James McCulloch (ed), *Cities and Global Climate Change*, Climate Institute, Washington DC, 1990, pp 66–89
92 WHO 1992, op cit
93 WHO 1992, op cit
94 McMichael and others 1996, op cit
95 McMichael and others 1996, op cit
96 McMichael and others 1996, op cit
97 IPCC, *Potential Impacts of Climate Change: Report to IPCC from Working Group II*, World Meteorological Organization and the United Nations Environment Programme, 1990
98 Scott 1994, op cit
99 di Pace et al 1992, op cit; Scott and others 1996, op cit
100 Scott and others 1996, op cit
101 In many countries they are not because they are based on old colonial codes or on inappropriate imported models – see Hardoy and Satterthwaite 1989, op cit
102 Scott and others 1996, op cit

Further Reading

Ecological Footprints

See *Our Ecological Footprint – Reducing Human Impact on the Earth*, Mathis Wackernagel and William Rees, New Society Publishers, 1995. Available from New Society Publishers, PO Box 189, Gabriola Island, BC, Canada V0R 1X0 or 4527 Springfield Avenue, Philadelphia PA 19143, USA

See also: Wackernagel, Mathis, 'The ecological footprint of Santiago de Chile', *Local Environment*, Vol 3, No 1, February 1998, pp 7–25

Creating a Sustainable London, John Jopling and Herbert Girardet, Sustainable London Trust, London, 1996

City-region Interactions

The Urban Environment, Ian Douglas, Edward Arnold, London, 1983. (A large-format book with many maps, figures and illustrations; although published over 15 years ago, this is still one of the most interesting introductions to the subject)

For one of the most interesting and detailed studies of city-region environmental interactions, see *Atlas Ambiental de Porto Alegre*, Rualdo Menegat (main co-ordinator), Universidade Federal do Rio Grande do Sul, Prefeitura Municipal de Porto Alegre and Instituto Nacional de Pesquisas Espaciais, Porto Alegre, 1998. This is a large-format and very detailed environmental atlas of the city and its surrounds which includes coverage of the natural systems – for instance, the geological evolution, all aspects of the regional ecology, climate, flora and fauna – and of the city's construction. It comes with a CD-Rom. Available from Secretaria Municipal do Meio Ambiente, Prefeitura Municipal de Porto Alegre, Avenida Carlos Gomes 2120, Porto Alegre CEP 90.480-OO2, RS, Brazil

For case studies of city-region interactions, see the originals of the papers or reports whose findings were summarized in boxes in Chapter 20:

Douglass, Mike, 'The environmental sustainability of development – coordination, incentives and political will in land use planning for the Jakarta metropolis', *Third World Planning Review* Vol 11, No 2, 1989, pp 211–238

Kreimer, Alcira, Thereza Lobo, Braz Menezes, Mohan Munasinghe and Ronald Parker (eds), *Towards a Sustainable Urban Environment: The Rio de Janeiro Study*, World Bank Discussion Papers No 195, World Bank, Washington DC, 1993

Kelly, Philip F, 'The politics of urban-rural relationships: land conversion in the Philippines' *Environment and Urbanization*, Vol 10, No 1, 1998, pp 35–54

See also: Satterthwaite, David, 'Environmental transformations in cities as they get larger, wealthier and better managed', *The Geographic Journal*, Vol 163, No 2, July 1997, pp 216–224

Atkinson, Adrian, 'The urban bioregion as a sustainable development paradigm', *Third World Planning Review*, Vol 14, No 4, November 1992, pp 327–354.

For details of the environmental impact of pollution on agriculture, see Conway, Gordon R and Jules N Pretty, *Unwelcome Harvest*, Earthscan Publications, London, 1991

Cities and Global Warming

Climate Change and Human Health, A J McMichael, A Haines, R Sloof and S Kovats, WHO, Geneva, 1996. Available from the World Health Organization, 1211 Geneva 27, Switzerland (WHO/EGH/

96.7). Although not specifically on cities, this contains a wealth of information about the climate system and the possible effects of climate change on, among other things, temperature, air pollution, disease-causing agents, food production, extreme weather events and sea-level rise. It also discusses stratospheric ozone depletion and its direct and indirect health impacts

Climate Change 1995; Impacts, Adaptations and Mitigation of Climate Change: Scientific-Technical Analyses, Robert T Watson, Marufu C Zinwowera and Richard H Moss (eds), published for the Intergovernmental Panel on Climate Change by Cambridge University Press, Cambridge, 1996, especially Scott, Michael J and others, 'Human settlements in a changing climate: impacts and adaptation', Chapter 12 (pp 399–426)

Cities at Risk, R K Turner, P M Kelly and R C Kay, BNA International, London, 1990

International Programmes

ICLEI: The International Council for Local Environmental Initiatives (ICLEI), City Hall, East Tower, 8th Floor, Toronto, Ontario M5H 2N2, Canada. European office: ICLEI, Eschholzstr. 86, D-79115 Freiburg, Germany. Web page http://www.iclei.org

The European Campaign of Sustainable Cities and Towns, Rue de Trèves/Trierstraat 49-51, B-1040 Brussels, Belgium,e-mail: campaign.office@skynet.be; web page: http://www.sustainable-cities.org

The Sustainable Cities Programme, U.N. Centre for Human Settlements and the U.N. Environment Programme, PO Box 30030, Nairobi, Kenya

Index

Other relevant publications from Earthscan

ENVIRONMENTAL PROBLEMS IN AN URBANIZING WORLD
Finding Solutions to City Problems in Africa, Asia and Latin America
Jorge E Hardoy, Diana Mitlin and David Satterthwaite

An updated and much expanded version of *Environmental Problems in Third World Cities*, describing the scale, nature and underlying causes of environmental problems in large and small cities – and who is most affected by them. It includes environmental problems with household and community-level impacts, and those with city-wide and regional impacts, and discusses the current and likely future impact of climate change on cities. It highlights the many innovative ways in which environmental problems are being addressed by low income communities, as well as by NGOs, local authorities, national governments and international agencies and considers the national and international framework needed to support local action.

£15.95   paperback   1 85383 719 9   forthcoming 2001 (prices subject to change)
£40.00   hardback   1 85383 720 2

THE CITIZENS AT RISK
From Urban Sanitation to Sustainable Cities
Gordon McGranahan, Pedro Jacobi, Jacob Songsore, Charles Surjadi and Marianne Kjellén

This book describes and analyses the changing nature of urban environmental risks, their distribution and how they arise, drawing on detailed case studies in Accra, Jakarta and Sao Paulo. It also considers how best to improve conditions for those living in fast growing cities and argues that environmental justice provides more meaningful measure and goal for urban environmental improvement than 'sustainability'.

£16.95   paperback   1 85383 561 7   forthcoming 2001 (prices subject to change)
£45.00   hardback   1 85383 562 5

SQUATTER CITIZEN
Life in the Urban Third World
Jorge E Hardoy and David Satterthwaite

'one of the best contemporary statements of what is occurring in the growth of urban places in the Third World' *Environment and Planning*

'a very readable book, containing a lot of well documented information' *Third World Planning Review*

Squatter Citizen is about the lives of the 'squatter citizens' in cities of Africa, Asia and Latin America and the problems they face in their struggle for survival. It describes how they develop their own homes and neighbourhoods and their other contributions to city development. This book also challenges many common assumptions about the urban change – for example that urban citizens live in very large cities and that cities are growing rapidly, or that city dwellers benefit from 'urban bias' in government and aid policies.

£13.95 paperback 1 85383 146 8

CITIES IN A GLOBALIZING WORLD
Global Report on Human Settlements 2001
United Nations Centre for Human Settlements (Habitat)

Successor to the 1996 Global Report, this is the only reliable and comprehensive assessment of the world's cities, and an essential tool and reference for academics, researchers, planners and public authorities and civil society organizations around the world. The 2001 report highlights the impacts of globalization and the influence of market forces on urban and housing policies. It examines the benefits in greater wealth and freedoms, and studies the increased isolation and marginalization of the urban and rural poor and other vulnerable social groups. It documents current housing and urban conditions, including access to basic services, and proposes policies and initiatives for improved quality of life across all sectors of urban society.

£20.00 paperback 1 85383 806 3 forthcoming 2001 (prices subject to change)
£55.00 hardback 1 85383 805 5

SUSTAINABLE CITIES IN DEVELOPING COUNTRIES
Cedric Pugh

The imperative of sustainability in the 21st century can be exacerbated by the challenges of development; if the pitfalls of urban planning are introduced then there is a clear need for this book, establishing as it does ground rules for the burgeoning sphere of urban studies from a comprehensive range of perspectives including economics, political science, theories of health, the impact of the built environment, the appraisal of environmental assets through to the very conceptual foundations of sustainability. All the key contemporary developments are dealt with: the growth in international law and agreements on controlling greenhouse gases; the effect of reforms in finance, governance and methods of appraisal on the areas of waste management; the theoretical advances in the community development aspects of health and the neighbourhood environment guided by the experiences of the World Bank, WHO and UNEP.

£17.95 paperback 1 85383 619 2
£48.00 hardback 1 85383 624 9

URBAN INFRASTRUCTURE IN TRANSITION
Networks, Buildings and Plans
Edited by Timothy Moss, Simon Guy and Simon Marvin

This book examines the mounting pressures for change on the infrastructure of cities, in particular the utilities for water, energy, sewage and solid waste. These pressures come from different quarters: liberalization and privatization of the markets for services; tighter environmental standards; new economic incentives; competing technologies; changing consumption patterns causing over-use or over-capacity. Sustainable use of energy and resources is vital if cities are to thrive or even function. The authors show how much potential improved management of infrastructure holds for improving environmental and service quality. More efficient technology has a part to play, but the really significant improvements in quality of life will be delivered when the flow of material and energy through a city is focused on achieving these goals in each city's local context.

£18.95   paperback   1 85383 689 3
£48.00   hardback   1 85383 694 X

MUNICIPALITIES AND COMMUNITY PARTICIPATION
A Sourcebook for Capacity Building
Janelle Plummer

Poor urban communities are increasingly involved in the delivery of services and infrastructure. The state has largely withdrawn leaving municipal authorities in charge of urban development policy. But they often don't have the organizational or resource capacity to cope. This Sourcebook presents a comprehensive idea of the capacities needed for community participation to work. It sets out the options, stages and kinds of participation involved in delivering services to urban residents. It also lays out the management structures, systems, skills and attitudes needed. A companion to *Municipalities and the Private Sector* (forthcoming).

£20.00   paperback   1 85383 744 X

URBAN DEVELOPMENT AND CIVIL SOCIETY
The Role of Communities in Sustainable Cities
Michael Carley, Paul Jenkins and Harry Smith

The state is no longer seen as providing effective urban management and public–private schemes have often failed to provide for the needs of the urban poor. Throughout the world, 'bottom-up' community initiatives have been proving more successful. This book examines the role of communities and how civil society can combine with local government and the private sector in achieving sustainable urban development. It sets out a theoretical framework and applies this to case studies drawn from all over the world – from the poorest, through rapidly urbanizing and transitional economies to some of the most developed cities of the world.

£14.95   paperback   1 85383 717 2
£40.00   hardback   1 85383 718 0

THE COMMUNITY PLANNING HANDBOOK
How People can Shape Their Cities, Towns and Villages in Any Part of the World
Nick Wates

An accessible how-to-do-it style, with tips, checklists and sample documents help readers to get started quickly, learn from others' experience and select the approach best suited to their situation. The glossary, bibliography and contact details allow them to find further resources and information. This handbook is essential for all those involved in shaping their local environment – planners, architects, community workers, local authorities and residents – and a useful reference for students.

£14.95 paperback 1 85383 654 0

SUSTAINABLE COMMUNITIES
The Potential for Eco-neighbourhoods
Edited by Hugh Barton

There is widespread acceptance of the principle of creating more sustainable communities that are responsive to local needs, but much vague and unrealistic thinking about what this might mean in practice. Current reality suggests more the death of local neighbourhoods rather than their creation, reflecting an increasingly mobile, privatized and commodified society.

Sustainable Communities examines the practicality of re-inventing neighbourhoods. It presents the findings of a worldwide review of eco-villages and sustainable neighbourhoods, demonstrating what is possible. The main thrust of the book is focused on the ordinary localities in which people live, looking at the changing nature and role of local place communities, at the technologies (of energy, food, water, movement) that help close local resource loops and the potential for subsidiarity in decision making down to the local level.

£17.95 *paperback* 1 85383 513 7

CITIES FOR CHILDREN
Children's Rights, Poverty and Urban Management
Sheridan Bartlett, Roger Hart, David Satterthwaite, Ximena de la Barra and Alfredo Missair

This book was written to help the different agencies and departments of city governments and international agencies to understand and respond to the rights and requirements of children and adolescents in urban areas. It includes discussions of housing and basic services, neighbourhood environments, child-care, schools, health care, juvenile justice and urban governance from the perspective of children and also considers issues such as street and working children.

£18.95 *paperback* 1 85383 470 X

CITY-REGION 2020
Integrated Planning for a Sustainable Environment
Joe Ravetz
Foreword by Professor Sir Peter Hall

City-Region 2020 offers a vision for how things can and should change – a direction of travel towards the future. Drawing from the most comprehensive and detailed case study project ever undertaken on sustainable development at the city and regional scale, this important guide translates principles into practice for the sprawling post-industrial conurbation of Greater Manchester, through integrated strategic management of the entire city-region. It also explores methods and tools such as sustainability indicators and appraisals that can be applied anywhere in the western world.

£19.95 *paperback* 1 85383 606 0

MAKING CITIES WORK
The Role of Local Authorities in the Urban Environment
Richard Gilbert and others

This important book shows how cities can be made to work sustainably if they are efficiently managed. It looks at the vital role which local authorities play in safeguarding and developing them and how potential environmental and social problems can be overcome.

£14.95 *paperback* 1 85383 354 1

GREENING THE BUILT ENVIRONMENT
Maf Smith, John Whitelegg and Nick Williams

'should be on every reading list on environmental politics as well as urban planning... a book that you must read!' *Environmental Politics*
　　Setting out the clearest possible specification of the problems involved, *Greening the Built Environment* covers the social, economic and environmental dimensions, examining in depth the construction industry, transport and planning, health and community, equity, and the economy.

£16.95 *paperback* 1 85383 403 3

HEALTHY CITY PROJECTS IN DEVELOPING COUNTRIES
An International Approach to Local Problems
Edmundo Werna, Trudy Harpham, Ilona Blue and Greg Goldstein

With the growth of cities and towns throughout the developing world have come significant health problems. The urban poor are particularly affected, faced with the worst of both worlds: urban problems such as pollution and stress, combined with infectious diseases common in both rural and urban areas. The Healthy City Project shows how to put health high on the agenda of urban officials, integrating it into all other planning and development decisions.

£15.95 *paperback* 1 85383 455 6

THE EARTHSCAN READER IN POPULATION AND DEVELOPMENT
Edited by Paul Demeny and Geoffrey McNicoll

Following in the best tradition of previous Readers, the editors present a collection of seminal articles that explore these issues, drawn from a literate middle ground lying between the simplified popular treatments that characterize much of the debate and the highly technical specialist literature. The material represents a wide range of positions within this highly-charged field.

£19.95 *paperback* 1 85383 275 8

Earthscan Publications Ltd

www.earthscan.co.uk